INFANCY
DEVELOPMENT FROM BIRTH TO AGE 3

Second Edition

Dana Gross
St. Olaf College

Allyn & Bacon

Boston Columbus Indianapolis New York San Francisco Upper Saddle River
Amsterdam Cape Town Dubai London Madrid Milan Munich Paris Montreal Toronto
Delhi Mexico City Sao Paulo Sydney Hong Kong Seoul Singapore Taipei Tokyo

Senior Acquisitions Editor: *Jeff Marshall*
Editorial Assistant: *Courtney Elezovic*
Executive Marketing Manager: *Nicole Kunzmann*
Senior Production Project Manager: *Patrick Cash-Peterson*
Manufacturing Buyer: *Debbie Rossi*
Editorial Production and Composition Service: *Amy Saucier, Laserwords Maine*
Photo Researcher: *Sarah Evertson*
Cover Administrator: *Joel Genderon*

Library of Congress Cataloging-in-Publication Data

Gross, Dana Lynn.
  Infancy : development from birth to age 3 / Dana Gross. — 2nd ed.
    p. cm.
  ISBN-13: 978-0-205-73419-1
  ISBN-10: 0-205-73419-7
    1. Infants—Development. 2. Toddlers—Development. I. Title.

  HQ774.G77 2011
  305.232—dc22

                                         2010031844
Printed in the United States of America
4 5 6 7 8 9 10 V092 16 15 14

Dedication

To John, Rolf, and Simon

CONTENTS

PREFACE

The focus of this book is on current research, theory, practice, and policy about development from birth to 3 years of age. It developed in response to my experience using other infancy books in my own courses with undergraduates. In trying to find a book that was appropriate in content and presentation, I discovered that many of the available texts were either too advanced or too basic. The overly advanced books tended to be encyclopedic in their coverage, often gave only minimal coverage to important practical topics, and seemed not to have been written with teaching and learning in mind. The overly basic books tended to leave out information about how research is conducted, focused almost exclusively on practical topics, and lacked advanced critical thinking approaches. Some books adopted a chronological approach that missed opportunities to highlight the coherence, continuity, and change in specific aspects of development from birth to age 3. This book offers a useful middle ground that provides students with enough information about research to understand methodological issues, explore both practically and theoretically important topics, and engage in thinking critically about development from birth to age 3.

THE CHALLENGE AND OPPORTUNITY OF REVISION

In responding to the challenge and opportunity to revise this book, I sought to retain and enhance the best features and qualities from the first edition (described below), while updating the research literature about topics originally included and adding exciting new content to reflect perspectives that had emerged or grown in prominence since the first edition was published. The new content includes:

- Institute of Medicine guidelines for weight gain during pregnancy (Chapter 3)
- More cross-cultural comparison of prenatal care, obstetrical procedures, and birth outcomes (Chapter 3)
- New ideas about the most optimal time to clamp and cut the umbilical cord (Chapter 4)
- Comparison of CDC and World Health Organization standards for charting growth (Chapter 5)
- New perspectives about the causes of growth failure (Chapter 5)
- Effects of maltreatment on brain development (Chapter 5)
- Practical tips for preventing Shaken Baby Syndrome (Chapter 5)
- Discussion of the United Nations Millennium Development Goals (Chapter 5)
- Increased coverage of ecological and dynamic systems theoretical perspectives (Chapter 6)
- More developmental neuroscience perspectives on perception (Chapter 6)
- Enhanced coverage of gaze following, joint attention, and theory of mind (Chapter 7)
- Expanded coverage of violation of expectations research and critiques of this approach (Chapter 7)
- More information from developmental neuroscience about cognition and learning (Chapter 7)
- Expanded discussion of parent-child reminiscing and autobiographical memory (Chapter 7)
- New information about joint attention in children with autism (Chapter 7)
- Information about near infrared spectroscopy (NIRS) (Chapters 7 and 8)
- Greater attention to the emergentist coalition model of language acquisition (Chapter 8)

- Addition of the REEL and ITL child language assessments (Chapter 8)
- Expanded coverage about the development of bilingual and multilingual children (Chapter 8)
- More attention to cultural differences in parent-child conversations (Chapter 8)
- New information about language and communication in children with autism (Chapter 8)
- Expansion of postpartum depression to include paternal depression (Chapter 9)
- Addition of the Lab-TAB assessment of early temperament (Chapter 10)
- Theory of mind perspectives on the understanding of emotion (Chapter 10)
- Discussion of the HOME assessment for studying early caregiving environments (Chapter 11)
- Inclusion of the Chicago Longitudinal Study (Chapter 11)
- Expanded discussion of pre-kindergarten (Chapter 11)
- New studies of the impact of TV/DVDs on parent-child interaction and early language development (Chapter 12)

ENGAGING, THOUGHT-PROVOKING CHAPTER OPENERS

Each chapter in this book begins with a thought-provoking, real-life scenario that highlights and introduces key issues and concepts. When I use this approach in my classes, it draws students into the topic from the beginning and enables them to relate subsequent material to specific questions raised at the outset. Examples of these scenarios include infants being sent to wet nurses in eighteenth-century Paris (Chapter 1), linguist Werner Leopold's classic longitudinal study of his infant daughter Hildegard's development as a bilingual child (Chapter 2), and health and physical growth—including brain development—in an infant adopted from an East European orphanage (Chapter 5). Chapter 9 begins with questions about baby shower gifts and the things that all infants need, Chapter 10 asks us to consider what it is that makes the thousands of infants who are named Jacob or Emma each year unique, and Chapter 12 invites us to ponder whether media and computers are among the things that every child needs.

THE BROADER HISTORICAL CONTEXT

In many of the chapters, historical information highlights how far we have come in our understanding of the first 3 years of life. This is seen most prominently in Chapter 1, which contains a comprehensive chronology and many examples of historical perspectives on childhood and the study of child development, but other chapters also contain the historical context for current practices. Chapter 2, for example, considers remarkable discoveries about genetics that have resulted from the Human Genome Project. Chapter 3 reminds us that we did not always understand the vulnerability of the prenatal period, while Chapter 4 discusses trends in childbirth procedures and options. Chapter 11 describes current research on early childcare and early intervention as well as trends in women's employment, parental leave policies, and childcare for infants and toddlers. Chapter 12, which focuses on the presence and role of music, media, and computers in the lives of the very youngest children, recounts the recent history of technology and programming aimed specifically at under-3 audiences.

POLICY CONSIDERATIONS

A number of chapters include policy considerations, in part because these are prominent issues in the field of child development and in part to answer important "so what?" questions. Students everywhere want to know more than just what the latest research shows—they want to know what we can *do* with our knowledge. In Chapter 5, for example, we learn that awareness of the harm caused by lead exposure led to changes in legislation regarding formulas for paint and gasoline, that public health campaigns to keep babies safer by placing them on their backs to sleep led to reductions in the rate of Sudden Infant Death Syndrome, and that awareness of the benefits of human milk led to the establishment of public health goals and hospital practices to support new mothers in breastfeeding. In Chapter 11, we compare the implications of parental leave policies in the United States and in a wide range of other countries, we learn about different ways of measuring the impact of early intervention, and we examine the question of universal pre-kindergarten. In Chapter 12, we explore issues surrounding television and other media for infants and toddlers, including a well-known policy statement from the American Academy of Pediatrics.

PRACTICAL AND THEORETICAL ISSUES

There is a balance in this book between practical and theoretical issues. In Chapter 6, for example, we consider the implications of motor and locomotor development for parents and caregivers who want to make the environment safe for active babies and toddlers. In Chapter 8, we learn about prelinguistic communication and the value of using gestures to help toddlers and caregivers communicate before real words or signs appear. Chapter 9 describes some of the factors that can smooth young children's transition to siblinghood and help to incorporate the new sibling system into existing family relationships.

DIVERSITY AND MULTICULTURAL EXPERIENCE

Students everywhere want and need to understand interconnections between cultural, institutional, familial, and personal experiences. To address these concerns, issues of diversity and multicultural experience are incorporated into virtually every chapter, illustrating how nature and nurture work together. In Chapter 5, we examine nutritional needs and dietary patterns in the United States as well as the effects of malnutrition, which is a significant problem for infants and toddlers in many other parts of the world. In Chapter 6, we learn that there are cultural differences in parents' beliefs about the experiences needed for healthy physical growth and motor development. Chapter 7 introduces the notion of diversity by comparing examples of guided participation in different cultures. As we see in Chapter 8, English is only one of the languages in the world, and many infants and toddlers grow up in a bilingual or multilingual community. Chapter 9 reminds us that there is also diversity in infant-caregiver relationships and that, across cultures, there are different expectations and beliefs about infants' development and the roles that mothers and fathers (and others) play in their care. Chapter 9 also considers several examples of a different kind of diversity: postpartum depression, maltreatment, and early institutionalization and social deprivation. In Chapter 11, our review of childcare discusses the inclusion of children with disabilities, and our examination of early intervention addresses the impact of poverty on development from birth to age 3.

PEDAGOGICAL ELEMENTS

Last, but certainly not least, I have included a number of pedagogical elements that I was not able to find in most of the other infancy books I had used or examined. Each chapter contains a chapter outline, summary and conclusion section, questions for reading and discussion, and clear definitions of key words. With critical thinking skills in mind, many of the questions at the end of each chapter invite students to apply their knowledge or consider it in light of other evidence.

I hope that you enjoy and learn from this book. We know so much about the first 3 years of life, but in many ways the study of infants and their development is still in its own infancy. As new discoveries are made, it is my wish that the chapters in this book will enable you to appreciate and make sense of that information, evaluating it and applying it to the babies and toddlers you know. I would love to hear from you, if you have comments or suggestions. Feel free to get in touch with me at grossd@stolaf.edu.

Dana L. Gross, Ph.D.

Professor of Psychology
St. Olaf College
Northfield, MN

ACKNOWLEDGMENTS

I would never have been inspired to write this book if it were not for all of the students who have joined me in exploring the fascinating journey from birth to age 3. I am grateful for the many ways in which they have made me a better teacher and for their comments on the first edition of this book. I feel fortunate to have received so many specific and useful suggestions from my anonymous reviewers; I tried to incorporate as many of their good ideas as possible. Finally, along the way, many people at Pearson/Allyn & Bacon provided guidance and assistance; I particularly want to thank Stephen Frail and Jeff Marshall for their support throughout the revision process.

Beliefs About Babies: Historical Perspectives on Children and Childhood

Suppose you heard about parents, living in a large city, who sent their newborn infant to live with an unrelated woman in the countryside until the age of 2 to 3 years, never paying a visit to their child during that time. The woman—the family's wet nurse—would have responsibility for all aspects of caring for the baby, especially nursing the infant with her own breast milk. Paid to care for several infants in this way, she might supplement their diet with a concoction called pap, consisting of a small amount of milk, simmered with flour, honey, and perhaps a bit of watered-down wine or beer. She might chew bread or meat, allowing the food to mix with her saliva, before placing it in the infant's mouth. If the infant became ill, the wet nurse might pray to a saint to provide a cure.

Would you approve of this diet and the care being provided? Would you have any concerns about the baby's well-being? How would you feel about the parents, knowing that they had made these arrangements partially in order to make it easier for the mother to return to an active social life and partially in order not to violate a taboo against sexual relations while nursing? Would your opinion of the parents change if you were told that 95 percent of children born in their city that year were nursed by wet nurses for similar reasons and under similar circumstances?

As someone living in the twenty-first century, you almost certainly find this scenario objectionable, but if you were living in Paris, France, in the eighteenth century, you probably would see very little to criticize (Fontanel & d'Harcourt, 1997). You might even feel envious or embarrassed if your family could not afford to hire a wet nurse. Moreover, in the absence of specialized pediatric medicine, which was not developed until the late nineteenth century, you probably would not find fault with the wet nurse's efforts to treat the infant's illness. These divergent views about the proper care and feeding of infants reflect prevalent popular and scientific beliefs then and now. Our focus in this opening chapter is on the events that have transformed, and continue to transform, our thinking about infancy and childhood. We consider historical changes in views about the nature of children and childhood itself, as well as transformations in family structure, health, and education. These evolving perspectives and practices are fascinating, but as we discuss next, they are not the only reason to study infants and their development from birth to age 3.

WHY DO WE STUDY INFANTS?

Why are you interested in studying development from birth to age 3? Do you want to understand a particular infant or toddler better? Are you planning to work with babies or young children in your future career? Do you want to learn how to be an effective parent? There are many good reasons to study infants.

Development as Transformation

One of the most basic reasons to study development during the first three years of life is the significant transformation that occurs in every developmental domain. Even a casual observer of the same child from birth to the age of 3 years would be able to identify dramatic physical changes that occur. Infants not only gain weight and grow in length, but they also learn new skills and demonstrate increasing coordination and intentionality in using those skills. Infants who initially can only swipe at toys that are attached to the front of their car seat or high chair are soon able to be selective in the way that they touch and manipulate those toys. By 3 to 4 months of age, initially immobile newborns learn to roll over, then crawl, and are on their way to independent walking by the time they celebrate their first birthday. The ability to communicate through language also emerges during the first three years of life, opening new opportunities to understand as well as influence young minds. Even before they can communicate through language, however, babies express their feelings and show preferences for parents and other caregivers, reflecting a capacity for memory and for forming special relationships. Which transformations during infancy do you find the most interesting?

Impact of Early Experience

A second reason to study infant development is to understand the impact of early experience on development. From birth to age 3, there is tremendous variability in infants' early experiences and the settings in which they spend time. Some infants are cared for at home by parents, grandparents, or other adults, whereas other infants enter full-time group childcare at an early age. How do parents' choices affect their children's early development? Are there long-lasting effects of early experiences? Does early enrichment, such as watching "brain boosting" videos and DVDs, make a difference later in childhood? Is it possible to overcome the negative effects of early deprivation and adversity, as experienced by infants living in orphanages and other institutional settings? Infants who are born preterm are more likely than ever before to survive; how does their early arrival affect their subsequent development? These and other examples that you may wonder about raise important questions about the degree to which humans are resilient early in life and the extent to which we remain open to the effects of experience during childhood and beyond.

Research Methods and Tools

A third reason to study infants is that we currently have more tools and information available to guide our inquiry than at any previous time. Imaging techniques provide glimpses of the developing fetus, and other prenatal tests give expectant parents and doctors more information than ever before. Advances in technology enable researchers to examine the infant brain and to understand how it is shaped by experience. New understanding of genetics offers intriguing possibilities to predict and even influence infants' health from the earliest point in development. As we discuss in Chapter 2 and throughout the rest of this book, researchers' selection of particular methods and tools enables them to ask infants profound questions long before the subjects of their studies are able to utter their first word.

Many infants and toddlers are cared for by their grandparents.

Interdisciplinary Collaboration

Fourth, this is an ideal time to study infants because there is heightened interest in interdisciplinary collaboration. Pediatricians, early childhood educators, social service providers, researchers in child development, and public policy makers have never been more open to sharing knowledge and working together to improve the conditions in which infants live and, hopefully, thrive. Economists have recently become involved in evaluating intervention programs for infants and toddlers in an effort to identify programs that are worthwhile and cost-effective. Historians, too, have taken an interest in understanding changes in children's experiences over time, as well as reconceptualizations of the nature of childhood and children (Elder, Modell, & Parke, 1993).

RECURRING THEMES IN THE STUDY OF CHILD DEVELOPMENT

As long as there have been infants, there have been beliefs about the factors that affect their development. These beliefs have been incorporated into formal theories in disciplines such as psychology and sociology as well as folk theories held by parents and the general public. Theories about child development are usually specific to particular developmental domains, which means that they tend to focus on topics such as language, memory, or emotion, rather than explain or unify multiple areas of development. For that reason, we introduce specific theories in the chapters about the domains to which the theories pertain. In this section we briefly touch on some of the factors that all developmental theories address—themes that we return to throughout our study of infant development.

The Path of Development: Stages Versus Continuous Change

The field of child development has many theories that describe development as occurring in a **stagewise** fashion, with qualitatively different abilities or characteristics emerging out of the transition from one stage to the next. Stage theories capture the sort of impression that infrequent observations of the same child over the first three years of life might create. At an early visit, the infant would appear to be focused inward, oriented toward his or her own fingers or toes; he or she might show a strong desire to remain close to the parents. A visit several months

Development from birth to age 3 may seem either abrupt or continuous, depending on how frequently children are observed.

later, by contrast, would reveal an infant who seems intent upon crawling or cruising away from the caregiver in order to explore the environment. In this sense, the child would appear to possess a qualitatively different set of motivations and abilities at the second visit than at the first. By the time of a third visit, when the child is 3 years old, the occasional visitor would notice the emergence of language abilities and new forms of play, suggesting that the child had entered a new stage of development.

To parents, or to an observer who sees the child more frequently, daily exposure to the infant would show that there were many subtle changes from birth to the time when independent crawling or walking began. In addition, they would know that the acquisition of new abilities did not occur all at once but was the result of days, weeks, or even months of practice and, initially, failure. Seen in this way, it would appear that development is relatively **continuous,** without clearly marked stages.

Theories differ in terms of whether they describe development as stagewise or continuous. Researchers' beliefs about whether development is stagewise or continuous may influence the measures and designs they use in their studies and the inferences they draw from their data. We examine some of these issues when we consider research methods in the next chapter.

Heredity and the Environment

In every domain of development, there has been debate about whether the amazing transformations during the first three years of life are the result of childrearing practices and experiences in the environment (**nurture**) or whether they occur relatively independently of experience (**nature**) and are the result of some predetermined "program," whether the source of that program is viewed as divine or biological. Researchers have moved away from the strong version of this debate, and no one would plausibly argue today that development is affected only by experiences parents provide. Nor would anyone seriously assert that parents' contributions are unimportant in children's development. Instead, the debate has become more nuanced, with both sides recognizing that there is an interaction of heredity and the environment.

This does not mean that the nurture camp has ceased exploring the effects of experience; indeed, it has become even clearer that there are many coexisting, interacting environmental influences in children's lives (Bronfenbrenner & Morris, 1998; Ramey, Ramey, & Lanzi, 2006). Children are influenced by environments in both direct and indirect ways, including settings in which they never spend time, such as their parents' workplace. Parents who have stressful jobs, for example, may be more impatient and less sensitive interacting with their infants at home than parents whose work is less emotionally draining. The quality of the care that infants receive is also affected by the wider neighborhood or community in which they live, as well as the cultural context and even the historical period.

The nature proponents, for their part, have also continued to provide new levels of analysis. Early research in embryology provided a foundation that has been built upon by modern-day studies of prenatal development, aided by high-tech tools that enable researchers to view the developing fetus with increasing clarity and precision. Early twentieth-century notions about the brain's development during infancy have been expanded and modified as well by recent advances in neuroscience.

Thanks to the Human Genome Project, we know more than ever before about the genetic material that provides a "blueprint" for development. The evidence is clear that even some aspects of development that appear to be "prewired" are influenced by experience. Dietary regulation, for example, can alter the effects of a genetic predisposition for the disease phenylketonuria (PKU), preventing cognitive disabilities that would occur otherwise. Exposure to alcohol during the prenatal

From birth, babies are prepared to respond to and elicit responses from parents and other caregivers.

period, as another example, can anesthetize the fetus, interfering with the movement of arms and legs and changing the normal course of the brain's development and later functioning. Children's biologically influenced characteristics, such as whether they are "easy" or "difficult" babies, also have an impact on the responses they elicit from parents and other caregivers. Despite their shared genes, identical twins exhibit different amounts of positive and negative social behaviors toward other children and adults if their parents consistently show more affection to one twin but are hostile and punitive toward the other child. As these examples and others throughout this book confirm, it is now clear that development occurs as a result of nature *and* nurture.

Active or Passive Development?

Throughout history, parents, philosophers, social reformers, and scientists have tended to view infants as relatively incompetent, passive creatures, playing only a minimal role in their own development. The childrearing advice given to parents tended to reflect this perspective, and parents were seen as the most important agents in the processes of education, socialization, physical development, and personality formation.

There is clear evidence, however, that from birth babies are prepared to respond to and elicit responses from parents and other caregivers. Even very young infants are capable of communicating many of their needs nonverbally by cooing, crying, and reaching. They also learn about the physical world as they act upon and explore it using different methods at different ages, first mouthing objects and later fingering, grasping, banging, and dropping them. Contemporary theories of infant development incorporate infants' surprisingly sophisticated capabilities, and many empirical studies measure changes that result from infants' own actions as well as the actions of their caregivers.

Normal and Atypical Development

Just as we now know that infants are much more capable than previously thought, it is also clear that infants develop at different rates. Parents of two or more children can usually report which one rolled over, sat up, or began walking first; when two or more parents are together, they inevitably make comparisons between their infants. Parents who conclude that their child is precocious may feel a sense of pride or validation of their parenting, even when the milestone is something over which they have no direct influence, such as the eruption of the child's first tooth. It can be worrisome, though, if the baby seems significantly slower to develop than other babies, and parents may wonder if their infant is within the normal range of development. Infants with atypical development, whether in the physical, cognitive, or socioemotional domain, present a challenge to parents and caregivers, but they also can and should be included in activities and programs with more typically developing children. In the chapters that follow, we consider recent research on atypical development in infancy, focusing on everyday issues as well as the implications for theories about normal development.

Culture and Context

Across contemporary cultures, there are many differences in the ways that parents care for and interact with their infants (DeLoache & Gottlieb, 2000; Harkness, Moscardino, Blom, et al., in press; Shore, 2004). In some cultures, in contrast to typical arrangements in the United States, infants and parents share the same bed, even when there would be room in the house for children to sleep elsewhere by themselves (Harkness & Super, 2001; Morelli et al., 1992). In addition, although many U.S. parents play games and engage in pretend play with their infants and toddlers, these practices are not universal (Parmar, Harkness, & Super, 2008; Roopnarine, Johnson, & Hooper, 1994). In the rest of this book, we examine some of these differences and consider what they reveal about the nature—and nurture—of early development.

We also endeavor to understand the richness and diversity of parenting practices within the United States. As we discuss family life, for example, we need to remember that, before European immigrants arrived in the New World, there were numerous and diverse Native American cultures. Daily family life and customs involving marriage, birth, and childrearing reflected worldviews that prevailed in each culture and geographical region. In some groups, each nuclear family functioned as a separate unit and lived in its own dwelling, but in others households consisted of several nuclear families sharing a common long house. In many Native American cultures, elaborate ceremonies involving members of the community were performed at the birth of a child, and other adults in the community were often responsible for guiding and supporting the child at significant milestones in life, practices that remain important today (Gill, 2002).

The diversity and validity of Native American family life has not always been recognized or supported in the United States.

The diversity and validity of Native American family life has not always been recognized or supported. For much of U.S. history, American Indians were encouraged or coerced to follow European patterns of childrearing, and differences among tribes were either dismissed or not recognized. It was not until 1978, when the Indian Child Welfare Act was passed, that the intrinsic value of American Indian cultures and extended families was recognized at the federal level. Although there are still concerns about interpretation and implementation, the law has resulted in fewer children being removed from their families, a practice that had occurred in the past for as many as 25 to 35 percent of all American Indian children (Goodluck, 1999).

A history of family disruption is also part of the experience of the majority of African Americans, a phenomenon that can be traced back to the practice of slavery. As historians have noted, however, there were also African Americans who were free while others were enslaved, and it is important to recognize differences in past experience as well as the great diversity in family structure and parenting style that exists among contemporary African American families (Hatchett & Jackson, 1999; McAdoo, 1999).

Similarly, whereas some Mexican American families and families of Spanish descent have been in the United States since the eighteenth and nineteenth centuries, there are also many who immigrated during the second half of the twentieth century from Mexico as well as Puerto Rico, the Caribbean, and Central and South America (McAdoo, 1999). Researchers now recognize that there are many different parenting styles among these groups (Chahin, Villarruel, & Viramontez, 1999; Martinez, 1999; Suárez, 1999).

Great diversity of experience, beliefs, and behaviors are also found among families who are often grouped together as Asian American. Chinese immigrants, for example, began arriving in the United States in 1820 but were actively prevented from coming to and being integrated into the United States after 1882, when the Chinese Exclusion Act was passed (Lin & Liu, 1999; Ou & McAdoo, 1999). Vietnamese families, by contrast, largely immigrated to the United States in three distinct waves during the 1970s and 1980s (Gold, 1999).

In recent years, refugees from unstable countries, such as Somalia, Sudan, and Myanmar (Burma) have found new homes in the United States, often in communities that bear little resemblance to the villages and cities from which they came (Office of Refugee Resettlement, 2007). Differences in family structure, social class, and educational background prior to immigration, as well as differences in community sponsorship and support, have had a significant impact on each of these groups' experience.

In summary, the United States is becoming a more diverse nation in an increasingly interconnected world. Awareness of cultural and ethnic diversity is essential if we are to understand the many different settings in which infants develop. This awareness also reminds us that ideas about proper childrearing practices are often a function of time and place. As we discuss next, historical comparisons, such as the image of an eighteenth-century infant being sent off to a wet nurse, may also help us perceive both change and continuity in perspectives on infants and their development.

HISTORICAL PERSPECTIVES ON INFANCY AND EARLY CHILDHOOD

Views about children and their development have changed throughout history. In the past, like today, there was not always agreement concerning the proper care of infants and the role of children in society. As we summarize major trends and turning points in perspectives on infants and their development, it is important to remove the sentimental lens through which we may view children and families, especially when we consider times that some now regard as "simpler" days. From the vantage point of the mid-twentieth century, for example, some historians (Ariès, 1962) painted a picture of medieval times as a freer, more equitable era for children. According to this perspective, children's lives may have been better before adults removed them from the working world and sequestered them in school for years of compulsory education. This nostalgic interpretation has been challenged, however, by historical research showing that children in the past were more likely to be killed, abandoned, exploited, and abused (Boswell, 1988; Clement, 1997; Hawes & Hiner, 1985).

Historical Studies of Children and Childhood

Given that parents and children who lived in earlier times cannot be observed or interviewed, how do historians know what their lives were like and what adults of the time thought about them? Three major sources of information have been used: (1) **literary evidence,** including parents' diaries and letters; childrearing advice written by midwives, ministers, and doctors; and children's books; (2) **quantitative archival evidence,** such as census data, tax records; and legislative and court records; and (3) **material culture,** such as toys, clothing, furniture, and works of art. When interpreting these sources, historians are aware—and we should be too—that many of the details about daily life probably were not recorded, because they were viewed as ordinary and unimportant. It is also possible that diaries included entries about problems that parents encountered with their infants, rather than successes, leading modern readers to assume that there was a greater prevalence of problems than successes (Pollack, 1983). Where records do exist, they generally represent families who were educated, wealthy, or prominent. It is also important to recognize that beliefs and behavior do not always match; as is true today, even when parents had childrearing manuals and were able to read them, it cannot be assumed that they followed the advice they contained (Colón & Colón, 2001; Hulbert, 2003; Pollack, 1983; Schulz, 1985).

Historians of childhood continue to debate the interpretation of evidence. Some have argued that, despite social and technological changes, examining available materials in their entirety reveals significant continuity and surprisingly little change in parent-child relationships, even when the time span considered covers the years 1500 to 1900. According to some historians, for example, far from tolerating or ignoring child abuse and abandonment, in the past most parents, and society as a whole, looked at these practices with horror and outrage, much as parents and other adults do today. There is also evidence that parents who sent their infants to wet nurses were emotionally attached to them and took steps to remove their children from these arrangements if they discovered conditions of neglect or abuse (Pollack, 1983).

There is compelling evidence that parents have always wondered about their children's development, even before birth, and have taken steps to promote their well-being. Views about proper childrearing methods and even definitions of childhood itself have often changed, however, because they are cultural inventions, constructions that reflect a society's basic shared beliefs and values at a particular point in time (Borstelmann, 1983; Cahan et al., 1993; Colón & Colón, 2001; Hulbert, 2003). The impermanence of childrearing beliefs and practices is reflected in a significant reversal that occurred by the nineteenth century in Paris; wealthy women began nursing their own infants, and poorer mothers who worked outside of the home were the ones hiring wet nurses (Colón & Colón, 2001).

Many scholars have documented the history of children and childhood, but a complete consideration of these historical studies is beyond the scope of this chapter. Instead, we focus on three key issues: changing views of children, family life, and education. In addition, although we consider some aspects of childhood in ancient Greece and Rome, as well as medieval and Renaissance Europe, our main focus is on the United States and the time from the nineteenth century to the present. Table 1.1 shows a chronology of events that affected children in the United States from the seventeenth century to the present time.

TABLE 1.1	A Chronology of Childhood and Child Development in the United States
1619	Poor English children are shipped to Virginia for their families' financial gain; indentured service and apprenticeships await them.
	Twenty Africans—the first slaves brought to the colonies—arrive in Virginia.
1624	In Jamestown, Virginia, the first African American child is born to slave parents.
1642	Massachusetts statute requires parents and masters to teach children to learn to read and to learn a trade.
1662	Virginia law specifies that a mother's status as slave or free person determines her children's status.
1688	The first formal antislavery resolution is passed by the Quakers of Pennsylvania.
1721	Inoculation for smallpox is introduced in Boston.
1776–1830s	Public schools are established in North Carolina, Vermont, Virginia, New York, Massachusetts, and Pennsylvania.
1777	Vermont is the first state to abolish slavery.
1819	Civilization Fund forces Native American people to cast aside their religious views, practices, and languages; Native American children are separated from their families and sent to off-reservation boarding schools in which their native language is forbidden.
1820s–1840s	Infant school movement is imported from Europe.
1824	Bureau of Indian Affairs is established.
1830	Indian Removal Act forces most of the Native American population in the southeastern United States to move to Oklahoma.
1833	American Anti-Slavery Society is created; leaders from 10 states meet in Philadelphia.
1836	Massachusetts is the first state to adopt a compulsory school attendance law.
1842	In Massachusetts and Connecticut, the working day for children under 12 years of age is limited to 10 hours.
1850s–1870s	Organizations for the protection of poor, abused, abandoned, and orphaned children are founded, including the New York Children's Aid Society, the New York Catholic Protectory, and the New York Society for the Prevention of Cruelty to Children.
1856	In Wisconsin, the first kindergarten opens, based on the philosophy of Frederich Froebel.
1863	Abraham Lincoln signs the Emancipation Proclamation, freeing slaves in all states.
1865	Slavery in the United States is outlawed when the 13th Amendment is ratified. The Bureau of Refugees, Freedmen, and Abandoned Lands is established to assist former slaves.
1882	The Chinese Exclusion Act limits immigration and integration into the United States.
1880s	Pediatrics becomes organized, with journals and professional societies established.
1890s	Milk stations (milk depots) are established in major American cities to dispense bacteria-free milk and advice about infant feeding and hygiene.
1897	National Congress of Mothers is founded (later renamed National Congress of Parents and Teachers).

TABLE 1.1	Continued
1906–1912	Organizations promoting the moral and physical well-being of children and youth are established, including the Playground and Recreation Association of America, Boy Scouts of America, Campfire Girls, and Girl Scouts of America.
1914	U.S. Children's Bureau, created in 1912, publishes *Infant Care,* a childcare manual urging parents to adopt a child-centered approach in which they place the child's welfare at the center of family life.
1918	Mississippi adopts compulsory school attendance law, the last state to do so.
1920	Fertility rate is 3.2 (average number of children born to white women).
1928	The National Foundation for Infantile Paralysis (later renamed the March of Dimes) is established to raise funds for research into the causes and prevention of poliomyelitis.
1934	Indian Reorganization Act is enacted to enable conservation and development of Native American lands and resources by and for Native American communities; required "pedigree papers" to be issued by each tribe.
1935	Social Security Act provides aid to dependent children, maternal and child health programs, disabled children's programs, and child welfare services.
1940	Inequalities among children, especially rural, low-income, migrant, and minority children, are noted in White House Conference on Children in a Democracy.
1946–1964	"Baby Boom" changes U.S. demographics in post–World War II period.
1950	Midcentury White House Conference on Children and Youth is held.
1953	Department of Health, Education, and Welfare is established.
	Dr. Jonas Salk reports success of polio vaccine.
1954	*Brown v. Board of Education* court case leads to end of racial segregation in schools.
1964	Head Start is established as part of the War on Poverty to serve low-income children between the ages of 3 and 5 years.
1972	Smallpox vaccination is discontinued in the United States due to eradication of the virus.
	American Indian Education Act incorporates Native American language and culture into education.
1973	Children's Defense Fund begins advocacy of children's issues, especially those concerning low-income and disabled children.
1977	Zero To Three is founded by child development experts to disseminate information about the significance of the first three years of life.
	World Health Organization (WHO) efforts result in the eradication of all smallpox viruses, except for samples stored for government research purposes.
1978	Louise Brown, first "test-tube" baby (from *in vitro* fertilization) is born in England.
	Pregnancy Discrimination Act prohibits employment discrimination on the basis of pregnancy or childbirth.
	Indian Child Welfare Act strengthens families by ending the practice of removing Native American children from their homes and placing them with non-Native American families off the reservation.

(continued)

TABLE 1.1	Continued
1979	Department of Health and Human Services (DHHS) is created when a separate Department of Education is established. Within the DHHS, the Administration for Children and Families is organized to oversee a number of programs and services, including Head Start.
1980	The WHO recommends that all countries stop vaccinating for smallpox.
1990	Americans with Disabilities Act (ADA) is passed to protect the civil rights of all individuals with disabilities. Children with disabilities are covered by the Individuals with Disabilities Education Act (IDEA).
	Native American Language Act is passed to preserve native languages.
1991	Poliomyelitis is eliminated from the Americas, leading the March of Dimes to refocus its efforts, becoming the March of Dimes Birth Defects Foundation.
1992	European Union mandates a paid 14-week maternity leave.
	American Academy of Pediatrics recommends that all infants be placed on their back or side to sleep to prevent Sudden Infant Death Syndrome.
	U.S. Family and Medical Leave Act is passed to enable up to 12 weeks of unpaid, job-protected leave to care for a newborn infant, a newly adopted child or a foster child, or a spouse or parent with a serious health condition.
1994	Early Head Start is established to serve low-income pregnant women and families with infants and toddlers from birth to age 3.
1996	American Academy of Pediatrics recommends that all infants be placed on their back to sleep to prevent Sudden Infant Death Syndrome.
1997	State Children's Health Insurance Program (SCHIP) is established to provide health insurance to children in families without other means of obtaining health insurance.
	White House Conference on Early Childhood Development and Learning is held.
1998	European Union institutes a three-month parental leave.
2000	Human Genome Project completes "working draft" of the human genome.
	Fertility rate (average number of children born to all women over a lifetime) is 2.1.
2001	Canadian Employment Insurance Act expands paid leave benefits from six months to one year for mothers as well as fathers.
2002	SCHIP coverage provides prenatal and delivery care for low-income women.
2004	California is the first U.S. state to enact a paid family leave policy.
2005	American Academy of Pediatrics endorses the use of pacifiers and back-sleeping for all infants and recommends that infants not sleep with parents in order to prevent Sudden Infant Death Syndrome.
2006	Institute of Medicine of the National Academies publishes *Preterm Birth: Causes, Consequences, and Prevention,* reporting disparities in preterm birth rates among different racial and ethnic groups.
2007	Improving Head Start for School Readiness Act reauthorizes Head Start through 2012, allowing for expanded funding of Early Head Start.
2008	Fostering Connections to Success and Increasing Adoptions Act is enacted to improve outcomes for children in foster care and promote more permanent and stable families by supporting relative caregivers and expanding access to funding and services for Native American and Native Alaskan tribal groups.

TABLE 1.1	Continued
2009	American Academy of Pediatrics recommends that the diagnosis Abusive Head Trauma be used in place of Shaken Baby Syndrome.
2009	New York is the first of many states to pass a Safe Baby Bottle Act banning bisphenol-A (BPA) in baby bottles, sippy cups, and other children's products, due to concerns about the effects of BPA on the hormonal system and links to later-life health problems and diseases.

Source: Based on Bremner et al., 1970; Christian, Block and the Committee on Child Abuse and Neglect, 2009; Harjo, 1999; Hawes & Hiner, 1985; Helfand, Lazarus, & Theerman, 2001; Hulbert, 1999; Low & Clift, 1984; Mathews, MacDorman, & Menacker, 2002; Noymer, 2002; Population Reference Bureau/Child Trends, 2002; and Silvey, 1999.

Views of Children

At many points in history, parents and other adults have debated the true nature of children, and at any given time, differing attitudes and opinions have coexisted. Some have regarded children as innocent, naïve, and unformed, whereas others have viewed them as possessing innate, sometimes undesirable characteristics and predispositions that need to be modified through parents' actions. Views of children at any given time determine the degree to which systems and policies are in place to protect them and promote their development.

ANCIENT GREECE AND ROME Stages of growth and development were noted in ancient times, and distinctions were made between infants, young children, and adolescents. Children in ancient Greece and Rome were valued as the future of society, but they were generally regarded as property and had few rights (Borstelmann, 1983). Boys in particular were valued as future warriors, and parents were required to have infant males inspected to be sure that they were healthy and sufficiently well formed to benefit from rigorous training and education. Infants who did not pass this inspection were abandoned and left to die of exposure (Colón & Colón, 2001).

Early Roman law required parents to raise all healthy male infants and at least one of the female infants born to them. Infants were abandoned for a number of reasons, including gender, poverty, illegitimacy, and birth defects (Boswell, 1988). Infanticide and maltreatment of infants and young children were practiced for many years before Roman emperors, beginning around the year 100 CE, acted to protect children through legal reforms (Colón & Colón, 2001).

MEDIEVAL EUROPE In medieval Europe (approximately 500 to 1300 CE), plagues killed many people, and fewer written records remain than from ancient Greece and Rome (Boswell, 1988). According to the documents that did survive this era, **infant mortality rates** (the number of deaths per 1,000 live births, before the age of 1 year) were high, and perhaps as many as one or two of every three children died in the first year of life (comparison statistics for infant mortality at other times in history are shown in Table 1.2). Parents used the only means available to them, usually charms and amulets of various kinds, to protect their infants from harm and sickness (Fontanel & d'Harcourt, 1997). One of the "ailments" that parents feared during the Middle Ages (and well into the mid-nineteenth century) was teething. Infants who were teething often suffered from fevers, convulsions, and diarrhea brought on by parasites, cholera, or respiratory diseases, so many parents erroneously believed that teething per se could prove fatal. Remedies for teething and its accompanying illnesses included placing leeches on the baby's gums, hanging amulets around the baby's neck, or following other superstitious

TABLE 1.2 Infant Mortality Rates in Historical and International Perspective[a,b]	
Historical Era	**Infant Mortality Rate**
Number of deaths per 1,000 live births by the age of 1 year:	
United States	
1920	100.0
1940	47.0
1945	38.3
1984	12.6
1990	8.9
2002	7.0
2000 International Comparisons[b]	
Number of deaths per 1,000 live births by the age of 5 years:	
Industrialized Countries[c]	6
Latin America/Caribbean	37
East Asia/Pacific	44
South Asia	100
Middle East/North Africa	64
Former USSR/Central Eastern Europe	38
Sub-Saharan Africa	175

Notes: (a) Based on information in Hawes & Hiner, 1985; and Mathews, MacDorman, & Menacker, 2002.
(b) Population Reference Bureau/Child Trends, 2002. (c) Western Europe, the United States, Australia, and Israel.

practices that were thought to transfer the baby's ailment to some other person or object (Fontanel & d'Harcourt, 1997; Howe, 1998).

Given the high rate of infant mortality, there was great concern about the souls of deceased infants. Parents whose infants became ill often went on a religious pilgrimage or prayed to the "first pediatricians of Christianity"—saints specializing in children and their illnesses, including Saint Quintin (whooping cough), Saint Blaise (sore throats), Saint Apollonia (toothaches), Saint Nicholas (colic and diarrhea), and Saint Medard (parasitic worms). One healing pediatric saint was Saint Guinefort, a greyhound who had been killed while defending his young. In praying to Saint Guinefort, parents hoped that he would remove the sick creature (a changeling) that had been left in their child's place by forest sprites and return their real child. If the child recovered, it was taken as proof that Guinefort had defeated the devilish forest sprites and their real child had been returned. If the child died, on the other hand, parents could tell themselves that the child had not been theirs (Boswell, 1988; Fontanel & d'Harcourt, 1997).

In early medieval Europe, just as in ancient times, infants were still abandoned and left to die of exposure, and laws even supported parents' rights to sell their children into servitude (Boswell, 1988). By the beginning of the seventh century, another form of abandonment—**oblation**—had been established. Oblation was the permanent "donation" of an infant or very young child to a monastery. The practice removed the requirement of servitude per se, but by law, oblates were required to remain in the monastery for the remainder of their lives. In comparison with other forms of abandonment, oblation offered parents assurance that their child would survive, be well fed, and even receive some education as part of a "family" in which all of the children were adopted (Boswell, 1988).

As early as the eighth century, religious leaders showed concern for abandoned infants by establishing asylums and orphanages. In response to alarm about the numbers of infants who were drowned or left to die of exposure, and to offer parents an alternative to infanticide, between 787 and 1421, infant asylums were founded, first in Italy and later in other major European cities (Boswell, 1988; Colón & Colón, 2001; Fontanel & d'Harcourt, 1997).

In some wealthy families, infant abandonment functioned as a way of reducing the number of possible heirs among whom the father's property and wealth would need to be divided. Changes in inheritance laws in some parts of Europe, such as England, allowed a single heir to be designated, resulting in a reduction in infant abandonment (Borstelmann, 1983). Among poor families, the practice of infant abandonment declined when opportunities developed for impoverished children to earn a living by becoming servants in the households of wealthy families. In other parts of Europe that did not experience an increase in prosperity, or where overpopulation was a problem, however, abandonment and infanticide, especially of illegitimate children, appear to have continued. Legislation in the thirteenth century focused on whether abandoned infants should be baptized. The main consequence for parents who knowingly abandoned their infants was loss of the right to control or reclaim the child in the future. Poverty-stricken parents (usually fathers) had the legal right to sell their children (Boswell, 1988).

THE RENAISSANCE   During the Renaissance (approximately 1300–1500), as in previous times, children continued to be abandoned and left at the doors of churches or in publicly run foundling homes. These institutions, which were the precursor to orphanages and children's hospitals, developed systems through which mothers could anonymously leave their newborns. In some cases, there was a depository with a revolving tray on which the infant could be placed and transferred indoors, out of the harsh elements (Boswell, 1988; Colón & Colón, 2001; Fontanel & d'Harcourt, 1997). Sadly, infants taken into these foundling homes may have been more likely to die than infants who previously had been abandoned surreptitiously and then rescued by adoptive parents. Records from the fourteenth century show that, as a result of poor hygiene and an absence of effective medical care, 20 to 40 percent of infants died within a year, many within a month, of arriving in the foundling home. By comparison, the mortality rate among infants sent to wet nurses during the same time was about 17 percent (Boswell, 1988).

Many Renaissance thinkers contemplated ways to create a perfect society, as exemplified by Sir Thomas More's *Utopia* (1516). More's book, like much literature from the late Renaissance, pondered human values, the difference between good and evil, and the path to virtue. Religious reformers in Europe asserted that parents had a duty "to produce good Christian souls, along with good, healthy human beings of limitless potential" (Colón & Colón, 2001, p. 284). The ideal child was described as pious, disciplined, obedient, and teachable. The debate about whether infants were inherently innocent or corrupt continued in Europe and was exported to Puritan colonies that were established in the New World by the middle of the seventeenth century.

COLONIAL AMERICA   For Puritans in the New World, infancy began in the womb and prayers were needed because infants were believed to be conceived in sin. Prenatal care, therefore, was both physical and spiritual (Beales, 1985). At birth, children were regarded as "innocent vipers," likely to commit evil but not yet able to understand the nature of their acts, ignorant of Scriptures and inherently sinful but capable of becoming enlightened and restrained. Pious parents had two tasks, instruction and discipline (Moran & Vinovskis, 1985). Puritan attitudes about these tasks are reflected in advice from John Robinson, minister of the Plymouth Colony (1625), who wrote, "And surely there is in all children, though not alike a stubbornness, and stoutness of mind arising from natural pride, which must, in the first place be broken and beaten down" (cited in Moran & Vinovskis, 1985, p. 26).

Despite the harshness of these words to our twenty-first-century ears, there is evidence that Puritan parents were devoted to and loved their children. Given the likelihood that at least some of their children would not live beyond their first year, parents showed love and concern for their infants' souls by baptizing them early, usually within one to two weeks of their birth. Other signs of Puritans' love for their children include expressions of grief in letters and diaries after a child had died and the common practice of naming subsequent children after deceased siblings. The care and training of children were the nuclear family's responsibility, but concerns about spoiling them with too much affection led some Puritan families to send their offspring to live with other Puritan families for a time (Beales, 1985; Hareven, 2000; Pollack, 1983).

Throughout the colonial period, epidemics of smallpox, diphtheria, scarlet fever, yellow fever, intestinal diseases, and influenza occurred in waves. Smallpox was particularly deadly, especially for young children; some parents inoculated their children against the disease after the practice was introduced in Boston in 1721, but the practice was controversial. Children also died of ordinary childhood diseases, including measles, whooping cough, and mumps. Slave children often suffered from malnutrition, with the result that the mortality rate for young black children was twice that of white children. In addition, because colonial children's homes were not "baby-proofed," many young children died or were seriously injured in accidents in and around the home (Colón & Colón, 2001; Schulz, 1985).

Unlike the Parisian parents described at the beginning of this chapter, most Puritan parents did not employ wet nurses (Finkelstein, 1985). Instead, mothers nursed their infants themselves, a practice that was thought to impart the mother's positive qualities and pious attitudes to the child early on. Coincidentally and fortuitously, antibodies in the mother's milk also afforded infants at least some degree of temporary immunity from the diseases surrounding them (Beales, 1985).

During the seventeenth and eighteenth centuries, Puritan parents' diaries became increasingly focused on childhood and childrearing as abstract concepts. Whereas earlier diaries noted children's specific misbehaviors and parents' responses to those actions, for example, later records described general approaches to childrearing and philosophies about discipline. Parents increasingly wrote about their efforts to train their children to think and behave in morally correct ways (Pollack, 1983).

During the nineteenth century, an increasingly romantic view of childhood emerged, and young children came to be seen as the redeemers of a more complex, possibly corrupt, industrialized society (Borstelmann, 1983). In a sense, childhood was discovered anew. The home was envisioned as a refuge from the outside world (Hareven, 1985, 2000), and the mother's role as moral guardian was sentimentalized and emphasized in numerous publications. In *The Mother at Home* (1834), for example, the Rev. John Abbott wrote, "O mothers! . . . There is no earthly influence to be compared with yours. There is no combination of causes so powerful, in promoting the happiness or the misery of our race, as the instructions of home" (p. 167).

Before the age of 5 or 6 years, children were regarded as creatures under the control of animal impulses. For this reason, infants and very young children were thought to need "guidance, not repression, activity rather than confinement, sensitive tutoring from a totally available, benevolent mentor" (Finkelstein, 1985, p. 124). Because mothers were viewed as inherently gentle and morally superior, they were seen by many as the ideal agents to protect children through a concentrated, socially isolated relationship in an environment that they controlled (Finkelstein, 1985).

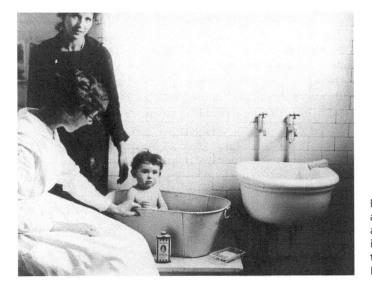

Beginning in the 1890s, advice about infant care, feeding, and hygiene was dispensed to immigrant parents in locations that included New York City's Ellis Island.

The sentimentality directed toward motherhood began to change toward the end of the nineteenth century, as scientific professionals emerged to assist mothers in making the right choices for their children. Mothers themselves played a central role in bringing about this collaboration. As early as 1888, for example, a group of affluent, educated New York City mothers established the Society for the Study of Child Nature. Soon after that, mothers' clubs and child study groups were formed across the country. The National Congress of Mothers (later renamed the National Congress of Parents and Teachers) was founded in 1897, as "the widespread mood of a closing century coalesced into a self-conscious institutionalized movement for a new era" (Hulbert, 1999, p. 21). At the 1899 National Congress of Mothers, Dr. Luther Emmett Holt, one of America's first pediatricians and author of *The Care and Feeding of Children* (1894), reflected this mood when he endorsed systematic, scientific study as the best way to promote children's health and development (Hulbert, 1999).

Holt's advice found a receptive audience because scientific study had shown that bacteria in urban milk supplies were the likely source of fatal infections and diseases in infants. To address this problem, child-health activists established milk stations, first in New York City during the 1890s, and later in other U.S. cities. As milk stations became more widespread, advice about infant care, feeding, and hygiene was dispensed along with the milk (Colón & Colón, 2001; Halpern, 1988).

As waves of new immigrants arrived in the United States and settled in urban areas with large populations, members of the clergy, educators, and social observers became concerned about the children. Disease and illness, including cholera, tuberculosis, and infant diarrhea, were rampant; hunger and malnutrition were common (Berrol, 1985). In response to these conditions, from 1800 until 1835, clergy members established protective settings, such as Sunday schools for infants in the factories where their parents worked (Finkelstein, 1985).

Another sign of concern for child welfare at the end of the nineteenth century was the emergence of the Progressive Movement, which was active from the 1890s until the 1920s. The available evidence suggests that Progressives were motivated by a mixture of feelings, including humanitarian altruism, concern, fear, confusion, and a desire to exert control over the changing urban environment (Cohen, 1985). Regardless of their motives, members of the Progressive movement were involved in the establishment of a growing number of private and public institutions, all of which existed to counteract the negative influence of the adult world on children (Finkelstein, 1985).

Public policy and interventions addressing the problems of children and families became established during the twentieth century, and many are now a familiar part of twenty-first-century life. Continuing their activities from the beginning of the twentieth century, women's organizations throughout the country called for and organized child study initiatives to document and solve child welfare problems. They also lobbied for federal support of studies of children's health and development. In 1912, they were rewarded by the establishment of the United States Children's Bureau, which was designed to serve as a clearinghouse for information about the best childrearing practices. In 1914, the Children's Bureau published the first edition of *Infant Care,* a manual distributed at no cost to millions of new parents (Cohen, 1985; Cravens, 1985). The federal government lacked the funds to produce significant change, however, and in the end philanthropic foundations formed partnerships with universities in support of the scientific study of children and their development (Cravens, 1985). We return to the scientific study of child development later in this chapter. For now, we consider some of the ways in which family life has varied.

Family Life

Immigrants to the New World in the early seventeenth century brought their old customs, beliefs, and childrearing practices with them. It is difficult to generalize about their experience in the American colonies because, like today, childhood and family life were affected by the characteristics of the local community (Beales, 1985; Schulz, 1985). The best records of colonial families come from Puritans who settled in New England.

In the seventeenth century, most New England women married in their late teens or early twenties and began having children within the first year of marriage. Women typically continued having children, at two-year intervals, until they were in their late 30s or early 40s (Beales, 1985). Families thus had a relatively large number of children, by today's standards, but the high rate of infant mortality (between 10 and 30 percent of infants did not survive beyond the age of 1 year) meant that the household itself was not necessarily that large at all times (Schulz, 1985). The basic family unit was the nuclear family, with kinship networks nearby providing an important source of support (Hareven, 1985, 2000).

The Industrial Revolution changed family life dramatically in the United States. At the beginning of this period, most children lived in rural areas and grew up farming with their parents and a relatively large number of siblings (in 1865, 82 percent of families had five or more children). By the mid-twentieth century, by contrast, most children had fewer siblings (in 1930, 57 percent lived in families with three or fewer children) and lived in urban areas with populations of 10,000 or more (Hernandez, 1997). The effects of the Great Depression on family life in the 1930s, are well documented but beyond the scope of this chapter. In general, it appears that children born during the years of greatest economic hardship were more negatively affected than children whose first years of life occurred when their families—and the country as a whole—were more affluent (Elder, 1974; Elder & Hareven, 1993). This finding, which is echoed whenever we discuss the effects of poverty and parenting stress due to financial hardship, reflects the unique vulnerability of the youngest children in families—infants and toddlers (Evans, 2004; Shonkoff & Phillips, 2000).

A defining demographic trend—the Baby Boom—occurred in the years following World War II (1946–1964), with the peak occurring in 1957. Babies born at this time, unlike those born during the Depression, entered a world in which the United States was experiencing a new child-centered period of prosperity. During the Baby Boomers' formative years, families, schools, and community life were transformed in important ways. There was an increase in the proportion of Americans marrying and a decline in the number of childless couples. The average age at which women married decreased from 21.5 in 1940 to 20.1 in 1956 (Strickland & Ambrose, 1985). For comparison, the corresponding age was 23 in 1970 and 25 in 2003 (Fox, Connolly, & Snyder, 2005). In addition, more couples were having their first child within 13 months of their marriage, and more than half of women marrying for the first time gave birth to their first child before they were 20 (Strickland & Ambrose, 1985).

Studies of childrearing patterns in the 1950s suggest that middle-class parents, especially young, first-time mothers, regarded their role in ways that were different from prewar parents. Many parents at this time were influenced by Dr. Benjamin Spock's (1946) *The Common Sense Book of Baby and Child Care,* which sold more than 28 million copies and, by 1976, had become the best-selling book in the twentieth century, after the Bible. In addition to medical advice, Spock urged parents to adopt a child-centered, "commonsense" approach for socializing children, intended to minimize confrontation and conflict in the family. He encouraged mothers to monitor their children's growth and development and to gently and tactfully guide them toward becoming a cooperative member of a happy family (Strickland & Ambrose, 1985). Spock's goals also included alleviating mothers' anxiety about childrearing, since he believed that anxiety itself could be harmful to children's development. Ultimately, the book was intended to help parents create a more democratic society (Hulbert, 2003; Strickland & Ambrose, 1985). As shown in Table 1.3, Spock's advice about toilet training also reflected attitude changes in the 1940s (Brazelton et al., 1999).

TABLE 1.3 Changes in Attitudes and Advice about Toilet Training	
Years	**Attitudes and Advice**
1920s/1930s	A rigid, parent-centered approach to toilet training was recommended. This view was in keeping with the theoretical positions of well-known child development experts, such as John B. Watson.
1940s/1950s	Experts, including Benjamin Spock, rejected absolute and rigid rules for toilet training. It was believed that rushing children or being too harsh with them might fail and lead to behavioral problems. Parents were advised to look for "signs of readiness" in their child and to communicate with them in order to enlist their cooperation before beginning training.
1950s/1960s	Pediatricians, such as T. Berry Brazelton, proposed a child-oriented gradual method. Based on notions of child readiness, this approach integrated physical, emotional, and cognitive elements. Child readiness was believed to be present in most children by the age of about 18 months. Surveys from 1951 to 1961 showed that approximately one-half of children were continent during the day by the age of 27 months, and nearly all children (98 percent) were fully toilet trained by the age of 36 months.
1960s/1970s	Experts, such as Nathan Azrin and Richard Foxx, used applied behavior analysis as the basis for structured-behavioral toilet training. In published reports, their method was said to achieve toilet training with normal, healthy toddlers in an average of 3.9 hours. The Azrin-Foxx method incorporated notions of child readiness with principles of applied behavior analysis.

Source: Based on Brazelton et al., 1999.

Spock's advice made an impression on parents in the late 1940s and 1950s. One review of the parenting literature of the time, for example, indicates that middle-class and working-class parents appear to have exchanged positions with respect to permissiveness with their children. Whereas middle-class mothers before 1945 had been less permissive than mothers of the working class, after 1945, the trend was in the other direction (Bronfenbrenner, 1958, cited in Strickland & Ambrose, 1985).

Spock's advice was not the only factor shaping middle-class parents' attitudes and child-rearing behaviors (Strickland & Ambrose, 1985). Postwar economic prosperity also affected patterns of childrearing (Elder et al., 1993; Potter, 1954, cited in Strickland & Ambrose, 1985). Greater affluence made it possible, for example, for families to buy washing machines and other conveniences. These trends suggest that parents who read Spock's advice may have followed it because it coincided with changing middle-class attitudes about children and families as well as economic and social conditions that made it possible for them to do so (Strickland & Ambrose, 1985).

By contrast and if they were aware of it, for families living in poverty, the new, child-centered approach probably did not seem very commonsensical. One study from the 1960s compared white and black mothers in Chicago in terms of their exposure to Spock's book. Whereas 77 percent of white, middle-class mothers had read *Baby and Child Care,* only 32 percent of black, middle-class mothers had. Similar patterns were found among working-class mothers, with 48 percent of white, working-class mothers reporting that they had read Spock's book, as compared to 12 percent of black, working-class mothers (Blau, 1971, cited in Strickland & Ambrose, 1985).

It is reasonable to assume that other groups who were not benefiting from postwar prosperity, such as migrant worker families, were also likely to be indifferent to or unaware of the new approach to childrearing. As shown in a landmark television documentary in 1960, *Harvest of Shame,* migrant children often began working in the fields by age 7 or 8 and experienced transience, poverty, and poor living conditions from birth. Middle-class Americans who saw this program were shocked to discover that only 1 out of every 500 migrant children finished grade school (Strickland & Ambrose, 1985).

There was growing public awareness that not all American children were being nurtured by parents who had the knowledge, skills, and time to implement the new, commonsense approach to childrearing. At the level of the federal government, there was increasing evidence of the harm being

In 1960, the landmark television documentary *Harvest of Shame* publicized the transience, poverty, and poor living conditions of many children in migrant worker families.

done to Baby Boom children growing up in environments filled with poverty, discrimination, and a lack of opportunity or hope. This awareness led to political support for a "war on poverty," an effort to create a "Great Society" in a United States that would be rid of poverty and racial injustice. As part of the "war" effort, Project Head Start was created in 1964 to serve preschool-age children of low-income families (we discuss the more recently established Early Head Start program for infants and toddlers in Chapter 11).

The compensatory model of Head Start sought to provide the best childrearing advice and comprehensive services for economically disadvantaged families. What was the nature of this advice, and what were the experts telling parents about infant development and care during this time? One review of the U.S. Children's Bureau *Infant Care* manual and *Parents* magazine from 1955 through 1984 shows that there was not a simple, direct relationship between what experts knew and the information that was communicated to parents (Young, 1990). Information about biological aspects of infant development (perception, cognition, and temperament) was most accurately and consistently communicated to parents, but coverage of the mother-infant relationship, childcare, feeding, and fathers grew, shrank, or remained the same as a function of the "broader cultural context and demographic changes" (Young, 1990, p. 17).

As shown in Table 1.4, advice concerning the mother-infant relationship from the mid-1950s until the early 1970s emphasized the mother's role over all other influences; by the 1970s, experts recognized that the mother-infant relationship is only one of many important relationships influencing the child's development. Advice about the father's role revealed another shift, from the 1950s and 1960s when "mothers were encouraged to include fathers in the care of the baby but not to expect fathers to share equally in the care of the infant," to the mid-1980s when "new parents were told that fathers could share in the role of primary caretaker" (Young, 1990, p. 23).

The postwar trends that produced the Baby Boom generation were not duplicated by young adults in the later 1960s and 1970s. As we noted previously, the average age for first marriage increased steadily, and many young adults postponed having children or even decided to remain childless. Between 1957 and 1976, marriage and parenthood came to be viewed as a personal choice and less as a "natural" accompaniment of adulthood. Social regard for families remained high, but there was more tolerance of a range of choices about whether and when to start a family (Arnett, 2000; Douvan, 1985).

Education

Popular press reports in recent years about brain development from birth to age 3 have heightened many parents' desire to expose their infants to stimulating experiences that will increase their intelligence. Despite the fact that brain development does not end at age 3, many new parents now feel pressure to make the most of their infant's first brain-building months and years. We turn now to examine historical evidence concerning parents' beliefs about the importance of educating very young children.

One of the most influential philosophers and educators in the late seventeenth and early eighteenth century, John Locke, believed that children could (and should) be educated as soon as possible. In Locke's *Essay Concerning Human Understanding* (1690), he described children as tabula rasa—"blank slates"—and argued that children's behavior and knowledge are derived from experience, rather than being innately predetermined. In *Some Thoughts Concerning Education*, Locke (1693) advised against forcing or coercing children or acting in any way that would discourage their natural curiosity (Hulbert, 1999; Moran & Vinovskis, 1985).

Another widely read publication, many years later, was Jean Jacques Rousseau's (1762) *Émile, or On Education.* In *Émile,* Rousseau asserted that parents need to be aware of and shape

TABLE 1.4	What Child Development Experts Told Parents (Usually Mothers) in *Infant Care*	
Topic	**1955**	**1980**
Newborns...	...are more passive than active.	...learn through their own actions, but parents need to provide stimulation.
Temperament...	...each baby is different.	...refers to your baby's distinctive style. Which type is your baby?
Feeding...	...your baby with breast milk is the natural way. The breast is the center of his emotional world.	...with sensitivity is more important than whether you give your baby breast milk or formula. Unless you feel strongly about not breastfeeding, however, you should plan to nurse your baby.
The Mother-Infant	...is the reason your baby is happy and secure. Your baby needs you as much as he needs food or air.	...is only one of several important relationship...influences on your baby's emotional health.
The Father-Infant	...can be a great help to you, but do not expect your baby's father to share equally in caring for him.	...provides a unique and necessary relationship...complementary relationship to the relationship that you have with your baby. Your baby's father can share the role of primary caregiver with you.
Nonparental Childcare...	...is like boarding your baby away from home.	...will not harm your baby as long as you choose the right setting. Use our checklist to judge your baby's childcare setting.
Infants...	...are able to see light and color. They have an awakening memory around the age of 6 months.	...are able to track objects, make associations between events, and discriminate patterns. They learn best when you interact with them and respond to their actions. Watch to see what your baby is interested in and take your cue from him or her.

Source: Based on Young, 1990.

children's natural tendencies in order to create morally desirable individuals embodying traits of humility, chastity, and honesty. Instead of confining infants in swaddling clothes, for example, Rousseau advised parents to adopt natural childrearing practices that would allow the infant to be active and free to move. These views gained favor in Europe as well as in the American colonies and influenced beliefs about child development and the role of parents by the end of the nineteenth century (Hulbert, 1999).

Puritan parents in the New England colonies taught their children to read very early in life, at least by 4 or 5 years of age. The preferred reading material was the Holy Scriptures, and their primary motivation was to improve their children's souls and moral character (Moran & Visnovskis, 1985). Males were usually better educated than females, so fathers at first played the dominant role in educating children in colonial New England. This appears to have changed in the mid-seventeenth century, as men became less involved in the church and were increasingly viewed as less suitable moral educators, while women continued church membership at high levels and became increasingly literate. By the late seventeenth century, Puritan ministers had become accepting of women as educators, inside the home and in local schools that were established as the population increased. At the end of the eighteenth century, public schools and churches in New England had primary responsibility for educating children, but the family was still expected to teach very young children the alphabet and provide them with the foundations of literacy (Moran & Visnovskis, 1985). As we discuss next, public and private institutions came to play an increasingly significant role in family life and in children's development.

Early in the nineteenth century, many educators believed that children as young as 18 months could be educated and taught to read at an early age; these educators strongly supported the **infant school movement** and imported it from Europe in the 1820s (Hareven, 2000). In the United States, infant schools offered poor children aged 2 to 4 years an early education as a way of compensating for their disadvantaged family life (Moran & Vinovskis, 1985). By the 1830s and 1840s, middle-class children were enrolled as well. In Massachusetts, as many as 40 to 50 percent of 3-year-olds attended infant schools, and most American parents believed that very young children could and should be taught to read (Moran & Vinovskis, 1985).

Not everyone supported the infant school movement. In the 1830s, physicians, educators, and authors of popular childrearing books began to express concerns about systematic efforts to encourage young children's intellectual development (Hareven, 2000). Some even warned that early childhood education would lead to insanity (Finkelstein, 1985). As a result, attendance began to drop at infant schools throughout the country, and by 1860, almost no 3- or 4-year-olds attended schools in Massachusetts or anywhere else in the United States (Moran & Vinovskis, 1985).

Between about 1840 and 1860, there was growing support for the expansion of schools and education for children, as long as it did not begin before the age of 6 or 7 years, and as long as it built children's character by providing a refuge from the adult world (Finkelstein, 1985). School attendance was not yet the norm, however, and only 50 percent of children ages 5 to 19 were enrolled in school in 1870 (Hernandez, 1997).

As shown in Table 1.1, laws concerning compulsory education, child labor, and the treatment of juvenile delinquents were enacted, although these changes were gradual and there was sometimes wide variation across the United States. Massachusetts, for instance, was the first state to pass compulsory school attendance laws in 1836, whereas Mississippi, acting in 1918, was the last state to do so (Bremner et al., 1970, 1971; Hawes & Hiner, 1985). One clear, if not surprising, result of this legislation was a sharp increase in school attendance. Enrollment rates for children ages 7 to 13, which had hovered around 50 percent in the mid-1800s, rose to 95 percent by 1940 and to 99 percent by 1949 (Hernandez, 1997).

By the beginning of the twentieth century, early childhood education had also taken root, as seen in the expanding kindergarten movement. The concept of the kindergarten, imported from Germany, was based on Friedrich Froebel's theories about the necessity and centrality of play in early childhood (Cohen, 1985). The first kindergartens in the United States were opened in the mid-1850s, with a curriculum that explicitly rejected the earlier infant school emphasis on precocious learning (Finkelstein, 1985). Instead, kindergartens were intended to protect impoverished children from the city streets and to facilitate immigrant children's assimilation into U.S. culture. Immigrant neighborhoods in many cities had private charity kindergartens as well as kindergartens in public schools. By the late 1870s, the organized play and socialization available in kindergartens came to be seen as a necessity for all young children, regardless of their family's economic resources (Cohen, 1985; Finkelstein, 1985).

Progressives directed some of their efforts at the youngest members of society, creating day nurseries for the young children of working, often destitute mothers and, in 1898, founding the National Federation of Day Nurseries (Cohen, 1985). The original purpose of these daycare settings was to contribute to the moral elevation of impoverished families and children, but, by the 1920s, public and private attitudes had changed again. Daycare came to be regarded as "a custodial place of last resort for needy, pathological families" (Ashby, 1985, p. 497).

As we have seen, views of childhood have evolved throughout history. Significantly, there is little debate today about whether children are inherently innocent or sinful. In fact, "the transition from a moral and religious to a more secular and scientific view of childhood is one of the great revolutions" of the twentieth century (Smuts & Hagen, 1985, p. 6). We look now at the fascinating transition to the scientific study of infants and children, from the perspective of those who studied them.

THE DEVELOPMENT OF CHILD DEVELOPMENT

During the twentieth century, parents increasingly turned to professionals with expertise in the field of child development to provide guidance and answer questions about childrearing. Increasingly, professionals in child development moved away from an examination of and intervention in children's external worlds and toward the consideration of children's internal, psychological experiences. To understand the history of the scientific study of infants and children requires some understanding of the emergence of child development and its introduction into the United States at the beginning of the twentieth century, as well as an awareness of the emergence of pediatric medicine, since many researchers in child development focused their attention on early physical growth and motor development.

It has become commonplace for parents to bring their infants and children to visit a pediatrician, not only in times of sickness but also for preventive well-child care. This is an experience that most children growing up in previous eras would not have had. Although parents sought advice from local experts, such as midwives, clergy, and older relatives, it would not have occurred to them to consult a pediatrician, because physicians who focused exclusively on children did not exist. In 1880, child specialists called themselves *pediatrists* rather than pediatricians, and there were fewer than 50 such specialists in the United States, none of whom saw children on a full-time basis. It was not until the 1930s and 1940s, in fact, that pediatrics emerged as a secure, established part of medicine (Cravens, 1985; Halpern, 1988).

As many historians have noted, pediatrics developed in response to health-related social problems, such as those we have already discussed concerning the children of immigrants (Halpern, 1988; Sears, 1975). The same influence of real-world problems was evident in the origins of helping professions such as education and social work and, to a great extent, in the discipline of child development. As one historian observed,

> [d]uring the first two decades of the twentieth century, these professions began relevant research to improve their abilities, but their main influence on the future science was their rapidly expanding services for children in the schools, hospitals, clinics, and social agencies. . . . [I]t was in the next decade, the 1920s, that scientists from several nonprofessionally oriented ("pure science") disciplines began to join the researchers from the child-oriented professions to create what we now view as the scientific field

of child development.... But ... child development is a product of social needs that had little to do with science qua science.... The field grew out of *relevance*. (Sears, 1975, p. 4, original author's emphasis)

We conclude this chapter with a closer look at several of the key figures in the history of child development and how they contributed to the scientific study of children in the United States.

G. Stanley Hall

In order to understand how scientific approaches to the study of child development were introduced into the United States, we need to consider the central role played by G. Stanley Hall, the first professor of psychology in the United States, the first president of the American Psychological Association, and an organizer of the Child Study Section of the National Education Association. Hall became aware of child psychology during post-doctoral studies in Germany with Wilhelm Wundt (who established the first psychology laboratory in 1879) and subsequently " ... did more than any other founder of U.S. psychology to develop the new ... child psychology" (Cravens, 1985, p. 423). Returning to the United States in 1880, Hall was convinced that the new science of psychology had the potential to create better individuals and thus a better society (Hulbert, 1999). He also believed that scientific research and the study of children could transform educational practices (Cairns, 1998). His contributions include the following:

- Using a questionnaire method to study children's thinking and to help teachers understand the concepts children had learned by the time they entered school.
- Appearing with Dr. Luther Emmett Holt (whom we discussed earlier in this chapter) to give speeches at numerous meetings of child study groups and at conferences held by organizations such as the National Congress of Mothers.
- Extending the views of European embryologists and other scientists to argue that the life cycle consists of stages of predictable and naturally unfolding maturation.
- Training many of the first child psychologists in America, including John Dewey, who later became one of the most influential psychologists in the field of education in the early twentieth century.
- Arranging a historic meeting in 1909 between Sigmund Freud and the leading psychologists in North America to discuss, among other topics, Freud's views that experiences early in life, especially infancy and toddlerhood, are of great consequence for subsequent development and functioning.

James Mark Baldwin

Like Hall, James Mark Baldwin was a pioneer in organizing psychological science in North America. Known primarily for his later theoretical work, in his early years Baldwin founded an experimental laboratory at the University of Toronto in which he began a research program on infant psychology (Cairns, 1998). Among the topics that Baldwin explored in the early 1890s were the ontogeny of movement patterns and handedness. In one study of handedness, Baldwin observed the development of his own infant daughter's reaching behavior under systematic, controlled laboratory conditions. In order to eliminate any hand preference that might result from the way that parents carry their infants, Baldwin even specified that his wife should give their daughter equal time in her left and right arms (Harris, 1985). Influenced by theories of evolution, Baldwin considered research on "handedness" in animals to be relevant to his study of human infants. Baldwin is also remembered for:

- Asserting, in 1895, that intellectual development in the individual could not be considered without also contemplating the evolution of the mind in the human species.
- Describing how development progresses from infancy to adulthood in a series of stages, the first of which he called the sensorimotor stage, a term that was later used by Jean Piaget in his theory of infant intelligence.
- Articulating, in 1897, the view that, beginning in infancy, social development occurs through a dialectical process in which the child moves from an initial, self-focused stage and eventually reaches a more empathic stage that incorporates the views of other people, a sociocultural approach that emerged again years later in the work of Russian psychologist Lev Vygotsky (Wertsch & Tulviste, 1992).

John B. Watson

As the United States became a major center, along with Europe, for the scientific study of children, the American public became more aware of the implications and applications of this new science as it entered their homes, schools, and communities. Not everyone in the United States shared Hall's enthusiasm for European traditions in psychology. One influential dissenter was John B. Watson, who carried out research at Johns Hopkins from 1916 until 1920 and then wrote books about the "purely American" psychological perspective of behaviorism. He also gained wide recognition in the 1920s and 1930s for popular-press publications in which he advised parents to apply behaviorist theory to the important job of childrearing. Here are some of the reasons that Watson remains a well-known figure:

- Watson rejected European traditions, including questionnaire research and the use of introspection (self-reflection) as a way of tapping the contents of the mind. In his view, the only way to produce scientific data was to employ behavioral, noncognitive methods—namely, observation.
- Watson observed infants, studying their behavioral and emotional responses to stimuli that he presented. Watson chose to study infants because he believed that the conditioning of basic emotions (love, fear, and rage) early in life provided the foundation for later behavior and personality.
- Watson believed that psychological science could and should be applied across a wide range of everyday settings, including the home. In a best-selling book, *Psychological Care of Infant and Child* (1928), Watson argued that parents, especially mothers, should avoid smothering their children with too much affection. The danger, he wrote, was that the child would become conditioned by this love, the result being an unhealthy dependence on and need for attention and affection from others. Watson urged parents to be emotionally cool with their children and to adhere to strict schedules. Despite an absence of empirical evidence, Watson's views were widely disseminated to the public, at least some of whom must have been impressed by their apparent scientific legitimacy.

The empirical study for which Watson is probably best known is a case study of conditioned fear in an infant he referred to as "little Albert" (Watson & Rayner, 1920). In his work with Albert, Watson paired the presentation of an aversive stimulus (a loud noise that made Albert fearful and upset) with a previously neutral stimulus (a white rat). Following a series of pairings, the rat alone began to elicit a fear response from the child, supporting Watson's behaviorist prediction.

Although the details of Watson's experiment have been embellished and even distorted over the years (Harris, 1979), it led to many subsequent studies by other psychologists, especially in the 1920s and 1930s, and remains a part of the standard coverage of behaviorism in many psychology courses.

Arnold Gesell

Arnold Gesell, a former student of Hall, founded a child study laboratory at Yale in 1911, in which he carried out methodologically rigorous and innovative studies of early physical growth and motor development. Through his research, Gesell came to the opposite conclusion than Watson did regarding the role of experience in early development, asserting that infants have an innate ability to develop in optimal ways, despite variability in experience. Gesell's accomplishments include the following:

- Being one of the first to compare the development of twins and to use motion pictures in his research.
- Publishing the results of his research in 1928, in *Infancy and Human Growth,* a book in which he charted and compared normal and "exceptional" infants in terms of their physical, motor, and perceptual development.
- Recognizing a key role for maturation in development, while also noting that experience may modify the functioning of some inborn maturational mechanisms.

Child Research Institutes: Research and Dissemination

As the discipline of psychology emerged and gained strength in America, child development experts became more interested in solving children's problems from within rather than through social engineering and public policy (Bornstein, 2006; Cravens, 1985). Child research institutes, including those at Columbia University, Yale University, and universities in Iowa and Minnesota, were established in

Arnold Gesell founded a child study laboratory at Yale University in 1911 and carried out innovative studies of early physical growth and motor development.

the 1920s and 1930s with funds provided by the Laura Spelman Rockefeller Memorial (Schlossman, 1985). The dual mission of these institutes was research and dissemination of useful findings to the general public, but more attention and resources were directed to basic research documenting the growth and development of "normal" children.

Each institute developed its own character, and researchers at each institute became known for carrying out particular kinds of studies. Researchers at Iowa, for example, studied growth and physical maturation, as well as the care and feeding of infants and children. Behavioral and emotional development were explored at Columbia, Johns Hopkins, University of Minnesota, University of California, and Washington University (St. Louis). Mental testing and studies of intelligence and IQ were associated with researchers at Iowa, Berkeley, Minnesota, and Stanford. Two institutes— Berkeley and Fels—began systematic longitudinal studies (Cairns, 1998).

A significant amount of research and theoretical work in child development during this time was influenced by Freud's (1910) psychoanalytic theory or variations of it (Emde, 1992). Social learning theory emerged as a hybrid of behaviorist and psychoanalytic thinking, and researchers sought to apply concepts from this new perspective (e.g., reinforcement, imitation, and observational learning) to problems like childhood aggression, usually focusing on school-age children.

In the years following the Depression (1930–1945), numerous federal agencies were established and legislation was enacted to address child welfare problems, especially those resulting from economic devastation caused by the Depression. In addition to child labor laws, federal daycare programs were established in the 1930s through the Works Progress Administration; the 1935 Social Security Act offered coverage for dependent, rural, and disabled children; free lunches were offered daily to poor children in New York City; and the Emergency Maternal and Infant Care (EMIC) Program was established in 1943 to provide free healthcare for the wives and infants of lower-ranking men serving in the military during wartime. Records show that the EMIC program was effective at reducing infant and maternal mortality rates; infant mortality, for example, fell from 47 per 1,000 live births in 1940 to 38.3 in 1945 (Ashby, 1985).

In the years following World War II, social learning theorists continued to study topics such as aggression but also explored the development of gender-role typing and conscience, as well as the relation between parental attitudes, beliefs, and childrearing practices and children's social development. These studies were unusual at the time for their multi-method approach, in which the researchers interviewed parents, observed children's play behavior, and observed parent-child interactions. Social learning research also highlighted the importance of studying the mutual, bidirectional influence of parent and child. This was a departure from previous approaches, which had assumed that the direction of influence flowed from parents to children (Bornstein, 2006; Cairns, 1998).

John Bowlby

In the 1950s and 1960s, work began on another fundamental topic, the infant-caregiver attachment relationship. Harry Harlow studied the formation and consequences of attachment in rhesus monkeys at about the same time that John Bowlby used his clinical observations of the mother-infant relationship to construct a theory of attachment in humans. Bowlby detailed his theory in several important books, including the multivolume *Attachment and Loss*, most notably, *Attachment* (vol. 1, 1969) and *Separation: Anxiety and Anger* (vol. 2, 1973). As we learn in Chapter 9, Bowlby's theory incorporated ideas from his own psychoanalytic background, from studies of imprinting and bonding in animals, and from theories of cognitive development in infancy (Bretherton, 1992).

Sharing the Results

Interest in scientifically derived information about parenting and child development continued to grow throughout the twentieth century. When *Parents Magazine* began publishing in the late 1920s, however, the success of the magazine surprised even its publishers (Schlossman, 1985). One reason for this enthusiastic reception may have been the magazine's initial affiliation with the Laura Spelman Rockefeller Memorial and, by association, the child development research institutes that the Memorial had funded.

Another sign of the growth of the field of child development was the establishment of a scholarly scientific journal, *Child Development,* in 1930. Soon after that, the Laura Spelman Rockefeller Memorial, in conjunction with the National Research Council, helped launch the Society for Research in Child Development (SRCD)—the interdisciplinary professional organization that became associated with *Child Development* (Cravens, 1985). The Memorial also funded programs to recruit future professionals and to develop parent education programs. Today, SRCD is a multidisciplinary professional association with approximately 5,500 members engaged in research, education, and practice in more than 50 countries (The Roots of SRCD, 2009). An Oral History Project was initiated in the late 1980s to document these events, as seen through the eyes of those who participated in them as child development researchers and practitioners (Cameron & Hagen, 2005). As results of this project become available, they are archived on the SRCD website for scholars, teachers, and practitioners to use.

The rest of the story of the study of infant development up to the present time is told in the remaining chapters of this book, as we consider this important period of the lifespan from a topical perspective. In Chapter 2, we discuss methods that researchers use to study infant development. In Chapters 3, 4, and 5, we learn about the biological beginnings of infancy, including prenatal development and health, nutrition, and physical growth from birth to the age of 3 years. Chapters 6, 7, and 8 bring us into the cognitive domain, where we explore sensation, perception, and motor development, as well as learning, intelligence, and language. The social world of emotions and relationships is the focus of Chapters 9 and 10, while Chapters 11 and 12 examine institutions that are now commonplace in the lives of children younger than 3—childcare, early childhood education, and electronic media.

WRAPPING IT UP: Summary and Conclusion

How have infancy and childhood changed over time? Children who lived in the distant past cannot be observed or interviewed, so our answers to this question are based on indirect sources, such as parents' diaries, childrearing books, toys, paintings, and records of births and deaths. As imperfect as these sources are, they reveal both differences and similarities between the present and the past. We know, for example, that parents in the past gave birth to more children than today, but that many of those children died in infancy. Despite high rates of infant mortality, parents in the past appear to have grieved over each loss, just as parents do today. Infant abandonment was once a common practice in many parts of the world, but that concern about the vulnerability of infants and children gradually led to institutional and legal forms of protection. Increasing awareness of the importance of infancy and early childhood gave rise to organized efforts to train and educate children early in life so that they would grow up to be moral, responsible, and capable adults.

We have seen that childrearing advice—now more typically referred to as parenting advice—has sometimes been inconsistent or faddish. As a result, it has often produced confusion among parents who merely want to know what the experts think

(Hulbert, 1999, 2003). Holt, the highly regarded pediatrician and author of *The Care and Feeding of Children* (1894), for example, warned parents about the health risks of kissing children and the dangers of making infants nervous and irritable by playing with them (Cairns, 1998). In popular magazines in the 1920s, the behavioral psychologist John B. Watson instructed parents to put their young children on strict schedules, to avoid being overly affectionate toward them, and to ignore their own emotional responses to their young children (Watson, 1928).

In the 1930s and 1940s, by contrast, experts recommended that parents respect their children as unique individuals, watch for signs of their natural unfolding, and ensure that their children's needs were met while avoiding intervention and conflict. These views were disseminated in childrearing books with titles such as *Babies Are Human Beings* (1938), *Keep Them Human* (1942), *Infant and Child in the Culture of Today* (1943), and *Our American Babies* (1944). Similar views were also presented in Dr. Spock's influential parenting book, *The Common Sense Book of Baby and Child Care* (1946).

Given the extreme positions that have sometimes been presented, it is reasonable to wonder how many parents actually followed the experts' advice—a question that is just as relevant today as it was when Watson urged parents to avoid expressing too much emotion in their interactions with their children. For a more recent example, consider the medium of television. When it became established, public television programs, like *Sesame Street* (which first aired in 1969), were developed with the

assistance of child development experts. Knowing that knowledgeable professionals had been involved in the production of these educational programs, many parents felt confident that they would have positive effects on their children. In recent years, electronic media, including public television programs, have been created with toddler and even infant audiences in mind. Although some of these programs have been designed by experts in child development, at least one other set of experts—the American Academy of Pediatrics—issued a policy statement advising parents not to use these forms of media with children under the age of 2 years. As in the past, therefore, parents may wonder which position is correct and how to apply the experts' recommendations in their own lives. There is, it seems, no end in sight to the search for information and advice about infants and young children.

This book is not a parenting manual, but periodically we consider how the findings might be interpreted and used by parents or adults who work with infants and toddlers. For some topics, there may be more than one right answer, the right answer may vary according to the characteristics of the children in question, or we may not know enough yet to be able to provide definitive answers for anyone. Like parents of infants, we acknowledge this uncertainty while continuing to ask questions. When evaluating answers, we presume that objective evidence is more valid than appeals to emotion, tradition, or unsupported beliefs. Above all, our focus is on current findings from systematic studies by researchers whose work uses recognized, accepted research methods, the topic of our next chapter.

THINK ABOUT IT: Questions for Reading and Discussion

1. Imagine that you are a historian in the twenty-*second* century and your topic is the history of infancy and early childhood. What sorts of literary evidence, quantitative evidence, and material culture—evidence and artifacts being created today—might you use to study parenting in the twenty-first century? What sorts of conclusions might be drawn from these sources about our current society's attitudes about infants and their development? What would be the

advantages and disadvantages of using these kinds of materials instead of observing infants directly?

2. Children in the United States and many other industrialized countries are becoming toilet trained at increasingly older ages (Bakker & Wyndaele, 2000; Brody, 1999). Whereas 92 percent of 18-month-olds were toilet trained in 1957, in 1999, only 2 percent of 2-year-olds, and 60 percent of 3-year-olds were reliably toilet trained.

(It is not until the age of 4 years that most U.S. children—98 percent—are finally out of diapers.) Use the information in this chapter to identify some of the factors that might be responsible for this trend.

3. What is the most surprising thing about the history of infancy and childhood that you have learned from this chapter? How does this information affect your views about infants and development from birth to age 3?

4. What do you think was the most important factor influencing the establishment and growth of the field of child development in the United States? Is this factor still important today? Are current conditions right to continue supporting the field of child development? Explain.

5. Do you think that today's parents would support an infant school movement? Why or why not?

6. Which of the recurring themes in the study of child development do you think is the most important? Explain.

7. When you think about the recurring themes in the study of child development, how do you tend to view the key debates? Do you tend to believe more strongly in nature or in nurture as an influence on development? Do you tend to view babies as active or passive participants in their own development? How important do you think culture and the historical era are? Compare your views with the views of others taking this course. In addition, after you have finished this book, take another look at your notes to see if your ideas have changed.

Key Words

Continuous (5)   Characterization of development as a gradual, smooth process of change.

Infant mortality rate (13)   Number of deaths per 1,000 live births, usually reported with reference to the age of 1 year.

Infant school movement (23)   An early nineteenth-century movement, imported to the United States from Europe, in which educators believed that children as young as 18 months could be educated and taught to read.

Literary evidence (9)   Written information, including parents' diaries and letters, childrearing advice written by ministers and doctors, and children's books.

Material culture (9)   Physical evidence, such as toys, clothing, furniture, and works of art.

Nature (5)   Biological factors influencing development.

Nurture (5)   Environmental and experiential factors influencing development.

Oblation (14)   Medieval European practice involving the permanent "donation" of an infant or young child to a monastery.

Quantitative archival evidence (9)   Official sources of written information and data, including census data, tax records, and legislative and court records.

Stagewise (4)   Characterization of development as occurring in distinct phases, with qualitative differences between stages.

Research Methods

All research begins with a question, and the questions that researchers address reflect the times in which they live. Like their predecessors working in the early twentieth century, contemporary researchers still investigate fundamental questions about the influence of nature and nurture on children's development. Today's researchers also have new questions to explore, however, such as the impact of media on very young children and the pros and cons of early childcare. At the same time that new research topics have arisen, research methods have also evolved over time. We highlight some of these changes in this chapter by weaving in the story of a pioneering study that involved two languages, two countries, and one little girl.

When Hildegard Rose Leopold was born in 1930, her father, a German linguist, took an immediate and intense interest in her language development. In family conversations, Werner Leopold spoke only German, while his American wife Marguerite spoke only English. Keeping detailed records, beginning when Hildegard was 8 weeks old, Werner Leopold sought to document the development of a child growing up in a bilingual home. The video- and audiotaping technology that is so prevalent and accessible today had not yet been invented, so Leopold took copious notes about Hildegard's vocalizations on slips of paper that he carried with him and spent weekends meticulously writing up and organizing the notes (Hakuta, 1986). Moreover, unlike most language researchers today, who tend to specialize in the study of just one aspect of language, such as the acquisition of word meaning or grammar, Leopold made observations about all aspects of his daughter's language development. The result, *Speech Development of a Bilingual Child: A Linguist's Record* (1939, 1947, 1949), was a four-volume publication covering nearly 900 pages.

Leopold's study provided an important foundation for research on childhood bilingualism, but his approach was extremely labor-intensive and, in the end, provided information about only one child. What alternative research methods might he have used to answer the same set of questions? In this chapter we consider the range of options available to researchers, whether the focus is on the development of language, cognition, perception, motor skills, or relationships. As we do, we encounter several classic studies that changed our understanding of the development of infants and young children. We also see that in the past, as is true today, choosing among the options requires researchers to make three major decisions about how they will explore their question: the type of setting, the research design, and the measures that they will use.

RESEARCH SETTINGS

Werner Leopold observed and made notes about his daughter's language development in ordinary settings, including their home in the United States and their living quarters during extended visits to Germany (Hakuta, 1986). Even without such easy access to infants, some researchers choose to carry out studies in their participants' homes and in other everyday settings rather than in a laboratory. In light of the extra effort involved, why do some researchers elect those settings, and how do they compare to laboratories?

Naturalistic Studies

In some studies researchers observe infants in **naturalistic settings**—their usual surroundings, such as their own home or their regular childcare center. In some naturalistic research, like a classic study of language acquisition that we discuss in Chapter 8 (Brown, 1973), children's spontaneous behavior is recorded as they interact with their parent or caregiver. This was also the case when Fernald and Morikawa (1993), in a cross-cultural study of Japanese and European American families, observed 6-, 12-, and 19-month-old infants and their mothers as they played with toys at home and compared the dyads' conversations and play themes. In many studies using **naturalistic observation,** researchers remain relatively passive observers in the sense that, apart from being physically present, they do not intervene in or try to influence the situation. One example of this is a study that took place in a health clinic and involved the observation of the type and duration of emotion expressions of 2- to 7-month-old infants in response to the acute pain of a diphtheria-pertussis-tetanus (DPT) inoculation (Izard, Hembree, & Huebner, 1987). Although the researchers in this study undoubtedly had an emotional reaction to observing babies cry in pain, they were careful not to show these feelings or to intervene in any way as the infants' parents comforted them.

If researchers are becoming familiar with the setting or gathering ideas for future studies, they may write a **narrative record**—a detailed description of the range of behaviors they observe. By contrast, to answer questions about specific, well-defined behaviors, they use techniques that allow them to focus on just those target behaviors. In **event sampling,** for example, a small number of behaviors are identified and the researcher notes each time they occur by making a mark on a prepared checklist. It is essential to have a clear **operational definition,** a concrete verbal description that enables researchers to measure target behaviors and outcomes accurately. Operational definitions help researchers differentiate between behaviors that may appear to be similar in a number of ways, such as aggression and rough-and-tumble play ("play-fighting"). In an observational study of children's physical interactions on the playground, for example, researchers, as well as the children's teachers, might want to compare the frequency of each type of behavior. To do this, aggression might be defined as "physical contact between two or more children, accompanied by angry facial expressions and resulting in physical injury, negative emotions, and the cessation of interaction between the children, perhaps with the intervention of teachers or other adults." Rough-and-tumble play, by contrast, might be defined as "physical contact between two or more children, accompanied by smiles and laughter, not resulting in physical injury or negative emotions, and leading to continued interaction between the children" (Pellegrini, 1998; Pellegrini & Smith, 1998).

Operational definitions are necessary whether studies take place in a naturalistic setting or in a laboratory. Training observers to use a single operational definition increases the likelihood that all members of a research team use the same criteria and minimizes **observer bias**—the phenomenon in which researchers' expectations or beliefs influence the way they record or interpret behavior. Researchers involved in one classic study of children in six cultures—the United States, India, Japan, Kenya, Mexico, and the Philippines—were able to compare interactions in settings in which children spent a typical day by specifying operational definitions for more than 30 possible behaviors, including "observing," "ignoring," "insulting," and "assaulting," as well as "helping," "nurturing," "suggesting," "commanding," "greeting," and "imitating" (Whiting et al., 1966).

In an observational study of the development of pride, researchers might use an operational definition that includes a set of predetermined behaviors, such as erect posture, smiling, and verbal expressions such as "I did it!"

Research need not be as ambitious as the six-culture study in order to benefit from clear operational definitions. In a laboratory study of toddlers' responses to their mother's verbal and nonverbal behavior during a challenging puzzle task, researchers coded children's display of feelings of pride and shame (Kelley, Brownell, & Campbell, 2000).

> *Pride* was coded when at least three of the following five behaviors occurred within 30 s[econds] following a child-produced success outcome: erect posture (i.e., shoulders back and head up), smile (either open or closed mouth), eyes directed at the experimenter or mother, points to outcome or applauds, or positive self-evaluation (e.g., "Yeah!" or "I did it!"). *Shame* was coded when at least three of the following five behaviors occurred within 30 s following a child-produced task failure: body collapsed, corners of the mouth down turned/lower lip tucked between teeth, eyes lowered with gaze downward or askance, withdrawal from the task situation, or negative self-statements. (p. 1065)

Pride and shame are such familiar emotions that differences between them may seem intuitive or obvious, but the use of clear operational definitions made it possible for different members of the research team to use the same criteria to categorize children's emotional displays. (Table 2.1 shows an example of a checklist that might have been used to record data about these behaviors.) Clear operational definitions also make it possible for subsequent researchers to make direct comparisons between their findings and those of the original researchers, whether they are studying pride and shame in a laboratory or in a naturalistic setting.

In some naturalistic studies, researchers take an active role and try to elicit particular child behaviors by creating specific experiences. Jean Piaget (1954), for example, whose research on cognitive development we discuss in Chapter 7, studied his own children in naturalistic settings but tested their reactions to the appearance and disappearance of objects that he selected and manipulated as well as objects that they encountered on their own.

Like Werner Leopold, Piaget recorded his observations in writing. Contemporary researchers in naturalistic studies take notes too, primarily to provide contextual information later, during the coding of audiotape or videotape records. In one study of infants' reactions to pictures in books, researchers both videotaped and took notes about children's manual exploration and vocalizations (DeLoache et al., 1998). Because this study compared infants in the United States and on the Ivory Coast of Africa, notes taken in these settings, especially entries about the presence and function of pictures and picture books in each culture, provided useful information later.

TABLE 2.1 Example of a Prepared Checklist for Use in Event Sampling

To code displays of *pride,* in the 30 seconds following a child-produced success outcome, make a mark for every instance of the behaviors listed.[a]

Success Outcome #	Erect Posture Smile	Eye Contact	Positive Self-Evaluation
1			
2			
3			
4			
5			

Source: (a) Adapted from information in Kelley, Brownell, and Campbell, 2000.

In one observational study of infants' reactions to pictures in books, researchers both videotaped and took notes about children's manual exploration and vocalizations.

Some naturalistic studies, like DeLoache and colleagues' picture book study, explore phenomena through **ethnographic research,** in which researchers make detailed observations or conduct interviews in everyday settings. Ethnographic research can be carried out in the researcher's own culture, as was done in a study of Girl Scout cookie sales in the United States (Rogoff et al., 2002). In most ethnographic research, however, researchers from one (usually Western) culture study behavior in a different (usually non-Western) culture. Ethnographic methods are a staple of anthropological research—Margaret Mead's famous (1928, 1930) studies of child and adolescent development in Samoa and New Guinea are an example of this tradition—but many psychologists, child development researchers, and pediatricians have also used this method to provide comparative data on topics such as sleeping, feeding, discipline, parent-infant interaction, and other infant care practices (Rogoff et al., 1993; Small, 1998; Winikoff, Castle, & Laukaran, 1988).

Results of ethnographic studies can be surprising to anyone who assumes that the way infants are cared for in their own culture is the "natural" or "best" way. One revealing ethnographic study compared infants' sleeping arrangements in rural Guatemala and in middle-class homes in the United States (Morelli et al., 1992). Whereas U.S. parents tended to promote their infants' independent sleeping at an early age, Mayan parents in Guatemala slept with their children in the same bed, typically until the next child in the family was born. In addition, whereas U.S. parents tended to express concerns about co-sleeping, Mayan parents regarded the typical U.S. practice as cold and neglectful. These findings are consistent with other research suggesting that, around the world, more families prefer the Mayan practice of co-sleeping than the U.S. sleeping arrangements.

Differences between cultures become even more apparent when members of distinct groups have an opportunity to come into contact with each other. This was demonstrated in an ethnographic study in which the researcher videotaped agrarian mothers in West Africa and urban, middle-class mothers in Germany as they interacted with their babies. In a clever twist, the

Co-sleeping is a less common practice in the United States than it is in many other parts of the world.

researcher showed the two sets of videotapes to all of the parents and interviewed them about the interactions they saw. This approach helped clarify differences and similarities in the underlying beliefs in each culture about optimal amounts of breastfeeding, body contact and stimulation, object stimulation, and face-to-face contact (Keller, 2003).

Ethnographic studies can also reveal aspects of development that are universal, occurring at about the same age or in the same way, regardless of cultural practices. As we discuss in Chapter 8, for example, there are cross-cultural variations in how much parents speak to their infants and in the degree to which they believe infants are capable of understanding language. Despite these variations, the process of language acquisition is remarkably similar across numerous cultures that have been studied (Slobin, 1985). In addition, as we discuss in Chapter 9, despite differences in beliefs and in patterns of interaction with infants, parents in countries as diverse as China, Colombia, Germany, Israel, Japan, and the United States tend to agree about the behaviors they believe an "ideally secure" child should exhibit (Posada et al., 1995).

Naturalistic studies are appealing for a number of reasons (see Table 2.2). First, once children become accustomed to the presence of researchers and their recording equipment, their behavior is likely to be representative of their usual behavior. Second, parents may be more at ease when observed in their own home rather than in an unfamiliar laboratory. Given that infants and toddlers respond to their parents' emotional cues, it is clearly preferable to observe parents and their young children in settings in which parents feel comfortable. A third reason some researchers use naturalistic settings is to generate ideas about spontaneous behaviors that could be studied further in a more controlled laboratory setting.

One researcher who used both naturalistic and laboratory settings was Mary Ainsworth, whose groundbreaking work we discuss in Chapter 9. Some of her earliest observations of infant-caregiver interactions were carried out in children's homes (Ainsworth, 1967), but her later research resulted in the development of the Strange Situation—a standard laboratory procedure for investigating the infant-caregiver relationship (Ainsworth et al., 1978).

Laboratory Studies

One potential problem with naturalistic settings is the degree to which they vary across dimensions that may make a difference in children's behavior. Parent-infant interactions in a home

TABLE 2.2 Comparison of Naturalistic and Laboratory Studies	
Naturalistic	**Laboratory**
Infants' behavior is likely to be typical	Strange environment may elicit strange behavior
Parents may feel comfortable in own home	Parents may feel anxious, self-conscious
Variations may exist across settings	Testing environment can be controlled, standardized for all participants
Good source of ideas for further study	Ideal for studying behavior that occurs only infrequently in naturalistic settings
Requires adjustment to equipment and researchers	Equipment and researchers can be hidden
High external validity, low internal validity	Low external validity, high internal validity
An integral part of ethnographic research	Ideal for normative studies and studies requiring specialized equipment and stimuli

where a boisterous older sibling is playing nearby or a television is turned on, for example, are likely to be different from interactions in a home in which there are few distractions and little background noise. By using a standard **laboratory setting**—a specially designed research space—researchers are able to eliminate extraneous nuisance factors, such as ringing telephones and barking dogs. This allows them to focus on the influence of selected **independent variables**—the conditions that they are interested in studying—in order to see how they affect the **dependent variable**—behaviors of interest. Researchers who want to study the effect of older siblings on infants' interactions with their mothers, for example, might use the independent variable of "group composition" to compare infant-mother pairs with infant-mother-sibling trios in terms of the amount of physical contact that occurs between the infant and mother (the dependent variable). In other studies using laboratory settings, researchers may intentionally vary other conditions, such as the presence and type of toys, or the amount of potentially distracting background noise. When these factors are systematically varied, their influence on the infant's

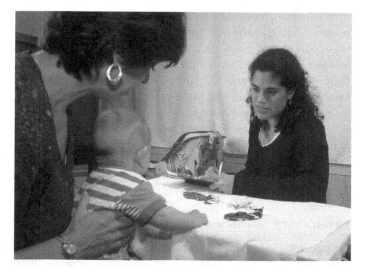

In laboratory settings, researchers have a high degree of control over the environment. This enables them to provide certain types of toys and observe how infants respond, as this researcher is doing.

behavior (the dependent variable) can be more clearly understood.

The focus of the investigation may also influence researchers' choice of a laboratory setting instead of a naturalistic setting. Researchers studying the development of perceptual abilities, for example, often show babies computer-generated video displays (e.g., Arterberry & Bornstein, 2002) or examine their crawling and walking in specially designed environments (e.g., Karasik et al., 2008). As we consider later in this chapter and in Chapters 4 and 6, researchers who study newborns' perceptual abilities often record behavioral measures, such as heart rate or sucking rate in response to carefully presented stimuli (e.g., Moon, Cooper, & Fifer, 1993). Similarly, as we discuss in Chapter 3, researchers who explore prenatal development or fetal responses to external stimuli depend on ultrasound scanners and fetal heart rate monitors. Studies like these require the presence of equipment that is not found in infants' homes, childcare centers, or other naturalistic settings.

Some researchers are interested in charting normative development, such as determining the average age for the development of walking or the acquisition of aspects of language. For greatest accuracy, these researchers usually need to observe large samples of infants in the same controlled laboratory situation.

Another advantage of laboratory settings is that recording equipment and observers can be disguised or hidden from view. As a result, infants in laboratory settings may not need to become accustomed to the visible presence of apparatus and a stranger and may interact with their parent in ways that are similar to their behavior at home.

A final advantage of laboratory settings is that they make it easier for researchers to study behaviors that occur infrequently in the natural environment. One researcher who wanted to understand the development of toddlers' responses to obstacles, for example, set up barriers of different heights and materials (e.g., opaque versus transparent) in a narrow laboratory hallway and asked parents to call to their children from the other side of the barrier, encouraging them to cross over it (Schmuckler, 1996). Parents of infants and toddlers often "baby-proof" their homes, removing furniture that affords climbing and installing safety gates at the top and bottom of staircases. It is unlikely, therefore, that the researcher would have been able to observe infants climbing and stepping over barriers in a naturalistic setting—especially since parents would normally actively discourage those behaviors.

Many researchers choose laboratory settings because they allow a significant degree of control over the conditions in which participants' behavior will be observed, such as ensuring that the temperature and background noise level in the room are the same for everyone. In laboratory settings, it is also easier for researchers to manipulate independent variables, such as the effect of a mother's presence versus absence on her young child's free play behavior. The greater the degree of control researchers have over independent variables, the more confident they can be that any differences they find between groups, such as differences in free play behavior between a mother-present and a mother-absent group of toddlers, may be attributed to the independent variable, in this case, the presence or absence of the mother. When researchers have this sort of control, their studies are said to have high **internal validity**—the degree to which differences in the dependent variable (free play behavior) are caused by differences in the independent variable (mother's presence versus absence). A study is said to have low internal validity when alternative explanations cast doubt on the effects of the independent variable. In our example, this might happen if an unintended difference existed between the mother-present and mother-absent groups of toddlers, such as the presence of familiar versus unfamiliar toys, that could have influenced the toddlers' motivation to play.

If internal validity is so desirable, why does research also take place outside of controlled laboratory settings? One reason is that the internal validity of a study is related to that study's **external validity**—the degree to which the findings can be extended, or generalized, to other samples and settings. If mother's presence versus absence has an influence on free play behavior for only one sample of toddlers, for example, but not other samples in subsequent studies, the original study would be said to have low external validity because the results apply so narrowly. Studies need to have both internal validity and external validity, so researchers must consider both when designing and carrying out their investigations.

As we have seen, the choice of a research setting has a significant impact on researchers' ability to conduct their studies and to draw conclusions from their data. When selecting a setting, researchers need to consider their specific goals, but the choice need not be an either/or one. Behaviors that are documented in both naturalistic and laboratory settings may ultimately be more convincing and informative than behaviors that are seen in only one setting.

RESEARCH DESIGNS

There are a number of alternative research designs that Werner Leopold might have used to study the language development of his bilingual daughter. Each design has its strengths and weaknesses, and researchers need to keep these characteristics in mind as they consider their options.

Case Studies and Single-Subject Research

The approach Werner Leopold took is an example of a **case study**—an in-depth examination of a single individual. Well-known case studies were carried out in psychology by Sigmund Freud and Jean Piaget. Susan Curtiss (1977) studied the language development of Genie—an abused, socially isolated, apparently nonverbal girl who came to the attention of authorities at the age of 13 years (also see Rymer, 1993). Another often-cited case study of an infant was published by Charles Darwin about his son, Doddy. Although Darwin was not the first to carry out detailed observations of his own child, when his article appeared in 1877 (based on notes he had taken while observing his son 37 years earlier), it gave legitimacy to the systematic study of children. As a celebrity of his time, Darwin's publication also inspired many parents to write their own **baby biographies** (observational records of their infants' early development). These parents probably did not realize that Darwin had followed in the footsteps of others, such as Dietrich Tiedemann (1787), who is generally acknowledged as having published the first psychological diary of longitudinal development in children (Cairns, 1998).

Parents who wrote baby biographies in the nineteenth century were also unaware of the methodological rigor that such studies need in order to be considered scientifically useful, but a number of researchers at that time began to use methods from other sciences to study individual infants' behavior and development. In the 1880s, William T. Preyer broke new ground by applying methods and concepts from embryology to the study of postnatal behavior and development. Preyer's work suffered from technological limitations and theoretical biases that led him to the erroneous conclusion that the normal human infant hears nothing at birth. Nevertheless, many of his observations about infant development were surprisingly accurate, and he is generally reported to have been a meticulous, careful observer (Cairns, 1998). Preyer outlined rules for his observations that are consistent with observational methodology used by researchers today, including comparing different people's observations in order to achieve accurate information.

Another well-known study of an individual infant's development was begun in 1893 by Millicent Washburn Shinn (the first woman to earn a Ph.D. in psychology from the University of California). Shinn's (1900/1985) book, *The Biography of a Baby,* was based on a day-by-day account of her niece Ruth's first year of life. Shinn was aware of Tiedemann's work and at first consciously modeled her biography on Preyer's records. Shinn also recognized that her niece did not represent all babies and might even differ greatly from others. Still, like her predecessors, she believed that the case study approach offered unique advantages, explaining, "If I should find out that a thousand babies learned to stand at an average of 46 weeks and two days, I should not know as much that is important about standing, as a stage in human progress, as I should after watching a single baby carefully through the whole process of achieving balance on his little soles" (p. 11).

In the case studies that we have considered so far, researchers documented the naturally occurring behavior and development of a single child, without intervening or otherwise manipulating the child's experience. In other case studies, researchers do intervene or study the effects of an experimental manipulation on a single participant; these studies are referred to as **single-subject research** (Miller, 1998). A good example of single-subject research is one-on-one therapy with children on the autism spectrum, using principles of operant conditioning (rewards and punishment) to reduce undesirable behaviors (e.g., temper tantrums, rocking, repetitive finger movements) and increase desirable behaviors (e.g., language, eye contact, playing with toys) (Lovaas & Smith, 1989; McEachin, Smith, & Lovaas, 1993).

To understand how this approach works, consider the goal of increasing appropriate play with toys. Working with one child at a time, researchers or special education workers record the initial, baseline level of contact with toys and then begin systematically rewarding the child each time he or she engages in that behavior. At first, rewards are given for even slight approximations of the target behavior, such as briefly touching a toy train. Eventually, rewards are given only for the complete behavior that is being targeted, such as connecting two or more parts of a toy train and pushing it along a track. Throughout the sessions, the duration of the child's appropriate play with the train is recorded and, if the treatment has been successful, it will be evident to anyone examining the record.

Single-subject research gives the researcher more control and internal validity than a case study that is primarily descriptive. As shown in Table 2.3, however, both types of studies have limitations, beginning with external validity concerns about the degree to which the individual being studied is representative of other people. Indeed, the more unique the subject of the study, the less likely the results can be tested and replicated in future research. Another concern is the possibility

TABLE 2.3 Comparison of Three Research Methods

Case Study/Single-Subject	Quasi-Experimental	Experimental
Permits in-depth study of a single individual	Compares pre-existing groups	Creates groups for comparison, using random assignment
External validity may be low, especially if individual is very unique	External validity is high	External validity may be low
Internal validity is high in single-subject experiments, but not in descriptive case studies	Internal validity may be low; inferences about cause and effect cannot be drawn	Internal validity is high; conclusions about cause and effect can be made
May suggest topics for research with larger samples	The only design available for many topics, where ethical or practical considerations make random assignment to groups impossible	The best design for topics that allow experimental manipulation and random assignment to groups

that the researcher may be theoretically biased when interpreting the data. Although the evidence with respect to Werner Leopold suggests that he was an objective observer (Hakuta, 1986), it is easy to imagine that case studies, especially those carried out by parents, might not always provide an accurate record. Case studies and single-subject research are valuable, however, for the detail that they provide about individual children. They may also point researchers to aspects of development that can be fruitfully studied with larger samples.

Quasi-Experimental Studies

Many researchers use a **quasi-experimental design** (also referred to as a nonexperimental design) to collect information about groups of participants that are already formed before the study begins. For practical reasons, this design is used in the investigation of preexisting group variables such as culture, race, ethnicity, and gender, where participants cannot be randomly assigned to a group. For ethical reasons, this design is the only option available for topics such as the effect of preterm birth, prenatal exposure to alcohol, or the impact of child abuse, since researchers cannot ethically induce these experiences (see Table 2.3). In quasi-experimental studies, researchers compare the groups they select in terms of dependent variables of interest, such as physical growth, motor development, or language acquisition.

If Werner Leopold had used a quasi-experimental design, he might have studied children whose parents had already decided to bring them up bilingually and compared their language development with the language development of children growing up in monolingual homes. (For both practical and ethical reasons, it would not be possible to randomly assign children and their families to monolingual or bilingual groups.) The results of this hypothetical study could indicate whether there is a relationship between the number of languages to which a child is exposed from birth and the rate of that child's language development.

If Leopold found that children in monolingual homes were more advanced in their language development than children from bilingual homes, he might conclude that learning more than one language during childhood is detrimental to language development. This finding would not permit him to infer, however, that early exposure to more than one language *causes* slower language development than early exposure to just one language. Alternative explanations would still need to be considered, such as the impact of other differences between the two groups of families. These differences might include the children's intellectual abilities, parents' attitudes about the language(s) they speak, families' economic resources, or even the amount of verbal interaction each child experiences.

Unless Leopold could rule out the effect of these other differences, a study like this one would suffer from low internal validity. There are some steps that could be taken to strengthen any causal inferences that might be drawn. One approach would be to equate the families in each group on other factors that could be related to child language outcomes. This would leave only the number of languages in the child's home—one or two—to vary between the families. Another approach would use statistical procedures to "partial out" the effect of nonlanguage differences between groups. Even with these adjustments, Leopold would never be able to remove the influence of all of the potentially important factors, and any causal conclusions would still need to be viewed as tentative.

Experimental Studies

In contrast to quasi-experimental studies, inferences about cause and effect can be drawn from studies using an **experimental design**—a design that examines the effect of an independent variable on a dependent variable (see Table 2.3). Experiments differ from quasi-experiments in employing **random assignment** (using a random number table or another nonsystematic procedure) to place each participant into one of two or more groups that represent different aspects of the independent variable. When random assignment is used, each participant has an equal chance of ending up in each of the groups being compared in the experiment. In our earlier discussion of laboratory studies, there were two conditions of the independent variable being compared—presence versus absence of the mother—and the dependent variable was the child's free play behavior. If children were randomly assigned to either the mother-present or the mother-absent condition, and if a greater quantity or higher quality of play behavior were found for children whose mothers were present, the researchers could conclude that the presence of a child's mother increases or improves the child's play behavior. In fact, the researchers in this example could be relatively confident that something about maternal presence *caused* the difference in play behavior between the two groups of children. They would still need to determine *how* maternal presence exerts its effects—through the mother's direct involvement in the child's play, as a result of suggestions that she makes to the child from the sidelines, or just by providing a comforting presence in the room.

How might Werner Leopold's study have been adapted to an experimental design? One way would be to bring young children growing up in bilingual homes into a laboratory setting and explore their ability to learn a set of new words, made up by the researcher (words like *bleg, thrip,* and *lart*). All of the children would be shown an object to accompany the new word, but half of the children would be taught the new word by their mother, whereas the other half would be taught by an unfamiliar person (the researcher). If Werner Leopold used random assignment, potentially important differences between the two groups of children might still exist, but their influence could be controlled through random assignment, ensuring that each child would have an equal chance of being taught by either a familiar person or an unfamiliar person. Random assignment would also ensure that potentially important differences across children would be distributed across the two teaching conditions. The results of this hypothetical experiment would indicate whether bilingual children learn new words better when the teacher is a familiar or an unfamiliar person.

As a result of random assignment, an experiment like this one would have a relatively high level of internal validity. It could be criticized for having relatively low external validity, however, because even if the findings were replicated in other samples of bilingual children studied by other researchers, the use of nonsense words would limit its generalizability to children's acquisition of real languages in naturalistic settings. The best plan, since no research design is without weaknesses, may be to use more than one approach and determine whether the results of different kinds of studies using different measures tend to agree or disagree (Brewer & Hunter, 1989).

RESEARCH DESIGNS FOR STUDYING DEVELOPMENT

Implicit in all developmental research is the goal of understanding how behaviors and abilities change with age and experience. When Werner Leopold studied his daughter's language development, he chose an intensive approach when she was a newborn and continued recording his observations into her adolescence. As Hildegard's father, Leopold's choice of a years-long design may seem like an obvious one. Numerous other researchers have also studied their subjects over a span of months or even years, although not all have gathered the staggering quantity of data that

TABLE 2.4	Comparison of Three Developmental Research Designs		
Longitudinal	**Cross-sectional**	**Microgenetic**	
Charts individual change or stability over time	Does not provide information about individual change or stability	Ideal for studying infants' rapidly developing skills, showing individual change or stability	
Can reveal relations between early functioning and later development; is ideal for showing long-term effects of interventions	Does not provide information about participants at later ages	Focuses on a short period of time, not usually linked to performance at later ages	
Time consuming, expensive, susceptible to attrition of participants over time	Economical and efficient, with lower chance of attrition	Time consuming and labor intensive study of a relatively small sample; likelihood of attrition is low	
Results may apply only to the cohort of participants studied	Does not differentiate between differences due to age and differences due to cohort	Results may apply only to individuals involved in study	

Leopold amassed. We look next at several classic examples of longitudinal studies and consider the advantages and disadvantages of this research design (see Table 2.4).

Longitudinal Research

In **longitudinal research,** investigators study the same sample of participants over time, measuring their behavior or ability at specified intervals. Longitudinal research enables researchers to chart individual change or stability over time, revealing relations between early functioning and later development.

Longitudinal designs can be used with a small number of participants, as illustrated by Leopold's case study and by a classic investigation of language development involving three children known as Adam, Eve, and Sarah. The research team in that study visited the children's homes approximately every two weeks, beginning when they were around 2 years of age, and audiotaped their interactions for approximately 2 hours on each visit. Although each child developed language at a different rate, they acquired aspects of language in a similar order (Brown, 1973).

It is more common for longitudinal studies to gather data from a relatively large number of participants. One pioneering longitudinal study observed approximately 700 Hawaiian children over a period of 30 years, identifying factors in some children's lives that helped them triumph over early adversity, poverty, and neglect (Werner, 1989, 2000). Participants in another landmark longitudinal study of the infant-caregiver relationship are now in their thirties; we discuss the evidence for long-term continuity and consequences of those early relationships in Chapter 9 (Sroufe, 2005; Sroufe et al., 2005).

In contrast to the findings of research on social and emotional development, longitudinal studies of intelligence have generally produced only modest evidence of continuity when measures in infancy are compared with measures in childhood and adolescence. One of the problems in this research is a lack of **measurement equivalence**—correspondence between the measures, or dependent variables, used at two different points in time (Miller, 1998). Whereas IQ tests in childhood and beyond typically rely on verbal ability, intelligence tests for babies tend to focus on nonverbal, motor abilities. We consider whether and how infant intelligence predicts later intelligence in Chapter 7.

Longitudinal designs are a good way to evaluate the effects of interventions on development. Ramey and his colleagues, for example, used a longitudinal design to study children from the time they were 6 weeks of age until they entered early adulthood (e.g., Ramey & Campbell, 1991; Ramey et al., 2000; Ramey & Ramey, 1998a). By comparing children randomly chosen to participate in an early childhood education program and children randomly chosen to receive pediatric and social work services, nutritional assistance, and home visits, the researchers were able to assess the influence of the education program in a number of developmental domains. We discuss this research program in greater detail in Chapter 11.

Longitudinal studies are not ideal for all researchers or all research questions. One disadvantage is that they are time consuming. In order to gather data about how a given behavior or ability changes across childhood and into adolescence, researchers need to commit themselves to studying the same group of individuals for nearly two decades. Researchers who have been involved in some of the most ambitious longitudinal studies, such as the Stanford Studies of Gifted Children, the Oakland (Adolescent) Growth Study, the Berkeley Growth and Guidance Studies, the Fels Research Institute Study, and the Seattle Longitudinal Study, have grown old with their subjects and in some cases have been outlived by them. This problem is obviously less relevant when studies examine development from birth to the age of 2 or 3 years, since intervals of even a few months can reveal dramatic developmental change (Miller, 1998; Tikotzky & Sadeh, 2009).

Keeping track of all of the participants in a longitudinal study over many years can be expensive, and some participants may decline to continue in the study or become unavailable for a variety of reasons. In some longitudinal studies, such as those investigating intelligence or cognitive abilities, it may be unclear whether participants' performance improves as a result of the development of more advanced abilities or as a result of repeated exposure to the measures of those abilities, a phenomenon known as a **practice effect.** Again, these problems tend to be of less concern for researchers studying developmental change over the period of infancy (Miller, 1998).

Finally, it is not always clear in longitudinal research whether the results obtained for a particular group or generation, known as a **cohort** of participants (such as infants born in the same year), are generalizable to other groups. The reason for concern about generalizability to other cohorts is especially evident when considering studies that were begun in the 1920s or 1930s. The individuals in these studies experienced a particular set of historic events, including the Great Depression, World War II, the Korean War, and the Vietnam War, and they lived in a society that has changed dramatically, especially in terms of technology and educational and work opportunities for girls and women. It is reasonable, therefore, to ask whether and how the course of their development compares to the development of children born in the 1960s, the 1990s, or the twenty-first century. In Chapter 12, we consider some of the ways in which infants born in the twenty-first century constitute a unique cohort.

Cross-Sectional Research

Given the practical limitations of longitudinal studies, it is not surprising that most developmental researchers choose to conduct **cross-sectional research.** In cross-sectional designs, two or more age groups of participants are compared in terms of their behavior or ability at the same point in time. If Leopold had used a cross-sectional design, he could have gathered data covering the same range of ages by comparing different groups of English–German bilingual children between 8 weeks and 14 years. Instead of spending 14 years, he could have finished his study in just one year.

Cross-sectional studies can provide important converging evidence for longitudinal findings. This was true of cross-sectional studies that later replicated the longitudinal description of Adam, Eve, and Sarah's early language acquisition. In comparison to longitudinal studies, cross-sectional research is typically less time consuming, less expensive, and more flexible because new variables can be explored in subsequent cross-sectional studies. The problems of participant loss and practice effects are of less concern in cross-sectional studies than in longitudinal research.

Even when cross-sectional studies reveal differences between age groups, it cannot be assumed that the differences are due to developmental change. If researchers are not careful when selecting their sample, they will have difficulty disentangling the influence of age from the influence of other "nuisance" variables. In Leopold's research, these nuisance variables might include differences in the families' economic resources or in the amount of English and German to which children in various families are exposed. Another potential problem, especially in cross-sectional studies comparing a wide range of ages and older samples, such as 10-, 20-, 30-, and 40-year-olds, is that age differences may reflect generational differences—**cohort effects.** Infancy researchers, fortunately, are probably safe in assuming that 12-, 18-, and 24-month-olds all represent the same cohort (Miller, 1998).

Microgenetic Research

Cross-sectional studies reveal age differences and suggest developmental differences, but they do not provide information about *how* development occurs. Researchers who want to understand developmental processes as they occur within the same individual have turned recently to what might be thought of as a very short-term longitudinal design—**microgenetic research.** In microgenetic studies, participants are observed in a relatively large number of sessions over a short period of time, with the researchers gathering a rich set of data on which fine-grained analyses can be performed. Microgenetic analyses are applicable across many different developmental domains and can be adapted to a wide variety of settings, including those outside of a laboratory (Siegler, 2006).

The microgenetic method has been used to shed light on older children's cognitive development and problem solving (Siegler, 2006; Siegler & Crowley, 1991). In a study comparing children with and without cognitive disabilities, the microgenetic approach was applied over a period of 12 weeks to document changes in the strategies used to solve math and reading problems. The results revealed a number of similarities between the two groups of children that had not been detected in other studies using less dense sampling (Fletcher et al., 1998).

In studies of infants, the microgenetic approach has proved especially fruitful in documenting learning and development—significant changes in behavior that often occur in a relatively brief period. The microgenetic approach has been used to investigate the onset of walking (Adolph, 1995) and reaching (Thelen & Smith, 1994; Thelen & Spencer, 1998), as well as the development of infants' manual and oral exploratory responses to objects presented over several sessions (Jones, 1996). Patterns of vocalization and emotional communication have also been analyzed in videotapes of mother-infant play made over a period of 4 to 7 months (Pantoja, Nelson-Goens, & Fogel, 2001).

If Leopold had been able to use modern technology to videotape samples of his daughter's language, and if his study had covered a vastly briefer period of time (e.g., 24 to 30 months of age), it would have been similar to some contemporary microgenetic studies. Microgenetic studies generally have a much smaller number of participants than cross-sectional studies. This is due to the dense sampling of behavior and detailed analysis of videotapes, which makes them both expensive and labor intensive. Still, the new insights they may provide make them an attractive option for many researchers today.

In addition to selecting a setting and design for their question, researchers also need to choose a response measure. The age and abilities of the research participants play an important role in this choice, and as we discuss next, infants present special challenges to researchers. There are advantages to studying infants, however, because unlike older children and adults, they are often unaware that they are participating in research. This means that researchers are more likely to see infants exhibiting typical behaviors, even in unfamiliar laboratory settings.

RESEARCH MEASURES

The specific question the researcher is asking influences the measures chosen in a study. In studies of infant-parent relationships, for example, it makes sense to measure behaviors that occur in the course of infant-parent interactions, such as play, emotional communication, and physical contact. In investigations of language development, by contrast, researchers quite reasonably focus on aspects of communication, both verbal and nonverbal. In this section we examine examples of the range of response measures that are used in studies with infants, as shown in Table 2.5. Some

TABLE 2.5 Response Measures for Studying Infant Behavior and Development	
Response Measure	**Examples**
Behavioral	
Psychophysiological	• Heart rate
Involuntary responses to stimuli and events in the testing environment.	• Cortisol level
	• Brain activity measured with electroencephalography (EEG) and event-related potential (ERP)
Visual Behavior	• Visual fixation
Spontaneous "looking time" responses to stimuli and events in the testing environment.	• Visual preference
	• Habituation/dishabituation
Conditioned Behavior	• Conditioned sucking
Responses to stimuli that are reinforced by contingencies in the testing environment. When infants learn that their behaviors produce a rewarding outcome, researchers can vary the stimuli and note whether the infant displays the conditioned behavior under those circumstances.	• Conditioned headturning
Parental Report	• Diary reports
	• Checklists
	• Rating scales
	• Questionnaires
Archival Research	• Census records
	• Vital statistics, such as births and deaths
	• Childcare manuals and parenting magazines
	• Equipment used to care for infants
	• Equipment used to care for infants

researchers choose to measure behaviors that infants display spontaneously, while others focus on behaviors that they teach infants to perform. In some studies, researchers forego direct observation of infant behaviors altogether and gather parental reports about their infants or examine data and records that other researchers have gathered.

Behavioral Responses

Newborn and very young infants are capable of making a number of simple behavioral responses, such as looking and sucking, that researchers can use to investigate their perceptual and cognitive abilities. Thus, if responses do not depend on more advanced behaviors, such as the ability to reach, crawl, or speak, it is possible to ask even very young infants specific questions and end up with useful, interpretable answers. Almost any behavior that infants display spontaneously can be used as a dependent variable.

PSYCHOPHYSIOLOGICAL MEASURES   Some researchers use psychophysiological measures to gauge infants' responses to stimuli. Heart rate is the most popular of these measures, primarily because it can be recorded in response to any sort of stimulus, whether it involves infants' vision, hearing, or sense of taste, touch, or smell (Miller, 1998). When infants are orienting and attending to stimuli, their heart rate tends to slow down. Heart rate is also attractive to researchers because it can be used with infants of any age and does not depend on motor skills. Changes in heart rate can be measured even when overt behavioral changes are not apparent (Bornstein & Lamb, 1992). Some researchers have combined measures of heart rate and other behavioral responses in the same study. These studies have shown, for example, that infants who do not show behavioral signs of stress when their parent leaves the room sometimes have changes in heart rate that are consistent with a psychological stress reaction.

Other studies using psychophysiological responses have measured levels of the stress hormone cortisol in the saliva of infants and young children (Andersson, Bohlin, & Hagekull, 1999; Larson et al., 1998; Watamura, Kryzer, & Robertson, 2008). Cortisol levels can be measured between 15 and 45 minutes after a stressful event, whether the stress is the result of a medical procedure like circumcision, a painful inoculation, a distressing separation from the parent, or interactions in a

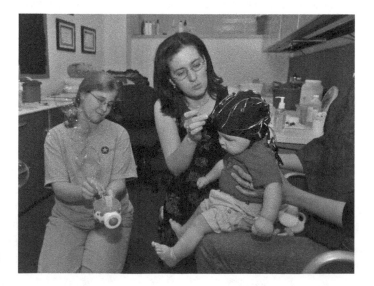

New technology allows researchers to measure electrical activity in the infant's brain, using electrodes that rest on the scalp in a special cap.

play group of unfamiliar children in an unfamiliar setting. Cortisol can be gathered from saliva that collects in flavored dental pads the child has chewed or sucked on. Cortisol levels fluctuate naturally during the course of the day, however, so researchers need to be aware of these normal rhythms when examining their data.

Some researchers measure electrical activity in the infant's brain, using sensitive electrodes that rest on the scalp. Recordings of the spontaneous natural rhythms of the brain are made using **electroencephalography, or EEG** (Johnson, 1998). The EEG procedure is attractive because it is both noninvasive and relatively inexpensive. It is not well suited to the study of cognition, because it does not reveal brain activity in response to particular stimuli, but it is sensitive to state changes and can be used in studies of social and emotional development (Nelson & Bloom, 1997). Electrical activity resulting from the presentation of discrete stimuli can be measured with the cortical **event-related potential, or ERP.** The ERP has been useful in studies of infants' cognitive abilities, including attention, memory, and language comprehension (Nelson, 1994, 1995; Nelson & Bloom, 1997). The primary difficulty in applying ERP methodology to infants is that muscle or eye movements can produce responses that are not related to the stimulus under study, and the results may lead researchers to disregard a participant's entire data set (Johnson, 1998; Nelson & Bloom, 1997; Shonkoff & Phillips, 2000). In Chapter 5, we examine brain development as well as more recently developed measures such as magnetic resonance imaging, or MRI scans, which are not well suited for use with alert, active infants and young children.

MEASURES OF VISUAL BEHAVIOR   Visual fixation—infants' spontaneous looking behavior—is commonly used in laboratory studies of perception and cognition; researchers present carefully constructed stimuli and note the direction and duration of infants' looking behavior. We discuss the development of perceptual abilities in Chapter 6. For now, it is sufficient to note that even newborn infants are able to shift their attention from one object or one display to another, and this ability improves with age. By noticing where and for how long infants gaze, researchers have been able to answer many fundamental questions about perceptual abilities in infancy (Aslin, 2007).

Much of contemporary research in infant perception is built on the pioneering work of Robert Fantz (1961), who developed the **visual preference method**—a technique in which infants' looking behavior is used to determine their ability to perceive and notice differences between stimuli presented in a laboratory setting. Fantz designed a special looking chamber in which infants lie on their back and look at two visual stimuli that are presented simultaneously, such as a bull's-eye and a solid circle. (The position of the bull's-eye and the circle are alternated so that the researcher can detect responding that is based on a preference for displays on the baby's right side, rather than a preference for pattern complexity.) The stimuli cannot be examined simultaneously, however, so infants are required to move their head slightly in order to look at the entire display. In Fantz's studies the dependent variable was the duration of the infants' look at each stimulus. (Looking down into the chamber, it is possible to see where the infant is looking during each moment of the session.) If infants looked longer at one stimulus, such as the bull's-eye, Fantz inferred that they preferred that stimulus. Using this method, Fantz—and many researchers after him—tested infants' ability to discriminate between pairs of stimuli varying in numerous ways, including complexity, familiarity, and symmetry.

The usefulness of the visual preference method is limited, however, if an infant does not show a clear preference for one of the two stimuli. The absence of a preference could reflect something as uninteresting as an infant's preference for stimuli that are shown on the right side; since the two stimuli appear equally often in the left and the right positions, a strong right-side preference would result in similar looking times for the two stimuli. Absence of a preference could also indicate that the infant could not tell the difference between the two stimuli or that the infant noticed the difference but did not prefer one more than the other. Automated eye tracking instruments have become more available, giving researchers the means of performing more fine-grained analyses of infants' looking (Aslin & McMurray, 2004; Miller, 1998).

Infants' spontaneous looking behavior is also a frequent measure in studies in which infants are shown just one stimulus at a time in a procedure known as the habituation and dishabituation method—the most commonly used method in the study of infant perception and cognition (Kellman & Arterberry, 1998). **Habituation** refers to the phenomenon in which infants gradually lose interest in a stimulus after repeated presentations. The first time the stimulus is shown, infants show an **orienting response** and may momentarily cease any ongoing activity in order to give close visual attention to the new stimulus (Haith & Benson, 1998; Miller, 1998). After numerous presentations, the orienting response weakens but can be reactivated by replacing the first stimulus with a different one. The recovery of attention when a new stimulus is introduced is known as **dishabituation.** Researchers infer, for example, that infants who become habituated to one stimulus, such as a photograph of a woman's face, and show dishabituation when that photograph is replaced by a photograph of a different woman's face are able to detect differences between the two stimuli.

If infants fail to show dishabituation, it may mean that they cannot detect a difference between the old and new stimuli. It may also indicate, however, that change in looking behavior was not a sufficiently sensitive measure of infants' orienting response. Because the orienting response is also characterized by subtler physiological changes, researchers may use heart rate or automated eye tracking equipment as an index of infants' habituation–dishabituation response (Aslin & McMurray, 2004; Miller, 1998). Other behaviors, such as sucking rate, can also be used to detect decreasing and increasing amounts of responsiveness to stimuli during habituation and dishabituation.

Habituation measures are valuable because they can be used with infants only a few months or even a few days old (Aslin, Jusczyk, & Pisoni, 1998). In addition, given that orienting responses, habituation, and dishabituation are naturally occurring behaviors, researchers do not have to teach infants to respond in these ways. Habituation–dishabituation measures do have some drawbacks, however, including attrition rates of 50 percent or higher. These rates reflect the requirement that infants remain in a stable state for as long as 10 to 15 minutes in order to complete all parts of the sequential task (Aslin et al., 1998; Kellman & Arterberry, 1998). Another potential limitation is the existence of individual differences among infants in how quickly they habituate and dishabituate. This variability may reflect individual differences in infants' ability to process information about the world, and as we discuss in Chapter 7, some researchers have reported finding correlations between infants' efficiency of habituation and cognitive abilities later in childhood (Colombo, 1993; Colombo & Janowsky, 1998; McCall & Carriger, 1993). The creative, evolving nature of research is exemplified by this application—a method that was developed primarily to study infant perception is now being used to explore the foundations of intelligence.

CONDITIONED BEHAVIOR   In some studies, researchers teach infants how to respond. A procedure known as **conditioned headturning** has been used to assess infants' ability to hear differences between auditory stimuli. When infants turn their head to look in the direction of a new sound or speech sample, they are rewarded with an entertaining sight, such as an animated toy moving inside a lighted display case. Infants who are rewarded with this sight every time they hear that sound or speech sample—and only when they hear that sound or speech sample— soon learn to turn their head after they hear it, in anticipation of the "show." Once this headturning response has been conditioned and is elicited reliably, a different sound (or speech sample) can be presented or alternated with the original one. Infants who do not turn their head in response to the new stimulus are assumed to be able to discriminate between the one used in conditioning and the new stimulus, whereas infants who turn their head, looking for the entertaining display, are thought not to be able to make this discrimination (Miller, 1998; Pelucchi, Hay, & Saffran, 2009).

The conditioned headturning procedure and its variations work because infants are able to notice and remember associations between their responses to specific events, such as the presence of a particular sound, and the consequences of their response. Some variations on the basic conditioned headturning procedure have made the task so complex that it cannot be used with infants younger than 4 or 5 months of age, but the simple version of the procedure has been used with infants as young as 2 to 3 months old. Once the conditioning phase is completed, the technique has the advantage of a low attrition rate and great flexibility in the stimuli that can be used (Aslin et al., 1998; Miller, 1998).

Parental Reports

Researchers working with infants and very young children typically see them for only brief periods of time. During that time, infants may not reveal their full range of abilities due to the interference of factors such as behavioral state changes or wariness in the presence of an unfamiliar researcher or strange laboratory setting. One way to gather more representative data is to use **parental reports,** data provided about infants' behavior and development by their parents or caregivers, who have almost unlimited access and opportunity to observe them. Werner Leopold may be the best example of a parent who used every opportunity to notice and record his child's development.

Some researchers have trained parents to keep diaries in which they systematically record observations about one aspect of the infant's development, such as memory, in everyday settings (Ashmead & Perlmutter, 1980). In other studies, parents provide researchers with reports, often in checklist form, about whether their child has achieved particular milestones in the development of motor skills, social interaction, or language and communication. As they use these measures, researchers need to keep in mind that parental reports do have some limitations. The principal disadvantage is that, for a variety of reasons, parents may misunderstand instructions or fail to give accurate reports about their children's behavior and development. As we note in Chapter 10, when we discuss approaches to studying infant temperament, it can be useful to employ multiple methods, such as direct observation in a laboratory setting as well as parents' ratings of their child's behavior in everyday contexts.

Archival Research

Some researchers are interested in understanding the period of infancy at different points throughout history. Infants from the past obviously cannot be compared directly with infants living today, but archival records can be used. **Archival research** may use official sources of information, such as census records or birth certificates from different points in time, to answer questions about changes in birthweight, family size, maternal age, and rates of infant mortality or infant growth. Archival research can also be based on information found in popular childcare manuals from the past, parents' diaries, or even cultural artifacts such as children's literature, works of art, advertisements, and furniture (Clement, 1997; Fontanel & d'Harcourt, 1997). As we noted in Chapter 1, examination of issues of *Parents* magazine revealed significant change in the advice being given to parents of infants from 1955 to 1984 (Young, 1990).

FIGURE 2.1 Nineteenth-century prints illustrating a turnstile and slide walker—devices used to hold infants in an upright position before they learned to walk independently.

Source: Reprinted by permission of Roger-Viollet Agence Photographique.

Archival studies often make fascinating reading and may reveal changes in beliefs about the essential nature of babies and their development. The history of devices used to restrain and prop up infants, for example, shows that parents in the Middle Ages, and even in the seventeenth and eighteenth centuries, "had no faith that children would come to walking of their own accord" (Calvert, 1992, p. 34). Parents believed that, without active intervention, babies might never abandon their animalistic form of crawling on all fours. As a result, they used contraptions of all kinds, like those shown in Figure 2.1, to hold infants upright and guide their first steps before they began walking independently. Histories of feeding practices, as another example, are rich in details about the practice of wet-nursing and the development of bottles, nipples, and alternatives to breast milk (Fontanel & d'Harcourt, 1997).

ISSUES IN RESEARCH WITH INFANTS

Infants' nonverbal responses can be illuminating, but babies are not always cooperative research participants. Moreover, researchers working with infants can never actually know what they perceive, feel, or remember—all response measures require inference and interpretation. Parents can sometimes help researchers interpret infants' behavior, but studies of infants entail special ethical concerns, and researchers need to take precautions to help parents understand their role as the child's advocate in the research setting.

Behavioral State

Unless researchers are studying sleep, they need participants to be awake and alert in order to provide data. Newborn infants, however, sleep an average of 16 to 17 hours each day and move in and out of as many as 10 different states of arousal (Freudigman & Thoman, 1998; Louis et al., 1997; Thoman, 1990). These **behavioral states** include four awake states, three transition states between sleep and waking, two sleep states, and one transition sleep state. Of these 10 states, the awake/alert state, in which the infant's eyes are open and the infant is engaged in attentively scanning the environment, is the most optimal one for nearly all research questions. Unfortunately for researchers, less than 10 percent of the average newborn infant's day is spent in this state (Louis et al., 1997; Thoman, 1990).

A regular, predictable pattern of sleep/wake states depends upon neurological development. This is one of the reasons it can take several months before an infant gets "on a schedule." Some infants show greater regularity at an earlier age than others (Freudigman & Thoman, 1998; Ingersoll & Thoman, 1999; White et al., 2000). One neonatal assessment that takes this variability across infants into account—the Brazelton Neonatal Behavioral Assessment Scale (NBAS)—uses it to help new parents become sensitive to their infant's behavioral patterns and capabilities (Brazelton & Nugent, 1995; Nugent, Petrauskas, & Brazelton, 2009). We discuss sleep/wake states and the Brazelton NBAS in more detail in Chapter 4.

Newborn infants who have been fed recently are likely to drift into a sleep state. Infants who are hungry are also unlikely to be attentive research participants. To compensate for these tendencies, if it will not interfere with the study, parents sometimes offer pacifiers to help their baby remain alert and nonfussy (Franco et al., 2000). It is also a good idea to make the experimental session as short as possible. Even with these steps, researchers who work with newborns must accept the reality that attrition of participants will be commonplace. Indeed, in some studies with newborns, as many as 50 percent of infants may not complete the procedure due to factors such as drowsiness, crying, needing a diaper change, or spitting up.

Inference and Interpretation

Another challenge facing researchers working with infants and preverbal children is the problem of inference and interpretation (Cohen & Cashon, 2006; Haith & Benson, 1998). The measures that researchers use to study infants are necessarily indirect, since participants cannot respond verbally to questions about what they perceive, think, or feel. Researchers rely on responses such as changes in heart rate and cortisol levels, as well as behaviors such as sucking, looking, and in some studies, reaching, crawling, or walking.

In many studies of infant perception and cognition, researchers measure the duration of infants' visual gaze toward stimuli, as shown in Figure 2.2. In these studies, which we discuss further in Chapters 6 and 7, differences in the amount of time infants spend looking at various stimuli are inferred to reflect their awareness of or preference for characteristics that the researcher has manipulated, such as size, complexity, and familiarity. In some studies, infants who look longer at "impossible" events—such as a solid object that appears to pass through another solid object—are described as expressing surprise. In other studies, the duration of infants' looking behavior when stimuli like dolls or small toys are introduced or taken away is said to reveal an early understanding of addition and subtraction. Inferences like these are not universally accepted, and researchers continue to debate the meaning of infants' behavioral responses.

FIGURE 2.2   In some laboratory studies, infants are shown side-by-side video displays and the amount of attention they give to them is compared to determine whether they prefer one display more than the other.

Ethical Concerns

All studies with human participants need to be concerned with **research ethics**—a set of principles and guidelines for conducting acceptable research activities. Before researchers conduct their studies, they must obtain approval from an independent Institutional Review Board (IRB). Members of the IRB are independent in that they must not be part of any research team whose proposal they review. In considering whether to approve proposals, the IRB determines whether the researchers' plans meet guidelines for ethical conduct in research, such as those developed by the American Psychological Association or the Society for Research in Child Development (SRCD, 2000). Guidelines from SRCD specify that researchers studying child behavior and development must use the least harmful and least stressful procedures whenever possible. The rationale for any proposed exposure to physical or psychological stress must be extremely clear and compelling; even then, the IRB may not give approval to studies if the risk imposed on participants is not outweighed by the potential value of the findings.

Ethical guidelines for research with humans require that participants give their **informed consent,** explicit agreement that is based on understanding the procedures involved in a study and any risks those procedures might entail and knowing that they are free to withdraw or decline to participate without any negative consequences. It is generally assumed that children cannot give informed consent, but children who can answer questions verbally are able to give their **assent**—or agreement—to participate in research (Thompson, 1990). Children who can speak are also able to indicate that they wish to discontinue participating through statements such as, "I don't want to play this game anymore."

In studies with infants, not even assent is possible, so researchers need to obtain the informed consent of participants' parents. Researchers must explain all procedures clearly, indicate any potential risks that may result from participation, and make clear the parents' right to stop participation on their infant's behalf. It is also essential that parents be told exactly how their rights to privacy will be maintained. If the infant's behavior is videotaped, for example, parents need to be told who will have access to the videotape, how their family's identity will be protected, how long the videotape will be kept by the researcher, and what will happen to the videotape after the study is completed.

Parents of the same infant do not always agree about the conditions under which they will allow their child to participate in research and whether they are willing to continue if a study involves multiple sessions over a period of months or years; to address possible differences of opinion, some researchers ask both parents to give their informed consent. The situation can also be complicated if one of the parents is a highly motivated infancy researcher looking for unlimited access to a young research participant in a naturalistic setting. In one such family, the father was a researcher who installed 11 video cameras and 14 microphones throughout the home in order to record his son's language development from birth to age 3. Given the potential threats to the child's privacy, as well as the privacy of other family members and guests, the IRB that reviewed the father's research application approved the study with certain conditions: Each camera and microphone needed to have an "off" switch, visitors needed to give their informed consent to be recorded, and portions of the tapes had to be erased if anyone, even the researcher's son after the age of 18 years, requested that their part of the total 250,000 recorded hours be destroyed (Belluck, 2009).

Regardless of whether they are related to the child being studied, researchers also need to make clear any benefits—or lack of benefits—associated with the study. Parents who bring their infants to participate in a study in a university setting or health clinic, for example, may also bring unfounded expectations that their infant's intelligence or health will be enhanced as a result of their participation. In studies involving infants who are at risk, due to conditions such as preterm birth or prenatal exposure to drugs or alcohol, researchers need to be extraordinarily clear when obtaining informed consent if infants will be randomly placed into either a potentially helpful treatment group or a comparison group that will not receive treatment. If, in the course of such a study, researchers become convinced that there is no doubt about a treatment's effectiveness, ethical guidelines direct them to offer the treatment to all participants.

Researchers need to be cautious when communicating with parents about any developmental problems that they suspect an infant may have, if those problems become evident during the course of a study. Because young infants' state of arousal has a significant impact on their ability to attend to stimuli, they may not always display their "best" performance. If parents express concerns about their child's development, researchers may provide information or referrals to qualified specialists. As a rule, however, unless researchers have the necessary expertise and are using recognized assessment tools, it is best if they give parents only general feedback about their infant's performance in the study. By contrast, researchers who strongly suspect that an infant has been abused or neglected must notify the local child protection agency.

Where Do Babies Come From?

Unlike researchers studying college students, who often participate in research as a requirement for an academic course or to receive extra credit, researchers studying infants have the additional challenge of finding participants. Some researchers utilize public announcements of births, while others recruit participants from childcare centers, parenting groups, health clinics, and hospitals. Still others place advertisements in newspapers or parenting magazines. In some studies, researchers may have funds with which to pay families for their participation. When researchers report the findings of their studies in published articles or at professional conferences, they provide summary information about the source and characteristics of their sample. This information is useful to the wider community of researchers, since it is informative about the external validity of the study and the ethnic, racial, linguistic, and socioeconomic diversity of the participants.

WRAPPING IT UP: Summary and Conclusion

Researchers make choices when they plan and carry out empirical research, accepting the trade-offs entailed in those choices. Naturalistic studies usually are more generalizable than studies carried out in laboratory settings, for example, but laboratories offer greater consistency and uniformity of experience across research participants. There are also different advantages and disadvantages when conducting case studies as opposed to studies with larger samples, quasi-experiments rather than experiments, and longitudinal versus cross-sectional approaches. Some researchers combine different approaches or turn to microgenetic research to illuminate the process through which development occurs over a relatively short period of time.

The specific question the researcher is asking influences the measures chosen. Some measures rely on infants' natural, spontaneous responses. Infants can also be conditioned to perform behaviors as a way of signaling that they detect differences between stimuli. Parental reports about infants' behavior and development can provide useful information, especially when researchers train parents to observe specific aspects of their child's development and systematically record these observations in structured diaries.

Researchers working with infants face special challenges, including the tendency for newborns to shift frequently between behavioral states. To the extent that researchers studying infants rely on indirect measures, they base their conclusions on inference and interpretation, and different researchers may have different interpretations of the same evidence. Ethical guidelines for research with children assist researchers in incorporating ethical practices into their studies. Infants are unable to give either informed consent or assent, so researchers need to obtain informed consent from parents.

The choices that researchers make are also affected by the availability of infants and, as illustrated in the case of Werner Leopold's study of Hildegard, the limitations of existing knowledge and technology. The methodological choices available to researchers are one indicator of how much is already known about a topic, so accepted measures and standard laboratory procedures are most likely to exist for topics that have been under investigation for many years. Even for well-established topics, there is room for innovation as new and more sensitive measures become available. It has been noted that "all methods must cope with the fact that human infants are nonverbal, relatively immobile, and only intermittently cooperative experimental subjects" (Kellman & Arterberry, 1998, p. 317). It is a testament to researchers' creativity and perseverance that so many choices exist today.

THINK ABOUT IT: Questions for Reading and Discussion

1. Which do you think are more valuable—naturalistic studies or laboratory studies? If you were the parent of an infant, would you allow a research team to observe you and your child in your home, or would you prefer to participate in a laboratory setting?

2. What are some of the ethical issues that researchers should consider when carrying out case studies, especially when the individual being studied is at risk or may have been deprived of normal care early in life? From an ethical standpoint, how would you evaluate Werner Leopold's study of his bilingual daughter?

3. Some researchers use deception in their studies. Under what circumstances do you think this is appropriate? Would you agree to participate—or have your child participate—in a study that you knew involved some sort of deception? Why or why not?

4. Some studies explore basic issues, such as infants' ability to discriminate between two speech sounds. Other studies investigate applied issues, such as the impact

of childcare on infants' development. If you were in charge of allocating funds, explain how you would divide the money between these types of studies.

5. What sorts of issues should ethnographic researchers be sensitive to when observing behavior and development in a culture other than their own?

6. Can you think of a way Werner Leopold could have carried out his study using ethnographic research methods? Could archival research have been used in a study like his? Would psychophysiological measures have been useful? Explain your answers.

Key Words

Archival research (51)   Research that replaces the direct observation or assessment of research participants with examination of records or artifacts.

Assent (54)   Verbal agreement to participate in research, obtained when participants are unable to give informed consent.

Baby biography (40)   Observational records made by parents or other caregivers of an infants' early development.

Behavioral state (52)   Any of 10 distinct levels of arousal observed in newborn infants, including four awake states, three transition states between sleep and waking, two sleep states, and one transition sleep state.

Case study (40)   Also referred to as the clinical method, this is an in-depth examination of a single individual.

Cohort (45)   A particular group or generation of participants, such as infants born in the same year.

Cohort effects (46)   A problem in cross-sectional research, in which age differences may actually stem from generational, or cohort, differences.

Conditioned headturning (50)   A technique in which infants are taught to turn their head every time they hear a particular signal—and only when they hear that signal. Once this headturning response has been conditioned and can be elicited reliably, a different stimulus is presented or alternated with the original signal. Infants who do not turn their head in response to the new stimulus are assumed to be able to discriminate between the signal used in conditioning and the new stimulus, whereas infants who turn

their head are thought not to be able to make this discrimination.

Cross-sectional research (45)   A developmental design in which two or more age groups of participants are compared in terms of their behavior or ability at the same point in time.

Dependent variable (38)   The main behavior or response of interest in a study, this is the researchers' measure of the impact of the independent variable(s).

Dishabituation (50)   Infants' recovery of attention when a new stimulus is introduced.

Electroencephalography (EEG) (49)   A measurement of electrical activity and spontaneous natural rhythms in the brain.

Ethnographic research (36)   A technique for exploring the interaction of culture and biology, in which researchers from a Western culture make observations or conduct interviews in everyday settings in non-Western cultures.

Event-related potential (ERP) (49)   A measurement of electrical activity resulting in the brain from the presentation of discrete stimuli.

Event sampling (34)   A technique in observational research in which a small number of behaviors are identified and the researcher makes a note each time they occur by making a mark on a prepared checklist.

Experimental design (42)   A design that examines the influence of an independent variable on a dependent variable.

External validity (39)   The degree to which the findings of one study can be extended, or generalized, to other samples and settings.

Habituation (50)   The phenomenon in which infants gradually lose interest in a stimulus after repeated presentations.

Independent variable (38)   Aspects of a research setting that researchers identify or vary, such as presence or absence of an infant's mother, in order to determine their effect on behaviors of interest.

Informed consent (54)   A key requirement in ethical research, based on research participants being able to understand the procedures involved in a study and any risks those procedures might entail and knowing that they are free to withdraw or decline to participate without any negative consequences.

Internal validity (39)   The degree to which differences in the dependent variable are actually due to differences in the independent variable.

Laboratory setting (38)   A specially designed research space that enables researchers to control or eliminate the influence of irrelevant or distracting factors.

Longitudinal research (44)   A developmental design in which investigators study the same sample of participants over time, taking measures of their behavior or ability at specified intervals.

Measurement equivalence (44)   Correspondence between the measures, or dependent variables, used at two different points in time.

Microgenetic research (46)   A developmental design in which participants are observed over a period of time, perhaps 10 or more sessions, with the researchers gathering a rich set of data on which fine-grained analyses can be performed.

Narrative record (34)   A detailed description of the range of behaviors researchers observe.

Naturalistic observation (33)   Studies in which researchers remain relatively passive observers in the sense that, apart from being physically present, they do not intervene in or try to influence the situation.

Naturalistic setting (33)   Studies in which researchers observe infants in their usual surroundings, such as their own home or their regular childcare center.

Observer bias (34)   The phenomenon in which researchers' expectations or beliefs influence the way they record or interpret behavior.

Operational definition (34)   A clear, concrete verbal description that enables researchers to measure target behaviors and outcomes accurately.

Orienting response (50)   Infants' behavior the first time a stimulus is presented, characterized by momentary cessation of any ongoing activity in order to give close attention to the new stimulus.

Parental reports (51)   Data provided about infants' behavior and development by their parents or caregivers.

Practice effect (45)   Improvement in participants' performance as a result of the repeated exposure to the measures of those abilities.

Quasi-experimental design (42)   A design in which researchers collect information about groups of participants that are already formed before the study begins.

Random assignment (43)   The equivalent of flipping a coin, this technique is used to ensure that each child has an equal chance of being placed into the different groups being compared on a specific dependent variable. As a result of this precaution, potentially important differences across children are distributed across the different groups.

Research ethics (53)   A set of principles and guidelines for conducting acceptable research activities.

Single-subject research (41)   A variation of the case study, in which researchers intervene or study the effects of an experimental manipulation within a single participant.

Visual fixation (49)   Infants' looking behavior at stimuli presented in laboratory settings.

Visual preference method (49)   A technique in which infants' looking behavior is used to determine their ability to perceive and notice differences between stimuli presented in a laboratory setting

Genetics, Conception, and Prenatal Development

All parents hope that their infant will be healthy at birth. Expectant parents can do much more than simply hope, however, if they want to increase the chance that their baby will have a healthy start in life. There are many ways to safeguard prenatal development, and as a result, the vast majority of pregnancies in the United States and other developed countries end with the birth of a healthy, full-term baby.

Recent advances in medical technology have made it possible for some pregnancies to get started by bringing together eggs and sperm from donors who usually will never meet the children their contributions helped create. In some countries, however, such as Sweden, Switzerland, Austria, The Netherlands, Australia, New Zealand, the United Kingdom, and the United States, knowledge about a person's biological lineage is now viewed as a basic human right, and various procedures exist to inform donors that their identity as the source of the egg or sperm may be revealed to any offspring making that request (Frith, 2001). Regardless of whether identity information is available, many prospective parents select donors who are described as possessing a particular set of physical characteristics, in an effort to have a child who resembles them in race, height, and eye and hair color. If information about the donor's education level or occupation is available, prospective parents may also use that information to include or exclude a potential donor. Prospective parents have many different reasons for using donor eggs or sperm and they feel different ways about donor anonymity. Rather than hide their child's biological origins, as was often done in the past, an increasing number of parents are opting to share this information as just one of many important aspects of their child's life.

Some parents go even further, using the donor's unique identification number to obtain additional sperm or eggs from the donor "bank" to create a family with siblings who are biologically related. In cases where a family has only one child, knowledge of the donor's identification number can be used to find that child's half-siblings through registries that facilitate contact between families who share the same donor. In some cases, families may discover that their "only" child has dozens of donor-shared siblings, some of whom—along with their parents—may be interested in meeting and developing a relationship. As shown in Table 3.1, there are many reasons parents search for their child's donor or donor siblings, including simple curiosity and wanting to have more information about their child's inherited medical history (Freeman et al., 2009).

Donor searches afford new definitions of family, while also raising interesting questions about genetics, conception, and human development. Is it really possible to influence the characteristics of donor offspring to the extent that some prospective parents desire? Are genetically related siblings necessarily more similar and compatible than unrelated siblings? How does each child's experience interact with his or her genetic potential to produce a unique person? As we

TABLE 3.1 Parents' Reasons for Searching for Their Child's Donor and Donor Siblings		
	One of the Reasons (%)	The Main Reason (%)
Reasons for searching for donor:		
For my child to have a better understanding of who he/she is	73	21
To give my child a more secure sense of identity	67	18
Curiosity about characteristics of my child's donor	71	10
Wanting to thank my child's donor	60	10
Medical reasons	36	7
To have a better understanding of my child's ancestral history and family background	60	5
My child asked me to	13	5
I want my child to know that I tried to find his/her donor	50	4
To have a better understanding of my child's genetic makeup	62	3
To obtain another vial of sperm or another egg(s)	5	3
Wanting to meet my child's donor	37	2
Unhappy not knowing who my child's biological father/mother is	14	2
To find out more about my child's donor's life and family	42	1
To find a new family member	5	1
To find another parent figure for my child	2	1
Desire to form a relationship	9	—
Interest in why my child's donor donated	20	—
Reasons for searching for donor siblings:		
Curiosity (e.g., about similarities in appearance and personality)	85	27
For my child to have a better understanding of who he/she is	66	18
To give my child a more secure sense of identity	61	17
For my child to have a sibling	33	11
I want my child to know that I tried to find his/her donor sibling(s)	47	4
Medical reasons	37	4
My child asked me to	7	3
Desire to form friendship with the family	37	3
To have a better understanding of my child's genetic makeup	44	3
To find another vial of my child's donor's sperm or another egg(s)	9	2
Interest in sharing experiences of donor conception with their parents	43	1
To have a better understanding of my child's ancestral history and family background	36	1
To find out more about my child's donor sibling(s)'s life and family	38	1
Unhappy not knowing who my child's donor sibling(s) is/are	7	—

Source: Freeman, Jadva, Kramer, & Golombok, 2009.

discuss in this chapter, prospective parents have a better chance of using genetic information to influence and understand their future child's health than his or her athletic ability or intelligence. Advances in the study of genetics, conception, and prenatal development make it clear that a person's genetic endowment is only one of multiple influences on development and behavior.

GENETICS AND THE HUMAN GENOME

All forms of life—plants, animals, and people—possess genetic information specifying their potential characteristics. Across the twentieth century, a number of significant milestones were achieved in the study of genetics. First, the cellular basis of heredity was shown to be **chromosomes,** physical structures consisting of **deoxyribonucleic acid (DNA).** The genetic code of a cell is carried by DNA, strands of four basic molecules—adenine (A), thymine (T), cytosine (C), and guanine (G). The molecular basis of DNA is a double-helix structure that resembles a twisted ladder, with molecules always paired together in the same way—A with T, and C with G—to form the rungs of the ladder. The sequence of the rungs varies, however, and provides a unique set of instructions for inherited characteristics. With this discovery in 1953 by Watson and Crick, it became possible to define a **gene** as a segment of DNA in a specific location on a chromosome.

Further studies showed that DNA duplicates itself during a lifelong process of growth through cell division known as **mitosis.** In mitosis, chromosomes in a cell are duplicated and a copy of each chromosome moves to either end of the cell. When the chromosomes are organized in this way, the cell then divides in two, producing two identical cells. The original cell and its copy each contain a complete set of the original cell's 46 chromosomes (Dennis & Gallagher, 2001).

Another phase of the science of genetics began when researchers determined the mechanism by which cells "read" the information in genes and created technologies of cloning and sequencing. The first animal to be cloned was a sheep named Dolly (Schnieke et al., 1997). Since then, other animals, including mice, cows, cats, and rabbits, have been cloned (Evans et al., 1999; McCreath et al., 2000; Shin et al., 2002).

All living things have their own way of packaging DNA in chromosomes; mosquitoes have six chromosomes, pea plants 14, cats 38, and dogs 48 (Dennis & Gallagher, 2001). Human cells usually contain 46 chromosomes, arranged in 23 pairs—one pair of **sex chromosomes** (XX in females and XY in males) and 22 pairs of **autosomes** (any of the chromosomes other than the sex-determining chromosomes). The arrangement of chromosome pairs, with one member of each pair coming from each parent, is shown in the karyotype (pictorial display of chromosomes) in Figure 3.1.

On June 26, 2000, scientists completed the Human Genome Project (HGP)—a "working draft" of the DNA sequence of the 30,000 to 40,000 genes in the human genome (Venter et al. 2001; Wolfsberg, McEntyre, & Schuler, 2001). This discovery ushered in an era of "postgenomic science," in which research efforts are focusing on ways to use genomic information to diagnose, treat, and even prevent inherited diseases (Baltimore, 2001). Subsequently, in 2001, a multinational group of researchers completed work on a human haplotype map, or HapMap, that describes more than 1 million markers of genetic variation (International Genome Sequencing Consortium, 2001).

Genetics and Disease

Genes influence many human characteristics, including eye color, the ability to perceive color, and even more importantly, physical development and health. There are many well-known hereditary diseases, but even rare conditions may significantly affect the lives of infants and their families. This was the case for one set of new parents who were not able to identify their daughter Gabby's condition—hereditary sensory autonomic neuropathy (HSAN) Type 5—until she

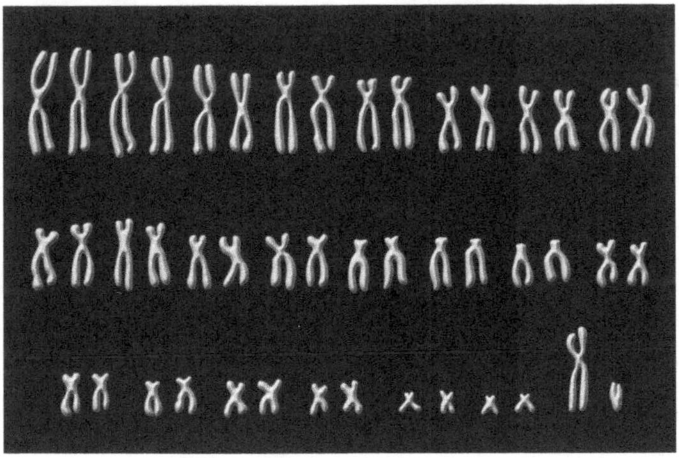

FIGURE 3.1 A karyotype shows the 23 pairs of chromosomes that humans usually have; this karyotype is from a male, as shown by the presence of one X chromosome and one Y chromosome in the 23rd pair.

reached the age of 1 year. Initially, they and Gabby's pediatrician thought that she simply had a high tolerance for pain because as a newborn she continued sleeping peacefully even when her heel was pricked to draw blood for a routine health screening. They would later discover that Gabby was unable to feel pain at all, despite having other senses that functioned normally.

As scientists learn more about human genetics, it may be possible to treat hereditary conditions such as HSAN Type 5 and predict which prospective parents are most likely to pass on genes for inherited disorders of all types (Herrmann, 2008). For now, because there is no cure, Gabby's parents watch her carefully and have her wear swimming goggles so that she will not accidentally poke, scratch, or otherwise damage her eyes (Freed, 2004).

How close are we to understanding the genetic basis of human characteristics—and to helping children like Gabby? The answer depends on which characteristics are examined. Table 3.2 shows examples of congenital human diseases (diseases present from birth) with a known genetic basis. A very small number of diseases, such as Huntington's disease and achondroplasia (both caused by genes located on chromosome 4), are inherited when a child receives a single dominant gene. All individuals inheriting this gene develop the disease and, if they have offspring of their own, have a high probability of passing it on to the next generation. (Huntington's disease is a degenerative neurological disease with symptoms not appearing until middle adulthood; achondroplasia is a form of dwarfism that is apparent from birth.) Other diseases, such as Tay Sachs disease (chromosome 15), Noonan syndrome (chromosome 12), sickle-cell anemia (chromosome 11), and a form of hearing loss in newborns (chromosome 13), occur only when a child receives two recessive genes for the disease, one from each parent. Still other diseases, such as hemophilia and Duchenne muscular dystrophy, are the result of **sex-linked inheritance** of recessive genes. These diseases (and harmless traits such as red-green color blindness) are transmitted when boys receive a single defective X chromosome from their mother. Girls receive a second, nondefective X chromosome from their father and thus do not usually inherit the characteristic.

Research is under way to discover whether and how the X chromosome might be involved in Autism Spectrum Disorders and Fragile X syndrome, both of which are more prevalent in boys. Autism and Fragile X are neurodevelopmental disorders, often diagnosed in infancy, that cause severe and pervasive deficits in cognition, emotion, language, and social functioning, although impairment can range from mild learning disabilities to more severe problems. This variability suggests that, even if a link to the X chromosome is discovered, there may be other

TABLE 3.2   Examples of Congenital Human Diseases with a Genetic Basis

Disease	Characteristics	Genetic Factors	Prevalence
Achondroplasia (dwarfism)	Disorder of bone growth, short stature, and shortened arms and legs	Chromosome 4, dominant trait	1 in 25,000 births
Asthma	Chronic respiratory disease	Chromosomes 5, 6, 11, and 14, recessive trait	1.4 percent of U.S. children
Cystic fibrosis	Overproduction of mucus, which interferes with lung function	Chromosome 7, recessive trait	1 in 2,000 births
Duchenne muscular distrophy	Muscle weakness and respiratory failure leading to death by early adulthood	X chromosome, recessive trait	1 in 3,500 males
Hemophilia	Excessive bleeding	X chromosome, recessive trait	1 in 10,000 births
Huntington's disease	Progressive neurological disease, usually appearing in middle adulthood	Chromosome 4, dominant trait	1 in 10,000 births
Noonan syndrome	Multiple malformations of the body and face, short stature, developmental delays, and learning disabilities	Chromosome 12, dominant trait	1 in 2,500 births
Phenylketonuria (PKU)	Metabolic disorder resulting in cognitive disabilities without a diet free of phenylalanine	Chromosome 12, recessive trait	1 in 10,000 to 1 in 25,000 births
Sickle-cell anemia	Deformation of red blood cells, resulting in oxygen deprivation and possible death	Chromosome 11, recessive trait	1 in 500 African Americans
Tay-Sachs disease	Progressive neurological disease, death by age 5	Chromosome 15, recessive trait	1 in 3,000 Eastern European Jews

Source: Adapted from National Center for Biotechnology Information, 2002.

genetic and environmental factors involved. Candidates being explored include chromosomes 7, 10, and 19 (NIH/NIMH Human Genetics Initiative, 2005).

Very few diseases and complex human traits are determined simply. Instead, most complex characteristics with a heritable component, such as intelligence, personality, and psychopathology, appear to be influenced by multiple genes, interacting in ways that are poorly understood at the present time. Part of the continuing work of the Human Genome Project, therefore, is the complete specification of the genes on all 24 human chromosomes. The first chromosomes to be mapped in this way were chromosome 22 (Dunham et al., 1999), chromosome 21 (Hattori et al., 2000), and chromosome 20 (Deloukas et al., 2001).

It has been known for many years that an extra chromosome 21 causes **Down syndrome.** Individuals born with Down syndrome have mild to severe cognitive disabilities and distinctive facial features. Many people with Down syndrome also have physical malformations, including heart defects and intestinal obstructions. The risk of Down syndrome increases with maternal age, but other, still unidentified factors are thought to play a contributing role as well.

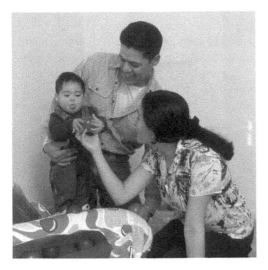

Infants born with Down syndrome have distinctive facial features and mild to severe cognitive disabilities; like other babies, they benefit from interactions with involved parents in a loving, stimulating environment.

Studies of twins and of families in which specific diseases are more common than in the population at large have contributed to our understanding of the genetic basis for many heritable conditions. It is now known, for example, that juvenile onset (Type I) diabetes (also known as diabetes mellitus) is a complex trait, a disease that is caused by mutations in several genes on chromosomes 6, 7, and 11. Genes on chromosome 20 are implicated in adult onset (Type 2) diabetes, obesity, cataracts, and eczema.

Even as the human genome becomes more fully understood, it is important to remember that most traits and abilities are produced through the process of **multifactorial transmission—** the interaction of genes and the environment. As a result, even identical twins, who inherit an identical genotype (genetic potential), may possess different phenotypes (the expression of characteristics that are possible for a given genotype), especially if their environments and experiences differ markedly. Consider the example of identical twins with the same genetic predisposition to develop Type 2 diabetes, a disease that is made worse by obesity. If one twin maintains a healthy weight, follows a nutritious diet, and exercises, but the other twin does none of these things, the second twin will be more likely to develop Type 2 diabetes.

Multifactorial transmission is also operating in schizophrenia, a form of psychopathology for which studies of families, twins, and adoptees have produced a compelling case for strong— but not deterministic—genetic factors. The rate of schizophrenia in the general population is relatively low (1 percent), as compared with the rate among children born to a schizophrenic parent (13 percent) and the rate among individuals with an identical twin who develops schizophrenia (48 percent). Even in the case of identical twins, however, their identical genetic inheritance produces different outcomes through unique interactions with environmental factors both before and after birth (Gottesman, 2001; International Schizophrenia Consortium, 2009).

New discoveries are reported almost daily about the genetics of various diseases, including diseases with childhood onset, such as juvenile idiopathic arthritis (Barnes et al., 2009), as well as diseases that may not develop until adolescence or adulthood, such as testicular cancer (Hovarth et al., 2009). In general, the more knowledge people have about their genetic predispositions, the more steps they may be able to take to prevent diseases that they may be at risk of developing. They may also be more likely to get regular screening tests for diseases that develop over time. If the disease is detected, they have a better chance of receiving early, effective treatment.

Genetics and Prenatal Development

Scientists are also learning more about the genetic basis of conception and prenatal development. Using animal models, researchers have made important discoveries about genes that determine the structure of specialized body structures, such as arms, legs, eyes, and parts of the brain (Cunningham et al., 2002). One group of scientists working with mice, for example, discovered a gene that controls the development of the hippocampus, a brain structure that is crucial for higher cognitive functions such as learning and memory (Zhao et al., 1999). The function of the gene was determined by inactivating it; when this was done, the researchers observed that embryos lacking the gene developed a malformed hippocampus.

Another group of researchers "knocked out" two genes in zebrafish and discovered that the resulting embryos failed to develop any sort of head or trunk—they were simply overgrown tails (Gonzalez et al., 2000). Researchers studying humans cannot perform these kinds of experiments, of course, but further investigation may yield evidence about the genetic basis of prenatal development and naturally occurring birth defects in a range of mammals, including humans. We discuss birth defects later in this chapter, but first let us consider the usual course of conception and prenatal development.

CONCEPTION

The basic process of fertilization is well understood yet remains a source of fascination, and researchers continue to learn about the **ovum** (female sex cell) and **sperm** (male sex cell). The ovarian structures that contain the genetic components of the ova are formed during the fetal period. As a result, a woman's follicles—ovarian structures containing immature eggs—exist even before birth. Sperm, by contrast, are made over a period of just 60 to 90 days, and new sperm are always being produced. The cells that nurture growing sperm—Sertoli cells—are formed primarily during the first six to nine months of life, however, which means that some male fertility problems may actually begin in the prenatal period, when the testes are still developing, rather than in puberty, or later, when mature sperm are produced (Timmons, Rigby, & Poirer, 2001).

Fertilization becomes possible when an egg matures in one of the ovaries, a process that occurs over a continuous 28-day cycle, due to the action of two proteins, ERK1 and ERK2 (Fan et al., 2009). During the first week in the cycle, the hypothalamus and pituitary release luteinizing hormone (LH) and follicle-stimulating hormone (FSH) into the woman's bloodstream. These hormones in turn bring about the production and secretion of ovarian hormones, including estradiol and progesterone. By the end of the first week of the cycle, the surge in these hormones results in the selection and subsequent growth of the follicle containing the egg that will be released during that cycle (Colón, 1997).

Initially, each unreleased egg has a full set of 46 chromosomes. By the end of two weeks, in response to a midcycle release of LH, the sex cells of the egg (also known as gametes) divide through the process of **meiosis.** Meiosis begins with duplication of the set of 46 chromosomes in the egg, as occurs in mitosis. The cells then divide twice, yielding four sex cells, each of which has one set of 23 chromosomes. Meiosis differs from mitosis in another way as well; the chromosomes in each sex cell are more than just a copy of the original chromosomes. This is because the pairs of chromosomes exchange pieces of their genetic material during the first meiotic division. This process produces chromosomes with new combinations of genes and, in offspring, new traits that may not have been present in either parent (Dennis & Gallagher, 2001).

A few hours after meiosis has ended, ovulation occurs: The egg is released from the ovary, and cilia (tiny hair cells) facilitate its travel through the fallopian tube, where it remains for one to two days. As the egg follows this path, the follicle in which it matured becomes a corpeus luteum and secretes hormones that prepare the uterine environment for possible implantation and pregnancy. The corpus luteum secretes these hormones for a period of only 14 days, however, and without fertilization it deteriorates (Colón, 1997; Gilbert, 2000). If the egg is not fertilized by sperm during this time, it too begins to disintegrate, and the woman experiences her typical monthly menstrual flow. The 28-day cycle then begins again.

If sperm are present, there is a chance that the egg will be fertilized. Although approximately 100 to 300 million sperm are released during a single ejaculation, only a few hundred travel as far as the fallopian tube, and only one sperm ultimately penetrates the membrane surrounding the egg. Their journey is possible because sperm have "tails" and can move through the cervix and the uterus, toward the fallopian tubes. Sperm locomotion is also assisted by hormones that affect the characteristics of the uterine environment. These hormones include estrogen, which is produced by the female's ovaries, and oxytocin, which is produced by the pituitary. The influence of the uterine environment is so strong that even sperm with deformed tails or other abnormalities may succeed in reaching and fertilizing the egg.

Sperm undergo the process of meiosis in the sperm-producing cells in the testes, before they are released through ejaculation. The mechanisms that determine which single sperm will join its 23 chromosomes with the 23 chormosomes of the egg are not completely understood (Colón, 1997). When a sperm penetrates the membrane of the ovum, the membrane itself changes, and no other sperm may enter the ovum thereafter. The cell that results when the ovum is fertilized is known as a **zygote.** Because an ovum always contributes an X sex chromosome, the sex of each zygote is determined by the sex chromosome carried by the father's sperm. If the sperm carries a Y chromsome, the resulting zygote will be XY, or a male. If the sperm carries an X chromosome, however, the zygote will be XX, or a female.

Twins and Other Multiples

Sometimes more than one ovum is released at ovulation (this is especially likely if the woman is taking fertility-enhancing drugs). When this happens, if each ovum is fertilized by different sperm, the resulting offspring are as closely related to one another as if they were siblings born years apart. Siblings resulting from two different eggs are referred to as **dizygotic twins** (two zygotes), or fraternal twins. Less frequently, a single fertilized ovum divides into two separate fertilized cells. Because these cells are fertilized by a single sperm, they are genetically identical, and the twins that result are referred to as **monozygotic twins** (one zygote), or identical twins. In approximately 40 percent of all twin pregnancies, only a single child is born. The "vanishing twin" phenomenon occurs in dizygotic twins when they carry different variants of a gene on chromosome 3 (PPAR-gamma), causing one twin to develop at the expense of the other. When twins have the same variant of this gene, they usually develop at the same pace (Busjahn et al., 2000; Landy & Keith, 1998). Monozygotic twins are always the same sex (two boys or two girls), but dizygotic twins, as well as triplets, quadruplets, and other multiples resulting from different sperm fertilizing each ovum, may be the same sex or different sexes.

Sex Chromosome Abnormalities

In some cases, the developing embryo has an abnormal number of chromosomes—either too many or too few—a condition known as aneuploidy. Instead of dividing evenly, the egg may have an extra X chromosome or the sperm may have both an X and a Y chromosome. For example, an egg with a normal X chromosome that is fertilized by a sperm with both an X and a Y chromosome produces a male with the XXY pattern, a condition known as Klinefelter syndrome. Klinefelter syndrome is the most common chromosomal abnormality, occurring as frequently as 1 in every 500 male births; males with this syndrome may have enlarged breasts, a lack of facial and body hair, and a rounded body type, as well as infertility and possible language impairment. As another example, a sperm cell with a normal X chromosome that fertilizes an egg with more than one X chromosome results in a female with an XXX pattern. This condition, known as triple X syndrome, occurs in approximately 1 out of every 1,000 female births and may be accompanied by tall stature, infertility, mild to moderate cognitive disabilities, and speech and cognitive delays. The risk of misalignment of chromosomes during meiosis increases with age and is more common among women over age 35 (Hodges et al., 2002).

Infertility and Assisted Reproduction

Approximately 2 percent of U.S. women of reproductive age have an infertility-related medical appointment each year, and 13 to 15 percent receive infertility services at some point in their lives. Approximately 7 percent of married couples in the United States in which the woman is of childbearing age report that they have not become pregnant, despite not using contraception for the previous 12 months (Centers for Disease Control & Prevention, 1995). In the past, these couples might have remained childless or created a family through adoption. Today, **assisted reproductive technology (ART)** makes it possible for many of these men and women to conceive their own biological children.

ART includes all fertility treatments in which both egg and sperm are handled. Intrauterine insemination (IUI, also referred to as artificial insemination), in which sperm is placed into a woman's uterus to facilitate fertilization, is thus not considered an ART procedure. As described in Table 3.3, a number of ART procedures are currently available. The procedure that received the most initial publicity was in vitro fertilization (IVF), which resulted in the birth of the world's first "test-tube" baby in 1978 (Steptoe & Edwards, 1978). Other ART procedures that have been developed include gamete intrafallopian transfer (GIFT), zygote intrafallopian transfer (ZIFT), and intracytoplasmic sperm injection (ICSI). Approximately 1 percent of all infants born in the United States each year are conceived through ART procedures (Sunderam et al. 2009; Wright et al., 2008).

TABLE 3.3 Number of Assisted Reproductive Technology (ART) Procedures Available to Achieve Conception Despite Fertility Problems	
ART Procedure	**How It Works**
In vitro fertilization (IVF)	An ART procedure in which eggs are removed from a woman's ovaries and fertilized outside of her body, with the resulting embryo transferred into the woman's uterus through the cervix
Gamete intrafallopian transfer (GIFT)	An ART procedure in which eggs are removed from a woman's ovary, combined with sperm, and transferred (still unfertilized) into the woman's fallopian tube through an incision in her abdomen
Zygote intrafallopian transfer (ZIFT)	An ART procedure in which eggs are collected from a woman's ovary and fertilized outside her body, with the zygote transferred into the woman's fallopian tube through an incision in her abdomen
Intracytoplasmic sperm injection (ICSI)	An ART procedure in which a single sperm is injected directly into a woman's egg in order to achieve fertilization

Source: Adapted from Centers for Disease Control & Prevention, 2001.

A woman's chances of becoming pregnant and having a live birth after using ART are influenced by a number of factors, including her age, the cause of infertility, the quality of the embryos, and the number of embryos that are transferred. Researchers are also investigating the influence of paternal age and patterns of alcohol and drug use as factors that may affect the success rate of ART (Klonoff-Cohen, 2005; Klonoff-Cohen & Natarajan, 2004). Success rates (defined as the percentage of egg retrievals that result in a live birth) for the most widely used ART procedures (IVF, GIFT, and ZIFT) are highest (54 percent in 2006) for procedures using fresh embryos produced from donor eggs (Sunderam et al., 2009; Wright et al., 2008). To maximize birth rates, physicians performing embryo transfer procedures often transfer more than one embryo. Although this increases the chance that a live birth will occur, it also increases the risk of multiple births. In fact, pregnancies achieved through ART, which uses drugs to induce ovulation, are more likely to result in multiple births than pregnancies occurring without intervention. These procedures are responsible for a marked increase in triplet and higher-order multiple births since the 1980s, and approximately 18 percent of multiple births in the United States each year begin through ART procedures (Centers for Disease Control & Prevention, 2000a; Sunderam et al., 2009; Wright et al., 2008).

ART procedures are generally safe for the babies conceived through them (Tournaye & Van Steirteghem, 1997). Complications during pregnancy and delivery and after birth may occur, however, when multiple fetuses are carried and when the babies are born too early in gestation (Colón, 1997; Goldenberg & Jobe, 2001; Koivurova et al., 2002; Schenker & Ezra, 1994).

Regardless of the number of ova, the sex of the zygote, and the process through which conception has been achieved, fertilization initiates a series of changes, culminating in the implantation of the egg in the mother's uterine wall and a period of prenatal development.

PRENATAL DEVELOPMENT

As late as the nineteenth century, the fetus was shown as a tiny, fully formed human being, frolicking in the mother's uterus. The period of gestation was viewed as a time when the miniature person simply grew larger and waited to be born. Many people believed that miscarriages and birth defects could be prevented by satisfying the cravings of pregnant women and protecting them from unnecessary emotional upsets. These beliefs influenced views of pregnancy as recently as the late nineteenth and early twentieth century. Doctors from this time placed prohibitions on expectant women that seem quite absurd today, including warnings about dancing, singing, swimming, riding on streetcars, and leaving the house after sunset. Most doctors of the time placed sexual intercourse off limits as well (Fontanel & d'Harcourt, 1997).

The stages of prenatal development are clearly understood today, and most pregnant women are advised to continue their normal activities—including work, travel, aerobic exercise, and sexual activity—until the first signs of labor begin (American College of Obstetricians and Gynecologists, 1994, 2003). Pregnant women who exercise regularly tend to have fewer problems during pregnancy and labor (Brankston et al., 2004; Chasan-Taber et al., 2009; Olson et al., 2009). There may even be sustained benefits after birth for children whose mothers exercised regularly during pregnancy (Clapp, 1996). Women with preexisting health problems and those experiencing complications during pregnancy need to follow their obstetrician's advice and limit their activities accordingly. As we discuss later, all pregnant women need to avoid **teratogens**—substances, such as alcohol, drugs, nicotine, and radiation, that are known to harm the developing fetus (Shepard et al., 2002). Table 3.4 shows some agents that are known or suspected to be teratogenic. Most teratogens produce their effects during specific critical periods of development, with the greatest damage typically occurring during the earliest part of pregnancy.

TABLE 3.4	Agents That Are Known or Suspected to Be Teratogenic

Teratogenic Agent

Drugs and Chemicals
Alcohol
Cigarette smoke
Cocaine
Cortisone
Diethylstilbesterol (DES)
Heroin
Lead
Methylmercury
Penicillamine (antibiotic)
Retinoic acid (Accutane, an acne medication)
Streptomycin
Tetracycline (antibiotic)
Thalidomide (sedative)
Trimethadione
Valproic acid (antiseizure medication)

Infectious Diseases
AIDS/HIV
Cytomegalovirus (CMV)
Herpes simplex
Parvovirus
Rubella (German measles)
Toxoplasmosis
Syphilis

Source: Adapted from Gilbert: Developmental Biology, Sixth Edition, Sinauer Associates, Inc. 2000; not all known or suspected teratogens are listed.

From the perspective of the expectant mother, pregnancy is usually experienced as three equally long trimesters, with the total period of gestation lasting 280 days, counting from the last menstrual period. From the perspective of the developing child, by contrast, the actual period of gestation is about 266 days (time since conception), and the three stages are unequal in length and characterized by unique events.

The Germinal Stage, Fertilization to 2 Weeks

The **germinal stage** begins with fertilization of an ovum by a sperm cell and ends at approximately 2 weeks. At approximately 30 hours postconception, the zygote divides in two via mitosis, forming two identical sets of chromosomes. The originals and the copy are then divided into two separate cells. At approximately 60 hours postconception, each of these cells undergoes the same mitotic process, resulting in a cluster of four identical cells. The process of mitosis repeats itself until, by about one week postconception, there are almost one hundred identical cells organized

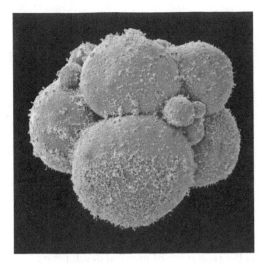

By approximately 1 week after conception, the process of mitosis has produced a hollow spherical cluster of cells called a blastocyst.

into a hollow spherical structure called a **blastocyst.** The cells in the blastocyst then begin to differentiate into an inner cell mass, which subsequently develops into the embryo, and an outer group of cells, the trophoblast (Gilbert, 2000).

During the process of early cell division and differentiation, the zygote travels through the fallopian tube to the uterus, where it begins the process of implantation in the uterine wall between the seventh and ninth day after conception. The mother's ovaries secrete hormones that maintain the uterine lining and prevent it from being shed. Hormones produced by the corpus luteum also help maintain the uterine lining, especially during the first trimester of the pregnancy. The germinal stage concludes at approximately 2 weeks postconception, after the blastocyst has become attached to the uterine lining, which provides it with nutrients and oxygen. As many as 55 percent of zygotes never reach this stage of development (Colón, 1997).

Sometimes implantation of the fertilized egg occurs outside of the uterus, a condition known as an ectopic pregnancy (also referred to as a tubal pregnancy). This potentially life-threatening condition is the leading cause of pregnancy-related deaths in the first trimester. There has been a fivefold increase over the past 20 years, with the result that approximately 10,000 ectopic pregnancies occur each year in the United States. The cause is often unknown, but tubal damage from sexually transmitted infections is thought to be responsible for many cases. The condition has also been attributed to fertility drugs, previous operations on the fallopian tubes, endometriosis (when uterine tissue implants outside the uterus), and cigarette smoking (Centers for Disease Control & Prevention, 1995).

The Embryonic Stage, 2 to 8 Weeks

A zygote that has become implanted is referred to as an embryo. The **embryonic stage** begins approximately two weeks after conception and ends in the eighth prenatal week, when the first bone cells replace cartilage in the embryo's skeleton. Major organ systems and structures develop during this stage, and the embryo is especially vulnerable to the effects of teratogens. The type of defect (the heart versus the eyes or palate) depends on which structures and organs are developing at the time of exposure to the teratogen.

Growth in the embryonic stage is rapid and follows two principles that are also evident in development after birth. According to the **cephalocaudal principle,** development occurs first in the

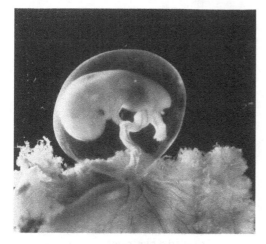

During the embryonic stage of prenatal development, major organ systems and structures develop, and the embryo is especially vulnerable to the effects of teratogens. At 8 weeks postconception, the embryo is 1 inch long and weighs about $\frac{1}{30}$ of an ounce.

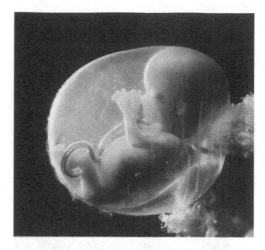

In the fetal stage of prenatal development, the major body parts and systems that were established during the embryonic stage grow and mature. At birth, the typical newborn is 20 inches long and weighs $7\frac{1}{2}$ pounds.

embryo's anterior region (head) and later in the direction of the embryo's posterior region (feet). In the early weeks of the embryonic stage, development of the embryo's lower regions lags behind development of the head, which is disproportionately large. Following the **proximodistal principle,** development begins in the center of the body and continues outward to the extremities. Thus fingers and toes develop later than and depend upon the earlier development of arms and legs.

As shown in Figure 3.2, a number of supporting structures begin to develop early in the embryonic stage. The **placenta** develops from cells in the trophoblast and from cells in the uterine lining; it contains a vast network of blood vessels and is connected to the embryo by the **umbilical cord.** Together, these structures bring oxygen and nutrients from the mother to the embryo and carry waste products from the embryo to the mother. The amniotic sac and its outer membrane, the chorion, envelop the embryo in amniotic fluid, which is replenished constantly during the pregnancy. The fluid acts as a barrier and a cushion and thus offers some degree of protection for the embryo at the same time that it helps to maintain a relatively constant temperature in the womb. The yolk sac is the source of red blood cells.

There is an invariant timetable for the development of major organs, systems, and body parts during the embryonic stage. In the third week after conception, the embryo's cells begin to differentiate. The upper layer of cells gives rise to the **ectoderm**—the source of the brain and spinal cord, sensory organs, and skin, nails, hair, and teeth. The brain and spinal cord develop from an ectodermal neural plate that thickens and then folds upon itself to become a neural tube. Later in the chapter we discuss neural tube defects, a common and serious malformation that originates at this point in gestation. The middle layer—the **mesoderm**—is the source of the circulatory and excretory systems, as well as muscles and the skeleton. The respiratory and digestive systems are formed from the lower layer, or **endoderm.**

In the fourth week after conception, the heart begins beating and the digestive system begins to develop. These changes are followed by the beginnings of arms, legs, eyes, ears, and tissue that develops into the lower jaw and larynx (week 5). During weeks 6 to 8, development occurs in the

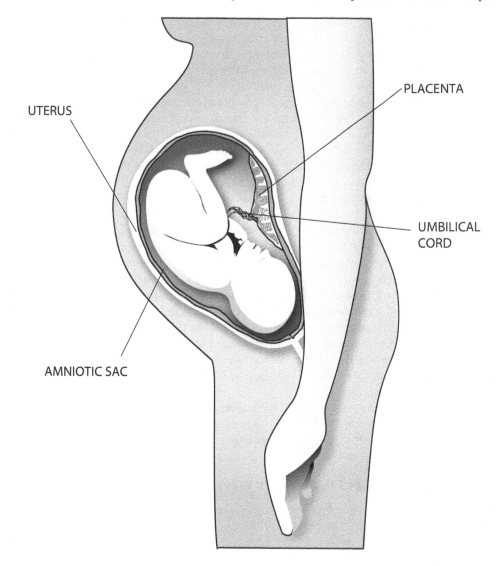

UTERUS

PLACENTA

UMBILICAL
CORD

AMNIOTIC SAC

FIGURE 3.2 Each part of this system plays an important role in maintaining the pregnancy and promoting the development of the embryo and fetus.

circulation system as well as in the nose, upper lip, tongue, palate, trachea, teeth, fingers, and toes. Eyelids begin to form, facial features continue to develop, and the gastrointestinal tract separates from the genitoruinary tract. Long bones begin to form, muscles are able to contract, and the umbilical cord is well developed (Gilbert, 2000).

One of the most significant developments during the embryonic stage—one that has a profound, lifelong impact from the moment of birth (or even earlier, if the parents learn the sex of their unborn child)—occurs when the embryo's reproductive system becomes differentiated as male or female. During the first six weeks of prenatal development, the primitive sex glands (known as gonads) of genetically male (XY) and genetically female (XX) embryos are undifferentiated. Then, at approximately 6 to 8 weeks, in response to the Y chromosome, the gonads in genetically male (XY) embryos begin developing into testes. The testes subsequently produce testosterone, the hormone that leads to the development of the male reproductive tract (the Wolffian duct system) and penis. At the same time, the testes also produce Müllerian Inhibiting Substance (MIS), a hormone that prevents the Müllerian duct system (the female reproductive tract) from developing (Ahmed & Hughes, 2002).

In genetically female (XX) embryos, in the absence of testosterone and MIS, the gonads begin developing into the Müllerian duct system, the Wolffian ducts degenerate, and the ovaries begin producing female hormones. For many years, it was believed that females are created by "default"—that female characteristics develop in the absence of a Y chromosome or if the embryo is not exposed to male hormones. Evidence in support of this view came from cases in the 1950s in which genetically female human embryos, whose mothers were treated with male hormones to prevent miscarriage before the third prenatal month, were born with masculinized external genitalia. By contrast, female embryos exposed to male hormones later, after the reproductive system had completed the process of differentiation, were not affected by those hormones and developed normally.

Recent discoveries about factors controlling embryonic growth and differentiation, however, have made it clear that normal female reproductive system development depends on the *presence* and functioning of specific genes and molecules. There is evidence that HOX genes are involved in the development of the Müllerian system and are necessary for both embryological reproductive tract development and adult function (Taylor, 2000). It is also becoming clear that molecules known as the Wnts are responsible for embryological growth and differentiation of the midbrain, central nervous system, kidney, and limbs and that some of these molecules are needed for normal development of the reproductive system. Without the influence of Wnt-4, Wnt-5a, and Wnt-7a, female (XX) embryos do not develop normally (Bernard & Harley, 2007; Heikkilä, Peltoketo, & Vainio, 2001; Heikkilä et al., 2005).

Taken together, these studies highlight the importance of timing in understanding the effects of experience on embryological development. They also show that sexual differentiation, like other aspects of prenatal development, is affected by genetic and physiological factors within the embryo as well as by the biochemical and hormonal environment in which the embryo is developing.

The Fetal Stage, 8 Weeks to Birth (38 Weeks)

During the **fetal stage** of prenatal development, major body parts and systems that were established during the embryonic stage grow and mature. The magnitude of growth that occurs during this last stage is readily apparent when comparing the 8-week-old fetus, which is approximately 1 inch long and weighs approximately 1/30 of an ounce, with the full-term newborn, which is typically 20 inches long and 7 1/2 pounds.

As in the embryonic stage, the timetable for development during the fetal stage is orderly and predictable, but the changes are more subtle. At about 9 to 12 weeks after conception, the fingers and toes are more clearly defined, tooth buds appear, and reflexes such as sucking and swallowing are developing. The eyelids close and will remain sealed shut until about the 28th week. The liver is now capable of producing red blood cells. Around 13 to 16 weeks, the fetus's head is covered with soft down known as lanugo, which will later cover the entire body; the skin on its body is almost transparent. Hair appears on the fetus's head, and eyebrows and eyelashes appear. The fetus swallows amniotic fluid, and meconium (a fetal waste product) is made in the intestinal tract. A 20-week-old fetus becomes increasingly active and has identifiable patterns of low and high activity, which may correspond to later sleep and wake states. Individual patterns of activity and responsiveness seem to correspond to differences in activity level and responsiveness after birth (DiPietro et al., 1996).

By about 24 weeks, fingerprints and toeprints are visible, as are fingernails, toenails, and nipples. The fetus's skin is protected by a waxy coating called vernix. With intensive care, survival is possible if the child is born at this stage. As we discuss in Chapter 4, infants born this early are extremely fragile and, if they survive, often have complications that affect their health and development for years. The fetus is able to hear and responds to sounds that are transmitted through the uterine wall. Fetuses often show an increase in activity and greater responsiveness to sounds between weeks 28 and 32, and their eyelids open and close. The fetus has a rudimentary ability to regulate body temperature. Bones at this stage are fully developed but are still soft.

A baby born at 36 weeks has an excellent chance of survival but is likely to be small. The average fetus at this stage weighs about 5 lb. 12 oz. to 6 lb. 12 oz. and is about 16 to 19 inches long. By 38 to 40 weeks, the fetus is considered full term.

Although brain development begins during the embryonic stage, with the formation of the neural tube and brain stem and the production of brain cells called **neurons** (approximately 250,000 to 500,000 per prenatal minute), the most rapid prenatal period of brain development occurs during the last two months. It is during this time that the number of brain cells increases most rapidly, and the interconnection of those cells begins. By about five months after conception, the majority of brain cells that make higher-level thinking possible are in place. The functional connections among those cells depend primarily on experience that occurs after birth, however, with the most significant connections being formed during the first two years of life (Black, 1998; Johnson, 1997; Shonkoff & Phillips, 2000). In this way, the brain differs from other major organs because it is not completely developed by the time the child is born, a point that we return to in Chapter 5.

Most pregnancies today are healthy, and infant mortality rates have dropped significantly, especially in the United States and in other developed countries. Complications still occur, however, sometimes for unknown reasons. In some cases, these complications are so serious that they lead to fetal death and endanger the mother. In other cases, the problems are evident in birth defects that may adversely affect the child's chances of survival and quality of life.

MISCARRIAGE   A pregnancy that ends before 20 weeks is called a miscarriage. Miscarriages that occur during the first trimester (12 weeks) are often due to problems in the fetus, such as chromosomal abnormalities. When such abnormalities exist, embryonic and fetal development do not progress normally; in some cases an empty amniotic sac may be formed around an embryo that never developed or that stopped developing in the earliest stages.

During the second trimester, problems with the woman's uterus are a more common cause of miscarriages, although chromosomal abnormalities still account for some cases. Uterine abnormalities that have been linked with miscarriage include a small or abnormally shaped uterus, or a uterus that has tumors or scar tissue from past surgeries. For some women with a history of miscarriage, treatment to increase the level of the hormone progesterone may help prevent subsequent miscarriages (Haas & Ramsey, 2008). Insufficient flow of blood in the placenta is another cause of some early miscarriage; for some women, repeat miscarriages may be avoided by taking low doses of aspirin and a blood-thinning drug called heparin (Badawy et al., 2008; Kaandorp et al., 2009; Laskin et al., 2009). Low levels of folic acid may be responsible for some early miscarriages; by adding 400 micrograms of folic acid to her daily diet even before becoming pregnant, a woman can reduce her chances of a miscarriage at the same time that she reduces the risk of a defect in the formation of the neural tube.

STILLBIRTH   When a fetus dies after 20 weeks, it is referred to as a stillbirth. Stillbirth is less common than miscarriage, occurring in approximately one in 200 pregnancies. As many as half of all stillbirths occur in pregnancies that appeared to be normal. The reasons for stillbirth are not always known, and in more than 30 percent of cases, the cause cannot be determined. One common cause of stillbirth is a placental problem, such as placental abruption, in which the placenta peels away from the uterine wall before delivery. This problem, which most frequently occurs around the 35th week of pregnancy, causes heavy bleeding and is life-threatening for both mother and baby. Fetuses who are small for gestational age or not growing properly may die from lack of oxygen; this problem is often seen in women who have high blood pressure. Fetal deaths that occur between 24 and 27 weeks are frequently caused by bacterial infections, which may go undetected if they cause no symptoms in the mother.

BIRTH DEFECTS

Most expectant parents today can assume that their baby will develop normally and be born healthy. However, approximately 120,000 babies out of approximately 4.3 million born each year in the United States are affected by birth defects (Centers for Disease Control & Prevention, 2006; Hamilton, Martin, & Ventura, 2009). This number represents a significant decline in the rate of birth defects since 1979, but they continue to be the leading cause of infant death in the United States (Centers for Disease Control & Prevention, 2006; Yang, Khoury, & Mannino, 1997). Babies born to foreign-born mothers are more likely overall to have birth defects than babies whose mothers were born in the United States. Rates vary across cultures and different types of defects, however, reflecting differences in mothers' socioeconomic status, education, and adoption of U.S. cultural beliefs and practices (Ramadhani et al., 2009). Researchers collect data about the prevalence of two major categories of birth defects: structural defects and birth defects resulting from chromosomal abnormalities. As shown in Table 3.5, the most common defects include those affecting the heart, the mouth and face, and the musculoskeletal system. The most common type of defect resulting from a chromosomal abnormality is Down syndrome (Centers for Disease Control & Prevention, 2006). We now take a closer look at two of these defects—those affecting the neural tube and the heart.

Neural Tube Defects

Neural tube defects (NTDs) are birth defects that involve abnormal development of the neural tube. As we noted earlier, the neural tube forms during the first few weeks of the prenatal

TABLE 3.5 Prevalence of Selected Major Birth Defects	
Category	**Estimated Prevalence**
Heart and circulation system	17 per 10,000 live births
Cleft lip/palate	17 per 10,000 live births
Down syndrome	14 per 10,000 live births
Muscles and skeleton	14 per 10,000 live births
Gastrointestinal tract	8 per 10,000 live births
Eye	2 per 10,000 live births
Club foot	58 per 100,000 live births
Anencephaly	10 per 100,000 live births
Spina bifida	19 per 100,000 live births

Source: Adapted from Centers for Disease Control & Prevention, 2006; and National Center for Health Statistics, 2001.

period and is the structure that eventually becomes the brain and spinal cord. In the United States, approximately 4,000 pregnancies per year are affected by NTDs, of which approximately 1,500 end in miscarriage or stillbirth. Several types of NTDs exist. Two types, spina bifida and anencephaly, make up 90 percent of all NTDs. A third type of NTD, encephalocele, accounts for the remaining 10 percent (Mathews, 2003).

Spina bifida is sometimes referred to as "open spine" because it occurs when the fetus's spine fails to close properly during the first month of pregnancy. Infants born with spina bifida sometimes have an opening on their spine, a condition that leads to nerve damage and varying degrees of permanent paralysis. Newborns with spina bifida usually need surgery to close the spinal opening within 24 hours of their birth in order to prevent further damage. Prognosis for infants with spina bifida depends on the number and severity of abnormalities (National Institute of Neurological Disorders and Stroke, 2001).

Anencephaly is a much more serious form of NTD, usually leading to stillbirth or death within a few hours or days after birth. In anencephaly, the anterior end of the neural tube fails to close; as a result, there is an absence of a major portion of the brain, skull, and scalp. Infants with this condition lack a forebrain and a cerebrum (the areas of the brain that are responsible for thinking). There may be a semifunctional brain stem, which makes it possible for the baby to breathe and respond to sound or touch reflexively. The brain tissue that exists may be exposed, without any bone or skin present (National Institute of Neurological Disorders and Stroke, 2001).

In encephalocele, the infant's brain tissue protrudes through abnormal openings in the skull. The symptoms vary in severity, with the prognosis depending on the specific brain tissue involved, the location of the skull openings, and whether there are other malformations of the brain. Babies born with encephalocele usually survive but may have cognitive disabilities (National Institute of Neurological Disorders and Stroke, 2001).

In 1992, after concluding that 50 percent or more of NTDs could be prevented if, prior to becoming pregnant, women consumed an adequate amount of folate (the B vitamin folic acid), the U.S. Public Health Service recommended that women of childbearing age increase daily consumption of folic acid to 400 micrograms (4,000 daily micrograms were recommended for women who have previously had an NTD-affected pregnancy). In 1998, the U.S. Food and Drug Administration required that all enriched cereal grain products have folic acid added (National Center for Health Statistics, 2002). How effective has this requirement been? Initial results suggest that it has had a positive impact (Centers for Disease Control & Prevention, 2004; Wolff et al., 2009). From 1995 and 1998, that there was an increase (from 64 to 75 percent) in folic-acid awareness among women who had recently delivered a live-born infant, as well as an increase in folate intake of U.S. women of childbearing age (Centers for Disease Control & Prevention, 2004; McDowell et al., 2008). As Figure 3.3 shows, the incidence of NTDs decreased between 1990 and 2006, when the rate of spina bifida reached the lowest level ever recorded (Centers for Disease Control & Prevention, 2004; Mathews, 2009).

Despite this progress, folic acid awareness still differs among groups of women. Women who have less than a high school education, those who are African American or Latina, those who receive no prenatal care during the first trimester, and those whose pregnancies were not intended are generally less aware of the benefits of folic acid (Ahluwalia & Daniel, 2001; Canfield et al., 2009; Farley, Hambidge, & Daley, 2002). Hope for changing these statistics comes from a study in 14 Texas-Mexico border counties in which the rate of NTDs was high. The study focused on women who had already had an NTD-affected pregnancy. After the intervention, a large percentage (89 percent) of the women who had had a subsequent pregnancy had taken folic acid before conception, and only 1 case of NTD occurred out of 124 pregnancies that resulted in

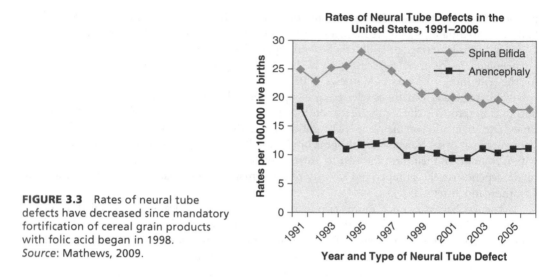

FIGURE 3.3 Rates of neural tube defects have decreased since mandatory fortification of cereal grain products with folic acid began in 1998. *Source*: Mathews, 2009.

live births (Centers for Disease Control & Prevention, 2000a). These findings suggest that even high-risk women can reduce their risk of NTDs if they are given clear information and guidance (Massi Lindsey et al., 2009).

Researchers have recently identified another potential risk factor, the level of vitamin B12 in a pregnant woman's diet. Results of a study of approximately 1,000 women in Ireland showed that offspring of women with the lowest levels of B12 had the highest rate of NTDs, independent of the effect of folic acid alone. Further study is needed, but these findings suggest that it may be important for women, especially those following a vegan diet, to consume adequate levels of B12 before becoming pregnant (Molloy et al., 2009).

Congenital Heart Defects

Approximately 7,000 babies are born each year with congenital heart defects (Centers for Disease Control & Prevention, 2006). The extent of the defect can range from mild and undetected to severe and life threatening. The defects can include holes in the chamber walls, inadequate blood flow, or abnormalities of the valves.

Congenital heart defects are often caused by environmental influences. Women with diabetes and women who contract rubella (German measles) during the first trimester of pregnancy have an elevated risk of having a baby with a heart defect (Wren, Birrell, & Hawthorne, 2003). Certain prescription medications have also been implicated, as well as alcohol and drugs such as cocaine. Advances in genetic research and studies of affected families also point to a role for genetics (Schott et al., 1998; Zhu, Kartiko, & Finnell, 2009).

Some heart defects may be diagnosed during the fetal stage. New diagnostic tests and surgical treatment over the past 40 years have led to improved survival rates for children with even the most serious heart defects. Half of the surgeries for congenital heart defects are now performed on children under the age of 2 years (Centers for Disease Control & Prevention, 2006).

In Chapter 4, we discuss another factor that has led to a reduction in deaths due to birth defects—new technology that has made it possible to save preterm infants and others born at risk. Overall, infant deaths due to birth defects have been reduced by half since 1960, largely as a result of new prenatal diagnostic and treatment options that we discuss next.

PRENATAL DIAGNOSIS AND TREATMENT

Expectant parents have a number of options available for assessing fetal development and detecting potential problems. In some cases, there are treatments, including hormones, medication, and even fetal surgery, that can correct defects before the child is born.

Advances in research on the genetics of human disease have led to the development of tests that offer expectant parents the chance to assess the health of a fetus and determine whether the child carries the code for a genetic disease, a disease for which the parents may not even realize they are carriers. However, prenatal genetic testing, especially for conditions that do not develop until adulthood, is controversial. The American Academy of Pediatrics (2000c) recommends that these tests be performed only when there are immediate medical benefits that can prevent the disease, delay its onset, limit its severity, or prevent secondary disabilities. Genetic tests are not without limitations, and not all genetic mutations that cause disease are understood or detectable at the present time. Counseling is thus an important part of any prenatal genetic testing procedures (Cunniff & Committee on Genetics, 2004).

Preimplantation Genetic Diagnosis (PGD)

When a couple has a known high risk of having a child with a serious genetic disorder, such as when both potential parents are carriers of a recessive gene mutation or when one parent has a dominant gene mutation, what can be done to avoid passing the same genetic potential to their offspring? One possible procedure is **preimplantation genetic diagnosis (PGD)**. In PGD, a biopsy is performed on blastocysts resulting from in vitro fertilization. Blastocysts that are not carriers of the genetic mutation for the disease are selected for transfer to the woman's uterus, while blastocysts that are carriers of the mutation, and those for which the genetic status cannot be determined, are not implanted.

In 1999, researchers used PGD for the first time to enable a couple, both carriers of the recessive genetic mutation for sickle-cell anemia to conceive a healthy (mutation-free) child. In that trial, three healthy embryos were transferred to the uterus, resulting in healthy twins delivered at 39 weeks gestation (Xu et al., 1999). Other applications of PGD have focused on a severe and usually fatal form of anemia called beta thalassemia (Chamayou et al., 2002). The number of disorders being tested using PGD has increased since its introduction in the late 1980s and now includes Huntington's disease, chromosomal abnormalities, and X-linked diseases (Basille et al., 2009; Chow et al., 2009; Kuliev & Verlinsky, 2008). PGD has also been used to select embryos free of a genetic mutation that causes early-onset Alzheimer's disease around age 40 to 50. Mutation-free embryos are selected for transfer, resulting in the birth of one or more healthy offspring (Verlinsky et al., 2004; Verlinsky et al., 2002).

In one family, PGD was used to produce their second child, selecting embryos that could serve as potential stem cell donors for an older sibling requiring treatment for Fanconi anemia (a recessive genetic defect that prevents cells from repairing damaged DNA or removing toxic molecules that damage cells) (Damewood, 2001; Verlinsky et al., 2001). Both parents were carriers of the mutation that causes the disease, and the only chance to save the first child was a stem cell transplantation from the umbilical cord blood of a healthy sibling. (Without such a transplant, children with Fanconi anemia usually die before they reach early adulthood.) Out of 30 embryos obtained in four IVF attempts, five compatible embryos were produced and, eventually, a healthy child was born, achieving the dual objective of saving the first child and producing a child that would be free of the life-threatening disease.

With a combined cost of $15,000 or more for each IVF and PGD, and no guarantee of success on the first attempt, these procedures are accessible by only a small segment of the population, at least at the present time. As genetic research unveils more about the genetic basis for an increasing number of human characteristics, however, many bioethicists note the potential for misusing PGD. What would prevent parents who want "perfect" children from using PGD to select other traits? Preimplantation sex selection of embryos conceived through IVF occurs in cultures in which families have a strong preference for sons rather than daughters (Almond & Edlund, 2008; Malpani, Malpani, & Modi, 2002). There are different opinions about this application of the procedure, but using PGD for sex selection for nonmedical reasons is prohibited in many countries (ESHRE PGD Consortium Steering Committee, 2002; Reproductive Health Technology Project, 2006; Savulescu & Dahl, 2000). Most clinics performing PGD use the procedure for serious diseases such as cystic fibrosis, Tay-Sachs disease, Huntington's disease, and sickle-cell anemia (Basille et al., 2009; Cunniff & Committee on Genetics, 2004).

Ultrasound

In **ultrasound** (also called ultrasonography), sound waves are bounced off the developing fetus and converted into an image called a sonogram that can be viewed on a special video monitor. The examiner holds an instrument called a transducer and moves it across the woman's abdomen. The most advanced ultrasound technology produces a detailed, three-dimensional image. Ultrasound has been used since the 1970s, across the prenatal period, without any identified risks for baby or mother.

Nearly 70 percent of pregnant women in the United States have an ultrasound exam (Centers for Disease Control & Prevention, 2006; Martin et al., 2005). An ultrasonogram can be used to identify a miscarriage, diagnose birth defects, check fetal well-being, and assist with other prenatal diagnostic tests, such as amniocentesis and chorionic villus sampling, which we discuss shortly (Cunniff & Committee on Genetics, 2004). Ultrasound is an effective early screening tool between 11 and 13 weeks for Down syndrome (Malone et al., 2005; Reddy & Mennuti, 2006).

Depending on the reason for the ultrasound, the procedure may take as little as 15 minutes or as much as several hours. One drawback is that it may miss some birth defects, perhaps as

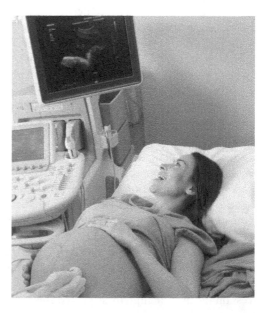

Many infants' first "baby pictures" are produced through ultrasound—a low-risk procedure in which sound waves are bounced off the developing fetus and converted into an image on a video monitor.

many as 25 to 50 percent (Grandjean, Larroque, & Levi, 1999). It may also lead to the opposite problem—a mistaken diagnosis of a birth defect that does not actually exist. The accuracy of an ultrasound diagnosis is affected by the training and experience of the examiner (Pathak & Lees, 2009; Reddy & Mennuti, 2006).

Maternal Blood Screening

The **maternal serum alpha fetoprotein (MSAFP) test,** also referred to as the triple screen, is used routinely and can detect neural tube defects, such as spina bifida or anencephaly. The test, which requires only a small blood sample from the mother, can also aid in the detection of Down syndrome. The blood sample is used to determine the level of alpha fetoprotein (AFP), a small amount of which normally crosses the placenta and enters the mother's bloodstream. High levels of AFP may indicate that the fetus has a neural tube defect, whereas low levels may signal Down syndrome. As part of the triple screen, the maternal blood sample is also analyzed for human chorionic gonadotropin (HCG), a hormone produced in the placenta, and estriol, an estrogen produced by both the fetus and the placenta. Abnormal levels of HCG and estriol may indicate fetal spinal defects and chromosomal abnormalities. The test is most accurate when performed between 16 and 18 weeks of gestation. If problems are suspected, a follow-up test or ultrasound may be used to gather more information (Cunniff & Committee on Genetics, 2004; Pilu & Hobbins, 2002).

In the late 1990s, researchers devised another form of noninvasive prenatal diagnosis using small samples of fetal DNA found circulating in maternal plasma (Maddocks et al., 2009). This approach, which can be carried out as early as 5 weeks gestation, is of greatest value for families with a high risk for heritable diseases, including X-linked diseases (Wright & Burton, 2009). Given that there are very few fetal DNA molecules and cells in maternal blood, researchers use special techniques to isolate and amplify that material, resulting in a more sensitive test (Sekizawa et al., 2007).

Chorionic Villus Sampling (CVS)

In **chorionic villus sampling (CVS),** a small amount of the chorion tissue surrounding the amniotic sac is extracted, using a needle guided by ultrasound. The test is usually performed between 10 and 12 weeks after the mother's last menstrual period. CVS can diagnose or rule out birth defects due to chromosomal abnormalities and is offered to women who will be 35 or older at the time of delivery, as well as to women with a previous child or pregnancy with a birth defect or chromosomal abnormality (Cunniff & Committee on Genetics, 2004). Studies of CVS have found that it is a safe and accurate procedure, especially when performed by experienced medical personnel (Evans & Wapner, 2005; Tabor, Vestergaard, & Lidegaard, 2009).

Amniocentesis

Amniocentesis is usually conducted in the second trimester (15 to 18 weeks postconception) of pregnancy. This test involves inserting a thin, hollow needle, guided by ultrasound, into the uterus and removing a sample of the amniotic fluid surrounding the fetus. The sample is analyzed for chromosomal disorders, including Down syndrome. Amniocentesis poses a small risk of miscarriage, however, and is not used for low-risk pregnancies. Given that the risk of Down syndrome increases as a function of maternal age (from 1 in 1,250 children born to mothers in their 20s to 1 in 100 children born to mothers age 40), amniocentesis is routinely offered to women who will be 35 or older at delivery. It may also be recommended if a woman has had a previous child or pregnancy with a birth defect or chromosomal abnormality, or if other prenatal screening tests suggest that a chromosomal abnormality or birth defect may exist. Amniocentesis has an accuracy rate of nearly 100 percent in diagnosing chromosomal abnormalities (American Academy of Pediatrics, 1994; Cunniff & Committee on Genetics, 2004).

Fetal Echocardiography

When a cardiac defect is suspected, fetal echocardiography—a special kind of ultrasonography that provides information about structural defects or rhythmic disturbances—can be used. This procedure is usually performed after 20 weeks gestation for cases in which a standard ultrasound has indicated potential malformations. It may also be performed when there has been prenatal exposure to a known teratogen, when there is a family history of congenital heart defects, or when a fetal chromosomal abnormality or disease has been diagnosed. The procedure may also be used to evaluate fetuses whose mothers have diseases associated with fetal structural heart defects, such as diabetes (Cunniff & Committee on Genetics, 2004).

Fetal Therapy

When defects are detected during the fetal stage, can anything be done to correct them before the child is born? The answer depends on the nature of the problem, but the options for fetal therapy—interventions carried out during the prenatal period in order to correct known defects or prevent health problems after birth—are expanding.

If the problem is a disease caused by faulty genes, it may someday be possible to perform gene therapy—inserting healthy genes into the cells of a person's body. Researchers studying severe combined immunodeficiency (SCID-X1), an X-linked condition, for example, reported successful treatment of this disease when they inserted healthy genes into the bone marrow of nine patients. Two of those patients, however, treated at 1 and 3 months of age, developed complications nearly three years later (Hacein-Bey-Abina et al., 2003). Results of studies with laboratory animals have been promising. Researchers working with diseased human lung cells grafted into a living mouse have had success "fooling" the body into repairing genetic codes that cause cystic fibrosis (Liu et al., 2002). Gene therapy has also been used to correct sickle-cell disease in mice that were bioengineered to contain a human gene for sickle-cell disease (Imren et al., 2004; Pawliuk et al., 2001). This form of gene therapy is known as somatic gene therapy because the targeted genes are in cells other than the sperm or eggs. Somatic gene therapy is still experimental, but if it becomes widely available in the future, it will help only the individual who has been treated. In order to prevent the genetic code from being inherited by the patient's offspring and all future descendants, germline gene therapy—changing the genes in sex cells—would be needed. This form of gene therapy entails numerous practical and ethical concerns, however, and is not being actively researched (Dennis & Gallagher, 2001).

Some health problems, such as HIV and heart rhythm disturbances, can be treated or prevented by giving drugs or other substances to the mother. Other potential problems, such as structural malformations, can be treated surgically before birth through fetal surgery—surgery performed on a fetus that remains connected to the placenta and is returned to the uterus following the procedure. Experimental trials were initiated in the 1960s but began in earnest in the 1980s. Since that time, with the development and refinement of ultrasound technology, operations on fetuses have succeeded more often, but there is still much about the physiology of the maternal-fetal-placental system that is not understood, and the field of fetal medicine is both technically challenging and ethically complex (Chescheir, 2009; Durkin & Shaaban, 2009). While some applications of fetal surgery, including repairing blocked urinary tracts, have produced such reliable results that they are now regarded as nearly routine procedures, others have not lived up to expectations and continue to generate controversy among doctors and medical ethicists (Evans et al., 2002; Wilson, 2002).

Despite the development of new surgical procedures, some conditions continue to be associated with very high fetal mortality rates, whether they are treated prenatally or after birth. In those cases, critics question the value of fetal treatment, since many babies need surgery after birth, even if they were operated upon prenatally (Harrison et al., 2003; Peek & Elliott, 2004). Critics also note that some open-uterus surgical procedures may lead mothers to risk their own lives in vain hope of saving their fetuses. Most fetal treatment facilities emphasize closed-uterus forms of treatment, with only a few medical centers actively engaged in research on open surgical techniques (Casper, 1998; Kunisaki & Jennings, 2008).

More consistently positive outcomes may be achieved through prevention efforts that promote healthy behaviors in pregnant women. As we have seen, a woman's nutrition, even before she becomes pregnant, may have a profound impact on the health and development of her unborn child. Besides having an adequate daily intake of folic acid, what can be done to achieve a healthy pregnancy and baby?

PRENATAL INFLUENCES

Pregnancy is not always apparent to women during the first trimester, especially if the pregnancy is unintended, as is true in as many as one-third to one-half of pregnancies in the United States (Alan Guttmacher Institute, 1999). Unintended pregnancy is more prevalent among women younger than 20 years, African American women, women with lower levels of education, and lower income women (Beck et al., 2002). In general, these are the same groups of women who, for a variety of reasons, are likely to receive prenatal care late or not at all (Beck et al., 2002; Martin et al., 2009).

Since 1990, the number of pregnant women seeking prenatal care during the first trimester has increased steadily. In 2006, the majority (68.3 percent) began prenatal care during the first trimester, but some women (8.2 percent) did not seek care until the third trimester or received no prenatal care at all. A higher percentage of non-Hispanic white women (76.0 percent) sought early prenatal care than either African American women (58.2 percent) or women of Hispanic origin (57.6 percent). Conversely, a higher percentage of African American women (11.9 percent) and women of Hispanic origin (12.2 percent) received late or no prenatal care than was found among non-Hispanic white women (5.3 percent) (Martin et al., 2009). Prenatal care that begins early in the pregnancy educates women about pregnancy and prenatal development. Without this information, women may be less likely to consume a healthy, nutritious diet and more likely to ingest alcohol or drugs and expose themselves (and their fetuses) to potentially harmful environmental influences.

Nutrition

Only a few generations ago, women were routinely advised by their doctors to gain no more than 15 pounds during their pregnancy. We now know that, on average, babies whose mothers gain fewer than 20 pounds are at greater risk of being preterm and are more likely to grow slowly during the prenatal period than babies whose mothers gain between 25 and 35 pounds (Ehrenberg et al., 2003; Martin et al., 2009). The amount of weight a woman should gain during pregnancy is best viewed in relation to her weight before becoming pregnant. Women who were underweight or overweight before becoming pregnant, as well as adolescents and women carrying twins or other multiples, may be advised to gain more or less weight (Martin et al., 2005; Schieve et al., 2000). Women whose pre-pregnancy body mass index (BMI, a measure of a person's weight for her height) is normal should usually gain between 25 and 35 pounds, whereas women who were underweight should gain between 28 and 40 pounds. Women in the overweight BMI category should usually gain between 15 and 25 pounds, while obese women should typically gain between 11 and 20 pounds (Committee to Reexamine IOM Pregnancy Weight Guidelines, 2009).

For all women, weight gain should be slow and steady. For a normal-weight woman, for example, the amount gained during the entire first trimester should be approximately 3 to 4 pounds, with 12 to 14 additional pounds added in the second trimester, about 1 pound per week during the seventh and eighth months, and only about 1 or 2 pounds for the entire ninth month. Women who gain more weight or gain a significant amount of weight early should consult their doctor to rule out any medical problems. Although they should be careful about the amount and type of food they eat thereafter, they should not try to lose weight during the remainder of their pregnancy. Losing weight before becoming pregnant, however, is a good idea because children born to women who are overweight or obese before becoming pregnant are more likely to have birth defects and to develop health problems that include a greater risk of becoming overweight by 2 to 3 years of age (Salsberry & Reagan, 2005; Watkins et al., 2003). Since 2003, the revised U.S. Standard Certificate of Live Birth has gathered information about maternal pre-pregnancy weight, height, weight at delivery, and age at last measured weight, data that may help doctors identify newborns who have a higher than average risk for these health problems (Menacker & Martin, 2008).

It is often said that pregnant women are "eating for two," but the second diner requires only about 300 extra calories each day. Just as it is important to gain the right amount of weight and to put it on at the right rate, it is also critical that the foods women consume are of high nutritional value (Kaiser, Allen, & American Dietetic Association, 2008). Many foods in the United States have been fortified since the 1930s, so pregnant women consuming recommended servings also receive the benefits of vitamins A and D in cow's milk, and thiamin, niacin, riboflavin, and iron in flour and bread products (Centers for Disease Control & Prevention, 2002a; United States Food and Drug Administration, 1996).

Salty foods should be eaten in moderation, and the salt pregnant women consume should be iodized because a deficiency of the micronutrient iodine interferes with normal functioning of the thyroid and the production of thyroid hormone. Low levels of thyroid hormone (a condition referred to as hypothyroidism) cause a range of serious problems, including miscarriage, still-birth, abnormalities in fetal brain development, and a form of cognitive disabilities known as endemic cretinism (Haddow et al., 1999; Hetzel, 1999).

Women in the United States generally get enough iodine, which has been added to salt since 1924 (Caldwell, 2009). Iodine deficiency still poses a significant risk of preventable brain damage in many parts of the world, however, and it is estimated that nearly 50 million people worldwide suffer from some degree of brain damage caused by iodine deficiency disorder. Fortunately, the number of countries with salt iodization programs has risen since 1991, and global rates of cognitive disabilities and cretinism have begun to fall (World Health Organization, 2001a, 2002b). Where iodized salt is not yet available, doses of iodized oil may be injected or administered orally to pregnant women, with the same preventive effects (World Health Organization, 1996).

To help develop the blood supply for fetus and mother, iron-rich foods should be consumed every day, eaten at the same time as foods rich in vitamin C to increase the body's absorption of iron. The need for iron is greater during pregnancy than at any other time in life, and many women in the United States and other developed countries take a daily prenatal vitamin supplement to ensure that their iron intake is sufficient. Iron deficiency is the most common nutritional disorder in the world. According to the World Health Organization (2002b), 50 percent of pregnant woman worldwide suffer from iron deficiency, a condition that contributes to preterm birth, low birth-weight, and 20 percent of all maternal deaths, primarily in developing countries.

For some nutrients, problems are caused by an excess. Women who consume more than twice the recommended daily amount of vitamin A in the first two months of pregnancy, for example, have a heightened risk of giving birth to babies with defects such as cleft lip or palate, hydrocephalus, or heart defects. The principal food that provides very high amounts of vitamin A is liver, so pregnant women are advised to limit their consumption (Rothman et al., 1995).

Alcohol and Drugs

The fetus and mother have separate circulatory systems, but small molecules, such as oxygen and nutrients, are able to cross through the cell membranes of the placenta. Unfortunately, alcohol and drugs are also able to pass through the placenta and may damage the developing child. The extent and type of damage that occurs depends on the timing, duration, and degree of exposure, with greater damage generally resulting from sustained exposure to larger doses earlier in the prenatal period.

It is difficult to obtain accurate reports, but experts believe that between 13 and 20 percent of pregnant U.S. women consume alcohol and more than 5 percent use illicit drugs, putting their fetuses at risk for a wide range of serious medical problems (Ebrahim & Gfroerer, 2003; Martin et al., 2005). There is ongoing debate about how to protect babies from these risks. On one side are those who advocate criminal punishment (for child abuse or child endangerment) for pregnant women who drink alcohol or take drugs. On the other side are those who argue that the best way to prevent or minimize damage to babies is to treat pregnant women for their addictions; according to this view, pregnant women will not seek this kind of help—or prenatal care—if they are in danger of being prosecuted as criminals. Although there is not agreement about the best way to address the problem of prenatal exposure to alcohol and drugs, everyone agrees that too much preventable damage is being done.

ALCOHOL   Prenatal exposure to alcohol is the leading preventable cause of birth defects, cognitive disabilities, and neurodevelopmental disorders (American Academy of Pediatrics, 2000b). Alcohol is used by more pregnant women than are drugs such as cocaine and marijuana, and it produces the most serious neurobehavioral effects in the fetus (National Organization on Fetal Alcohol Syndrome, 2002). **Fetal alcohol syndrome (FAS),** first clinically described in 1973, is a constellation of physical, behavioral, and cognitive abnormalities caused by prenatal exposure to alcohol (Jones & Smith, 1973). Children with FAS typically have small brains and growth deficiencies before and after birth, as well as poor coordination, attention-deficit hyperactivity disorder, and distinctive facial abnormalities. FAS is the leading known cause of cognitive disabilities in the United States (Gilbert, 2000; Jacobson & Jacobson, 2000). As many as 12,000 infants are born with FAS each year, and another 50,000 show signs of other fetal alcohol effects, including conditions referred to as alcohol-related neurodevelopmental disorder (ARND) and alcohol-related birth defects (ARBD) (American Academy of Pediatrics, 2000b; Jacobson & Jacobson, 2000; National Organization on Fetal Alcohol Syndrome, 2006).

Attempts to increase public awareness of alcohol's prenatal effects have reached many but not all women of childbearing age (Ebrahim & Gfroerer, 2003; Martin et al., 2005). The highest rates of self-reported alcohol use among pregnant women are found in the 35- to 44-year-old age group (17.7%), followed by college graduates (14.4%), employed women (13.7%), and unmarried women (13.4%) (Centers for Disease Control and Prevention, 2009a). These trends suggest that many women still do not understand the irreversible harm that can be done by consuming

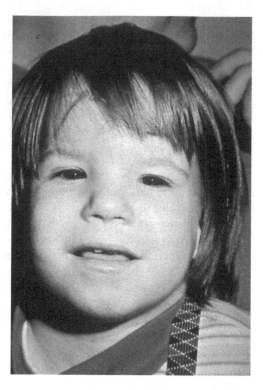

Prenatal exposure to alcohol produces fetal alcohol syndrome—a constellation of physical, behavioral, and cognitive abnormalities that are typically accompanied by the distinctive facial features seen in this child.

alcohol during pregnancy. Effects of prenatal alcohol exposure vary according to the timing, amount, and duration of exposure, with binge drinking being especially harmful to fetal brain development (Centers for Disease Control and Prevention, 2009a). Studies using animal models are shedding light on the mechanisms of fetal damage at different stages of development. It is clear, however, that there are differences among women in the effects of alcohol on their fetuses, even when the timing, amount, and duration of exposure are similar. No amount of alcohol, therefore, is regarded as safe.

ILLICIT DRUGS   Determining the effects of individual illicit drugs, such as cocaine, marijuana, methamphetamine ("speed," or "ice"), and heroin, on prenatal development can be difficult because pregnant women taking these substances often expose their fetuses to more than one drug, as well as alcohol and nicotine (Lester et al., 2004; Messinger et al., 2004). They are less likely to receive early prenatal care or consume a healthy diet, and the fathers of their babies are also more likely to have a history of drug and alcohol use as well as physical abuse (Della Grotta et al., 2009; Frank et al., 2002). Experiments with animals can reveal the effects of drugs in isolation, but even correlational (nonexperimental) evidence from research with humans indicates that illicit drugs are potent teratogens, causing miscarriage, stillbirth, and birth defects, as well as developmental problems in infancy and beyond. Valuable longitudinal studies—the Maternal Lifestyle Study and the Infant Development, Environment, and Lifestyle (IDEAL) Study—are each charting the development of babies who were exposed to cocaine, methamphetamine, and other drugs during the prenatal period (Della Grotta et al., 2009; Lester et al., 2002).

Women who use cocaine or methamphetamine during their pregnancy are at increased risk of giving birth to babies who are preterm or low-birthweight, effects that increase with greater exposure (Chiriboga et al., 1999; Smith et al., 2006). Cocaine-exposed babies tend to have a smaller head circumference and are at greater risk of dying from Sudden Infant Death Syndrome (SIDS) than are unexposed babies. Prenatal cocaine exposure is also associated with lower arousal, poorer quality of movement and self-regulation, greater excitability, and abnormal reflexes at the age of 1 month (Lester et al., 2002). Children exposed to cocaine in utero frequently have significant delays in mental skills by the age of 2 years and behavior problems, learning difficulties, and a need for special educational services when they reach school age (Bada et al., 2007; Levine et al., 2008).

Experiments with animals show that cocaine interferes with the development of neural systems in the fetal brain, with the most serious alterations seen during the period corresponding to the first trimester of pregnancy (Levitt, Reinoso, & Jones, 1998). Damage may also occur when cocaine constricts the vascular system, decreasing blood flow through the placenta, and producing low levels of oxygen in the fetus (Eyler et al., 1998; Singer et al., 2002). Developmental delays due to prenatal exposure to cocaine are most prevalent in infants who were also low birthweight and experienced nonoptimal caregiving after birth (Messinger et al., 2004). These findings offer hope that at-risk newborns—those who are known to have been prenatally exposed to cocaine or other substances—may be helped through early interventions (Frank et al., 2002).

Heroin abuse can also cause serious complications during pregnancy, as well as postnatal problems with learning and attention underlying cognitive development (Moe & Smith, 2003). Pregnant women trying to detoxify from heroin are at increased risk of miscarriage or preterm delivery; treatment with methadone (a safer, synthetic form of heroin) for the remainder of the pregnancy is recommended instead (National Institute on Drug Abuse, 2002). Evidence about the effects of prenatal exposure to marijuana are less clear, but heavy use has been linked to birth defects, low birthweight, and neurological disturbances (Dreher, Nugent, & Hudgins, 1994).

Babies born to drug-addicted mothers are often addicted themselves and suffer withdrawal symptoms at birth. Women who inject drugs are at risk of becoming infected with the HIV virus and may pass the virus on to their babies. For a variety of practical and ethical reasons, it is not always easy to determine how a particular substance affects prenatal development in humans. As we discuss next, however, just because a drug or other substance is legal does not mean that it is safe (Thompson, Levitt, & Stanwood, 2009).

MEDICATION   During pregnancy, women need to decide how to relieve symptoms of colds and other short-lived illnesses. Some herbal treatments and dietary supplements, despite being "natural" products, may be unsafe for the developing fetus. Certain over-the-counter medicines, such as aspirin and ibuprofen, should be avoided in the last three months of pregnancy because they may cause problems in the fetus or complications during delivery (Koren, Pastuszak, & Ito, 1998; Meadows, 2001).

Until the 1960s, some women took a tranquilizer called thalidomide to treat morning sickness. Sadly, thalidomide—even as little as one tablet—caused numerous birth defects in more than 7,000 infants. The drug's specific effects varied depending on when in the critical period it was taken (teratogenic effects were produced only during days 34 to 50 after the mother's last menstruation). After the link between the drug and birth defects was documented, it was withdrawn from the market. The mechanisms through which thalidomide causes birth defects remain unclear—research is hampered because the only animal models for the drug are primates—but it is beginning to be prescribed again, this time to treat tumors, autoimmune problems, and leprosy (Gilbert, 2000; Raje & Anderson, 1999).

The dangers of prescription medication are not always apparent during the prenatal period and may not be known for many years. In the 1940s and 1950s, millions of women were prescribed a synthetic estrogen called diethylstilbestrol (DES) to prevent miscarriage. Babies—boys as well as girls—born to these women experienced a high rate of genital-tract structural abnormalities and cancers as they reached adulthood. Many DES daughters have had reproductive problems, including a higher incidence of infertility, miscarriage, and preterm delivery (Swan, 2000; Trimble, 2001; Troisi et al., 2007).

For women who have chronic health conditions, not related to pregnancy per se, questions about the safety of prescription medications for those conditions can be a significant source of concern. According to current guidelines, medical conditions such as diabetes, epilepsy, and high blood pressure should continue to be treated and kept under control during pregnancy. Women taking psychoactive drugs to modify mood and behavior in the treatment of psychiatric illnesses, such as schizophrenia, depression, and obsessive-compulsive disorder, should also keep those conditions under control. Changes in the woman's physiology during pregnancy can influence the effectiveness of the pre-pregnancy dose, however, requiring adjustments. Studies of how the body absorbs, distributes, metabolizes, and excretes drugs may help doctors determine the optimal doses of medications to help pregnant women stay physically and mentally healthy (Meadows, 2001).

The effects of medication on the developing fetus are often unclear or unknown, and ethical issues limit the experimental testing of medications on pregnant women (American Academy of Pediatrics, 2000c; Brent, 2004; Meadows, 2001). What options are available, then, to women who must take medication during pregnancy? If there are concerns about a new drug's safety, an older version can be prescribed, since an absence of safety concerns in a long-used drug can provide some reassurance. Some drugs that are known to be harmful only during a particular stage of pre-natal development can be withheld until the vulnerable period has passed. This has been done with the antibiotic tetracycline, which can cause permanent staining of a baby's teeth if taken before 24 weeks. The psychoactive drug lithium carries a small risk of heart defects, so women who use lithium may be advised to stop taking it during the time when the baby's heart is forming. Third trimester use of antidepressant medication carries an increased risk of preterm birth and other adverse birth outcomes (Källen, 2004). Clearer labeling being developed by the Food and Drug Administration may help pregnant women and their doctors make decisions about the risks and benefits of various medications (American Academy of Pediatrics, 2000d; Meadows, 2001).

NICOTINE   Tobacco use during pregnancy has declined over the years, but in 2006, approximately 13 percent of all pregnant women in the United States reported smoking cigarettes. Smoking rates were higher among non-Hispanic white women (18.1 percent) and African American women (10.6 percent) than among women of Hispanic origin (2.8 percent) (Martin et al., 2009). Smoking during pregnancy is most prevalent among women under age 25, women with lower levels of education, and women with lower incomes (Hamilton et al., 2005; Higgins et al., 2009).

Cigarette smoke contains more than 2,500 chemicals, and the effects of these substances on prenatal development are not known, so pregnant women who smoke are putting their unborn children at significant risk. Cigarette smoking during pregnancy tends to result in low-birthweight babies (weighing less than 5.5 pounds) because nicotine depresses the mother's appetite at the same time that it reduces her ability to supply oxygen to the fetus (Martin et al., 2005; Ventura et al., 2003). Nicotine is also associated with infertility, miscarriages, ectopic pregnancies, infant mortality, preterm delivery, child morbidity, and an increased incidence of asthma and ear infections (Centers for Disease Control & Prevention, 2002a; Lieu & Feinstein, 2002). Studies of laboratory animals have found that nicotine exposure affects breathing in newborn mice and may thus play a role in Sudden Infant Death Syndrome in humans (Eugenín et al., 2008). Maternal smoking during pregnancy is also associated with intellectual and behavioral problems during childhood, but the effects of nicotine appear to depend on which parts of the brain are developing at the time of exposure (Dwyer, McQuown, & Leslie, 2009; Eskenazi & Castorina, 1999).

Efforts to reduce smoking rates among women during and after pregnancy have been more effective than campaigns to prevent women from smoking before they become pregnant (Tong et al., 2009). This is an important finding because, if women stop smoking by the 16th week of pregnancy, they are no more likely to have a low-birthweight baby than women who never smoked. Even women who stop smoking only in the third trimester of pregnancy can improve their baby's growth. Secondhand smoke also appears to be harmful to pregnant women and their fetuses, suggesting that all smokers in the home should try to quit or stop smoking around the mother.

CAFFEINE   One legal stimulant frequently consumed before and during pregnancy is caffeine, which is found in coffee, tea, colas, and chocolate. Many women curtail their caffeine consumption during pregnancy, but it appears that a moderate level (fewer than 5 cups per day) is not teratogenic (Hinds et al., 1996; Johansen et al., 2009; Linnet et al., 2009; Santos et al., 1998; Vestergaard et al., 2005). Although it is not clear how to apply the results of experiments with animals to humans, some laboratory studies have found that daily prenatal exposure to moderate levels of caffeine leads to reduced body length and weight, as well as impairments in caradiovascular function and growth (Momoi et al., 2008).

Disease

Diseases carried by the mother can adversely affect fetal development. Some of these diseases can be treated before birth, but others cause permanent defects and disabilities or lead to miscarriage or stillbirth.

HIV AND OTHER INFECTIONS   Between 6,000 and 7,000 U.S. women infected with HIV give birth each year. Perinatal HIV infection occurs when women with HIV pass the virus on to their baby during pregnancy, delivery, or breastfeeding. Drug treatment during pregnancy can dramatically reduce the risk that the virus will be passed on if women with HIV take zidovudine (ZDV) during the second and third trimesters of pregnancy and during labor and delivery. Guidelines from the U.S. Public Health Service also recommend giving ZDV to newborns for the first six weeks of life, even if the newborn has not yet been diagnosed with HIV; medication is stopped when tests show that the baby does not have HIV (Centers for Disease Control & Prevention, 2000c, 2002). Worldwide, many HIV-infected women who give birth do not receive these drugs. As a result, perinatal HIV and pediatric AIDS continue to be a significant public health threat in many developing countries (Lindegren et al., 1999; March of Dimes, 2002).

Another infection, toxoplasmosis, is caused by a parasite that can be avoided by eating only cooked meat, peeling or washing all raw fruits and vegetables before eating, and avoiding contact with cat or rabbit feces that may contain the parasite. If a woman develops toxoplasmosis during pregnancy, tests can determine whether the fetus is infected as well; if so, the infection can be treated by giving medication to the mother. The most serious effects tend to occur when infection occurs early in the pregnancy and include miscarriage or stillbirth, severely impaired eyesight, cerebral palsy, and seizures (American College of Obstetricians and Gynecologists, 2000).

Women who contract rubella (German measles) during pregnancy, especially during the first trimester, may give birth to a baby with congenital rubella syndrome—a collection of birth defects that includes eye defects, hearing loss, heart defects, cognitive disabilities, and sometimes movement disorders. Congenital rubella syndrome is rarely seen when infection occurs after 20 weeks of pregnancy because the development of nearly all vulnerable organs is complete by that time (Shonkoff &

Phillips, 2000). Some infected babies have short-term health problems, while others may not develop noticeable problems with vision, hearing, learning, and behavior until childhood. More than 30,000 babies were born with birth defects in an outbreak of the disease in 1963 to 1965 that also resulted in thousands of miscarriages and stillbirths (Gilbert, 2000). Major outbreaks of rubella no longer occur in the United States, thanks to routine vaccination in childhood.

PREEXISTING CHRONIC DISEASES Most women with preexisting chronic diseases should continue treating and controlling their symptoms after they become pregnant. The chance of having a chronic disease or developing a medical condition during pregnancy increases as a woman's age goes up (Martin et al., 2005). With proper medical care, however, including early prenatal care, most women with chronic diseases can expect to have healthy babies.

About 1 percent of women of childbearing age have diabetes before pregnancy, and another 3 to 5 percent develop gestational diabetes, a form of diabetes that develops during pregnancy (Martin et al., 2009). If left untreated, diabetes can damage organs, including blood vessels, nerves, eyes, and kidneys. Daily insulin injections can prevent these complications. Diet and exercise can also help control blood sugar levels (Brankston et al., 2004; Chasan-Taber et al., 2009). Women with poorly controlled diabetes prior to pregnancy are more likely than nondiabetic women to have a baby with neural tube defects or heart defects. They are also at greater risk of miscarriage and stillbirth (Wren et al., 2003). Most women are routinely screened for gestational diabetes between the 24th and 28th week of pregnancy, since gestational diabetes tends to develop relatively late in pregnancy. Although women with this form of the disease usually do not have an increased risk of giving birth to a baby with birth defects, treating even mild cases (often with just diet and exercise) reduces birth complications (Landon et al., 2009).

Extra sugar in the mother's blood crosses the placenta and goes to the fetus; this is why women with poorly controlled diabetes of either type tend to give birth to babies who are very large, perhaps 10 pounds or more. The most serious birth defects related to diabetes occur in the early weeks of pregnancy, so women with preexisting diabetes should consult their doctor before pregnancy. Some oral diabetes medications have been associated with birth defects, and these medications need to be replaced by insulin before and during pregnancy. Close monitoring is also important because physiological changes in the woman's body during pregnancy may change the dose of insulin that is needed. Women with gestational diabetes usually do not need to take insulin (Kjos, 1999).

Some women have chronic hypertension (high blood pressure) before they become pregnant and many develop pregnancy-induced hypertension. Although hypertension usually causes no obvious symptoms in the mother, it can slow fetal growth by constricting the blood vessels that supply oxygen and nutrients. Hypertension is also a risk factor for conditions that place the mother and fetus at risk, including placental abruption (separation of the placenta from the uterine wall), preeclampsia (high blood pressure accompanied by protein in the urine), and eclampsia (a rare but life-threatening condition that causes convulsions and coma). Most women with chronic hypertension have healthy babies, but it is important to seek medical advice about whether the form and dose of medication they usually take is safe during pregnancy.

RH DISEASE Some diseases, like Rh disease, do not develop until a woman becomes pregnant. Rh disease is defined as an incompatibility between the blood of the mother and her fetus. Without treatment, the incompatibility causes destruction of fetal red blood cells and can lead to stillbirth. In newborns, Rh disease can cause jaundice, anemia, brain damage, heart failure, and death. The mother's health is not affected.

Most people have Rh-positive blood and produce Rh factor, a protein found in their red blood cells. Rh-negative individuals lack the Rh factor but are just as healthy as those who are Rh-positive. A baby conceived by a mother who is Rh-negative and a father who is Rh-positive may inherit the father's Rh-positive blood type. As we noted earlier, the fetus and mother have separate circulatory systems. During labor and delivery, and sometimes during pregnancy, however, some of the baby's Rh-positive blood cells may enter the mother's bloodstream, triggering an immune system response and production of antibodies. In a first pregnancy, Rh-positive babies are at little risk, but subsequent Rh-positive fetuses are endangered by the mother's Rh antibodies, which can cross the placenta and destroy fetal blood cells. (Babies conceived by two Rh-negative parents are not at risk for Rh disease.) A simple maternal blood test prior to pregnancy can reveal whether a woman is Rh-negative and whether she has been sensitized to Rh factor in a previous pregnancy. All babies born to Rh-negative women are tested for their Rh type at birth or, in some cases, with amniocentesis, but a maternal blood test offers a safer, less invasive way to determine fetal Rh status (Chan et al., 2006; Lo, 2005, 2006).

Before 1968, approximately 20,000 babies in the United States were born with Rh disease each year. With the development of a purified blood product called Rh immune globulin (RhIg), that number has fallen to approximately 4,000 babies each year. When Rh-negative mothers receive an injection of RhIg within 72 hours of delivery, the production of antibodies can be prevented in nearly all cases. Because some women develop antibodies during pregnancy, RhIg injections are also given at about 28 weeks of pregnancy. RhIg prevents the production of Rh factor antibodies by destroying any Rh-positive fetal cells in the mother's bloodstream. Treatment with RhIg must be repeated with each pregnancy and in any situations in which fetal blood cells might mix with the mother's blood, including miscarriage, ectopic pregnancy, and amniocentesis. Fetuses that are known to have Rh disease can be treated with blood transfusions as early as the 18th week of pregnancy (Grab et al., 1999). These treatments are usually successful, and most treated babies with severe Rh disease survive.

Stress

Prenatal exposure to stress has been linked to complications during pregnancy as well as behavioral abnormalities after birth (DiPietro, 2004; Kofman, 2002; Mulder et al., 2002). When animals and humans perceive threats or other aversive environmental events, there are rapid changes in heart rate and blood pressure. Stress also activates the hypothalamic-pituitary-adrenal (HPA) axis, producing higher levels of adrenaline and stress hormones, such as cortisol. The placenta buffers the developing fetus to a degree, but increased levels of these hormones in the mother's body are known to increase fetal exposure (Talge et al., 2007).

The attack on the World Trade Center on September 11, 2001, induced high levels of stress in residents of New York City, including those who were in utero at the time. To examine the effects of this stressful prenatal event on fetal growth and subsequent health and development, researchers compared birth outcomes for infants born to 300 women who were pregnant on September 11. Infants whose mothers were in the first trimester of pregnancy at the time of the World Trade Center event and lived within a two-mile radius of the World Trade Center had significantly briefer gestations, lower birthweights, and shorter birth lengths than infants whose mothers were in the second or third trimester when the attack occurred (Lederman et al., 2004). Although these findings indicate that the effects were greatest during the earliest period of prenatal development, it is not clear that they were the result of stress alone. It is possible, for example, that they were due to exposure to air pollution caused by the towers' collapse, another negative influence on fetal development and growth (Brent & Weitzman, 2004; Perera et al., 2002).

Experiments with laboratory animals show that fetuses exposed to high levels of stress hormones tend to develop fewer receptors in the brain for those hormones. This deficit may explain later behavioral and emotional difficulties that are observed after birth, including problems coping with and recovering from stress (Huizink, Mulder, & Buitelaar, 2004; Huizink et al., 2002; Talge et al., 2007). A review of more than 250 animal and human studies of the effects of maternal stress found that the most common consequences in offspring were impairments in learning, motor development, and emotional reactivity (Huizink et al., 2004).

It is difficult to know whether the findings from studies of animals, such as rats and monkeys, can be directly generalized to humans (Brent, 2004). Whereas maternal stress in humans is typically investigated by assessing levels of self-reported psychological stress and anxiety encountered on a daily basis, in studies of animals, stress is usually induced by exposure to environmental events, such as prolonged or repeated periods of loud noise. Given significant differences in the types of stressors used in human versus animal studies, some researchers assert that caution must be used in drawing inferences about the effects of prenatal stress in humans.

Research focusing solely on humans is also challenging to interpret, in part because of the tendency to use maternal reports rather than independent measures both to measure anxiety during pregnancy and to rate infants' behavior after birth (DiPietro, 2004). One recent study with humans addressed this issue by creating stressful experiences in the laboratory. The researchers asked pregnant women to complete a challenging cognitive task and also showed them graphic scenes from a video about labor and delivery (DiPietro et al., 2002). Surprisingly, women who experienced higher levels of stress during these tasks had infants who had better scores on assessments of their development. These results suggest that relatively mild prenatal stress is not necessarily harmful and may even be beneficial for later development—a finding that has also been observed in animal studies involving mild stress (DiPietro, 2004; Fujioka et al., 2001). Stress that is specific to a woman's pregnancy, however, may contribute to lower birthweight and other negative birth outcomes more than other sources of stress. This is particularly true if women respond to pregnancy-specific worries by smoking and failing to consume a healthy diet (Lobel et al., 2008).

One promising approach to studying this complex topic involves objectively measuring the effects of a stressor experienced by all pregnant women living in a particular community. In one such study, Project Ice Storm, researchers in Québec, Canada, are following 150 children whose mothers experienced an objectively stressful natural disaster. Measures taken at age 2 years suggest that children whose mothers experienced higher levels of stress exhibited poorer cognitive and language development, with the severity of the impairment affected by the timing of exposure during the prenatal period (King & Laplante, 2005).

Environmental Hazards

While some potential hazards come from within, others exist in the external world. Pregnant women should avoid exposure to environmental hazards such as radiation and paint fumes, since these agents are known to be teratogenic. Dental X-rays should be skipped during pregnancy, and another adult should complete any home improvement projects, including painting the baby's room. If there are hazards in the mother's workplace, such as paint fumes, she should try to find a different, less risky assignment or another job entirely, if possible.

A noisy work environment, in which the mother is exposed for hours at a time to loud machinery, for example, is also regarded as a potential hazard for the fetus. Studies of women who reported consistent exposure to workplace noise during pregnancy have found that their offspring are at increased risk for high-frequency hearing loss. In addition, although the evidence is mixed, prenatal noise exposure may be associated with preterm birth and intrauterine growth retardation. This is an area in which human experiments are not possible, but studies with animals suggest that the risks of prenatal noise exposure should not be overlooked (Brent & Weitzman, 2004).

Environmental hazards in the places where food is raised can also have teratogenic effects. Fish is a good source of low-fat protein, but during pregnancy it is a good idea to limit the type of fish consumed. Babies who are exposed prenatally to chemical pollutants such as polychlorinated biphenyls (PCBs) or large amounts of mercury may suffer brain damage resulting in developmental delays or even cerebral palsy, seizures, and cognitive disabilities (Hubbs-Tait et al., 2005). Most fish from grocery stores and in restaurants are safe for pregnant women to eat, and ocean fish are less likely to be contaminated than river and lake dwellers. Some fish are known to pose a greater risk than others, however; experts recommend that pregnant women avoid eating bluefish, striped bass, and freshwater fish from contaminated sources. Women should also curtail their consumption of swordfish, shark, tuna, and halibut during pregnancy, since these fish tend to contain the highest concentrations of mercury (Oken et al., 2005).

Pesticide regulations vary from one country to another, so it is a good idea to read labels and choose fruits and vegetables carefully. In the United States, two pesticides that were previously approved for household use—chlorpyrifos and diazinon—were banned by the federal government in 2000 after animal studies showed that exposure during pregnancy impaired growth and brain development in offspring. Additional supporting evidence of the potential harm caused by these pesticides came from The Mothers & Children Study in New York City, which was initiated in 1998 to study health effects of exposure to air pollutants, tobacco smoke, pesticides, and allergens. Analysis of approximately 400 births suggested that higher levels of prenatal exposure to chlorpyrifos were associated with smaller head circumferences. Given that small head circumference tends to predict delays and other problems with cognitive development, this finding suggests that the pesticide probably affects brain development in humans as well as in other animals (Berkowitz et al., 2004). Fortunately, the beneficial effects of the ban on these pesticides are already evident. A study in New York City showed that whereas infants born before the ban had higher levels of exposure and weighed an average of half a pound less than infants with no detectable pesticide levels, exposure levels decreased after the ban and were no longer associated with growth problems (Whyatt et al., 2004). Continuing and expanded monitoring of children's exposure to environmental contaminants may lead to other bans and the prevention of many childhood health and developmental problems that begin before birth (Goldman et al., 2004; Hubbs-Tait et al., 2005).

In many regions of the world, pregnant women may not be aware of or able to avoid toxic chemicals and pollutants that permeate the food, water, and air around them. These substances have been linked to higher levels of infertility (Fei et al., 2009). In regions of the former Soviet Union, such as Kazakhstan, where industrial production was unregulated for years, high concentrations of lead, mercury, and zinc in drinking water, vegetables, and air appear to be responsible for a twofold increase in the incidence of birth defects since 1980 (Edwards, 1999; Gilbert, 2000). Radioactive fallout from the Chernobyl nuclear power plant disaster of 1982 has also been implicated in an increase in the rate of anemia and birth defects in regions of the former Soviet Union where exposure was the highest (Petrova et al., 1997). Researchers are concerned about environmental pollution in Eastern Europe and in countries undergoing rapid industrial growth, but even in cities in the United States, there is evidence that fetal development and growth are adversely affected by exposure to environmental contaminants (Adibi et al., 2003; Jedrychowski et al., 2004; Perera et al., 2004b).

Paternal Influences

Pregnant women are not the only ones who need to be concerned about the teratogenic effects of environmental hazards, including those that exist in the workplace. A number of agents, such as lead and radiation, can affect men's reproductive health by lowering the number of sperm or producing abnormally shaped sperm that have trouble swimming or lack the ability to fertilize the egg (Bellinger, 2005; Parker et al., 1999). Researchers are beginning to understand the risks posed by these chemicals and the potentially harmful effects on the health of family members who are exposed to chemicals brought home on the worker's skin, hair, clothes, shoes, tool box, or car (Klemmt & Scialli, 2005). Lead that is brought home in this way, for example, can cause severe lead poisoning among family members and neurobehavioral and growth effects in fetuses (National Institute on Occupational Safety and Health, 2002).

Men who use cocaine are also putting their offspring at higher risk for birth defects, since the drug appears to interfere with the production of normal sperm (George et al., 1997; Li et al., 1997; Yazigi, Odem, & Polakoski, 1991). Paternal use of certain medications, such as amphetamines and diet pills, has been linked to mutations that increase the risk of leukemia in children (Shu et al., 2004). Infants born to fathers who use marijuana during conception, pregnancy, and after birth have also been found to have a higher risk of dying before the age of 1 year (Klonoff-Cohen & Lam-Kruglick, 2001). Experiments with laboratory animals, comparing mice fathered by cocaine-exposed males with mice whose fathers were not exposed to cocaine, have found that mice with cocaine-exposed fathers had more difficulty learning the course through a maze (He, Lidow, & Lidow, 2006).

Men who smoke cigarettes in the home create a hazardous environment for mothers and children, including those not yet born. Babies whose fathers smoke tend to be lower birthweight than those without prenatal exposure to secondhand smoke, and they have a higher rate of childhood cancer (Ji et al., 1997). Effects of prenatal exposure to secondhand smoke on birthweight and head circumference are amplified for children with prenatal exposure to other environmental pollutants, such as those often found in cities (Perera et al., 2004a).

These findings indicate that both expectant parents can be involved in giving their baby a healthy start in life. As we discuss in Chapter 4, fathers as well as mothers have a role to play at their child's birth and during the newborn period.

WRAPPING IT UP: Summary and Conclusion

We know more than ever before about the genetic basis for many hereditary conditions, including those that may compromise prenatal development and the chance for a healthy birth and childhood. Most diseases and complex characteristics are influenced by multiple genes interacting with each other and with environmental influences.

Genetic researchers using animal models have discovered genes that determine the development of specialized body structures and parts of the brain. Understanding the genetic basis of conception and prenatal development may help couples experiencing infertility by offering new options to help them conceive a child and maintain a pregnancy. One increasingly common option, assisted reproductive technology, is associated with a higher rate of multiple births and the complications those births entail.

The stages of prenatal development—the germinal stage (0 to 2 weeks postconception), embryonic stage (2 to 8 weeks postconception), and fetal stage (8 weeks to birth, or approximately 38 weeks)—differ in terms of their duration as well as the key events taking place. With intensive care, a fetus born at 24 weeks may survive. Brain development begins during the embryonic stage, but the most rapid prenatal period of brain development is during the last two months. Unlike other major organs, the brain is not completely developed at birth.

Birth defects are less common today than in the past but continue to be the leading cause of infant death. Neural tube defects in the United States have been reduced through folic acid fortification of cereal grain products. Congenital heart defects range in severity, but even children with the most serious defects are more likely to survive as a result of new diagnostic and treatment options.

A number of options exist for prenatal diagnosis and treatment. Low-risk ultrasound images and maternal blood screening are used routinely. Chorionic villus screening and amniocentesis are used only in specific circumstances to diagnose or rule out defects and chromosomal abnormalities. Couples with a known high risk of having a child with a serious genetic disorder may consider using preimplantation genetic diagnosis (PGD).

Fetal therapy options are expanding, and many fetal problems already are treated or prevented by giving drugs to the mother or by choosing a cesarean delivery. Fetal surgery has been perfected for some defects but is still considered experimental for most other conditions.

With early prenatal care, women are more likely to consume a healthy, nutritious diet during pregnancy. Alcohol and drugs damage the developing child by crossing the cell membranes of the placenta. Prescription medications, like illicit drugs, may have permanent teratogenic effects on the fetus, so alterations in the specific amount or type of medication may be necessary.

Fetal development can be adversely affected by preexisting chronic conditions and by infectious diseases carried by the mother. Environmental hazards may exist in the mother's or the father's workplace and are sometimes found in the foods the mother eats. Taken together, these potential dangers may seem overwhelming, but parents and prospective parents who are aware of risks can take steps to avoid them or minimize their impact. As a result, most pregnancies in the United States and other developed countries end with the birth of a healthy, full-term baby—the focus of our next chapter.

THINK ABOUT IT: Questions for Reading and Discussion

1. Compare the reasons parents search for their children's donors with the reasons they search for their children's donor siblings. What are the pros and cons of carrying out these searches?

2. Would you want to know if you, your parents, your future spouse—or your future children—carried genetic mutations for disease? Why or why not? If so, when would you want to have this information and how would you use it?

3. Discuss the assisted reproductive technology (ART) options available to couples facing infertility. If friends of yours were considering ART or other methods of becoming parents, what advice and information would you give them?

4. Many prohibitions placed on pregnant women in the past are now known to be unnecessary. Besides those discussed in the chapter, what other "old wives tales" have you heard about things women (and men) should avoid during pregnancy? Did you find any support in this chapter for those ideas?

5. Compare the three stages of the prenatal period in terms of length, major events, and vulnerability to teratogens.

6. Which items would you put on a Top Ten list of steps that expectant parents could (or should) take to help their baby have a healthy start in life?

7. Compare the relative importance of nutrition, alcohol and drugs, disease, and environmental hazards on prenatal development. If you could focus on only one of these influences, which would it be and why?

8. Which assessment, diagnostic, and treatment options would you want to use if you and your spouse or partner were expecting a child? If there are some options that you would avoid, what are they and why would you avoid them?

Key Words

Amniocentesis (81)   A procedure for prenatal diagnosis in which a small sample of fluid is taken from the amniotic sac and used to detect any genetic or chromosomal abnormalities.

Assisted reproductive technology (ART) (68)   Fertility treatments in which both egg and sperm are handled.

Autosomes (62)   Any of the chromosomes other than the sex-determining chromosomes.

Blastocyst (71)   The hollow, spherical structure comprised of approximately 100 identical cells formed through mitosis during the first week after conception.

Cephalocaudal principle (71)   The pattern of growth in which development begins in the anterior (head) and later occurs in the posterior (tail) of the organism.

Chorionic villus sampling (CVS) (81)   A procedure for prenatal diagnosis in which cells are collected from the chorion, the fetal membrane that gives rise to the placenta.

Chromosomes (62)   Physical structures consisting of DNA and supporting proteins.

Deoxyribonucleic acid (DNA) (62)   Strands of molecules that carry the genetic code of a cell.

Dizygotic twins (67)   Siblings resulting from two different eggs, also known as fraternal (DZ) twins.

Down syndrome (65)   A congenital syndrome, also referred to as trisomy 21, in which there is an extra chromosome 21; individuals with Down syndrome have distinctive facial features and other physical characteristics and have mild to severe cognitive disabilities.

Ectoderm (72)   The upper layer of the inner cell mass, which gives rise to the brain and spinal cord, sensory organs, and skin, nails, hair, and teeth.

Embryonic stage (71)   The second prenatal stage, lasting from two weeks to eight weeks.

Endoderm (72)   The lower layer of the inner cell mass, from which the respiratory and digestive systems develop.

Fetal alcohol syndrome (FAS) (85)   A constellation of physical, behavioral, and cognitive abnormalities caused by prenatal exposure to alcohol.

Fetal stage (74)   The third prenatal stage, lasting from 8 weeks until birth.

Genes (62)   Units of hereditary information; each gene is a segment of DNA in a specific location on a chromosome.

Germinal stage (71)   The first prenatal stage, beginning at conception and ending at approximately 2 weeks.

Maternal serum alpha fetoprotein (MSAFP) test (81)   A screening test in which the level of alpha fetoprotein in the mother's bloodstream is measured; also known as the triple screen because it measures the amount of estriol and HCG present in the mother's blood.

Meiosis (66)   The process through which sex cells divide at conception.

Mesoderm (72)   The middle layer of the inner cell mass, from which the circulatory and excretory systems, muscles, and skeleton develop.

Mitosis (62)   The life-long process of cell division in which a cell divides into two identical cells.

Monozygotic twins (67)   Siblings resulting from a single egg, also known as identical (MZ) twins.

Multifactorial transmission (65)   The interaction of genes and the environment that produces most complex human characteristics.

Neural tube defects (76)   Birth defects that involve abnormal development of the neural tube during the first few weeks of the prenatal period.

Neuron (75)   Nerve cell in the brain, comprised of a cell body, axons, and dendrites.

Ovum (66)   Female sex cell.

Placenta (72)   A network of blood vessels, formed from cells in the trophoblast and from cells in the uterine lining, the function of which is to convey oxygen and nutrients to the embryo and carry away waste products.

Preimplantation genetic diagnosis (PGD) (79)   A procedure in which a biopsy is performed on blastocysts resulting from in vitro fertilization, with the purpose of selecting blastocysts that are not carriers of genetic mutations for disease for transfer to the woman's uterus.

Proximodistal principle (72)   The pattern of growth in which development begins in the center of the body and moves toward the extremities of the organism.

Sex chromosomes (62)   The pair of sex-determining chromosomes that each human possesses: XX in females and XY in males.

Sex-linked inheritance (64)   Transmission of characteristics via the mother's X chromosome; sons but not daughters inherit the trait.

Sperm (66)   Male sex cell.

Teratogens (70)   Substances, such as alcohol, drugs, nicotine, and radiation, that are known to cause harm to the developing fetus.

Ultrasound (80)   A prenatal diagnostic tool, also referred to as ultrasonography, that uses sound waves to create moving images of the fetus and detect any structural abnormalities.

Umbilical cord (72)   The structure through which the embryo is connected to the placenta.

Zygote (67)   The cell that results when an ovum is fertilized by a sperm cell.

Birth and the Newborn

The children's book *On the Day You Were Born* is about a baby named Calla (Frasier, 1991). Through colorful paper collages and poetic prose, the book illustrates the joyful anticipation with which Calla's family, along with animals, trees, the oceans, the sun, the moon, and the Earth itself, await her arrival. Reading this book with their parents, young children often ask about the day *they* were born. The story that they hear is a special one because it is their story, unlike anyone else's.

In many families, children's birth stories are accompanied by pictures showing the moments after, and sometimes during, their birth. For children born at home—a rare event in the United States but a relatively common occurrence in other parts of the world—the pictures are likely to show surroundings that are familiar and people they recognize. For all children, the pictures are also likely to reflect how their parents viewed their birth—as a public act; an event for which siblings, other relatives, and even close friends should be present; or as a more private experience, something to be shared with others only after the baby was born.

Underlying this uniqueness, all birth stories share a common plot, since childbirth is a physiological process with predictable, universal stages. We begin this chapter by considering the fundamental aspects of the story of human birth that we all share. We examine the typical birth experience for healthy, full-term infants and explore the normal variability that exists in the birth process. We also consider some of the complications associated with childbirth and measures that are used to gauge newborn infants' health. In addition, because childbirth is an event that occurs within a particular context, we examine childbirth practices from historical and cultural perspectives and consider options that are available to expectant mothers and fathers today.

THE BIRTH PROCESS: STAGES OF CHILDBIRTH

Long before the birth process began to be explained by scientists, it inspired a great variety of practices and folk theories (Todman, 2007). Women in seventeenth- and eighteenth-century Europe appealed to saints to initiate and ensure a safe delivery. They also relied upon childbirth sachets, tied onto or placed upon the woman's belly in the days or hours before labor began. These sachets, filled with medallions, rosary beads, and tiny parchments covered with religious writings and magic formulas, were often handed down from one generation to the next. To coax a reluctant baby from the womb, birth assistants often untied all knots in the home. They also tried to stimulate labor by shaking or frightening the mother, or putting pepper in her nostrils to cause sneezing and contractions (Fontanel & d'Harcourt, 1997).

Traditional views in Bali, by contrast, regarded the onset of labor as the result of actions taken by four "sibling spirits" of the fetus. These "siblings," believed to be present in the blood, the amniotic fluid, the placenta, and umbilical cord, and the waxy vernix caseosa covering the infant at birth, were said to open the cervix and push the infant from behind (DeLoache & Gottlieb, 2000). In some respects, this view was fairly accurate. As we discuss next, one of the "sibling spirits" (the placenta) does in fact play a role in initiating labor.

The First Stage: Contractions, Dilatation, and Effacement

Approximately 266 days after conception, hormones produced by the placenta and the developing fetus trigger the onset of labor (Grammatopoulos & Hillhouse, 1999; Mendelson, 2009). The first stage consists of regular, progressive uterine contractions and **dilatation,** or widening, of the cervix from its normal, closed position to a full 10 centimeters. Not all women experience labor in the same way. For some women, dilatation (also referred to as dilation) occurs over a period of one or two days, but for others it is accomplished within one or two hours.

One common sign that labor is imminent is the loss of the mucous plug sealing the cervix during pregnancy. The ensuing "bloody show" is an imprecise indicator, however, and the first contractions could still be days or weeks away. In about 2 to 3 percent of pregnancies, the mother's "water" breaks before contractions begin, a phenomenon referred to as **premature rupture of the membranes,** or **PROM** (Martin et al., 2005). When this happens, the membranes surrounding the amniotic sac break open, and amniotic fluid is released, sometimes in a dramatic gush and other times as a slow, steady leak (the fluid continues to be replenished even after the membranes rupture). Contractions often begin within 12 to 24 hours, and most women experiencing PROM give birth within 72 hours. If labor does not progress after the membranes rupture, both mother and baby may be vulnerable to infection, and delivery may be hastened. In high-risk situations, however, as when PROM occurs before the baby would be expected to survive outside of the womb, every effort is made to maintain the pregnancy as long as possible (Mercer, 2003).

The first stage of labor consists of a latent phase and an active phase. In first labors, the **latent phase** usually lasts less than 20 hours, fewer hours in subsequent pregnancies. Uterine contractions during the latent phase often begin 5 to 30 minutes apart and last between 15 and 40 seconds. These contractions typically are not painful for the mother, and she is able to rest between them. In the **active phase,** contractions come closer together, perhaps 2 to 5 minutes apart, and they last approximately 45 to 60 seconds. In addition to the more intense and frequent contractions, the rapid opening of the cervix in the active phase makes it the most difficult and painful part of labor.

As the cervix widens, it also begins to thin out—a process known as **effacement**— preparing for the next stage of labor, in which the baby begins to enter the birth canal. As the baby descends, the mother often feels increased pressure and the urge to push. If her cervix is adequately dilated, she will be allowed to follow these urges, if she wishes. Although it is commonly believed that the mother's pushing is essential to delivery, the real work is performed by uterine contractions and, depending on the mother's position, the force of gravity.

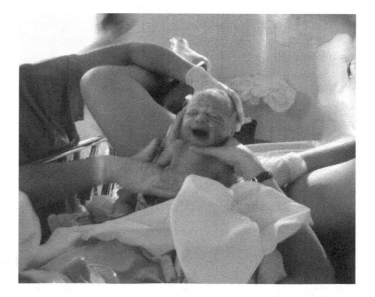

In a normal vertex delivery, the baby's head emerges first.

The Second Stage: Delivery of the Infant

The second stage of labor typically lasts less than two hours in a first birth and is even briefer in subsequent births. During this stage, the baby is gradually pushed out, usually in the head-first **vertex position.** Some babies may need to be turned or guided during labor. As the baby's head begins to emerge, it may show signs of compression and molding as a result of being squeezed through the birth canal. This elongation is normal and occurs because the skull bones have not yet fused together; it is only temporary and usually diminishes within a few days after birth (Persing et al., 2003). In some cultures, the birth attendant actively shapes and smooths the newborn's head with her hands rather than waiting for this to occur on its own (DeLoache & Gottlieb, 2000).

The Third Stage: Placental Expulsion

In the third stage of childbirth, the placenta separates from the uterine wall and is expelled through a final set of contractions. Attendants clamp and cut the baby's umbilical cord and examine the mother's vagina for any tears or bleeding. Practices vary, but many maternal health experts advocate active management of the third stage of labor, an approach that combines massage of the woman's abdomen with administration of drugs to stimulate uterine contractions and expulsion of the placenta (Winter et al., 2007). Although most attention from this point on is focused on the baby and mother, attendants inspect the placenta to make sure that it has been completely expelled; any tissue remaining in the uterus could be a source of postpartum hemorrhage, bleeding that is the cause of approximately 25 percent of all maternal deaths (World Health Organization Department of Making Pregnancy Safer, 2006).

Many doctors practicing today were trained to clamp and cut the umbilical cord as quickly as possible. New research shows, however, that this procedure should normally be delayed. Waiting as little as 3 minutes allows blood from the placenta to be transfused to the baby and, especially in resource-poor settings, reduces the risk of anemia (iron deficiency) for up to six months after birth (Hutton & Hassan, 2007; Van Rheenen & Brabin, 2006; Van Rheenen et al., 2007).

COMPLICATIONS OF CHILDBIRTH

In many developing countries, maternal and neonatal mortality rates are high, as shown in Figure 4.1 and Table 4.1 (McClure, Goldenberg, & Bann, 2007; United Nations, 2008a). According to the United Nations, every minute, a woman dies from complications of pregnancy and childbirth, resulting in more than 500,000 deaths per year, principally in developing countries and regions such as South Asia and sub-Saharan Africa. Making progress toward the UN's Millennium Development Goal—reducing maternal deaths in developing nations to three-quarters of the 1990 level by the year 2015—will require the presence of many more trained health workers with skills and equipment to deliver emergency obstetric care (United Nations, 2008b). Most newborns and mothers in developed countries, including the 4.3 million babies born in the United States each year and their mothers, have access to this kind of care and thus survive the experience with few, if any complications (Martin et al., 2009; Worley, McIntire, & Leveno, 2009).

Failure to Progress

For some women who reach term (37 weeks gestation) and experience premature rupture of the membranes (PROM), labor begins and then fails to progress (Sheiner et al., 2002). When this happens, expectant parents may feel impatient, disappointed, discouraged, and worried.

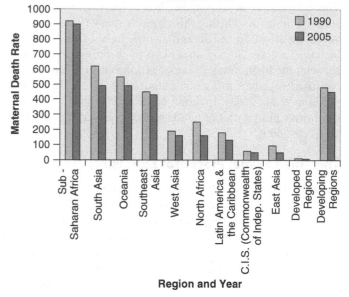

FIGURE 4.1 Maternal deaths per 100,000 live births, 1990 and 2005. (CIS consists of Armenia, Azerbijan, Belarus, Georgia, Kazakhstan, Kyrgystan, Moldova, Russia, Tajikistan, Turkmenistan, Ukraine, and Uzbekistan.) *Source:* United Nations Millennium Development Goals Report, 2008.

Labor contractions sometimes subside in response to pain medication that is administered to the mother, but the reasons labor fails to progress during the first stage are not always known.

According to some childbirth experts, failure to progress is a reflection of normal variability. As long as neither the fetus nor the mother is in danger, they argue, labor should be allowed to follow its own natural time course (Kennedy & Shannon, 2004). Many hospitals, however, have a policy of using synthetic hormones to induce labor if spontaneous contractions have not begun within 12 hours. (We discuss labor induction in more detail in the section on medical interventions.) There is equivocal evidence of links between labor induction following PROM and better neonatal and maternal outcomes. Some studies suggest that labor that is induced is more likely to end in a cesarean (surgical) delivery than is labor that starts on its own (Alexander, McIntire, & Leveno, 2001; Cammu et al., 2002; Rayburn & Zhang, 2002; Sheiner et al., 2002). Other studies, by contrast, including some in which women have been randomly assigned to receive early versus later induction after failure to progress, have found no group differences in birth outcomes or rates of complications (Dencker et al., 2008; Heimstad et al., 2007).

Childbirth experts also have different opinions about the effects of prolonged labor during the second stage (the time from full cervical dilatation to delivery). In a study of 1,200 vaginal deliveries in Germany, comparing women whose second stage of labor lasted less than two hours with women who labored in that stage for more than four hours, there was no significant difference in the health of their newborns (Janni et al., 2002). Canadian researchers, by contrast, who examined a database containing information about more than 63,000 low-risk, full-term births found a higher rate of adverse outcomes for both mothers and newborns when Stage 2 labor lasted longer than three hours in women giving birth for the first time and longer than two hours in women who had given birth previously (Allen et al., 2009). Additional studies of neonatal outcomes following prolonged labor are needed to provide guidelines for when intervention should occur and when it is not necessary (Kawasaki et al., 2002).

TABLE 4.1	Selected Stillbirth Rates, Maternal Mortality Rates, and Obstetrical Care Indicators		
	Stillbirth Rate (per 1,000 births)	Maternal Mortality Ratio (per 1,000 deliveries)	Skilled Attendant at Delivery (%)
Developed Countries			
Argentina	6	.70	99
Australia	3	.06	100
Canada	3	.05	98
Denmark	5	.07	100
Developing Countries			
Brazil	8	2.60	88
China	19	5.60	97
Egypt	10	.84	69
India	39	5.40	43
Ivory Coast	53	6.90	63
Malaysia	41	.03	97
Malawi	13	18.00	61
Pakistan	22	5.00	20
Zimbabwe	17	11.00	73

Source: McClure, Goldenberg, & Bann, 2007.

Breech Presentation

During the last weeks of the prenatal period, most fetuses settle into an inverted position, which allows for a head-first birth. In approximately 5 percent of singleton pregnancies, however, the fetus is in a **breech presentation,** with the feet or buttocks emerging first in a vaginal delivery (Martin et al., 2009). Babies born preterm are more likely to be in a breech position, as are twins and other multiple pregnancies. Vaginal deliveries of breech babies are dangerous because of the risk that the umbilical cord will be compressed, robbing the infant of oxygen during delivery (Uygur et al., 2002).

Current guidelines direct obstetricians and midwives to attempt to turn the fetus in utero at about 37 weeks gestation in a procedure known as external cephalic version (American College of Obstetricians & Gynecologists Committee on Obstetric Practice, 2002). This procedure is most successful when drugs are used to relax the mother's uterus (Hofmeyr, 2002). Even when external cephalic version is successful, the pregnancy continues to be high risk, with a greater likelihood of fetal distress, failure to progress in labor, and cesarean delivery (Chan et al., 2002). If the fetus's position cannot be changed, the preferred option is a cesarean delivery before labor begins (Hutton, Hannah, & Barrett, 2002).

Preterm Birth

As worrisome as labor that does not progress quickly may be, a more serious concern is labor that begins before the end of normal gestation. In the year 2006, 12.8 percent of all babies—the highest figure ever reported in the United States—were born **preterm** (before 37 weeks gestation). Approximately 70 percent of all preterm births occur between 34 and 37 weeks gestation (Engle,

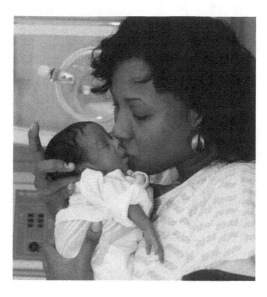

Preterm birth rates have continued to rise in the United States, but survival rates have also increased, thanks to the development of neonatal intensive care units.

Tomashek, Wallman, and the Committee on Fetus and Newborn, 2007). Approximately 2 percent are born **very preterm** (before 32 weeks gestation) (Martin et al., 2009). As shown in Figure 4.2, the proportion of infants born preterm or very preterm has increased in recent years. Progress at reducing the incidence of preterm birth has been hampered by lack of full understanding of the causes (Ashton et al., 2009; Behrman & Butler 2006).

Preterm birth is the leading cause of neonatal death in the United States and in other industrialized countries (Goldenberg et al., 2001). Hospital care for preterm infants is expensive; in 2005, the average cost per preterm baby was approximately $52,000 (Behrman & Butler, 2006). For these reasons, there is widespread agreement that preterm labor should be stopped, if possible, by giving the mother steroids or other drugs that temporarily end uterine muscle contractions (Belteki & Smith, 2009; Williamson et al., 2008). Women who give birth preterm have a slightly greater frequency of early contractions than women who give birth after the 35th week, but researchers have not been able to use this tendency to make accurate predictions about which women will have a preterm delivery (Goldenberg et al., 2008; Iams et al., 2002).

Preterm birth is more common for twins and other multiple pregnancies than for pregnancies involving just one fetus, and it is associated with PROM and medical induction of labor (Goldenberg et al., 2008; Martin et al., 2009). In some cases, preterm labor and birth may be the result of maternal infections or abnormalities of the placenta or uterus (Goldenberg et al., 2008; Romero et al., 2001). Many people believe that sexual activity late in pregnancy may cause preterm delivery, because the contraction-inducing hormone oxytocin is released during orgasm. Researchers studying patients in prenatal clinics, however, found that frequency of intercourse or orgasm during late pregnancy was not associated with an increased risk of preterm delivery (Sayle et al., 2001).

Mothers living in poverty have a higher rate of preterm birth than women with more resources, and researchers are investigating the hypothesis that chronic and acute psychological stress, including the stress of racial discrimination, causes the placenta to secrete labor-inducing hormones (Kramer et al., 2001; Osypuk & Acevedo-Garcia, 2008). The rate of preterm birth varies as a function of race and ethnicity and is highest among African American infants (18.5 percent), followed by American Indian (14.2 percent), Hispanic/Latino (12.2 percent), non-Hispanic white (11.7 percent), and Asian/Pacific Islander (10.9 percent) infants (Martin et al., 2009). Across all

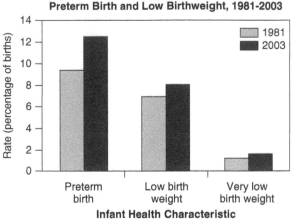

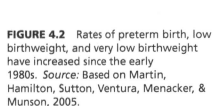

FIGURE 4.2 Rates of preterm birth, low birthweight, and very low birthweight have increased since the early 1980s. *Source:* Based on Martin, Hamilton, Sutton, Ventura, Menacker, & Munson, 2005.

groups, existing medical and public health strategies have been relatively ineffectual in reducing preterm birth (Ashton et al., 2009; Goldenberg et al., 2008).

Unlike the prevention rate, the *survival* rate for preterm infants has improved dramatically since the 1970s (from 10 percent to 45 percent for babies weighing 2 lb. or less), thanks to the development of **neonatal intensive care units (NICUs)** (described in Table 4.2). Methods that were introduced, especially in the 1970s and 1980s, include improved delivery room care and resuscitation, assisted ventilation, monitoring of blood oxygen levels and heart rate, intravenous nutrition, and drugs and other treatments to improve the functioning of preterm infants' immature lungs (Craig et al., 2009). In 1989, the Centers for Disease Control and Prevention began collecting data on a subset of neonatal intensive care practices. These data show that the rate for assisted ventilation, a treatment for respiratory distress syndrome in preterm infants, increased from approximately 11 out of every 1,000 births in 1989 to 22 per 1,000 births in the year 2000 (Martin et al., 2002a).

Despite this progress and an improved chance of survival, extremely preterm infants are still at greater risk of developing life-threatening infections, respiratory distress syndrome, and brain hemorrhages than are full-term infants (L.E. Mouradian, Als, & Coster, 2000). Treatment with steroids prior to preterm delivery diminishes some of these risks by causing fetal tissues to mature, but treatment must be brief enough to avoid potentially undesirable side effects, including impairment of fetal growth (Belteki & Smith, 2009; Goldenberg & Jobe, 2001).

Every effort is made to extend pregnancy as close as possible to full term because development within the uterine environment has measurable advantages. Survival rates increase with infant age; in one study, whereas only 56 percent of babies born at 24 weeks survived until discharge from an NICU, nearly 70 percent of those born at 25 weeks survived (Effer et al., 2002). Infants born very preterm (before 32 weeks) are more likely to die during the first year of life than are infants born either moderately preterm (32 to 36 weeks) or at term (37 to 41 weeks) (Field et al., 2009; MacDonald & the Committee on Fetus and Newborn, 2002). Preterm infants, even when they are healthy, show less mature sucking and feeding behaviors at 40 weeks than full-term (same chronological age) infants at birth (Medoff-Cooper, McGrath, & Shults, 2002; L.E. Mouradian et al., 2000). The immaturity of their lungs makes them vulnerable to respiratory distress, although this problem can be treated with a substance called surfactant (Engle & the Committee on Fetus and Newborn, 2008). Smaller and less mature infants have the most profound complications, but research examining children up to 2 years of age indicates that even infants who are born between one and four weeks preterm have more health

TABLE 4.2	Technologies and Procedures in the Neonatal Intensive Care Unit[a]

Vital Signs Are Monitored
Blood pressure
Heart rate
Lung function
Respiration
Temperature

The Environment Is Optimized
Ambient noise and light are reduced
Continuous positive airway pressure keeps lungs functioning
Feeding and nutrition are provided through intubation or an IV line
Mechanical ventilation is provided via an endotracheal tube and respirator
Pain relief is administered through an IV line
Parents are encouraged to be involved in care and to provide skin-to-skin contact
Phototherapy is used to treat jaundice
Supplemental oxygenation is administered through an oxygen hood or nasal tube
Temperature is controlled through an overhead warmer or in an isolette chamber

Tests Are Performed
Blood sample analysis
CT scanning
Electrocardiogram (EKG)
Electroencephalogram (EEG)
Eye and retinal exam
Genetic analysis
Hearing screening
MRI imaging
Spinal fluid analysis
Ultrasound
X-rays

Note: (a) Not all infants experience all of these technologies and procedures.
Source: Some information is adapted from Horbar and Lucey, 1995, p. 141.

problems than full-term infants, as well as an increased risk of delay in developmental milestones, such as crawling and combining words (Engle et al., 2007; Hediger et al., 2002).

Preterm infants who survive have a higher rate of neurological impairments, including cerebral palsy, and the effects of these impairments may be long lasting (Engle et al., 2007; Hack, Klein, & Taylor, 1995). One review of research showed that children born preterm had lower cognitive test scores and a higher incidence of attention-deficit hyperactivity disorder (ADHD) and other problem behaviors at age 5 compared to full-term children (Bhutta et al., 2002). In a study of preterm birth in Ireland and the United Kingdom, children born at or before 25 weeks gestation had lower levels of academic achievement and required more special education at age 11 years than their full-term schoolmates (Johnson et al., 2009).

The most serious developmental outcomes and neurological impairments are usually seen among very low birthweight infants (those weighing less than 3.25 lb.) who grow up in a deprived environment (Draper et al., 2009; Hack et al., 1995), but intervention research suggests that some of these problems may be treatable. The Infant Health and Development (IHD) Program (1990), a controlled intervention study that we discuss further in Chapter 11, provided educational enrichment and parental support for approximately 1,000 preterm, low-birthweight infants and their families. The IHD Program, which used random assignment to either an enrichment program or pediatric follow-up care, found that children in the enrichment group had higher IQ scores at age 3 than their matched counterparts in the control group. The intervention made the greatest difference—at least in the short term—for infants whose mothers had the fewest years of education (Hack et al., 1995).

Some researchers think that it may be possible to produce even more positive and longer lasting outcomes for preterm infants by making modifications in the NICU and at home (Als et al., 2003; Holsti et al., 2004; L.E. Mouradian et al., 2000). The Newborn Individualized Developmental Care and Assessment Program (NIDCAP) was designed to address one of the most important differences between extremely preterm infants and full-term infants—preterm infants' brains have not yet undergone the rapid growth that normally occurs during the last trimester of pregnancy. As a result of their brain's greater immaturity, preterm infants tend to respond more dramatically to external stimuli, such as noise and bright lights, and they become more easily fatigued because they have more difficulty calming themselves after they become stimulated. A number of studies have found that preterm infants benefit from NIDCAP care that recognizes these fragile infants' need for interactions that are calmer, slower, and quieter than those that typically occur in traditional NICUs (Als et al., 2003; Kleberg et al., 2008; Mouradian & Als, 1994). NIDCAP care also uses specialized accessories, such as natural sheepskins for babies to lie on and extra-soft pacifiers.

While many studies have produced promising results, more research is needed before NIDCAP individualized care can be recommended as the preferred method of caring for all preterm infants (Ariagno et al., 1997; Jacobs, Sokol, & Ohlsson, 2002; Maguire et al., 2008). Regardless of whether they endorse NIDCAP care, neonatal experts agree that the number of painful procedures in the NICU must be minimized and that sick newborns need to be treated with drugs or other effective therapies for the prevention of pain (American Academy of Pediatrics Committee on Fetus and Newborn, Section on Surgery, and Section on Anesthesiology and Pain Medicine, Canadian Paediatric Society Fetus and Newborn Committee, 2006).

Low Birthweight

The mean birthweight in the United States in the year 2006 was 7 lb. 5 oz., or 3,298 grams (Martin et al., 2009). Approximately 8 percent of all babies born each year are considered **low birthweight (LBW)** because they weigh less than 5.5 lb., or 2,500 grams. Approximately 1.5 percent are **very low birthweight (VLBW)**, weighing less than 3.25 lb., or 1,500 grams, at birth (Martin et al., 2009). (Figure 4.2 shows recent trends in LBW and VLBW.) Low birthweight in a full-term infant may be the result of maternal illness during pregnancy, especially conditions that interfere with circulation in the uterus and placenta. Some forms of fetal growth disturbance are caused by fetal genetic or chromosomal abnormalities, and still others occur, as we discussed in Chapter 3, when the fetus is exposed to teratogens such as alcohol and cocaine. In many cases, the cause of fetal growth impairment is unknown. Women carrying multiple fetuses are more likely to give birth preterm, and their babies have a higher incidence of LBW and VLBW. Older women are more likely to have multiple pregnancies and thus the risk of LBW and VLBW increases with maternal age (MacDorman & Kirmeyer, 2009).

The incidence of LBW, like the incidence of preterm birth, varies as a function of race and ethnicity. The rate of LBW in the United States is significantly higher among African American infants (14.0 percent) than among American Indian/Alaskan Native (7.5 percent) infants, non-Hispanic white infants (7.3 percent), Hispanic/Latino (7.0 percent) infants, and Asian/Pacific Islander (1.1 percent) infants. The highest rate of VLBW (3.1 percent) is also found among African American infants (Martin et al., 2009).

Mortality rates are strongly influenced by infants' birthweight. Around the world, 98 percent of all neonatal deaths occur in developing countries, often as a consequence of preterm birth and low birthweight (Moss et al., 2002). In the United States, the majority of VLBW infants (weighing less than 1,500 g) survive, but approximately 25 percent die before the age of 1 year, as compared with 2 percent of LBW infants (weighing between 1,500 grams and 2,499 grams) and only 0.03 percent of infants weighing 2,500 grams or more at birth (MacDorman & Kirmeyer, 2009; Martin et al., 2005). In comparison with normal birthweight children, LBW and VLBW children are at greater risk for cognitive disabilities, cerebral palsy, blindness, deafness, psychomotor problems, school failure, subnormal growth, and health problems (Martin et al., 2002; Powls et al., 1997). Some of these problems respond to interventions that include parental support and environmental enrichment, so there is more hope than ever before for tiny, fragile babies (Wilson-Costello et al., 2007).

Postdate Birth

Some babies are born past their due date and weigh considerably more than average. At the upper end of the range are **macrosomic births,** babies weighing more than 8 lb. 13 oz., or 4,000 grams, at birth. As the percentage of preterm and LBW births has increased in recent years, the percentage of postdate and macrosomic births has decreased (Martin et al., 2009).

In 2006, approximately 33 percent of all births occurred at 40 weeks and later, as compared with 48 percent in 1990. During the same period, the proportion of births taking place between 37 and 39 weeks increased from 41 percent to 54 percent. These figures reflect an increase during that period in the proportion of managed deliveries and the use of induction and cesarean deliveries (Martin et al., 2009).

When labor has not begun by 40 weeks gestation, expectant parents may ask that labor be induced. If they are planning to give birth in a hospital, where the standard practice typically is to induce labor after 41 weeks gestation, they are likely to have their request granted. Given some estimates that as many as 70 percent of postdate pregnancies (pregnancies extending beyond 41 weeks gestation) are actually normal-term pregnancies for which there was an error in estimating the date of conception, the decision to induce is considered in conjunction with other measures of the fetus's age (Rooks, 1997).

How do postdate babies fare, in comparison with babies born "on time"? Some postdate babies have malformations and others suffer from malnutrition and asphyxia as the aging placenta begins to function less effectively and the level of amniotic fluid begins to drop (Caughey & Musci, 2004). Post-term, or postdate, infants tend to be longer than full-term babies, and they tend to have drier, looser skin and longer fingernails and body hair. National studies comparing mortality rates for postdate and full-term **neonates** (infants younger than 1 month of age) also suggest that postdate births carry a higher risk of infant death (Caughey & Musci, 2004). A review of 16 studies using randomized controlled trials showed that the rate of cesarean delivery was higher for post-term pregnancies that were not induced at 41 weeks, possibly due to their large size (Sanchez-Ramos et al., 2003). Despite these potential complications, the majority of post-term babies are normal and healthy at birth.

Twins and Other Multiple Births

The number of births of twins or higher multiples has increased dramatically in recent years. The rate of twin births increased from 19 per 1,000 total births in 1980 to approximately 32 per 1,000 births in the year 2006 (Martin et al., 2009). The rate of triplet and other higher order multiple births increased from 37 per 100,000 live births in 1980 to approximately 193 per 100,000 births in 1998 and 153 per 100,000 births in 2006 (Martin et al., 2009). More triplets were born between 1990 and 1995 than during the entire decade of the 1980s (Martin et al., 1997).

What accounts for these trends? One factor is the increasing availability and success of assisted reproductive technology (ART). Almost one-half of all triplets born in 1998, for example, were born to parents who used ART (Centers for Disease Control and Prevention, 2002h).

Another reason for the increased rate of twin and multiple births is the older age of childbearing in the United States. Birth rates for women in their late 30s and older have increased dramatically since 1980 (Martin et al., 2009). Women in their 30s and 40s are more likely than women in their 20s to have a multiple pregnancy, even without the use of ART or fertility-enhancing drugs. In fact, in the year 2006, approximately 20 percent of all births to women 45-54 years of age and over were twin births, as compared with 2 percent among women 20-24 years of age (Martin et al., 2009). As we noted in Chapter 3, parents using ART are strongly encouraged to try to achieve pregnancies involving no more than two fetuses, primarily because twins and multiple pregnancies tend to be higher risk than single-ton pregnancies. The recent decline in the proportion of triplet and higher order births is a reflection of this awareness and of improved ART procedures that allow a smaller number of embryos to be implanted and survive (Martin et al., 2009).

The twin birth rate has increased for each of the three largest racial and ethnic groups in the United States. There are differences across these groups, however, with the highest rates of twin births occurring among African American women (36.8 per 1,000 births) and non-Hispanic white women (36.7 per 1,000 births) and the lowest rate among Hispanic/Latina women (21.8 per 1,000 births) (Martin et al., 2009). For reasons that are not well understood, Asian women are less likely to give birth to twins and other multiples.

Twin and other multiple pregnancies are usually more complicated than singleton pregnancies, and the birth process itself tends to be more difficult. Twins and other multiples have an elevated risk of preterm birth, low birthweight, and other complications, such as breech position.

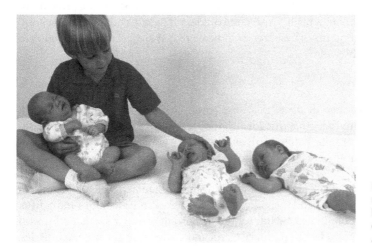

For a variety of reasons, the number of births of twins or higher multiples has increased dramatically since the 1970s and 1980s.

Twins and other multiples also face a higher risk of death during infancy than do singleton births (Martin et al., 2009).

Singleton infants born to mothers older than 35 tend to have an elevated risk of preterm birth, low birthweight, and mortality. This risk is not seen, however, among twins and other multiples born to older mothers. One likely reason is that older mothers with twin and triplet pregnancies tend to have more financial resources than younger mothers, including better access to early prenatal care. Older women are more likely to have used ART to conceive multiple-gestation pregnancies, and fetuses produced using ART are less likely than their naturally achieved counterparts to share a placenta or amniotic sac, reducing the risk of complications involving these structures. It is also possible that donor eggs, which are usually from younger women, may lead to healthier multiple-gestation pregnancies in ART than might occur in comparable pregnancies involving older women's own eggs (Zhang et al., 2002).

The degree of potential control entailed with ART and other fertility treatments is unprecedented in human history and raises ethical and technological questions for prospective parents to consider. The array of childbirth options that are now available in most developed countries has expanded as well, and expectant parents have numerous options to consider regarding the setting, participants, and obstetrical procedures.

CHILDBIRTH OPTIONS

More often than not, throughout history and across diverse cultures, birth has taken place in a woman's own home, with other, more experienced women serving as birth attendants. In the mid-twentieth century, however, especially in the United States and other developed nations, childbirth and pregnancy began to be treated by many in the medical community as a disease to be cured (Cosans, 2004; Hausman, 2005; Kennedy & Shannon, 2004). Childbirth came to be regarded as a process with which only doctors were qualified to assist. For a time, as this view became predominant in Western culture, midwives were chastised and even prosecuted for practicing medicine without a license (Borst, 1995; Rooks, 1997).

Today, trained nurse midwives are part of the obstetrical team in many hospitals in developed countries. Obstetricians predominate at births in the United States, but there is a trend toward greater use of midwives and nonmedical birth assistants. In developing countries, traditional childbirth practices still exist but are increasingly augmented by Western obstetrical procedures (DeLoache & Gottlieb, 2000). Moreover, it is now assumed that fathers will not only be present but will play an important role in their child's birth. Expectant couples often take childbirth classes and learn about specific childbirth techniques. These trends indicate that the experience of childbirth varies not only across but also within cultures.

Medical Interventions

Expectant parents today have a range of obstetrical procedures to consider and thus play an important role in writing their child's birth story. Ideally, they will have a chance to learn about these procedures well in advance of their baby's birth and become aware of potential advantages and disadvantages for baby and mother. (Figure 4.3 shows recent trends in obstetric procedures.)

INDUCTION OF LABOR   If labor fails to progress in a full-term pregnancy or fails to begin in a postdate pregnancy, the expectant parents and their obstetrical team may consider **labor induction.** If this choice is made, labor can be initiated by intravenously administering a synthetic form of oxytocin, a hormone normally released by the pituitary gland and a stimulant for uterine muscles.

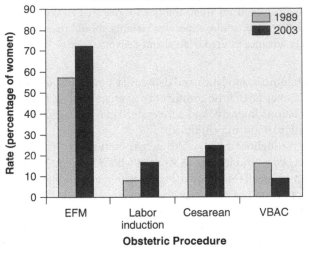

Obstetric Procedures, 1989–2003

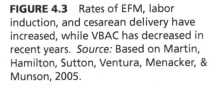

FIGURE 4.3 Rates of EFM, labor induction, and cesarean delivery have increased, while VBAC has decreased in recent years. *Source:* Based on Martin, Hamilton, Sutton, Ventura, Menacker, & Munson, 2005.

(Naturally secreted oxytocin is also involved in the production of breastmilk.) In the year 2006, labor was induced in 22 percent of all U.S. births, a rate that is more than double the rate of 9.5 percent in 1990 (Martin et al., 2009).

An association between induced labor and childbirth complications was demonstrated in a study involving more than 15,000 births in Belgium (Cammu et al., 2002). In comparison with women whose labor began spontaneously, women with elective induced labor had a higher rate of cesarean delivery, delivery using instruments such as forceps, and pain medication. Babies born to mothers with electively induced labor were also slightly more likely than comparison babies to be transferred to a neonatal hospital ward for special care. One potential problem with electively induced labor is that, if the gestational age has been miscalculated, the infant could be born preterm. Another consideration is that induction of labor does not always work, especially if the woman's cervix is not ready. Approximately 20 percent of women who are induced fail to go into labor within 24 hours and ultimately require a cesarean delivery (Pandis et al., 2001).

ELECTRONIC FETAL MONITORING   If contractions have begun, **electronic fetal monitoring (EFM)** may be used to monitor contractions and the infant's heart rate. External sensors, attached to a belt placed across the mother's abdomen, may be used, but a more sensitive procedure involves introducing a wire into the mother's vagina and placing a sensor on the infant's scalp. If the mother's labor has failed to progress or if there are concerns about possible complications, internal EFM can alert the obstetrician to fetal distress (Feinbloom, 1993). According to data collected in 2003, the majority of births in the United States (85 percent) used at least one form of electronic fetal monitoring (EFM) (Martin et al., 2005). Despite the widespread use of EFM, critics of the procedure question its value. They assert that, because the meaning of certain fetal heart-rate patterns is not always clear, fetal distress may be overdiagnosed and subsequently responded to with unnecessary medical interventions (Feinbloom, 1993).

Mothers and fathers, like childbirth experts, sometimes have conflicting feelings about EFM. In-depth interviews with 15 married couples before and after the birth of their first child showed that fathers felt a greater sense of involvement in and control over labor and delivery when EFM was used. Mothers, by contrast, often reported feeling that the EFM information and technology minimized their role in labor and delivery and diminished the importance of their active participation and awareness. Some women resented their husband's fascination with the EFM readings or were bothered by the restrictions EFM equipment placed on their ability to move freely (Williams & Umberson, 1999). These findings suggest that, if possible, expectant parents should discuss their feelings about medical interventions well in advance of actual labor and delivery.

PAIN RELIEF   Pain is a normal part of childbirth, and labor and delivery last merely hours out of an entire lifetime. Knowledge of these facts may be of little comfort to a woman in labor, however, as the pain becomes stronger and contractions intensify and accelerate. There are a number of options available to help women cope with pain during childbirth.

One option that has been in use throughout history and across cultures is to have the woman change position, as often as is necessary and helpful. A woman who is lying on her back may find relief by turning on her side, getting on all fours, squatting, kneeling, or standing up and walking around. Massage and pressure applied to her back may also provide some relief.

Women who take childbirth education classes may learn about a second option — relaxation and breathing techniques to alleviate pain. A major goal of these techniques, based on approaches pioneered in the 1940s by Grantly Dick-Read in England, Ivan Pavlov in Russia, and Ferdinand Lamaze in France, is to short-circuit the links between a laboring woman's fear, tension, and pain by teaching her a distracting pattern of controlled breathing. Childbirth educators today do not universally endorse these breathing patterns, and many now argue that breathing normally in response to the body's own needs is preferable. Some experts note that shallow, controlled breathing may result in hyperventilation, reducing the amount of oxygen in the blood, which may affect the baby (Feinbloom, 1993). A Swedish study of women randomly assigned to childbirth education classes that included instruction about breathing techniques versus women who did not have this preparation found no group difference in the use of pain relief medication or in the amount of stress parents reported about the birth experience (Bergström, Kieler, & Waldenström, 2009).

A third option is to use medication to manage pain during childbirth. As early as the mid-1800s, physicians began experimenting with chloroform and other substances. By the early 1900s, injections of narcotics were being used, with harmful side effects occurring for some mothers and infants (Walker & O'Brien, 1999). The medication options available to women in labor today are less dangerous, and approximately two-thirds receive medication to help manage pain during childbirth (Beilin, 2002).

Analgesic medication can be used to reduce pain without eliminating it. These drugs are usually injected and act quickly. Side effects may include drowsiness and euphoria. Analgesics pass through the placenta to the fetus and can interfere with the infant's responsiveness and feeding for hours after birth. To minimize these effects, analgesics are usually given during the first stage of labor, when birth is still hours away.

In contrast to analgesics, **anesthetic medication** works by eliminating pain entirely. In the past, general anesthesia was often used to enable the obstetrician to deliver the baby while the mother "slept." Although women were spared the pain of childbirth, they missed out on positive aspects of the experience, such as seeing the baby emerge and holding their newborn child in the moments after birth. General anesthesia also complicates recovery after childbirth because it affects the mother's entire system. With the exception of emergencies, general anesthesia is no longer used in labor and delivery.

Women in labor who choose anesthetics may select a drug that blocks the nerves that send pain messages to the brain. The most widely used of these anesthetics are spinals and epidurals. Spinal anesthetics temporarily block the sensory and motor nerves in the mother's pelvic area and legs, so the woman is unable to feel or move. Her ability to push during contractions is eliminated, and the contractions themselves often decrease in force. Additional interventions (which we discuss shortly) may be required to deliver the baby.

Spinal blocks cannot be given for vaginal deliveries until the cervix is fully dilated. This means that they provide no relief during the most painful and intense stage of labor. For this reason, and because spinal anesthesia may be risky for the mother's health, some childbirth experts recommend that spinal anesthesia not be used (Rooks, 1997).

Epidural anesthetics are a popular alternative to spinal blocks. Epidurals numb the woman's pelvis and legs but can be administered at levels that preserve her ability to walk and change positions (Wilson et al., 2009). In addition, in contrast to spinal blocks, epidurals can be given during the active phase of the first stage of labor. A catheter is left in place in the woman's back so that more anesthesia can be delivered as needed, with administration often controlled by the woman herself (Halpern & Carvalho, 2009). Epidural blocks are not without risk. If they are started too early, they may stop labor. Like spinal blocks, epidurals tend to decrease uterine contractions, possibly leading to the use of forceps or cesarean section to deliver the baby (Ros et al., 2007; Sharma et al., 2002; Walker & O'Brien, 1999).

Another form of analgesia injects intrathecal opioids (narcotics) into the fluid of the spinal canal early in labor. Intrathecal analgesics offer pain reduction for up to 10 hours with almost no impairment of muscle control (Feinbloom, 1993). A review of clinical trials found that intrathecal opioids provide early labor analgesia that is comparable to epidural blocks (Bucklin, Chestnut, & Hawkins, 2002). However, another study in which women chose the type of pain medication they wanted to use revealed that intrathecal injections provided less effective, briefer pain relief than continuous epidural blocks. Intrathecal injections appear to work most effectively for women who give birth within two to three hours of the injection (Fontaine, Adam, & Svendsen, 2002). Some investigations of intrathecal opioids have found that they are associated with fetal heart rate abnormalities, although those "nonreassuring" patterns did not result in a greater number of cesarean deliveries or neonatal problems (Van de Velde, Vercauteren, & Vandermeersch, 2001).

FORCEPS AND VACUUM EXTRACTION Uterine contractions sometimes decrease in force during delivery, becoming less effective at pushing the baby out of the birth canal. When this happens, if the baby has descended far enough, the obstetrician may use instruments, such as forceps or a vacuum extractor, to help with delivery. Forceps are metal instruments that reach into the birth canal, grasp the infant's head, and pull the infant out. The vacuum extractor is a plastic cup with which the obstetrician applies suction to the baby's scalp. When assistance is needed during a vaginal delivery, vacuum extraction is a good replacement for forceps, since it causes less damage to the mother and is associated with a lower need for anesthesia and a lower incidence of cesarean delivery (Johanson & Menon, 2000). As the cesarean rate has increased, the combined rate of forceps and vaccum extraction has declined from 9.5 percent in 1994 to 4.5 percent in 2006 (Martin et al., 2009).

EPISIOTOMY When it appears that the mother's vaginal opening may not be large enough to accommodate the infant without tearing, many obstetricians perform an **episiotomy** (De Leeuw et al., 2008). In an episiotomy, an incision between the vagina and the anus widens the opening before the baby's head emerges. Critics of this procedure assert that women with episiotomies tend to have worse outcomes than those without them; one randomized study reported that women with vaginal tears healed better than women who had had episiotomies (Feinbloom, 1993; Klein et al., 1992).

In light of controversy about the necessity and value of the procedure, overall episiotomy rates declined between 1983, when they were 70 percent, and 2000, when they dropped to 20 percent.

Episiotomies are most likely to be performed in deliveries using forceps (Goldberg et al., 2002; Hudelist et al., 2005). They are also more frequently performed for non-Hispanic white women and for women with private health insurance (Weeks & Kozak, 2001).

To minimize the need for an episiotomy, childbirth educators recommend that women give birth in an upright position, since tearing seems to occur more frequently among women giving birth while lying on their back. It is also helpful to avoid pushing too strenuously. Instead, uterine contractions can be allowed to do most of the "heavy lifting" during delivery, allowing the birth to proceed at its own pace, as long as mother and child are doing well.

CESAREAN DELIVERY   **Cesarean delivery** is a surgical delivery, performed with the mother under spinal or epidural anesthesia. General anesthesia is used in emergencies, when other forms of anesthesia would take too long to begin working. Some cesarean deliveries (also referred to as C-sections) are performed in response to a medical emergency, either before or during labor, but others are scheduled before labor ever begins. In addition to having had a prior cesarean delivery, other common reasons for scheduling cesarean sections are when the baby is in a breech position, when there are twins or higher multiples, and when the baby is too large to pass through the birth canal.

Cesarean delivery rates in the United States have increased significantly since 1970, when only 5.5 percent of all births were cesarean. By the year 1988, rates had soared to 25 percent of all births and critics questioned whether all cesareans were medically necessary (Martin et al., 2002). Rates then began to decline, before rising again in the 1990s. Since 1996, the rate of primary cesarean deliveries (first-time surgical deliveries) and the rate of repeat cesarean deliveries have increased. As a result, in 2007, the rate climbed to 31.8 percent of all births, an all-time high (Hamilton et al., 2009).

At the same time that cesarean rates were increasing, the rate of vaginal births after cesarean (VBAC) fell markedly, from 28.3 percent in 1996 to 8.5 percent in 2006 (Martin et al., 2009). This trend reflects changes in medical advice after a large study indicated that women attempting VBAC were three times as likely to experience a uterine rupture during spontaneous labor and 15 times as likely to suffer this life-threatening complication if labor was induced. Infants in these VBAC cases were 10 times as likely to die as infants delivered by cesarean (Martin et al., 2005; Smith et al., 2002).

Cesarean rates overall increased in the year 2006 for all racial and ethnic groups (Martin et al., 2005). In that same year, as in previous years, there was a higher total rate of cesarean deliveries among older women than among younger women (47.6 percent for those between 40 and 54 years of age versus 22.2 percent for those ages 20 to 24) (Martin et al., 2009). One reason older women have more cesareans may be that they have higher rates of induced labor. In addition, older women are more likely than younger women to have a cesarean when there is failure to progress and when the fetus is in distress (Ecker et al., 2001).

Cesarean deliveries are generally safe, but there are some risks involved. Women who give birth via cesarean are more likely to develop infections and complications of anesthesia, and they are slightly more likely to die than are women who give birth vaginally (Liu et al., 2007; Ophir et al., 2008). Some experts suggest, however, that women who die following a cesarean are more likely to have preexisting health conditions that are the real reason for their higher mortality rate. Even without life-threatening complications, cesarean delivery is a major surgical procedure. In addition to being more expensive than vaginal delivery, a cesarean requires a longer hospital stay and adds at least one week of recovery time for the mother following the birth (Declercq et al., 2007).

How do cesarean deliveries affect newborns' health? A study of 29,000 U.S. births between 1992 and 1999 found that full-term infants delivered by scheduled cesarean section were nearly five times more likely to develop serious lung problems than infants delivered vaginally. This finding suggests that there may be a physiological benefit for otherwise healthy infants to undergo labor and vaginal delivery (Levine et al., 2001). Canadian researchers analyzing a database of 143,000 full-term deliveries from 1988 to 2002, however, found that vaginal deliveries in which forceps and vacuum extraction were used resulted in more birth trauma (such as bruising, bleeding on the brain, and damage to the spinal cord) than either unassisted vaginal deliveries or cesarean deliveries. Overall, infants delivered via cesarean had more respiratory problems and longer stays in the NICU than infants delivered vaginally (with or without assistance of forceps and vacuum extraction). The most serious problems occurred in cesarean deliveries that were carried out after labor had begun (Liston et al., 2008).

Women and their doctors need to take these findings into consideration when deciding whether to try to achieve a vaginal delivery or opt for a cesarean. This is particularly true regarding a new trend, cesarean delivery on maternal request, in which women with uncomplicated pregnancies ask their doctors to perform a cesarean when their baby is full term, before they have gone into labor. According to the small amount of research on this phenomenon, as many as 6 percent of births in the United States may now be the result of cesarean by maternal request (Bettes et al., 2007; Gossman, Joesch, & Tanfer, 2006, 2009). Given the cost and longer recovery time associated with these procedures, as well as the generally excellent outcomes for vaginal births, the reasons for and responses to these requests deserve further investigation (Fenwick et al., 2008; Gamble et al., 2007).

In addition to the United States, rates of cesarean deliveries have increased dramatically in many other parts of the world, especially in developed countries (Belizá, Althabe, & Cafferata, 2007; Carayol et al., 2007; Kwee et al., 2007; Lehmann et al., 2007; Tollånes et al., 2007). It is important, therefore, that childbirth educators work with all expectant parents, not just those considered high risk, to prepare them for the possibility of a cesarean birth and the more complicated recovery it entails. Without this kind of counseling, women who give birth by cesarean section may have less positive feelings about the experience, themselves, and their infants; there is also some evidence that they are more likely to exhibit less optimal parenting behaviors and may be at higher risk for postpartum depression and other mood disturbances than women who give birth vaginally (Lobel & DeLuca, 2007).

Whether parents experience childbirth as joyful depends, in part, on the context and setting in which their child is born. Parents in the twenty-first century have a range of experiences, often as a consequence of choices that they make about the setting for and participants in their child's birth.

Hospital, Home, or Birth Center?

Until the middle of the twentieth century, most women chose to give birth at home. In fact, the earliest maternity hospitals functioned primarily as charities, and only the very youngest, most destitute, and socially isolated women delivered their babies in them (Meier, 1999). Most births occurring at home before the middle of the twentieth century were attended by women from the community. In the southeastern United States, these women were sometimes referred to as granny midwives. Granny midwives were typically trained through apprenticeship to older midwives, but some received additional training from state health departments. In Texas and the southwestern United States, *parteras* from the community assisted Latina women in childbirth, just as Native American women usually were assisted by experienced—but not medically trained—Native American women (Rooks, 1997).

BIRTH ATTENDANTS AND SETTINGS   Today, 99 percent of all U.S. births take place in a hospital, with a physician—usually an **obstetrician,** a doctor trained to assist and perform procedures during labor and delivery—in attendance in the vast majority of births (91.5 percent in 2006). In 1975, only 1.0 percent of all births were attended by a **certified nurse-midwife (CNM),** a figure that increased to 7.9 percent in 2006 (Martin et al., 2009). Certified nurse-midwives are registered nurses who have completed nurse-midwifery education programs and met criteria for certification by the American College of Nurse-Midwives. They are licensed to practice throughout the United States

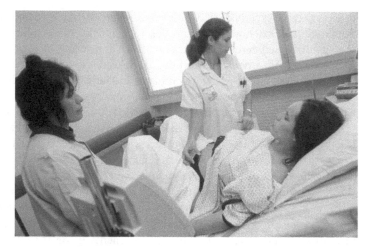

Although doulas perform no medical procedures during childbirth, they play an important role as the mother's advocate and provide her with guidance, encouragement, and reassurance.

and attend births in all settings, but most work exclusively in hospitals. Almost half (46 percent) of all midwives in industrialized countries are nurses (Rooks, 1997).

Some expectant parents, including those who opt for a hospital delivery with an obstetrician, choose to have the additional assistance of a **birth doula,** a trained layperson who guides, encourages, praises, and reassures the woman but performs no medical procedures during childbirth. Some doulas provide postpartum care for the family, offering breastfeeding support and advice, cooking meals, and running errands (Doulas of North America, 2002).

HOSPITAL VERSUS HOME BIRTH   Home births have begun to increase recently in some developed countries, including Denmark, England, Germany, and New Zealand. Among developed countries, the Netherlands has the largest number—approximately 30 percent. These home births are attended by trained and regulated midwives who provide continuous support during labor, delivery, and the infant's first week. Home births in the Netherlands are generally safe for mother and baby; there is a low incidence of complications and consequently a low rate (less than 5 percent) of cesarean deliveries (Tew & Damstra-Wijmenga, 1991). Studies of home birth safety in a number of other countries, including England, Scotland, Wales, Australia, and Canada, provide similar results (Rooks, 1997; Symon et al., 2009).

In the United States, there is mixed evidence about the safety of planned home births. Studies are hampered by the fact that, for both practical and ethical reasons, random assignment of pregnant women to a home versus a hospital birth setting cannot be done. Another research challenge is that, unlike in the Netherlands, there is often variation in the United States from one home birth to another, in terms of the attendant's experience (Johnson & Daviss, 2005).

Some research using birth and death certificates has shown higher infant mortality rates during labor and in the neonatal period for births occurring in hospitals than in homes. This pattern, however, probably reflects the greater tendency for high-risk pregnancies to be directed to hospitals. Among infants born at home, deaths during labor or in the neonatal period occur most frequently when there are undiagnosed congenital abnormalities, such as heart defects, or when there are known risks, such as breech presentation, twins or other multiples, or postdate birth. When women with these risks are excluded from data analysis, some studies report mortality rates for home births that resemble those associated with low-risk hospital births, approximately 2 to 3 deaths per 1,000 live births (Johnson & Daviss, 2005; Rooks, 1997; Symon et al., 2009).

The safety of home births is affected by the level of training of the attendant, with greater risk associated with lower levels of training. Physicians and certified nurse-midwives are rarely present at home births, and lay midwives are not allowed to be the primary attendant at hospital births. As a result, direct comparisons of birth attendants with different levels of training in the same settings are generally not possible (Pang et al., 2002). Researchers in Norway, however, were able to compare midwife-led births with conventional births in different wards of the same clinic. Although they were not able to use random assignment, results showed that more women in the conventional setting than in the midwife-led setting had episiotomies, received epidural blocks, and were given nitrous oxide anesthesia, while more women in the midwife-led ward were given opiates and nonpharmacological pain relief and were assisted in using a range of positions throughout labor and delivery. Rates of emergency cesarean deliveries and vaginal deliveries requiring forceps or vacuum extraction were similar in the two wards (Eide, Nilsen, & Svein Rasmussen, 2009).

Given the number of studies suggesting that home births for low-risk pregnancies are generally as safe as births that take place in hospitals (Symon et al., 2009), why don't more expectant parents choose home birth? One reason may be lack of information about birth outcomes and safety. In addition, in the United States, the healthcare system is based on the assumption of a hospital birth, and a woman's healthcare insurance may not cover birth that is planned to take place in another setting or with an attendant other than a physician or certified nurse. Expectant parents may also worry about potential complications, even in a low-risk pregnancy, and choose to have the latest medical technology available nearby in the event that an emergency arises.

Parents who choose a home birth have good reasons, too. For women without adequate healthcare insurance, cost may be a strong motivating factor, since a home birth attended by a midwife may cost as much as 30 percent less than a hospital birth attended by an obstetrician. Women living in remote rural areas may lack transportation and a place to stay near the hospital while waiting for labor to begin. In some cases, women have had prior negative experiences with hospital births or want to have a birth experience that is "natural" and under their control, occurring without medical interventions. Finally, the familiar, private home environment appeals to some women because it makes them feel more comfortable and secure.

In recognition of the desire to give birth in a relaxed, private setting, most hospitals in the United States and in other developed countries now offer expectant parents a homelike atmosphere, with labor and delivery occurring in the same room (Fannin, 2003). Analysis of labor and birth outcomes in a large database of women who gave birth either in a homelike setting or in a conventional hospital maternity ward showed that women in the homelike setting used less pain medication, were less likely to have a cesarean delivery, and expressed greater satisfaction with their care (Hodnett, 2001; Hodnett et al., 2005).

In some hospitals, certified nurse-midwives support the woman throughout labor and delivery (Hatem et al., 2008). Studies of this kind of continuous care, including randomized controlled studies of thousands of women in Australia, Canada, and the United States, indicate that it provides mothers (and fathers) with support and technical expertise that results in a greater sense of control and a more positive birth experience than labor and delivery attended by a series of nurses they have not met before (Eide, et al., 2009; Hodnett et al., 2002; Homer et al., 2002).

Women who receive continuous care from an attendant who is known to them also tend to require less pain medication and have fewer medical interventions performed, including cesarean deliveries (Klaus & Kennell, 1997). These benefits appear to accrue even when continuous care is provided by a doula, rather than a nurse-midwife (Keenan, 2000; Scott, Berkowitz, & Klaus, 1999; Scott, Klaus, & Klaus, 1999). In addition to providing a continuous physical presence, doulas help women in labor try a variety of nonpharmacological pain-relief techniques, such as relaxation, massage, and changing position (Doulas of North America, 2002).

Many hospitals have responded to patients' interest in natural and alternative treatments by exploring acupuncture and herbal treatments during pregnancy, labor, and delivery. The medical community in the United States has drawn the line, however, at a controversial practice known as water birth (American Academy of Pediatrics Committee on Fetus and Newborn, 2005). Proponents of water birth, which is more common in Switzerland and other European countries, assert that women who submerge themselves during labor are able to achieve pain relief without using medication. Advocates of water birth also report that women who deliver underwater require fewer medical-surgical interventions, use less pain medication, and have a lower rate of cesarean section (Geissbuhler & Eberhard, 2005; Geissbuhler, Stein, & Eberhard, 2004).

These claims have been challenged by medical experts who question the methodological rigor of existing studies of water births (Nikodem, 2004; Woodward & Kelly, 2004). Even if the purported positive effects for laboring mothers were substantiated through randomized control trials (the "gold standard" for evaluating the efficacy and safety of new health and mental health treatments), there would still be a lack of evidence that water births are better for babies or are as safe as traditional "land births" (Gilbert, 2002). Documented complications from water births include drowning and near drowning, asphyxiation, seizures caused by water intoxication, respiratory distress syndrome, pneumonia, and other infections (American Academy of Pediatrics Committee on Fetus and Newborn, 2005; Bowden et al., 2003; Nguyen, Kushel, & Teele, 2002). Expectant parents should be aware, therefore, that there does not appear to be sufficient evidence that the alleged benefits of water births outweigh the potential dangers (American Academy of Pediatrics Committee on Fetus and Newborn, 2005).

BIRTH CENTERS   An increasing number of expectant parents in the United States and in many other countries are choosing to give birth in a birth center, a freestanding site that may be affiliated with a hospital. In the United States, birth centers are typically licensed and regulated by the states in which they operate, and a set of national standards has been developed to allow for accreditation and comparability in terms of quality of care, birth outcomes, and cost (National Association of Childbearing Centers, 2002).

Giving birth in a birth center is generally less costly than in a hospital, in part, because lay midwives, rather than more expensive CNMs or obstetricians, typically attend the birth (Stone et al., 2000). Midwives in birth centers generally wait for labor to begin on its own, avoid the use of pain medication, and perform intermittent rather than continuous electronic fetal monitoring, which leaves the woman free to move about throughout labor. Episiotomies are performed in only about 12 percent of birth center deliveries, as compared with 20 percent of hospital births (Lubic, 2002).

Comparisons of birth outcomes for low-risk pregnancies have typically found little difference between hospitals and birth centers. A recent two-year study in Norway of more than 1,200 women who started labor in birth centers found that they generally fared well; only 4.5 percent of the women had to be transferred to a hospital (Schmidt, Abelsen, & Øian, 2002). A study in Australia showed no significant difference in the cesarean rate for women in birth centers (3.5 percent) and women in hospitals (4.3 percent) (Homer et al., 2000). Another Australian study of 200 women who were randomly assigned either to a birth center or a hospital found no differences in birth outcomes, but women in the birth center group had higher levels of satisfaction with their birth experience and felt greater encouragement to breastfeed immediately after birth (Byrne, Crowther, & Moss, 2000).

NEONATAL ASSESSMENT

Newborn infants are unaware of their parents' preferences and choices. They come into the world without any notion of where they are or who was present at their birth, but they arrive ready to interact with and respond in numerous ways, often to the surprise and amazement of their parents.

Assessment at Birth

In the moments after birth, all parents want to know how their baby is doing. Some first-time parents may be shocked at how red, wrinkled, and misshapen their child looks. Fluid and mucous may need to be suctioned out of the infant's nose and mouth. The infant's body is usually covered in vernix caseosa, an unappealing waxy coating that protects the skin from exposure to amniotic fluid in utero. The baby may have a thick head of hair or appear to be bald at birth, and the genitals and breasts of newborns, both boys and girls, tend to be swollen as a result of stimulation by the mother's hormones.

Birth attendants also want to know how the baby is doing. They find out by using a quick screening procedure named after the doctor who developed it, Virginia Apgar (1953). The **Apgar Score** provides an immediate profile of the infant's physical health at 1 and 5 minutes after birth. As shown in Table 4.3, the scale measures five dimensions that are a convenient mnemonic for the name of the assessment—*A*ppearance (color), *P*ulse (heart rate), *G*rimace (reflex irritability), *A*ctivity (muscle tone), and *R*espiration (breathing). The infant receives a score of 0, 1, or 2 for each dimension, with a total possible Apgar score ranging from 0 to 10. Scores from 7 to 10 are considered normal, scores of 4 to 6 intermediate, and scores between 0 and 3 indicate that the infant is in need of medical attention or even resuscitation. Although the Apgar dimensions are listed separately, they are actually part of a physiological cycle or system, with the infant's respiratory efforts affecting each of the other dimensions (Pinheiro, 2009).

The Apgar score at 5 minutes after birth is a useful indicator of the baby's condition, particularly if it is different than the 1-minute rating (Martin et al., 2009). Apgar scores do not provide specific, reliable information about the child's future neurological functioning or indicate the cause of congenital conditions such as cerebral palsy. Irrespective of race and ethnicity, the Apgar score for the color component is based on the color of mucous membranes of the mouth; of the whites of the

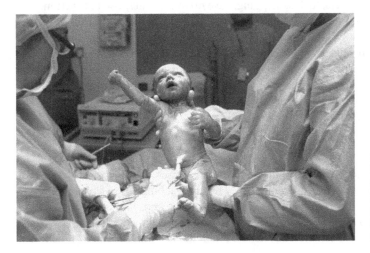

Some first-time parents may be shocked to see how red, wrinkled, and misshapen their newborn infant looks. They may also be surprised to see how alert their baby is in the moments after birth.

TABLE 4.3	Apgar Components and Scores		
		Scores	
Components	**0**	**1**	**2**
Appearance (Color of arms, legs, and body)	Blue	Blue limbs, pink body	Pink
Pulse (Heart rate in beats per min.)	None	Slow (under 100 bpm)	Rapid (100 to 140 bpm)
Grimace (Coughing, sneezing)	None	Weak	Strong
Activity (Muscle tone, arm and leg movements)	None	Weak	Strong
Respiration (Breathing)	None	Irregular	Strong, regular

Source: Adapted from Apgar, 1953.

eyes; and of the lips, palms, hands; and soles of the feet. Apgar scores are affected by maternal medications and infant conditions, including preterm birth and low birthweight, and thus need to be interpreted in conjunction with other available information about the pregnancy, labor, and delivery (American Academy of Pediatrics, Committee on Fetus and Newborn, American College of Obstetricians and Gynecologists, & Committee on Obstetric Practice, 2006).

Of the 48 states reporting Apgar scores in the year 2006, only 1.6 percent of U.S. newborns had Apgar scores below 7 at 5 minutes after birth, a statistic that has not changed significantly since 1990. The stability of this statistic, in the context of an increasing number of preterm and LBW infants, is evidence of the success of most neonatal resuscitation efforts (Martin et al., 2009).

Reflexes

Newborn infants are equipped to respond to their environment. Touch is the first sense to develop prenatally, and a number of preadapted **reflexes** can be stimulated through touch. Some of these reflexes are described in Table 4.4 and include rooting, sucking, grasping, stepping, and the Babinski. Other reflexes, such as the Moro, are stimulated when the infant's vestibular sense responds to the loss of physical support. Some of these reflexes, such as rooting (which prepares the infant to nurse), are of obvious survival value, but others, such as stepping, have no immediately useful function.

Many of the reflexes that are present at birth diminish over the next few months and then disappear. This is evidence of maturation of centers in the brain that control voluntary movements. When these reflexes persist or are delayed in disappearing, the reason may be a neurological problem, such as cerebral palsy, so further assessment should be performed (Other reflexes, such as blinking in response to an object approaching the eyes, continue to function throughout the life span). As we discuss in Chapter 6, at least one reflex that seems to disappear—stepping—can actually be activated at later ages than was once thought possible.

Sensory Abilities

Infants are able to use all of their senses at birth, but not all of their senses are equally well developed. Newborns are able to distinguish between different tastes. They have a built-in preference for sweet tastes (a preadaptation that makes breastmilk, which is naturally sweet, especially appealing) and an innate aversion to bitter tastes. The sense of smell is also very well developed at birth. Newborns quickly learn their mother's scent and can even discern the difference between the smell of their own

TABLE 4.4	Examples of Reflexes Present at Birth
Reflex	**How It Works**
Babinski response	The infant's big toe flexes and all of the other toes spread out when the sole of the foot is stroked lengthwise.
Incurvation (Gallant response)	When held horizontally and facing down so that the arms and legs are free, the infant's lower body swings to the side when a finger runs along the spine.
Moro reflex	A startle response in which the infant's arms and legs extend and then are pulled in toward the body after a sudden bump to the infant's crib or a slight loss of support (as might happen when a short parent or babysitter is unable to reach all the way over the crib rail when placing the sleeping baby in his/her crib).
Palmar grasp	The infant grasps a finger that is placed into his/her hand, pressing on the palms.
Rooting Response	The infant's head turns and the mouth opens when the cheek or corner of the mouth are touched by a finger or nipple.
Stepping or walking reflex	When held upright, the infant's feet make stepping movements if he/she is placed on a table or other solid surface.
Sucking response	The infant begins to suck when a finger, nipple, or pacifier is placed in the mouth.

Source: Based on information in Brazelton & Nugent, 1995.

amniotic fluid and the amniotic fluid from another newborn (Marlier, Schaal, & Soussignan, 1998; Schaal, Marlier, & Soussignan, 1998). The sense of hearing is functioning well before birth. Newborns are able to distinguish between their mother's voice and the voice of another woman, and they recognize the contours of the language their mother speaks and notice differences between that language and other languages to which they were not exposed in utero.

The least well-developed sense at birth is vision, but newborns do respond to different levels of brightness. They look away from light that is very bright and toward areas of dark-light contrast. We discuss the development of vision, as well as sensation and perception, in greater detail in Chapter 6.

Adaptations during the Neonatal Period

In the moments following birth, infants need to adjust to a number of sudden changes. For the first time, they move in a light-filled, nonaqueous environment, regulate their own body temperature, and breathe air into their lungs. Having never experienced hunger before, they must also adapt to sucking and swallowing as they nurse or drink from a bottle. Sounds that previously were muffled through the uterine wall are now heard more clearly and at greater volume.

Newborns who have a chance to receive "kangaroo care" (skin-to-skin contact achieved by placing the infant directly on the mother's chest or abdomen) shortly after delivery appear to adapt to these changes more quickly than newborns who receive standard care. Kangaroo care was originally developed in Colombia in the late 1970s for use with LBW and preterm infants there and in other developing countries and resource-poor settings. Since then, the practice has expanded into developed countries and has been evaluated in controlled studies using random assignment. When compared with standard crib care, in which there is minimal skin-to-skin contact, kangaroo care appears to offer physiological benefits for infants and psychological benefits for their parents (Hall & Kirsten, 2008). Babies receiving kangaroo care tend to sleep longer, in a quieter sleep state, and exhibit more relaxed movements and postures following stressful procedures in the NICU (Ferber & Makhoul, 2004, 2008; Johnston et al., 2009). Preterm infants who are able to conserve their energy in this way tend to gain weight faster and go home sooner than babies who experience ongoing stress, pain, and disrupted, disorganized sleep. A study in Colombia suggests that the benefits of kangaroo care may also extend to the home environment up to one year later, especially when fathers participate (Tessier et al., 2009).

Within a day or two, newborn infants begin to show regularities of behavior, including **states of arousal,** or distinct levels of alertness within which behaviors occur (Ingersoll & Thoman, 1999). Even before birth, as early as 29 weeks into the prenatal period, there are predictable patterns of activity and relative inactivity, corresponding roughly to active sleep, quiet sleep, and wakefulness (Mirmiran et al., 1992). In the newborn period, infants' time awake can be further differentiated into drowsy or semi-dozing, quiet alert, active alert (which can include fussing), and crying (Brazelton & Nugent, 1995; Gnidovec, Neubauer, & Zidar, 2002). When asleep, the typical newborn alternates between active and quiet sleep every 15 minutes, waking up every one to six hours, although distinctive, consistent patterns are evident across babies. States are one measure of an infant's central nervous system maturation. Newborns initially spend more than two-thirds of their time asleep or drowsy, and much of their time awake is spent fussing, crying, or moving between states. Over the course of the subsequent weeks and months, infants spend an increasing amount of their time awake in a quiet alert state, providing parents and other caregivers with new opportunities for interaction (Becker & Thoman, 1983; Thoman, 1990).

States provide parents with information about infants' needs, including their receptivity to interaction. It is not always easy, however, for new parents to differentiate between their newborn's changing states. One helpful tool is the **Brazelton Neonatal Behavioral Assessment Scale (NBAS)** (Brazelton & Nugent, 1995; Nugent et al., 2009), a structured interactive examination used with infants until the end of the second month of life. The goal of the exam is to elicit from infants their best performance possible, noting their predominant state of arousal.

The NBAS consists of 28 behavioral items and 18 reflex items that are "packaged" into sets of related items administered in a particular sequence. Beginning with a 2-minute observation of the infant in a sleep state, the examiner notes the sleeping baby's reactions to auditory, visual, and tactile stimulation. When parents are present, they may be surprised to see their baby startle in response to the sound of a ringing bell but quickly become habituated to the stimulus and continue sleeping. The examiner subsequently tests the infant's reflexes, responses to being undressed, and social interactive behaviors. Crying or fussing during the exam is not unusual and provides an opportunity to assess the infant's consolability, including self-consolability.

A single NBAS assessment is useful as a screening instrument for gross neurological or behavioral dysfunction. Several consecutive assessments can be used to study the effects over time of maternal substance use and other risk factors. The greatest value of the NBAS, however, may be as a teaching and intervention tool for parents. The examiner can help parents see that their infant has many capabilities for both shutting out and interacting with people and objects in the world. The examiner can highlight changes in the baby's alertness and motor movements as a function of state changes—behaviors that can help parents notice and adjust to the infant's needs at that moment. Parents can be invited to test the infant's reflexes and use their voice to help console the baby. Seeing the infant relax when the sucking reflex is stimulated also helps parents understand the importance of oral comfort for very young infants (Brazelton & Nugent, 1995; Nugent et al., 2009).

Infants born preterm often respond differently to caregivers and the environment than fullterm infants. In order to measure these differences more precisely, and in order to differentiate among low- and high-risk preterm infants, researchers developed the **Assessment of Preterm Infants' Behavior (APIB)** by modifying items from the NBAS (Als et al., 1982, 2005). The APIB has been used in many studies of preterm infants and can be used to gauge the effects of interventions and treatments on motor, state, and other neurobehavioral responses (Als et al., 2003; Mouradian & Als, 1994; L.E. Mouradian et al., 2000).

Other researchers working with at-risk infants, primarily those believed to have been exposed prenatally to cocaine or other harmful substances, developed the **Neonatal Intensive Care Unit Network Neurobehavioral Scale (NNNS)** to assess their functioning (Lester et al., 1994). The NNNS is similar to the NBAS in that it measures a range of neonatal behaviors sometimes referred to as the "four As of infant behavior": arousal, attention, affect (including social interaction), and action (motor patterning) (Lester et al., 2004). Using the NNNS, researchers are able to assess birth outcomes and neonatal functioning in high-risk pregnancies (de Moraes Barros et al., 2008; Lester et al., 2004).

WRAPPING IT UP: Summary and Conclusion

Childbirth is safer today in the United States and other developed countries than at any previous time. Childbirth experts disagree about some issues, such as whether delivery should be hastened when there is failure to progress, but they agree about many others, including the value of educating expectant parents about childbirth and including them in the entire process.

Preterm birth rates have remained high, and more research is needed to clarify the reasons for racial and ethnic differences in this birth outcome. Advances in neonatal intensive care have led to better survival rates for tiny, fragile babies. The rate of twin and multiple-infant births has increased dramatically, as a result of increased use of fertility treatments and increases in maternal age at birth. Pregnancy, labor, and delivery are riskier when twins or other multiples are involved.

Many births in developed countries use medical and surgical interventions during labor and delivery. The incidence of cesarean delivery has continued to increase and occurs in approximately one-third of all births in the United States. Nearly all births in the United States take place in a hospital with a physician or certified nurse-midwife in attendance.

The Apgar Score reflects the newborn's condition immediately after birth. Most infants have a score indicative of good health by 5 minutes.

Neonates possess innate reflexes, many of which disappear within the first few months of life. Newborns' senses are functional at birth, enabling them to feel, taste, smell, and hear with surprising precision. Vision is the least well developed sense at birth.

Newborns make many adaptations to the external world. States of arousal, including sleep-wake states, change during the first months after birth. These changes affect infants' ability to interact with parents and other caregivers and to learn from the environment.

The Brazelton Neonatal Behavioral Assessment Scale (NBAS) assesses newborn infants' capabilities, showing parents how well they are preadapted to interact and learn. Other assessments have been developed to assess preterm infants (APIB) and infants with prenatal exposure to drugs (NNNS). These assessments can help pediatricians understand infants' needs and provide them with the most appropriate care and treatment. The NBAS and other neonatal assessments are not a substitute for other assessments of infant health and well-being, however, and they cannot be administered reliably beyond the first months of life. In the next chapter, we consider measures that can be used in this way—aspects of health, nutrition, and physical growth that constitute the milestones and targets for development from birth to age 3.

THINK ABOUT IT: Questions for Reading and Discussion

1. Which aspects of labor and delivery do you think first-time expectant parents would be most surprised to learn about?
2. Why have rates of preterm birth and low birthweight increased so much since the 1970s? What are the short- and long-term outcomes of preterm birth and low birthweight?
3. How might the recent increase in the rate of twins and other multiple births affect our society?
4. How should doctors respond to women who request cesarean delivery for a healthy, full-term pregnancy? What are the risks and benefits?
5. Indicate which birth setting you would choose—hospital, home, or birth center—and explain your choice.
6. What do you think is the most important neonatal characteristic for new parents to understand? How might you help them learn about this characteristic?

Key Words

Active phase (100)   The second phase of labor, with increasingly painful contractions coming more frequently as the cervix opens.

Analgesic medication (112)   Drugs that reduce pain without eliminating it.

Anesthetic medication (112)   Drugs that eliminate pain by blocking nerves that send pain signals to the brain.

Apgar Score (119)   An assessment used at 1 and 5 minutes after birth to provide a profile of the infant's physical health.

Assessment of Preterm Infants' Behavior (APIB) (123)   A modification of the NBAS that is designed to gauge the effects of interventions and treatments on preterm infants' motor, state, and other neurobehavioral responses (see Brazelton Neonatal Behavioral Assessment Scale).

Birth doula (116)   A trained layperson who provides nonmedical assistance during labor and delivery.

Brazelton Neonatal Behavioral Assessment Scale (NBAS) (122)   A structured examination that is used with infants from birth until the age of 2 months to assess reflexes and social interactive behaviors.

Breech presentation (103)   A birth in which the infant emerges feet or buttocks first.

Certified nurse-midwife (CNM) (115)   Registered nurses who are trained to assist during labor and delivery.

Cesarean delivery (114)   A surgical procedure performed when a vaginal delivery would be too dangerous for mother, baby, or both.

Dilatation (99)   Widening and opening of the cervix during labor.

Effacement (100)   The thinning out of the cervix during labor.

Electronic fetal monitoring (EFM) (111)   The use of external or internal sensors to monitor contractions and detect signs of fetal distress.

Episiotomy (113)   A procedure in which an incision is made to widen the vaginal opening.

Labor induction (110)   A procedure in which a hormone is administered in order to initiate uterine contractions leading to labor and delivery.

Latent phase (100)   The initial phase of the first stage of labor, marked by widely spaced contractions that are not painful.

Low birthweight (LBW) (107)   A birthweight of less than $5\frac{1}{2}$ lb., or 2,500 grams.

Macrosomic birth (108)   A birthweight of more than 8 lb. 13 oz., or 4,000 grams.

Neonatal Intensive Care Unit (NICU) (105)   A specialized hospital setting for the care of medically vulnerable infants, including those born preterm and very preterm.

Neonatal Intensive Care Unit Network Neurobe-havioral Scale (NNNS) (123)   A measure designed to assess the functioning of at-risk infants, primarily those believed to have been exposed prenatally to alcohol, cocaine, or other teratogens.

Neonate (108)   Newborns and infants younger than 1 month of age.

Obstetrician (115)   A physician trained to assist and perform procedures during labor and delivery.

Premature rupture of membranes (PROM) (100)   Condition occurring when the amniotic sac breaks open before contractions begin.

Preterm (103)   A birth that occurs before 37 weeks gestation.

Reflexes (120)   Involuntary responses to stimuli, present at birth and gradually diminishing during the first few months of life.

States of arousal (122)   Distinct levels of alertness within the general behavioral categories of active sleep, quiet sleep, and wakefulness.

Vertex position (101)   A birth in which the infant is delivered head first.

Very low birthweight (VLBW) (107)   A birthweight of less than $3\frac{1}{4}$ lb., or 1,500 grams.

Very preterm (104)   A birth that occurs before 32 weeks gestation.

5

Physical Growth, Health, and Nutrition

When Nadia was adopted from an austere Russian orphanage at the age of 15 months, she weighed only 13 pounds and her head fit into a cap intended for 6-month-olds. She couldn't sit up on her own, didn't know how to feed herself, and didn't play with the toys her adoptive parents had bought for her. After being spoon-fed and cared for in her new home, Nadia began to gain weight and her head circumference increased. She also learned to pick up small pieces of food with her fingers and eventually fed herself with a spoon. By the age of 3 years, Nadia was still considerably smaller than most children her age, but she was a healthy, energetic child—a little girl who most people would not have guessed began life facing great adversity and deprivation.

From time to time, Nadia's parents wondered how her experience in the orphanage would affect her future growth and development. More frequently, however, they marveled at her progress and, like most parents, thought about the topics that we focus on in this chapter—steps that parents can take to keep infants and young children safe and healthy.

PHYSICAL GROWTH

Growth during the first three years is faster than at any other point after birth (Behrman, Kliegman, & Jenson, 2000). Most infants lose about 10 percent of their birthweight during the first week, but this weight is usually regained by the time the baby is about 10 days old. Growth occurs in spurts, rather than at a steady rate (Lampl, 2009; Lampl & Thompson, 2007). Birthweight typically doubles by about 5 months and triples by 12 months. If children's weight continued to triple each year, the average 3-year-old would weigh approximately 200 pounds. Fortunately, the rate of weight gain decreases after the first year and does not increase again until adolescence.

Besides adding weight, infants also grow in length. By the end of the first year, most babies are about 10 inches longer than they were at birth. Increases in length slow down by one-half during the second year and by one-third by the age of 3 years (American Academy of Pediatrics, Shelov, & Hannemann, 1998). Body proportions change as well. Whereas the newborn infant's head is approximately one-fourth of overall body length, the typical 3-year-old child is less top-heavy and has a slimmer build. Growth rates vary across children, however, and many 3-year-olds still have a big tummy even if their arms and legs have begun to slim down. Changes in body proportions, along with increases in strength and coordination, have implications for motor development, a topic that we consider in Chapter 6.

Significant brain growth and development occur after infants are born. The newborn's skull grows rapidly too, increasing more during the first 4 months than at any other time in life (American Academy of Pediatrics, Shelov, & Hannemann, 1998). Head circumference correlates well with postnatal brain growth and is one of several measures available to track early physical growth and development.

Three-year-olds may seem like giants next to their younger siblings.

Measuring and Predicting Growth

Pediatricians use growth charts to compare individual infants' weight, length, and head circumference with the measurements of other children of the same age. These charts—first constructed by the National Center for Health Statistics (NCHS) in 1977—are a series of percentile curves showing the distribution of body measurements in children in the United States. Commonly used measurements for infants up to 36 months include length-and-weight-for-age, head-circumference-for-age, and weight-for-length. Separate charts are used for boys and girls because boys tend to be slightly longer and heavier. Height (as opposed to body length) can be reliably measured after age 2; there are separate sets of charts for children between 2 to 5 years of age, and for ages 2 to 20 years, tracking height-for-age, weight-for-age, and weight-for-height.

The original set of NCHS growth charts was based on a sample of white, formula-fed, middle-class infants from Ohio in the 1970s and did not accurately reflect the cultural and racial diversity of the United States then or now. In 2000, the Centers for Disease Control and Prevention (CDC) addressed these shortcomings by creating new growth charts. The CDC used information from the National Health and Nutrition Examination Survey (NHANES), based on physical examinations of a representative sample of the U.S. population, including a mixture of breastfed and formula-fed infants (Kuczmarski et al., 2000; Ogden et al., 2002).

Approximately half (54%) of the mothers in the NHANES sample initiated breastfeeding; of those infants, however, only 21 percent were exclusively breastfed for four months, while about 10 percent were partially breastfed for four months, and 24 percent had been completely weaned from breast milk by that age. Breastfed babies tend to grow differently than babies who are not breastfed, gaining weight more quickly in the first two months and then more slowly for the remainder of the first year, while their rate of increase in length tends to be greater than the rate observed in infants who are not breastfed. As a result of these differences, breastfed babies are typically leaner and longer, and the CDC growth charts are not entirely adequate for monitoring their growth (de Onis, Garza, Onyango, & Borghi, 2007; de Onis & Onyango, 2003).

Unlike the earlier NCHS growth charts, the 2000 CDC charts contain information about body-mass-index-for-age for ages 2 to 20 years. **Body mass index (BMI)** is a measure of weight in relation to height and is calculated for adults by dividing an individual's weight in pounds by the square of his or her height in inches and multiplying the result by 703 (adults with BMIs ≥ 30 are considered obese). Instead of calculating a BMI for young children, the CDC defines obesity as age- and gender-specific weight-for-height scores at the 95th percentile or above. Overweight and obesity have become a significant health problem in many developing countries, affecting children as well as adults. As shown in Figure 5.1, the prevalence of childhood overweight and obesity in the United States more than doubled for 2- to 5-year-olds as well as for school-age children from 1976 to 2004. Rates among low-income 2- to 5-year-old children are even higher, and increased from 12.4 percent in 1998 to 14.5 percent in 2003; because rates for this subgroup remained at 14.6 percent in 2008, some health experts believe that the trend may have stabilized (Sharma et al., 2009). To reduce the prevalence of childhood obesity and overweight, pediatricians must work with parents and other caregivers to track the amount and rate of weight children gain, and, from an early age, encourage healthy levels of activity and a nutritious diet (Federal Interagency Forum on Child and Family Statistics, 2009; vanDijk & Innis, 2009).

The World Health Organization (WHO) developed a different approach to measuring growth. Unlike the 2000 CDC charts, which describe how representative samples of U.S. infants and children grew over a particular period of time, the 2006 WHO Child Growth Standards are a statement about how children everywhere *should* grow (de Onis et al., 2007). Through its Multicentre Growth Reference Study (a longitudinal study of 8,440 exclusively breastfed infants

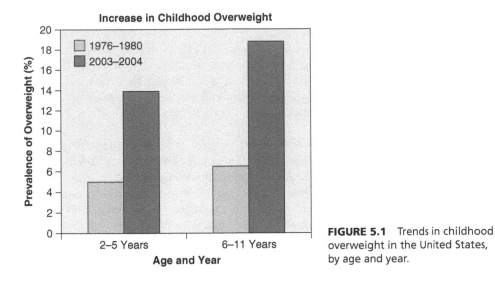

FIGURE 5.1 Trends in childhood overweight in the United States, by age and year.

in Brazil, Ghana, India, Norway, Oman, and the United States), the WHO found that environmental factors are the main cause of disparities in physical growth, both within and between countries. When children's health and nutrition needs are met, they have a similar capacity to grow and develop to within the same range of height and weight for age. With this evidence, health professionals around the world may be able to work together more effectively to advocate for additional resources and the right of all children to achieve this potential (Kerac et al., 2009; WHO, 2009).

Health researchers around the world have begun to compare the WHO standards with other measures, most commonly the 2000 CDC charts. Researchers in Bahrain, Canada, and Mexico concluded that the WHO standards should be used in those countries (Al-Raees et al., 2009; Ponce-Rivera et al., 2008; vanDijk & Innis, 2009). Health experts in Belgium, by contrast, determined that a locally developed growth chart was superior (Roelants, Hauspie, & Hoppenbrouwers, 2009). A research team in South Africa noted that the WHO standards offer many advantages, but adopting them widely will require additional resources and coordination among already-strained healthcare systems (Kerac et al., 2009; Norris et al., 2009). The WHO encourages pediatric associations and health agencies in all countries to evaluate existing evidence and conduct further studies to make the most appropriate recommendations for measuring child growth in their populations (WHO, 2009).

At the individual level, infants' physical growth is influenced by genetics. The extent to which a child's genetic potential is expressed, however, is affected by multiple, interacting conditions, and a child's health and nutrition are always experienced within a particular caregiving environment and broader psychosocial and cultural context.

Failure to Thrive

When infants' growth falters significantly, doctors may diagnose a condition known as **failure to thrive (FTT)**. Most cases of FTT are caused by a lack of adequate nutrition (Black et al., 2006; Block, **Krebs, the Committee on Child Abuse and Neglect, & the Committee on Nutrition,** 2005). Infants may fail to get enough nutrients because parents have difficulties breastfeeding or preparing formula correctly, choose unhealthy foods, or do not use effective feeding techniques. Some babies, especially those born preterm or with other health problems, have oral or motor conditions that complicate feeding, while others have strong negative reactions to some or many kinds of food, based on texture, flavor, or unknown qualities (Block et al., 2005; Chatoor et al., 2004). In a small number of cases, infants have a disease that prevents their body from absorbing nutrients in breast milk, formula, or other food they consume (Dimmock et al., 2007; Wright, Parkinson, & Drewett, 2006a, 2006b). Parental anxiety about feeding difficulties and children's stunted growth may exacerbate the situation, fostering dynamics at mealtime that become another part of the problem (Wright et al., 2006a, 2006b).

In some cases, referred to as **psychosocial short stature,** children are underweight and extremely short for their age, and FTT may be a sign of neglect or emotional and psychological trauma (Block et al., 2005). Early studies of children with psychosocial short stature reported dramatic growth spurts when children were moved to a new, caring environment, a surge most likely due to improvements both in diet and in growth hormone secretion (Widdowson, 1951). More recently, this pattern has been observed among infants adopted from orphanages. Like Nadia, the majority of these children are below normal weight and height; more than one-third are below the 3rd percentile for length, weight, and head circumference. Growth data from orphanages in Eastern Europe and China indicate that children lose an average of one month of linear growth for every three months spent in an institutional setting. Growth stunting in these children is influenced by prenatal experience and postnatal diet as well as a psychosocially induced factor—abnormal growth hormone secretion due to stress and poor quality of care (D.E. Johnson, 2000).

Catch-up growth is typical among previously institutionalized adoptees, with the greatest increase usually occurring among children who were adopted before the age of 6 to 8 months (D.E. Johnson, 2000; Rutter, 1998). In a study of Romanian adoptees younger than 18 months of age, nearly 80 percent of growth-stunted children were in the normal range for height-length within nine months of their adoption (Johnson et al., 1993). There are limits, however, in the extent to which previously deprived children recover from the effects of earlier institutionalization (Gunnar, 2000; Gunnar et al., 2001; Gunnar & Quevedo, 2007).

Studies of preterm infants may shed light on the abnormal production of growth hormone among institutionalized infants and children. As we learned in Chapter 4, preterm, LBW, and VLBW infants benefit from skin-to-skin kangaroo care. Controlled studies have also found that fragile, underweight babies thrive in response to another form of tactile/kinesthetic stimulation, gentle infant massage (Field, Hernandez-Reif, & Freedman, 2004; Mendes & Procianoy, 2008). In some of these studies, massaged preterm infants have gained up to 53 percent more weight than unmassaged comparison infants receiving the same number of calories (Field et al., 1986; Field, Diego, & Hernandez-Reif, 2007; Gonzalez et al., 2009). Touch, including infant massage, appears to work by increasing the release of gastrointestinal food absorption hormones, serum insulin, and insulin-like growth factor-1 (IGF-1); it may also activate growth genes, just as lack of caring touch in orphanages may interfere with the normal action of these hormones and genes (Field et al., 2007, 2008; Massaro et al., 2009).

Brain Development

Like other aspects of physical growth, brain development occurs rapidly after birth. The newborn brain is approximately one-fourth the size of an adult's brain but grows to about 80 percent by 3 years and 90 percent by age 5 (Nelson & Luciana, 2008; Shonkoff & Phillips, 2000). Unlike other aspects of physical growth, the developing brain cannot be seen by the casual observer—or interested parent. Yet, with the assistance of **electroencephalograms** (**EEGs,** which measure the brain's activity through external electrodes placed on the scalp) and imaging tools, such as

positron emission tomography (**PET,** which shows the amount of activity, such as glucose uptake, in the brain), or **magnetic resonance imaging** (**MRI,** which reveals the brain's structure), researchers have documented profound changes occurring in the months and years after birth.

Brain development begins prenatally with the generation of neurons. By birth, most of these neurons have migrated to areas where they will perform specialized functions, such as those involved in processing sensory information and controlling motor movements. In order to perform these functions, neurons must become interconnected to a network of other neurons by forming **synapses,** or connections. The brain's growth after birth is thus primarily the result of new projections from each neuron—the axons and dendrites that form synapses with other neurons' axons and dendrites. As shown in Figure 5.2, **axons** carry electrical messages away from

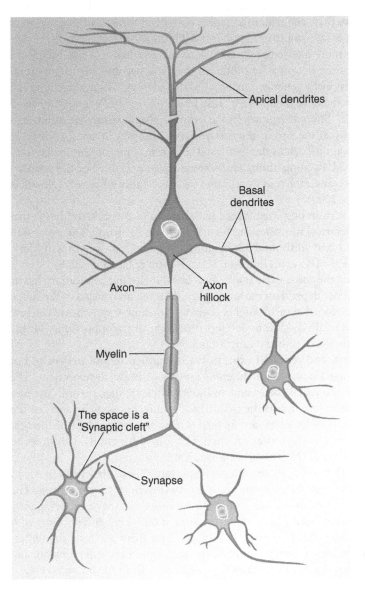

FIGURE 5.2 Axons and dendrites connect neurons together in a network.

the neuron cell body, and **dendrites** bring those signals to the cell body. In the space between one neuron's axon and the next neuron's dendrites, biochemicals called **neurotransmitters** are released from **vesicles** (or storage spaces) at the end of the axon and taken up by the next neuron's dendrite.

There is regional variation in **synaptogenesis** (the formation of synapses), with the most rapid increase and peak density of synapses in different areas occurring at different ages. Before 5 weeks of age, the most active areas appear to be in the sensorimotor cortex, thalamus, brainstem, and parts of the cerebellum. Between 3 and 4 months, there is a rapid increase in the number and density of synapses in the visual cortex, with the peak density found between 4 and 12 months. The prefrontal cortex (an area involved in higher forms of thinking), by contrast, is slower to develop and synapse density does not peak until after the first year. During the most active period of its development, 2 million new synapses are created every second in the cerebral cortex, and by 2 years of age more than 100 trillion synapses have been formed in this region of the brain (Johnson, 2001; Nelson & Luciana, 2008; Shonkoff & Phillips, 2000).

The brain's development is more like sculpting a block of marble than it is like building a snowman. This is because many more neurons are produced than will become part of an established network, and some of the originally generated material is "carved away." Beginning at the end of the first year, many synapses in the developing brain cease functioning. The "pruning" of these synapses occurs at different ages in different regions. In the primary visual cortex, the number of synapses per neuron begins to drop at the end of the first year, but synapses in areas involved in higher forms of learning and reasoning, such as the prefrontal cortex, may not be eliminated until adolescence, or even into adulthood. Pruning ultimately removes about one-third of the synapses between early childhood and adolescence; the result is a brain that works more efficiently (Nelson & Luciana, 2008; Shonkoff & Phillips, 2000).

Axons in the synapses that remain become covered with **myelin** (a dense, fatty sheath that enhances the speed with which electrical messages can be sent between neurons). The process of myelination has been documented into adulthood but begins during the first two years of life. It is complete in many areas by the age of 4 years (Johnson, 2001; Nelson & Luciana, 2008).

Early survival and control of the most basic bodily functions, including respiration, heartbeat, circulation, sleeping, and reflexes, depend on the lower brain. This region consists of the spinal cord and brain stem and is well developed at birth. Higher regions—the limbic system and cerebral cortex—are immature at birth and relatively slow to develop, providing ample opportunity for the influence of experience on the brain's structure and functioning.

Experience activates neurons, and repeated experiences strengthen neural networks, but the role of experience is not always the same for different aspects of brain development. The majority of neural connections in the visual cortex and auditory cortex are made within the first several months after birth, for example, whereas the majority of connections in the areas of the brain responsible for certain aspects of language are formed during the second half of the first year. By contrast, the prefrontal cortex, the center for higher cognitive functions, continues to develop and remains open to experience (Nelson & Luciana, 2008).

Some aspects of brain development are **experience-expectant;** these structures seem to "expect" to have certain kinds of stimulation and are ready to develop once they receive it. The visual cortex, for example, "expects" to receive signals from both eyes but depends on receiving early visual stimulation to develop normally—with equal representation of both eyes. Infants born with a congenital cataract in one eye (an opaque covering that blocks light from reaching the retina) require corrective surgery. Without early treatment, input from the normal eye will stimulate and take over regions of the visual cortex that would ordinarily process input from the occluded eye.

Many other, **experience-dependent** aspects of brain development function differently. These structures and systems develop as a result of each person's experiences, such as learning to play a musical instrument or ice skate. These experiences determine whether particular brain functions are developed and reinforced. Unlike experience-expectant aspects of brain development, experience-dependent abilities are generally open to change throughout an individual's lifetime, enabling new skills to be learned at any age (Nelson & Luciana, 2008; Shonkoff & Phillips, 2000).

Not all experiences exert a positive influence on brain development. Early physical and psychological stress produces abnormal functioning in areas of the brain (the hypothalamus and brainstem) that regulate fundamental aspects of healthy growth and development. The extent of the abnormalities is influenced by factors such as the length of exposure to inadequate caregiving and children's unique genetic characteristics.

Maltreatment, the Brain, and Shaken Baby Syndrome

Maltreatment, defined by the National Child Abuse and Neglect Data System (NCANDS) as neglect, medical neglect, physical abuse, sexual abuse, or psychological maltreatment, affects large numbers of children in the United States annually. According to NCANDS, in 2007 approximately 794,000 children (10.6 per 1,000 children of all ages) were identified as victims of child abuse or neglect. Approximately one-half (46.1%) of all victims were non-Hispanic white, 21.7 percent were African American, and 20.8 percent were Hispanic. One-third (31.9%) were under the age of 4 years, with the highest incidence of maltreatment (21.9 per 1,000 children) found among the youngest children, those younger than 1 year. As shown in Figure 5.3, the highest rate of fatalities occurred among children younger than 1 year of age. The majority of perpetrators were parents, relatives, or unmarried partners of parents (Schnitzer, & Ewigman, 2005; U.S. Department of Health and Human Services, Administration on Children, Youth and Families, 2009).

The amygdala, the area of the brain that registers and responds to fear and anxiety, is relatively mature at birth and appears to be fully functional by the age of 1 year. Other neurobiological components of stress-response systems also develop and become organized in the early months of life, meaning that infants are capable of experiencing fear, anxiety, and psychological stress (Gunnar & Quevedo, 2007). For children who survive maltreatment, what are the effects on the developing brain?

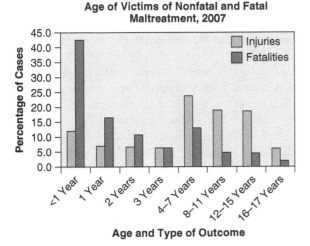

Age and Type of Outcome

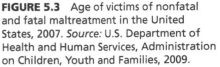

FIGURE 5.3 Age of victims of nonfatal and fatal maltreatment in the United States, 2007. *Source:* U.S. Department of Health and Human Services, Administration on Children, Youth and Families, 2009.

Until relatively recently, evidence regarding the effects of early abuse and neglect came primarily from studies of animals. Experiments with rodents and nonhuman primates showed that in the absence of adequate maternal care, early overstimulation of the amygdala results in an animal version of post-traumatic stress disorder that lasts into adulthood. Infant rhesus monkeys, for example, deprived of normal maternal care, become fearful, anxious adult animals that show exaggerated physiological stress responses. These animals produce higher levels of stress hormones and anxiety-related brain neurochemicals than monkeys reared with adequate maternal care (Shonkoff & Phillips, 2000; Suomi, 1991). Encouragingly, some studies have found that even brief, early exposure to a nurturing or stimulating environment may reduce the long-term impact of adversity and deprivation (Francis et al., 2002; Parker et al., 2006).

Clinical studies of severely neglected or abused children have documented profound disturbances of normal development, including delays and abnormalities in cognitive, emotional, social, and physical development. In a pioneering study, Spitz (1945) showed that young children placed in foster care and given sensitive, nurturing care had better developmental outcomes. Clinical studies have not focused on the effects of early adversity on the developing brain per se, but new evidence from developmental neuroscience is beginning to provide some insights (Goldsmith, Pollak, & Davidson, 2008; Gunnar & Quevedo, 2007; Shirtcliff, Coeb, & Pollak, 2009).

Threats to physical or psychological safety change the brain's functioning, including the functioning of areas involved in food intake, digestion, growth, and respiration. MRI scans indicate that maltreated children suffering from post-traumatic stress disorder have significantly smaller brains than children who have not been abused. Brain volume appears to decrease as duration of abuse increases, with the areas most closely involved in physiological stress responses more affected than other regions (Beers & De Bellis, 2002; De Bellis et al., 1999). Children who experience the most global neglect, involving minimal exposure to language, touch, and social interaction, usually fare the worst (Perry & Pollard, 1998).

Early traumatic experiences affect the way that children attend to their surroundings and monitor socially relevant information, especially concerning other people's emotions. One study using event-related potentials (ERPs) and other physiological measures compared physically abused and nonabused children. Whether presented with faces or voices, physically abused children showed stronger ERP and physiological responses to expressions of anger than did nonabused children; the groups did not respond differently to expressions of happy and sad emotions. A history of physical abuse thus appears to increase children's physiological and perceptual sensitivity to cues about anger, a heightened awareness that may be adaptive in an unpredictable, abusive home (Shackman, Shackman, & Pollak, 2007).

Early adversity also appears to challenge children's immune system, with effects that are seen at least until the age of 9 to 14 years. One recent study compared two kinds of adversity: physical abuse in children's own homes and deprivation in institutional settings in Romania, Russia, other Eastern European countries, and China. When researchers analyzed saliva samples from children who had experienced one of these forms of early adversity, they found evidence of continuing stress—higher-than-normal levels of an antibody for the herpes simplex virus. This indicator of ongoing stress was not unexpected in the physically abused children because they were still living with their families of origin. It was notable, however, that the effects of early trauma and deprivation were still evident in the previously institutionalized children's compromised immune functioning as many as 13 years after adoption and placement in a more optimal caregiving environment (Shirtcliff et al., 2009).

Early adversity does not necessarily lead to the same outcome in all children, and some studies have found evidence of resilience. Researchers using a laboratory assessment of social stress compared cortisol (stress hormone) levels and electrocardiogram (ECG) responses in three groups of children: an early adoption group, who had experienced moderate early life stress as a result of being cared for in foster care in their country of origin before being adopted by the age of 8 months; a later adoption group, who had experienced severe early life stress as a result of being cared for in an orphanage until they were at least 1 year old; and a nonadopted (no early life stress) group living with their families of origin. More than half of the later adoption group and approximately one-fifth of the early adoption group had had a severe growth delay at the time of adoption, but the two groups were similar in height and weight by the age of 10 to 12 years. Most interestingly, there were large variations in cortisol level within the later adopted group, suggesting that neurobiological effects of severe early life stress are not inevitable (Gunnar et al., 2001, 2009).

Many of the participants in these studies have been school-age children who experienced abuse and other forms of early trauma, but researchers believe that the findings are applicable to younger children (Gunnar & Quevedo, 2007; Pollak, 2008). In addition, although more research is needed, the evidence strongly suggests that animal models of early adversity and deprivation are relevant to humans.

There is no question that an infant's brain is vulnerable to sudden injury in **shaken baby syndrome (SBS),** a subtype of abusive head trauma due to maltreatment, in which an angry or frustrated adult shakes an infant violently (Christian et al., 2009). Many cases of SBS occur when a parent or caregiver reacts out of frustration to a crying baby (Lee et al., 2007). Some adults shake babies in the mistaken belief that it is less damaging than spanking or hitting an infant. In fact, whiplash motions are more harmful because infants' heads are heavy and large, but their neck muscles are relatively weak.

During shaking, parts of the brain—which has been compared to a bowl of gelatin—may separate as it slams into the front and then the back of the skull with a force five to 10 times greater than if the child had simply tripped and fallen (Wiggins, 2000). Physicians diagnose SBS when they find bleeding in the retina of the infant's eyes, blood on the brain, and increased head size caused by fluid build-up in the brain. There may also be damage to the spinal cord and broken ribs. Shaken infants are often brought for medical attention after losing consciousness, having difficulty breathing, or developing seizures; some caregivers report to medical authorities that the baby was shaken during resuscitation efforts (Altimier, 2008; Christian et al., 2009). In 65 percent to 90 percent of cases, the perpetrator is an adult male in his early 20s—often the baby's father or the mother's boyfriend. Female perpetrators are more likely to be a babysitter or childcare provider rather than the infant's mother (Dias et al., 2005; Sinal et al., 2000).

Abusive head trauma is the leading cause of infant death from injury in the United States each year. As many as 30 percent of all affected babies die, and many milder cases of SBS go undetected or are misdiagnosed. Infants who do not die from the abuse nearly always sustain permanent damage that may include partial or complete loss of vision, hearing impairments, seizures, or cerebral palsy, as well as cognitive impairments and behavior problems (Altimier, 2008; Dias et al., 2005).

Given that brain damage occurs with shaking that lasts as little as 20 seconds, some parents worry that they might unintentionally damage their infant's brain during active, physical play. Experts caution against rough play that is age-inappropriate, but adults twirling, spinning, tossing, or bouncing infants are unlikely to cause SBS injuries. Educational materials and classes are a good way to increase new parents' awareness of the dangers of shaking a baby. Prevention efforts are especially effective when they provide tips for coping with an inconsolable baby and information explaining that it is normal for infants to follow a pattern described as the Period of PURPLE, an acronym reminding parents that there is a *Peak* age (2–4 months) for inconsolable crying, that long crying bouts can be *Unexpected*, with infants being *Resistant* to soothing, showing a *Pained* facial expression, and crying for a *Long* time, often in the late afternoon or *Evening* (Barr et al., 2009; Dias et al. 2005).

HEALTH AND SAFETY

Nearly all newborns receive an Apgar Score in the minutes after birth, while assessments, such as the Brazelton NBAS, check reflexes and other abilities during the first days and weeks. Newborns' health is also screened in all 50 states and the District of Columbia, although the number of disorders and conditions assessed varies.

Newborn Screening

Mandatory screening exists nationwide for three conditions: phenylketonuria, or PKU (an inherited metabolic disorder leading to accumulation of the amino acid phenylalanine, developmental delay, cognitive disabilities, and autistic-like behavior); congenital hypothyroidism (an inadequate production of thyroid hormone that can lead to cognitive disabilities and a growth disorder); and galactosemia (a metabolic disorder that can result in failure to thrive, cognitive disabilities, and death). Several states screen for 20 or more other conditions (Mitka, 2000; Rose et al., 2006). Newborn screening is usually accomplished within 24 hours of the infant's birth by analyzing a blood sample obtained by pricking the baby's heel. Tests are currently available for about 30 conditions, and some experts advocate screening for any condition for which a test and treatment are available, even rare diseases, if the information would make a difference to the child (Kaler et al., 2008). Critics argue that enthusiasm for screening needs to be tempered by an assessment of the availability of resources for treatment (Kaye & the Committee on Genetics, 2006; Mitka, 2000).

In many congenital disorders, early diagnosis enables intervention to begin earlier, usually leading to better outcomes. This is often true for hearing deficiencies at birth, which affect as many as 12,000 infants born in the United States each year (National Center on Birth Defects and Developmental Disabilities, 2007). Without newborn screening, the average detection of hearing loss occurs at 14 months, an age by which fundamental problems with the acquisition of speech and language may have developed (American Academy of Pediatrics Task Force on Newborn and Infant Hearing, 1999). Since 2005, newborn hearing screening has been required before hospital discharge in all 50 states and U.S. territories (American Academy of Pediatrics Joint Committee on Infant Hearing, 2007). The most frequent assessment, otoacoustic emissions (OAE), involves placing a miniature microphone in the infant's ear and measuring sound waves produced in the cochlea (inner ear) in response to clicks or tones. Another technique, auditory brainstem response (ABR), involves pasting electrodes on the infant's scalp in order to measure electroencephalographic (EEG) waves in response to clicks or other sounds. Despite achieving screening for 95 percent of U.S. newborns, approximately 50 percent of infants who do not pass the initial screening fail to receive follow-up assessments to determine whether they have a hearing problem, how severe it might be, and what sorts of interventions and other services might be appropriate (American Academy of Pediatrics Joint Committee on Infant Hearing, 2007).

Screening for Lead Poisoning

Children living in homes built before 1978 (especially those with deteriorating paint or ongoing remodeling projects) should be screened for their exposure to lead, a highly toxic metal that causes brain damage, behavioral problems, learning disabilities, seizures, and even death. In 1978, lead-based paints were banned for use in housing, but experts estimate that 4 million homes (25% of U.S. homes with children younger than 6 years) currently have deteriorated lead paint or elevated levels of lead-contaminated house dust (Binns, Campbell, & Brown, for the Advisory Committee on Childhood Lead Poisoning Prevention, 2007; Jacobs et al., 2002).

The effects of lead exposure are cumulative and initially cause no obvious symptoms, although some children may be lethargic or complain of abdominal pain. Screening is usually targeted rather than universal, and children at risk can be evaluated through a simple test checking the level of lead in their blood. Children with the greatest exposure to older, poorly maintained housing—low-income urban children—have the highest rates of lead poisoning. Children from low-income families are eight times more likely to have elevated blood lead levels than children from high-income families. Approximately 310,000 U.S. children under the age of 6 years (down from 13.5 million in 1978) have blood lead levels exceeding the recommended limit (Binns et al., 2007; Jacobs et al., 2009). Figure 5.4 shows that, although the percentage of young children with unacceptably high blood lead levels has decreased since 1988, there are still racial and ethnic group differences (Hubbs-Tait et al., 2005; Schwemberger et al., 2005).

Lead affects every system in the body, and infants and very young children are at greatest risk because they tend to put their fingers, toys, and other objects—and any lead dust on them—into their mouths. Lead also finds its way into children's blood and is deposited in their bones when they eat lead-based paint chips. Children younger than 3 years of age are especially vulnerable to these effects because they are growing rapidly and their bodies absorb more lead than the bodies of adults with the same exposure (Children's Environmental Health Initiative, 2002).

The effects of lead on cognitive functioning may be only partly reversible (Hubbs-Tait et al., 2005). It is best, therefore, to prevent ingestion in the first place. Lead-based paint that is peeling or flaking should be removed, but improper removal of lead-based paint can actually increase the risk

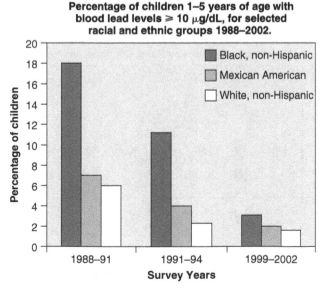

FIGURE 5.4 Blood lead levels as a function of race/ethnicity and year. *Source:* Schwemberger, Mosby, Doa, Jacobs, Ashley, Brody, et al., 2005.

to children by spreading paint chips and dust. To minimize the spread of lead dust in potentially contaminated areas, damp mops and cloths, rather than brooms or vacuum cleaners, should be used to clean floors and windowsills.

Children's hands and toys should be washed frequently and their play needs to be supervised to ensure that they do not ingest household items made of lead, such as drapery weights, since that form of sudden lead poisoning may not be diagnosed in time to save the child's life. Children's metal jewelry and painted toys may contain lead, so parents need to be aware of these potential dangers (VanArsdale et al., 2004).

Exposure to lead can also be reduced by making sure that food is not prepared or served in pottery that may be glazed with a lead-based finish. Using cold water for food preparation is helpful, since hot water is more likely to carry lead from plumbing in older houses in which lead pipes have not been replaced with copper or other safe alternatives (Binns et al., 2007).

For children with elevated blood lead levels, nutritional interventions offer additional protection. Iron and calcium supplements, for example, reduce absorption of ingested lead, as does a low-fat diet (Binns et al., 2007; Hubbs-Tait et al., 2005). With increased awareness and efforts to prevent contamination in high-risk communities, it may be possible to eliminate this serious threat to children's physical and intellectual well-being.

Infant Mortality

In most parts of the developed world, **infant mortality rates (IMRs),** (the number of infants who die before reaching the age of 1 year) are significantly lower than in the past. From 1980 to 2006, infant mortality in the United States (expressed as the number of deaths per 1,000 live births) declined from 12.6 to 6.71. There was little change, however, from 2000 and 2006, due to an increase in the number of infants born preterm and at low birthweights (Callaghan et al., 2006; MacDorman & Mathews, 2008).

Although IMRs dropped between 1995 and 2005, as shown in Figure 5.5, they still vary by race and ethnicity. Significant advances will be required in order to reduce disparities among racial and ethnic populations and move all Americans closer to the Healthy People 2010 objective of an overall IMR of 4.5 (Luke & Brown, 2006; MacDorman & Mathews, 2008).

The three most common causes of infant deaths are congenital malformations, disorders related to preterm birth and low birthweight, and sudden infant death syndrome (SIDS). Infant

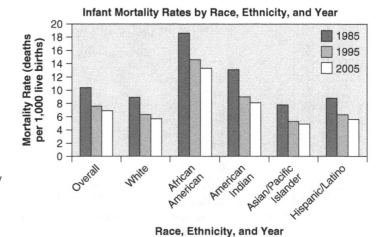

FIGURE 5.5 Infant mortality rates vary by race, ethnicity, and year. *Source:* National Center for Health Statistics, 2009.

death in the United States is more likely to occur for infants whose mothers had no prenatal care, were teenagers, had less than 12 years of education, were unmarried, or smoked during pregnancy. Male infants are at greater risk than are female infants, and there is a higher mortality rate for preterm and multiple births (Kugelman et al., 2007; MacDorman & Kirmeyer, 2009; Singh & Kogan, 2007).

How do these findings compare with IMRs in other parts of the world? As Table 5.1 shows, rates vary significantly between developed and developing countries (Bhutta et al., 2005). According to UNICEF, the highest mortality rates in the year 2007 (reported for children under the age of 5 years as the number of deaths per 1,000 live births) were found in Sierre Leone (262), Afghanistan (257), Chad (209), and Equatorial Guinea (206); 33 other countries had rates of 100 or higher. Across these settings, infant mortality is linked to the same basic factors—poverty, inadequate prenatal care, and complications of pregnancy, exacerbated by health-compromising conditions such as malnutrition and scarcity of clean drinking water. Low rates of immunization are also found in the countries with the highest IMRs (Bhutta et al., 2005; UNICEF, 2009; United Nations, 2008a).

The United Nations Millennium Development Project seeks to reduce the under-5 mortality rate by two-thirds by the year 2015. Given that 37 percent of those deaths occur in the first month of life, improved neonatal and maternal care are high priorities (United Nations, 2008b). By implementing proven interventions throughout the first three years, this outcome could be achieved by saving 6 million lives in the 42 countries in which 90 percent of child deaths occur. The cost of reaching this goal is high—approximately $5.1 billion, or $887 per child—but so is the cost of failing (Bryce et al., 2005).

TABLE 5.1	International Rankings for Infant Mortality Rates in Selected Countries, 1960 and 2005	
Country	**1960 Ranking (Rate)**	**2005 Ranking (Rate)**
Australia	5 (20.2)	21 (5.0)
Austria	24 (37.5)	15 (4.2)
Canada	15 (27.3)	25 (5.4)
Denmark	8 (21.5)	17 (4.4)
England and Wales	9 (22.4)	21 (5.0)
Finland	6 (21.0)	5 (3.0)
France	16 (27.7)	9 (3.6)
Hong Kong	26 (41.5)	2 (2.4)
Japan	19 (30.7)	4 (2.8)
Norway	3 (18.9)	6 (3.1)
Singapore	21 (34.8)	1 (2.1)
Slovakia	17 (28.6)	31 (7.2)
Spain	28 (43.7)	14 (4.1)
Sweden	1 (16.6)	2 (2.4)
Romania	33 (75.7)	36 (15.0)
United States	12 (26.0)	30 (6.9)

Note: Countries with the same IMR receive the same rank.

Source: National Center for Health Statistics, 2009.

Common Illnesses and Immunizations

Approximately 60 percent of U.S. newborns become clinically jaundiced, meaning that the infant's immature liver is unable to contribute to the normal breakdown of oxygen-carrying red blood cells, causing the skin and whites of the eyes to turn yellow, usually by the second or third day of life. This condition, which is more common in preterm infants, begins to subside within 10 days. Jaundice also occurs more frequently and may last longer among infants who are breastfed than among formula-fed babies but is rarely cause for concern. A more serious condition, pathologic jaundice, is rare but extremely dangerous because it develops quickly (within 24 hours after birth) and may lead to brain damage or death if not treated. Mild cases of normal jaundice are often left untreated, but infants with more serious cases receive phototherapy under special ultraviolet lamps (American Academy of Pediatrics Subcommittee on Hyperbilirubinemia, 2004; Ip et al., 2004; Morris et al., 2008).

Most illnesses affecting infants and toddlers do not result in hospitalization. Children get their first cold around the age of 6 months and have an average of seven or eight colds per year until the age of about 5 years. Infants with colds frequently develop a fever as high as 100 to 104 degrees. Fever is a sign that the body's immune system is functioning, however, and most fevers below 105 degrees are not harmful. Exceptions are a child who is having convulsions or who otherwise acts or looks very sick. After the age of 2 months, acetaminophen can be given to reduce a fever if the child is very uncomfortable. Aspirin should not be used to treat children's fevers, because it may cause a severe brain infection known as Reye's syndrome (American Academy of Family Physicians, 1996).

Compared with infants cared for at home, infants in group childcare tend to have higher rates of intestinal infections and upper respiratory infections, with the biggest difference in rates occurring among infants younger than 12 to 18 months (Kamper-Jørgensen et al., 2008; Lu et al., 2004) Infants and toddlers, like older children and adults, become ill through person-to-person transmission or through airborne exposure; infection rates can be decreased when childcare providers are conscientious about hand washing and disinfection of surfaces and toys. Children in high-quality childcare settings tend to have lower rates of illness than children attending poorer quality programs, possibly because staff in high-quality settings tend to be more knowledgeable about health promotion and are more likely to have opportunities and resources with which to educate children's parents about hygiene practices they can follow at home (Gupta et al., 2005; Lu et al., 2004). These precautions cannot prevent all infections, so parents may be heartened to know of correlational evidence suggesting that babies who develop infections often have fewer allergies later in childhood than those with fewer early illnesses (Johnston & Openshaw, 2001).

In addition to having an immature immune system, infants and toddlers are especially susceptible to contagious illnesses because they have poor personal hygiene and frequently place their hands, toys, and other objects in their mouth. Viruses, bacteria, and parasites are responsible for the most common contagious illnesses: skin infections (e.g., chickenpox, fifth disease, impetigo, and lice), respiratory infections (e.g., bronchitis, croup, strep throat, and whooping cough), intestinal infections (e.g., diarrhea and hepatitis A), and other infections (e.g., pinkeye).

Some contagious diseases, such as whooping cough, mumps, measles, and hepatitis A and B, can be prevented through immunization. Infants in the United States receive a combined series of eleven vaccines, with the first dose for most of these vaccines given at the age of 2 months (Committee on Infectious Diseases, 2009). As a result, vaccine-preventable childhood diseases—and the disabilities and deaths they cause—are at record lows in the United States and in countries with similar rates of immunization (National Center for Health Statistics, 2009; UNICEF, 2009). Infants and toddlers in licensed childcare programs have consistently high rates of immunization.

New vaccines have been added to the recommended schedule in recent years, including a vaccine for varicella (chickenpox), influenza, and rotavirus (Centers for Disease Control and Prevention, 2009b; Committee on Infectious Diseases, 2009). Most infants' immune system can safely assimilate multiple vaccines. Even in rare cases where children develop high fevers or seizures as a reaction to vaccines, there is no greater incidence of speech delays, developmental problems, or autism (Barlow et al., 2001; Offit et al., 2002). Recent reviews of more than 2,000 studies of millions of children also show that neither the measles-mumps-rubella (MMR) vaccine nor a preservative used in some vaccines cause autism or other diseases and disabilities (Institute of Medicine Immunization Safety Review Committee, 2004; Tozzi et al., 2009).

Immunization rates for some individual vaccines are as high as 95 percent for some population subgroups (National Center for Health Statistics, 2009). One paradoxical outcome of the development and widespread use of vaccines is that some parents decide to benefit from so-called "herd immunity" and choose not to have their children immunized, since there is no apparent threat of contracting polio or other once-prevalent childhood diseases (Armstrong et al., 2007). Many vaccine-preventable diseases exist in other parts of the world, however, and may be carried to the United States by travelers. Without vaccines, epidemics could return and pose a threat once again, causing serious illness, disability, and death (Gawande, 2004). Even with high immunization rates in the United States, there are still outbreaks of vaccine-preventable childhood diseases, such as pertussis (whooping cough) and chickenpox, which can prove fatal among nonimmunized children, especially babies younger than 6 months (Glanz et al., 2009).

Vaccines may soon be available for infections of the middle ear (otitis media)—a common problem in infancy that is frequently treated with antibiotics (O'Brien et al., 2009; Poehling et al., 2007). Intermittent, temporary hearing loss caused by fluid that collects in the ear does not appear to interfere with receptive language or expressive language through 2 years of age (Roberts, Rosenfeld, & Zeisel, 2004). Ear infections are often painful, however, and many parents must take time off from work to bring their children to a health clinic and care for them at home. To address these problems, some infants and toddlers with frequent ear infections may have tiny plastic ventilation tubes surgically inserted through the eardrum to allow fluid to drain and reduce the likelihood of subsequent ear infections. The tubes often fall out after about one year but sometimes need to be surgically removed. Parents can help reduce the number of ear infections their baby experiences by making sure they are not exposed to tobacco smoke in the home or at childcare. Besides ear infections, secondhand smoke is associated with a higher rate of sore throats, sinus infections, colds, respiratory infections, asthma, and sudden infant death syndrome (Lieu & Feinstein, 2002; Richter & Richter, 2001).

Ear infections are sometimes suspected when babies begin teething, typically between 5 and 9 months of age. As new teeth push their way through, the gums become swollen and red. Some infants temporarily change their nursing behavior, cry more, and have difficulty sleeping. In previous centuries, teething was believed to be potentially fatal (Fontanel & d'Harcourt, 1997). Even today, many parents believe that teething causes fevers and other illnesses. These other problems are unrelated to teething, but the coincidental timing makes it tempting to assume that there is a causal relationship (Macknin et al., 2000).

Infants' first teeth typically erupt between the ages of 5 and 9 months, contributing to a gradual transformation from "baby" to "child."

A more serious problem is premature loss of primary teeth due to decay—the most common chronic disease of childhood, especially among lower-income children whose families do not have dental insurance or who are unaware of the importance of preventing oral diseases (Mouradian, Wehr, & Crall, 2000). Given the clear links between oral health and overall health throughout the lifespan, following oral health practices beginning in infancy can make a difference (Satcher, 2000). As soon as the first tooth erupts, parents should use a soft cloth or baby toothbrush to keep it clean. After the age of 2 years, a pea-sized amount of fluoridated children's toothpaste may be used. Some infants have primary teeth pulled as a result of early decay, but this can usually be prevented by making sure they do not take bottles of milk, formula, or juice to bed during a nap or at night (the liquid pools around the baby's teeth and leads to baby-bottle caries) (Lott, 2002).

Accidental Injuries

Every 1.5 minutes, an infant under the age of 12 months is seen in an emergency room for treatment of a nonfatal accidental injury (Mack, Gilchrist, & Ballesteros, 2008). Many unintentional injuries in childhood can be prevented through education, changes in the environment or in products, and legislation or regulation (The Future of Children, 2000). Knowledge of child development can also help parents and other caregivers recognize and prepare for risks at each age and stage.

Unintentional injuries are the major reason for death among infants and young children, with the most common causes being suffocation, motor vehicle accidents, fire, drowning, and choking (Overpeck et al., 1999). Many accident-related deaths can be prevented by using properly installed child car seats, as required by law in all 50 states (Winston et al., 2004). Deaths due to fire can be prevented through adult supervision and by never allowing children to play with matches, lighters, or lighted candles. Open flames should be kept out of children's reach, and sleepwear should be flame-retardant.

Drowning and near-drowning are significant problems, especially in states where there are many pools or bodies of water (Hwang et al., 2003). Children should always be supervised in these situations, and pools should be fenced in with childproof locks on gates. Contrary to some popular beliefs, providing children younger than 4 years of age with swimming lessons does not appear to increase the risk of drowning and may offer some protection, although it does not eliminate the need for adult supervision (Brenner et al., 2009; Yang et al., 2007). Infants should never be left alone in a bathtub. Those who are able to sit upright in a bath chair may slip through the harness into the water, and even babies who sit well on their own may lose their balance and be unable to right themselves (American Academy of Pediatrics Committee on Injury and Poison Prevention, 1993).

As babies and toddlers develop and gain new skills, parents need to be aware of and anticipate new hazards (Mack et al., 2008). The ability to use a pincer grip to pick up tiny objects, such as pieces of dry cereal, between thumb and finger develops in most infants between 8 and 10 months of age. Infants of this age learn through oral exploration, so objects that are picked up usually are carried to the mouth, enabling infants to experience the joy of feeding themselves. Infants' windpipes are quite narrow (any object that fits inside a circle 1.7 inches or 4.3 cm in diameter should be considered a choking hazard), however, so parents need to ensure that pieces of food are small enough to be swallowed without blocking the child's airway or causing him or her to choke (e.g., grapes should be cut into two to four pieces). Given that infants use their new manipulative skills to learn about the world beyond their high chair, parents also need to be vigilant about picking up small objects—including older siblings' toys.

Baby walkers (wheeled devices that hold pre-walking infants upright with their feet in contact with the floor) have been the cause of serious injuries, most commonly sustained when the infant falls down the stairs in the apparatus. These falls are especially harmful because the walker's wheels accelerate the speed at which the infant falls. New standards for baby walkers, along with parent education, reduced the number of walker-related injuries in children under the age of 15 months, from 23,000 annually in the mid-1990s to 5,100 in 2001 (American Academy of Pediatrics Committee on Injury and Poison Prevention, 2001b; Brown, 2000; Shields & Smith, 2006). Design improvements have not prevented all walker-related accidents; some injuries occur when infants have access to hazards they would not otherwise be able to reach from a crawling or sitting position on the floor. After reviewing the scientific evidence, the Canadian government concluded that the risks outweighed the benefits and banned the sale of baby walkers in their country (Injury Data Analysis Leads to Baby Walker Ban, 2004).

The safest place for an infant or toddler inside a car or van is in a car seat that is properly installed in the back seat.

Prior to taking their first steps, babies who are not in walkers or other "containers" are able to move independently by rolling, crawling, and pulling themselves up to a standing position. Each of these milestones creates the need for parents to reevaluate the safety of the environment. Getting down on the floor can help parents and other caregivers see their home—including its potential hazards—from the child's perspective.

To prevent injuries due to falling, childproof safety gates should be installed at the top of stairs. Access to balconies, porches, and decks also needs to be controlled. Building codes throughout the United States require that all new construction include railings that are at least 36 inches high and spaced no more than 4 inches apart. In older homes, it is up to parents and caregivers to check to make sure that these features are present.

Falls from low heights, such as a low deck or even down a staircase, may cause injury but are almost never fatal (Mack et al., 2008). In fact, a large injury database in California suggests that the incidence is less than 1 death per 1 million children per year (Chadwick et al., 2008). The possibility of child abuse is always considered, therefore, in children with serious injuries from unwitnessed falls reportedly from low levels. Falls from heights of two stories or more, by contrast, are a life-threatening problem for children living in urban areas in older, multistory housing. Infants and young children are more likely than older children to fall from windows, and boys are more likely to fall than girls. Falls from windows tend to occur most in warm climates and in summer months, when windows are open in homes without air conditioning (Mack et al., 2008).

Prevention efforts include close supervision and modification of the environment. In addition to railings on balconies, decks, and porches, window guards can be installed on all windows. In cities where window guards are required by law, there have been sizable reductions in the number of injuries and fatalities caused by falls. In many other urban areas, window guards are not mandatory, which means that prevention efforts are the responsibility of parents and caregivers rather than landlords. Education about potential problems and solutions, such as moving the child's crib and other furniture away from windows, can increase awareness of ways to keep young children safe from falls at home (American Academy of Pediatrics Committee on Injury and Poison Prevention, 2001a).

Not all falls and injuries occur at home, of course, so parents need to think about safety in other settings where their child spends time. When evaluating play areas in public parks, for example, parents should look for soft rather than hard play surfaces underneath climbers and other playground equipment; distinct, age-appropriate play areas for older and younger children; and fences to separate play areas from bicycle and vehicle traffic.

Some parents may prefer not to think about the potential hazards facing their infants and toddlers. With a little effort, however, they can follow the three As—Assess the settings in which their children spend time, Anticipate potential problems, and Act to remove them. If they do, they can celebrate and support their children's development, knowing that they have created a safe environment for playing, eating, bathing, exploring, and, as we learn next, sleeping.

Sudden Infant Death Syndrome

The American Academy of Pediatrics (AAP) recommends that babies be placed on their back to sleep, due to the clear association between prone (facedown) stomach-sleeping and **sudden infant death syndrome (SIDS)**. SIDS, the leading cause of death in infants between 1 month and 1 year of age, is the diagnosis given when an infant younger than 1 year dies and a complete investigation is unable to identify a specific cause (Centers for Disease Control and Prevention, 2008). The AAP advises parents to avoid other identified risk factors for SIDS, particularly, soft bedding, bed-sharing, and exposure to secondhand cigarette smoke. Infants sleeping in an overheated room or wearing two or more layers of clothing while they sleep also have an increased risk of SIDS (American Academy of Pediatrics, 2000a; Malloy & Freeman, 2004; Task Force on Sudden Infant Death Syndrome, 2005). It is possible that pacifier use may reduce the risk of SIDS, but the evidence is correlational and not universally accepted (Hauck, Omojokun, & Siadaty, 2005; Task Force on Sudden Infant Death Syndrome, 2005; Vennemann et al., 2009a).

Infants sleeping in adult beds are approximately 20 times more likely to suffocate, compared with infants sleeping in cribs (Scheers, Rutherford, & Kemp, 2003). Bed-sharing among parents and infants in the United States increased from 5.5 percent in 1993 to 12.8 percent in 2000. It is especially prevalent (48 percent) among unmarried, low-income African American mothers living in urban areas (Brenner et al., 2003; Hauck et al., 2008; Shapiro-Mendoza et al., 2009; Willinger et al., 2003). Proponents of bed-sharing assert that it promotes breastfeeding (Chen & Rogan, 2004); opponents highlight the increased risk of suffocation, especially when it occurs along with maternal cigarette smoking, recent parental alcohol consumption, and parental exhaustion. The AAP advises parents to breastfeed infants because, in addition to other health benefits, it has been found to reduce the risk of SIDS by 50 percent (Vennemann et al., 2009b). When parents keep young infants close at night for breastfeeding, however, the AAP recommends providing a separate sleeping space (e.g., a bassinet or crib) in the same room (Hauck et al., 2008; Task Force on Sudden Infant Death Syndrome, 2005; Vennemann et al., 2009a).

The peak age for SIDS is between 2 and 4 months. Boys are more likely to be victims than are girls, and most deaths occur in the fall or winter, when infants are most likely to be dressed in multiple layers or covered with blankets and comforters. There is a higher incidence among infants whose mothers were less than 20 years old at the time of their first pregnancy as well as among infants whose mothers received late or no prenatal care (Iyasu et al., 2002; Phipps, Blume, & DeMonner, 2002). Preterm and low birthweight infants also have a higher risk for SIDS than full-term babies (Witcombe et al., 2008). Among African Americans and Native Americans, SIDS rates are two to three times higher than rates for white babies (Shapiro-Mendoza et al., 2009).

A public health campaign called Back to Sleep, launched by the National Institute of Child Health and Human Development (NICHD) in 1994, led to a significant reduction in the number of SIDS deaths, from about 6,000 each year to approximately 2,200 in the year 2004 as shown in Figure 5.6 (Heron, 2007; Kochanek et al., 2004). According to the National Infant Sleep Position Study (NISP), about 80 percent of parents surveyed in 1997 to 1998 said that they had received back-sleeping advice from a physician or nurse or had learned of the recommendation from reading materials or radio and television. Caregivers who said that they had received this advice from all sources were six times more likely to follow the recommendation (Willinger et al., 2000).

A study in Chicago, covering the years from 1993 to 1996, found that a higher percentage of African American babies were placed on their stomach to sleep than were babies from all other ethnic and racial groups included in the study (43% versus 12%). The study also found that African American parents were less likely than white parents to have been told by healthcare providers to avoid placing babies on their stomach to sleep, a difference that may help explain why 75 percent of SIDS cases were African American, whereas only 13 percent were white Hispanic and 12 percent non-Hispanic white (Hauck et al., 2002). In response to these trends, the National Black Child Development Institute joined forces with NICHD and other organizations

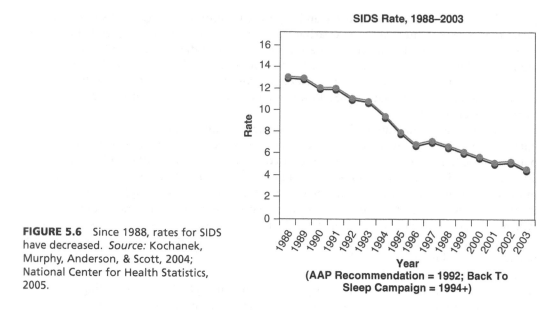

FIGURE 5.6 Since 1988, rates for SIDS have decreased. *Source:* Kochanek, Murphy, Anderson, & Scott, 2004; National Center for Health Statistics, 2005.

to spread the important Back to Sleep message and help all parents and caregivers become aware of the power they have to prevent SIDS (see Table 5.2).

It is vital that nonparental caregivers place babies in the familiar back-sleeping position because cases of SIDS have occurred in childcare settings when infants were placed in the unfamiliar prone position (Moon, Calabrese, & Aird, 2008; Moon, Kotch, & Aird, 2006; Moon, Patel, & Shaefer, 2000; Vennemann et al., 2009a). The importance of discussing safe sleeping practices

---

TABLE 5.2 Recommendations to Reduce the Risk of SIDS

Place infants on their backs every time they go to sleep.

Use a firm sleep surface and do not place soft materials or objects under a sleeping infant.

Keep soft materials or objects such as pillows, quilts, comforters, sheepskins, and stuffed toys out of the infant's crib.

Do not smoke during pregnancy and avoid exposing infants to secondhand smoke.

Avoid bed-sharing but provide a crib or other separate sleeping environment in the same room as the parents.

Consider using a pacifier at nap time and bedtime.

Avoid overheating by dressing infants lightly for sleeping and keeping the bedroom temperature comfortable.

Avoid commercial devices that claim to reduce the risk of SIDS.

Do not use home monitors as a strategy for reducing the risk of SIDS in otherwise healthy infants.

Minimize positional plagiocephaly (flattening of the back of the head) by encouraging "tummy time" when infants are awake and being observed by a caregiver.

Support the Back to Sleep campaign and share these recommendations with all caregivers of infants, including child care providers, grandparents, foster parents, and babysitters.

Source: Based on Task Force on Sudden Infant Death Syndrome, 2005.

when childcare arrangements are first being made is highlighted by the finding that approximately 30 percent of SIDS-related deaths in childcare occurred in the first week, with half of those deaths occurring on the first day (Mitchell et al., 1999).

We know more than ever about specific actions to take and practices to avoid, but even the best outreach programs and the most conscientious caregiving are unlikely to prevent all SIDS deaths. This is because some cases may be linked to conditions that are beyond the control of parents. For some infants, the problem may be a brain abnormality, such as a defect in a portion of the brain involved in controlling breathing and waking during sleep (Kinney et al., 2003). These abnormalities alone probably do not cause SIDS, but they may make infants with the defects less able to cope with a lack of oxygen and elevated levels of carbon dioxide, possible outcomes of respiratory infections or rebreathing air that is trapped in soft bedding during stomach-sleeping. Other SIDS deaths may be the result of genetic predispositions to underlying metabolic disorders that disrupt breathing and heart functioning (Opdal & Rognum, 2004).

NUTRITION AND FEEDING

In some cultures, infants are fed traditional herbal preparations or prechewed solid foods almost from birth, whereas in other cultures, breast milk is the only food given until the infant is several months old. Cultures differ in whether they value the mother's first milk for its unique health-giving properties or discard it because it is regarded as undigestible or even harmful to the infant. There are also differences in beliefs about whether infants should be fed whenever they show signs of hunger or according to a set schedule (DeLoache & Gottlieb, 2000; Fjeld et al., 2008). When caregivers from older generations disagree with parents, or when cultural traditions and beliefs differ from current research-based recommendations, it may not be easy for parents to determine which practices to follow.

Nutritional Requirements in Infancy

Infants require the greatest amount of energy per pound of body weight, and children under the age of 2 years need more fat in their diets than any other age group. In addition, because infants' brains, bones, and other body structures and systems are developing rapidly, malnutrition in infancy or early childhood has different—and more damaging—effects than malnutrition at other points in the life span (Napier & Meister, 2000; Pollitt et al., 1993).

The typical newborn wakes up 10 to 12 times during every 24-hour period, ready to be fed. Regular feeding is so important during the first two weeks that babies should usually be awakened for feeding if they sleep more than four hours at a time. After a feeding and diaper change, most newborns fall back to sleep. As infants begin to spend more time in a quiet alert state in the first weeks and months after birth, however, parents no longer need to assume that time awake should be used primarily for feeding. Instead, they can learn to read their infant's cues for signs of hunger, such as bringing hands to the mouth, rooting or pressing the face against the adult's body, and facial grimacing. Feeding is likely to proceed more smoothly if parents can feed their infant when these signs appear, before fussing and crying—the last indicators of hunger—begin (American Academy of Pediatrics/Work Group on Breastfeeding, 1997; National Center for Education in Maternal and Child Health, 2002).

Babies also show signs of fullness, if parents know what to look for: turning their head away from the nipple, closing their mouth, and showing interest in things other than eating (National Center for Education in Maternal and Child Health, 2002). Experts advise against coaxing infants to finish a bottle, since this behavior may set up a pattern of overfeeding and unhealthy weight gain that could predispose the child to overweight or obesity (Napier & Meister, 2000; Taveras et al., 2004). Parents can feel confident about their infant's milk consumption as long as the baby is swallowing, producing between six and eight wet diapers daily, and gaining weight (National Center for Education in Maternal and Child Health, 2002).

During the first year of life, infants require the same nutrients that are part of a healthy diet for older children and adults—energy, protein, calcium, iron, vitamins, and micronutrients. Until the age of about 4 to 6 months, they can get all of these requirements through breast milk or infant formula. In fact, because newborns have a gag reflex that causes them to push solids out of their mouth with their tongue, and do not develop the ability to chew and swallow until the second half of the first year, a liquid diet is ideal (Napier & Meister, 2000).

Breast Milk

Human milk is the preferred form of feeding for infants, even those who are preterm or ill, because it fulfills their nutritional needs, just as the milk of all other mammals is ideally suited to meet the nutritional needs of their offspring (Furman et al., 2003). Cow's milk, evaporated milk, or any substitutes other than commercially made infant formula are not easily digested and may cause health problems.

Nursing should begin as soon as possible after birth. The first milk, **colostrum,** is a thick, yellowish fluid, richer in protein and protective antibodies than the milk that is produced a few days later. Both colostrum and breast milk contain disease-preventing proteins—lactoferrin and lysozyme—that help fight bacteria and promote growth and maturation of the intestinal tract (Napier & Meister, 2000).

Human milk reduces the risk of many diseases and lowers the risk and severity of diarrhea and infections of the lower respiratory system, middle ear, and urinary tract. Breastfeeding may also protect infants against SIDS, diabetes, allergies, asthma, digestive diseases, and high

Mother's milk contains disease-preventing substances and is the most natural and least expensive way to provide nourishment for human infants.

cholesterol levels in adolescence (Chen & Rogan, 2004; Horta et al., 2007; Owen et al., 2002; Singhal et al., 2004). Breast milk contains two hormones, leptin and adiponectin, that help regulate appetite and metabolism; this may be one reason babies who are breastfed tend to have lower levels of childhood obesity (Horta et al., 2007; Li, Fein, & Grummer-Strawn, 2008).

Studies in countries where mothers breastfeed their infants for longer durations than most U.S. mothers suggest that breastfeeding may enhance cognitive development. Researchers in Denmark found an association between duration of infant breastfeeding and intelligence in young adulthood (Mortensen et al., 2002). Norwegian and Swedish researchers reported that full-term, small-for-gestational-age (SGA) infants (those weighing 6 pounds or less) scored an average of 11 points higher on IQ tests if they were exclusively breastfed for the first six months, in comparison to SGA infants who were fed formula or solid food before the age of 6 months (Rao et al., 2002). Studies of normal-size, full-term infants have reported similar trends, although the IQ advantage for breastfed infants at 5 years of age may be relatively small (Horta et al., 2007). Given that these studies are correlational, it is possible that other differences between Nordic countries and the United States also contributed to the findings.

Mothers benefit from breastfeeding, both during the postpartum period and across their adult years. In the hours and days following birth, breastfeeding triggers the release of the hormone oxytocin, which helps the uterus return to its original size and reduces postpartum bleeding. Breast-feeding burns up approximately 500 calories per day, helping new mothers return more quickly to their pre-pregnancy weight. Other apparent benefits for nursing mothers include a reduction in hip fractures in the postmenopausal period, and a reduced risk of other health problems, including hypertension, cardiovascular disease, ovarian cancer, premenopausal breast cancer, and rheumatoid arthritis (Pikwer et al., 2009; Schwarz et al., 2009).

Ideally, infants should be breastfed exclusively for the first six months after birth. If this is not possible, pediatricians advise mothers to breastfeed as long as they can in order to maximize health benefits for both infant and mother. The AAP recommends that infants who are weaned from breast milk before the age of 12 months be switched to a commercially prepared infant formula, with cow's milk given after the age of 1 year (American Academy of Pediatrics/Work Group on Breastfeeding, 1997; Hatsu, McDougald, & Anderson, 2008).

In the United States, the popularity of breastfeeding declined during the twentieth century until about 1970; rates then fluctuated during the 1980s and 1990s before increasing again (Wright & Schanler, 2001). A national survey in 2005 found that approximately 73 percent of new mothers had ever breastfed at the time of hospital discharge. Only 39 percent of infants were still being breastfed at 6 months, however, and only 20 percent until 1 year (Centers for Disease Control & Prevention, 2005b). Although initial breastfeeding rates have moved closer to the target of 75 percent set by the Healthy People 2010 initiative, they fall short of the goal of having at least 50 percent of mothers continuing to breastfeed for five to six months and 25 percent for 1 year (U.S. Department of Health and Human Services, 2000a). White and Latina women breast-feed at higher rates than African American women, and the highest rates of breastfeeding in the United States are found among higher-income, college-educated women who are at least 30 years of age. Women in this demographic group initiate breastfeeding at rates of more than 80 percent, with nearly 65 percent continuing to breastfeed for three months (Grummer-Strawn et al., 2006; National Center for Health Statistics, 2009; Ryan, Zhou, & Acosta, 2002).

Educating young, low-income mothers about the benefits of breastfeeding is both important and challenging (Grummer-Strawn et al., 2006; Guise et al., 2003). A study of participants in the nationwide Women, Infants, and Children Supplemental Nutrition Program (WIC) in 2002–2003 found that 47 percent of WIC mothers younger than 20 years of age initiated breastfeeding in the hospital (as compared with 57% of WIC mothers between 30 and 34 years of age), and only 14 percent were still breastfeeding after six months (as compared with 27% of 30- to 34-year-olds) (Ryan & Zhou, 2006). If these younger women were similar to their counterparts in a previous WIC study, many of them may have stopped breastfeeding as soon as 19 days after their infant's birth (Baydar et al., 1997).

Given that human milk is the ideal form of nutrition for infants, why do some mothers choose not to breastfeed? Studies of WIC participants, who breastfeed at lower rates and for a shorter period of time at all ages, suggest that one important factor may be the program's practice of giving infant formula to all breastfeeding mothers within two weeks of their child's birth and providing them with food supplies that many women regard as less desirable than the food given to mothers using infant formula (Holmes et al., 2009).

In some cases, the benefits of breastfeeding are outweighed by the risk that the infant might contract an infectious disease that the mother carries, such as HIV, herpes simplex virus type 1, or West Nile virus (Centers for Disease Control & Prevention, 2002d; Miotti et al., 1999; World Health Organization and UNICEF, 2009). In the United States and other developed countries, mothers with HIV are advised to give their babies formula rather than breast milk. In sub-Saharan Africa and other developing countries, by contrast, women who are HIV-infected have fewer clear alternatives, making breastfeeding their main option. It is encouraging, therefore, that researchers in Zambia recently found that rates of HIV infection were similar for infants whose HIV-positive mothers had stopped breastfeeding early (by 5 months) and for those whose mothers continued breastfeeding as long as 12 months. These findings mean that most HIV-positive mothers in these settings can continue to breastfeed (avoiding contamination that might occur by adding unsanitary water to powdered formula), giving their babies the known benefits and health-promoting antibodies in breast milk (Kuhn et al., 2008). At the same time, researchers are continuing to search for new combinations and doses of drugs that might lessen the risk of transmitting HIV through breastfeeding (Kumwenda et al., 2008).

Women taking certain kinds of medication should usually avoid breastfeeding, at least temporarily. These medications include drugs that may cause side effects such as drowsiness and altered breathing, certain forms of iodine, and chemotherapy (World Health Organization and UNICEF, 2009).

Some women get discouraged and switch to formula within weeks or even days of their child's birth when they have more difficulty establishing breastfeeding than they had anticipated, an experience that may be magnified and overrepresented in media reports about breastfeeding (Brown & Peuchaud, 2008). Mothers who combine formula with breast milk have a high likelihood of discontinuing breastfeeding when they notice their milk supply beginning to decrease. They may lose confidence in their ability to sustain the infant on their own, despite the fact that the mother's body responds readily to the infant's needs (Li et al., 2008; Shealy et al., 2008). If several feedings each day use formula in place of breast milk, the milk supply decreases but will usually increase again if the mother nurses her child more frequently.

Women who are overweight or obese tend to breastfeed at lower rates than other women, in part because their bodies respond more slowly to the effects of suckling. They are more likely than other women to have prolonged labors and cesarean births, which also delay the initiation of lactation and may make it more difficult to establish breastfeeding. Given that African American women have the highest rates of obesity in the United States, this is a problem that affects their infants more than the infants of Hispanic and white women (Jevitt, Hernandez, & Groër, 2007; Mok et al., 2008). Many hospitals employ lactation consultants who can educate all new mothers in the hours after their baby is born, addressing a wide range of initial concerns as well as providing assistance later as questions arise, such as how to continue breastfeeding after returning to work (Guise et al., 2003).

In Denmark, Norway, and Sweden, as well as in Australia and many other countries in which new mothers have paid, job-protected maternity leaves during part or all of their child's first year of life, breastfeeding initiation rates are high (94 percent or more). In general, women with longer leaves from work tend to continue breastfeeding longer, with as many as 20 percent of mothers still engaging in breastfeeding until their baby is 12 months old (Ekström, Widström, & Nissen, 2003; Lande et al., 2003; Michaelsen et al., 1994; Scott et al., 2006).

Women without such generous maternity leaves can still provide breast milk for their baby when they return to work. Effective strategies include having on-site childcare, telecommuting (working from a home office, with the infant nearby), keeping the infant at work, allowing the mother to leave work to go to the infant, or having the infant brought to the work site (Fein, Mandal, & Roe, 2008). If these arrangements are not possible, a breast pump can be used at work to express milk for other caregivers to give to the baby. Employees who are supported in continuing to breastfeed are less likely to miss work, in part because their infants are less likely to become ill (Cohen, Mrtek, & Mrtek, 1995).

Away from work, people who are not well informed about the value of breastfeeding for at least six months may question or actively discourage women who continue nursing rather than switch to formula and bottle-feeding. Some mothers nursing in public have even been charged with indecent exposure. To ensure that a woman's right to breastfeed is not infringed upon, most states have passed legislation to clarify the differences between indecent exposure and breastfeeding (Baldwin, 2001; Vance, 2006).

The WHO has studied breastfeeding rates and practices in many countries around the world. In regions where water is unsanitary and other hygiene risks exist, it is usually safer for mothers to breastfeed their infants than to use bottles and formula. According to the WHO (2000) Global Data Bank on Breastfeeding, however, only 35 percent of infants worldwide are exclusively breastfed until 4 months of age. Mothers who initiate breastfeeding within the first hour after birth are more likely to establish and continue nursing, but this practice occurs at low frequencies in many Eastern European (17%) and Central Asian (17%) countries, as well as in many parts of South Asia (25%) and Asian-Pacific regions (33%) (Jana, 2009).

The Baby-Friendly Hospital Initiative (outlined in Table 5.3) and other health education campaigns have increased breastfeeding rates and duration, suggesting that further increases are possible (Abolyan, 2006; Kramer, Chalmers, et al., 2001; World Health Organization/United Nations Children's Fund, 1989). More than 16,000 Baby-Friendly hospitals have been designated in nearly 200 countries (83 existed in the United States as of July 2009) (BFHI USA, 2009). The more elements of Baby-Friendly practice that women experience while still in the hospital, the more likely they are to continue breastfeeding after they are discharged (DiGirolamo, Grummer-Strawn, & Fein, 2008; Merewood et al., 2005; Merten, Dratva, & Ackermann-Liebrich, 2005; Nyqvist & Kylberg, 2008).

Infant Formula

The same feelings of warmth and physical closeness that are experienced through breastfeeding can be approximated by holding infants being fed with formula rather than propping up the bottle. Close contact also makes it easier to pay attention and respond to the infant's signals.

Infant formula available today is the best alternative to breast milk that has ever existed. Parents who choose to give their babies formula can feel confident that no other substance

TABLE 5.3	Practice Guidelines in Baby-Friendly Hospitals

Have a written breastfeeding policy that is routinely communicated to all healthcare staff.

Train all healthcare staff in skills necessary to implement this policy.

Inform all pregnant women about the benefits and management of breastfeeding.

Help mothers initiate breastfeeding within one hour of birth.

Show mothers how to breastfeed and how to maintain lactation, even if they should be separated from their infants.

Give newborn infants no food or drink other than breast milk unless medically indicated.

Practice "rooming in" by allowing mothers and infants to remain together.

Encourage breastfeeding on demand.

Give no artificial teats, pacifiers, or soothers to breastfeeding infants.

Foster the establishment of breastfeeding support groups and refer mothers to them on discharge from the hospital or clinic.

Source: World Health Organization/United Nations Children's Fund, 1989.

would be safer or healthier, in part because infant formula is monitored and regulated by the U.S. Food and Drug Administration (Birch et al., 2000). Ensuring that infant formula remains safe and healthy after purchase is up to parents. A national study of nearly 1,500 mothers' feeding practices from birth to 1 year raised questions about parents' ability to fulfill this important responsibility, given that the majority of mothers said they had not been instructed about how to handle formula safely. Between 30 percent and 55 percent of the sample reported following unsafe practices, such as not always washing their hands with soap before preparing formula, failing to adequately wash bottle nipples between feedings, and using a microwave to heat formula in bottles. A small percentage (6%) stated that they did not always discard left-over formula, even if more than two hours had passed since it had been prepared and first used. These findings suggest that more parent education may be necessary (Labiner-Wolfe, Fein, & Shealy, 2008).

Most infant formula is made from modified cow's milk, but there are also soy-based alternatives available. Parents who are vegetarians may choose a soy-based formula for its compatibility with a non–animal-based diet (Bhatia, Greer, & Committee on Nutrition, 2008). In addition, although there is little evidence of its protective value, some parents switch to a soy-based product because they believe their infant is allergic to other types of formula, even if a pediatrician has not been consulted to diagnose the allergy (Greer et al., 2008; Luccioli et al., 2008). Regardless of the base, infant formula should be enriched with iron to ensure that babies do not become iron deficient (American Academy of Pediatrics Committee on Nutrition, 1999; Napier & Meister, 2000).

The end of exclusive breastfeeding or formula-feeding marks the beginning of **complementary feeding,** a gradual transition that the AAP recommends parents not initiate until the baby is 4 to 6 months of age. In the United States, the first solid food is often iron-fortified baby cereal, made from rice or another single grain and mixed with breast milk or formula. At first, the consistency is quite thin; as they get older, and their digestive systems become more mature, infants can tolerate increasingly thicker cereal and other pureed foods (National Center for Education in Maternal and Child Health, 2002). Despite the AAP recommendation, the Feeding Infants and Toddlers Study (FITS, a cross-sectional survey of parents of 2,900 U.S. children aged 4 to 24 months) found that solid food had been introduced to 40 percent of the babies before the age of 4 months. Infants who were fed solid foods earlier were twice as likely to have discontinued breastfeeding by 6 months and to have been fed fatty or sugary foods, such as sweet drinks, french fries, candy, cookies, and cake, at 12 months. These patterns are problematic because they introduce unhealthy food choices at an early age, while also reducing the amount of immunity-boosting breast milk babies consume (Grummer-Strawn, Scanlon, & Fein, 2008).

Ideally, infant cereal is followed by simple, single-ingredient foods, such as pureed fruits and vegetables. Pureed meats are a good source of iron at this age. By choosing fruits and vegetables that are rich in vitamin C, parents can help their infant's body absorb the iron in their diet. It is not necessary to sweeten or otherwise season these foods in order to make them more enticing. Many foods need to have multiple introductions, perhaps as many as 15 to 20, before infants accept them (National Center for Education in Maternal and Child Health, 2002).

Foods that may cause an allergic reaction are wheat, eggs, nuts, and citrus fruits. By introducing one new food at a time, parents can determine whether their infant is allergic to it, but delaying the introduction of these foods will not protect babies from developing allergic reactions to them (Greer et al., 2008).

The balance between breast milk or formula and solid foods begins to shift toward solid foods after the age of 6 months. A small amount of fruit juice can be offered, but breast milk or formula should still be the main sources of liquid food. To provide sufficient energy, snacks should be given in midmorning and afternoon (National Center for Education in Maternal and Child Health, 2002).

In the second half of the first year, babies can tolerate thicker foods and foods containing a mixture of ingredients. They often begin to participate more actively in feeding by reaching for the spoon, and they show interest in the food being eaten by the rest of the family. To enhance the infant's social and language development, meals should be relaxing occasions in which parents and other family members enjoy food and conversation together. Unless the main meal is very spicy or presents choking hazards, small pieces of each dish should be shared with the infant. As fine motor skills and hand-eye coordination improve, small pieces of soft finger foods can be given to infants to encourage self-feeding. Foods to be avoided for their choking potential include nuts, hot dogs, raisins, raw carrots, whole grapes, popcorn, and peanut butter or any other thick, sticky foods. Honey may contain harmful bacteria and should not be given to infants before the age of 1 year (Fox et al., 2004; Napier & Meister, 2000).

Nutritional Requirements in Toddlerhood

During the second year of life, growth slows down, but toddlers still need energy to support their increasing levels of activity. Toddlers can feed themselves with increasing success, brought about by improvements in fine motor skills and the appearance of more teeth. Toddlers have smaller and less consistent appetites than infants, which some parents find worrisome. Parents can be assured, though, as long as a healthy variety of foods are offered, and provided that the child continues to grow, gain weight, and develop normally. Nutrition experts suggest that 1- to 2-year-olds be given serving sizes of approximately 1 tablespoon for each year of age (Fox et al., 2004; Napier & Meister, 2000).

Children ages 2 to 3 years generally have healthier diets than children between the ages of 4 and 9 years, and only 4 percent have a diet that the USDA Healthy Eating Index (HEI) would rate as poor. Even so, only 36 percent of 2- to 3-year-olds consume a diet that is considered good according to the HEI, and the majority (60 percent) have a diet that needs improvement. According to another dietary "report card," the percentage of 2- to 3-year-olds consuming

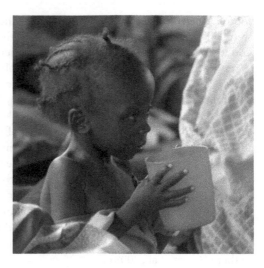

This young girl, suffering from malnutrition, is receiving medical treatment in a refugee camp in Darfur.

recommended amounts of each of the major food groups—grains, vegetables, fruit, milk, meat, and total fat—is too low (Carlson et al., 2001; Fox et al., 2004).

The nutrients that are most frequently missing from U.S. toddlers' diets at the recommended daily levels are iron, zinc, and calcium. Unless iron deficiencies are severe and exacerbated by other illnesses, they can be addressed by giving toddlers more iron-rich foods, including meat, and combining them with foods that are rich in vitamin C (Dee et al. 2008).

Meat is also a good source of zinc, as are dairy products, eggs, and whole-grain cereals. Without adequate amounts of zinc, the immune system does not function properly and growth may be delayed. Zinc deficiencies also cause impairments in attention and learning (Hubbs-Tait et al., 2005; Rao & Georgieff, 2000).

As many as one-third of U.S. toddlers fail to consume enough calcium (Fox et al., 2004; Napier & Meister, 2000). Children who drink too much juice or other beverages rather than milk are at greatest risk of not having adequate calcium intake. Calcium is essential for the development of healthy bones, skin, and teeth. Besides milk, other good sources of dietary calcium are dairy products such as yogurt and cheese, broccoli, tofu, and dried beans and peas. These foods are especially important for children with problems digesting milk, due to lactose intolerance (Greer, Krebs, & Committee on Nutrition, 2006).

Some children grow up in a family that, for cultural, religious, ethical, or health reasons, follows a vegetarian diet. Although it is difficult to generalize across the range of vegetarian diets, existing evidence indicates that children's nutritional needs can be met if parents are knowledgeable about healthful combinations of foods and give their children vitamin and mineral supplements, if they are needed (O'Connell et al., 1989).

The Problem of Malnutrition

Throughout this chapter, we have noted that overweight and obesity are health problems affecting an increasing number of young children in the United States. Worldwide, however, many more children (perhaps as many as 40 percent of those under the age of 5 years) suffer from problems related to an insufficient amount of food or an inadequate intake of essential nutrients (World Health Organization, 2002b). Many children first become malnourished as they make the transition to complementary feeding. For infants whose mothers do not have access to a healthy diet during their pregnancy, malnutrition is part of their lives even before birth.

Researchers working with rodents and other animal models are beginning to learn more about the effects of isolated nutrient deficiencies (deUngria et al., 2000; Hubbs-Tait et al., 2005; Johnson, 2005; Rao & Georgieff, 2000). The timing of deprivation or supplementation of nutrients affects the influence of those substances on the developing brain. In addition, whereas the very same micronutrients promote normal development at recommended levels, higher levels often produce toxic effects (Hubbs-Tait et al., 2005; Rao & Georgieff, 2000). As informative as these findings are, as we consider some of the major problems of malnutrition affecting infants and young children, we should remember that nutrient deficiencies rarely occur in isolation. Instead, they are usually compounded by environmental hazards and stressors such as poverty, poor prenatal care, and nonoptimal caregiving (Hubbs-Tait et al., 2005).

The most common form of malnutrition, **protein-energy malnutrition (PEM),** affects children who do not consume enough protein and calories. Children with PEM are susceptible to marasmus (a wasting disease in which fat and muscle are depleted) and kwashiorkor (a disease that occurs in response to a sudden deprivation of food, marked by apathy and swelling of the extremities, torso, and face). According to the WHO (2002b), PEM is responsible for half of all child deaths and affects approximately 25 percent of children worldwide. The majority of children suffering from PEM live in Asia and Africa.

Infants and young children are more susceptible to PEM-caused growth impairment than are older children because of their high energy and protein needs and their vulnerability to infection. Infants who experience PEM have reduced IQ scores and lower verbal and spatial abilities (Rao & Georgieff, 2000). Nutritional supplementation appears to reverse some of the cognitive impairments associated with PEM, with some benefits lasting several years after supplementation (Pollitt et al., 1993, 1996).

To be healthy, all humans need enough protein and calories, as well as a number of micronutrients, such as vitamins, iron, and zinc. The effects of **micronutrient deficiencies** on the brain and body include damage to cell structure and impairment in cell metabolism that affects fundamental processes such as DNA and RNA synthesis, myelination, and neurotransmission (Johnson, 2005; Rao & Gerogieff, 2000). Two particularly serious forms of malnutrition are deficiencies of the micronutrients iron and vitamin A.

Worldwide, iron deficiency is the most common nutritional disorder after PEM. Iron deficiency anemia affects as many as 40 percent of children under age 5 around the world, mostly in developing countries. In many developing countries, the effects of iron deficiency anemia are magnified by malaria and worm infections that lead to blood loss (World Health Organization, 2002b). Iron-deficiency anemia causes fatigue, restlessness, irritability, and a poor attention span—problems that contribute to delays and abnormalities in cognitive and social development. It also interferes with the development of motor skills, such as standing and walking (Hubbs-Tait et al., 2005; Napier & Meister, 2000; Rao & Georgieff, 2000, 2001). Although the effects in developed countries are rarely as severe as those seen in developing countries, approximately one-fourth of breastfed babies have no supplemental iron source at 6 months, and nearly three-fourths receive fewer iron-rich foods or iron supplements than recommended (Dee et al., 2008).

Children with vitamin A deficiencies develop severe visual impairment and blindness as well as life-threatening illnesses and infections (Rao & Georgieff, 2000). Because breast milk is a natural source of vitamin A, one of the best ways to combat a deficiency is through breastfeeding. Doses of vitamin A can also be given to children in liquid or capsule form (Klemm et al., 2008). Given that the effects last only four to six months, the best approach is to promote and provide a diet that is rich in vitamin A foods, such as carrots, sweet potatoes, and fruit (World Health Organization, 2001b).

The human body, specifically, our skin, is able to make vitamin D after exposure to UV-B light outdoors. Concerns about links between UV exposure and skin cancer, however, have reduced the amount of time that many people, including children, spend outdoors, and parents are advised not to expose babies to direct sunlight before the age of 6 months (American Academy of Pediatrics Committee on Environmental Health, 1999). Deficiencies of vitamin D may lead to rickets, a serious disorder in which the bones lose calcium and become soft and weak, causing skeletal deformities that are often irreversible. The peak incidence for rickets is between 3 and 18 months, but it can be prevented by giving infants a daily vitamin D supplement, beginning at birth; this is especially critical for breastfed babies, since infant formula is fortified with vitamin D. Many dairy products contain vitamin D, so separate supplements are not usually needed once children begin drinking cow's milk, eating yogurt, and consuming other foods, such as certain types of fatty fish, that are natural sources of vitamin D (Wagner, Greer, & the Section on Breastfeeding and Committee on Nutrition, 2008).

In the United States, the federally funded WIC nutrition program promotes the health and nutritional status of low-income women, infants, and children by offering supplemental nutritious foods as well as nutrition education and counseling. Studies of WIC outcomes since the program's inception in 1974 indicate that pregnant women who participate have longer, healthier pregnancies, fewer preterm births, and fewer infant deaths, but lower rates of breastfeeding. Children participating in WIC programs have better diets overall, however, as well as a higher intake of iron and other key nutrients, than comparable nonparticipants (U.S. Department of Agriculture, 2002).

In other parts of the world, programs to end malnutrition are administered by a variety of governmental and nongovernmental organizations, including UNICEF and WHO. The greatest needs are in countries suffering from food shortages or famine due to emergencies, war, or agricultural problems caused by extreme drought or flooding. In addition to working to ensure that there is enough healthy food available, successful childhood malnutrition programs focus on supporting prenatal nutrition, promoting breastfeeding, and educating parents about appropriate nutrition for infants and children. The problems are daunting, but community-based interventions in many parts of the world have proven effective at reducing malnutrition (Pollitt et al., 1996; Santos et al., 2001; World Health Organization, 2001b). These aid efforts are critical because, as we have seen in this chapter, developing infants and young children cannot wait.

Setting infants on a course for healthy development begins with experiences during the prenatal period and continues when the caregiving environment is nurturing and safe. In our next chapter, we see that infants also benefit from an environment that stimulates all of their senses and allows them to explore freely.

WRAPPING IT UP: Summary and Conclusion

Growth during the first three years is faster than at any other point after birth. Infants whose nutritional intake is inadequate, as well as those who are deprived of caring physical contact, tend to grow slowly and fail to thrive. Dietary and caregiving interventions often reverse these problems, giving babies and toddlers a chance for rapid "catch-up" growth.

Postnatal brain growth primarily consists of the interconnection of neurons and the formation of synapses. Pruning of synapses begins at the end of the first year and helps make the child's brain work more efficiently and quickly. Experience activates neurons, and repeated experiences strengthen neural networks. Experiments using animal models and studies of maltreated children suggest that early adversity, stress, and deprivation leave their mark on the developing brain.

Mandatory newborn health screening exists nationwide for three conditions and for congenital hearing problems; states vary in the number of additional diseases included in newborn screening. The effects of lead poisoning are cumulative and may result in brain damage, behavior problems, learning disabilities, seizures, and even death.

As with many environmental influences on health, infant mortality rates in the United States vary by race and ethnicity. Globally, infant mortality is linked to poverty, inadequate prenatal care, complications of pregnancy, malnutrition, lack of clean drinking water, and low rates of immunization against childhood illnesses and diseases. The major causes of early childhood death in the United States are from unintentional injuries, many of which are preventable.

Sudden infant death syndrome (SIDS) is the leading cause of death in infants before the age of 1 year. The risk of SIDS can be reduced by placing babies on their back to sleep and by avoiding the use of soft bedding. Other environmental risks have been identified, but some cases of SIDS may be linked to an abnormality in the portion of the brain involved in controlling breathing and waking during sleep.

Until the age of about 4 to 6 months, infants' nutritional requirements can be provided through breast milk or formula. Overweight and obesity are growing concerns in the United States. Worldwide, however, infants and young children are more likely to suffer from problems related to an insufficient amount of food or essential nutrients due to a diet low in protein and calorie content.

THINK ABOUT IT: Questions for Reading and Discussion

1. How does experience shape the postnatal development of the brain?
2. What do you think is the most significant reason for the decline in infant mortality rates in the United States and other developed countries?
3. What would you need to do to make your own home, apartment, or dormitory room safe for an infant? What would you have to do to make it safe for a toddler or preschooler? Which age do you believe faces the greatest risk from accidental injuries? Explain.
4. What instructions should parents give their infant's caregivers to prevent shaken baby syndrome? To prevent sudden infant death syndrome?
5. What are the benefits of breastfeeding? Why don't all mothers breastfeed their infants as long as the experts recommend? What could be done to increase the rate of breastfeeding?
6. Explain which health problem you think is more serious for infants and very young children—overnutrition (obesity and overweight) or undernutrition (malnutrition).
7. What can be done to address and remedy racial, ethnic, and socioeconomic disparities in infant health?

Key Words

Axon (131)   A branchlike structure that conveys electrical messages outward from a neuron's cell body and toward the synapse.

Body mass index (BMI) (128)   A measure of weight in relation to height.

Colostrum (148)   A thick, yellowish fluid, richer in protein and protective antibodies than the breast milk that is produced a few days after birth.

Complementary feeding (152)   The transition from exclusive breastfeeding or formula-feeding to the inclusion of solid food in an infant's diet.

Dendrites (132)   Branchlike structures that convey electrical messages from the synapse and toward a neuron's cell body.

Electroencephalogram (EEG) (130)   A measure of the brain's activity that uses external electrodes placed on the scalp.

Experience-dependent (133) Aspects of brain development that develop solely as a result of a person's experiences.

Experience-expectant (132) Aspects of brain development that "expect" to have certain kinds of stimulation and are ready to develop once they receive it.

Failure to thrive (129) A condition, usually due to inadequate nutrition, in which a child's growth falters and weight gain is not as rapid as would be expected for his or her age.

Infant mortality rates (138) Statistics representing the number of infants who die before reaching the age of 1 year.

Magnetic resonance imaging (MRI) (131) An imaging technology that reveals the brain's structure.

Maltreatment (133) Neglect, medical neglect, physical abuse, sexual abuse, or psychological abuse.

Micronutrient deficiency (155) A form of malnutrition that occurs when insufficient amounts of minerals and vitamins are consumed in the diet.

Myelin (132) A fatty covering that insulates axons and increases the efficiency of neural functioning.

Neurotransmitters (132) Biochemical substances that transmit information between neurons through release and uptake at synapses.

Positron emission tomography (PET) (131) An imaging technology that shows the amount of activity in the brain.

Protein-energy malnutrition (PEM) (155) A form of malnutrition that occurs when insufficient amounts of protein and calories are consumed in the diet.

Psychosocial short stature (130) A type of failure to thrive in which a child is both underweight and extremely short, often as a result of neglect or emotional and psychological trauma.

Shaken baby syndrome (SBS) (135) A subtype of abusive head trauma due to maltreatment, in which an angry or frustrated adult shakes an infant violently, resulting in brain damage or death.

Sudden infant death syndrome (SIDS) (144) The diagnosis given when an infant younger than 1 year dies and a complete investigation is unable to identify a specific cause.

Synapses (131) Spaces between neurons, in which biochemical messages are released and absorbed.

Synaptogenesis (132) Formation of synapses in a network of neurons.

Vesicles (132) Neurotransmitter storage spaces at the end of the axon.

Sensation, Perception, and Motor Development

Every morning in villages in Africa and the Caribbean, mothers and babies engage in an important interactive routine. Placing the baby on her lap facing toward her, the mother grasps the infant's hands in hers, and extends both sets of arms straight up over her head. The baby's body stretches out and remains in that posture as the mother raises their arms together, lifting her young child in front of and above her. After a moment, she lowers their arms and repeats the sequence several more times. The mother also bounces her knees up and down, and the baby's legs bend and straighten in response to these movements, launching the tiny body upward as the mother raises their arms once again. The mother performs this routine, as did her mother before her, because she believes that it will accelerate her baby's growth and enable her child to learn to sit, crawl, stand, and walk. In a few months, she will introduce other activities to stimulate these basic motor skills.

When researchers from Germany visited Nso villages in West Africa and showed videos of urban German mothers who placed their infants on their backs and left them there, even when they were wide awake, Nso mothers expressed concern about how German babies would achieve motor milestones without targeted stimulation of their muscles and joints. They also found it curious that German mothers held their babies in their arms instead of carrying them on their backs and hips as is done in their society. German mothers, for their part, were surprised to see videos of Nso mothers engaged in such vigorous physical activities with such small infants. Unlike those mothers, they assumed that simple growth and maturation would promote their babies' motor development without any special intervention or stimulation. Rather than leading infants through predetermined sequences, German mothers were more concerned with finding out what their babies were interested in doing and responding to their cues (Keller, 2003).

These different perspectives and practices may be surprising because, at first glance, physical development appears to be one of the most culturally universal, biologically based aspects of growth during the first three years. After all, healthy, well-fed babies everywhere gain weight, develop muscle strength and control, and learn to walk independently, usually around the time they celebrate their first birthday. Nevertheless, recent cross-cultural research, such as the study of Nso and German mothers, shows that even apparently simple growth and maturation take place in a caregiving context that is influenced by parents' beliefs (Keller et al., 2004; Keller, Yovsi, & Voelker, 2002).

After babies are born, the whole world is able to witness a series of amazing physical transformations. Initially immobile infants learn to coordinate their limbs and maintain balance to roll over, sit upright, stand, and begin to walk, often in time for their first birthday. The toddler and preschool years see many other achievements, including the ability to run, hop, and walk up and down steps. There is also significant improvement in the ability to pick up and manipulate small objects, with the result that very young children become able to use tools found in their culture, such as crayons, zippers, and chopsticks. The predictable progression of these abilities suggests that there is an underlying maturational timetable directing development. We learn in this chapter, however, that they are also influenced by experience. We begin by considering the development of sensory and perceptual abilities and the perception-action system that contributes to maintaining balance, reaching for and manipulating objects, and moving through space.

SENSORY ABILITIES AND PERCEPTUAL DEVELOPMENT

At birth, infants are able to see, hear, feel, taste, and smell. As shown in Table 6.1, these abilities are not equally well developed, but they all provide newborns with information about the people and objects in their world. Some of these senses, such as hearing, are activated during

TABLE 6.1	Infants' Sensory and Perceptual Abilities
Sense	**Examples of Abilities**
Vision	Newborns notice objects and people in motion. Between 8 and 14 weeks, infants improve in their ability to use smooth eye movements to track moving targets.
	Newborns prefer looking at patterns with high contrast. They find the human face particularly attractive.
	Infants younger than the age of 4 weeks have a very limited ability to distinguish between different colors and initially perceive the difference only between red and white. By 8 weeks, color vision is still not mature, but most infants are able to discriminate between white and a number of other colors. By 4 months, infants' color vision is comparable to that of adults.
	Newborns can perceive objects and surfaces around them, but their visual acuity is estimated to be 20/400. By about 8 months, visual acuity is nearly as good as it would be in an adult with "perfect" 20/20 vision.
	The visual cortex is immature at birth, and accurate vision depends on unimpeded stimulation and visual experience.
Hearing	Newborns and young infants turn toward the source of a sound, but they have more difficulty than older children and adults in locating the precise origins of sounds, especially when they are very brief.
	Newborns pay special attention to the sound of the human voice. They prefer listening to their own mother's voice and the language that they heard her speaking before they were born.
	Newborns are not able to hear the full pitch range that adults perceive, but this perceptual ability improves significantly by the age of 6 months. Infants tend to become interested and attentive when they hear high-pitched sounds and voices. Low-pitched sounds, by contrast, tend to have a soothing and calming effect.
Touch	Infants need touch and physical contact with caregivers in order to grow and thrive.
	Most of the neonatal reflexes are triggered by the sense of touch.
	Newborn infants are able to feel pain, although they may not always cry or move in ways that clearly reflect their discomfort. Swaddling is effective because it affects newborns' sense of touch. Skin-to-skin contact with a parent or other caregiver is another reliable way to comfort newborns. Sucrose solutions alleviate mild pain.
	Many parents use massage with younger infants, but it can also be used with older infants and toddlers to provide an important emotional connection.
Taste	Newborns are able to differentiate between sweet-, salty-, sour-, and bitter-tasting substances. They prefer sweet flavors but dislike sour and bitter flavors. Salty substances rarely elicit negative reactions.
	Prenatal and postnatal exposure to flavors influences infants' acceptance and enjoyment of those flavors.
Smell	Newborns appear to have a preference for sweet aromas and a dislike of odors that older children and adults find unpleasant.
	Olfactory learning begins during the prenatal period and continues from the moment of birth.
Other Senses	The vestibular sense as well as the proprioceptive and kinesthetic senses provide infants with information about the body's position and movement. This feedback contributes to motor development and motor learning.

the prenatal period, whereas others, such as vision, receive their first stimulation after birth. Although the senses are interconnected—newborns turn their head in the direction of a sound, especially if the sound is their mother's voice—we focus most of our discussion on one modality at a time.

Theories of Infant Perception

Research conducted over the last few decades has shown that infants are relatively competent perceivers, able to detect, discriminate, and respond to sights, sounds, tastes, aromas, and textures. Before valid and reliable research procedures were developed, however, the accuracy of infant perception was questioned.

EMPIRICIST PERSPECTIVES   Debates about infant perception began long before the field of child development emerged in the twentieth century. As shown in Table 6.2, philosophers pondering adults' knowledge about the world probed the origins of this knowledge in newborns. Late seventeenth- and early eighteenth-century British empiricist philosophers, such as Berkeley (1709/1901), believed that this knowledge had to be constructed since it was not contained in the information picked up by the retina and other sensory receptors. Only through experience, and by piecing together the individual bits of information conveyed by those specialized receptors, could meaning be imposed on and perceived in the meaningless sensations (Kellman & Arterberry, 1998; Spelke & Newport, 1998).

NATIVIST PERSPECTIVES   A contrasting viewpoint came from thinkers favoring nativist explanations. Philosophers like Kant (1781/1924), in the late eighteenth century, refuted the notion that accurate associations and meanings could be built up during infancy with only a limited amount of sensory experience. Instead, nativists asserted, the ability to perceive the world must be innate.

A particularly intriguing issue for many early theorists was the development of **depth perception**—the ability to perceive the world in three dimensions. The logical problem with which they grappled was how the retina, which is flat, could convey the world in 3D. Empiricist philosophers asserted that infants could only perceive depth after they had accrued enough experience with different two-dimensional views to be able to combine and interpret them as different aspects of the same view. Empiricists also thought that indirect perception—learning through association—occurred as infants became aware of the different eye muscle movements involved when they focused at near versus far distances (Kellman & Arterberry, 1998).

GESTALT PERSPECTIVES   Gestalt psychologists, active from the 1930s until the 1950s, believed that the brain is designed to perceive information from the flat retinal image in three dimensions (e.g., Koffka, 1935). Given their assertion that two-dimensional information is inherently meaningless and needs to be translated and organized into accurate three-dimensional representations, Gestalt views were congruent with other theories in existence at that time (Kellman & Arterberry, 1998).

ECOLOGICAL PERSPECTIVES   Beginning in the 1960s, psychologists endorsing a new perspective—the **ecological theory of perception**—proposed something quite different, the idea that the visual system perceives meaningful information directly, without intermediate steps to interpret it. As we discuss later, the ecological theory regards vision as just one component of a perceptual system in which all of the senses are inherently coordinated. The best-known proponents of this ecological view,

TABLE 6.2	Theoretical Views of Infant Perception	
Theoretical View	**Key Theorist**	**Assumptions**
Empiricist	Berkeley	Knowledge about the world must be constructed because sensory receptors, such as the retina, do not provide direct, accurate information about the properties of objects in the world. Infants are not able to perceive the world in three dimensions until they have learned to associate different eye muscle movements with the act of focusing on objects that are near versus far.
Nativist	Kant	Accurate perception of the world is possible from birth or with only a limited amount of experience because knowledge about objects and their properties is innate. Infants are able to perceive the world in three dimensions because they are born with the ability to interpret information for depth and distance.
Gestalt	Koffka	The world is perceived accurately from early in life because the human brain is designed to enhance and interpret information that it receives from the sensory receptors. Perception of depth and three-dimensionality is the result of the brain's inherent ability to transform and organize the limited information conveyed to it by the flat retina.
Ecological	Gibson	The perceptual system perceives information about the world directly and accurately, without any intervening interpretive steps, because it has evolved to extract regularities from the organized patterns that exist in all settings. Infants are able to perceive depth and distance in the world because they are sensitive to a rich array of cues in the environment, such as the receding texture of a floor pattern from near to far, or different views of the same object as they move around it.
Dynamic Systems	Thelen	New skills and other forms of behavior emerge due to self-organization and interactions of the components of a complex system operating on multiple levels. A child's development is affected by mutual, continuous interactions occurring at all levels and across a wide range of timescales, with no single part of the system—neither nature nor nurture—exerting an inevitable or isolated influence. Perceiving the world in 3D reflects an evolutionary foundation for that ability, as well as the influence of a child's own cumulative experience and a number of other factors that can be understood by manipulating them under controlled experimental conditions.

Source: Based on Kellman & Arterberry, 1998, 2006.

J. J. Gibson (1966, 1979) and E. J. Gibson (1969, 1984), held that information in the world is organized in meaningful ways and humans, like all other animals, have evolved the ability to perceive and make use of this organization. According to the ecological view, the ability to discern available information may improve with experience, and increasingly subtle differences may be detected, but infants do not need to learn to impose meaning per se.

How does the ecological perspective explain the development of the ability to see the world in 3D? One answer is that humans, like other animals, move about the world and, as they do, make use of abundant, meaningful information in the environment. They perceive the boundaries of objects and are able to determine the relative locations of a set of objects by noticing how their views of those objects change. In this way, for example, as infants crawl around a playroom, they are able to perceive that toys that are closer to them cover up more of the view of toys that are farther away. Even without moving around the entire set of toys, infants—like all perceivers—are able to gain a changing array of meaningful and informative views of the toys and perceive their relative positions in the room simply by adjusting their posture and moving their head.

DYNAMIC SYSTEMS PERSPECTIVES   A somewhat different answer to the classic nature-nurture question comes from **dynamic systems theories,** perspectives that describe development as the emergence of new forms of behavior due to self-organization and interactions of the components of a complex system operating on multiple levels. According to dynamic systems theories, development is affected by mutual, continuous interactions occurring at all levels and across a wide range of timescales, with no single part of the system—neither nature nor nurture—exerting an inevitable or isolated influence. The unique characteristics of dynamic systems theories have been illustrated through the metaphor of a fast-moving mountain stream, in which the flow of water is affected by the contours of the stream bed and the temperature and other current weather conditions, as well as the mountain's geological history and long-range climate patterns. Ongoing changes, such as the addition of rocks or dams, also affect the rate and path of the stream's flow, but those influences cannot be considered independent of the other components of the system (Thelen & Smith, 2006).

Dynamic systems theorists assert that full understanding of the emergence of new behaviors in perceptual and motor development requires consideration of a wide range of relevant components, including evolutionary, environmental, social, cognitive, and biological factors, as well as other potentially modifiable variables. To explain the development of the ability to see the world in 3D, for example, researchers informed by dynamic systems theories might consider the evolutionary origins and value of that ability, as well as the influence of a host of other factors. In experiments, they might systematically provide infants of different ages with particular kinds of visual, tactile, or aural experiences with real or virtual objects that adults perceive as three-dimensional—the perceptual equivalent of introducing rocks or other built structures into a stream—in order to gauge the effect on infants' looking at or reaching toward them. Dynamic systems theories are potentially informative across domains and ages, but they have been applied most frequently in studies of perceptul, motor, and cognitive development in infancy and early childhood (Thelen & Smith, 2006).

Where does the theoretical debate about the development of perception stand now? While some echoes of the debate between the empiricists and the nativists continue, many researchers are instead actively testing predictions of ecological theory and dynamic systems theory. The specific mechanisms that the Gestalt psychologists posited are viewed as implausible by today's experts, but there is support for the general notion that nature and nurture work together, with evolved predispositions and unlearned organizational tendencies providing an important foundation for subsequent perceptual development (Kellman & Arterberry, 1998; Spelke & Newport, 1998; Thelen & Smith, 2006).

Vision

Vision is the most studied but least well-developed sense at birth. Researchers make inferences about infants' ability to perceive a range of visual stimuli, based on changes in their rate and pattern of sucking, heart rate, and brain activity, as well as the length and direction of their gaze in habituation or preferential looking procedures. Several decades of sophisticated experiments have shown that a number of fundamental visual abilities are either present at birth or develop rapidly in infancy.

NEWBORN ABILITIES   One robust finding is that newborns notice and pay attention to objects and people in motion. By the age of 8 weeks, infants are able to distinguish between moving and stationary objects, even while they themselves are in motion (Kellman & von Hofsten, 1992). They have difficulty before the age of 2 months using smooth eye movements to track objects, especially if the object is moving swiftly (Aslin, 1981). Instead of keeping up with a toy as it moves, infants younger than 2 months tend to lag behind or make a series of jerky eye movements (saccades) that fall short of where the moving target is positioned. The accuracy of these saccadic eye movements improves by the age of 11 to 14 weeks (Kellman & Arterberry, 1998; Shea & Aslin, 1990).

Newborns prefer some patterns more than others; the human face and face-like configurations are particularly attractive and salient (Kellman & Arterberry, 2006; Nelson, 2001). Newborns are able to discriminate among static line drawings or photographs of faces as well as among moving images of the faces of their mother and a stranger (Sai, 2005; Slater & Quinn, 2001). Areas of high contrast, such as a person's hairline or dark wood trim at the edge of a light-colored ceiling, draw newborns' attention (Fantz, Fagan, & Miranda, 1975). Although newborns scan the edges of faces more than their interior features, by the age of 1 month, they are able to discriminate their mother's face from that of a stranger, even if they are unable to see the edges of either face (Pascalis et al., 1995).

Certain patterns, such as black-and-white checked mobiles and toys, seem to be especially attractive to *parents*, who may buy them because they have heard that newborns cannot perceive color. "Color," however, is actually comprised of three attributes: brightness (the light intensity of an object), hue (the wavelength of an object), and saturation (the distribution of wavelengths of an object). Early studies of infant color perception were often inconclusive because stimuli that were used varied in more than one of these attributes. Infants who appeared to respond differentially to different hues, such as red and green, might actually have noticed and responded to differences in brightness. More recent research has been able to match levels of brightness while varying the hues of paired stimuli (Kellman & Arterberry, 2006).

These experiments have found that infants younger than 4 weeks of age discriminate between red and white but not between white and other hues (Adams, Courage, & Mercer, 1994). By the age of 8 weeks, many infants are able to discriminate between white and a number of colors, specifically, red, orange, blue, certain greens, and certain purples but not between white and yellow or yellow-green (Teller, Peeples, & Sekel, 1978). This pattern suggests that an early form of color vision exists but is different from adult color vision. Very young infants' failure to discriminate between hues may be due to a lack of **cones** (photoreceptors in the eye that respond to specific hues, or wavelengths of light) or other immaturities in the visual system (Kellman & Arterberry, 2006; Kellman & Banks, 1998). Color vision continues to develop, and by about 4 months of age, parents and their infants have a fairly similar ability to perceive a spectrum of distinct colors (Adams, Courage, & Mercer, 1991; Kellman & Arterberry, 2006).

How clearly can newborns see? **Visual acuity** (the smallest spacing that can be perceived between parts of a pattern) is significantly worse at birth than "perfect" 20/20 vision. In adults, visual acuity is measured with the Snellen scale, which compares how well a person sees letters on an eye chart at 20 feet to the distance at which a person with good vision would see the letters with the same degree of clarity. An adult whose vision is 20/60 thus sees at 20 feet what a person with good vision is able to see at 60 feet. To study visual acuity in infants, researchers replace eye charts displaying letters of the alphabet with gratings (patterns of stripes spaced at varying distances) or other high-contrast patterns. Because infants tend to look at the more complex of two visual stimuli, researchers present two gratings and measure the amount of time the infant looks at each.

In a variation on this procedure, called **forced-choice preferential looking,** infants are shown two targets—a screen displaying a grating with a particular spacing between the stripes and another screen that is uniformly blank. Infants who are able to perceive the grating prefer looking at it, but infants who are unable to detect the pattern perceive it as another uniform field and show no clear preference (Kellman & Banks, 1998).

Some researchers have used electrophysiological measures, such as the visual evoked potential, to study visual acuity and **contrast sensitivity,** which is the ability to perceive differences among the elements of an image or pattern under varying degrees of contrast between the pattern and its background (e.g., black patterns on a white background versus a grayish background). For both visual acuity and contrast sensitivity, high-tech measures tend to be more sensitive than behavioral measures in estimating infants' abilities (Kellman & Arterberry, 2006).

Newborn visual acuity is estimated to be approximately 20/400. Practically speaking, newborns are able to perceive objects and surfaces in their environment but miss many of the finer details, such as texture and intricate patterns. By the age of about $5\frac{1}{2}$ months, visual acuity improves to approximately 20/100 and to nearly adult levels by the age of about 8 months. At the same time that visual acuity improves, contrast sensitivity also develops. One reason for these improvements is the eyeball's rapid growth during the first year of life. As the size of the eye increases, the greater distance from the front of the eye to the retina at the back creates a larger, clearer image on the retina (Kellman & Banks, 1998). In comparison with adult vision, visual acuity and contrast sensitivity are initially particularly poor in the **fovea** (the center of the eye), in part because newborns' foveal photoreceptors, which transmit light signals to the optic nerve, are spaced about four times farther apart than those of adults. Peripheral vision, by contrast, is not significantly different for infants and adults; at all ages, acuity and contrast sensitivity are relatively poor at the periphery and under low-light conditions (Kellman & Arterberry, 1998; Kellman & Banks, 1998).

Another reason for newborns' initially poor vision lies in the brain. The **visual cortex,** which processes visual information, is immature at birth. Whereas in the mature visual system, the optic nerve sends messages first to the lateral geniculate nucleus and then to the visual cortex, visual processing during the first several weeks after birth relies primarily on a subcortical visual system that provides information from the periphery rather than the fovea. Subcortical pathways dominate visual processing until higher cortical areas become specialized and more efficient (Johnson, 2000; Kellman & Arterberry, 1998).

Vision problems are relatively rare among infants, although some groups, such as those born preterm or with a family history of eye problems, are at greater risk (American Academy of Pediatrics Section on Ophthalmology, American Academy of Ophthalmology, & American Association for Pediatric Ophthalmology and Strabismus, 2006; Repka, 2002b). Early detection and treatment are essential because the visual cortex depends on stimulation in order to develop normally. With unimpeded **binocular vision** (input from two aligned eyes that move together), signals are received from both the left and right visual fields. These signals stimulate the development of columns of neurons that respond specifically to the signals received from either the left or the right eye. The integration of the slightly different view that each eye sees underlies the ability to perceive a three-dimensional world.

When the visual system does not function correctly, the allocation of neurons in the visual cortex changes to reflect the child's visual experience (Birch & Wang, 2009). If, for example, one of an infant's eyes is crossed (as occurs in conditions known as amblyopia and strabismus), areas of the visual cortex that normally would register signals from the misaligned eye are taken over and respond to stimulation that the other, uncrossed eye receives. Children with these conditions often have normal (20/20) vision in one eye but significantly worse (20/200) vision in the other eye. Amblyopia and strabismus are usually treated by covering the stronger eye with a patch during the child's waking hours and using glasses to strengthen the weaker eye (Maples & Bither, 2006). Treatment regimens traditionally specified that the normal eye should be patched for 6 hours each day, but patching for only 2 hours a day may be just as effective (Pediatric Eye Disease Investigator Group, 2006; Repka et al., 2003, 2005). Special eyedrops can be used to blur vision temporarily in the normal eye, with results that are comparable to patching (Menon et al., 2008; Repka, 2002a; Stewart et al., 2007). These new options are easier to comply with, and parents report less concern about the potential social stigma of patching.

Infants with congenital cataracts are at risk for vision problems, if the cataract is not surgically removed (Ellemberg et al., 2000; Lloyd et al., 2007; Putzar et al., 2007). Follow-up care for these children typically involves patching the normal eye and correcting the vision in the eye that was operated on (Maurer et al., 1999; Valenti, 2006). If vision problems are not corrected early, the brain's ability to receive signals from the weaker or occluded eye diminishes and eventually ceases (Maurer, Mondloch, & Lewis, 2007). Given the importance of early treatment, experts recommend that all infants have their vision checked at the age of 6 months, using a simple red reflex exam to detect any asymmetries in the amount and pattern of light reflected from the back of the eyes (American Academy of Pediatrics Committee on Practice and Ambulatory Medicine and Section on Ophthalmology, 2002a; American Academy of Pediatrics Section on Ophthalmology, 2002b).

PERCEIVING OBJECTS   Accurately perceiving ordinary objects in everyday situations, such as a ball on the floor or a cup on a high chair tray, requires determining where each object begins and ends. It also depends on the ability to perceive edges and internal elements of objects as belonging together. Many of these abilities are present in very young infants.

In detecting the edges of objects, infants must determine the significance of ambiguous markings (such as shadows) and assign each boundary or edge to a specific object or surface. It is well documented that infants notice areas of high contrast (which often coincide with edges) from a very early age (Fantz et al., 1975). From birth, they also recognize objects seen from different angles (Kellman & Arterberry, 1998, 2006; Slater & Morison, 1985). Together, these abilities imply that very young infants perceive the edges of objects.

Movement appears to help infants perceive edges and objects. In a number of studies, infants have been habituated to displays in which two arrangements of elements on a video screen (e.g., fields composed of patterns of dots) move back and forth in various ways. In some conditions, the **accretion and deletion** of elements creates a display that adults judge to show overlapping fields with distinct edges or an object moving against a stationary background. In these and other studies, infants as young as 2 to 3 months show renewed visual interest when they see patterns of elements moving in different ways that adults do not perceive as depicting objects or fields with moving edges (Granrud et al., 1984; Johnson & Mason, 2002; Kellman & Arterberry, 2006).

In solving the problem of object unity—perceiving entire three-dimensional objects, rather than a set of separate elements—infants benefit from the tendency for most objects to be composed of homogeneous substances. Balls, for example, tend to be made out of rubber, plastic, or metal, but not all three substances. In addition, the substance of an object, such as a woven basket, is often different from the surface on which it rests, such as a polished stone countertop. Object unity is also specified by the tendency for object properties, such as texture, color, or pattern, to be consistent across an object but "disappear" abruptly at its edges. The ability to use this kind of information about texture, color, and other properties of objects and their surroundings in order to perceive discrete objects emerges later than the ability to detect edges. Studies using homogeneous and heterogeneous objects suggest that at least 5 months of perceptual experience may be necessary before infants are able to use properties such as color and texture as information for object unity (Johnson, 1997b; Kellman & Arterberry, 2006; Spelke et al., 1993).

Differences between the characteristics of objects and their surroundings become more salient, however, as objects and infants move around. Infants watching a ball roll across a floor, for example, have information that infants watching a motionless ball do not have. Even a slight change in posture and head position may highlight the fact that the surface of a plastic laundry basket responds differently to changes in the reflected ceiling light than does the texture of the tiled floor on which it sits (Kellman & Banks, 1998). The effectiveness of movement has been shown in experiments with partially occluded objects. Infants are first habituated to a display that adults perceive as a single, partially hidden object moving behind a stationary rectangle (display A, shown in Figure 6.1). If infants show renewed interest in display B, researchers infer that they perceive two separate objects behind the occluder in display A. Dishabituation to display C, by contrast, is regarded as evidence that infants perceive a unitary object behind the occluder in display A. The ability to perceive the initial display as a single, unified object has been found in infants as young as 2 months (Johnson & Aslin, 1996; Kellman & Spelke, 1983; Slater et al., 1996).

When shown continuous transformations of a three-dimensional object, 4-month-old infants are able to recognize it later in a different orientation, whereas infants who see only static "snapshots" of the same display do not (Kellman, 1984). By the age of 3 to 4 months, infants are better able to recognize unfamiliar faces when they are presented as moving (videotaped) stimuli than as static photographs (Otsuka et al., 2009). At approximately the same age, infants

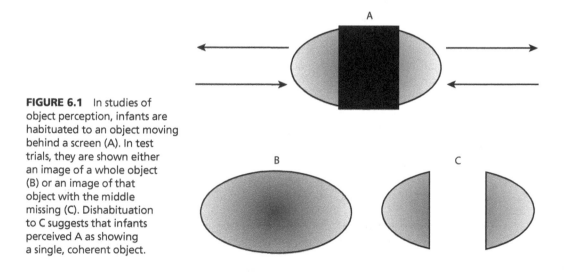

FIGURE 6.1 In studies of object perception, infants are habituated to an object moving behind a screen (A). In test trials, they are shown either an image of a whole object (B) or an image of that object with the middle missing (C). Dishabituation to C suggests that infants perceived A as showing a single, coherent object.

discriminate faces presented in videotaped displays accompanied by a soundtrack (Bahrick, Hernandez-Reif, & Flom, 2005).

Movement also enables infants to perceive human actions in experiments using point-light displays, which are created by using special lighting to illuminate white dots strategically applied to an actor's arms, legs, and torso. When babies as young as 4 months of age view these displays on videotape (but not as static displays), they discriminate between upright and inverted human figures engaged in particular movements, such as walking and running (Bertenthal, Proffitt, & Cutting, 1984). Experiments with 2-day-old infants show that they are able to use the motion in point-light stimuli to discriminate between displays of walking and random motion (Simion, Regolin, & Bulf, 2008). The superiority of dynamic information over static information, and of multiple viewpoints over single viewpoints, for both social and nonsocial objects, suggests that the perceptual system may have evolved to notice and respond to motion-carried information (Kellman & Banks, 1998; Kuhlmeier, Troje, & Lee, in press; Mash, Arterberry, & Bornstein, 2007).

PERCEIVING DEPTH   One classic study of infants' depth perception used an apparatus known as the visual cliff, a specially devised table with a clear plastic top. Although the surface of the table was completely continuous, researchers created the illusion of a drop-off by placing a checkerboard pattern underneath the plastic on one end of the table and another checkerboard pattern farther below the surface on the other end. Infants who ventured onto the "deep" end of the table were described as lacking depth perception, whereas those who were reluctant to move beyond the "shallow" end were credited with that ability (Gibson & Walk, 1960; Walk & Gibson, 1961). Another possible interpretation is that infants who were willing to cross over the edge of the "cliff" used tactile information to assess the situation, in addition to or instead of visual cues, and concluded that it was safe to crawl across the table's surface. The visual cliff was used in a number of experiments but yielded inconclusive results about very early development due to its limited ability to measure depth perception in precrawling infants (Kellman & Arterberry, 2006).

As shown in Table 6.3, infants initially rely on a subset of the information that older children and adults can use to perceive depth. The information infants use earliest, **kinematic depth cues,** is carried by motion. One type of kinematic depth cue that came up in our earlier discussion of edge detection—accretion and deletion of texture—also provides information about which of two edges is closer. In an experiment with video displays of moving dot patterns, 5- and 7-month-old infants reached more frequently to the display that adults judged to appear closer (Granrud et al., 1984). Another type of kinematic depth cue, **optical expansion and contraction,** refers to the increase and decrease of the size of an object's image on the retina. When older children and adults see a two-dimensional image, such as a shadow, increase in size symmetrically (in all directions), they perceive the approach of an object. By contrast, when the size of a shadow form decreases, older children and adults perceive an object moving away from them. As early as 1 month of age, infants who are shown rapidly symmetrically expanding two-dimensional forms blink their eyes in a defensive response, much as they would if a three-dimensional object approached at the same rate. They do not show this response when two-dimensional forms expand asymmetrically (in just one direction) or when they contract, suggesting that optical expansion and contraction convey information about the position of objects relative to the self from the first weeks of life (Nanez, 1988; Nanez & Yonas, 1994).

Between the ages of 2 and 4 months, infants begin to use another source of information— **stereoscopic depth information**—to perceive depth. Stereoscopic information is produced by **binocular disparity,** the difference between the image on each retina. In experiments using

TABLE 6.3	Development of Sensitivity to Depth Cues	
Depth Cue	**Age**	**Examples**
Kinematic	1 month	A two-dimensional shadow form increases and decreases in size, producing optical expansion and contraction. The viewer perceives a three-dimensional form moving toward and then away from them.
	5–7 months	Two random-dot patterns move on a video monitor, producing systematic, unified accretion and deletion of the dots. The viewer perceives the dots as belonging to two separate shapes, with the leading edge of one shape moving in front of the other shape.
Stereoscopic	2–4 months	Two slightly different two-dimensional images of the same picture create binocular disparity. The viewer perceives a single, three-dimensional image.
Pictorial	5 months	Height-in-the-picture-plane: Objects that are closer to the horizon are judged to be more distant than objects that are farther away from the horizon.
	5–7 months	Relative size: A smaller-looking, more distant stroller is judged to be the same size as a larger-looking stroller that is closer to the viewer.
	5–7 months	Linear perspective: Railroad tracks converge toward the horizon, suggesting distance and depth.
	5–7 months	Texture gradient: Floor tiles gradually appear to get smaller toward the horizon.
	5–7 months	Interposition: A nearby shoe covers part of the view of a ball that is farther away from the viewer.

Source: Adapted from Arterberry, 2008; Kellman & Arterberry, 2006.

preferential looking, 4-month-olds looked longer at displays containing disparity that adults judged to show depth (Held, Birch, & Gwiazda, 1980). Other experiments using a range of response measures have found corroborating evidence for the development of stereoscopic sensitivity by about 4 months of age (Kellman & Arterberry, 2006). The underlying change that makes stereoscopic perception possible is the maturation of disparity-sensitive cells in the visual cortex—alternating columns of cells that receive stimulation from either the left or the right eye (Kellman & Banks, 1998). The timetable for this maturation, from birth to 6 months, is the reason that visual problems interfering with input from either eye should be detected and treated as early as possible (Maurer et al., 2007).

Infants become sensitive to a third source of depth information—**pictorial depth cues**—between 5 and 7 months of age. Pictorial depth cues make it possible for artists to convey information for a three-dimensional scene on a two-dimensional surface. These cues include relative size (showing objects at different sizes and distances from the viewer), linear perspective (showing parallel lines converging toward the horizon), texture gradients (showing surface elements gradually getting smaller toward the horizon), interposition (showing closer objects in front of objects that are farther away), and height-in-the-picture-plane (placing more distant objects closer to the horizon, which is usually higher in the picture plane).

In studies of pictorial depth cues, researchers typically eliminate depth information that might be carried via binocular disparity by covering one of the infant's eyes with a patch.

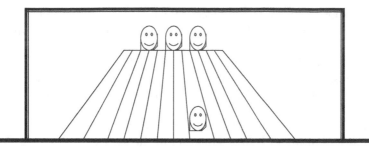

FIGURE 6.2 Researchers use a preferential reaching procedure and interpret infants' reaching toward objects or displays as evidence that they perceive those objects as being closer. Pictorial depth cues create the illusion of a horizontal surface receding in depth.

Researchers use a preferential reaching procedure and interpret infants' reaching toward objects or displays as evidence that they perceive those objects as being closer, as shown in Figure 6.2 (Kellman & Banks, 1998). The results of numerous experiments with a range of pictorial depth cues indicate that sensitivity tends to emerge between 5 and 7 months of age, although there is variability in the timing (Arterberry, 2008; Yonas, Elieff, & Arterberry, 2002). Macaque monkeys develop sensitivity to pictorial depth cues at an age that is approximately equivalent to the age at which sensitivity emerges in human infants (Gunderson et al., 1993). The ability to perceive pictorial depth cues thus appears to be the result of maturation of the visual system as well as experience with the cues.

Hearing

The vast majority of research in infant perception, like the bulk of this chapter so far, has investigated the development of vision. We turn now, however, to consider evidence regarding the development of the sense of hearing, attending briefly to a topic of particular interest—speech perception—that we discuss further in Chapter 8.

LOCATING SOUNDS   From birth, infants turn in the direction of sounds, as if searching for the source. **Auditory localization**—the ability to detect the location of sound sources—appears to undergo a U-shaped developmental change. Whereas newborns respond reliably, turning their head toward the sound of a rattle that is shaken to one side, 1- to 3-month-olds respond less strongly and less frequently. By the age of 4 to 5 months, infants once again respond consistently and accurately. This pattern is thought to be the result of a shift in control of the response from subcortical to cortical brain structures (Muir & Hains, 2004).

When newborns and young infants turn toward a sound, they are significantly less able than older children and adults to locate the precise origins of sounds, especially if the sounds are very brief (Clarkson & Montgomery, 2000). One study with 2- to 7-month-olds compared their ability to reach toward objects in one of four conditions: an invisible noise-making object, a glowing visible object, a single object that could be both seen and heard, and two objects (one visible and the other audible) in different locations. At all ages tested, infants were slower and less accurate in reaching for unseen objects that they could hear than for visible-but-silent objects (Stack et al., 1989). These findings indicate that pinpoint localization develops more gradually than other aspects of audition.

PERCEIVING SPEECH   Newborns pay special attention to the human voice and prefer it to other sounds (Vouloumanos & Werker, 2004, 2007). They are particularly attuned to the sound of their mother's voice and are able to discriminate between her voice and the voices of other women (DeCasper et al., 1994; Kisilevsky et al., 2003; Saffran, Werker, & Werner, 2006). They are even able, at just 2 days after birth, to detect the difference between their native language (the language that they have heard their mother speaking in utero) and other languages (Moon et al., 1993).

Mothers, as well as fathers and other caregivers, usually speak to infants in a high-pitched voice. This modification draws infants' attention to the speaker and may facilitate language learning. As many parents and caregivers know, low-pitched sounds, such as those in most lullabies, tend to have the opposite effect—soothing and quieting infants, rather than arousing their attention and interest. Newborns are not able to hear the full pitch range that adults perceive, but over the first six months of life they become more skilled in their ability to detect differences between a wider variety of pitches (Clarkson, 1996; Clarkson, Martin, & Miciek, 1996; Saffran et al., 2006).

Infants as young as 4 months of age prefer melodies that adults find pleasant sounding, such as those with consonant rather than dissonant intervals and more regular rhythms (Trehub, 2002). In a study comparing original consonant versions of European folk songs with modified dissonant versions, 4-month-olds looked longer at loudspeakers playing consonant versions and also fussed less and were calmer and more attentive when they heard those renditions (Zentner & Kagan, 1996). By 5 to 6 months of age, infants discriminate high- and low-pitched nonspeech sounds and seem to prefer those that are higher pitched (Trainor & Zacharias, 1998). Studies of 6- to 10-month-olds have shown that infants also prefer listening to naturally segmented excerpts of music (those with a pause at the end of a musical phrase), as opposed to excerpts that are unnaturally segmented (with a pause in the middle of a musical phrase) (Jusczyk & Krumhansl, 1993).

Most spoken utterances are continuous streams of speech, without obvious pauses and markers between words and phrases, which makes speech perception a complex task for first language learners. Considered in objective terms, infants hear sentences like *hilittlebabylet'sgotothepark* but must learn to perceive them as a series of distinct words and phrases. At the same time, infants need to learn to ignore differences in the speech stream that mature speakers can easily disregard, such as the subtle difference between the /p/ sound in the words *pin* and *spin*. Infants also need to be able to perceive multiple examples of a speech sound as the same sound, despite differences between speakers in dimensions such as pitch, intonation, and speed. For example, although there are objective acoustical differences in the way that parents, older siblings, and grandparents pronounce an infant's name, the infant needs to be able to ignore the variations and hear these utterances as the same name. Fortunately, this ability is well developed by 4 to 6 months of age and may even be present in 1-month-olds (Kuhl, 1987; Kuhl & Miller, 1982; Saffran et al., 2006). If this were not the case, the task of learning to produce speech sounds would be difficult, if not impossible, since infants would need to try to match the infinite number of variations produced by different speakers uttering the same speech sounds.

Adding another layer of complexity, languages differ in the speech sounds that they use. Native speakers of Japanese, for example, produce sounds that approximate /r/ and /l/ in English, but the Japanese language does not make a distinction of meaning in that range of speech sounds. As a result, native speakers of Japanese have great difficulty *hearing* /r/ and /l/ as two distinct elements of spoken English (Iverson et al., 2003; Zhang et al., 2005). As another example, native speakers of English are not sensitive to a contrast in Hindi between /Da/ and /da/; instead of two functionally different speech sounds, they perceive only one—/da/ (Werker & Tees, 1984).

From birth, infants are able to perceive speech sounds categorically and, like adults, discriminate between categories such as /ba/ and /pa/ (Gerken & Aslin, 2005). Unlike adults, young infants are able to perceive speech categories from all human languages. The speech sounds that individual languages use are only a subset of all possible speech sounds that could be used, however, and in the course of acquisition, language learners become specialists at perceiving and producing that subset. As they do, it becomes more difficult to discriminate between contrasts that are not linguistically meaningful in their native language. We return to this topic in Chapter 8, where we describe the process through which infants become language specialists.

Babies have difficulty becoming language specialists (for spoken languages) if they have an undiagnosed or untreated hearing impairment. These problems often can be avoided if families, doctors, and audiologists work together to follow the "1-3-6 Plan," guidelines that call for newborn hearing screenings by 1 month of age, diagnosis by 3 months, and intervention (if needed) by 6 months (American Academy of Pediatrics Joint Committee on Infant Hearing, 2007). As we learned in Chapter 5, despite achieving hearing screening for nearly all U.S. newborns, about half of the infants who do not pass the initial screening fail to receive follow-up assessments. According to a six-year, multi-hospital study, a variety of factors affect screening follow-up, with the most significant reasons being the family's type of health insurance and the specific type of hearing loss (Spivak et al., 2009). Another reason identified by the American Speech-Language-Hearing Association (2008) is a shortage of practitioners qualified to work with deaf and hearing-impaired infants and their families, providing audiological services that also take into account each family's social, cultural, and linguistic background.

To protect hearing, the American Academy of Pediatrics Committee on Environmental Health (1997) recommends shielding infants, and children of all ages, from extremely loud noises. In addition to obvious sources, such as lawnmowers and loud music, parents need to consider their children's toys as a potential source of damaging noise.

Touch

Infants need touch and physical contact with caregivers in order to grow and thrive, and they are born prepared to respond to stimulation of this sense. One sign of their readiness is the set of neonatal reflexes, many of which are triggered by the sense of touch.

REFLEXES   Stroking the sole of a newborn's foot elicits the Babinski reflex, in which the foot flexes and the toes fan out. Touching the infant's cheek elicits the rooting reflex, in which the head turns and the mouth opens, as if searching for a source of food. Supporting the infant and placing the feet on a flat surface produces a stepping reflex.

Researchers have long wondered about the connection between reflexes, such as the stepping reflex, and later motor patterns, such as walking. Early views were that the reflexes disappeared as a result of development of the motor cortex. Contemporary research informed by dynamic systems theory shows, however, that this assumption must be questioned (Bertenthal & Clifton, 1998; Thelen & Smith, 2006). Taking into account the rapid growth and weight gain during the first months after birth, researchers instead proposed that the stepping reflex diminishes in response to biomechanical constraints, such as the increasing weight of the infant's leg and muscle strength that is no longer adequate to perform the stepping movement. They tested this hypothesis by putting weights on the legs of infants who were still exhibiting the stepping reflex at a high rate. With the added weight, the reflex disappeared. They also partially immersed babies who had stopped exhibiting the stepping reflex on dry land. With the effects of gravity reduced in the water, the reflex reappeared (Thelen, Fisher, & Ridley-Johnson, 1984).

PAIN   Another sign of newborns' sense of touch is their ability to feel pain. Although some neurologists formerly thought that newborns could not feel pain, more than 40 infant pain assessment scales are now available, and pediatricians routinely use local anesthetics and other forms of medication for infants undergoing surgery as well as procedures that are more common, such as heel-sticks to draw blood samples (American Academy of Pediatrics Committee on Fetus and Newborn, Committee on Drugs, 2000; Simons et al., 2003). Contrary to earlier views, a lack of crying, facial grimacing, or changes in bodily movement cannot be assumed to indicate an absence of pain (Peters et al., 2003).

Relatively few studies have examined pain in fragile babies, such as those born very preterm or at extremely low birthweight, but it appears that these infants—who typically must undergo many uncomfortable procedures as part of their care in the NICU—may respond differently (less strongly) than healthy, full-term newborns (Gibbins et al., 2008; Hummel & van Dijk, 2006). A study comparing infants born at 28–31 versus 32–34 weeks found that babies born at earlier gestational ages were more physiologically reactive to pain caused by heel-stick blood draws. The more preterm babies' overt behavioral responses did not reflect their greater physiological reactivity, however, indicating that evaluation of pain in this population requires careful assessment using multiple measures (Lucas-Thompson et al., 2008).

Even among healthy infants, relying on facial expressions may not be sufficient because facial responses to pain may change with age (Williams et al., 2009). In one longitudinal study of infants' responses to an event that elicits acute pain—the DPT inoculation—2-month-olds cried and showed facial expressions of "emergency pain." As the sample of infants returned for booster shots at 4, 6, and 18 months of age, they continued to cry, but their facial expressions of pain became mixed with fear and anger, as their increasing cognitive abilities enabled them to anticipate the inoculation (Izard, Hembree, & Huebner, 1987).

Skin-to-skin contact and swaddling are simple ways to comfort newborns by affecting their sense of touch (Gray, Watt, & Blass, 2000). Infants who are comforted by a parent during inoculations often recover more quickly than babies who are not held or touched in a soothing way. Giving breast milk or formula may also help if the pain is mild; newborns given a sweet solution

This toddler is comforted when she sucks her thumb and feels the familiar texture of her favorite blanket.

following a routine heel-stick blood draw cry less and show less physiological distress than infants who are not given sucrose to drink (Blass & Hoffmeyer, 1991; Harrison, 2008; Smith & Blass, 1996). The combination of a pacifier and sweet solution has also been found effective at reducing stress responses to the pain of immunization at 3 months of age (Mörelius, Theodorsson, & Nelson, 2009). Newborns with more intense or long-lasting pain require medication, however, and may be more distressed, even at later ages, by subsequent painful events than infants who have not experienced similar levels of pain neonatally (Grunau, Weinberg, & Whitfield, 2004; Ruda et al., 2000; Taddio et al., 2009).

The sense of touch continues to be important for older infants and toddlers, many of whom find emotional comfort when they stroke a special corner of a favorite blanket, hug a stuffed animal, suck their thumb, or twirl their hair. In addition, while many parents use massage with younger infants to soothe them and create an emotional connection, this contact and other forms of touch, such as back rubs, can also be used with toddlers and older children.

Taste

Despite the importance of the sense of taste, in comparison with studies of vision, hearing, and touch, relatively little research has been directed at understanding its origins and functioning in infancy. The first stimulation of this sense occurs prenatally, when flavors of food the mother consumes may be passed on to the fetus in the amniotic fluid, which is a salty liquid.

INNATE PREFERENCES   As shown in the phenomenon of sucrose analgesia, the sense of taste is involved in young infants' response to mild pain (Ramenghi, Evans, & Levene, 1999). Newborns' sense of taste also contributes to their survival, since they have an innate preference for high-energy, sweet-tasting substances, such as breast milk.

Studies of infants' sense of taste up to the age of about 4 months usually involve giving water or another liquid to which flavoring has been added, while older infants may be given either flavored liquid or flavored solid food, such as bland rice cereal. Infants' responses are most frequently gauged from their facial expressions, sucking rates, or quantity of liquid or solid food that is ingested (Harris, 1997). The intensity of those responses depends, in part, on the strength of the solution—*how* sweet, salty, sour, or bitter it is. A very dilute solution generally produces a less extreme response than a solution that is more concentrated.

Newborns differentiate between sweet-, salty-, sour-, and bitter-tasting substances. They dislike sour and bitter flavors, as shown in their negative facial expressions and limited consumption of substances with these flavors. Sweet-tasting substances, by contrast, typically produce placid facial expressions, and infants suck faster and more steadily, consuming relatively large quantities. Infants tend to have moderate responses to salty solutions and begin to prefer them between the age of 3 and 6 months (Beauchamp et al., 1994). Even at birth, salty substances rarely elicit negative facial expressions, and infants usually do not refrain from ingesting them, perhaps a reflection of their in utero exposure to amniotic fluid (Harris, 1997; Harris, Thomas, & Booth, 1990).

EFFECTS OF EXPERIENCE   Infants who are breastfed are exposed to the flavors of foods their mother eats, and some researchers have found that this early exposure—paired with the sweetness of the breast milk—increases the likelihood that those other flavors will be received favorably when solid foods are introduced (Mennella & Beauchamp, 1999; Mennella, Jagnow, & Beauchamp, 2001). Babies who are formula fed also develop taste preferences as a result of their early postnatal exposure. Infants in one study who had been fed soy formulas, for example, were more likely as preschoolers to prefer broccoli and bitter-flavored apple juice compared with children who had been fed milk-based formulas (Mennella & Beauchamp, 2002; Mennella, Kennedy, & Beauchamp, 2006).

In an experiment that tested the specificity of flavor learning, one (prenatal exposure) group of pregnant women drank carrot juice during pregnancy and water while breastfeeding, a second (early postnatal exposure) group drank water during pregnancy and carrot juice while breastfeeding, and a third (control) group drank water during pregnancy and while breastfeeding. Later, when infants began complementary feeding (making the transition to eating solid food), and before they had ever been fed foods or juices containing the flavor of carrots, they were given cereal prepared with carrot juice as well as cereal prepared with water. Videotapes of the infants' facial expressions were consistent with mothers' ratings that, unlike the control group, infants who were exposed prenatally to the flavor of carrots enjoyed the carrot-flavored cereal more than plain cereal. Infants who had been exposed to the flavor of carrots only through breastfeeding showed fewer negative facial expressions when eating carrot-flavored cereal than infants who had never tasted carrots before. These findings show that prenatal and early postnatal exposure to flavors may enhance infants' subsequent acceptance and enjoyment of those flavors (Mennella et al., 2001; Nicklaus, 2006).

Infants' taste preferences continue to change as a result of experience. When 6-month-olds in one experiment were given salted and unsalted rice cereal, they preferred the salted version. The magnitude of their preference for the salted cereal correlated positively with the number of times they had eaten salted foods during the previous week. After the age of about 12 months, infants and toddlers showed a preference in new foods for salted over unsalted versions. For familiar foods, however, they preferred versions that were similar to the way they usually had experienced those foods, whether that was with or without salt (Harris, 1997).

With age, cognitive factors play an increasingly important role in children's taste preferences. In the second year of life, children tend to eat more of foods that they have watched others eating or foods with which they have positive emotional associations. In addition, over time, food that is presented in a way that emphasizes its instrumental role tends to become less preferred (Harris, 1997). Parents can minimize this tendency by being careful not to create the impression that the principal reason to eat broccoli is to earn a cookie.

Infants' temperament may also affect the degree to which they accept or reject new tastes. As we discuss in Chapter 10, infants differ in their response to novelty, such as unfamiliar toys or unusual sights. Just as some infants have strong negative emotional reactions to these stimuli, while other infants show interest and positive emotions, new flavors, textures, and aromas may elicit different responses—negative, neutral, or positive—in different infants as a function of whether they are "conservative" or "sensation-seeking" eaters (Harris, 1997).

Smell

The ability to taste depends, in part, on the ability to smell, a sense that is well developed at birth. Exposure to odors, like experience with flavors, influences infants' behavior and physiology in both immediate and long-lasting ways.

INNATE PREFERENCES   Without direct prior exposure, newborns appear to have a preference for sweet aromas (such as vanilla) and a dislike of odors that older children and adults find unpleasant (such as fish and ammonia). They wrinkle their nose and even cry when exposed to the latter but not the former (Wilson & Sullivan, 1994). Studies using EEG recordings have also found that infants and adults respond similarly to lavender and rosemary (Sanders et al., 2002).

Pleasant odors appear to have a soothing effect on infants' behavioral states, and some parents apply principles of aromatherapy at bath time or bedtime, exposing their babies to scented lotions and bath products to help them feel calm and relaxed.

Newborn humans, like many nonhuman animals, appear to be particularly receptive to biological odors, including their mother's milk (Nishitani et al., 2009; Schaal et al., 2009). Newborns in one experiment, for example, were significantly less distressed following a heel-stick blood draw if they were presented with the smell of either their mother's breast milk or vanilla (Rattaz, Goubet, & Bullinger, 2005). Babies in a Japanese study who had been separated from their mothers for 10–14 days (due to the absence of a maternity ward in the hospital where the study was carried out, many mothers routinely were not able to be with their newborns until they were discharged) sucked more vigorously during bottle feeding when they could smell the odor of their mother's expressed breast milk than when they were exposed to the odor of formula or plain water (Mizuno & Ueda, 2004).

EFFECTS OF EXPERIENCE   Although there are innate reactions to specific aromas, it is also clear that olfactory learning begins during the prenatal period and continues from the moment of birth (Browne, 2008). As a result, newborn infants are able to recognize the smell of their own amniotic fluid (Schaal, Marlier, & Soussignan, 1998, 2000). In addition, when they are just days old, they are able to detect the difference between breast milk produced by their own mother and breast milk from another lactating woman, an ability that may contribute to the development of the infant-parent relationship (Marlier & Schaal, 2005; Porter & Winberg, 1999). Two- and four-day-old infants who are bottle-fed, however, show a preference for the prenatal odor of amniotic fluid rather than the postnatal odor of the formula they are being fed (Marlier, Schaal, & Soussignan, 1998). The specificity of prenatal olfactory learning was also demonstrated in a study in which infants whose mothers consumed licorice while pregnant subsequently preferred the odor of anise (a licorice-flavored plant), whereas infants without prenatal exposure showed aversive or neutral responses (Schaal, Marlier, & Soussignan, 2000).

Taken together, these findings have practical implications, the first being that new parents may want to plan to avoid using products that mask potentially important biological cues (Browne, 2008; Varendi, Porter & Winberg, 1992). Second, it may be helpful to remember that young children who develop a special attachment to a favorite blanket or stuffed animal may derive just as much comfort from its unique, soothing odor as they do from the way it looks and feels. The olfactory sense and aromatic properties of the environment should thus be considered potentially important influences on behavior and mood during infancy and beyond.

Other Senses

Some of the neonatal reflexes that we discussed in Chapter 4 are stimulated by other senses, including the **vestibular sense,** which conveys information about balance and support. One example of how this sense works is the Moro reflex, activated when neonates feel a loss of support and fling their arms and legs out quickly before drawing them in toward the center of the body. As infants become mobile, and throughout the rest of the life span, the vestibular sense provides important feedback that helps maintain equilibrium. The **proprioceptive** and **kinesthetic senses** provide information from muscles, tendons, and joints about the body's position and movement. These senses work together with the visual system, contributing to the ability to reach toward an object, adjust the speed and direction of the arm as it is extended, and grasp the object with the appropriate amount of force while bringing it back toward the body.

In an experiment testing the integration of infants' proprioceptive and visual senses, 5- and 7-month-olds saw two side-by-side video monitors, each showing a point-light display of an infant's legs moving. (In each display, the infant wore long black socks painted with dots of white paint, and only the dots appeared in the video.) Each infant saw a live (contingent) display of its own legs moving and a recorded (noncontingent) display of another infant's legs. (Seated with their legs extending underneath a table, the video display was infants' only source of visual information about their legs.) At both ages, infants looked longer at the noncontingent display, suggesting that they noticed it did not match the proprioceptive information about their own legs' movements (Schmuckler & Fairhall, 2001). A similar study using ordinary video displays found that 5-month-olds also looked longer at noncontingent displays showing recordings of either their own or another infant's legs instead of a live, contingent display of their own legs (Bahrick & Watson, 1985). These findings show that coordination of visual and proprioceptive information supports infants' perception of the world and contributes to the developing awareness of a coherent, enduring physical self. As we discuss next, intersensory coordination also facilitates infants' perception of a coherent, dynamic world.

Intermodal and Cross-Modal Perception

An infant watching her bathtub being filled with water from a hand-held shower hose is witnessing a multimodal sensory event. She sees the spray of water at the same time that she hears it hit the plastic tub. If her father holds her close enough, she may also feel the water spraying on her hand and notice its warmth. If the baby puts her fingers in her mouth, she may notice that the water tastes different than the milk and rice cereal she just finished eating. The baby's father experiences bath time as a unified event, one in which the sight and sound of the water, and its other properties, not only coincide, but unmistakably belong together. Does his young daughter share this perception?

According to researchers influenced by J. J. Gibson's (1966) ecological theory of perception, which regards the senses as an inherently coordinated system, there is every reason to believe that infants perceive multisensory events as coherent and unified. Guided by this ecological view, their experiments differ from most of those we have learned about so far, in that they typically explore more than one sense modality at a time (Bahrick, Lickliter, & Flom, 2004; Gibson, 1966). Many of these studies examine infants' **intermodal perception**—the ability to integrate multiple simultaneous sources of sensory information.

INTERMODAL ABILITIES   Most everyday experiences contain redundant information across multiple sensory modalities, corresponding to the rate, rhythm, intensity, and duration of ongoing events; researchers refer to these characteristics as **amodal properties** (Lickliter & Bahrick, 2000). In contrast to characteristics that are specific to just one sense modality, such as the color of a bath toy (visual), the temperature of water (tactile), or the pitch of a parent's voice (auditory), amodal properties may be perceived through more than one sense. In the bath time example, amodal information about the rate and intensity of the water's movement is conveyed redundantly, present both in the sound of each spurt of water hitting the plastic tub and in the sight of each short, synchronized blast.

From an early age, infants are able to coordinate visual and auditory information in multimodal events. In a frequently used experimental procedure, infants are presented with two different videotaped events side-by-side, while a single, centrally located soundtrack plays. Infants who look longer at the display that matches the soundtrack are assumed to have noticed the redundancy of the information provided by each sensory modality. In one study, for example, infants who saw two displays—several small marbles being shaken inside a plastic tube and one large marble being shaken inside an identical tube—looked longer at the display matching the collision soundtrack (Bahrick, 1987). Seven- and 9-month-olds in another study watched side-by-side videos of two musicians playing different musical instruments and heard a soundtrack matching only one instrument. Although infants had had little or no prior experience with the woodwind, brass, and string instruments in the displays, they looked longer at the video in each pair for which they heard a soundtrack (Pick et al., 1994). Other studies using this procedure have found that infants are able to match faces and voices on the basis of a speaker's age, gender, and affect (happy and angry expressive behaviors) (Bahrick, Netto, & Hernandez-Reif, 1998; Soken & Pick, 1992).

Based on the accumulating evidence, some researchers have proposed an **intersensory redundancy hypothesis.** As shown in Table 6.4, this hypothesis asserts that multimodal events promote perception of amodal properties, whereas unimodal events enhance perception of modality-specific information (Bahrick, Lickliter, & Flom, 2004). Support for these ideas comes from experiments with young infants: 3- and 5-month-olds who were first habituated to a video-taped event (such as a toy hammer tapping), for example, noticed changes in amodal properties of that event (such as the rhythm or tempo of the tapping) when they were able to both see and hear those events; they failed to notice those changes, however, when they could only see or hear them. Consistent with the intersensory redundancy hypothesis, infants were more attentive to changes in unimodal properties (such as the position of the toy hammer), when they saw silent videotapes than when the tapes had an accompanying soundtrack (Bahrick, Flom, & Lickliter, 2002; Bahrick & Lickliter, 2000).

Early sensitivity to amodal information in multimodal events may facilitate accurate perception, helping young infants notice and respond to fundamentally important characteristics of those events, such as their rate and intensity. With perceptual experience, however, infants are able to use unimodal and multimodal sources more flexibly, and by the age of about 7 months, babies perceive changes in amodal properties even when they are presented in just one modality (Bahrick et al., 2004; Bahrick, Lickliter, & Flom, 2006; Flom & Bahrick, 2007). For example, whereas 4-month-olds in one study of affect were able to perceive amodal properties only when they were presented in

TABLE 6.4	Predictions of the Intersensory Redundancy Hypothesis		
		Stimulus Property	
		Amodal	**Modality-Specific**
		Properties such as tempo, intensity, rhythm, and duration	Properties such as color, pattern, position, and pitch
Stimulation Available for Exploration	*Multimodal* Video display <u>with</u> a soundtrack	Attention is **facilitated** (+)	Attention is **attenuated** (−)
	Unimodal Video display <u>or</u> a soundtrack	Attention is **attenuated** (−)	Attention is **facilitated** (+)

Source: Based on Bahrick, Lickliter, & Flom, 2004.

video displays accompanied by a soundtrack, 7-month-olds were equally sensitive to that information when it was presented either visually or aurally (Flom & Bahrick, 2007).

More studies of the development of intermodal perception are needed, covering a broader range of ages. The addition of neuroscience methods is another potentially fruitful direction, given that experiments with cats and monkeys have shown that cells in certain areas of the brain respond to more than one sensory modality, provided that the animal has sufficient postnatal experience in a multisensory environment (Neil et al., 2006; Wallace & Stein, 2000, 2007).

Multisensory events are part of everyday experience, but the full range of sights and sounds, as well as other sensory information, is not always available to be perceived. The baby in her bedroom, for example, hearing her father's voice announcing bath time as he walks upstairs, expects to see him, not her mother or a stranger, appear in her doorway. When the baby's father reaches into her diaper bag to find her favorite teething toy, he may try to locate it just by feeling around. If, during his groping, he encounters other items, such as a pacifier or extra diapers, he is likely to recognize—through touch alone—that they are not his daughter's toy. These experiences are evidence of cross-modal perception.

CROSS-MODAL ABILITIES   As noted in the previous examples, **cross-modal perception** is the ability to perceive information about a person or object from one sense, such as vision, and use it when encountering the person or object later using a different sense modality, such as hearing or touch. One recent study of 9- to 12-week-old infants documented the cross-modal neural representation of speech sounds by comparing ERP responses in different experimental conditions. In the first phase, babies in a video-only condition watched a silent videotape of a person pronouncing a vowel, while babies in a comparison condition heard a soundtrack of that vowel and saw a video in which the speaker's mouth was not visible. In an auditory-only test phase, both groups of infants heard a soundtrack that either matched or differed from the vowel that had previously been presented. Both groups of infants had similar ERP responses: When the vowel in the test phase was a mismatch, they noticed the difference; when it matched the original vowel, they noticed that as well. These findings show that babies in the video-only condition had access to a representation of the speech sound that they were able to use in the auditory-only condition, even though their sole prior experience with it was in the visual modality (Bristow et al., 2008).

Babies are also able to coordinate visual information with **haptic information**—exploratory mouth or hand movements that go well beyond mere tactile contact with an object. In one well-known study, 1-month-old infants haptically explored a pacifier that was either bumpy or smooth by sucking on it. The researchers made sure not to allow the babies to see the pacifier as it was being placed in and later removed from their mouth. When the infants later saw two pacifiers—one bumpy, the other smooth—they looked longer at the pacifier that matched the one on which they had previously sucked, suggesting that they were able to transfer haptically derived texture information to the visual modality (Meltzoff & Borton, 1979).

Investigations of cross-modal transfer involving visual and manual exploration have yielded less consistent results. In some studies, infants as young as 2 months who explored an object only with their hands perceived that object as familiar in a later visual test, but transfer in the other direction—from visual familiarization to manual recognition—has not been found. This pattern and other inconsistencies may reflect very young infants' limited ability to explore objects systematically with their hands (Kellman & Arterberry, 1998; Rochat, 1989; Streri & Molina, 1993). By $5\frac{1}{2}$ months of age, infants who manually explore a ball that they are not allowed to see are nevertheless able to use that tactile experience as a basis for responding to subsequent visible events involving the ball (Schweinle & Wilcox, 2004).

Sensory and perceptual abilities, together with physical growth and change, contribute to major milestones of motor development from birth to age 3. The ability to explore the world through reaching, grasping, and manipulating undergoes significant change during infancy, enabling children to act in new ways, expanding their play repertoire, and developing self-care skills that include eating and dressing.

MOTOR DEVELOPMENT

Across a wide range of motor skills, from reaching and manual exploration to crawling and walking, there is an intimate link between perception and action. This link was evident in visual cliff studies that we learned about earlier in this chapter. Some infants, hesitating before deciding whether to crawl across the clear plastic table top, felt it with their hands and looked closely at the surface (Gibson & Walk, 1960). The more crawling experience infants had gained, the more likely they were to draw back from the virtual edge of what appeared to be a deep drop-off. When the drop-off was adjusted to appear to be about the distance from one stair step to the next, however, infants with stair-crawling experience sometimes turned around and attempted to descend backwards down the illusory staircase. More recent studies have provided further support for the notion of a dynamic perception-action system.

Assessing Motor Development

Major motor milestones typically appear in a predictable fashion during the first three years (shown in Table 6.5). For this reason, although there is variation in specific test content and administration, motor milestones are assessed in many developmental inventories, such as the Denver Developmental Screening Test II. One common assessment, designed for infants from birth to 42 months of age, is the **Bayley Scales of Infant Development-Second Edition (BSID-II)** (Bayley, 1993); a briefer version, the Bayley Short Form-Research Edition (BSF-R), is also widely used (Flanagan & Park, 2005). These assessments do not correlate well with children's later scores on intelligence tests, a point we discuss in Chapter 7. Both instruments, however, allow researchers and practitioners to compare individual children's abilities to a set of normative ages for a range of **fine motor skills,** such as grasping objects between finger and thumb, and **gross motor skills,** including the achievement of balance and postural control that enables infants to sit alone, stand without support, and move on to more advanced skills, such as walking up stairs and jumping. The timing of these motor skills highlights the cephalocaudal direction (from the head to the trunk and lower body) in which infants typically gain control over and stabilize body movements. Researchers now recognize that these predictable motor skills are part of a dynamic perception-action system, one that adapts to properties of the environment and changes in the infant's own body (Adolph, 2008; Thelen & Smith, 2006).

Even before infants are able to move around well on their own, they adjust their posture in response to visual information, even when the visual system conflicts with other cues about the stability and supportability of surfaces. In a classic study involving 13- to 16-month-old infants, researchers designed a room that moved around a standing infant, creating the illusion of movement in the absence of kinesthetic information for movement (similar to the sensation of moving that a person sitting in a parked car experiences as cars on either side begin to move). The majority of infants lost their balance or moved to compensate for the apparent movement indicated by the moving walls (Lee & Aronson, 1974). Similar results have been found at younger ages in studies involving new walkers whose movement was affected by their passage through a moving hallway

| TABLE 6.5 | Approximate Ages for the Appearance of Fine and Gross Motor Milestones | |

Milestones	Age	Examples
Fine Motor Skills		
Prereaching	Present at birth	Neonates extend their arms toward nearby objects.
Coordinated reaching	3–4 months	Infants hold objects and examine them visually before bringing them to their mouth.
Smooth reaching	5–6 months	Infants make one or two targeted movements, instead of several jerky movements, as they reach for objects. They can pass objects back and forth between their hands.
Adjusting hand position	6–8 months	Infants adjust their hands in order to grasp different types of objects and objects in different orientations. Visual feedback from their own hands is not necessary at this age.
Increasing specificity	8–9 months	Infants grasp objects and explore them manually with increasing specificity. Whole-hand grasping is replaced by a fingertip grasp involving opposition of the thumb to the other fingers.
Handedness	11 months	Infants show a clear preference for using one hand or the other in activities such as self-feeding.
Manipulating objects	10–20 months	Fine motor skills are used to perform a variety of increasingly complex activities, including scribbling and "drawing" with markers, painting with paintbrushes, and building with blocks.
Gross Motor Skills		
Head control	3 weeks–4 months	Infants hold their head steady when their body is supported and held upright.
Upper body control	3 weeks–2 months	When placed on their stomach, infants begin to raise their head and use their arms to push their upper body off of the surface on which they are lying.
Rolling	3 weeks–5 months	By rolling, infants can move from their side to their back.
Rolling over	2–7 months	Infants can roll over when placed on their back.
Independent sitting	5–9 months	Infants can sit upright by themselves.
Crawling	5–11 months	Infants begin to crawl, using a variety of postures and approaches as they learn about balance and coordination.
Climbing stairs (crawling)	10–13 months	Infants crawl up stairs, often prior to learning to descend.
Pulling up	5–12 months	Infants grab onto furniture and pull themselves up to a standing position. Side-stepping cruising is common.
Independent walking	9–17 months	Infants begin taking steps in an upright position. With experience, they adjust their body posture and leg position and learn to maintain their balance while in motion.
Running	18–24 months	Children gain sufficient balance and coordination to run.
Galloping and hopping	24–36 months	As leg muscles become stronger and balance improves, children begin to engage in other gross motor skills.

Source: Based on Adolph & Berger, 2006; Bayley, 1993; Berger, Theuring, & Adolph, 2007.

(Schmuckler & Gibson, 1989), prewalking infants who adjusted their posture while seated in a moving room (Butterworth & Hicks, 1977), and 3-day-old infants whose stepping reflex was elicited by the sight of a virtual surface that appeared to be moving (Barbu-Roth et al., 2009).

Reaching, Grasping, and Manipulating Objects: Fine Motor Skills

The ability to reach for, grasp, and manually explore objects is an important motor skill that develops over the first year of life. Newborns display prereaching movements and extend their arms toward nearby objects, suggesting that the foundation for this skill is present at birth (Ennouri & Bloch, 1996; Rönnqvist & von Hofsten, 1994).

Many studies, including an intensive longitudinal study of four infants from 3 weeks to 1 year of age, have shown that younger infants' reaches typically consist of several movements, rather than just one or two targeted movements, as occurs in older infants' reaches. Younger infants' reaches also tend to be less directly aimed at their target, and they often have less control over the speed (Bhat, Heathcock, & Galloway, 2005; Thelen & Spencer, 1998; von Hofsten, 1991). Reaching movements vary, however, as a function of the type of action. When young infants are trying to bat at an object, rather than grasp it, for example, they are able to make smoother, more accurate arm movements (Berthier, 1996). Object size makes a difference, too; 4- to 6-month-old babies make more adjustments and corrections when reaching for a small object than for a big one (Rocha, dos Santos Silva, & Tudella, 2006).

Repeated experience with familiar objects facilitates infants' ability to reach for, grasp, and manipulate those objects. This was shown in an experiment with 9-, 12-, and 15-month-olds, in which infants initially examined a set of objects that were identical except in color and weight. Infants were then presented with two new test objects for which the original color-weight correspondence was reversed (e.g., a lightweight blue object and heavy orange object from the familiarization phase appeared as heavy blue and lightweight orange objects in the test phase). Throughout the study, sensors on babies' arms measured the force of their actions, revealing that they relied on their previous experience (the original color-weight correspondence) to anticipate and produce the force that they expected to need in the test phase (Mash, 2007).

Infants' characteristics are another important factor. Longitudinal data collected weekly from four babies showed that the emergence of reaching varied according to differences in body strength, general activity level, prior motor skill development, and motivation. As a result, despite the common goal of reaching and grasping objects, they accomplished this task in different ways, responding to different challenges. Some exuberant babies, for example, had to learn to reduce the force of their arm movements, whereas others had to learn to produce more muscle force; too much speed was a problem for some babies, whereas too little was a problem for others. These findings are consistent with dynamic systems theories, which assert that motor development is "always a continual dialogue between the nervous system, the body, and the environment" (Thelen & Spencer, 1998, p. 513).

Coordination of reaching and grasping develops rapidly over the first six months of life, facilitated by increasing postural control (Bhat et al., 2005; Rocha & Tudella, 2008). Infants are able to bring their hands to their mouth from a very early age; by the age of about 4 months, infants typically study objects visually before bringing them to their mouth for oral exploration (Bertenthal & Clifton, 1998; Rochat & Senders, 1991). These actions are affected, however, by the stability of babies' posture and their ability to change positions, freeing both hands to grasp and explore nearby objects (Rocha & Tudella, 2008; Thelen & Spencer, 1998). In one experiment, 6-month-olds who were not yet able to sit independently made smoother reaching movements when placed in an infant seat that facilitated postural control than when they did not have this support (Hopkins & Rönnqvist, 2002). As infants begin walking, around the age of 12 months, they often return to two-handed reaching. This decline is only temporary, however, and coordinated reaching with one hand typically resumes once a stable walking gait is established (Corbetta & Bojczyk, 2002).

Early studies of infants' grasping and manual exploration identified three distinct stages from 20 to 32 weeks of age: a whole-hand grasping stage, an intermediate stage involving the thumb's opposition to the palm, and a finger-tip grasp involving opposition of the thumb to the other fingers (Halverson, 1931, 1932). More recent research has validated the notion of a general developmental progression for various grips during infancy (Siddiqui, 1995), but it is also clear that infants as young as 6 months adjust their grasp in response to the properties of objects, including their size, shape, weight, substance, and noise-making propensity (Gibson & Walker, 1984; Palmer, 1989). Visual information guides grasping and manual exploration with increasing specificity; by the age of 8 to 9 months, infants are able to anticipate object shape and size, adjusting their finger and thumb positioning well in advance of contact with the object (Bertenthal & Clifton, 1998). Infants' reaching and grasping strategies become more flexible by 10 months of age but are also affected by an emerging hand preference (Fagard, Spelke, & von Hofsten, 2009).

By the second half of the first year, infants make adjustments in order to grasp objects in different orientations, even if they are not able to see their own hands (Bertenthal & Clifton, 1998; Clifton et al., 1994). Infants are also able to catch moving objects at various speeds and lighting conditions, adjusting their reach in anticipation of the object's trajectory (Robin, Berthier, & Clifton, 1996; von Hofsten, 1983). These findings indicate that young infants use proprioceptive information to guide arm and hand movements.

Toward the end of the first year, infants begin using simple tools, such as spoons. By the age of about 11 months, most infants have developed a clear hand preference for self-feeding. Between 11 and 17 months of age, infants typically try out a variety of grips before settling on the most successful approaches (Connolly & Dalgleish, 1989). Longitudinal studies indicate that early tool use develops gradually, reflecting individual infants' unique experiences and evolving physical abilities, and has much in common with other components of the perception-action system (Lockman, 2000).

By the age of about 11 months, most infants have developed a clear hand preference for self-feeding.

Crawling and Walking: Gross Motor Skills

In the 1930s and 1940s, descriptions of substages in the development of crawling and other motor abilities supported the prevailing view that changes in these skills were due to the maturation of neural structures. Differences in the rate of development were thought to reflect genetic differences in the timing of cortical control of movements previously under reflexive control, rather than variations in experience (Gesell, 1946; McGraw, 1935, 1940). More recent studies, guided by dynamic systems theories, have challenged this assumption, documenting a variety of ways in which independent locomotion develops; these theories also highlight the contributions made by infants' own adaptive responses as they move through the environment (Adolph, 2008; Adolph & Berger, 2006).

One longitudinal study of 28 infants, for example, started with their first attempts at crawling (around 7 to 8 months of age) and continued until they began independent walking (at about 12 months). A variety of crawling postures were observed, but there was no evidence of a strict sequence of stagewise development. Approximately half of the infants crawled on their bellies before crawling on hands and knees, while the other half began with hands-and-knees crawling (Adolph, Vereijken, & Denny, 1998).

As infants become more expert at crawling, they pull themselves up to stand and begin cruising—walking with support, usually stepping sideways. Initially, infants hold onto furniture, moving one limb at a time, but later they develop a more complex pattern of movement involving two or three limbs simultaneously and become more stable—less wobbly. They often continue to use several distinct patterns of limb and body movements, however, rather than settle on just one combination. This adaptive solution allows for greater flexibility when cruising in a range of settings requiring different degrees of involvement by the trunk and arms relative to the legs (Haehl, Vardaxis, & Ulrich, 2000).

Infants with stairs in their home usually learn to crawl up stairs earlier (at about 10 months of age) than infants without everyday opportunities to learn this skill, in part because parents in homes with stairs tend to provide babies with explicit lessons. Learning to crawl down stairs develops slightly later and, by contrast, appears to emerge at about the same age (approximately 13 months) for babies with and without stairs in their home, possibly because parents in both settings prevent infants from trying to descend stairs until they believe that they are ready to do so. Most babies try out a variety of strategies for descending stairs, including turning around and backing down (Berger, Theuring, & Adolph, 2007).

When infants begin to walk without support, they fall down frequently, in part because there is great variability in their gait. From one moment to the next, their legs may be close together or far apart; their leading foot may be followed more or less quickly by their other foot. Infants initially achieve stability by raising their arms and taking slow steps that are relatively wide apart—a "Frankenstein's monster" style of walking. After two to three months of practice, leg muscles become stronger and the limbs are better coordinated; infants' gait becomes more stable and consistent. Whereas beginning walkers have both feet planted on the ground for as much as 60 percent of the time (for adults, the comparable figure is 20 percent), experienced walkers become better able to maintain their balance as their weight shifts from one foot to the other and the distance between steps increases (Adolph & Berger, 2006; Adolph, Vereijken, & Shrout, 2003; Badaly & Adolph, 2008).

Infants often make the task of walking more challenging by picking up and carrying toys or other objects of varying size and weight. In addition, infants' bodies continue to grow and change, requiring ongoing adjustments in order to maintain balance and coordination. Some researchers have studied these adaptations by attaching loads to babies' bodies or having them

To the delight of their parents, infants' first independent steps are often taken around the age of 12 months. This remarkable motor milestone is the result of a vast amount of previous locomotor experience.

wear vests containing weights. Less experienced walkers are usually more disrupted by these loads than are more experienced walkers, especially if the loads are placed asymmetrically on their body or if they are also required to negotiate a challenging surface, such as a slope (Adolph & Avolio, 2000; Garciaguirre, Adolph, & Shrout, 2007; Vereijken, Pedersen, & Størksen, 2009).

Walking experience helps infants and toddlers learn about their own physical abilities and the suitability of those skills for particular, sometimes novel situations, such as climbing over barriers of varying heights (Schmuckler, 1996) or moving through doorways of varying widths (Adolph, 1997). In numerous studies, locomotor experience—not children's height, weight, or other body-size characteristics—appears to underlie accurate perception of the ability to climb over barriers, squeeze through openings, and negotiate variable terrain.

Children become more adept at using visual input to guide their locomotion, adjusting to information about whether the terrain surrounding them is rigid enough to support walking or would be better negotiated by crawling (Gibson et al., 1987; Stoffregen et al., 1997). Infants and toddlers adjust their crawling and walking in response to their perception of the slope of an incline, the support offered by a handrail, and the width of a platform (Berger, Adolph, & Lobo, 2005).

Infants do not always transfer learning from one posture to another. This was shown in a study in which newly crawling babies, who accurately perceived that they could not safely reach across a wide gap, attempted to crawl headlong into the opening (Adolph, 2000). Studies also show that lessons learned while crawling in specific settings are not necessarily carried over to walking and may need to be relearned (Adolph, 2000, 2008; Adolph, Vereijken, & Shrout, 2003; Berger & Adolph, 2003). Keeping this in mind may help prevent accidental injuries if, for example, parents and caregivers realize that infants who have learned to crawl up and down stairs will not necessarily be able to navigate those stairs safely when they first begin to do so in an upright, walking mode.

Implications for Parents and Caregivers

There is considerable variation across cultures in how parents handle prewalking infants and encourage their motor development (Gardiner, Mutter, & Kosmitzki, 2002; Hewlett et al., 1998; Hopkins & Westra, 1990; Rogoff & Morelli, 1989). In many parts of the world, infants are carried on the mother's back, secured in place with a blanket or strips of cloth, leaving the mother's hands free to cook, weave, tend to crops, or perform other daily tasks (Keller, 2003; Pretorius, Naudé, & Van Vuuren, 2002). In the United States and in most developed countries, by contrast, infants are more likely to be strapped into strollers and wheeled, rather than carried. In these contexts, parents often give their infants "tummy time" on a blanket on the floor and baby-proof the home to enable their children to crawl and explore in safety. In contexts where parents have concerns about sanitation or safety, lying on or crawling across the floor may be discouraged or even forbidden (Wong, 2009). Finally, in some cultures, infants are discouraged from walking before the age of 1 year, whereas in other cultures, including the United States, many infants spend time in devices that parents hope will encourage early independent walking (DeLoache & Gottlieb, 2000; Garrett, McElroy, & Staines, 2002).

How do these different practices affect patterns of motor development? The answer depends on the type of early experience and the specific ability in question (Gardiner, Mutter, & Kosmitzki, 2002; Super, 1976). Infants in traditional cultures strapped onto their mother's back, for example, do not appear to crawl or walk later than infants who are not confined in this way and may even begin walking without the benefit of extensive crawling experience (Gardiner, Mutter, & Kosmitzki, 2002; Wong, 2009). Babies who spend significant amounts of time in walkers or other infant equipment, however, appear to begin walking later than babies who are not placed in those devices—the opposite result that parents are often trying to achieve (Abbott & Bartlett, 2001; Garrett, et al., 2002; Siegel & Burton, 1999). If, as many researchers have found, infants explore and test out a variety of crawling, cruising, and walking postures on their way to becoming more skilled in these forms of locomotion, it is possible that infants confined in walkers are actually missing out on opportunities to develop a flexible repertoire of relevant skills (Adolph & Berger, 2006).

Infants who are assisted in performing specific locomotor skills, including stepping, reaching, and crawling, appear to benefit from the practice (Adolph et al., 1998; Lobo et al., 2004; Vereijken & Thelen, 1997). In a study of Jamaican infants who were assisted in sitting upright from an early age, independent sitting appeared earlier than among a comparison group of English infants without early assistance with this skill (Hopkins & Westra, 1990). In another study, researchers who systematically activated young infants' stepping reflex over a period of

This Mexican mother carries one child on her back while she sorts tomatillos with her other child.

weeks reported that these babies began to walk earlier than a comparison group who did not receive this extra stimulation (Zelazo et al., 1993). A three-week study of 9- to 21-week-old infants, in which parents were instructed to emphasize social, postural, or object-oriented experiences, showed that babies with postural and object-oriented training displayed more advanced reaching and haptic exploration of objects than babies in a social interaction condition (Lobo & Galloway, 2008).

What are the implications of these findings for parents and caregivers? As we have discussed, motor abilities—even "automatic" motor milestones, such as crawling and walking—develop gradually as a result of repeated experience. Before learning to roll over by themselves, infants benefit from practice coordinating their limbs with the movements of their head and body. Structured infant exercise programs and equipment are not necessary, however, for the development of healthy infants (American Academy of Pediatrics Committee on Sports Medicine, 1988). Instead, infants should be in a safe environment that stimulates their senses and enables them to participate actively. While parents can make occasional use of infant "containers," such as bouncy seats, playpens, and strollers, babies need ample time every day to move and explore. To the extent possible, there should be a range of toys and other child-safe objects made out of a variety of substances with different noise-making capabilities.

For toddlers and preschoolers, experts recommend that, during waking hours, children should not be sedentary for more than one hour at a time (National Association for Sport and Physical Education, 2002). Beginning in the toddler years, children benefit from both structured physical activity and unstructured free play and should have time for both kinds of activities every day. Although normal motor development can occur across a wide range of contexts and opportunities, the ideal environment at these ages is one that gives children objects to ride, push, pull, throw, and catch, and structures that they can climb through and on. Above all, these activities should be fun for the children involved and provide them with a foundation for lifelong physical activity.

WRAPPING IT UP: Summary and Conclusion

Infants are able to see, hear, feel, taste, and smell at birth. Traditional empiricist theories assumed that infants are initially unable to perceive the world accurately, whereas nativist theories challenged the empiricist notion that initially meaningless sensory information could become meaningful as a result of experience during infancy. Gestalt theories asserted that the brain is designed to translate and organize sensory information that would otherwise be meaningless. According to the more recently developed ecological theory, the perceptual system perceives meaningful information about the environment accurately and directly. Dynamic systems theories describe development as the emergence of new forms of behavior due to self-organization and interactions of the components of a complex system operating on multiple levels.

Vision is the least well developed sense at birth. Newborns notice and pay attention to objects and people in motion. Their attention is drawn to areas of high contrast, and they prefer some patterns more than others. Visual acuity is poor at birth but improves to nearly adult levels by the age of about 8 months. Visual problems, although relatively rare among infants, can be detected with early screening. Early treatment is necessary to prevent permanent impairment and promote normal development of the visual cortex. Perceiving objects and perceiving depth improve during the first six months of life.

Newborns pay special attention to the human voice and seem to prefer it to other sounds. Infants are aroused by high-pitched speech and soothed by low-pitched sounds. Innate sensitivity to all language sounds diminishes as infants become more attuned to the sounds that are meaningful in their native language.

Most neonatal reflexes are activated through the sense of touch. The ability to feel pain is present from birth; mild pain can often be alleviated through physical comforting and swaddling; sucrose analgesia is also effective for pain that is not too intense or long lasting.

Infants have an innate preference for high-energy, sweet-tasting substances but dislike sour and bitter flavors. The foods that pregnant women consume influence babies' reaction to flavors and odors during the early postnatal period. Infants respond to aromas in ways that are similar to adults' responses. They recognize salient biological odors, such as amniotic fluid or their own mother's breast milk.

Infants' vestibular sense conveys information about balance and support, and some neonatal reflexes are activated by stimulation of this sense. The proprioceptive and kinesthetic senses provide information from muscles, tendons, and joints about the body's position and movement.

Intermodal perception is facilitated by infants' ability to perceive amodal properties of events. Cross-modal perception is possible soon after birth, as shown by studies of visual-haptic transfer.

Fine and gross motor skills develop in a predictable order and are part of a dynamic perception-action system that enables infants to adapt to their environment. Visual information guides infants' locomotion, and locomotor experience helps them learn about their own physical capabilities. Across cultures, there is variation in how prewalking infants are handled and in the role parents play in encouraging locomotor development. Beginning from infancy, children need opportunities every day to move, explore, and develop their perceptual and motor abilities.

THINK ABOUT IT: Questions for Reading and Discussion

1. How would you decorate a room for an infant or toddler in order to optimally stimulate all five senses?
2. In what ways is motor development part of a perception-action system?
3. Why do you think that movement is such a salient source of visual information for infants? Compare the potential value of knowing an object's location or trajectory with the potential value of knowing its color, shape, or size.
4. How does independent mobility affect infants' lives? What impact does it have on their parents?
5. Describe the ideal environment for supporting and stimulating motor development during infancy.
6. What could we learn by studying sensation, perception, and motor development across a range of cultural contexts? Suggest a specific topic or question and outline how it might be investigated.

Key Words

Accretion and deletion (167)   The apparent appearance and disappearance of elements of a visual stimulus, such as its texture or pattern.

Amodal properties (178)   Information that exists redundantly across sense modalities, rather than being specific to just one modality, such as the synchrony of a sight and its accompanying sound.

Auditory localization (171)   The ability to detect the location of sound sources.

Bayley Scales of Infant Development-Second Edition (BSID-II) (181)   A widely use assessment that includes scales for measuring motor development from birth to 42 months of age.

Binocular disparity (169)   Slightly different retinal images that are produced when a viewer looks at a single object or visual stimulus.

Binocular vision (166)   Visual input from two eyes that are aligned and move together.

Cones (165)   Photoreceptors in the eye that respond to specific hues, or wavelengths of light.

Contrast sensitivity (166)   The ability to perceive differences among the elements of an image or pattern under varying degrees of contrast between the pattern and its background (e.g., black patterns on a white background versus a grayish background).

Cross-modal perception (180)   The ability to transfer information about an object from one sense, such as vision, and use it when encountering the object later using a different sense, such as touch.

Depth perception (162)   The ability to perceive a three-dimensional world.

Dynamic systems theories (164)   Perspectives that describe development as the emergence of new forms of behavior due to self-organization and interactions of the components of a complex system operating on multiple levels.

Ecological theory of perception (162)   A theory that assumes that the visual system perceives meaningful information directly from the properties of the environment.

Fine motor skills (181)   Skills, such as grasping small objects, that involve movements of the fingers and hands.

Forced-choice preferential looking (166)   A research procedure in which infants are shown two visual stimuli simultaneously and the total amount of time they spend looking at each display is compared.

Fovea (166)   The center of the eye.

Gross motor skills (181)   Skills, such as crawling and walking, that involve movements of the whole body and large muscle groups.

Haptic information (180)   Exploratory mouth or hand movements that go well beyond mere tactile contact with an object.

Intermodal perception (178)   The ability to integrate multiple simultaneous sources of sensory information, such as sights and sounds produced by a single object or event.

Intersensory redundancy hypothesis (179)   The theoretical notion that intersensory redundancy in multimodal events promotes perception of amodal information, whereas unimodal events enhance perception of modality-specific properties.

Kinematic depth cues (169)   Information about perceptual depth that is carried by motion.

Kinesthetic sense (177)   A sense that conveys information about the body's position and movement.

Optical expansion and contraction (169)   The increase and decrease in the size of an object's image on the retina.

Pictorial depth cues (170)   Information about perceptual depth that is used in two-dimensional representations of the three-dimensional world, including relative size, linear perspective, texture gradients, and interposition.

Proprioceptive sense (177)   A sense that conveys information from muscles, tendons, and joints about the body's position and movement.

Stereoscopic depth information (169)   Information about perceptual depth that is produced by binocular disparity.

Vestibular sense (177)   A sense that conveys information about physical balance and support.

Visual acuity (165)   The smallest spacing that can be perceived between parts of a pattern.

Visual cortex (166)   The area of the brain that processes visual information.

7

Cognition, Learning, and Intelligence

Between 6 and 12 months of age, infants become able to use a spoon to feed themselves, showing increasing skill and a consistent hand preference by the age of about 11 months. As thrilled as parents are by this achievement, in the second year of life something even more amazing happens—very young children begin to use spoons to *pretend* to feed themselves. Approaching their second birthday, children become increasingly adept at employing familiar objects and realistic props to simulate a

This young boy's pretend conversation might not occur without the presence of such a realistic prop.

range of actions, such as giving a doll a bath or putting their teddy bear to sleep. If the ability to feed oneself depends on perceptual-motor development, what underlies the ability to act *as if* imaginary food is being eaten?

Children pretending to feed a stuffed animal follow the routine they have observed parents enacting with them: picking up a spoon, moving it toward the "baby's" mouth, and offering encouraging commentary about the delicious food. At a minimum, the ability to engage in pretense depends on being able to notice these events, remember their components, and perform the same actions in a different context. As we discuss in this chapter, these are all cognitive abilities that appear and improve during the first three years of life. They are advances that enable children to acquire, organize, and use knowledge about the world, in short, to behave intelligently. We review these aspects of cognitive development, comparing different, often conflicting theoretical and methodological approaches. We also summarize efforts to define and measure intelligence in infancy and to use those measures to predict intelligence later in childhood. The focus of this chapter is on cognitive development, but the skills and knowledge that we discuss are acquired and used in a physical, social, and cultural context. To illustrate this, we begin by considering the development of play—a pervasive childhood activity that both depends upon and contributes to early cognitive development.

THE DEVELOPMENT OF PLAY

Children's play may not look very different from other everyday activities. How do we know, therefore, that a child putting a doll to sleep is playing—pretending that it is bedtime—rather than acting on the belief that the doll is actually tired? According to most definitions of **play,** in contrast to other activities, it is intrinsically motivated, characterized by attention to means rather than ends, and distinguished from purely exploratory behavior. Unlike organized games, play also tends to be free from externally applied rules (Rubin, Fein, & Vandenberg, 1983). Children pretending that it is naptime for their doll, therefore, often initiate this activity on their own, rather than have it suggested or organized for them by an adult. Although some steps may be omitted, to the extent that children have noticed and can remember their own routines, they are likely to give the doll a snack or drink before taking off its shoes, laying it down with a pillow and blanket, and finally reading a story or singing a lullaby. Play is not always logical or directly derived from everyday experience, however, and very young children also pretend about scenarios that no adult would suggest, such as unrolling a toilet-paper "snake" into the toilet or "vacuuming" the kitchen table with an apple slice.

Play with Objects

Play is influenced by the materials and opportunities available. In communities with relatively few resources, promoting young children's play may be overshadowed by parents' efforts to meet more basic needs, such as providing food and shelter. Children in developed countries, by contrast, often have access to toys that are designed to be safe, developmentally appropriate, educational, and, increasingly, activated by a tiny computer chip. While these features may make toys attractive to adults who buy them, infants do not notice or care if their toys are expensive and smart. Across many different contexts, play develops chiefly as a function of children's evolving motor, cognitive, and social skills. As Table 7.1 shows, play with objects changes during the first three years of life.

TABLE 7.1 Types of Object Play from Birth to Age 3

Type of Play	Ages	Characteristics and Examples
Exploratory	Birth to 4 months	Repetitive motor movements, focused on the infant's own body: kicking the legs, reaching for and sucking on the toes, practicing moving and rolling over.
Relational	4 to 12 months	Bringing together and manipulating objects that are not related to each other, such as a piece of silky fabric and a plastic measuring cup. Repeatedly banging objects or putting them into containers and dumping them out are favorite activities.
Functional	12 to 18 months	Infants discover how their own actions create reactions, and play with objects becomes more intentional. After discovering that a toy can be activated by pushing a button or pulling a string, infants repeat this action.
Functional-relational	12 to 18 months	Objects are increasingly used in ways that show understanding of their intended use: Children roll objects with wheels, pretend to drink out of empty cups, and "talk" on toy telephones. They bring together related objects, such as a bowl and spoon or a doll and the doll's bed.
Gross motor play	12 to 24 months	As gross motor skills develop, children use them to push toys such as small carts or pull toys that have strings. Children also enjoy play that involves climbing, sliding, swinging, spinning, or moving their whole body through containers such as play tunnels, gigantic cardboard boxes, and ball crawls (shallow vats of large plastic balls).
Fine motor play	24 to 36 months	As children's fine motor skills develop, they are able to play with fingerpaint and Play-Doh®. They also enjoy filling and emptying containers with dried beans, uncooked pasta, sand, and water. Fine motor skills can also be used to string beads, put together simple puzzles with large pieces, and build towers and other structures with wooden blocks or age-appropriate Legos®.

Source: Based on information in Garner, 1998.

Babies learn about the world as a result of their exploratory play with objects. With as little as 30 seconds of initial play and physical contact, infants develop expectations about toys' characteristics. If researchers subsequently modify salient, functional properties (such as eliminating their noise-making capability), 13-month-old infants persist in trying to reproduce the original effects (Baldwin, Markman, & Melartin, 1989).

As children become more skilled at walking, between the ages of 12 and 24 months, much of their play uses gross motor skills. In addition, because 2- to 3-year-old children less frequently put objects in their mouth, they become more likely to use fine motor skills to play with a variety of materials. As they near the age of 3 years, most children can use scissors, glue sticks, and paintbrushes with increasing control, although the focus of these activities still tends to be on playful manipulation and exploration.

Social Play

An increasing array of computer software designed for very young children has extended play to include objects and characters in a virtual reality. The best "object" to interact with, however, is still a responsive human playmate. In many parts of the world, parents and adult caregivers play simple, repetitive games with young infants, eliciting and responding to their smiles, coos, limb movements, and changes in visual attention (Fernald & O'Neill, 1993; Roopnarine et al., 1994). Adult-infant play often consists of pat-a-cake and other singing games with hand and arm movements, give-and-take games (trading toys back and forth), pointing-and-naming games, and peekaboo. As infants get older, they assume an increasingly active role, initiating play as well as responding to adults' behaviors (Fogel, Nwokah, & Karns, 1993). Adult-infant play is not universal, however; in some cultures, play is regarded as unimportant or appropriate only for child participants, such as the infant's older siblings and peers (Bornstein et al., 1999; Farver & Howes, 1993; Gaskins, 1999; Tamis-LeMonda & Bornstein, 1996).

In cultures where adult-infant play is common, parents often adopt the role of their child's teacher. Mothers are more likely than fathers to use play as an opportunity for teaching infants about words and routines, whereas fathers tend to play more physically and "just for fun" (Barnard & Solchany, 2002; Parke, 2002). The ways in which mothers and fathers interact and play with their infants vary, however. Even within the same culture, parent-infant play is affected by factors such as parents' employment status, knowledge of child development, and involvement in their infant's daily care (Fisher et al., 2008; Tamis-LeMonda, Chen, & Bornstein, 1997).

Cross-culturally, mothers who view play as contributing to cognitive development are more likely to provide props and specific suggestions than are mothers who regard play as a primarily social or entertaining activity (Farver, Kim, & Lee, 1995; Farver & Wimbarti, 1995; Tudge, Lee, & Putnam, 1998). Children in collectivist (group-oriented) cultures are often guided in mother-child play to use toys to promote social interaction, whereas children in individualist cultures (like the United States) are more often prompted to focus on the characteristics of the toys themselves. In a study comparing Argentine and U.S. mothers, Argentine mothers (who are part of a collectivist culture) encouraged their 20-month-olds to pretend to perform social routines, such as feeding or sharing with others, but U.S. mothers encouraged their children to use the same set of toys in functionally different ways, such as stacking a set of cups or dialing a toy telephone (Bornstein et al., 1999).

Japanese mothers tend to emphasize social routines during play ("Feed the teddy" or "Say thank you"), whereas American mothers more frequently use play as an opportunity to teach infants about objects' names and functions ("That's a dump truck" or "Push the car"). Given that

Japanese culture is built on a foundation of interdependence and mutual empathy, whereas U.S. culture tends to emphasize independence and individual achievement, these different patterns suggest that parents use play to socialize infants and young children, reinforcing prevailing cultural beliefs and practices (Fernald & Morikawa, 1993; Tamis-LeMonda et al., 1992).

In contrast to cultural variation in adult-infant play, play among peers and siblings appears to be nearly universal. From a very early age, most babies respond with enthusiastic interest whenever there is a chance to interact with other infants or children (Howes, 1996). Infants with autism—a developmental syndrome that we discuss in greater detail in Chapter 8—are one notable exception. They tend not to show typical signs of social interest, such as making eye contact with or imitating other people, and they often play alone, using toys in unusual ways, such as arranging and rearranging them repeatedly (Frith, 2003; Preissler, 2006). Most infants, by contrast, initially demonstrate social interest through visual gaze at other children, excited vocalizations, and reaching or other movements of the hands, arms, and body—a behavioral repertoire that some parents describe as "species recognition." If they are close enough, precrawling infants reach for each other, examining the other child or fingering the same toys. With independent mobility, infants crawl toward each other and in the direction of toys and sights that draw their attention. Toddlers' more advanced locomotor skills enable them to carry toys and other objects and use these items in social play. Infants and toddlers who spend time together on a regular basis show clear preferences for specific play partners within a larger group of children. Experience with coordinated, complementary play activities— like chasing and give-and-take games—during the early toddler years is a foundation for more complex forms of social pretend play during the third year of life and beyond (Garner, 1998; Howes, 1996).

Pretend/Symbolic Play

Pretend/symbolic play usually emerges after the first birthday, when children behave in a nonliteral way, acting *as if* they were performing familiar routines, such as eating, going to sleep, or washing their face. The earliest pretend actions tend to be brief and unrelated to children's other ongoing behavior. They may, for example, add sound effects ("vroom, vroom") and motions that transform a piece of toast into a car just before eating it. With age, children combine pretend actions into a coherent sequence, such as washing a doll's hands before feeding her lunch.

Children's pretend play is initially dependent on the presence of realistic props, such as a toy telephone, and they have difficulty using substitutes with little resemblance to the real object, such as a wooden block, until nearly 3 years of age. Children younger than age 3 also avoid using props that already have specific functions, such as a shoe, to symbolize other objects, such as a telephone (Garner, 1998).

As early as 15 months of age, however, infants are able to notice patterns and inconsistencies in others' pretend actions, even if they involve unusual objects. Fifteen-month-olds appear surprised (look with increased interest), for example, if they observe a person pretending to pour liquid into one cup and then pretending to drink from another cup. They also appear surprised if they observe a person pretending to pour liquid into one shoe and then pretending to drink from another shoe, provided that they previously saw the person pretend to pour liquid into and drink from a single shoe (Onishi, Baillargeon, & Leslie, 2007). Although infants of this age would not typically use such an unusual prop in their own play, their looking behavior in these studies may indicate that they are able to ignore an object's identity and focus on the coherence of the pretend sequence.

Young children's pretend play is initially focused on the self but gradually expands to include other participants. A 13-month-old who places a bowl on his head, for example, pretending that it is a hat, is unlikely to place the bowl/hat on a parent's head unless asked to do so. By the age of about 15 months, children begin to engage in parallel pretend play—sitting near each other and occasionally making eye contact, as both children rock their own baby doll or push their own small train along a wooden track.

Pretend play becomes more social between 2 and 3 years of age, and children begin to coordinate their pretend actions with those of playmates. At first, this tends to occur through nonverbal imitation, such as pretending to drink from a cup after seeing playmates pretending to drink from their own cups. Later, children also begin to respond by verbally imitating play partners and producing their own play-related speech (Eckerman & Didow, 1989). The ability to comprehend pretend play in others advances significantly after the second birthday (Harris & Kavanaugh, 1993). As a result, a child whose playmate knocks over an empty cup and exclaims over the "spilled milk" may respond by pretending to dry off the table or refill the cup from an empty pitcher.

Two- and 3-year-olds begin to construct basic narratives about their play, often drawing on past experiences (Kavanaugh & Engel, 1998). Children's developing verbal skills enable them to comment on their own actions and coordinate them with others as part of a larger play theme (Lloyd & Goodwin, 1995). They use words to specify the setting ("This is a bus"), their roles ("I drive the bus"), and those of their play partners ("You ride the bus"). Shared, cooperative pretend play (also called sociodramatic play) reveals children's understanding of the world, including everyday scenes (e.g., making dinner at home), less frequent events (e.g., a checkup at the doctor's office), and relatively rare experiences (e.g., flying on an airplane).

Parents do not explicitly teach children how to pretend, but they do offer inspiration and encouragement by providing toys, props, and opportunities to play. Many parents support their children's pretense by using unique verbal and nonverbal behaviors, such as higher pitched speech, exaggerated actions, and a greater incidence and duration of sound effects, smiling, and direct eye contact (Lillard & Witherington, 2004; Ma & Lillard, 2006; Reissland & Snow, 1996). In an experiment with 18-month-olds, for example, mothers pretending to eat Cheerios® and drink juice talked more about those actions than when they were actually eating and drinking, and they made more sound effects (e.g., "mmmm"). These behaviors help very young children recognize and learn about the pretend mode (Lillard & Witherington, 2004).

The duration and quality of play often increase when parents join in (Bornstein et al., 1996; Harris & Kavanaugh, 1993; Kavanaugh & Engel, 1998). When mothers become involved, more time is spent setting up make-believe episodes, clarifying roles, finding props, and specifying the sociodramatic play theme. Once pretend play is under way, mothers ask questions, make suggestions, and give demonstrations. These behaviors appear to facilitate children's play, as long as the parent's involvement is not intrusive or insensitive to children's interests (Garner, 1998; Harris & Kavanaugh, 1993; Stilson & Harding, 1997).

Joint make-believe with older siblings also enhances young children's pretend play. Young children playing with an older sibling engage in more role-playing than when they play alone or even with their mother and sibling together. Explicit, sometimes heated discussion of each sibling's role contributes to young children's understanding of others' feelings and beliefs (Youngblade & Dunn, 1995), a topic that we discuss in more detail later. We turn now to examine the theory and legacy of Jean Piaget—one of the first scientists to study the development of children's play and children's minds.

PIAGET'S THEORY: CONSTRUCTING AND REPRESENTING KNOWLEDGE

According to Piaget (1896–1980), a Swiss researcher who observed his own three children beginning at birth, the capacity for pretense depends on the emergence of specific cognitive abilities, including **mental representation**—the ability to remember and think about objects and events, even when those objects and events are not present. Piaget asserted that this ability develops during the last half of the second year of life (between 18 and 24 months of age) as the culmination of a series of qualitatively distinct stages.

Piaget (1936/1952, 1937/1971, 1946/1962) developed a theory of cognitive development that describes four discrete periods of intelligence. Infancy (birth to 2 years) is the period of **sensorimotor intelligence,** early childhood (2 to 6 years) the **preoperational thought** period, middle childhood (6 to 12 years) the period of concrete operations, and adolescence (12 years and older) the period of formal operations. At each stage, according to Piaget, the child thinks about the world in a qualitatively unique way, developing the capacity for logical, abstract reasoning in the final stage. Our focus here is on the sensorimotor period and the very early preoperational stage.

Sensorimotor and Preoperational Intelligence

Piaget is known as a constructivist. Departing from the simple dichotomy of nativism versus empiricism, his theory proposes that knowledge is neither innately given nor provided through passive experience; instead, it is constructed and derived from children's own actions and adaptations to the environment. As we saw in Chapter 6, when infants encounter new objects and surfaces, exploration yields potentially useful information, such as which toys can be grasped and which surfaces are suitable for walking across. Given a new object that looks like a ball, children may use actions—which Piaget termed **schemes**—similar to those they have used previously to touch or push other balls. During the sensorimotor period, schemes are primarily physical—based on sensory and motor acts—but during the later three periods, schemes may also be conceptual, as when ideas are either reinforced or modified by experience.

In Piaget's view, infants engage in **assimilation** when they employ previously used actions to explore an object, whereas they use **accommodation** when they adjust their exploratory actions to an object's novel characteristics. Assimilating a new ball, for example, might consist of rolling it in the same manner as other balls previously encountered. In accommodation, by contrast, infants might shake a new ball if they discover that doing so produces music or animal sounds or makes the ball light up. This discovery might occur as a result of their own explorations or by watching and imitating another person's actions. With both modes simultaneously available (but one process predominating), the complementary processes of assimilation and accommodation modify schemes as a result of experience.

Piaget (1937/1971) believed that the foundation for all knowledge begins in infancy. In his view, infants are **egocentric,** initially understanding the world as it is filtered through their own sensory and motor acts. Across the first two years of life, infants gradually become more aware of others' perspectives, but egocentrism continues to affect children's thinking into early childhood. The incremental nature of cognitive development is evident in the six distinct stages (shown in Table 7.2) into which Piaget divided the sensorimotor period.

From birth to 1 month of age (Stage 1), **reflex schemes** provide infants with a set of initial responses to the world. Learning during this stage is limited because reflex schemes are unchanging across different sources of stimulation, showing little accommodation or modification. The same

TABLE 7.2	Piaget's Six Stages of Sensorimotor Intelligence	
Stage	**Ages**	**Characteristics and Examples**
1. Reflex schemes	Birth to 1 month	Infants respond reflexively to sensory stimulation. Grasping, sucking, and other reflexes provide infants with a set of schemes for initial learning.
2. Primary circular reactions	1 to 4 months	Infants learn about the world through chance activation of schemes. Grasping or sucking on toes initially occurs as a result of random movements but is subsequently repeated "just for fun."
3. Secondary circular reactions	4 to 8 months	Infants intentionally use schemes to repeat actions and achieve specific outcomes. Pushing a button occurs repeatedly and intentionally in order to activate a musical toy.
4. Coordination of secondary schemes	8 to 12 months	Infants coordinate two separate schemes in order to produce a specific outcome. An obstacle in front of a toy is moved before the toy is picked up and manipulated.
5. Tertiary Circular reactions	12 to 18 months	Infants "experiment" with schemes to discover how they work. Banging on a toy xylophone with a small mallet makes "music," whereas using fingers or a plastic cup produces a different sound.
6. Mental combinations	18 to 24 months	Toddlers are able to think about and select schemes to achieve desired outcomes. After looking at vertical crib bars, the child modifies his grasp on a toy in order to pull it through the first time.

Source: Based on information in Piaget, 1937/1971.

rooting reflex, for example, is elicited whether the infant's cheek is touched by the stroke of a finger, a nipple, or a rubber pacifier.

From 1 to 4 months of age (Stage 2), infants exhibit **primary circular reactions,** and sensory and motor schemes occur by chance. Although schemes are discovered by chance, infants work hard to recreate those schemes, intentionally moving their hand to their mouth and then sucking on their fingers. Infants' repeated (circular) actions are used for "entertainment" rather than to provide information about the world; in Piaget's view, this shows that infants are still egocentric and focused inward.

From 4 to 8 months of age (Stage 3), **secondary circular reactions,** schemes are less egocentric and infants focus on repeating actions to achieve specific outcomes. The events that infants initiate and repeat in this stage—such as dropping Cheerios® over the side of their high chair and watching them land on the floor—are often accompanied by signs of enjoyment. Piaget's daughter Lucienne reportedly squealed with laughter each time she kicked her legs and made a mobile over her crib move (Crain, 2000).

Infants 8 to 12 months of age (Stage 4) show **coordination of secondary schemes** and engage in means-end problem solving when they combine two separate schemes in order to produce an interesting outcome. Piaget observed his son, Laurent, move an obstacle (Piaget's hand) out of the way in order to reach a matchbox. Laurent's coordination of two schemes (moving and grabbing) was not the first solution he tried as he attempted to grab the matchbox, but it was the most successful one (Crain, 2000). Piaget inferred from this behavior that his son had begun to develop a basic understanding of spatial relationships—the notion that some objects are in front of others—as well as the relevance of the order in which the two schemes were used, since grabbing the matchbox could not occur until the hand had been moved out of the way. Infants' conception of space is still egocentric at this stage, and they are unaware of the spatial relations among objects in the world, independent of their direct contact with those objects.

From 12 to 18 months (Stage 5), **tertiary circular reactions,** infants try out different schemes to discover the effects of those actions. Infants in this stage are like little scientists, performing "experiments" on the people and objects around them.

From 18 to 24 months (Stage 6), **mental combinations,** children are able to think about their actions and select schemes to achieve an outcome. Piaget's daughter Lucienne discovered a solution for retrieving a small chain from a matchbox in which her father had placed it. Piaget noted that Lucienne first tried turning the box over and then attempted to squeeze her finger into the closed box. When these schemes failed, she reportedly opened and closed her mouth, while looking intently at the matchbox, and then quickly slid back the cover to make the opening of the matchbox wide enough to retrieve the chain (Crain, 2000).

The ability to imitate facial gestures (such as mouth opening and tongue protrusion) during face-to-face interaction is present in both newborn humans and nonhuman primates and appears to be an innate response to certain kinds of motion (Anisfeld, 1996; Ferrari et al., 2009; Meltzoff & Moore, 1983). By contrast, according to Piaget, the capacity for **deferred imitation** (repeating actions observed earlier, in the absence of a model for those actions) depends on Stage 6 mental representation. One well-known example comes from Piaget's daughter Jacqueline, who had a temper tantrum in her playpen that exactly mimicked a temper tantrum she had witnessed in another child the previous day. Fortunately, children also show deferred imitation of behaviors that parents find desirable and praiseworthy, including hugging and sharing.

Mental representation is evident in many other achievements at this age. It underlies the use of gestures, words, and signs to communicate ideas, as well as the use of numbers to count. Mental representational ability also contributes to children's emerging self-concept, and as we noted previously, their ability to engage in pretend play.

According to Piaget, whereas the first symbols appearing at the end of the sensorimotor period are representations of actions, the symbols that children use in the subsequent preoperational period may be either action-based or linguistic. Around the age of 2 years, children begin to use language to represent and talk about past and present experiences, as well as desires for the future. A child giving his stuffed animal a turn on his riding toy, for example, may narrate the activity, saying, "ride, bear." A child who accompanies her grandmother to the airport at the end of a visit together may tell her babysitter the next day, "Nanny go bye-bye."

Object Permanence

One of the best-known examples of the development of sensorimotor intelligence is **object permanence,** Piaget's term for infants' gradually developing understanding that objects continue to exist even when they are not in sensory or motor contact with them. If infants younger than 4 months drop a toy, for example, they do not actively look for it. In Stage 3, infants look for toys and other objects they have dropped, but their searches are short-lived, suggesting that they are not sure the objects still exist. Piaget tested object permanence by placing an ordinary object (his pocketwatch) under a blanket. He noted that, unless some part of the watch remained visible, Stage 3 infants typically failed to lift up the blanket and retrieve the hidden object.

In Piaget's theory, object permanence begins to develop around 8 months of age (Stage 4). In this stage, infants who watch a toy being hidden under a cloth or inside a container successfully use means-end problem solving to search for and retrieve it. Their understanding of object permanence is not yet complete, however. Stage 4 infants tend to make the **A-not-B error,** a mistake that occurs when infants watch an object being hidden repeatedly in one location (A) and successfully retrieve it from that location, but continue to search for the object there even after they have seen it being hidden at a different location (B). According to Piaget, the A-not-B error reflects infants' belief that their own actions will cause the object to appear at the location where those actions were previously successful.

In Stage 5, Piaget noted that infants are able to search for and retrieve an object at any location, regardless of whether they have previously searched at that spot. This new flexibility in search behavior depends, however, on the child having observed the object being moved and hidden in its final location. Piaget granted 18- to 24-month-olds (Stage 6) full object permanence. At this stage, children search flexibly and persistently until they find the object.

Overall, Piaget's observations and theory emphasized qualitative change in cognitive development and painted a picture highlighting infants' cognitive deficits and shortcomings. That picture has faded over the years, as more recent research has focused on continuity in development and assertions that some aspects of many cognitive abilities exist earlier than Piaget reported. One reason for these contradictory conclusions is that Piaget used different methods than subsequent researchers have employed. (Examples of different procedures used to study object permanence are shown in Table 7.3.)

Piaget's object permanence task depends on infants engaging their cognitive and motor abilities in means-end problem solving: they must remember that the hidden object still exists and recall its location, and they must also be able to lift the blanket or remove the cover of a container before they can retrieve the object. Unless they are given explicit, repeated practice, many infants younger than 12 months have difficulty coordinating and sequencing these movements (Bojczyk & Corbetta, 2004).

In one experiment using a modified search task with 14-month-olds, researchers allowed infants to watch while an object was hidden in a container but prevented them from searching for it for 24 hours. Some infants returned to the same room and searched correctly; infants who were brought to a different room, however, tended not to search, even though the original

TABLE 7.3	A Variety of Procedures Have Been Used to Study Object Permanence	
Procedure	**Researcher**	**Principal Findings**
An object is hidden underneath a cloth or inside one of two opaque containers.	Piaget	Full object permanence, without the A-not-B error, develops between 18 and 24 months.
An object is "hidden" by darkness.	Goubet & Clifton	Infants search for objects in the correct location, based on an auditory cue, by $6\frac{1}{2}$ months.
An object is involved in an "unexpected" event, such as disappearing after being placed behind an occluding screen or fitting inside a too-small container.	Baillargeon	Infants as young as $2\frac{1}{2}$ to $3\frac{1}{2}$ months look "surprised" because their expectations about object existence and object properties such as solidity are violated.

When this infant uncovers the hidden toy, he is showing his understanding that objects continue to exist even when they are not visible.

container with the object inside it had been moved to the new setting. These findings suggest that infants may be guided by the notion that objects have a unique identity. Like older children and adults, they search for a specific object in the setting where it disappeared and do not assume that they will find the object in an identical container in a different location (Moore & Meltzoff, 2004).

Other experiments have tested infants' ability to search for an object hidden by darkness, rather than under a blanket or inside a container (Clifton et al., 1991; Goubet & Clifton, 1998; Hood & Willatts, 1986). In one such study, $6\frac{1}{2}$-month-old infants first watched a ball drop down a tube a number of times and learned that it would emerge from the tube in one of two locations, each of which made a distinctive sound when the ball landed there. During the next phase, which was carried out in the dark, the ball was dropped and infants heard one of the two auditory cues. Unable to see the ball, they nevertheless reached for it in the correct location, suggesting that they remembered its existence even when they could not maintain visual contact with it (Goubet & Clifton, 1998).

Is it possible that infants might know that a hidden object continues to exist but fail to search for it because they do not have the necessary motor skills? Eliminating manual search and a reaching response entirely, some researchers have asked whether infants understand that objects are both solid and continuous, that one solid object cannot pass through another solid object, that objects exist despite changes in location, and, if unimpeded, move without interruption or changing direction (Baillargeon, 2002; Baillargeon, Spelke, & Wasserman, 1985). As we discuss next, these studies use looking time as the primary measure of infants' physical reasoning about objects.

Babies in these studies participate in a familiarization phase before being shown one of two types of test events. In studies of infants' reasoning about containment, for example, they are first shown an object being moved into and out of a container that easily accommodates its size and shape (as shown in Figure 7.1). This brief familiarization phase usually consists of several repeated steps, such as the container first being presented alone, then the object appearing and the hand of an unseen experimenter moving it into the container (which is briefly obscured by an opaque screen), and finally (with the screen moved out of the way) the appearance of the container with the object already inside of it.

To test babies' reasoning about the size of objects and containers into which they can be placed, some infants see an "expected" event, similar in most respects to the familiarization event,

Familiarization Event

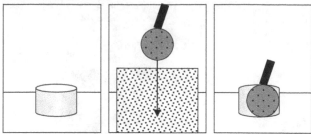

Test Events

Unexpected (Impossible) Narrow Container Event:

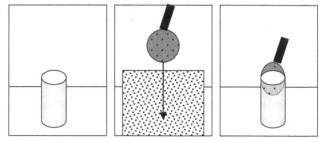

Expected (Possible) Wide Container Event:

FIGURE 7.1 Infants in violation-of-expectation experiments see a familiarization event before being tested about their expectations in subsequent events. *Source:* Based on Aguiar & Baillargeon, 2003.

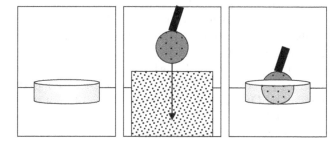

but involving a different-looking container; other infants see an "unexpected" event, in which the final step in the sequence appears to show the object fitting inside a too-narrow container. If infants in the unexpected event condition look longer at that display than infants in the expected event look at their test event, researchers infer that they possess knowledge about physical events involving containment. Heightened attention and interest in the unexpected event condition is taken as evidence that infants' expectations about physical containment have not been supported, giving this research method the name **violation-of-expectation (VOE) procedure** (Aguiar & Baillargeon, 2003).

Numerous studies using the VOE procedure have shown that infants as young as $2\frac{1}{2}$ to $3\frac{1}{2}$ months of age look longer at some unexpected (impossible) events involving objects, but not all object properties are understood at the same age. It is not until $5\frac{1}{2}$ to $6\frac{1}{2}$ months of age, for example, that infants respond to violations of expectations about object support, as when a box appears not to fall, despite being pushed almost all the way off of a platform (Hespos & Baillargeon, 2008). Infants of this age also begin to look longer at unexpected collisions, as when a wheeled toy moves farther after being bumped by a small object than by a bigger object, and they respond differently to events involving inert versus self-propelled objects (Luo, Kaufman, & Baillargeon, 2009). Around the same age, infants look longer when they see a toy that they observed being hidden in one spot in a sandbox emerge from a different spot (Baillargeon, 1994b; Newcombe & Huttenlocher, 2006; Newcombe, Sluzenski, & Huttenlocher, 2005). In other studies, infants as young as 5 months of age are said to understand another aspect of objects—their numerosity following addition and subtraction—if they look longer at unexpected (impossible) than expected (possible) transformations involving the appearance and disappearance of objects (McCrink & Wynn, 2004; Simon, Hespos, & Rochat, 1995; Wynn, 2000).

Interpreting the findings of VOE studies, some researchers have asserted that infants possess innate beliefs about objects and object properties, while others have hypothesized that infants possess innate learning mechanisms that help them accurately interpret their experience with objects from an early age. According to the innate-belief account, infants are born with a core set of principles about the physical world, principles upon which they subsequently build a more complete understanding (Spelke et al., 1992; Spelke & Kinzler, 2009; Wynn, 2000). Advocates of the innate-learning-mechanism explanation, by contrast, propose that infants find certain kinds of experiences particularly salient and pay attention to them, learning about the physical world as they observe toys, food, and other objects being supported or falling, rolling freely or bumping into obstacles, being given to them or taken away, and disappearing under a couch or reappearing on the other side (Baillargeon, 1994a, 2002). Although these theoretical interpretations are not identical, they both portray infants more as passive observers of the world than as the active investigators Piaget described (Müller & Giesbrecht, 2008).

Some critics challenge the interpretation of VOE studies, questioning whether infants' looking behavior actually reflects an early understanding of object concepts. One fundamental problem is that, compared with expected stimuli, unexpected events do not always elicit prolonged attention (Aslin, 2007; Kagan, 2008). In addition, given subsequent failure to replicate findings of earlier VOE studies after varying characteristics of the stimuli, it is possible that infants in the earlier studies were responding to perceptual—not conceptual—differences between the initial familiarization phase and the subsequent test events (Casasola, Cohen, & Chiarello, 2003; Cohen & Marks, 2002; Mix, Huttenlocher, & Levine, 2002; Moore & Cocas, 2006; Wakeley, Rivera, & Langer, 2000a, 2000b). Critics also reject VOE researchers' use of the word "surprise" to explain infants' longer looking times and the words "reason, believe, judge, and realize" (Haith & Benson, 1998). In response, VOE researchers have stated that they assume infants' reasoning is carried out without explicit awareness, and that the word "surprise" is simply a "short-hand descriptor, to denote a state of heightened attention or interest induced by an expectation violation" (Luo et al., 2009, p. 443).

Interpretation of infants' looking time in VOE studies might be illuminated more fully by adding other response measures, such as vocalization and changes in facial expression, heart rate, and event-related potentials (ERPs). VOE studies might also be improved by incorporating microgenetic and longitudinal approaches, enabling researchers to understand short-term learning in context as well as continuity and change from infancy to childhood (Campos et al., 2008; Kagan, 2008; Quinn, 2008; Spencer & Perone, 2008).

The A-not-B Error

Piaget's A-not-B error has been replicated many times. As we discuss next, there is supporting evidence for more than one explanation (Marcovitch & Zelazo, 1999; Newcombe & Huttenlocher, 2006; Ruffman et al., 2005).

According to some accounts, infants make the A-not-B search error, even when they can see the "hidden" toy inside a transparent container, because they are confused by the contradiction between their ability to see the toy and tactile information that a barrier is in the way (Diamond, 1991). As early as 8 months of age, however, babies in the standard A-not-B procedure glance at the correct location before searching at the incorrect spot (Ahmed & Ruffman, 1998; Hofstadter & Reznick, 1996). This could indicate that infants know a toy is hidden at location B but have difficulty restraining themselves from performing a previously successful motor act at location A (Diamond, 1991; Newcombe & Huttenlocher, 2006; Zelazo, Reznick, & Spinazzola, 1998). Support for this explanation comes from an experiment in which 24-month-olds watched a puppet search for an object in an incorrect location, despite having searched correctly on previous trials. Although children had difficulty performing the same search correctly, they showed heightened attention to the puppet's search failure, suggesting that their understanding about the object's location may have been more accurate than their manual search behavior indicated (Mash et al., 2006).

Evidence against the inhibition explanation—and in favor of the view that infants search in accordance with their beliefs about an object's location—comes from a study of 8- to 12-month-olds who searched in a modified A-not-B task. The object was placed twice inside location A and then deposited into a hidden compartment at either location A (AAA) or B (AAB); as a result, whether infants peered into location A or B, they found no sign of the object. Researchers compared the amount of time infants persisted in searching at each location and found that they searched at A in both types of trials but were more diligent in searching at A when they had seen the object hidden only at A (AAA trials). Next, AAB trials were compared with AAB-next-to trials, in which the object was twice placed next to location A before being hidden in the secret compartment at location B. Given that infants had never seen the object placed inside location A, they focused their searching at location B rather than A, suggesting that errors in the standard A-not-B task may be guided by infants' beliefs about where the object is most likely to be found (Ruffman et al., 2005).

Infants' inexperience with the motor skills required to use both hands to lift the cover of a container and then retrieve a toy may explain some A-not-B errors, especially given that additional experience improves performance (Munakata, 1998; Newcombe & Huttenlocher, 2006). In an experiment with 9- to 21-week-old infants, three weeks of object-oriented experiences with parents led to higher rates of reaching, object exploration, and means-end behaviors (Lobo & Galloway, 2008). In a microgenetic study with $6\frac{1}{2}$-month-olds, infants were given weekly exposure to a task that required coordinated, two-handed movements to retrieve a toy from a box. Infants explored the box manually—scratching, banging, and pushing on it—and eventually discovered how to retrieve the toy. Infants who interacted with a semi-transparent box benefited from sustained visual contact with the toy and made this discovery one month sooner than infants with an opaque box (Bojczyk & Corbetta, 2004). Repeated exposure to the A-not-B task, even over a brief period of time, is also helpful. The more opportunities infants have to find a toy when it is hidden at the second location, the less likely they are to make the A-not-B error (Spencer, Smith, & Thelen, 2001). Taken together, evidence of the association between infants' exploratory actions and success on the A-not-B task lends some support to Piaget's claims that infants' own sensorimotor activities contribute to the development of means-end behavior and other aspects of cognitive functioning.

The A-not-B error may also be explained by young infants' immature memory system. The error is more prevalent when there is a delay of even 5 seconds between the time when the object is hidden at location B and the time when the infant is allowed to search. As memory ability improves, the length of delay that infants can tolerate before making the search error increases. During the first year of life, the ability to inhibit reaching to previous locations over longer delays develops as connections form between the prefrontal cortex and areas of the brain that control motor movements (Diamond, 1991; Diamond, Werker, & Lalonde, 1994; Paterson et al., 2006).

Although the A-not-B error becomes less frequent with age, search errors continue into the early preschool years (Butler, Berthier, & Clifton, 2002; Hood, Cole-Davies, & Dias, 2003; Newcombe & Huttenlocher, 2006). This is perhaps to be expected, given that even cognitively mature adults looking for lost keys or other misplaced items sometimes return to a previous location, despite having searched in that spot unsuccessfully.

Understanding and Using Representations of Space

Very young infants perceive a three-dimensional world in which objects vary in distance from one another, with some objects within reaching distance and others beyond their grasp. Although Piaget believed that infants do not *understand* that objects exist independent of their own physical presence until the end of the sensorimotor period, subsequent studies have not uniformly supported his view.

Some studies of infants' ability to keep track of their position in relation to a location in space have trained babies to expect to see a particular toy or person's face in a specific location whenever they hear an auditory signal. Following training, infants are moved in the room and the signal is presented without any event occurring. If infants use an **egocentric framework** (relying on the direction in which they previously turned to see the event), they end up looking in a different location during the test phase. If, on the other hand, they use an **allocentric framework** (using cues in the room, such as a distinctive color or pattern in the original location), they look at the same spot as they did during the training phase (Acredolo, 1978).

Studies using this procedure have found that infants begin to use landmarks (distinctive features in a room) as cues about spatial relationships toward the end of the first year of life (Acredolo, 1990; Bushnell et al., 1995; Newcombe & Huttenlocher, 2006). When there is a single direct landmark, infants as young as 8 months of age are able to use it to locate the target after their own position in the room has changed (Keating, McKenzie, & Day, 1986; Rieser, 1979). If there is more than one landmark, or if a landmark is indirect (occupies a spot other than the target location), however, infants typically have difficulty using information in the environment before the age of 11 months.

In one series of experiments investigating the use of direct and indirect landmarks, 12-month-olds searched for toys that they saw being hidden either beneath or near cushions that varied in their distinctiveness. As expected, infants benefited from the presence of a direct landmark (when the toy was hidden under a unique-looking pillow) but performed worse when there was an indirect landmark (when the toy was hidden near an equally distinctive pillow) than when there was no landmark at all. Infants' difficulty with indirect landmarks may reflect the greater cognitive challenge involved in keeping track of a two-step solution—first, remembering to use the distinctive pillow, and second, once they arrive at that spot, remembering where, in relation to that location, they will find the hidden toy (Bushnell et al., 1995).

The ability to use indirect landmarks may depend on maturation of the hippocampus—a part of the brain that underlies the spatial memory system (Diamond et al., 1994; Mangan et al., 1994). A study with children ranging in age from 16 to 36 months supports this explanation (Newcombe et al., 1998). As children watched, researchers hid toys by burying them in a sandbox filled with sand. In some conditions, the sandbox was completely surrounded by a uniformly plain curtain. In other conditions, the curtain was opened, and children could use features in the room to guide their search. Before starting to search, children's parents escorted them to the other end of the sandbox. With the curtain drawn, all children had difficulty but still performed above chance levels when retrieving the hidden toys. Without the curtain, children older than 21 months of age searched more accurately, presumably because they were able to use indirect landmarks in the room. Improvement in the use of indirect cues was dramatic and abrupt—absent at 16 months but present at 21 months. A neurological maturation explanation for these findings is supported by comparable findings in studies of brain development in young rats learning to use indirect landmarks to navigate through mazes (Seress, 2001).

Children gradually become more skilled at using information about spatial relationships, including representations such as photographs, video images, and scale models. Children as young as 24 months understand that a photograph or video image can be a symbol for something else, such as a particular space. When shown an image of a room and given a description of a toy's hiding place in that room, children of this age are able to retrieve the toy when they are allowed to search in the actual space (Suddendorf, 2003).

Some studies have reported a low level of performance overall among 24-month-olds because they tend to succeed on first searches but not on subsequent trials when the same toy is hidden in different locations in the same room (DeLoache & Burns, 1994; Sharon & DeLoache, 2003). Reminiscent of the A-not-B error, 24-month-olds tend to search in previous hiding spots in the room, rather than in the most recent location. When these sorts of incorrect searches are prevented, however, by using four different toys hidden in four different, distinctively furnished rooms, performance levels are significantly better, suggesting that they were able to understand the relation between a photograph of each space and the space itself (Suddendorf, 2003).

Representational insight, awareness of the relation between a space and a symbol for that space, is still uneven at 30 months; children have greater difficulty using three-dimensional symbols, such as a scale model of a room, than two-dimensional representations, such as a photograph or video image of the same space. It is not until the age of about 36 months that children are consistently able to use scale models to find hidden toys in spaces that the models represent (DeLoache, 2000; Newcombe & Huttenlocher, 2006).

Young children also make scale errors in both laboratory studies and everyday settings, attempting to perform actions on objects that are too small, such as trying to sit in a small-scale chair or climb into a small-scale car (DeLoache, Uttal, & Rosengren, 2004; Rosengren et al., 2009). The processes that contribute to the development of representational insight, which eventually enables older children to understand and learn from abstract representations, such as maps and globes, are not well understood. Children's failures at younger ages may be the result of an inability to shift attention from one representation (e.g., of a space, object, or model) to another and to enact or inhibit appropriate actions (DeLoache, 2000; DeLoache et al., 2004).

We turn now to an influential theory articulated by Lev Vygotsky that places cognitive development and learning in the context of social interactions. As widely accepted as this perspective is now, it was overshadowed for many years by Piaget's theory. Unlike Piaget's emphasis on the child's own developing mind, Vygotsky regarded cognitive development as the result of social interaction and children's internalization of their culture's organization and communication of knowledge.

VYGOTSKY'S SOCIOCULTURAL THEORY: LEARNING AS A SOCIAL ACTIVITY

Lev Vygotsky (1896–1934) was a Russian psychologist who built his theory on the assumption that cognitive abilities develop in and are shaped by children's **sociocultural contexts**—home, school, and other settings in which they spend time. From his perspective, knowledge is created through children's interactions with others, primarily parents and teachers, rather than being innate or discovered through their own actions or self-reflection. In Vygotsky's theory, the most significant psychological tool for children's acquisition of knowledge is the speech of those around them. According to this view, the 18-month-old child whose mother makes up a song to narrate the steps involved in putting on his shirt (e.g., "right arm, left arm, over the head, and pull it down") becomes a 3-year-old who sings the same song aloud as he tries to dress himself. Vygotsky (1934/1986) described the child's verbal behavior at the later age as **egocentric speech,** speech that is directed to himself or herself rather than to others, with the purpose of enhancing his or her own concentration on goals and strategies while performing a task or solving a problem. Eventually, through the process of internalization, the child no longer needs to utter the words out loud; he or she retains the narrative as inner speech that represents the steps involved in getting dressed. In this way, young children whose parents provide a rich speech environment are laying an important foundation for the subsequent development of skills and understanding of the world, including the child's past experiences.

When discussing previous experiences, some parents use a high-elaborative reminiscing style that includes many details and asks children to provide new information, often by posing open-ended questions, such as "What did we see at the park?" Other parents use a less elaborative style that covers fewer topics in less depth (Fivush, Haden, & Reese, 2006). In addition to within-culture variation, there are also differences in reminiscing style across cultures. European and European American parents, for example, tend to reminisce with their children in ways that highlight their individuality and independence more than is typically true of Asian parents (Wang, 2006). Children whose parents use a more elaborative style tend to have more memories and remember more details about their personal past (Fivush et al., 2006; McGuigan & Salmon, 2004). A one-year longitudinal intervention study that began when children were $1\frac{1}{2}$ to $2\frac{1}{2}$ years old showed that parents who initially use a low-elaborative style can learn new strategies for reminiscing, increasing the quantity and quality of their children's autobiographical memories (Reese & Newcombe, 2007).

The Zone of Proximal Development

As a psychologist who focused primarily on school-age children's learning, Vygotsky was interested in enhancing each child's potential. After observing the effects of teachers on children's performance, he described the concept of the **zone of proximal development (ZPD),** the distance between a child's actual developmental level—the ability to solve a problem alone—and the level of potential development—how much better the child can solve the problem when assisted or guided by a more capable individual. Vygotsky did not provide a full account of the ZPD or explain how internalization occurs, but more recent researchers have adapted and expanded upon these ideas (Wertsch, 1979, 1985). Some applications of his theory might surprise Vygotsky, who generally ascribed little importance to young children's play and asserted that imaginary (pretend/symbolic) play was essentially impossible before the age of 3 years (Lambert & Clyde, 2003; Vygotsky, 1933/1978). Nevertheless, his notion of the profound influence of social interaction and sociocultural context is reflected in many current investigations of early play and learning.

When this girl's mother offers helpful hints and encouragement, she is able to complete a puzzle that was too challenging to complete on her own.

The concept of the ZPD has been extended, for example, to describe parent-child interactions during problem solving, as when a 3-year-old girl guided by her father is able to complete a 20-piece puzzle that she would not be able to put together alone. Building on Vygotsky's notion of the ZPD, Wood, Bruner, and Ross (1976) coined the term **scaffolding** to describe the process through which tutors structure tasks to boost children's performance, such as "removing" parts of the task that are beyond the child's ability. Critical steps in the process of scaffolding are recruiting the child's interest in the task, simplifying the task to enable the child to recognize the parts that he or she can perform, maintaining the child's interest, highlighting relevant aspects of the child's response so that he or she can judge its accuracy, and demonstrating correct solutions (Wood, Bruner, & Ross, 1976). The father scaffolding his young daughter's puzzle play may show her the front of the box (e.g., "Look at this picture of Big Bird. After we make this puzzle, we'll have the same picture") or put aside the more complicated middle pieces and ask her to begin by finding the four corners. He may also draw her attention to the part of the picture that can be seen on each piece, asking her to find specific elements (e.g., "I see one of Big Bird's feet. Can you find it?"). To maintain his daughter's interest in the puzzle, he may provide encouraging feedback about her performance (e.g., "You did it! Now look for his other foot.").

Many researchers have extended Vygotsky's theory and the concept of scaffolding to describe the contributions that parents and older siblings make to young children's play (Bodrova & Leong, 1996, 1998). Mothers of 21-month-olds in one study, for example, successfully scaffolded their children's play as a function of their knowledge about how play typically develops during infancy and toddlerhood; those who were the most knowledgeable about the development of play provided their children with the most developmentally appropriate structure, guidance, and verbal commentary (Tamis-LeMonda, Damast, & Bornstein, 1994). Parents' assumptions about the goals and process of effective scaffolding also reflect the characteristics of the culture in which they live (Abels et al., 2005; Bornstein et al., 1999).

Guided Participation

In the Vygotskian tradition, learning is regarded as a social activity, yet around the world cultures vary in terms of how much time children and parents spend together and the types of activities they engage in during the course of a typical day (Tudge et al., 2006). In the United States and other developed countries, children of employed parents almost never accompany their parents to their place of work, and they rarely see their parents engaged in the work for which they are paid. When adults—parents or paid caregivers—interact with them, they tend to focus on child-centered activities, such as playing, reading, eating, and cleaning up. In many other cultures, however, infants are carried on their mother's back and observe her while she works in the home or in the fields. Toddlers in these cultures are often cared for by older siblings, and they are more likely than most U.S. children to spend the day near their mother, observing and even assisting her as she performs tasks such as cooking, cleaning, sewing, and making baskets (Maynard, 2002; Rogoff, 1998).

Despite obvious differences, children in all cultures learn through social interaction and structured activities, a process known as **guided participation** (Rogoff et al., 1993, Rogoff, 1998). In guided participation, an extension of Vygotsky's ZPD, "individual development is regarded as occurring during joint problem solving with people who are more skilled in the use of cultural tools, including inventions such as literacy, mathematics, mnemonic skills, and approaches to problem solving and reasoning" (Rogoff et al., 1993, p. 6). Guided participation encompasses explicit and implicit instruction as well as nonverbal demonstrations provided by more skilled members of a community. In this way, the concept of guided participation goes beyond Vygotsky's emphasis on verbal instruction as the foundation of learning.

A multitude of cross-cultural studies of mother-child interaction show that guided participation reflects childrearing goals and beliefs in particular cultural contexts (Abels et al., 2005; Bornstein et al., 1999; LeVine et al., 1994). In a study of parents and toddlers ranging in age from 12 to 25 months in Guatemala, India, Turkey, and the United States, researchers interviewed parents about their child's development, behavior, and daily routines, including feeding, dressing, and sleeping, and asked about the kinds of play and social games the child enjoyed. They also observed how parents showed their child a set of novel objects—a pencil box with a sliding lid, a jumping-jack doll, a metal embroidery hoop, a clear plastic jar covered with a lid and containing a small toy, and a peek-a-boo puppet—and tried to have him or her use the objects.

As anticipated, there were differences in guided participation (shown in Table 7.4). In communities where children were usually kept apart from adults' daily work (the United States

TABLE 7.4 Differences Observed in Guided Participation across Four Communities	
Community	**Guided Participation**
Middle-class	
United States and Turkey	Parent gives specific verbal instructions to child.
	Parent motivates child during structured, playful interactions.
	Parent engages child in conversation as a peer.
Non–Middle-class	
Guatemala and India	Parent uses nonverbal communication (gestures, shared visual attention) with child.
	Parent stands to the side, ready to help the child, if needed, during exploration.
	Parent remains in adult role rather than becoming engaged with child as a peer.

Source: Based on information in Rogoff, Mistry, Göncü, & Mosier, 1993.

and Turkey), parents tended to take charge of the interaction with each object, providing verbal commentary and joining in the exploration with their child. In communities where children were integrated into adults' daily social and work activities (Guatemala and India), by comparison, parents tended to support toddlers' inclination to explore without specific prompting and instruction. In both types of communities, parents guided young children in ways that were consistent with local institutions and structures (Rogoff et al., 1993).

It is clear that learning in a social context begins in infancy, long before the school years on which Vygotsky focused his attention. Contemporary research supports Vygotsky's concept of the ZPD, the position that children's learning is enhanced by social interaction that takes into account their developmental level and the culture in which they are living. Depending on the cultural context and goals, specific verbal instruction is not always a necessary feature of learning in a social context; there are many ways in which young children can gain valuable knowledge that prepares them to function effectively in their community.

COGNITIVE SCIENCE PERSPECTIVES

In contrast with the Vygotskian and Piagetian traditions, contemporary studies of early learning and memory place infants' development within the framework of cognitive science, an approach that combines traditional questions with newer information processing and neuroscience methodology. Like Piaget's pioneering research, these newer approaches investigate cognitive functioning at the behavioral level, but many also incorporate physiological and neurological measures, such as changes in heart rate and brain activity (Saxe & Pelphrey, 2009).

After electrodes are attached to this special cap, the researchers will study this infant's brain activity in response to visual stimuli.

Attention

Infants' visual attention—the amount of time they spend looking at a stimulus—has been used in habituation, preferential looking, and VOE procedures to answer questions about early sensory, perceptual, and cognitive functioning. In recent years, attention itself has become the focus of research.

Initially, most studies of attention used habituation or preferential looking procedures and measured the duration of infants' looking at static stimuli, such as geometric patterns. Subsequent experiments have gone further, comparing infants' looking at a wider array of stimuli over a broader age range. These studies generally have supported previous findings: duration of looking changes across the first year of life. After an initial increase in attention from birth to 8 or 10 weeks of age, there is a steady decrease from approximately $3\frac{1}{2}$ months to 6 months. After the age of about 6 months, looking time is increasingly influenced by stimulus complexity (Colombo & Mitchell, 1990). Researchers think that infants' looking time declines between $3\frac{1}{2}$ and 6 months of age because babies become more efficient at scanning and processing the features of the stimulus (Colombo, 2001, 2002; Colombo & Mitchell, 1990). As children get older, beginning between 12 and 18 months of age, longer looking times in complex tasks are an indicator of the increasing ability to self-regulate attention while processing information (Colombo, Kannass, et al., 2004).

In an experiment with 3- to 12-month-olds, infants saw 20-second static and moving displays that included white dots on a black background, videotaped faces, and excerpts from a *Sesame Street* video (Courage, Reynolds, & Richards, 2006). As shown in Figure 7.2, peak-looks (the duration of the longest look) were highest at 14 weeks of age and dropped until the age of 26 weeks. From 26 to 52 weeks of age, looking time remained stable or declined slightly for simple displays such as a high-contrast dot pattern; it increased slightly for more complex stimuli such as faces; and it increased even more for extremely complex stimuli such as a *Sesame Street* video clip. At all ages, moving stimuli elicited longer looking than did static versions.

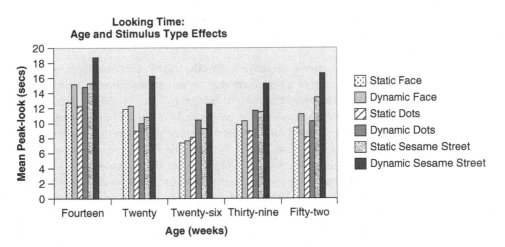

FIGURE 7.2 Looking time varies as a function of infant age and stimulus complexity. *Source:* Based on Courage, Reynolds, & Richards, 2006.

In general, the more unexpected and unfamiliar a display, the longer infants look at it. Many studies have shown, however, that there is not an absolute or direct correspondence between familiarity and duration of attention. In one experiment, for example, 4-month-olds looked longer at a more familiar stimulus (a photo of their parent) than at a simultaneously presented picture of an unfamiliar adult. Four-month-olds also looked longer at a face showing typical features than at a face with scrambled features; 12-month-olds, by contrast, looked longer at the scrambled face (Kagan, 2002, 2008).

Duration of looking varies among infants of the same age, and these individual differences tend to be stable over time (Colombo & Mitchell, 1990; Courage & Howe, 2001). Young infants with shorter, more efficient looking patterns typically perform better on other tasks tapping visual recognition memory than infants with more prolonged looking patterns. According to some views, rather than being more involved in active information processing of the stimulus, babies with prolonged looking during habituation have greater difficulty disengaging their attention from the stimulus (Colombo, 2002). An experiment with 3- and 4-month-olds provided some support for this account (Frick, Colombo, & Saxon, 1999). Researchers first assessed look duration using a habituation procedure and then tested infants' ability to shift their attention from a centrally located display to one on the periphery of their visual field. The display in the center continued to be illuminated, requiring that infants disengage their attention in order to focus on the new peripheral stimulus. Infants who had habituated more quickly were also faster at shifting their attention than were infants with longer habituation times. The efficiency of infants' information processing, including speed of habituation, may contribute to subsequent performance on some intelligence tests, a point we return to later (Colombo et al., 2004; McCall & Carriger, 1993; Rose et al., 2005).

Differences between infants who show shorter versus longer looking times during habituation have also been found when patterns of change in a physiological measure—heart rate— are compared. When a visual stimulus is first presented, infants' heart rate typically decelerates, coinciding with greater and more active engagement in examining and processing the stimulus. Infants with longer looking times during habituation tend to show an initial heart rate deceleration, but while their gaze remains fixated on the stimulus, their heart rate then returns to levels that reflect the end of attention. By augmenting behavioral measures of looking with measures of change in heart rate, this study and others like it have shown that longer duration of looking does not necessarily indicate more thorough processing of a stimulus (Colombo, 2001, 2002; Courage et al., 2006; Richards, 2001).

Another potentially informative approach involves the use of event-related potential (ERP) recordings to chart the development of a waveform that represents attention to stimuli. To study ERPs in infants, researchers use a special lightweight helmet to place dozens of small electrodes (sometimes more than 100) on the surface of the baby's scalp. After an initial baseline phase, a visual or auditory stimulus is presented and a record is made of the brain's activity while the infant attends to the sight or sound. The ability to shift attention improves during early infancy (between 3 and 6 months of age); studies using ERPs indicate that this ability is supported by increasing function of the prefrontal cortex and maturation of pathways involving the parietal lobe (Richards, 2001, 2005; Vaughn Van Hecke & Mundy, 2007). In the future, measures of these waveforms may be used to identify and possibly treat attention-related deficits early in life (Jankowski, Rose, & Feldman, 2001; Nelson & Monk, 2001). Current directions in the study of attention also include exploration of the influence of infant nutrition and other potentially modifiable factors on visual information processing (Colombo, Kannass, et al., 2004; Colombo, Shaddy, et al., 2004).

Gaze Following, Joint Attention, and Theory of Mind

Newborns prefer looking at faces with open eyes that are focused on them, rather than closed or averted (Batki et al., 2000; Farroni et al., 2002). This preference, which is supported by subcortical areas of the brain, including the amygdala, is an important foundation for mutual gaze during face-to-face interaction (Johnson, 2005; Johnson & Farroni, 2007). We discuss mutual gaze and emotional communication in Chapters 9 and 10. Here, we highlight the development of coordinated visual attention and its role in infant learning.

Gaze following is a characteristic of social interaction in which one person shifts his or her visual attention in the direction another person has turned to look. In everyday situations, this shift is typically accompanied by head movement, with the eyes focused on a specific target, such as a wall clock, another family member, or a telephone that begins ringing. In laboratory settings, infants sit across from an experimenter who shifts his or her gaze to a predetermined target. Researchers have modified this basic procedure to investigate the influence of the type of shift (eyes only, head only, or eyes and head together), the features and spatial location of the target, and characteristics of the infant-experimenter interaction (Moore, 2008).

As early as 3 months of age, babies follow the direction of another person's gaze and head movement to objects that are nearby. They tend to have difficulty until the age of about 9 months if multiple targets are present and may become "stuck" on the first one they look at, rather than moving their gaze to a more distant object on which the experimenter is focusing (D'Entremont et al., 2007).

Some researchers have hypothesized that a specialized eye direction detector innately predisposes infants to follow an eye gaze shift, with this behavior further reinforced when it leads them to observe interesting sights (Baron-Cohen, 1995). Studies show, however, that very young infants usually do not follow a shift in eye gaze that occurs without a head turn. Moreover, it is not until approximately 9 to 12 months of age that they reliably follow another person's gaze to find targets behind them or on the periphery of their visual field. Even at these ages, eye gaze alone is less effective than gaze combined with other cues, such as pointing toward an object (D'Entremont et al., 2007; Deák, Flom, & Pick, 2000; Moore, 2008).

Other researchers have claimed that robust gaze following depends on spatial representational abilities that may not develop until the age of 18 months (Butterworth, 1995). There is ample evidence, however, for simpler perceptually based accounts; infants as young as 9 months benefit from multiple, redundant cues, such as gaze shift combined with vocalizing and large, obvious gestures, including pointing (Flom et al., 2004; Flom & Pick, 2007). Multiple cues and salient, distinctive targets help even younger infants disengage their attention from another person's face and toward a target (D'Entremont et al., 2007; MacPherson & Moore, 2007).

Babies who follow another person's gaze toward an object learn about that object. This was the conclusion of a study in which 4-month-olds saw a video of an adult looking at one of two toys; later, when shown a video of just the two toys, infants looked longer at the one the adult had not looked at (Reid & Striano, 2005). ERP measures in a similar experiment provided converging neuropsychological evidence that infants had become more familiar with one of the toys simply by watching the adult look at it (Reid et al., 2004).

Toward the end of the first year, infants begin to understand the role of the eyes in attending to the environment; as a result, gaze following is increasingly influenced by the experimenter's behavior. As infants become more skilled at responding to another person's gaze by looking and pointing in the same direction, they also learn when *not* to attend. Whereas 9-month-olds shift their gaze in the same direction as an adult's head turn, for example, even if that person's eyes are closed, 10-month-olds tend to look or point in the same direction only if the adult's eyes are open. Twelve-month-olds' understanding is more developed but still incomplete; they follow the head movement of an adult wearing a blindfold as often as they do when the blindfold is worn as a headband across the adult's forehead. Infants 14 months of age and older discriminate between an adult wearing a headband, a blindfold with eye openings in it, and a solid blindfold, following head movements only when the adult's eyes are not covered. Similar levels of performance and apparent understanding can be elicited in 12-month-olds, if they first experience the effects of the blindfold on their own vision (Brooks & Meltzoff, 2002, 2005; Meltzoff & Brooks, 2007).

Taken together, studies of gaze following show that, from early in life, infants follow adult head movements and become increasingly sensitive to the direction of another person's gaze shift. Initially, infants do this without understanding that looking is a deliberate behavior, that attending to a target will provide them with knowledge about it, and that they will see the same sight as the adult whose gaze and head movement they are following (Poulin-Dubois, Demke, & Olineck, 2007). Nevertheless, the development of gaze following is a critical step toward understanding other people as active perceivers, thinkers, and communicators.

Gaze following supports infants' ability to engage in **joint attention**—shared perceptual exploration during social interaction, in which gaze alternates between some aspect of the environment and another person involved in the interaction. Our focus here is on the contribution of joint attention to the development of object knowledge; we discuss links to language and emotional communication in Chapters 8, 9, and 10.

Researchers distinguish between two types of joint attention. Responsive joint attention (RJA) consists of infants' gaze following and coordinating attention in response to another person's gaze shifts, head turns, and other behaviors such as vocalizing and pointing. Initiating joint attention (IJA), by contrast, refers to infants' spontaneous use of eye contact, gesturing, and vocalizing to elicit another person's attention. Existing research indicates that RJA is supported by the brain's "attention" system (the subcortical amygdala and posterior superior temporal sulcus), whereas the source of IJA is the "social brain" system (which includes the dorsal medial prefrontal cortex and anterior cingulate). Both types of joint attention contribute to the development of cognition, language, and social competence (Hoehl et al., 2009; Paterson et al., 2006; Vaughn Van Hecke & Mundy, 2007). Researchers still have much to learn about the neuropsychological processes involved in joint attention. One recently developed noninvasive imaging method, near infrared spectroscopy (NIRS), is just beginning to be used to study brain activity of young, alert infants, and affords exciting new possibilities for comparisons with fMRI studies of adults (Lloyd-Fox et al., 2009).

In most studies of RJA, an experimenter engages the infant in direct eye contact during a face-to-face interaction before shifting his or her gaze to a target in the room. Infants' behavior is compared with their response when the experimenter has not coordinated attention in this way. Based on infants' tendency to look longer at an experimenter who has made eye contact with them, some researchers have concluded that the foundation for RJA is present by 3 months, and perhaps as early as $1\frac{1}{2}$ months of age (Striano et al., 2007). Young infants do not learn as much as older infants, however, about the objects they encounter in RJA contexts (Striano, Reid, & Hoehl, 2006). In a study of 4- and 9-month-olds, only 9-month-olds differentiated between a novel toy (looking longer at it in a subsequent test condition) and the toy an experimenter had looked at and commented on while sharing attention with them (Cleveland & Striano, 2007).

Older infants, between 10 and 13 months of age, are better able to discriminate a novel toy and one that an experimenter has looked at during shared attention if the experimenter provides verbal commentary rather than silently alternating attention between the infant and the toy (Parise et al., 2007). An experiment with 18-month-olds showed that they engaged in joint attention toward an object when a parent looked and pointed and also when the parent used verbal information alone, such as "Look at the ball," provided that the object was familiar. For unfamiliar objects, by contrast, verbal information alone was ineffective, whereas the combination of verbal information, pointing, and shared attention promoted more sustained joint attention and learning. Infants looked longer, for example, when the parent made eye contact, pointed and looked at an unfamiliar object, and said, "Look at the pliers" (Flom & Pick, 2003). From 18 to 30 months of age, words and other symbols increasingly are incorporated into parent-infant interactions involving joint attention, contributing to language development (Adamson, Bakeman, & Deckner, 2004).

Some studies have examined babies' responses in situations in which an adult shifts attention between them and another person. In an experiment with 3- and 6-month-olds, infants of both ages were able to shift their attention between two other people. Moreover, as they shifted their gaze between the two adults, both 3- and 6-month-olds exhibited behaviors suggestive of IJA—smiling, vocalizing, and making mouth and body movements when they were momentarily excluded during a conversation between the two adults. In a follow-up study, in which an adult turned away from the infant to look at and talk to an object instead of another person, babies produced fewer IJA behaviors overall and directed them to the person rather than the object (Tremblay & Rovira, 2007). Sensitivity to differences in these situations reflects infants' early social experience and, as we discuss shortly, is an important foundation for developing an understanding of other people's states of mind, including their attention, knowledge, beliefs, and feelings.

So far, we have considered typical development. Infants and children with the developmental syndrome autism, by contrast, often show little interest in looking at other people's faces, and they tend not to respond spontaneously to gaze shifts with or without head movement (Osterling & Dawson, 1994; Volkmar & Mayes, 1990). Children with autism also seem not to understand the use of eye gaze in communicating a person's interest or intentions (Gernsbacher & Frymiare, 2005; Gernsbacher et al., 2008; Hoehl et al., 2009). Researchers using neuroscience methods to explore the absence of typical joint attention behaviors in autism have found evidence of differential neural processing (Akechi et al., 2009). Given that children with autism tend to have more severe deficits in IJA than RJA, one critical difference may lie in the "social brain" rather than in the "attention" system (Hoehl et al., 2009; Vaughn Van Hecke & Mundy, 2007).

While research continues into the underlying causes of these differences, joint attention behaviors have been incorporated into assessments for 2- to 4-year-old children (MacDonald et al., 2006). These measures (shown in Table 7.5) may help researchers identify subgroups likely to benefit from interventions (Leekam, Lopez, & Moore, 2000). Given that few approaches have produced long-lasting changes, however, especially for IJA, some researchers have proposed a markedly different approach. Asserting that children with autism simply use different, covert means to process joint attention cues and initiate joint attention, they recommend that parents, teachers, and others learn to interpret those behaviors, rather than try to extinguish or reshape them (Akhtar & Gernsbacher, 2008; Gernsbacher et al., 2008). Even with greater acceptance and understanding, communication and interaction may still be challenging, due to the difficulty many individuals with autism have understanding others' perceptions, knowledge, beliefs, and feelings.

TABLE 7.5	Examples of Measures Used to Assess Joint Attention		
Type of Joint Attention	**Type of Event**	**Examiner's Actions**	**Child's Behavior Indicating Joint Attention**
Responsive (RJA)			
	Following a point to pictures	Examiner opens a small booklet with one picture on each page. He/she points with an index finger to a picture and waits 5 seconds maximum for a response before turning the page and repeating for the next picture.	Child looks at the picture to which the experimenter is pointing.
	Following a point to targets	Examiner points to a predetermined target in the assessment room, such as a picture on the wall behind the child, and says, "Look," waiting 5 seconds maximum for a response.	Child looks at the target to which the experimenter is pointing.
Initiating (IJA)			
	Toy activation (table)	Examiner uses a remote control to activate a mechanical toy animal 3 feet away on a table in front of the child. The toy remains activated for 15 seconds.	Child alternates gaze between the experimenter and the toy and/or points toward the toy and/or verbalizes about the toy.
	Toy activation (floor)	Examiner uses a remote control to activate a mechanical toy animal 4 feet away on the floor diagonally across from the child. The toy remains activated for 15 seconds.	Child alternates gaze between the experimenter and the toy and/or points toward the toy and/or verbalizes about the toy.
	Book prompt	Examiner opens a picture book and asks, "What do you see?"—allowing the child to look at, touch, or turn the pages for 20 seconds.	Child looks at the picture to which the experimenter is pointing and/or points to and/or verbalizes about it.

Source: Based on information in MacDonald, Anderson, Dube, Geckeler, Green, Holcomb, et al., 2006.

The capacity for joint attention underlies the ability to understand others' states of mind—a cognitive achievement called **theory of mind (ToM).** One widely used ToM laboratory task that assesses understanding of false beliefs asks children to predict where a story protagonist will search for an object that has been moved from the location where the protagonist last saw it. After seeing pictures or video of the object being moved from its original location, children who are able to think about another person's knowledge and beliefs state that the protagonist will search in the original location. Children guided by their own knowledge of the object's location, by contrast, assert that the protagonist will search in the new spot. Most children, with the notable exception of those with autism, succeed on false belief and other ToM tasks by the age of 4 to 5 years (Peterson, Wellman, & Liu, 2005; Wellman, Cross, & Watson, 2001).

A vast and expanding research literature indicates that ToM emerges gradually during infancy and the toddler years and is apparently supported by several interrelated skills and early social experiences. Toddlers whose parents frequently engage them in joint attention or in conversations about the mental states of family and friends, for example, tend to have more advanced performance on ToM tasks as preschoolers (Nelson, Adamson, & Bakeman, 2008; Ruffman, Slade, & Crowe, 2002). Children's ability at ages 2 to 4 years to regulate attention and control motor impulses also appears to contribute to ToM performance (Carlson, Mandell, & Williams, 2004; Flynn, O'Malley, & Wood, 2004; Hughes & Ensor, 2007). These skills are components of an ability called executive functioning, which is supported by development of the prefrontal cortex and other brain regions whose development is the focus of ongoing neuroscience research (Liu et al., 2009; Sabbagh et al., 2009; Zelazo et al., 1997).

In an effort to reveal the underpinnings of ToM, some researchers have employed the violation of expectation (VOE) method. Infants watch a familiarization event in which an association is created between an experimenter and an object; the experimenter may repeatedly reach for or perform the same action on that object. Subsequently, for infants in a false belief condition, while the experimenter is absent, turned away, or otherwise unable to see the display, another person, a puppet, or a gloved hand performs an action that would be expected to mislead the experimenter; the object may be moved to a different location, its appearance may be altered, or it may be replaced with a different object. When the experimenter returns or is once again able to look at the display, researchers observe where and how long infants look. If they understand that the experimenter is likely to act on a mistaken belief about the object's location or identity, they should look longer at the correct location or object when the experimenter unexpectedly reaches for it. For infants in a true belief control condition, in which the experimenter remains present and observes changes being made to objects in the display, looking times should be longer when the experimenter unexpectedly reaches for the incorrect object or location.

Using this basic procedure, VOE studies have reported that infants as young as 13 to 18 months of age are able to attribute false perceptions and false beliefs to other people (Luo & Baillargeon, 2007; Scott & Baillargeon, 2009; Song & Baillargeon, 2008; Song et al., 2008). According to VOE researchers, these findings support the notion of an innate psychological reasoning system that enables very young infants to notice and interpret other people's actions in light of unconscious assumptions about their motivation and other internal mental states. The principal reason children fail at traditional ToM tasks until the age of about 4, these researchers assert, is that they have difficulty simultaneously thinking about another person's false belief and selecting the correct response when asked a question about that person's false belief; immaturity of the connections between brain regions supporting these two abilities may be the underlying limitation (Scott & Baillargeon, 2009).

Not all researchers agree with this conclusion; previously discussed methodological and epistemological issues in the interpretation of infant cognition have also been raised here (Kagan, 2008; Müller & Giesbrecht, 2008; Southgate, Senju, & Csibra, 2007). Due to the important connections between ToM and many other aspects of cognition and learning, it remains an area of intense and lively inquiry.

Memory

The ability to remember previously encountered stimuli underlies nearly all aspects of infant cognition as well as the majority of methods used in the studies we have reviewed. Formerly, because most people's earliest memories extend back only as far as the age of about 3 years (a phenomenon referred to as infantile amnesia), many researchers believed that infant memory operated differently than memory in older children and adults and that the onset of language was the key event that enabled infants to create and retrieve representations of past events. Evidence against this notion is widely available, however, including an experiment with 2-year-olds who were able to use words to describe preverbal memories for a specific event when prompted by physical reminders of the event (Morris & Baker-Ward, 2007).

Researchers today have more tools than ever before to document and chart the growth of early memory, and recent studies have shown that the organization of the memory system is highly similar in infants, older children, and adults (Bauer, 2002, 2006; Rovee-Collier, 1999). Aspects of both **explicit memory** (conscious awareness of specific information, such as events and facts) and **implicit memory** (unconscious learning, including conditioning and aspects of motor learning) exist early in life.

Infants cannot provide verbal answers to questions about their **long-term memory,** information that is stored and available to be retrieved repeatedly over time, but researchers use other methods to determine whether they recall past experiences. Infants who are habituated to a display until they no longer show a high level of visual interest in it, for example, are inferred to have a memory for that display if they look longer at a different display. The type of memory tested in these studies is known as **recognition memory,** the ability to remember a previously presented stimulus or event when it is presented at a later time.

Infants' long-term memory can also be explored using conditioning techniques. In one well-known procedure used primarily with 2- to 6-month-olds, researchers tie a ribbon onto the infant's leg and connect it to an overhead mobile; when the infant kicks, the mobile moves. Later, the infant is placed in the same situation, but without the ribbon in place. Babies who kick their legs when they see the mobile are assumed to recognize the situation and remember the effect of their kicking during the previous session. To test memory between 6 and 18 months of age, researchers use a different task, in which pressing on a lever makes a toy train move around a track. Subsequently, when the lever is deactivated, infants who continue pressing it at a high rate are credited with memory for the task (Rovee-Collier, 1999).

Newborns are able to create a memory for visually presented information and retrieve it, even when tested a few days later. The period of time over which memories can be retrieved increases with age, from just a few days in newborns to a few months in 18-month-olds. At the youngest ages, even small changes in the setting (such as the color or pattern of the mobile) can inhibit memory retrieval. Memory can be enhanced, however, if infants are given brief glimpses of the display periodically (Rose, Feldman, & Jankowski, 2001; Rovee-Collier, Hartshorn, & DiRubbo, 1999; Schneider, & Bjorklund, 1998). In showing the beneficial effects of practice and familiarity, these studies indicate that infant memory is affected by the same factors as memory at later ages (Hayne, Barr, & Herbert, 2003; Rovee-Collier, 1999).

Piaget asserted that deferred imitation did not develop until 18 to 24 months of age, but more recent experiments suggest that it emerges during the last half of the first year of life, perhaps as early as 9 months of age (Bauer, 2006; Klein & Meltzoff, 1999). In a widely used procedure, infants observe an experimenter demonstrate how to perform a simple action with a novel object, such as making a small box sitting on a table light up by bending forward and gently pressing his or her forehead on its top. After a predetermined delay, infants are given the opportunity to handle the object and imitate the experimenter's actions, if they can remember them (Meltzoff, 1988a, 1988b; Meltzoff & Moore, 1998).

Researchers studying older infants and toddlers have explored long-term memory abilities in imitation tasks by first demonstrating novel, multistep sequences during an initial laboratory session and then observing their spontaneous performance with the same props during a subsequent visit. In some studies, a verbal description of the objects and actions accompanies the experimenter's demonstration and the infant is then given a chance to practice the same actions. In other studies, no verbal labels are provided and the infant does not have an opportunity to practice the actions until their return visit. Children who are allowed to practice actions immediately are better able to imitate them later and are aided more by verbal reminders than are children who are not allowed to practice (Hayne et al., 2003; Hudson & Sheffield, 1998). Given that the props in these studies are completely novel, successful performance depends on deferred imitation—the ability to reproduce the sequence based on long-term memory for the order of events (Bauer, 2005, 2006). These experiments test **recall memory,** the ability to remember a previously presented stimulus or event in the absence of current, ongoing perceptual support. This task is difficult because it involves more than simply recognizing a set of props; the previously demonstrated multistep sequence can only be enacted if it is recalled and recreated from memory.

As is true for older children and adults, infant memory is enhanced if there are **enabling relations**—a logically or practically necessary order among the steps in a sequence—rather than **arbitrary relations**—a sequence that may be performed in any order because the steps are not logically or practically linked (Bauer, 2002, 2006). It is easier, therefore, for infants and toddlers to recall how to build a gong (a sequence in which the gong must be hung up before striking it) than it is for them to remember the exact order in which blocks were previously placed into a container (a sequence in which the outcome is unaffected by the order in which red, yellow, and blue blocks are selected).

Despite evidence of the capacity for deferred imitation before the age of 12 months, it is an ability that is affected by a number of factors, including the type of sequence and the length of delay. Only about half of 9-month-old infants in one experiment, for example, reproduced the correct sequence of steps after a one-month delay, and then only if they had had multiple exposures to the sequence before attempting to reproduce it (Bauer et al., 2001). By the age of 13 months, by contrast, the majority of children in another study were able to reproduce a similar sequence of steps after a one-month delay. By the age of 20 months, they could reproduce the sequence after a 12-month delay (Bauer et al., 2000).

Different degrees of maturation of the hippocampus, an area of the brain involved in long-term recall memory, are one reason 9- and 13-month-olds perform at such different levels (Bauer et al., 2003). Although portions of the hippocampus are active from birth and enable infants to be conditioned to suck in response to an auditory stimulus or kick their legs in response to a visual display, the full neural network does not begin to function until the end of the first year of life (Nelson, Thomas, & de Haan, 2006).

Individual differences in the maturation of the network appear to affect same-age infants' ability to encode information during demonstration sessions and use it later to guide deferred imitation. This account is consistent with the findings of an experiment with 9-month-olds, in which less than half of the infants (46 percent) reproduced at least one of three demonstrated two-step sequences in the correct order one month later. ERP recordings made when infants saw photos of the steps in the sequence immediately after the demonstration and again one week later indicated that babies who were subsequently able to recall the sequences correctly showed evidence of greater functional maturity of the hippocampus than was evident in the other infants (54 percent) who failed the memory test (Bauer et al., 2003). In light of longitudinal research showing a relation between infants' capacity for deferred imitation at 9 months of age, joint attention at 14 months, and scores on tests of cognitive abilities at 4 years, researchers are interested in learning more about factors that might support maturation of the hippocampus and other parts of the memory system (Reznick et al., 2004; Strid et al., 2006).

Information stored in long-term memory was once active in **short-term memory**—a limited storage system that holds information for only a few seconds if the information is not actively rehearsed (Baddeley, 1992, 2000). The existence of long-term memory thus implies that infants also possess short-term memory, a conclusion that has been verified in numerous experiments (Rose et al., 2001; Ross-Sheehy, Oakes, & Luck, 2003).

In a study with 4- to 13-month-olds, infants saw rapidly changing displays of colored squares (ranging in number from one to six squares) on side-by-side video monitors. Visual memory capacity increased over the first year of life; whereas 4- and $6\frac{1}{2}$-month-old infants were able to retain short-term memory only for displays of one square, 10- and 13-month-old infants were able to notice changes in displays with as many as four squares, a level that was similar to adults' performance when tested using the same procedure (Ross-Sheehy et al., 2003).

As we discussed earlier, short-term memory for the spatial location of objects also improves at this age. In studies in which infants watch as an object is hidden at one of two or more locations and are then allowed to search after a brief delay, the number of locations that infants can remember and use to search accurately increases between 6 and 10 months (Diamond, 1998; Newcombe & Huttenlocher, 2006). Developmental neuroscientists are working to incorporate noninvasive ERP and NIRS measures into future studies of the origins and development of memory (Nelson & Monk, 2001; Nelson et al., 2006; Nelson & Webb, 2002).

Categorization

In Piaget's view, **categorization**—the ability to group objects, people, or events into similar categories based on shared attributes—does not develop until infants achieve mental representation, at approximately 18 to 24 months. More recent researchers have reported that even infants as young as 3 and 4 months of age discern categorical differences. In some of these studies, infants are habituated with examples from one category and then tested to see if they increase their visual attention when shown an example from a different category. In other studies, a familiarization/novelty preference procedure is used: Infants are first shown examples from one category and then given two displays to look at simultaneously, one a new example from the category and the other an example from a different category (Cohen & Cashon, 2006). In an experiment with 3- and 4-month-olds, for example, babies saw photographs of cats. After seeing many different images of cats, they were shown two new photographs, one of a cat and the other of a dog. Infants looked longer at the photograph of the dog, suggesting that they had formed the category of "cat" based on their previous exposure (Quinn, Eimas, & Rosenkranz, 1993). An eye-tracking study of 6- to 7-month-olds' ability to categorize cats versus dogs found that infants may possess a preexisting bias that leads them to focus on an animal's head (Quinn et al., 2009).

Other researchers have used object manipulation tasks to infer categorization. Infants are presented with a diverse set of small objects, such as toy animals and doll house furniture, and researchers observe the order in which they manipulate the intermingled objects. Babies who display sequential, within-category touching—manipulating first a pig, then a sheep, and finally a horse before touching a chair, a table, and a bed—are said to possess distinct categories, in this example, for animals and furniture (Mandler, 1998). In some studies, 6- to 7-month-olds have discriminated between categories at the global level (e.g., animals versus vehicles) but not between categories at a more basic level (e.g., dogs versus rabbits); basic-level discriminations within the category of animals did not appear until the end of the first year of life (Mandler & McDonough, 1998). Based on the results of these and similar experiments, some researchers have concluded that infants develop basic-level categories later than they develop categories at the global level, perhaps as a result of learning to notice

Selecting several blocks to play with, while ignoring the other toys nearby, suggests that this baby possesses an early ability to categorize objects.

correlations among features both between and within members of categories (Rakison & Poulin-Dubois, 2002).

The finding of cat-dog differentiation in 3- to 4-month-olds may appear to contradict the observation that infants younger than 12 months have difficulty making distinctions within the category of animals. One explanation for this difference may lie in the different research methods; even the same experimenters do not always find converging evidence when they use different procedures (Oakes & Madole, 2000). Different tasks may tap different levels of processing, with visual familiarization tasks involving low-level perceptual categorization and object manipulation tasks requiring higher-level conceptual categorization (Mandler, 1992). It is also possible that infants who are allowed to manipulate objects, rather than simply inspect them visually, are more likely to form categories based on the functional possibilities of those objects, such as whether they make noise when they are shaken or roll when they are pushed (Cohen & Cashon, 2006; Horst, Oakes, & Madole, 2005).

Another possible explanation is that infant categorization reflects learning about specific pictures or objects presented during an experiment (Oakes & Madole, 2000). Support for this account comes from studies in which infants intentionally have been presented with different examples of stimuli in order to determine whether and how their categorization might be affected (Quinn & Bhatt, 2009; Wilcox, Woods, & Chapa, 2008). When 10-month-olds in one experiment were presented with a series of perceptually similar items within the category of "land animals" (e.g., horse, dog, and cow), for example, they subsequently differentiated that category from the category of "sea animals." When the items within the category of "land animals" were more perceptually variable (e.g., rabbit, bear, ram), however, infants treated all of the items as examples of the category of "animals" (Oakes, Coppage, & Dingel, 1997).

By the age of 10 to 11 months, infants are able to use real-world knowledge to group objects and, like older children, may ignore opportunities to categorize objects according to their perceptual similarity (Pauen, 2002). These findings still do not identify the specific basis for categorization, and researchers continue to explore the mechanisms involved in this fundamental cognitive ability (Cohen & Cashon, 2006; Gelman & Kalish, 2006; Oakes & Madole, 2000).

DEFINING AND TESTING INTELLIGENCE IN INFANCY

Most intelligence tests include questions designed to tap memory, quantitative abilities, logical reasoning, pattern recognition, analogical reasoning, vocabulary knowledge, and verbal comprehension. Different, nonverbal tests have been constructed to assess intelligence in the first three years of life. In this final section, we briefly consider how intelligence is defined and measured in these tests, whether these tests are valid and reliable measures of infant and toddler intelligence, and whether researchers can use them to predict later performance on traditional intelligence tests. We also examine information processing approaches to the assessment of infant intelligence.

Traditional Tests

One of the best-known measures, the **Bayley Scales of Infant Development (BSID)** (Bayley, 1969, 1993), was developed by Nancy Bayley in the early decades of the twentieth century. The BSID assesses sensation, perception, motor, cognitive, memory, language, and social abilities from 1 month to 42 months of age. Items are grouped into three major scales: a motor scale for sensorimotor coordination and fine and gross motor skills; a mental scale measuring perception, memory, and vocal/verbal behavior; and a behavior rating scale using information provided by the parent.

Although the BSID provides a profile of infants' current functioning, scores often vary considerably from one testing time to another. This variability may reflect variations in individual infants' states of arousal and motivation, or as some researchers have suggested, it may indicate that intelligence itself is variable during infancy (Bornstein et al., 1997). The BSID is notoriously poor at predicting later performance on traditional intelligence tests, a limitation that Bayley herself reported in an early longitudinal study comparing BSID performance with intelligence scores at age 18 years (Bayley, 1949). Items on the BSID mental scales measure perceptual and motor development (e.g., "uses eye-hand coordination in reaching"), whereas intelligence tests for older children and adults do not assess these abilities (Bornstein et al., 1997). It should not be surprising, therefore, that infant measures do not predict later performance. In fact, as Bayley and others have found, it is not until the age of about 5 years that intelligence test scores are significantly associated with later test scores.

Information Processing Assessments

Growing awareness of the limitations of traditional tests of infant intelligence led researchers to reconsider assumptions about the measurement of early cognitive abilities. The resulting assessments focus on specific information processing components—visual-perceptual skills involved in attending to and examining stimuli so that information may be stored in and later retrieved from memory. As we noted earlier, studies of infant attention, habituation, and visual recognition memory have shown that information processing varies as a function of the complexity of stimuli and generally becomes more efficient with age (Colombo, 2002). We also know that there are individual differences in infants' information processing skills (e.g., some infants are "short lookers" in habituation procedures, whereas others are "long lookers") and that infants who are at risk for cognitive delay tend to process information less efficiently than normally developing infants (Bornstein et al., 1997; Colombo, 2002; Rose et al., 2005).

Information processing measures tend to be fairly reliable, especially when measures are taken close together in time (Bornstein, 1988). These measures have also been reported to be moderately successful as predictors of later intelligence. That is, the efficiency of infants' information processing during the first six months of life appears to be linked to their subsequent performance on tests of cognitive abilities and intelligence between 2 and 12 years of age—"short lookers" tend to have higher scores in childhood than do "long lookers" (Colombo & Janowsky, 1998; Rose & Feldman, 1997; Rose et al., 2005).

These findings suggest that there are initial, possibly genetic, individual differences in the neurological basis for information processing (Colombo & Janowsky, 1998; Reznick, Corley, & Robinson, 1997). The findings do not indicate, however, how information processing efficiency is affected by other factors, such as infants' reaction to the novel laboratory setting; it is possible, for example, that some babies settle more quickly and are thus able to perform more efficiently than others. In addition, findings of early individual differences do not negate the importance of environmental influences on cognitive performance and development (Reznick et al., 1997) nor preclude the possibility of modifying infants' information processing behavior (Colombo, 2002; Jankowski et al., 2001). Indeed, as we discuss in Chapter 11, early interventions, as well as everyday interactions with parents and caregivers, have significant short- and long-term impacts on infants' cognitive development.

WRAPPING THINGS UP: Summary and Conclusion

Today's researchers are indebted to Piaget and Vygotsky for framing fundamental issues and providing a foundation of detailed, systematic observations. Contemporary researchers, however, tend to be guided less by grand theories that attempt to explain numerous aspects of development than they are by "mini-theories" and the desire to understand specific developmental phenomena as they unfold over time and in different contexts (Haith & Benson, 1998; Oakes, 2009). Even as new approaches and questions emerge, however, it is possible to be impressed by how much we have learned.

Play during the first three years of life depends on the development of motor, cognitive, and social skills. Play also promotes skills in these domains by enabling infants and toddlers to learn about themselves, other people, objects, and events. The participants, materials, and content of play are affected by the social and cultural context in which it occurs.

Piaget's theory asserts that infants operate at the level of sensorimotor intelligence until the age of about 2 years and are active participants in their own learning. Key ideas are the incremental development of understanding of object permanence, spatial relationships, and categorization. Mental representation and the capacity to use words and other symbols is a hallmark of the transition to the preoperational stage.

Vygotsky's theory assumes that cognitive abilities develop in and are shaped by children's sociocultural contexts. Interactions with more advanced individuals help children learn within their own zones of proximal development. Contemporary researchers have adapted Vygotsky's concepts and introduced notions of scaffolding and guided participation to describe the process through which young children learn.

Cognitive science perspectives offer new levels of analysis that may be fruitfully combined with traditional behavioral measures. Infants' information processing abilities function from an early age and undergo important changes during the first year of life. Gaze following and joint attention promote learning about the environment and foster a developing theory of mind. Measures of the allocation of attention, speed of habituation, and visual recognition memory provide new insights into individual differences in these abilities.

The memory system functions from birth and is influenced by many of the same factors that affect memory in older children and adults. Significant neurological development beginning during the end of the first year of life supports increasing efficiency and flexibility in the infant's memory system. Short- and long-term memory enables infants to discern categories "online" during experiments as well as interpret stimuli in light of prior knowledge.

Traditional measures of infant intelligence tend not to yield stable profiles of cognitive abilities, nor do they predict later performance on intelligence tests. Information processing tasks, by comparison, offer more stable measures of infant intelligence, but individual differences in infancy do not negate the importance of early environmental and experiential influences.

As we have seen, preverbal infants are able to notice and remember a surprising amount of information about the people, objects, and events they encounter. This information influences their behavior and interactions on a daily basis and over time. The acquisition of language, however, provides a fascinating and useful window into young children's minds. We examine the profound changes in the domain of language in our next chapter.

THINK ABOUT IT: Questions for Reading and Discussion

1. What sorts of toys would you recommend that parents provide for their infant at each of the following ages: 6 months, 12 months, 18 months, 24 months, 30 months, 36 months? Explain the basis for your recommendations.
2. If new parents wanted to know whether and how they should join their child in play during infancy, the toddler years, and beyond, what would you recommend?
3. How would parents who endorse Piaget's theory of cognitive development interact with their child, as compared with parents who support Vygotsky's theory? What sorts of behaviors and situations might they create (or avoid)?
4. What can we do with the new findings about infants' cognitive abilities? What are the implications for parents and caregivers?
5. Should infant intelligence be assessed? Why or why not?

Key Words

Accommodation (197)   Piaget's term for adjusting exploratory actions in response to an object's novel characteristics.

Allocentric framework (205)   Spatial orientation that is based on external cues in the environment.

A-not-B error (200)   Piaget's term for the tendency, first seen around 8 months of age, for infants to search for objects at locations from which they previously successfully retrieved objects, even though they saw the object being hidden at a different location.

Arbitrary relations (219)   Steps in a sequence that may be performed in any order because they are not logically or practically linked.

Assimilation (197)   Piaget's term for employing previously used actions to explore an object.

Bayley Scales of Infant Development (BSID) (222)   A measure that is used to assess infant intelligence through motor, mental, and behavior rating scales.

Categorization (220)   The ability to group aspects of the world according to shared attributes.

Coordination of secondary schemes (198)   Piaget's fourth substage of the sensorimotor period, in which infants perform two separate schemes in order to produce a desired outcome.

Deferred imitation (199)   The ability to remember and repeat an action that was observed earlier in the absence of a model for those actions.

Egocentric (197)   Piaget's term for infants' tendency to understand the world through their own sensory and motor acts.

Egocentric framework (205)   Spatial orientation that is based on one's own body and physical actions.

Egocentric speech (207)   Verbal behavior that is directed toward oneself rather than others, with the purpose of enhancing concentration and performance during an activity.

Enabling relations (219)   A logically or practically necessary order between steps in a sequence.

Explicit memory (218)   Conscious awareness of specific information, such as events and facts.

Gaze following (213)   A characteristic of social interaction in which one person shifts his or her visual attention in the direction another person has turned to look.

Guided participation (209)   Patterns of social interaction and structured activity during joint problem solving involving people with different levels of skills and knowledge.

Implicit memory (218)   Unconscious learning, including conditioning and aspects of motor learning.

Joint attention (214)   Shared perceptual exploration during social interaction, in which gaze alternates between some aspect of the environment and another person involved in the interaction.

Long-term memory (218)   Information that is stored and available to be retrieved repeatedly over time.

Mental combinations (199)   Piaget's sixth substage of the sensorimotor period, in which infants are able to think about their actions and select schemes in order to achieve a desired outcome.

Mental representation (197)   The ability to remember and think about objects and events, even when those objects and events are not physically present.

Object permanence (199)   Piaget's term for infants' gradually developing understanding that objects continue to exist even when they are not in sensory or motor contact with them.

Play (192)   Activity that is intrinsically motivated, focused on means rather than ends, different from purely exploratory behavior, nonliteral, and free from externally applied rules.

Preoperational thought (197)   Piaget's second stage of cognitive development, from 2 to 6 years of age.

Pretend/symbolic play (195)   Play that emerges after 12 months of age, in which children behave in a nonliteral way.

Primary circular reactions (198)   Piaget's second substage of the sensorimotor period, in which sensory and motor schemes are activated by chance.

Recall memory (219)   The ability to remember a previously presented stimulus or event in the absence of ongoing perceptual support.

Recognition memory (218)   The ability to remember a previously presented stimulus or event when it is presented at a later time.

Reflex schemes (197)   Piaget's first substage of the sensorimotor period, in which infants respond to the world with a limited set of preadapted behaviors.

Representational insight (206)   Awareness of the relation between a space and a symbol for that space.

Scaffolding (208)   The process through which more capable individuals structure tasks to boost less capable individuals' performance.

Schemes (197)   Piaget's term for actions used to explore and interact with the physical environment.

Secondary circular reactions (198)   Piaget's third substage of the sensorimotor period, in which infants repeat schemes in order to achieve specific outcomes.

Sensorimotor intelligence (197)   Piaget's first stage of cognitive development, from birth to 24 months of age.

Short-term memory (220)   A limited storage system that holds information for only a few seconds if the information is not actively rehearsed.

Sociocultural contexts (207)   Settings in which children spend time, including home, childcare, and school.

Tertiary circular reactions (199)   Piaget's fifth substage of the sensorimotor period, in which infants try different schemes to discover the effects of those actions.

Theory of mind (ToM) (216)   A cognitive achievement that emerges around the age of 3 years, enabling children to understand others' feelings and beliefs.

Violation-of-expectation procedure (202) A procedure in which infants are shown possible and impossible events in order to test their understanding of physical phenomena and object properties.

Zone of proximal development (ZPD) (207) Vygotsky's term for the distance between a child's ability to solve a problem alone and how much better the child can solve the problem when guided or assisted by a more capable individual.

Language and Communication

It is just another day in the Tiny Tugboat room, childcare setting for a group of 20- to 30-month-olds. Simon, who is 2 years old, responds quickly and directly to a child who has just bitten his friend, Andrew, in a struggle over a toy. While the teacher makes her way over to intervene, Simon emphatically tells the perpetrator, "We don't bite our friends! That's not okay!" When the teacher arrives, she utters a nearly identical statement. Then, tears are dried, the dispute is discussed, and snack-time begins, followed by a story and art project. Just another day in which the Tiny Tugs hear language used by teachers to comfort, question, read to, and guide them. Just another day in which they are encouraged to "use their words"—instead of their teeth—to share thoughts and feelings.

Simon's response shows that he has been paying attention, acquiring new vocabulary words and learning when and how to use them. As a baby, Simon also heard lots of language and learned from it, but it would have been more difficult for him to produce evidence of his developing language skills. Still, Simon's caregivers knew that the words he heard every day, and their responses to his earliest efforts to communicate, would have an impact on his subsequent ability to understand and use language. Researchers who study language acquisition know this as well and, as we learn in this chapter, have identified a multitude of coexisting factors operating from birth to age 3.

STUDYING LANGUAGE DEVELOPMENT

After exploring preverbal infants' capabilities—including gestural communication and speech perception—we discover how babies progress from uttering single words to combining these elements in increasingly sophisticated ways. Given that many infants and toddlers around the world live in bilingual households and multilingual communities, information about their development appears throughout the chapter. We also review evidence about the causes of language delay and other aspects of atypical development, with a special focus on children with autism. We begin by noting some of the reasons language is so important and outlining the theoretical foundation for research in this domain.

These 2-year-olds are learning about literacy, a valued skill in their culture.

Why Language Matters

Language is a multipurpose tool that promotes learning as well as social and emotional development. Parents and caregivers use words and signs to draw infants' attention to specific objects, people, and events. The repetition of consistent labels provides infants with symbols with which to refer to aspects of their experience, including internal states. A positive emotional tone encourages infants to pay attention to and participate in ongoing activities, whereas a harsh or negative tone discourages them from doing so. Children who participate in conversations about others' feelings, beliefs, and desires gain insight into those perspectives, which supports developing theory-of-mind knowledge. Early exposure appears to be critical; the more experience children have with language and verbal interaction during the first two years, the more advanced their language skills are when they reach school age.

Language contributes to young children's developing sense of self by providing descriptions and evaluations of their characteristics and abilities. Parental rules and standards are conveyed through language, and adults' comments about children's compliance with these standards support the development of self-regulation and an early sense of morality. Young children use language with peers and siblings to specify and negotiate play activities. As early as the age of 3 years, they participate in family conversations, even turning the topic of conversation from others to themselves. Like other aspects of parent-child interaction, patterns of conversation vary across cultures, revealing a range of parental beliefs and expectations about child development. For these reasons and others that we discuss in this chapter, language matters.

Systems of Language

Traditionally, researchers have subdivided language into systems corresponding to the sound patterns of language (**phonology**), the meanings of words (**semantics**), rules for combining words (**grammar**), and the practical uses of language (**pragmatics**). As the examples in Table 8.1 suggest, a wide array of methods has been used to study production and comprehension of elements of these systems.

Studies of phonological development often rely on infants' looking behavior. New technology, such as event-related potential (ERP) and near infrared spectroscopy (NIRS), is beginning to be used to measure infants' brain activity in response to a variety of speech sounds. These measures can be especially informative when infants fail to show an overt behavioral response, such as preferential looking. Although the focus has been on responses to auditory stimuli, some researchers explore the speech sounds that infants produce, recording samples of cooing, crying, and babbling, as well as recognizable words.

In testing competing theoretical hypotheses about semantic development, researchers working with young infants tend to use measures of looking behavior and attention. Studies of older infants and toddlers more often use interactive measures. Many researchers incorporate nonlinguistic and contextual aspects of word learning, including joint attention with adults, into their studies.

At the level of grammar, there is a vast range of expressive and receptive phenomena to explore, from grammatical markers that create the past tense of a verb to the order of words in a sentence. Although cross-linguistic studies have the potential to yield valuable knowledge about early grammatical development, they are used less frequently than single-language approaches.

At the most basic level, pragmatic awareness enables children to recognize that people use language to refer to things in the world. As children develop this understanding further, they learn that language can be used for a variety of specific purposes, including informing, entertaining,

TABLE 8.1	Examples of Research Methods for Studying Systems of Language	
	Procedures	**Questions**
Phonology: Sound patterns of language	Infants are habituated to a particular speech sound, such as *pa*.	Do infants show renewed interest and alertness when a different speech sound, such as *ba*, is played?
	Infants are familiarized to speech sounds emanating from a prominent loudspeaker.	How much time do infants spend looking at the loudspeaker when familiar versus novel speech sounds are played?
	Infants are conditioned to turn their head when they hear a change in a speech sound or other auditory stimulus, such as from *bih* to *dih*.	When new speech samples are played, do infants turn their head to indicate awareness of differences in those stimuli?
	Infants hear sentences with recurring patterns consisting of invented words like *boga, giku, kuga,* and *gapi*.	How long do infants look at a loudspeaker playing samples of familiar elements and patterns versus samples with elements that violate previously heard patterns?
Semantics: Meanings of words	Infants' spontaneous speech is audiotaped; for infants learning sign language, spontaneous manual actions are videotaped.	What are infants' first words or signs? To what do their words or signs refer? How does the social context influence infants' word/sign use?
	Infants interact with an experimenter, who uses an invented word, such as *zop* or *dax*.	What do infants understand about the meaning of invented words they hear? To which aspects of the setting do they link those words?
	Infants participate in an audiovisual habituation procedure in which words and objects are paired.	Do infants look longer when word-object pairings are switched during test trials?
Grammar: Rules for combining and modifying words to communicate different meanings	Young children's conversations are recorded in the home or in other naturalistic settings.	What sorts of grammatical errors do young children make spontaneously? How do parents respond to those errors?
	Young children interact with experimenters who utter words or phrases that are either grammatically correct or incorrect, such as "feet" versus "foots."	How well can young children judge which words or phrases in a set of utterances are grammatically correct versus incorrect?
	Young children hear an experimenter produce a sentence using an invented word, such as *bod,* and are asked to modify that word.	How well can young children apply rules of grammar, forming the past tense when the word is used as a verb (e.g., *bodded*) or producing a plural form when the word is used as a noun (e.g., *bods*)?

TABLE 8.1	Continued	
	Infants and toddlers look at side-by-side videotaped displays accompanied by a single narration describing one of the displays. For example, when shown an elephant bumping a ball on one screen and a ball rolling into an elephant on the other screen, children may hear "the elephant bumped the ball" or "the ball bumped the elephant."	At what age do children comprehend the phrases or sentences that they hear? How much time do children spend looking at the display matching the narration versus the other display?
Pragmatics: Practical uses of language	Toddlers observe or interact with an experimenter who utters a novel word, such as *modi,* while looking at an unfamiliar object. In other conditions, the experimenter utters the novel word while looking away from the object. The experimenter may subsequently show the child several objects, including the unfamiliar one, and ask him or her to pick up the *modi.*	Do children understand that a fundamental purpose of language is to use words to refer to things in the world? Do they look at the object the experimenter is looking at? Do they pick up the unfamiliar object?

comforting, and (as Simon did) reprimanding other people. Experiments using joint attention and gaze shifts suggest that 18-month-olds seek out information about others' attentional focus and intentionality, using that information to acquire new vocabulary words. Studies in both laboratory and naturalistic settings show that children younger than 3 begin to use utterances selectively and appropriately to achieve specific social goals.

Theoretical Foundations

At one time, the study of language acquisition was a debate between theorists strongly favoring a learning explanation and those staunchly advocating a nativist account. Table 8.2 shows examples of evidence consistent with each of these perspectives. The psychologist B. F. Skinner was a key proponent of learning theories, while the linguist Noam Chomsky was associated with the nativist perspective. In Skinner's (1957) view, children learn language in much the same way they learn other behaviors—through imitation and reinforcement. He asserted that children acquiring language are actually learning to produce specific modeled and reinforced combinations of words, while suppressing other combinations that are neither modeled nor reinforced. Simon's word-for-word production of his teacher's utterances in previous biting incidents shows that imitation plays a role in young children's language acquisition.

Chomsky (1958), however, might have noted that children also utter many novel sentences that no one has produced before, indicating that there is more than simple imitation involved. Naturally occurring language tends to be complex, making it impossible for very young children to keep track of all of the reinforcement probabilities for different words and word orders as a basis for determining which words can be used as verbs as opposed to nouns and adjectives. Moreover, if the frequency of words children hear predicts their acquisition, then often-used

TABLE 8.2 Evidence Supporting Learning and Nativist Views of Language Acquisition	
Evidence Supporting Learning Views	**Evidence Supporting Nativist Views**
Children learn the language that is spoken around them, including a particular dialect and vocabulary.	Children progress through the same prelinguistic stages as they learn language.
The amount and variety of early exposure to language is predictive of children's later acquisition of both semantics and grammar.	Rate of acquisition varies across children, but there is a similar order for the acquisition of grammar.
Children learn about pragmatics as a result of language experience.	Children make errors they have never heard in adult speech.
Parents frequently modify their speech, simplifying the infant's language processing task.	Children are able to apply rules of grammar to words they have never heard before, including invented words.
Parents often create and take advantage of naturally occurring opportunities to label objects and actions for infants and to expand their young children's earliest utterances.	Deaf children being reared without exposure to formal sign language invent their own rule-governed, gestural systems of communication.
Monozygotic twins are not linguistically identical.	Newborns prefer listening to speech rather than other sounds.
	A genetic component underlies some forms of language delay.
	Humans possess a unique variant of the *FOXP2* gene, which supports the ability to articulate and produce speech; children without this variant have atypical language development.

parts of speech, like articles ("a" and "the"), should be acquired early; as we note shortly, these are almost never among children's first words. Another problem for the strong learning explanation is that, because parents and caregivers do not always produce complete, grammatical sentences, children do not always hear good models of language. Even when their own speech is grammatically correct, parents do not always react to young children's grammatical mistakes. Instead, they frequently overlook those errors and focus on the content and meaning (Brown & Hanlon, 1970; Hirsh-Pasek, Trieman, & Schneiderman, 1984).

Given that children are able to acquire much of the grammar in the language they are learning by the age of about 2 years, Chomsky asserted that infants are born possessing a universal set of grammatical rules for learning to understand and produce speech (Chomsky, 1965, 1980, 1986). Some support for this argument comes from studies of deaf children who develop their own sign language in the absence of an adult model in the environment (Goldin-Meadow, Mylander, & Franklin, 2007; Senghas & Coppola, 2001; Senghas, Kita, & Özyurek, 2004).

Over the years, as researchers amassed evidence for one side or the other, information processing models appeared and emphasized more general cognitive underpinnings of language acquisition (McMurray, 2007; Rose, Feldman, & Jankowski, 2009). Today, the learning-nativist debate is essentially over. Most theorists accept the role of learning and also recognize evidence for built-in constraints, biases, and abilities that facilitate the process of acquiring a first language

(Kuhl, 2000, 2004). It is obvious that there are intimate connections between the sounds, meanings, forms, and uses of words (Hollich, Hirsh-Pasek, & Golinkoff, 2000; Saffran, 2003). In addition, the dynamic social context in which language develops plays a more prominent role in many current theories (Spencer et al., 2009; Tomasello, 2007; Tomasello, Carpenter, & Liszkowski, 2007). The picture that emerges is thus a complex one, but this complexity does not deter babies from embarking on and succeeding at the task of language acquisition.

PRELINGUISTIC COMMUNICATION

Infants "listen" long before they can understand words, responding from birth to the human voice and, within just a few months, coordinating their vocal activity and body movements in response to another person's verbal and nonverbal rhythmic patterns (Feldman, 2006; Jaffe et al., 2001). During the first year of life, infants learn how to take turns in routines and games, such as peek-a-boo, preparing them for later turn-taking in conversations (Rochat, Querido, & Striano, 1999).

Infants "send messages" long before they can speak. The earliest messages—newborns' cries—are sent without any conscious intent to communicate and convey information about hunger, pain, and other internal states. Infants also produce nondistress vocalizations, social signals that often elicit contingent responses from parents and promote further interaction (Goldstein, Schwade, & Bornstein, 2009; Hsu & Fogel, 2003). These forms of prelinguistic communication lay a foundation for later language development.

Receptivity to Language

Like young birds and other animals, human infants are most responsive to the sounds produced by members of their own species (Aslin et al., 1998; Vouloumanos & Werker, 2004, 2007). Speech directed to infants is an especially attractive signal, even for babies just a few days or weeks old (Cooper & Aslin, 1990; Pegg, Werker, & McLeod, 1992). Known as **infant-directed (ID) speech** (formerly "motherese"), this form of language differs from adult-directed (AD) speech: ID utterances are shorter, more repetitive, higher-pitched, more variable in pitch, and less complex in vocabulary and grammar (Aslin et al., 1998). Speech directed to infants also tends to be more focused on emotional communication than AD speech (Trainor, Austin, & Desjardins, 2000).

Parents in some cultures believe that it is either unwise or unnecessary to speak to infants, and they are thus unlikely to use ID speech (DeLoache & Gottlieb, 2000; Schieffelin, 1990). ID speech has been found in so many languages and cultures, however, that some researchers regard it as practically universal (Kuhl et al., 1997). Infant-directed communication also appears to be universal in another way. Just like parents who use spoken language, parents who use sign language modify their signs when addressing an infant, using exaggerated hand and arm movements, displaying more emotional facial expressions, slowing down the rate of signing, and repeating signs more than they would when addressing an adult. Not surprisingly, deaf infants show a preference for ID over AD sign language (Erting, Prezioso, & O'Grandy Hynes, 1990; Masataka, 1996).

Infants respond to ID speech even in an unfamiliar language; 4- and 9-month-old English-learning infants listening to Cantonese, for example, prefer ID samples (Werker, Pegg, & McLeod, 1994). A cross-linguistic preference for ID language has also been found across modalities; 6-month-old hearing infants not previously exposed to sign language prefer the slower, more exaggerated and repetitive motions of ID sign language (Masataka, 1998).

ID speech functions like a set of introductory language lessons, exaggerating information about the sound system of the infant's native language, more effectively separating sounds into categories and providing a more distinctive basis for the child's imitation (Liu, Kuhl, & Tsao,

2003; Thiessen, Hill, & Saffran, 2005). Researchers working in a number of countries, including the United States, Russia, Sweden, and Japan, have found that mothers of 2- to 5-month-old infants produce more extreme vowels when speaking to their infant than when they address an adult. ID speech thus "stretches" the vowel space, providing information about sounds that are the foundation for words (Kuhl et al., 1997; Vallabha et al., 2007; Werker et al., 2007).

In addition to simplifying language, the singsong, rising and falling intonation pattern of ID speech engages and maintains infants' attention, increasing the likelihood that they will notice, attend to, and learn from speakers (and signers) using that style (Fernald & Mazzie, 1991; Kaplan et al., 1995; Thiessen et al., 2005). ID speech also carries information about speakers' emotions (Fernald, 1993; Trainor et al., 2000). Babies hear very different acoustic information when they are being praised ("good!") than when they are being warned ("stop!" or "no!"). Even though young infants do not understand the meaning of the words "good" and "stop," the short, sharp exclamation typically accompanying the word "stop" is more likely to keep them from touching a forbidden or dangerous object.

Of all the sounds surrounding babies every day, they respond to and eventually imitate human language, rather than doorbells or the sounds their pets make. What is the basis for this behavior? How does experience affect infants' developing speech and auditory processing abilities? Since the early 1970s, researchers have worked to find answers to these questions, illuminating many aspects of this fascinating process.

Speech Perception

In all spoken languages, there are variations of sound that function as speech units called phonemes. **Phonemes** are linguistically meaningful categories that signal differences in words through combinations of vowels and consonants. In English, for example, the difference between the words *back* and *pack* is a function of which of two phonemes, /b/ or /p/, is present. The **phonetics,** or set of vowels and consonants, that a particular language uses is only a subset of all possible speech sounds. The sounds that speakers produce may be phonetically different while still being perceived as belonging to the same phonemic category. For example, when analyzed in terms of acoustical physical energy, the /p/ in *pin* is not objectively identical to the /p/ in *spin*. Nevertheless, English speakers listening to these words report hearing the same phoneme /p/.

As we learned in Chapter 6, newborns are able to perceive phonetic categories from all human languages but lose much of this ability by the end of the first year, a sign of increasing specialization for the sounds of the language spoken around them. At 6 months of age, infants are able to discriminate native as well as nonnative consonant contrasts, but by 10 to 12 months, the ability to perceive nonnative contrasts decreases significantly (Aslin et al., 1998; Kuhl, 2004; Saffran, Werker, & Werner, 2006). Change in sensitivity to nonnative vowel contrasts occurs slightly earlier than consonants, possibly because vowels tend to be longer and louder (Iverson & Kuhl, 1995; Polka & Bohn, 1996; Polka & Werker, 1994). Bilingual babies, who become specialists for two sets of phonetic categories, briefly worsen at perceiving both sets around 8 months, despite hearing the contrasts regularly; by 12 months of age, however, they appear to discriminate speech sounds from both languages (MacLeod & Stoel-Gammon, 2005; Sebastián-Gallés & Bosch, 2005).

The potential value of this perceptual fine-tuning is reflected in a longitudinal study that tested infants at 7, 14, 18, 24, and 30 months of age. Babies who were better at discriminating native-language speech sounds at 7 months showed accelerated language ability at later ages, whereas those who were better at nonnative-language discrimination at 7 months showed reduced language abilities (Kuhl et al., 2005b; Tsao, Liu, & Kuhl, 2004). As another example of how speech perception "bootstraps" early language development, 17-month-old infants who excel at noticing subtle phonetic changes in pairings of new words with objects perform at higher levels than less phonetically sensitive infants on tests of language production and comprehension as preschoolers (Bernhardt, Kemp, & Werker, 2007; Werker & Yeung, 2005).

Infants use visual information as well as acoustic cues to become language specialists, becoming more sensitive to facial displays of articulation for the language(s) they are learning (Teinonen et al., 2008). In a study with 4-, 6-, and 8-month-olds, infants watched a silent video of bilingual speakers using either French or English. Following habituation, infants saw (but did not hear) the same speakers reciting sentences in the other language; infants whose looking time increased were assumed to have noticed the change in language. Comparison of monolingual English and bilingual French-English infants revealed the differential effects of early language exposure. At 4 and 6 months of age, all infants noticed the change in language, based on the visual information provided. At 8 months, however, monolingual infants had lost this ability, whereas bilingual babies continued to discriminate between the visual characteristics of the two languages to which they were regularly exposed, an ability they presumably used to continue learning those languages (Weikum et al., 2007).

Researchers initially believed that declines in sensitivity were an example of the "use it or lose it" principle. Phonetic feature detectors for all human languages were thought to be present from birth but to atrophy without stimulation from language input (Eimas & Corbit, 1973). This view was later undermined by experiments showing that adults can regain the ability to distinguish nonnative contrasts, if they have sufficient training (Lively, Logan, & Pisoni, 1993; Lively et al., 1994). In addition, English-speaking adults exposed early in life to a language they never used, such as Hindi or Zulu, are able to perceive phonetic contrasts in that language many years later, whereas adults without early exposure are unable to do so (Bowers, Mattys, & Gage, 2009).

Recent experiments, including some using ERP and NIRS measures, have shown that language exposure affects auditory processing through neural commitment to frequently occurring patterns in the native language (Iverson et al., 2003; Petitto, 2007; Zhang et al., 2005). With cumulative exposure to native language, perceptual sensitivity to nonnative contrasts is not lost. Instead, in a phenomenon known as the **perceptual magnet effect,** sensitivity shifts to favor phonemes in the native language, "pulling in" acoustically more distant speech sounds that were initially perceived as peripheral examples (Kuhl, 1991; Kuhl et al., 1992). Exposure to native language thus warps and contours the initial acoustic space. The resulting pattern of neural commitment is evident in most infants before the age of 12 months (Kuhl, 2004; Rivera-Gaxiola, Silva-Pereyra, & Kuhl, 2005; Saffran, Werker, & Werner, 2006).

Even brief encounters with the sound patterns of another language may make a difference, as shown in an experiment with 9-month-old English-learning infants exposed to native Mandarin Chinese speakers. After 12 laboratory sessions (approximately five hours of exposure), infants showed a reverse of the usual decline in sensitivity to Mandarin phonetic contrasts, whereas a control group of infants not exposed to Mandarin continued to lose their sensitivity to the nonnative language. The performance of infants exposed to Mandarin was comparable to the level found in infants living in Taiwan, indicating that even short-term exposure is effective at this age (Kuhl, Tsao, & Liu, 2003). Further studies are needed to explain how babies who live in bilingual or multilingual homes and communities maintain sensitivity to different sets of phonetic contrasts (Burns et al., 2007; Werker & Byers-Heinlein, 2008).

Recent experiments suggest that experience with language is important in another way. According to the theory of **constrained statistical learning,** infants perform a sort of statistical analysis that enables them to extract recurring patterns. In these studies, 7- to 9-month-old infants hear continuous sequences of syllables containing words from an invented language. After being familiarized with multiple repetitions of a sequence from that language, such as *golabup-abikututibubabupugolabupabikututibubabupu* . . . , researchers play individual words that were part of the sequence, such as *gola* or *bupa.* They compare infants' looking time at a loudspeaker playing one of those words with their looking time at a loudspeaker playing a word that was not part of the original sequence, such as *bugo* or *kubi.* If looking times differ, researchers infer that infants were able to discriminate the words being played and were able to use phonological regularities in the original sequence to extract word boundaries (Saffran & Estes, 2006; Saffran, Senghas, & Trueswell, 2001).

A number of studies have documented this statistical ability using artificial speech samples, suggesting that infants are able to use their cumulative language experience to *find* words in a continuous speech stream before they begin to learn their meaning (Kuhl, 2000; Saffran, 2003; Saffran & Thiessen, 2003; Saffran, Werker, & Werner, 2006). Infants presumably perform the same sort of analysis on real language. After months of experience, for example, infants extract the words *pretty* and *baby* (but not *tyba*) from the continuous speech stream *prettybaby.* This is because they have previously encountered the combination of *pre* and *tty* in other speech streams, such as *prettybig* and *prettygirl,* and the combination of *ba* and *by* in utterances such as *goodbaby* and *that'smybaby.* By comparison, they have less frequently heard the combination *ty* and *ba.* A recent experiment with English-learning 8-month-olds showed that, with as little as 2 minutes' exposure, babies of this age were sensitive to regularities ("transitional probability cues") in natural samples of fluent, infant-directed Italian speech—a language they had not previously heard (Pelucchi, Hay, & Saffran, 2009). Further studies may identify the learning mechanisms infants use in tasks with both real and artificial language samples (Marcus et al., 1999; Maye, Weiss, & Aslin, 2008; Thiessen & Saffran, 2003, 2007).

Despite the strong, accumulating evidence for this ability, statistical analysis alone is unlikely to explain the entire complex process (McMurray, Aslin, & Toscano, 2009). One reason is that, like categorical speech perception, constrained statistical learning has been found in monkeys, suggesting that it may be a more general learning ability (Hauser, Newport, & Aslin, 2001). Nevertheless, it is clear that the capacity to notice a variety of properties of language is present at birth, and experience with the native language shapes infants' attention to those properties, supporting their ability to process and segment the speech they hear (Nazzi, Jusczyk, & Johnson, 2000; Saffran, 2003; Saffran, Werker, & Werner, 2006). These findings have led a number of researchers to speculate that languages themselves may have evolved to match these perceptual-learning abilities. If true, this may help explain why most infants acquire language so easily (Kuhl, 2004; Saffran, 2003; Werker & Yeung, 2006).

Early Production: Babbling

For the first few months of life, infants coo and vocalize randomly, but around 3 to 4 months of age, their vocalizing begins to approximate the contours of **syllables,** combinations of consonants and vowels, such as *baba* and *mama.* Infants' vocalizing resembles mature speech sounds more if an adult vocalizes just after the infant does (Bloom, Russell, & Wassenberg, 1987). These experiences support infants' ability to notice similarities between the sounds they produce and the sounds they hear and may be important in guiding the development of connections in the brain for the eventual approximation of speech sound categories (Bloom, 1998; Kent & Miolo, 1995).

Between 6 and 9 months of age, vocalizing increases as infants engage in **babbling,** patterned but meaningless sequences of reduplicated sounds, such as *bababababa* and *mamamama.*

The most frequent sounds in infants' babbling repertoires (/b/, /d/, /g/, /p/, /t/, /k/, /m/, and /n/) are those that tend to occur most often in the language they hear and that reflect the infants' developing speech system (Bloom, 1998; Taylor, 1990). Initially, babies everywhere produce highly similar babbling patterns, regardless of the language spoken by those around them (Blake & de Boysson-Bardies, 1992; Locke, 1983). Even deaf babies begin to babble at approximately the same age as hearing babies (Lenneberg, Rebelsky, & Nichols, 1965; Smith, 1982). Continuation and elaboration of vocal babbling depends, however, on infants hearing the speech sounds that they and others around them produce (Oller & Eilers, 1988).

For deaf infants born to deaf parents, manual babbling begins around the same age as vocal babbling in hearing infants (Petitto, Holowka, et al., 2001; Petitto & Marentette, 1991). With exposure to sign language, deaf infants babble with their hands and fingers and show hand movements that are the manual equivalent of the phonetic and syllabic patterning in hearing children's vocal babbling. Hearing infants whose parents are profoundly deaf and thus communicate with them only in sign language also exhibit silent manual babbling (Petitto, Katerelos, et al., 2001; Petitto, Holowka, et al., 2004). Both vocal babbling and manual babbling are controlled by the brain's left hemisphere (Holowka & Petitto, 2002; Petitto et al., 2000). These findings are compelling evidence that infants are able to extract visual as well as auditory patterns from the environment and, moreover, that speech is only one possible form of language.

Gestural Communication

For many years, most researchers focused on vocal behavior, but recent studies of young children's gestures have expanded the definition of language development to include early manual communication. Beginning at birth and continuing into the second half-year, infants cry, coo, and use their face and body in an unintentional way, although caregivers often interpret these behaviors as reflecting communicative intentions (e.g., "Do you need a new diaper?" and "You sound hungry"). From 6 to 9 months of age, babies exhibit increasing coordination of vocalizations and movements, especially movements of the arm; they also begin to produce a rhythmic, temporal pattern that is similar to adults' coordinated speech and gesture (Iverson & Fagan, 2004).

At approximately 8 to 10 months of age, infants begin to use gestures in an intentional way to signal their desires and to indicate their interests to those around them (Goldin-Meadow, 2006; Messinger & Fogel, 1998). In this stage, babies raise their arms to indicate that they wish to be picked up, and they reach toward objects that they want, even when those objects are not close enough to be touched. These early deictic gestures are closely tied to the context (Acredolo et al., 2000; Goodwyn, Acredolo, & Brown, 2000). As caregivers respond to infants' pointing and reaching by fulfilling their nonverbal requests, routines involving sharing and trading of objects frequently emerge. The communicative nature of these gestures and routines is reflected in infants' tendency to vocalize and visually check with the caregiver. Although gestures initially appear without vocalizations, consistent vocal patterns (e.g., *wa* for water) begin to accompany gestures (Carpenter, Nagell, & Tomasello, 1998; Goldin-Meadow, 2006; Iverson & Fagan, 2004).

During the period between the onset of gestures (around 10 months) and the point in development when spoken words are plentiful (about 24 months), infants increasingly use symbolic gestures, such as bringing the thumb to the mouth for *bottle*, to represent objects and events. These gestures may be modeled by adults who use them during joint attention as tools for communication and as visual accompaniment to children's songs, such as "Twinkle Twinkle Little Star" or "The Itsy Bitsy Spider." Even when parents and children use the same gestures, they do not always use them in the same way. One analysis of child-parent interactions from 14 to 22 months of age, for example, showed that children were more likely than parents to use gestures such as pointing to reinforce (*bike* + point at bike), disambiguate (*that one* + point at bike), and supplement (*ride* + point at bike) their words (Özcaliskan & Goldin-Meadow, 2005a, 2005b).

Pointing supports subsequent language development (Goldin-Meadow, 2009; Tomasello et al., 2007). Longitudinal studies have found, for example, that the greater the number of different objects to which children point at 14 months, the larger their vocabulary at 42 months (Goldin-Meadow, 2007; Rowe, Özcaliskan, & Goldin-Meadow, 2008). One reason for this correlation may be that pointing, like other gestures, often prompts parents to follow children's shifts of attention, responding by "translating" with relevant words and sentences (Goldin-Meadow et al., 2007; Iverson & Goldin-Meadow, 2005). A child who points to an interesting sight, such as a street-sweeping truck, may thus enlist her father's attention and elicit the name of the vehicle and a brief description of its function.

Symbolic gestures alleviate the frustration that may arise before children have the ability to produce many words. In addition, children using symbolic gestures tend to advance faster in verbal development, progress that probably reflects their parents' tendency to gesture and speak more to them. The more symbolic gestures children have in their communication repertoire by 14 months, and the more gestures their parents use, the larger their verbal vocabulary at ages 2 and 4 years (Namy, Acredolo, & Goodwyn, 2000; Rowe & Goldin-Meadow, 2009; Rowe, Özcaliskan, & Goldin-Meadow, 2008).

In a study of 11-month-olds, parents interacting with their infants were instructed to promote symbolic gesturing by adding gestures to spoken words, using any physical motions that made sense to them. Children used symbolic gestures to request specific foods and activities, to share their feelings, and to elicit parental clarification of words. Measures of language acquisition beginning at 15 months showed a clear advantage for the sign training (ST) group over two control groups, especially early on. Although ST children were no longer ahead of control group children at the 36-month comparison, early benefits for the ST group included easier and more positive communicative interactions (Goldin-Meadow, 2006; Goodwyn & Acredolo, 1998; Goodwyn, Acredolo, & Brown, 2000).

Cross-linguistic studies show that there are both similarities and differences across languages and cultures in parent-infant gestural communication (Mayberry & Nicoladis, 2000). In laboratory studies, for example, both English-speaking and Italian-speaking parents modify their nonverbal communication with 20-month-olds, simplifying gestures (e.g., referring to visible objects by pointing toward them) to disambiguate spoken language (O'Neill et al., 2005). A longitudinal study in the homes of U.S. and Italian infants from 10 to 24 months, however, found differences in gestures and words produced during free-play and snack-time. American, English-speaking infants tended to use a preponderance of concrete, deictic gestures, such as pointing and reaching. Italian infants, by contrast, produced more symbolic gestures, such as bringing empty hands to their mouth to communicate "eating," possibly reflecting the influence of the gesture-rich Italian culture. In light of Italian infants' more advanced ability to use symbolic gestures to communicate, it may not be surprising that they produced fewer spoken words than did American infants (Iverson et al., 2008).

Some infants do not learn language from their parents, yet they use pointing and other gestures in much the same way that other children do. Young deaf children in hearing families, for example, who have not had an opportunity to learn sign language, nevertheless are able to create gestures and combine them in structured, sentence-like strings (Goldin-Meadow, Mylander, & Franklin, 2007; Senghas & Coppola, 2001; Senghas, Kita, & Özyurek, 2004). This was shown in a study of eight deaf 2- to 4-year-old children in Taiwan and the United States (four in each country) who had not been taught a signed language; their parents, who were not deaf, communicated with them using a combination of words and improvised gestures. Based on that input, children

When this infant and his mother engage in joint attention—looking at and pointing to the same picture on the wall—they are communicating through words, actions, and emotions.

independently invented unique gesture systems that shared many properties with natural language. Children's gestures surpassed their parents' in clarity and specificity, however, and were not directly derived from their parents' nonverbal actions (Goldin-Meadow et al., 2007). Although it is difficult to generalize from small samples, these findings may indicate that children are predisposed to learn to communicate in structured, language-like ways, using nonverbal means, even if they receive impoverished input (Goldin-Meadow, 2007).

SEMANTIC DEVELOPMENT

Whether infants are exposed to spoken language, sign language, or both, they become aware that patterns of speech sounds or signs have consistent meanings and contexts for use. Out of this awareness, children's first words emerge, augmenting their prelinguistic and nonverbal repertoire with new tools for learning and communication.

Milestones in the Acquisition of Meaning

The milestones of semantic development—the acquisition of vocabulary and word meaning—are well documented. Children's first words appear around the age of 12 months. Word learning begins gradually and then accelerates as children approach the end of the second year. Infants acquire words in the context of interactions with particular people and objects, guided by the perceptual qualities of those people and objects, such as their size, shape, texture, and color (Bloom, 1998). Infants and toddlers comprehend words before they can produce them, responding with excitement, for example, to parents' conversations about their favorite foods long before they can name them or ask for them with words (Hirsh-Pasek & Golinkoff, 1996). Language production is relatively straightforward to measure because it is directly observable. Researchers interested in language comprehension, however, face the challenge of studying a mental event that must be inferred from overt behavior and the context in which it occurs (Fernald et al., 1998).

In some studies, researchers assess infants' speech comprehension by asking parents to provide reports. In the MacArthur Communicative Development Inventories, for example, which we discuss later, parents use vocabulary checklists to indicate the words that they believe their children comprehend (Fenson et al., 1994). This indirect measure is only informative if parents are aware of and give accurate reports about the words their infants know. In other studies, infants' own behavior provides information about their receptive vocabulary. In these studies children are asked to choose a named object from among a number of alternatives (Woodward, Markman, & Fitzsimmons, 1994). Although this is a relatively direct measure, there are also practical and motivational limitations, such as infants becoming fatigued, bored, or distracted.

Another limitation of both parent-report and object-choice measures is that they do not provide information about the process of word recognition or how that process changes with age and experience. To address this limitation, some researchers study word recognition by tracking infants' eye movements as they look at pictures in response to familiar spoken words—*doggie, baby, ball,* and *shoe.* Babies see pictures of two of these objects at a time and hear ID-speech–style sentences ("Where's the _____?" "See the _____."), and researchers measure how long it takes them to look at the picture matching the spoken target word. Speed and efficiency of verbal processing increase dramatically over the second year. Whereas 15-month-olds usually do not seek out the correct picture until after the target word is spoken, 24-month-olds tend to shift their gaze to the correct picture before the word has been completely uttered, much as adults do in similar tests. During the first year of life, infants become nearly as fast as adults at shifting their gaze. Age-related differences in response time found in this experimental procedure, therefore, probably reflect differences in speed of linguistic processing rather than maturation of the visual-motor system (Fernald, Perfors, & Marchman, 2006; Fernald et al., 1998; Golinkoff et al., 1987).

Parents often report that babies as young as 8 months of age understand words (Bates, Dale, & Thal, 1995; Bloom, 1993, 1998). Many infants are able to recognize highly frequent words, such as their own name, by the age of 4 months (Mandel, Jusczyk, & Pisoni, 1995). It is not always possible for researchers to know how much previous exposure infants have had to their name or other words, but in some studies this experience has been precisely controlled. One team of investigators repeatedly visited 8-month-olds in their homes and played recordings of children's stories. After two weeks, infants heard lists of words that either occurred frequently or did not occur in the stories. Infants listened longer to lists of story words, whereas a control group, with no exposure to the stories, did not show a preference (Jusczyk & Hohne, 1997; Jusczyk et al., 1993). These findings indicate that 8-month-olds can remember words they have heard for a period of at least two weeks, even when there is no visible referent for those words (Aslin et al., 1998; Gerkin & Aslin, 2005).

When this infant is shown two different images, will he look at the image matching the word for the object that is shown—the ball instead of the shoe?

Experiments using an audiovisual habituation procedure called the Switch Task have documented the development of infants' ability to use speech perception skills to learn new words (Werker et al., 1998). In the Switch Task, babies are presented with two word-object pairings, one at a time, consisting of novel (experimenter-created) objects on a video screen accompanied by spoken labels, such as *bih* or *neef*. After being habituated to these pairings, babies are tested in a Same trial (consisting of one of the word-object pairings to which they were habituated) and a Switch trial (in which one of the previously seen objects is paired with the other object's word). Infants who have not learned the association between words and objects look equally long at objects in the Same and Switch test trials, whereas babies who have noted the initial correspondence look longer at the object when that association is violated in the Switch trial.

Studies of monolingual infants have found that 14-month-olds respond with "surprise" (look longer) during the Switch test trial when the words are quite dissimilar (e.g., *bih* and *neef*) or if they consist of similar-sounding words already in their vocabulary (e.g., *ball* and *doll*) (Fennell & Werker, 2003; Werker et al., 2002). When the words are less different and unfamiliar (e.g., *bih* and *dih*), however, they do not respond to the switch until the age of about 17 months (Pater, Stager, & Werker, 2004). These findings suggest that, during the second year of life, infants do more than simply respond to phonetic differences in the speech they hear; they begin to assume that different-sounding words refer to different objects. Thus, when they hear familiar words accompanied by a picture of the associated objects, they expect them to be pronounced in much the same way they have always heard them (i.e., *ball* is not supposed to sound like *doll*). For unfamiliar words, by contrast, they accept slightly different-sounding versions of words learned in the initial phase of the Switch Task (apparently deciding that *bih* is close enough to *dih*) when it is presented with one of the experimenter-created objects (Yoshida et al., 2009). As shown in Figure 8.1, bilingual infants appear to make the shift from phonetic to phonemic analysis in the Switch Task at a slightly later age (20 months) than monolingual infants. Researchers think that, although bilingual infants know as many words overall as monolingual babies, they know fewer words in each of the languages they are learning; as a result, they continue to use phonetic rather than phonemic processing in the Switch Task until they acquire additional words in each language (Fennell, Byers-Heinlen, & Werker, 2007). More studies comparing different types of bilingual infants are needed to test this explanation further.

Whether they are learning one language or more, children's first words typically refer to visible objects and people. Parents as well as researchers credit infants with knowledge of a word when their vocalization meets specific criteria, including "its phonetic shape, consistency, frequency, and

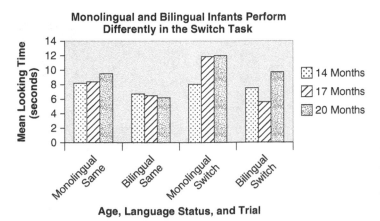

FIGURE 8.1 Monolingual and bilingual infants perform differently in the Switch Task. *Source:* Adapted from Fennell, Byers-Heinlein, & Werker, 2007.

meaningfulness in relation to something going on in the situation" (Bloom, 1998, p. 321). Infants who consistently utter *da* whenever a dog appears (but never make this sound when they see any other object or animal), for example, are likely to be granted the word *dog* as part of their productive vocabulary.

Most children experience a vocabulary spurt, becoming "vacuum cleaners" for words (Pinker, 1994). By the age of 18 to 19 months, most infants have learned about 50 new words (Bates et al., 1995; Bloom, 1998). The rate of productive vocabulary growth increases so rapidly beginning at about 18 months of age that some researchers have referred to it as a "naming explosion" (Bloom, 1973; Goldfield & Reznick, 1990). During this time, some children are reported to learn as many as 40 new words per week, and many go from having only 10 to 20 words to well over 100 within a month or two (Dromi, 1986; Goldfield & Reznick, 1990; Woodward & Markman, 1998).

Among young deaf infants learning sign language, first referential signs and a naming (signing) explosion occur at approximately the same ages as spoken vocabulary growth in hearing infants (Bloom, 1998; Folven & Bonvillian, 1991). Contrary to some popular beliefs, bilingual infants follow a similar timetable, whether they are acquiring two spoken languages, such as French and English, or one spoken and one manual language, such as French and Langue des Signes Québécoise (Holowka, Brosseau-Lapré, & Petitto, 2002; Petitto & Kovelman, 2003; Vihman et al., 2007). As noted earlier, bilingual and monolingual infants usually have vocabularies of similar size, when words from both of bilingual babies' languages are counted together (Pearson & Fernández, 1994).

One-Word Utterances

Across many different languages, including English, Spanish, Dutch, French, Hebrew, Italian, and Korean, children's first words often refer to nouns, such as animals, vehicles, food, clothing, toys, body parts, people, household items, places to go, things outside, actions, games, and routines (Bornstein et al., 2004; Nelson, Hampson, & Shaw, 1993; Waxman & Lidz, 2006). Not all researchers agree, however, that these first words should be categorized as if they were parts of speech in sentences produced by older children and adults. Although it is true that many of children's first words could be described as nouns—names for objects, like *ball, cookie, bottle,* and *dog*—there are also reasons to use caution when applying abstract grammatical categories to children's earliest utterances.

This 2-year-old girl and her mother communicate through American Sign Language. Research has shown that children learning sign language progress through the same stages as children learning a spoken language.

Focusing on the nouns in children's early language production may be misleading because children are also learning many other kinds of words, like *more, down, pretty,* and *open.* In fact, in one well-known study of 1-year-olds, object names made up only about one-third of the words children uttered (Bloom, Tinker, & Margulis, 1993). Even in a classic study reporting that more than half of some children's first words were nouns, some of the words named events like *lunch,* or transient "objects" like *lap* (Bloom, 1998; Nelson, Hampson, & Shaw, 1993).

Assigning children's first words to formal speech categories is also difficult because names for objects are often used to communicate other meanings (Bloom, 1994; Waxman & Lidz, 2006). These **holophrases** allow children who can produce only one word at a time to use each word in a more flexible way. The word *cookie,* therefore, might mean "That's a cookie," "I want a cookie," "I want another cookie," or even "I dropped my cookie," depending on the context in which it is uttered and the accompanying emotion.

Another problem is that, when children first learn new words, they do not always use them in the same way that older children and adults do. One common error, **overextension,** occurs when children use a word, such as *dog,* to refer to other objects, such as cats or rabbits, that may be perceptually or functionally similar to the word's correct referent (Anglin, 1977; Rescorla, 1980). In one well-known example of creative overextension, the young son of two language researchers overextended the name of their English sheepdog, Nunu, to a variety of objects, including other dogs, fuzzy slippers, and even a salad garnished with two large black olives that resembled their dog's nose (de Villiers & de Villiers, 1978). Although it is more difficult to detect, children sometimes make the opposite error of **underextension**—applying a word only to a specific instance, such as using the word *dog* for the family collie but not applying it to poodles, dalmatians, or dogs in general.

Individual Differences in Language Experience

Children differ in the timing of their first words and in the rate at which they acquire subsequent words (Smith, 2000). In one study, the range in age for first words was from 10 to 17 months, and the vocabulary spurt occurred as early as 13 months and as late as 25 months (Bloom, 1993). One factor contributing to this variability is the amount and variety of language that infants hear every day.

Consistent associations have been found between the quantity and quality of language input and infants' socioeconomic background (Bates, Bretherton, & Snyder, 1988; Bates et al., 1995). In one longitudinal study that began when infants were 7 to 9 months old, researchers found that parents in lower-income families talked less often to their children than parents in higher-income families; they also made fewer efforts to engage their children in conversation and gave verbal feedback that was more frequently corrective or critical than affirmative or encouraging. Children in lower-income families received less than one-half the language experience of children in middle-income families (616 versus 1,251 words per hour) and less than one-third that of children in higher-income families (2,153 words per hour). At the age of 30 months, children in lower-income families had smaller vocabularies than children in higher-income families (an average of 357 versus 766 words), suggesting that language input may have been a contributing factor (Hart & Risley, 1995, 1999). Another potentially impor-tant contribution to early language development—use of gesture—also differs as a function of socioeconomic background, with infants and toddlers in higher-income families being exposed to more gestural communication than children in lower-income families (Rowe & Goldin-Meadow, 2009).

Other studies have also found links between naturally occurring variations in infants' early language environments and their later language skills (Hoff, 2003; Hoff-Ginsberg, 1997).

Even within middle-class samples, there may be a wide range in the amount that parents talk to their 16-month-olds (from 700 to 7,000 words per hour) and, correspondingly, in children's vocabulary at age 26 months (from 200 to 800 words) (Huttenlocher, 1998; Huttenlocher, Levine, & Vevea, 1998; Huttenlocher et al., 2002). Well-documented links between children's early language development and their readiness for school highlight the potential implications of extreme differences in early language environments (Forget-Dubois et al., 2009). As a result, as we discuss in Chapter 11, researchers and early childhood educators are pursuing language and literacy interventions to ensure that all children are cognitively and linguistically prepared to learn.

In addition to the amount and variety of speech that children hear, parental responsiveness may influence the timing of milestones in children's early expressive language (Tamis-LeMonda, Bornstein, & Baumwell, 2001). A study involving 9- and 13-month-olds and their mothers found that parents' responsiveness during free play was related to children's first imitations, first words, attainment of 50 words in expressive language, combining words, and using language to talk about the past. Affirmations (e.g., "Nice job") and descriptions (e.g., "That's your Big Bird") were especially helpful at 9 months, supporting children's explorations and providing labels for objects and events that they had noticed. At 13 months of age, children's language development benefited when mothers responded to children as more advanced communicative partners—imitating their child's vocalizations (e.g., saying "doll" after the child said "da") and expanding on their child's communicative efforts (e.g., saying "Where did the ball go?" after the child said "ba?"). These findings suggest that infants benefit most when parents are responsive in ways that are relevant to their abilities and attention focus at different developmental stages.

Cultural and Linguistic Influences

Efforts to generalize about children's first words may not fully succeed because there is great diversity in the words in young children's early productive vocabularies. Out of 11,000 words that one researcher recorded from 14 children, for example, only five words appeared in the vocabularies of all the children (*baby, ball, down, juice,* and *more*). This diversity reflects the different sorts of topics that attract different children's attention. It also reflects the specific words that parents use in conversation, goals that they have for different kinds of conversations, and expectations about conversations with sons versus daughters (Bloom, 1993; Fivush et al., 2000; Smith, 2000). As we saw in Chapter 7, when talking about the past, some parents ask their child many questions and provide a large amount of information about specific events, whereas other parents ask fewer questions and provide less information, or focus more on the child's feelings during the events than on objective facts about the experience. These styles contribute to differences in children's ability to remember past events as well as the content of those memories (Fivush et al., 2006; Wang, 2006).

Across cultures, parents differ in the topics they discuss with their children and how they use language to socialize them. Beng parents in the West African nation of Ivory Coast, for example, emphasize teaching infants appropriate greetings and words for all of their relatives as early as possible. The Beng also believe that it is important for babies to gain further pragmatic understanding—learning how to tease and even playfully insult their relatives (Gottlieb, 2000).

Cross-cultural comparisons of parent-child conversations about past events have found that American parents tend to focus on building self-esteem and supporting young children's developing sense of themselves as unique individuals (Cho, Miller, & Bracey, 2009; Cho et al., 2005). Chinese parents, by contrast, tend to use these conversations as opportunities to reinforce children's awareness of standards for appropriate behavior as well as their obligations and connectedness to the family (Miller et al., 1997; Wang, 2004).

Cultures vary in the extent to which they encourage talkativeness in children. Japanese mothers in one study used verbal and nonverbal cues to shorten young children's personal narratives, creating minimally descriptive reminiscences that the researchers compared to haiku poetry. These interjections taught children that empathy and shared understanding with listeners are valued more than detailed recitations in which one person holds the floor to a significantly greater degree than another. Given that talkativeness is considered especially undesirable for males in Japan, mothers responded differently to boys than girls, interjecting more often in an effort to discourage their sons from speaking too much. English-speaking Canadian mothers, by contrast, tended to ask a greater number of questions, encouraging sons and daughters alike to speak more and provide additional descriptive details. These distinctive approaches reflect the different value that each culture places on individual self-expression in dyadic conversation (Minami & McCabe, 1995).

Cross-cultural studies also indicate that not all parents engage infants in the reciprocal vocalizing and object labeling that is so characteristic of dyadic interactions in middle-class cultures, such as those found in North America and parts of Europe (Bloom, 1998; Crago, Annahatak, & Ningiuruvik, 1993). Given the evidence we have already noted about the role of language experience and a rich language environment, how do infants with less face-to-face verbal interaction acquire language? One answer seems to be that infants in such cultures are often raised in multifamily, multiparticipant conversational contexts in which they are exposed to language. From the very beginning, infants are surrounded by and overhear adults' speech to older children of various ages and stages of language acquisition. The success with which children in these cultures acquire language suggests that overheard speech can serve as an important resource in first language acquisition (Akhtar & Tomasello, 2000; Oshima-Takane, Goodz, & Derevensky, 1996). Another potentially helpful form of language modeling occurs in some cultures when parents "speak for" their babies by holding them up and answering for them, saying, "I'm fine" in response to the question "How are you?" (Gottlieb, 2000).

Bilingual children acquire new words from both languages and usually use their first words in ways that show their awareness of different contexts for use (Holowka et al., 2002; Kovács & Mehler, 2009; Petitto & Kovelman, 2003). A child addressing his English-speaking childcare provider, for example, may use the word *milk*, but when communicating with his Spanish-speaking grandmother, would be more likely to use the Spanish word for milk—*leche* (Yavas, 1995). Just like monolingual children, bilingual children begin to put together two words sometime after the age of 18 months (Bhatia & Ritchie, 1999).

Explaining Early Word Learning

How readily do young children learn new words? A few minutes of training by an unfamiliar experimenter in a laboratory setting appears to be sufficient to enable 18- and even 13-month-olds to recognize novel labels for novel objects (Woodward et al., 1994). This finding suggests that children make significant progress in word learning before the naming explosion occurs, but how do infants solve the problem of matching individual words with the objects, people, events, and feelings to which they refer? A number of theories have been proposed for the acquisition of children's first words. Table 8.3 shows that some explanations focus on adjustments parents use when communicating with infants, whereas other accounts emphasize contributions made by infants themselves. Laboratory studies of word learning explore controlled language input that enables researchers to test specific assertions of competing theories. It is

TABLE 8.3	Theories of Early Word Learning	
Theory	**Assumptions**	**Examples**
Social/Pragmatic	Infants learn language in order to communicate with other people, share emotions, and locate the self in a social world.	Infants learn when they and their caregivers give joint attention to objects, people, or events. Infants use speakers' referenial cues to learn which words and referents go together.
Constraints/Principles	Infants are able to build their vocabulary with relative ease because they are guided by a set of assumptions about the possible meanings of new words.	The whole object assumption biases infants to assume that new words refer to whole objects rather than actions, spatial location, or parts or features of objects. The taxonomic assumption biases infants to extend a new word for one kind of object to other examples of that kind of object.
Mutual exclusivity	Infants assume that objects have only one name.	Infants map new words onto new objects whose names they do not know. They avoid using a new word for an object whose name they already know.
Grammatical cues	Children use grammatical cues in utterances they hear to narrow down the possible meanings of new words.	Children use the presence or absence of an indefinite article ("a") to infer whether a new word refers to a specific, unique object or all objects of that type.
Semantic contrast	Children learn the meaning of new words by contrasting them with known words from the same domain.	Children who are asked to bring the "navy" pants, not the "green" ones, are able to guess the meaning of the word "navy."

important to remember, however, that most early language learning environments are considerably richer, with multiple cues available (Golinkoff & Hirsh-Pasek, 2007, 2008; Tomasello, 2006; Waxman & Lidz, 2006).

SOCIAL AND PRAGMATIC CUES   Social/pragmatic theories begin with the observation that language learning occurs in a social context, such as a dyadic interaction between an infant and caregiver. According to this view, infants' primary motivation for language learning is to achieve emotional sharing with the caregiver, locating the self in a social world (Akhtar & Tomasello, 2000; Tomasello, 2007). Through joint attention—achieved through nonverbal adjustments in posture, gaze, and head orientation—infants and caregivers communicate and share understanding. Eventually, shared emotional and nonverbal communication becomes shared in speech (Bloom, 1998; Graham, Nilsen, & Nayer, 2007; Sabbagh, Henderson, & Baldwin, 2007).

Infants learn through joint attention and instruction from a more skilled person. After this infant's father demonstrates and talks about how to use the hammer, he will give his son a chance to try it out.

Many parents use "follow-in" labeling, providing names for objects to which their babies are attending (Masur, 1982). Children whose parents use this approach often have more advanced vocabularies than children who do not experience this kind of language input (Akhtar, Dunham, & Dunham, 1991; Tomasello & Farrar, 1986). Parents are not always aware of what their babies are looking at or interested in, however, and they engage in this form of labeling only 50 to 70 percent of the time (Baldwin, 1991). How, then, do infants avoid making semantic errors when parents do not establish joint attention with them?

Infants do not appear to follow a simple rule of association (Baldwin & Tomasello, 1998; Sabbagh et al., 2007). This was shown in an experiment with 16- to 19-month-olds, in which infants were taught a novel object label in either a follow-in labeling condition or a condition in which the experimenter provided an object label only when the baby and experimenter were looking at different objects. Babies at both ages learned the label in the follow-in condition; when the experimenter uttered the label in the absence of joint attention, 16-month-olds failed to learn the new word but did not make mistakes by mapping the new word onto the object they had been playing with and looking at (Baldwin, 1991).

Even when they are not sharing attention, speakers often provide potentially informative **referential cues**—gaze, facial expression, head orientation, and other verbal and nonverbal behaviors that reflect an individual's attentional focus, intentions, or expectations (Graham et al., 2007). Young language learners monitor these cues and use that information to map words to objects the speaker is looking at. Two-year-olds, for example, are sensitive to another person's referential intent; they assume that a speaker who says he is looking for a *crug* has found it if he shows a gleeful expression, looks wide-eyed, and exclaims "Ah!" upon encountering an object. If the speaker displays signs of unhappiness or disappointment, by contrast, 2-year-olds conclude that the found object is not a *crug*. Two-year-olds are also able to use speakers' nonverbal behavior to determine whether an intended action, described by a novel verb, such as *dax*, has occurred (Tomasello, 2000; Tomasello & Barton, 1994).

Young children are also capable of monitoring the success of their own communicative efforts, as shown in a study in which 30-month-olds requested particular toys. When these requests were deliberately misunderstood by an experimenter, children clarified their requests, indicating that they were keeping track of the experimenter's comprehension (Shwe & Markman, 1997).

In summary, there is support for the social/pragmatic view of word learning. Many parents, particularly in middle-class cultures, monitor infants' attentional and nonverbal cues, providing opportunities for teaching babies new words for objects and actions in which they are interested and simplifying the task of word learning. For their part, by about 18 months of age children are able to "read" speakers' subtle referential cues when determining which objects, object properties, and events are being discussed.

CONSTRAINTS AND PRINCIPLES   When children hear a new word, such as *gerbil,* how do they learn the meaning of that word? How do they decide that gerbil refers to the entire animal in front of them and that it does not mean feet, tail, furry, scamper, or any of the other things they might see at the moment they hear someone utter the word gerbil? One answer to this fundamental question (Quine, 1960) is that the human mind must be equipped with constraints or principles to eliminate at least some possible meanings. In fact, according to the constraints/principles view, children are guided by a set of default assumptions, of which the whole object, taxonomic, and mutual exclusivity assumptions are the best known (Hollich et al., 2000; Waxman & Lidz, 2006; Woodward, 2000).

The **whole object assumption** guides children to assume that new words refer to whole objects (identified principally by their shape), rather than actions, spatial location, or other parts or characteristics of objects (Gershkoff-Stowe & Smith, 2004; Hollich et al., 2000). Evidence for this bias includes the finding that young language learners, even 1- and 2-year-olds, tend to regard a new word, such as *bix,* as if it refers to an object as an entire bounded shape, as opposed to its substance, color, or parts (Booth & Waxman, 2009; Hollich, Golinkoff, & Hirsh-Pasek, 2007; Markman, 1989). Characteristics of an object are sometimes relevant, however, and may alter the tendency to focus on a whole object rather than its features. For some objects, like certain kitchen gadgets, for example, 2-year-olds tend to assume that a new word refers to the entire object, but they are much less likely to make this inference for less complex objects and nonsolid substances, such as a foamy pile of shaving cream (Imai & Gentner, 1997). An experiment with 3-year-olds found that children were better at learning new, invented words for complex novel objects when those objects were described in terms of how they function rather than when they were simply told about an object's characteristics. When shown a picture of a device called a *gulla,* for example, children who were told that it was used to grind up food performed better than children who were informed that it had a part made out of gold inside of it (Booth, 2009). These findings reflect the close association between word learning and conceptual knowledge, and more generally between language and cognition.

Some researchers think that object labels may be easier for children to learn because objects are more perceptually obvious than actions, relations between objects, or social cues about a speaker's intent (Gentner, 2007; Golinkoff & Hirsh-Pasek, 2008; Pruden et al., 2006). When 1- to 1½-year-olds in one study were given significant exposure to eight new object labels and eight new action words, for example, they learned and produced the object labels more quickly than the action words (Schwartz & Leonard, 1980). Experiments involving 14- to 17-month-olds indicate that toddlers perceive and respond to different kinds of events, but researchers are just beginning to understand how these perceptual abilities contribute to verb learning (Golinkoff & Hirsh-Pasek, 2008; Pulverman et al., 2008).

Some researchers assert that, if objects are particularly salient to infants, it is because parents tend to emphasize them more than actions in their speech. One structural property of language—word order—influences whether parents' speech highlights nouns. English-speaking parents, for example, tend to end utterances with nouns because English tends to follow a subject-verb-object structure, as in the sentence "the girl read the book." Languages like Korean and Japanese, however, have a verb-final sentence structure and utterances tend to end with verbs, as in "the girl the book read." Korean-speaking parents tended to end utterances with verbs, whereas English-speaking parents more frequently finished with nouns. Despite this difference, there is little difference in the proportions of nouns and verbs in English versus Korean parental speech; 15- to 24-month-olds in both settings tend to have many more nouns than verbs in their vocabularies (Au, Dapretto, & Song, 1994). Other cross-linguistic studies have also found a greater prevalence of nouns in the speech of 20-month-olds (Bornstein et al., 2004).

Evidence for this conclusion is mixed, however. A study of Korean- and English-speaking parents and their 12- to 26-month-old infants found that English-learning infants produced many more nouns than verbs, but Korean-learning infants produced nearly equal numbers of labels for objects and actions (Choi & Gopnik, 1995). In addition, although English-speaking mothers tend to focus on teaching children object names, whereas Japanese-speaking mothers tend to talk more about ongoing actions and social routines, both Japanese- and English-learning children at 12 and 19 months of age produce approximately twice as many nouns as verbs (Fernald & Morikawa, 1993). Additional cross-linguistic studies may shed further light on the significance of these patterns.

Studies examining children's first 50 words also raise questions about the relative prominence of nouns and verbs in children's speech. Children learn words for whole objects, but they also acquire words that are adjectives, action terms, and prepositions, and there is often variability across different children of the same age (Naigles, Hoff, & Vear, 2009). In one longitudinal study of 14 children, for example, monthly observations showed that object words comprised as few as 10 percent for some children and, at most, 50 percent for other children (Bloom, 2000; Bloom et al., 1993; Nelson et al., 1993).

The **taxonomic assumption** guides children to assume that new words should be extended to objects that are related to the category of the originally named object (Behrend, Scofield, & Kleinknecht, 2001; Hollich et al., 2000; Markman & Hutchinson, 1984). According to this view, the taxonomic assumption is at work when young children are taught a word for one kind of bird (e.g., calling a purple bird a *sud*) and then extend that new word to other kinds of birds but not to a bird's nest. The research literature provides support for this constraint on preschool children's word learning (Golinkoff et al., 1995). Studies of 9- to 20-month-olds suggest that this constraining assumption is operating at even earlier ages (Booth & Waxman, 2009; Waxman & Hall, 1993; Waxman & Markow, 1995).

The **mutual exclusivity assumption** leads children to assume that objects will have only one name. It also guides them to search for a nameless object referent as soon as they hear a novel word. In studies of this assumption, researchers typically present children with a familiar object, such as a ball, and an unfamiliar object, such as a shoe horn. The experimenter then asks the child for one of the objects, using a novel label, such as *glorp*. Children who follow the mutual exclusivity assumption select the novel, unnamed object rather than the ball when asked for the *glorp*. After the age of 2 years, children map novel labels to novel objects and novel actions (Behrend, 1995; Golinkoff et al., 1995; Merriman & Schuster, 1991).

By the age of about 12 months, infants are able to learn word-object associations for invented words and objects, even if those associations change. Researchers in one experiment showed infants drawings of pairs of novel shapes accompanied by pairs of spoken words, such as *bosa* and *manu*; shape-word combinations changed during the 4-minute session, but some shapes and words were paired more often than others. When infants subsequently saw a display of two shapes and heard a single spoken word, they looked longer at the shape that had more frequently appeared with that word. Analogous to the mutual-exclusivity effect observed in slightly older children, infants in this experiment were able to coordinate information across separate naming events and did not behave as if they thought the single word could refer to both of the shapes being displayed (Smith & Yu, 2008). Although the basis for this response requires further study, the results are consistent with the notion that constraints and biases direct children's word learning from an early age.

The mutual exclusivity assumption predicts that children should resist learning second labels for objects that already have names. In controlled word learning experiments, monolingual children typically resist redundant labeling well before their second birthday. Researchers studying 16-month-olds taught them a novel label either for an object with a name they already knew or for an object whose name they did not know. Consistent with the mutual exclusivity prediction, infants applied the labels only when they were presented for previously unnamed objects (Liittschwager & Markman, 1994). Arguments against this point, however, include the fact that children can and do learn more than one word for the same object. Bilingual children, for example, are willing to use a novel label to refer to an object for which they already know the name, if they believe that the two labels are from different languages. Consistent with the mutual exclusivity assumption, they resist applying a novel label to an already labeled object if they believe that the two labels come from the same language (Au & Glusman, 1990).

GRAMMATICAL CUES   At the same time that children acquire vocabulary, they are also learning about the rules of grammar for the language they are acquiring. Children's emerging understanding of these rules provides additional cues about the meaning of new words. As a classic study showed many years ago, preschool-age children use grammatical cues, such as word endings, to interpret unfamiliar words (Brown, 1957). They guess, for example, that *wugging* refers to an activity, whereas *wug* refers to an object. These findings have been widely replicated, including in studies showing that children as young as 2 years use grammatical cues to narrow down the possible meanings of new words (Gleitman, 1990; Hall, Lee, & Belanger, 2001; Naigles, 1996; Waxman & Kosowski, 1990).

In one series of experiments, toddlers aged 20 to 37 months learned a novel label for a doll. For some children, the doll was presented using a proper noun—"This is ZAV"—and for other children the doll was presented using a count noun—"This is a ZAV." A second identical doll was then placed nearby and the children's task was to choose one of the two dolls as a referent for the novel word, responding to one of two questions, either "Where is ZAV?" or "Where is a ZAV?" By the age of 24 months, children were more likely to select the first, labeled doll if they heard a proper name (ZAV) than if they heard a count noun (a ZAV) (Hall et al., 2001).

CONTRASTING SEMANTIC RELATIONS   As children's vocabularies increase, they use words they already know to guess the meaning of new words, a phenomenon known as **lexical contrast** (Carey & Bartlett, 1978). As a result of lexical contrast, children who hear adults ask for "the khaki pants, not the blue ones" become aware of the color to which the word *khaki* refers. This hypothesis was tested by using a lexical contrast approach to teach 3- and 4-year-old children a novel color word—*chromium*—to describe the color olive. After just a single session and a one-week delay, about one-half of the children showed some learning of the term *chromium* (Carey & Bartlett, 1978). Subsequent research has used more sensitive measures, including a larger array of color choices and additional domains, such as shape and texture, to investigate young children's ability to learn from lexical contrast. Two-year-olds in one such experiment learned novel words, such as *granular,* on the basis of hearing them contrasted with known words, such as *smooth,* from the same domain (Heibeck & Markman, 1987).

After decades of searching for a single theory to explain semantic development, researchers from different camps increasingly endorse the need to consider the multiple cues and sources of information that infants use to learn new words (Hall & Waxman, 2004; Hollich et al., 2000; Woodward & Markman, 1998). One hybrid perspective that seeks to find a middle ground and integrate competing explanations is the **Emergentist Coalition Model (ECM),** a theory that places existing evidence into a new framework. According to the ECM, before the age of approximately 12 months, infants learn new words by relying on attentional cues, such as the perceptual saliency of objects and temporal pairings of words and objects or events. Beginning at about 12 months, children become more dependent on social and linguistic cues, such as eye gaze, social context, and grammar (Golinkoff & Hirsh-Pasek, 2007, 2008; Hollich et al., 2000).

THE ACQUISITION OF GRAMMAR

In addition to word order, languages differ in whether and how they mark concepts such as the past, gender, and relationship status. An English-learning child can simply refer to his *brother,* but if he were learning Mandarin Chinese, he would need to choose between two different words— *didi* (younger brother) and *gege* (older brother). How early do children become aware of the rules of the language that is spoken around them? How does experience interact with innate constraints to guide young children's acquisition of grammar?

Multiword Utterances

Long before children put two or more words together, they infer meaning from word order. This has been shown in studies with infants as young as 17 months, who have not yet moved beyond the one-word level of production. When researchers showed infants of this age two simultaneous video displays of different actions (e.g., Ernie washing Cookie Monster versus Cookie Monster washing Ernie) and played an audiotaped sentence that described one of the two actions (e.g., "Look! Ernie is washing Cookie Monster!"), they found that infants tended to look at the display that matched the sentence (Hirsh-Pasek & Golinkoff, 1996). These findings show that infants of this age have already learned to use one grammatical marker—word order—to interpret sentences they hear.

Around 18 to 24 months, children begin to produce two-word utterances, using words they have already learned to say individually (Bloom, 1998). Children now say things like "mommy sock," "more juice," and "give me shoe," leaving out the little grammatical markers, like articles, plural endings, prepositions, and auxiliary verbs. Given their brevity, children's utterances at this stage are often referred to as **telegraphic speech** (Brown, 1973).

Children's early two-word utterances communicate a range of meanings, including agent + action (e.g., "Daddy eat"), action + object (e.g., "Eat cookie" and "Throw hat"), agent + object (e.g., "Mommy car"), object + attribute (e.g., "Big doggie"), recurrence (e.g., "More juice"), and nonexistence (e.g., "No cookie"). The order of the words in these phrases is usually fixed, reflecting the order in which children hear the words combined with other words in adult speech (Bloom, 1973, 1998; Brown, 1973). As a result, English-learning children rarely say things like "Cookie eat" or "Hat throw."

Grammatical Morphemes

Some early two-word utterances, such as "all gone" or "go byebye," are derived from familiar activities and routines, and are phrases learned as single units or formulas. Their existence does not indicate that children have learned how the order of the individual words determines the meaning relationships between them (Bloom, 1998). Another important fact about tracking children's grammatical development is that simply counting words is not always a useful index. Instead, language researchers compute the **mean length of utterance (MLU),** a measure based on the number of morphemes in children's speech. **Morphemes** are the minimal meaningful units in speech and they come in two varieties, free and bound. Free morphemes are words or parts of words that can function on their own, such as *boy, girl, walk, ocean,* and *call.* By contrast, bound morphemes are grammatical tags or markers that cannot stand alone; these include word endings like *-est, -s, -ing,* and *-ed.* When attached to free morphemes, bound morphemes modify the meaning. In English, for example, adding *-ed* to *walk* changes the meaning to the past tense. To compute the MLU for a particular child, researchers count up the number of morphemes (both bound and free) per utterance in a sample of the child's speech and divide that total by the number of utterances in the sample.

To illustrate, the utterance "Mommy sock" has two morphemes, whereas "Mommy's sock" has three; "Kitty eat" has two morphemes, whereas "Kitty is eat-ing" has four. As MLU increases, the number of words in an utterance increases, but even more importantly, the presence of more morphemes makes the child's speech seem more adultlike, less telegraphic.

As shown in Figure 8.2, several distinct stages of early language development have been described in terms of MLU. In the 1970s, researchers began to pay special attention to Stage II, when children first produce morphemes with which they can fine-tune communication. Researchers focused on three children's acquisition of 14 grammatical morphemes, including the present progressive ending *-ing* (driv*ing*), prepositions *in* and *on,* the regular plural *–s* (birdie*s*), past tenses of irregular verbs (*came, fell, broke, sat, went*), possessive *'s* (baby*'s*), articles *a* and *the,* past tense of regular verbs *–ed* (push*ed*), regular third person *–s* (jump*s*), irregular third person (*does, has*). Beginning at the age of about 2 years, spontaneous language samples were recorded in the children's homes approximately every two weeks as they interacted with their mothers and, sometimes, with the researchers. Although the three children acquired the 14 morphemes at different rates, they followed a nearly identical order (Brown, 1973). Cross-sectional study of the same morphemes with 21 English-speaking children confirmed the order of acquisition (de Villiers & de Villiers, 1973).

After these results became known, linguists wanted to know why children acquire these morphemes in essentially the same order. If some of the morphemes were phonologically easier, that could explain the pattern of acquisition. Arguing against this sort of account, however, is the finding that children showed a different order of acquisition for three *-s* morphemes that sound alike but are grammatically different. Across the studies of these morphemes, the plural (*pigs*) almost always preceded the possessive (*pig's*), and these, in turn, were followed by the third-person singular verb ending (*jumps*).

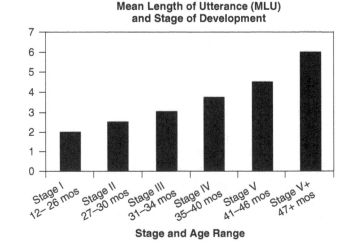

FIGURE 8.2 Early language development can be described in terms of the mean length of utterance (MLU). *Source:* Adapted from Owens, 1984.

Another possible explanation is that the frequency with which morphemes occur in adult speech determines the order of acquisition. Analysis of parental speech showed, however, that although articles (e.g., *the* and *a*) were among the most frequently produced morphemes, they were not among the first morphemes children acquired (Brown, 1973).

The most widely accepted explanation for the nearly invariant order of morpheme acquisition is that the complexity of the morpheme itself determines the ease with which children acquire it. As linguists define complexity, it refers both to semantic and grammatical characteristics, including the amount of information children must keep in mind in order to produce a correct utterance. Using the past tense verb *were*, for example, requires considering the subject, the number of the subject, and when the event occurred. The ending for regular plurals *-s*, by contrast, requires only that the child keep track of number. The difference in complexity, therefore, is one plausible explanation for the finding that the regular plural *-s* is acquired in Stage II, whereas the past tense plural verb form *were* is not acquired until Stage V.

Overregularization

Once young children acquire rules of grammar, they are able to use them to modify new words. This was first shown in the *wug* test, a classic experiment in which children heard and completed fill-in-the-blank statements like, "I know a man who likes to *bod*. He did the same thing yesterday. Yesterday he _____." Children who reliably mark the past tense in their own speech by adding the morpheme *-ed* to verbs readily supply the word *bodded*, demonstrating that they have learned a rule for generating new utterances, rather than simply memorizing verbs as they encounter them (Berko, 1958).

In English, most verbs apply the suffix *-ed* to form the past tense, but there are approximately 180 irregular verbs, exceptions to the *-ed* rule, which form the past tense in idiosyncratic ways (Marcus et al., 1992). As young children begin learning these words, they show a U-shaped pattern in which they initially produce a high proportion of them correctly. Subsequently, they begin to make **overregularization** errors, applying grammatical morphemes to words for which English makes an exception. As they make this error, they produce forms that they never hear adults utter, such as *mouses*, *foots*, *falled*, and *goed*. Eventually, children once again correctly produce a large proportion of irregular verb forms and irregular plurals.

These well-known errors were explored in an analysis of more than 11,000 irregular past tense utterances in the spontaneous speech of 83 children whose transcribed language samples are part of an archive known as the Child Language Data Exchange System (ChiLDES) (MacWhinney & Snow, 1990). Although the study confirmed previous reports of a U-shaped pattern of acquisition, it also produced some unexpected results. Despite the salience of overregularization in young children's speech, the errors turned out to be relatively rare, occurring in approximately 2.5 percent of irregular past tense forms produced. Overregularization remained at roughly the same low rate from the age of 2 years into the school-age years. In addition, the more often a parent correctly used an irregular form (e.g., *came*), the less often the child overregularized it (e.g., *comed*).

Individual Differences in Early Grammar

When study after study showed striking similarity in the order of acquisition of English morphemes, despite variations in children's language experience, many researchers concluded that children learn grammatical rules in similar ways. This assumption of universality has been tempered, however, by studies showing differences in the routes children take on their way to acquiring grammar (Bates et al., 1995; Bates et al., 1994; Bloom, 1998). In one study of three children, for example, two children's utterances combined verbs with nouns and used nouns to mark possession (e.g., *eat meat, throw ball,* and *mommy sock*), whereas the third child combined verbs with pronouns (e.g., *eat it* and *do this one*) (Bloom, 1970).

Whether children begin by combining verbs or objects of possession with nouns (e.g., *ride on the bus*) or start by combining these parts of speech with pronouns (e.g., *ride on it*) may be related to variation in children's single-word vocabularies or to differences in caregivers' speech to children (Goldfield, 1987; Hampson & Nelson, 1993; Shore, 1995). Regardless of which pattern children use initially, their use of nouns and pronouns becomes more similar by the end of the second year (Bloom, 1998).

Cross-Linguistic Studies of the Acquisition of Grammar

Until fairly recently, child language researchers focused on the acquisition of English grammar (Maratsos, 1998; Slobin, 1985, 1992). In English, active sentences follow a basic pattern: agent-action-patient (or subject-verb-object). This pattern, as in *the girl drank the milk,* seems "natural" and "direct" to most English speakers. Moreover, children learning English both comprehend and produce sentences possessing this pattern by the age of about 24 months. Not all languages use this pattern, however, so children learning languages that do not use fixed word order need to learn other ways to communicate about agents and patients (Maratsos, 1998).

Children learning Turkish, for example, hear agents, patients, and actions in all possible orders (Slobin, 1992). To express the idea *Simon hugged Andrew,* words may appear in any order, but the noun for the patient must have the suffix *-/u/* attached: *Andrew-u hugged Simon* (Maratsos, 1998). Children learning Turkish as their first language are not given explicit instructions about this system, but they hear older children and adults around them speaking and acquire the relevant rule. Although this may seem like a complex system, at least to English speakers, Turkish children use it correctly by or before the age of 2 years (Aksoy & Slobin, 1985). In addition, just as children learning English almost never make word-order errors (e.g., saying *Cookie eat baby* instead of *Baby eat cookie*), children learning Turkish rarely make errors in suffixation (e.g., adding *-/u/* to the agent instead of to the patient).

Other languages communicate agent-patient relations in other ways. Although English speakers may regard these as more difficult systems, young children learning those languages easily acquiring these rules and usually do so with very few errors by 2 years of age. In light of cross-linguistic findings, language researchers are reconsidering and updating "the assumption that what is complicated for adults to think about is necessarily complicated for children to acquire" (Maratsos, 1998, p. 434).

ATYPICAL LANGUAGE DEVELOPMENT

Children of the same age may understand and produce different numbers of words. Given the wide range for first words, the naming explosion, and other milestones of language development, parents of infants and toddlers who are slower than their peers may wonder if their child's development is still on track. In this final section, we consider several tools available for measuring whether a child's early language development is progressing normally. We also briefly explore new evidence about atypical language development, focusing on two examples—early language delay and autism.

Measuring Language Development

Of the more than 40 language-screening instruments available, only a small number are designed specifically to assess children younger than 2 years of age (Sturner et al., 1994). These instruments entail different advantages and disadvantages. Assessments based on parental report are subject to criticism, for example, since some parents may misunderstand instructions or fail to give accurate reports about their children's language development. Parental reports are less time-consuming and less expensive than evaluations performed by clinicians, however, so reliable, valid measures for very young children are needed to achieve the earliest diagnosis and follow-up treatment possible.

The Language Development Survey (LDS) (Rescorla, 1989) is a parent-report instrument for children between 12 and 24 months of age. In the LDS, parents write out three of the child's longest recent sentences or phrases and respond to a 310-word expressive vocabulary checklist. Evaluations show that the LDS is a valid and reliable screening device (Fenson et al., 1994; Rescorla & Alley, 2001).

The Rosettti Infant-Toddler Language Scale (Rossetti, 1990) is used primarily to detect delays in language skills from birth through 3 years of age. The assessment examines preverbal and verbal communication through a parent questionnaire and direct observation. The scale incorporates assessments of infant-parent interaction, pragmatics, gestures, play, language comprehension, and language expression.

Standardized tests include the Sequenced Inventory of Communication Development-Revised (SICD-R) (Hedrick, Prather, & Tobin, 1984), the Reynell Developmental Language Scales-U.S. Edition (Reynell & Gruber, 1990), the Preschool Language Scale-3 (PLS-3) (Zimmerman, Steiner, & Pond, 1991), and the Receptive-Expressive Emergent Language Test-Second Edition (REEL-2) (Bzach & League, 1991). Limitations are that these tests sample only a small set of language behaviors and need to be administered by highly trained examiners using a specific and fairly inflexible procedure (Fenson et al., 1994).

Assessment of children's language in naturalistic settings, such as the home, presents different sorts of challenges. These samples may be more likely than a standardized assessment to yield a representative language profile for a particular child, if the child is motivated to interact and speak. However, transcription and analysis require special skills and a significant investment of time—from 3 to 10 hours just to transcribe a 30-minute language sample (Fenson et al., 1994).

Some general developmental screening instruments include scales for assessing language. These include the Denver Developmental Screening Test (DDST) (Frankenburg, Dodds, & Archer, 1990) and the Minnesota Child Development Inventory (MCDI) (Ireton & Thwing, 1974). The DDST provides very little information about language development, based on a small number of items at each age level. The MCDI, by contrast, is more comprehensive, with 64 expressive language items and 67 receptive language items (Fenson et al., 1994).

One widely used tool for assessing both expressive and receptive abilities—the MacArthur Communicative Development Inventories (CDI)—shares many positive features of previously mentioned tests while also providing a detailed, representative sample of language in approximately 30 minutes (Fenson et al., 1994). The CDI is based on parent reports and checklists. As shown in Table 8.4, there is one form for infants between 8 and 16 months of age and another for toddlers between 16 and 30 months of age.

Researchers in one study used the CDI to describe language growth trends in 1,800 children between the ages of 8 and 30 months (Fenson et al., 1994). They found wide variability across children in the time of onset and course of acquisition of language and communication skills. Individual children, however, showed significant stability in the rate of language development. The

TABLE 8.4 Comparison of the Infant and Toddler Forms of the MacArthur CDI	
Infant Form	**Toddler Form**
396-word vocabulary checklist	680-word vocabulary checklist
Assesses understanding and production of early words, sound effects, and animal sounds.	Assesses production of specific words, sound effects, and animal sounds.
Checks infant's understanding of familiar words, such as their own name, and phrases, such as "no no" and "there's mommy/daddy."	Checks frequency of child's multiword utterances/ sentences, as well as use of grammatical morphemes, such as word endings used to form the plural –s and past tense of regular verbs –ed.
One section focuses on actions and gestures; parents indicate whether their child plays patty cake, points to interesting objects or events, and engages in pretend play.	Parents list three of the longest sentences that they have heard their child say recently.

Source: Based on Fenson et al., 1994.

predictive power of the CDI is low for infants between 8 and 16 months but increases when used with children 16 months of age and older (Fenson et al., 2000). Current research using the CDI is exploring the potential value of combining reports from children's preschool teachers with parent reports, particularly for low-income and bilingual children (Vagh, Pan, & Mancilla-Martinez, 2009).

In Chapter 7, we noted that some researchers have used measures of information processing in infancy to predict performance on tests of intelligence and cognitive functioning in childhood. Researchers studying language development have also examined information processing precursors in this domain. Using a procedure described earlier in this chapter (Fernald et al., 2006), for example, researchers found unique correlations between speed of language processing and CDI measures of children's vocabulary at 25 months of age and cognitive and expressive language abilities at 8 years (Marchman & Fernald, 2008). Other researchers, using a battery of information processing measures of memory at 12 months, found links between those measures and CDI reports at 12 and 36 months; information processing measures at 12 months also predicted expressive and receptive language abilities at 36 months (Rose et al., 2009). These findings support the position that common, domain-general abilities underlie the development of some aspects of language and cognition. Although this is a controversial conclusion, researchers on both sides of the issue agree that understanding the causes of early language delay is a high priority.

Early Language Delay

The majority of 2-year-olds with language delay have normal language abilities by the age of 3 or 4 years. In those cases, children may simply be at the extreme low end of the normal range of development. Nearly all children who have language impairments in later years, however, had some sort of prior language delay (Dale et al., 1998, 2003). One way to identify risk factors for early language delay is to study speech delays in children of normal intelligence without hearing deficits or neurological disabilities. Researchers examining a number of possible factors have found that boys are at higher risk than girls, especially if they have a family history of developmental communication disorders and if their mother has not completed high school (Campbell et al., 2003). Other studies also support the view that language delays may be the result of both genetic predispositions and environmental factors.

Studies of more than 3,000 pairs of 2-year-old twins have documented a strong genetic influence in some cases of early language delay, as well as in the development of vocabulary and grammar (Bishop et al., 2003; Dionne et al., 2003). These investigations indicate that, when one twin in a pair has a CDI vocabulary score in the lowest 5 percent, the other twin is also very likely to have a similar degree of language impairment, with a stronger association for monozygotic than for dizygotic twins. As CDI vocabulary scores increase, however, similarity between twins decreases. Researchers believe that children with a significant degree of impairment may have a genetically distinct language disorder, whereas those with even modestly higher scores—at the 10th rather than the 5th percentile—may be more influenced by environmental factors (Dale et al., 1998; Stromswold, 2006). Studies of families with severe expressive and receptive disorders have led to discoveries about the role of specific genes, such as FOXP2, in language development (Konopka et al. 2009).

Recent studies of clinical syndromes have yielded potentially important information about the representation of language in the brain. One promising cognitive neuroscience tool, near infrared spectroscopy (NIRS), is beginning to be used to study language processing in young infants. Initial studies indicate that infants as young as 4 to 5 months of age process phonetic information conveyed in infant-directed speech by using special linguistic mechanisms instead of general perceptual mechanisms. In the future, after typically developing babies' brains have been studied with this new instrument, it may be possible to use NIRS to identify infants at risk for early speech delay and other language disorders, with the possibility of intervening significantly earlier than is currently feasible (Petitto, 2007). Although much more work remains to be done, researchers have uncovered compelling data that now must be incorporated into any explanation of mind-brain relations.

Language and Communication in Children with Autism

Autism is a syndrome characterized by atypical social interactions and problems with language and communication. Estimates of its prevalence vary, but autism is thought to affect approximately 1 in 150 children, with a higher incidence among boys (Yeargin-Allsopp, Rice, & Karapurkar, 2003). It is a genetically based brain disorder, believed to develop during the first few weeks of fetal growth (Chakrabati et al., 2009; Fombonne, 2003; U.S. Department of Health and Human Services, 2009).

Although autism exists from birth, it may not be diagnosed until 18 to 36 months of age, or even later. One reason for the delay is that appropriate screening tools were not always widely available (Filipek et al., 2000; Lord et al., 2006). This is changing, however, in part due to studies that involved retrospective analyses of early home videos of infants later diagnosed with autism (Dawson et al., 1998; Osterling & Dawson, 1994; Werner et al., 2000). As early as 8 to 10 months of age, infants with autism display fewer social and joint attention behaviors than typically developing infants (Vaughn Van Hecke & Mundy, 2007). In particular, as we noted in Chapter 7, infants with autism rarely point in order to show objects to others, look at others, or respond to their own name (Baron-Cohen, 1995; Loveland & Landry, 1986; Mundy et al., 1986). As a result, even prior to a time that parents report autistic symptoms to their child's pediatrician, they tend to use compensatory strategies to engage their infants and attract their attention (Baranek, 1999). Awareness of signs of atypical prelinguistic development increases the likelihood of earlier diagnosis.

Five different diagnoses currently exist under **autism spectrum disorder (ASD):** Autistic Disorder, Asperger's Syndrome, Pervasive Developmental Disorder Not Otherwise Specified, Rett's Syndrome, and Childhood Disintegrative Disorder (U.S. Department of Health and Human Services, 2009). As shown in Table 8.5, these syndromes vary in terms of the severity of

TABLE 8.5	Autism Spectrum Disorder (ASD) Comprises Five Possible Diagnoses
Diagnosis	**Characteristics**
Autistic Disorder	Children exhibit poor language skills, withdrawn behavior, repetitive patterns of behavior, and the inability to engage in imaginative play.
Asperger's Syndrome	Children display similar general symptoms as children with Autistic Disorder but usually have well-developed language skills and normal or near-normal IQ.
Pervasive Developmental Disorder, Not Otherwise Specified	Children do not fall within the realm of other ASDs but show signs of a severe developmental disorder with autistic symptoms.
Rett's Syndrome	Affects only girls; development appears normal until approximately 6 to 18 months of age, when children lose language and motor abilities.
Childhood Disintegrative Disorder	Children show normal development until 2 years of age, then rapidly lose acquired skills, usually between 36 and 48 months of age.

Source: Based on information in U.S. Department of Health and Human Services, 2000.

language skill deficits, children's measured IQ level, and the appearance and course of symptoms. The heterogeneity of diagnoses posed a problem for early studies because the same criteria were not always used for including children in an autistic sample. To ensure that comparisons between different studies are appropriate and interpretable, researchers now use two valid and reliable diagnostic tools: the Autism Diagnostic Interview-Revised (Lord, Rutter, & LeCouteur, 1994) and the Autsim Diagnostic Observation Schedule-Generic (Lord et al., 2000; Tager-Flusberg, 2004).

Approximately 9 percent of children with autism never develop any functional language, and many have delayed speech that includes echolalia (direct repetition of speech) and reversal of pronouns, such as *I* and *you* (Hus et al., 2007). For higher functioning children with autism, acquisition of vocabulary and grammar tends to proceed as it does in typically developing children; a longitudinal study of grammatical morpheme acquisition, for example, found that the order of acquisition for autistic children was similar to the order reported for typically developing children (Tager-Flusberg, 1993). Children with autism also appear to follow the principle of mutual exclusivity in word learning experiments (Markman, Wasow, & Hansen, 2003). Children with autism tend to show relatively normal ability to articulate language sounds. Their use of stress and intonation may be unusual, however, and their speech may sound harsh, shrill, or hollow (Travis & Sigman, 2000).

For autistic individuals who are verbal and produce phrases, if not entire sentences, pragmatic deficits are common. Children (and adults) with autism often have awkward conversations, in which they may transmit and receive facts accurately while failing to achieve the smooth exchange of information that is found in most normal conversations (Travis & Sigman, 2000). Rigid, stereotyped patterns of expression may be used, as well as invented or idiosyncratic words and phrases (Volden & Lord, 1991). Maintaining a topic and responding contingently to another person during a conversation may also be problematic for children with autism (Hale & Tager-Flusberg, 2005).

The deficit in pragmatic development has been interpreted by some researchers as evidence that individuals with autism suffer from a specific inability to understand mental states in themselves and in others (Leslie & Roth, 1993; Hale & Tager-Flusberg, 2005). Lacking a "theory of mind"—awareness of the relation between mental states and behavior—children with autism fail to notice the emotional signals of others and are unable to share joint attention, engage in pretend play, entertain false beliefs, or use rules of politeness and contingency in conversation (Kasari et al., 1990; Sigman & Ruskin, 1999; Vaughn Van Hecke & Mundy, 2007). Not all autism researchers endorse this interpretation. Critics note that identifying a deficit in theory of mind does not indicate a causal connection with autism (Klin, Volkmar, & Sparrow, 1992).

Compared with the past, the incidence of significant language impairment appears to be lower in children currently being diagnosed with ASD (Anderson et al., 2007; Chakrabarti & Fombonne, 2001; Charman et al., 2003). Some recent experiments involving children with ASD have found that they are not as socially impaired as previously reported; they are able to use attentional social cues to learn new words but fare worse than typically developing children on tasks requiring processing of speaker intent (Luyster & Lord, 2009; Parish-Morris et al., 2007).

Brain imaging and ERP measures are beginning to offer greater insight into the neurocognitive basis of social and linguistic behavior in autism (Dawson et al., 2002; Hadjikhani et al., 2004). Initial intriguing findings indicate that the brains of children with ASD process social and linguistic stimuli differently from comparison samples that are matched in terms of chronological age or IQ. Children with ASD, for example, show a preference for nonspeech signals rather than speech samples. They also differ from comparison children in failing to show ERP changes in response to changes in syllables (Kuhl et al., 2005a). Future studies employing longitudinal designs, beginning when infants are first diagnosed, are needed in order to advance our understanding of the heterogeneity of ASD and links between genetics, cognitive abilities, social behavior, language, and brain development.

WRAPPING IT UP: Summary and Conclusion

Young children's communication and language skills are an important foundation for learning, development, and social interaction. Infants' early experience listening to or, in the case of deaf infants, watching their native language sensitizes them to the phonetic contrasts and rhythmic patterns in that language.

Children's first words appear around the age of 12 months and are usually followed by a vocabulary spurt at about 18 months of age. The rate of children's semantic development is influenced, in part, by the amount and variety of language they are exposed to, especially if it is responsive and attuned to their interests and abilities. Infants use multiple cues and sources of information to expand their vocabulary. Social and pragmatic factors play an important role, but infants also benefit from guiding constraints as they learn new words.

Children's earliest multiword utterances reflect their acquisition of grammatical rules, including word order. Cross-linguistically, all children are able to acquire grammatical rules for their native language and usually do so with very few errors by 2 years of age.

Language development can be assessed and compared to normative growth trends. Genetic studies of language delay and other communication problems indicate that there is often a heritable component. Investigation of autism has yielded information about the representation of language in the brain and the relation between language development and cognitive ability.

Language develops rapidly during infancy, and babies make the most of the opportunities available. Face-to-face interactions with familiar, responsive partners are an ideal learning environment. As Simon's experience in the Tiny Tugboat room showed, relationships provide the words, motive, and opportunity to learn and use language. In addition to being the principal vehicle for language development, however, they are important in their own right, as we discuss in Chapter 9.

THINK ABOUT IT: Questions for Reading and Discussion

1. What can parents do to help their newborn infant acquire language? How should their approach change as their baby becomes a toddler and then a young child?

2. Although it is possible to learn the vocabulary and grammar of many languages other than one's first language, it is often difficult to sound like a native speaker of those languages. How do studies of speech perception help explain this difficulty?

3. If you designed a language assessment for the first three years of life, which abilities would you include and how would you assess those abilities?

4. What can be learned by studying the acquisition of languages other than English? If you know more than one language, compare them in each of the major systems discussed in this chapter—phonology, semantics, grammar, and pragmatics.

5. How does the acquisition of language affect children and their families, especially parent-child interactions? How does atypical language development affect those relationships and interactions?

Key Words

Autism (257)   A syndrome characterized by disordered social interactions and problems with language and communication.

Autism spectrum disorder (ASD) (257)   A cluster of five related syndromes that vary in terms of language skill deficits, children's IQ, and the appearance and course of symptoms.

Babbling (236)   Patterned but meaningless sequences of reduplicated sounds, such as strings of syllables.

Constrained statistical learning (235)   The ability to extract recurring patterns from repeated experience with stimuli.

Emergentist Coalition Model (ECM) (251)   A theory about early word learning that describes children shifting at approximately 12 months of age from a reliance on attentional cues such as perceptual saliency and temporal continuity to a greater dependency on social and linguistic cues such as eye gaze, social context, and grammar.

Grammar (229)   Systems of rules for combining words or signs.

Holophrase (243)   Infants' first one-word utterances that name objects but also communicate other meanings.

Infant-directed (ID) speech (233)   Modifications that adults make when speaking (or signing) to infants, producing language that is shorter, more repetitive, higher-pitched, more variable in pitch, and less semantically and grammatically complex than language addressed to adults.

Lexical contrast (250)   The ability to learn a new word's meaning by comparing it to words that are already known.

Mean length of utterance (MLU) (251)   A measure of grammatical development that is based on the number of morphemes in speech.

Morphemes (251)   Minimal meaningful units in speech, such as words, parts of words, or word endings.

Mutual exclusivity assumption (249)   A constraint on learning that guides children to assume that objects will have only one name and to look for a nameless object when they hear a new word.

Overextension (243)   A common error in which children use a word to refer to other objects that may be perceptually or functionally similar to the word's correct referent.

Overregularization (253)   An error in which children apply grammatical morphemes to words for which a language makes an exception to the rule.

Perceptual magnet effect (235)   A phenomenon in which acoustic space is altered as a result of increasing sensitivity to native language phonemes and declining sensitivity to nonnative language phonemes.

Phonemes (234)   Linguistically meaningful phonetic categories that signal differences in words through combinations of vowels and consonants.

Phonetics (234)   A set of vowels and consonants that a particular language uses.

Phonology (229)   Sound patterns of language.

Pragmatics (229)   Using language for particular purposes in specific social contexts.

Referential cues (247)   Verbal and nonverbal behaviors, such as gaze, facial expression, and head orientation, that reflect an individual's attentional focus, intentions, or expectations.

Semantics (229)   Meanings of words or signs.

Syllables (236)   Combinations of consonants and vowels, such as *baba* and *mama*.

Taxonomic assumption (249)   A constraint on learning that guides children to assume that new words should be extended to objects within the same category rather than thematic associates.

Telegraphic speech (251)   Early two-word and multiword utterances that sound like telegrams because they lack grammatical markers and extra words, such as articles, plural endings, prepositions, and auxiliary verbs.

Underextension (243)   An error in which children apply a word only to a specific instance or fail to use it to refer to other referents for which the word would be correct.

Whole object assumption (248)   A constraint on learning that guides children to assume that new words refer to whole objects rather than actions, spatial location, or parts or features of objects.

Relationships and Social Development

If you were invited to a baby shower, what sort of gift would you bring? Would you select an item that reflects your ideas about the things every infant needs—clothing, toys, blankets, or perhaps a device for carrying or soothing the newborn? Would you choose a gift from a registry compiled by the expectant parents, a glimpse into their beliefs about the things their child needs most? In either case, the gift you choose would almost certainly be influenced by culture, climate, historical period, and even the baby's sex, if known in advance.

The things that all babies need most, however, are never found on gift registry lists for the simple reason that they are not "things" but experiences that come from relationships between infants and those who care for and interact with them. According to *Ten Things Every Child Needs* (Robert R. McCormick Foundation, 1997), the top three needs—interaction, touch, and a stable relationship—come directly from infants' social world. The remaining needs—a safe/healthy environment, self-esteem, quality childcare/preschool, communication, play, music, and reading—are typically experienced in a social context.

Relationships are important in infancy and across the lifespan. They influence development and functioning in social, cognitive, and emotional domains. From an evolutionary perspective, relationships are adaptive, affecting physical health and well-being through their influence on basic biological processes (Reis & Collins, 2004). Relationships affect children's development, and children's development, in turn, transforms their relationships (Hartup, 1989, 1996).

In this chapter we consider "vertical" relationships—those involving children and adults, in which there is an asymmetry of social power, skills, and experience. Vertical relationships serve important functions of protecting children when they are young and fostering the development of basic physical, social, and cognitive skills. The most important vertical relationship is the early infant-caregiver relationship, which has an impact on infants' and toddlers' development as well as contributing to development in early childhood and beyond. We also explore "horizontal" relationships—those characterized by partners (siblings, peers, and friends) who are relatively similar in their roles, abilities, and knowledge. In horizontal relationships, children refine and apply basic skills, learn about cooperation and competition, and eventually achieve psychological intimacy (Hartup, 1989, 1996).

We begin with a look at the foundation for infant-caregiver relationships—caregivers' beliefs about infants as social beings. Behavioral neuroscience studies of humans and other mammals have shown that universally adaptive parenting behaviors exist and are influenced by biology (de Jong et al., 2009; Kozorovitskiy et al., 2006; Wynne-Edwards, 2001; Wynne-Edwards & Reburn, 2000). Our focus, however, is on the ways in which social and cultural factors shape universal tendencies to produce different parenting strategies.

INFANT-CAREGIVER RELATIONSHIPS

Many people regard the infant-parent relationship as the primary social bond, augmented by a small number of peripheral relationships, but this view is not universal. Around the world, entire villages may be involved in childrearing, with each household's connection to the newest member of the community reinforced by a visit to the newborn's home within hours of the birth. In some societies, infants are raised by a large group of extended kin or are adopted by other families in the village and develop close, open relationships with both their adoptive and their biological kin (DeLoache & Gottlieb, 2000; Nsamenang, 1992).

In the United States, approximately 70 percent of all children, including those under the age of 3 years, live in a household with two married parents. The very youngest children, however, are more likely than other age groups to live with two parents who are not married (10 percent of infants younger than 1 year and 7 percent of children 1 to 2 years versus 4 percent of children 3 to 5 years and 2 percent of children between the ages of 6 and 11). As Figure 9.1 shows, among children younger than 5 living with unmarried parents, the least frequent arrangement is with a single father. Figure 9.2 shows that children's living arrangements differ across categories of race

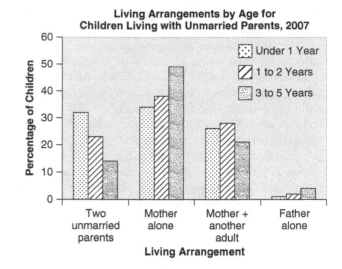

FIGURE 9.1 Living Arrangements for Children Living with Unmarried Parents, 2007. *Source*: Adapted from Kreider & Elliott, 2009.

and ethnicity. Whereas relatively few Asian, white non-Hispanic, and Hispanic children from birth to 5 years of age live with a single parent (usually the mother), this arrangement is much more common for African American children (Kreider & Elliott, 2009). Regardless of the makeup of a child's household, infants and toddlers develop most optimally when they grow up in a "village" of some sort—when their parents have support from other adults, ask for help when it is needed, and live in a community in which there are caring, involved neighbors who monitor and supervise all children, not just those to whom they are related.

Parents often begin to relate to their child before birth when they choose a name for their baby. Names under consideration may link the child to previous generations, as when a son has

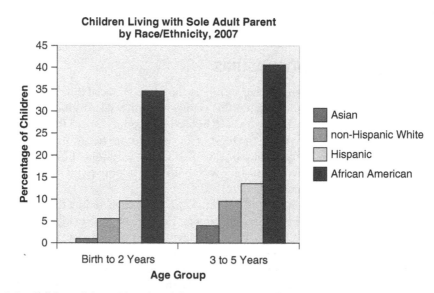

FIGURE 9.2 Children Living with Sole Adult Parent by Race/Ethnicity, 2007. *Source*: Adapted from Kreider & Elliott, 2009.

the same name as his father or grandfather. Potential names may embody qualities that parents hope their child will have, such as strength, courage, beauty, or grace. In some cultures, children are not named until they reach a significant milestone, such as the age of 100 days, and grandparents or even unrelated elders in the community—not the child's parents—may have the responsibility of bestowing names. Regardless of the variation in naming practices, parents everywhere anticipate what their child will be like and how their lives will be interconnected. They develop beliefs about their unborn child and envision a future role in the family and community (DeLoache & Gottlieb, 2000).

Patterns of Care and Interaction: Beliefs about Infants

In some cultures, often those in which subsistence farming is common, the prevailing pattern of care is **proximal parenting.** Parents maintain close, nearly constant physical contact by carrying babies on their body and by practicing co-sleeping (sharing either the same bed or the same room). Being nearby most of the time enables parents to respond quickly when the baby cries or is hungry. Beginning in infancy, cultures that use proximal parenting typically highlight the importance of social connections and interdependence among members of the family (Abels et al., 2005). Very young children, for example, may be taught the names of all members of the community—a sign that social relationships outside of the immediate family are important (DeLoache & Gottlieb, 2000). In other cultures, including much of middle-class North America and Europe, **distal parenting** is more typical. In comparison with the proximal approach, parents using a distal style have less physical contact with babies but more face-to-face verbal and vocal interaction; they are also more likely to encourage infants to look at toys or other objects while they talk about and manipulate them together. From infancy, the distal parenting approach reinforces the value of independence and self-reliance, encouraging distressed infants to try to comfort themselves, for example, by not immediately responding to their cries or other signals (Keller, 2003; Keller et al., 2009; Super & Harkness, 2009).

Proximal and distal parenting styles are guided by **ethnotheories,** implicit, coherent ideas about parenting and child development that reflect cultural communities' desired balance of characteristics such as independence/interdependence, competitiveness/compliance, and self-expression/deference to others (Kärtner et al., 2007; Keller et al., 2007; Rothbaum et al., 2000). Ethnotheories reflect changes occurring within cultures and thus require ongoing study of beliefs and practices across different generations and social groups (Eickhorst et al., 2008; Fogel, 2000; Lamm et al., 2008; Super & Harkness, 2009).

Parents' ethnotheories affect nearly all aspects of caregiving, including the amount of body contact, play with objects, face-to-face contact, and arousing stimulation they provide for babies during the first postnatal months (Harkness et al., in press; Harkness et al., 2007; Keller, 2003). In a study comparing beliefs and practices in the United States and the Netherlands, Dutch parents emphasized rest and regularity, whereas U.S. parents focused on providing stimulating interaction. At 6 months of age, Dutch babies went to bed earlier than U.S. babies (7:00 p.m. versus 8:30 p.m.) and averaged two hours more sleep per day. Mothers in the United States spent more time talking to their babies and touching them. These different caregiving contexts may be the reason U.S. infants spent more time in an active alert state, whereas Dutch infants spent more time in a state of quiet arousal (Super et al., 1996).

Studies of young children's sleep in a range of countries, including Australia, England, Israel, Italy, Japan, and the United States, have found links between parents' beliefs and sleeping practices (Hayes et al., 2007; Tikotzky & Sadeh, 2009). In one such investigation, families in Italy and Japan, as well as African American families in the United States, reported co-sleeping with their children.

Italian and Japanese parents in particular tended to view sleep problems sympathetically as evidence of the child's legitimate need to be with the mother. White non-Hispanic parents, by contrast, more frequently reported trying to ignore their child's cries and protests during the night so that self-comforting could be established early. These patterns suggest that African American and some non–North American families tend to emphasize interpersonal relatedness through close physical contact, whereas white non-Hispanic families more often reinforce notions of early independence and individuality (Wolf et al., 1996). There is a range of perspectives on co-sleeping within cultures, however, and even mothers and fathers in the same family do not always agree about the optimal frequency and duration of co-sleeping with babies and young children (Germo et al., 2007; Goldberg & Keller, 2007; McKenna & Volpe, 2007).

Researchers observing Central African foragers and farmers found distinctive patterns of childcare among neighboring groups, patterns reflecting different ethnotheories (Hewlett et al., 1998). The foragers—nomadic Aka pygmies—lived in physically close, interdependent community groups in which babies were usually carried in a sling on their mother's left side. During observations at the ages of 3 to 4 months and again at 9 to 10 months, Aka babies were more likely to be held, fed, and spent more time asleep or drowsy; they were also more often in close physical contact with their caregivers. Ngandu infants, on the other hand, were more frequently left alone and spent more time fussing, crying, smiling, vocalizing, and playing. Infants of the Ngandu people—farmers who remain in the same dwellings and work the same fields several years in a row—were more often put down; when they were carried, they were usually strapped to their mother's back. Ngandu parents socialized their infants to become more independent by interacting with them at a greater distance and allowing a greater period of time to pass before comforting them. Aka infants, by contrast, were usually surrounded by others and attended to more quickly; they also more often observed adults sharing caregiving responsibilities as well as food and other physical resources. These findings indicate that parenting strategies reflect socialization goals, beliefs, and values and may vary, even among

Patterns of caregiving reflect socialization goals. This infant is growing up in a culture that values interdependence, which his mother promotes by keeping him physically close to her during much of each day.

traditional cultures living in relatively close proximity to one another (Hewlett et al., 1998; Keller et al., 2004a; Super & Harkness, 2009).

Infants themselves influence the kinds of interactions they experience. Even in the earliest days and weeks, social interaction is **bidirectional**—involving reciprocal behaviors and responses. Newborn infants who sleep for several hours in a row, for example, elicit a different type of care than babies who spend more time awake or who are fussier. Whereas some infants may be soothed by rocking, others may find singing and vocalizing more effective. In addition, although there is often stability in individual infants' behavior patterns and cycles, there is also change and even day-to-day fluctuation (St. James-Roberts & Plewis, 1996). Mothers and fathers who notice their baby's tendencies, preferences, and developing capabilities may use their evolving understanding to provide more appropriate and effective care.

Caregivers and infants develop their own style of interaction, often leading to **dyadic synchrony**—caregiver-infant interactions characterized by mutual attention and affective matching or regulation (Harrist & Waugh, 2002). One example of dyadic synchrony is the back-and-forth sharing of emotions or vocalizations. An infant coos or gurgles and gazes at the mother, who returns her child's visual gaze and responds with words or sounds that seem to mirror the infant's behavior. Another example would be an interaction in which an infant looks away from the mother, who responds by pulling back or reducing the intensity of her speech or physical contact with the infant until the infant looks back at or vocalizes to her.

Most parents learn to read and respond to their baby's signals as they gain experience with him or her over the first days and weeks after birth. This learning process can be facilitated through parent education, including approaches using the Neonatal Behavioral Assessment Scale (NBAS), a standardized procedure that has been adapted for parents in many different cultural contexts (Nugent, Petrauskas, & Brazelton, 2009). A study carried out in Brazil, for example, found that mothers of newborns who saw a video based on the NBAS (Brazelton & Nugent, 1995), emphasizing infants' competencies and the importance of sensitive, face-to-face interaction, showed more dyadic synchrony involving vocal exchanges, looking to the partner, and physical contact during home observations one month later than did mothers of newborns who saw a video describing basic caregiving practices for infants. Mothers who saw the NBAS video were also more responsive to their infant's crying and involuntary responses (Wendland-Carro, Piccinini, & Millar, 1999). Many studies suggest that caregivers who are responsive and engage in synchronous interactions set the stage for a good infant-caregiver relationship.

Interactions between children and their caregivers are not always synchronous; in fact, the typical rate of such closely attuned interactions is probably below 50 percent of all interaction time (Harrist & Waugh, 2002). This does not mean that dyadic synchrony is unimportant. Indeed, dyadic synchrony is believed to serve several main functions in infancy. First, it provides opportunities for infants to experience and process multisensory input. The infant waving his arms, for example, has the chance to notice the corresponding rhythm and patterning of his mother's voice. Second, dyadic synchrony helps infants develop the capacity for self-regulation; by responding to the infant's level of arousal and activity, caregivers assist infants in learning to move from one state to another in the earliest months of life.

A third function of dyadic synchrony is helping the infant experience **effectance**—the feeling of influencing others or having an impact on the immediate environment, often in the pursuit of specific implicit or explicit goals (Crockenberg & Leerkes, 2005; Gianino & Tronick, 1988; Goldstein et al., 2009). Fourth, dyadic synchrony provides a foundation for the evolving relationship between infant and caregiver. Infants who experience a sense of effectance and come to expect that their caregiver will respond to them in positive, predictable ways are likely to develop a sense of trust in that caregiver.

For young infants, dyadic synchrony typically consists of a maintained, shared focus of attention and coordination of the timing or rhythm of body movements, vocalizing, and other behaviors. Caregivers, rather than infants, tend to achieve synchrony by noticing and responding to signals from their baby. Caregiver responses are not mere imitation, however; the intensity and rhythm of an infant's arm movements, for example, may be matched by the parent's tone of voice and rate of speech instead of being reflected in identical arm movements (Harrist & Waugh, 2002).

From a very early age, infants notice the contingency between their own actions and their caregivers' verbal and nonverbal responses (Kärtner et al., 2008; Leerkes, Blankson, & O'Brien, 2009). This was demonstrated in an experiment in which 2- and 3-month-olds first interacted with their mothers through live, closed-circuit video and then saw a recording of their mother's behavior from the first session. Infants responded with interest during the session when their mother's behavior was actually in response to their own behavior. They turned away from the video during the recorded session, suggesting that they noticed the lack of contingency (Murray & Trevarthen, 1985). Over time, babies learn that their behaviors influence social partners; 5-month-olds, for example, intensify their efforts to elicit responses from caregivers as well as from unfamiliar adults who do not respond to their vocalizing (Goldstein et al., 2009).

During the toddler years, caregivers continue to bear primary responsibility for facilitating synchrony, but children play an increasingly active role. Dyadic synchrony facilitates new aspects of child-parent interactions, supporting children's growing communicative competence, autonomy, and self-control (Harrist & Waugh, 2002). Parents and children who are attuned to one another have more conversations about objects and events that are the focus of shared attention. Dyadic synchrony at this age also makes it easier for parents to keep track of children as they become increasingly interested in exploring and testing their own abilities and limits. With dyadic synchrony present in a relationship, parents who pay attention to their toddler's actions are likely to have children who notice if their parents approve of their independent efforts. As we discuss in more depth in Chapter 10, joint attention and coordination of behavior also underlie the development of conscience and compliance with parents' requests and expectations (Kochanska, 2002).

Infants and their parents achieve dyadic synchrony when they share attention and communicate similar emotions at the same time.

The degree to which parents and other caregivers are attentive to infants' signals, accurate in their perceptions, and responsive to their child's needs is referred to as **sensitivity** (Ainsworth, Bell, & Stayton, 1972). Sensitive caregivers are able to detect and respond quickly and appropriately to signs of distress, thereby protecting infants from physical and emotional hardship while promoting their survival and sense of effectance (Leerkes et al., 2009; Lorber & Egeland, 2009). Parental sensitivity varies across settings and at different points in development (Lohaus et al., 2004, 2005). Parents can be sensitive when trying to comfort a baby who is upset, but they can also be sensitive in other circumstances, such as when trying to engage a toddler in play, reading, or other dyadic activities, noticing whether the child is interested in the activity, distracted by nearby sights and sounds, or otherwise unable or unwilling to participate.

Sensitive caregivers tend to be those whose own social, emotional, and physical stress are low or managed through supportive interactions and relationships with other adults (De Wolff & van IJzendoorn, 1997; Thompson, 1998; Valenzuela, 1997). Sensitivity may be enhanced through parent education, as was demonstrated in a study of low-income mothers of irritable newborns. Mothers were randomly assigned to either an intervention program focusing on maternal sensitivity and responsiveness or a control program. Nine months later, mothers in the intervention group were more responsive and stimulating than mothers in the control group; mothers in the intervention group were also more likely to have more harmonious and effective relationships with their infants (van den Boom, 1994).

Sensitivity is present in many different cultures, but it is influenced by culturally specific beliefs, goals, and practices. In countries as diverse as Cameroon, Chile, China, Colombia, Germany, India, Kenya, Mexico, and the United States, responsiveness varies in terms of whether it is predominantly physical, verbal, or visual (Kärtner et al., 2008; Keller et al., 2008; Posada et al., 2004). A study of the Gusii people of Kenya, for example, showed that they were physically responsive, touching and holding their 9- and 10-month-old infants when they cried, whereas mothers in Boston tended to use visual and verbal—but not physical—responses when their same-age infants showed distress (Richman, Miller, & LeVine, 1992). The Boston mothers, with higher than average levels of education, had been socialized to employ verbal methods that would engage infants in emotionally arousing conversational interactions. Gusii mothers, by contrast, used methods consistent with their culture's tendency to define competent parenting in terms of the ability to soothe and comfort infants and with the Gusii notion that it is unnecessary to speak to preverbal infants. The researchers saw "no indication in this evidence that one group of mothers is more responsive than the other, only that they are responsive in different ways to their infants' signals" (Richman et al., 1992, p. 620). We turn now to explore some of these differences further, considering mother-infant and father-infant interactions separately.

Cross-Cultural Differences in Mothers' Involvement

Many comparisons between white non-Hispanic mothers and Latina mothers have found that Latina mothers tend to emphasize politeness, control, and obedience in their children, whereas white non-Hispanic mothers more typically focus on their children's individuality and independence (Harwood et al., 1996, 2002). When mothers were videotaped interacting with 12- to 15-month-olds during feeding, social play, free play, and in three teaching tasks, Puerto Rican mothers tended to direct and structure infants' activities and to physically position and restrain them more than white non-Hispanic mothers did. White non-Hispanic mothers, by contrast, more often used verbal praise and made suggestions to influence children's behavior. Differences were also found in mothers' comments about socialization goals and strategies; whereas Puerto Rican mothers indicated a preference for direct teaching and control in order to instill a sense of proper demeanor, white non-Hispanic mothers said that they would try to maximize the child's autonomy and sense of personal accomplishment (Harwood et al., 1999). Over time, maternal expectations and behavior may encourage Latino children to strive for cooperation and interdependence, considering how their actions relate to other people's needs and wishes. European American children, by contrast, become increasingly likely to think about their own thoughts and desires, displaying behavior that reflects self-reliance and independence (Bornstein et al., 2008; Harwood et al., 1999; Ispa et al., 2004).

Cultural patterns of interaction and caregiving beliefs are derived from parents' culture of origin, but they also reflect influences of the mainstream culture if it is different from the culture of origin. Mothers' tendency to respond verbally during interactions with infants, for example, reflects their previous experience in school. In a study of the influence of acculturation on parenting beliefs and strategies, more and less acculturated Mexican American families, as well as white non-Hispanic and African American infant-mother dyads, were observed when infants were 15 months old and again at 25 months of age (Ispa et al., 2004). Acculturation status was determined by generational status (mothers born in the United States to U.S.-born parents were the most acculturated, followed by mothers born in the United States to Mexican-born parents and then mothers born in Mexico) and language usage (greater acculturation was ascribed to mothers who spoke English rather than Spanish at home). White non-Hispanic mothers displayed high levels of warmth and relatively low levels of control over their infants' actions, whereas less acculturated Mexican American mothers showed lower levels of warmth and higher levels of control. When more acculturated Mexican American mothers played and read with their toddlers, they showed an intermediate combination of warmth and control. These findings are consistent with other studies of immigrant parents that have demonstrated the cumulative effects of exposure to mainstream dominant culture on immigrants' parenting behaviors (Hill, Bush, & Roosa, 2003; Howes, Guerra, & Zucker, 2007; Parke & Buriel, 2006).

Father-Infant Caregiving and Interaction

Father involvement in children's lives is often measured in terms of accessibility (presence and availability), engagement (direct contact and interaction with children), and responsibility (participation in tasks such as taking children to the doctor, arranging play dates, and monitoring their activities). On all of these dimensions, father involvement in the United States increased during the last half of the twentieth century, and there is more variety across families than in the past, but many fathers still interact with young infants less than mothers do (Pleck, 1997; Pleck & Masciadrelli, 2004; Yeung et al., 2001). Mothers tend to spend more time than fathers engaged in basic routines and daily caregiving activities, including feeding, bathing, and soothing (Hossain & Roopnarine, 1994; Lamb, 1997; Martinez et al., 2006). As a result, some researchers have concluded that, with the exception of single-father households, "research has yet to identify any childcare task for which fathers have primary responsibility" (Pleck, 1997, p.73).

Whereas single fathers are compelled to be accessible, engaged, and responsible by necessity, observational studies suggest that fathers in two-parent families often defer to mothers the primary responsibility for tasks such as bathing, diapering, and dressing, even though they are able to perform those tasks as well as mothers when asked to do so, or when they are the sole parent on hand. When both parents are employed outside of the home, fathers tend to be more engaged in childcare tasks, but the proportion of interactions that are playful typically remains higher among working fathers than among working mothers (Lamb, 1997; Lamb & Lewis, 2004).

Fathers are more likely to interact in more physically stimulating ways than mothers, one likely reason that some infants and toddlers prefer their fathers as play partners (Lamb, 1997; Lamb & Lewis, 2004).

Mothers and fathers in the United States often behave differently when interacting with their children (Huston & Holmes, 2004; Ryan, Martin, & Brooks-Gunn, 2006; Stolz, Barber, & Olsen, 2005). Fathers tend to play in challenging and physical ways, such as gentle wrestling; they are also less likely to read to young children on a daily or even monthly basis (Martinez et al., 2006). Mothers, by contrast, are more likely to infuse their play with "teaching moments" in which they provide vocabulary words for toys or activities or offer suggestions about their children's play (Lamb & Lewis, 2004; Parke & Buriel, 2006).

Is it possible that these patterns reflect unlearned biological differences? Some researchers think so because many nonhuman primate fathers engage in more boisterous, physical play with their offspring than do nonhuman primate mothers. The applicability of these findings to humans is less clear, however, when we consider evidence of cross-cultural differences in human fathers' play styles. Studies of fathers in Sweden, Israel, Malaysia, India, and parts of Africa, for example, have found that they are not more likely to play in a physical way than are mothers in those cultures (Parke & Buriel, 2006; Roopnarine, 2004).

Many fathers become more involved during the toddler period, after their children begin to walk and talk. Fathers' greater involvement also coincides with an increase in young children's independence and testing of rules and limits (Woodworth, Belsky, & Crnic, 1996). Unlike young babies, for example, independently mobile infants create new opportunities for parental interaction by walking over to the family's television and pushing the buttons on its front while also looking directly at a nearby parent to see how they will respond.

Fathers' own characteristics also influence their involvement with children younger than age 3. Men with more social and economic resources are often able to spend more time interacting with their child than fathers without these resources. They are also more likely to play with young children and use affirming, age-appropriate words when they speak to them (Tamis-LeMonda et al., 2004; Woodworth et al., 1996).

Most children benefit when fathers are involved in their lives (Engle & Breaux, 1998; Parke & Buriel, 2006). One study of low-income African American families found that, whether they lived with their fathers or not, 3-year-old children whose fathers had positive attitudes about parenting, were employed and contributing financially to the family, and interacted in nurturing ways during play had better cognitive and language skills and fewer behavior problems than children of the same age whose fathers did not share these characteristics (Black, Dubowitz, & Starr, 1999). This finding is consistent with other evidence of the positive effects of the presence of the father and sensitive, responsive caregiving on young children's social and emotional development (Shannon, Tamis-LeMonda, & Cabrera, 2006; Tamis-LeMonda et al., 2004; Trautmann-Villalba et al., 2006; Vogel et al., 2006).

With these benefits in mind, family educators have developed programs to increase fathers' involvement in infant care during the transition to parenthood, particularly when the daily work of feeding, diapering, bathing, and responding to a baby is no longer hypothetical (Fivaz-Depeursinge & Corboz-Warnery, 1999). New parents' relationship with each other also influences the coordination and sharing of daily infant care tasks (Schoppe-Sullivan et al., 2006). Fathers participating in a program that combined information about infant care and development with opportunities to discuss the couple's relationship, issues of fairness, and the value of fathers' involvement in household work were more likely to change diapers, feed their baby, put the baby to sleep, and get up with the baby during the night than fathers in programs that focused exclusively on infant development and health and safety concerns. Fathers who participated in the dual-focus program did not engage in complete co-parenting, however; their involvement in daily caregiving tasks increased from a few times a month to a few times a week (Hawkins et al., 2008).

Fathers who wish to be more involved while their children are still very young sometimes find it difficult to do so. The reason may be institutional or structural, as when a father who would like to take his baby to a health clinic for well-child visits finds that clinic hours conflict with his work schedule and his employer will not grant him time off for routine check-ups. Other potential barriers to father involvement include fathers' lack of confidence in their parenting abilities and parents' different opinions about maternal and paternal responsibilities and skills (Garfield & Isacco, 2006; Russell & Hwang, 2004).

Men and women with egalitarian relationships as a couple often expect to be relatively equally involved in performing childcare tasks after the birth of a child. Commonly, however, the reality is different from those prebirth assumptions, with the mother carrying more of the burden than the father. This discrepancy may lead to diminished marital satisfaction as well as less well coordinated and positive caregiving, with one parent, for example, undermining the other's efforts to comfort a distressed infant (Khazan, McHale, & Decourcey, 2008).

Notions about co-parenting and the division of childcare labor typically originate before a child is born and influence the transition to parenthood (McHale et al., 2004; Talbot, Baker, & McHale, 2009). Researchers studying maternal "gatekeeping" behavior—efforts to encourage or discourage fathers' interaction with their infant—have found that prebirth beliefs and expectations, including mothers' idealization of relationships in their own family of origin, predict more negative, inhibitory behavior toward the father at $3\frac{1}{2}$ months postpartum and lower father involvement during observations of play involving the infant and both parents (Cannon, Schoppe-Sullivan, Mangelsdorf, Brown, & Sokolowski, 2008). When mothers have more realistic views of their own childhood and display positive gatekeeping, by contrast, engaging in low levels of criticism and high levels of encouragement, fathers tend to be more involved with their infant during laboratory observations and, very likely, in other settings as well (Schoppe-Sullivan et al., 2008).

Overall, although fathers often engage in more physical play with sons than with daughters and are slightly more likely than mothers to encourage sex-typed activities (e.g., urging boys to play with trucks rather than dolls), fathers and mothers tend to be highly similar in the behaviors they use to nurture, discipline, and teach very young children (Lamb & Lewis, 2004; Lytton & Romney, 1991; Martinez et al., 2006). Moreover, when caring for young infants, fathers tend to use the same pattern of interaction—distal or proximal—as mothers in the same cultural community (Eickhorst et al., 2008). In light of these findings, researchers have increased their focus on culture as an influence on fathers' caregiving and interaction (Cabrera et al., 2000; Sun & Roopnarine, 1996; Tamis-LeMonda et al., 2004).

Cross-Cultural Differences in Fathers' Involvement

In some cultural communities around the world, father-absence is the norm, and fathers typically do not live in the same house as their children. Mothers and children live in a separate residence, sometimes in the maternal household of origin, especially if the father has multiple wives and families. Fathers in these communities confer social status on their children but are not responsible for feeding or nurturing them; there may even be taboos against fathers having contact with infants. Instead, the father's primary role is one of disciplinarian and authority figure in the clan (Nsamenang, 1992; Townsend, 1997).

The majority of children in the United States live with two married parents, but, as noted earlier, group differences exist. Nearly 60 percent of African American children have a nonresident father, while comparable figures for Hispanic and white non-Hispanic children are considerably lower (30 percent and 21 percent, respectively) (Kreider & Elliott, 2009). Approximately 40 percent of children whose fathers live outside of the home have no contact with them, and about half of such children have never set foot in their father's home; the 60 percent who have contact with nonresident fathers see them for an average of just 69 days per year (Halle, 2002).

Despite these trends, it is difficult to generalize about father-child relationships in the African American population. In families with lower levels of education and economic resources, for example, it is not unusual for household membership to change or for children to experience multigenerational family life, with assistance and support given by grandparents, other relatives, and unrelated father figures. Father involvement ranges from infrequent, intermittent visits to "daily contacts with appreciable time investment" (Roopnarine, 2004, p. 65). The existing research clearly indicates that across socioeconomic classes, age categories, and family structures, high percentages of African American fathers show interest in, care for, and support their children, beginning in infancy.

Across different racial and ethnic groups in the United States, there are a variety of reasons some nonresident fathers in low-income families have little contact with their children, including estrangement from the child's mother. Federally funded fatherhood initiatives in the 1990s led to the creation of programs such as the Young Unwed Fathers Project, Responsible Fatherhood Programs, and Partners for Fragile Families. These programs differ in many ways, but all attempt to address a host of complex issues, obstacles to father involvement such as low levels of education, high rates of unemployment, health and mental health issues, substance abuse, housing instability, lack of transportation, the existence of other children with different mothers, and, in some cases, criminal records and incarceration. Being a good father is important to many nonresident fathers, but overcoming these challenges may be difficult, and programs often struggle simply to recruit and retain participants. For those who do enroll and remain involved in such initiatives, peer support and parent education have proved beneficial, especially for men whose own fathers may have been absent during their childhood (Martinson & Nightingale, 2008; McBride & Lutz, 2004; McLanahan & Carlson, 2004; National Fatherhood Initiative, 2009).

Traditionally, Latino fathers have provided discipline and economic resources, while mothers played the primary role in caring for and nurturing infants and young children. In some parts of the world, including in the United States, the traditional Latino father role is changing due to urbanization and acculturation. Latino fathers vary widely as a function of education, socioeconomic status, and country of family origin (Cabrera & Garcia Coll, 2004; Halgunseth, 2004; Harwood et al., 2002; Ispa et al., 2004).

Studies of immigrant families in the United States suggest that, with acculturation and new roles in the paid workforce for mothers, fathers often become more involved with young children than is typical in their culture of origin. In an observational study in families' homes, fathers who immigrated from India, for example, spent more time teaching their 18- to 44-month-olds skills and helping them socialize with family and friends if they had retained fewer traditional beliefs about family relationships, had less frequent contact with extended family members and friends still living in India, and reported less yearning to be in India. Fathers whose attitudes and behaviors revealed a stronger emotional and psychological connection to India, on the other hand, simply took care of their children's basic needs, such as feeding and cleaning them and responding if they became distressed. Regardless of their degree of acculturation, fathers did not often relate to young children as playmates, a role that fathers in India and many other parts of the world do not value highly (Jain & Belsky, 1997).

Urbanization and the widespread prevalence of dual-worker couples are changing father-hood in China, where families traditionally had many children and fathers served as stern disci-plinarians and breadwinners, while mothers provided care and nurturance in the home. Fathers rarely held young babies or interacted with them before the age of 6 months; both men and women generally believed that men could not care competently for infants (Ho, 1987; Jankowiak, 1992). With higher levels of education for men and women, as well as the one-child policy, new expectations for fathers of infants in China appear to be taking hold, reflecting the higher value that is placed on fathers' contributions to their only child's development (Engle & Breaux, 1998; Shwalb et al., 2004).

Fathers in Japan traditionally have not been closely involved in caring for infants and young children. Even today, despite higher levels of urbanization and education and fewer offspring, they may be relatively remote figures in their children's lives. In recent years, the Japanese government has implemented policies and slogans ("A man who does not participate in childrearing is not a father") to promote greater father involvement, and more Japanese fathers are present at their child's birth than in the past. Nevertheless, many Japanese fathers today are not actively involved. This is due, in part, to the long distances that fathers in urban Japan often commute to work. Complementary parental roles are further reinforced when women leave the paid workforce to become mothers and devote themselves to nurturing and educating children (Allison, 1996; Shwalb et al., 2004; Shwalb, Shwalb, & Shoji, 1996).

Government policies and initiatives in many countries use a combination of incentives to support mothers and families by promoting coparenting and father involvement. New fathers in Norway, for example, may take a 10-week paid, job-protected leave following the birth of a child (Ray, 2008). We discuss parental leave policies in more detail in Chapter 11.

Among the Aka pygmies of Central Africa, whom we discussed earlier, the traditional role for fathers provides a striking contrast with fathers' roles elsewhere. Without the benefit of formal, government-sponsored policies and incentives, the Aka are "the most nurturant fathers yet observed," (Engle & Breaux, 1998, p. 5). Aka fathers, for example, tend to hold their infants and nurture them at higher rates (20 percent versus 4 percent) than in other hunter-gatherer cultures that have been observed (Hewlett, 1987, 2004; Hewlett et al., 1998). Aka fathers' style of interaction is also less physically stimulating than fathers' play in other cultures. As a result, from birth, Aka children experience care from two nurturing, attentive parents who play generally reinforcing rather than complementary roles (Engle & Breaux, 1998).

Many questions about father-infant involvement are still unanswered, in part because family life is evolving in many parts of the world as a result of changes in education, economic systems, and patterns of maternal employment. In countries such as the United States, where nearly one-fourth (22 percent) of U.S.-born children live with at least one foreign-born parent, immigration trends are an increasingly important factor to explore (Federal Interagency Forum on Child and Family Statistics, 2009).

DISTURBANCES IN INFANT-CAREGIVER RELATIONSHIPS

There is no single right way for parents to care for infants. Across a broad range of patterns, informed by different ethnotheories, parents act to nurture children and promote healthy devel-opment. Some infant-caregiver relationships and patterns of interaction are unequivocally harmful, however. We turn now to consider three examples: postpartum depression, maltreatment, and early institutionalization.

Postpartum Depression

Being the parent of a newborn can be an exhausting and overwhelming experience. Both parents suffer from the effects of sleep deprivation and new daily routines, and first-time mothers as well as fathers may feel ambivalent about the demands of their new roles and changes in their previous relationship as a couple. Women in particular may worry if they do not feel an immediate "maternal instinct" or positive emotional connection to their child. As many as 50 to 80 percent of new mothers experience postpartum sadness within the first 10 days that is so well known it is referred to as the "baby blues." These feelings usually diminish without treatment as new parents recover physically, become more confident in their caregiving ability, and have time to get to know their baby (Onunaku, 2005).

For 8 to 15 percent of all new mothers in developed countries, negative feelings do not lessen with time, and women experience **postpartum depression**—a sense of despair and sadness so pervasive that it affects their ability to care for and interact effectively with their baby (Onunaku, 2005; Seifer & Dickstein, 2000). Rates of maternal depression may be even higher (estimates range from 15 to 57 percent) in poor, developing countries in which families tend to be large, with many children born close together. Women in these countries are also more likely to suffer from depression when they experience chronic health problems, domestic violence, lack of participation in family decisions, or are blamed for giving birth to daughters in a culture that strongly prefers sons (Wachs, Black, & Engle, 2009).

Although most research has focused on women, men may also experience postpartum depression but deny their feelings or fail to identify them as depression. The strongest predictors of paternal postpartum depression are a history of depression and having a partner with postpartum depression. During the first postpartum year, the incidence of paternal depression appears to range from 1 to 25 percent overall but is estimated to be 24 to 50 percent among men whose partners experience postpartum depression (Goodman, 2004; Schumacher, Zubaran, & White, 2008). More systematic study and public health education are needed, but the negative effects of paternal postpartum depression on children's development are similar to the effects of maternal depression during infancy and childhood (Ramchandani, O'Connor, et al., 2008; Ramchandani & Psychogiou, 2009; Ramchandani et al., 2005; Ramchandani, Stein, et al., 2008).

One widely used screening tool, the Edinburgh Postnatal Depression Scale, asks parents to answer 10 questions about their feelings in the past seven days (Cox, Holden, & Sagovsky, 1987; Wisner, Parry, & Piontek, 2002). When diagnosing depression in the context of childbirth, clinicians use the Diagnostic and Statistical Manual of Mental Disorders (DSM-IV) criteria to assess changes in mood, sleep, appetite, energy, concentration, decisiveness, and the ability to feel pleasure in daily life; warning signs also include feelings of worthlessness, despair, and thoughts about harming oneself or the baby.

Studies of postpartum depression in developed countries show that any woman may be susceptible, but mothers of sick newborns and mothers without economic or emotional support are especially vulnerable (Petterson & Albers, 2001; Smith & Howard, 2008). Many depressed mothers with supportive, nondepressed husbands who are involved in caregiving are able to interact positively and sensitively with their children (Cummings & Davies, 1999; Goodman & Gotlib, 1999). Nevertheless, even in low-risk, married, middle-class samples, depressed mothers interact differently with their infants than do nondepressed mothers. In addition to interacting less and being less sensitive and responsive, they are less likely to smile at, touch, and talk to their babies or engage them in joint attention (Campbell et al., 2004; Lovejoy et al., 2000; Paulson, Dauber, & Leiferman, 2006). Some depressed mothers show a different pattern and are physically intrusive with their infants (poking or prodding them, sometimes roughly), rather than withdrawn (Field, 1998b; Field et al., 2003; Tronick & Weinberg, 1997).

The effects of postpartum depression on infants vary according to its duration, with the most negative effects seen for babies whose mothers are chronically, persistently depressed. Mothers in one study, for example, whose depression lasted at least six months were less positive and interactive during feeding, face-to-face contact, and toy play. Women whose depression ended earlier were more positive and engaging, even at times when they met criteria for depression (Campbell, Cohn, & Meyers, 1995).

Infants who experience maternal depression show negative, "depressed" behavior themselves, even when interacting with nondepressed adults (Field et al., 1988). This finding, from a study of 3- to 6-month-olds, suggests that babies generalize interaction styles, especially patterns of visual attention and gaze, at a very early age. Unexpectedly, nondepressed adults in this study were negatively affected by their interactions with "depressed" infants and showed less optimal interactive behavior with them than with infants of nondepressed mothers, despite being unaware of the mothers' depression.

Overcoming "depressed" infants' behavioral tendencies may be challenging, given evidence that their brains may process emotional information differently than the brains of nondepressed infants. Studies using EEG measures have shown that as early as 11 months of age, infants of depressed mothers show unusual frontal brain electrical activity when they are interacting with their mothers and even when they are interacting with other adults in emotionally positive ways. In contrast to infants of nondepressed mothers, who show more activity in the left versus the right frontal region of the brain in response to negative emotions, infants of depressed mothers show reduced left frontal activity. This atypical pattern suggests that interacting with a depressed mother may modify infants' processing and experience of positive as well as negative emotions (Dawson & Ashman, 2000; Dawson et al., 1997, 1999).

Other evidence suggests that this brain asymmetry is present considerably earlier, perhaps even during the neonatal period (Field, Diego, & Hernandez-Reif, 2006; Field et al., 1995; Jones et al., 1997). Other explanations for EEG asymmetry need to be considered, therefore, including the possibility that at least some infants of depressed mothers are born predisposed to respond to emotions in unusual ways. Additional studies are needed to disentangle the relative contributions of prenatal factors and postnatal environmental influences.

Without intervention, depression-related disturbances in early infant-mother interactions are associated with poorer cognitive outcomes at 18 months and less secure parent-child relationships in infancy and early childhood (Carter et al., 2001; Martins & Garffan, 2000; Toth et al., 2009). Children whose mothers experienced depression when they were younger than 3 years of age are also at increased risk at ages 5 to 11 years for attention-deficit/hyperactivity disorder and anger management problems that may result in aggressive and antisocial behavior (Hay et al., 2003; Wright et al., 2000).

Several promising interventions offer hope for depressed mothers and their infants. One approach involves coaching depressed women and showing them how to touch infants during face-to-face interactions, a technique that can be tailored specifically for withdrawn mothers as well as those who are more intrusive. Withdrawn mothers, for example, are encouraged to touch their infants more often, whereas intrusive mothers are coached to slow down and imitate their infant's behaviors (Malphurs et al., 1996; Peláez-Nogueras et al., 1996). Counseling, psychotherapy, and antidepressant or anti-anxiety medication can be used to relieve some forms of depression. Alternative, nonpharmacological interventions that directly target mothers' mood states through massage or music therapy may also be effective (Field, 1998a, 1998b; Field et al. 1996). Alleviating mothers' symptoms, however, does not automatically enhance mother-infant interaction or eliminate the need to provide infants of depressed mothers with sensitive and emotionally responsive face-to-face interaction (Hay et al., 2003).

Therefore, given that infants of depressed mothers who are cared for by a nondepressed person are more likely to be able to engage in positive interactions, it is helpful if the father, grandparents, or other nondepressed caregivers can actively participate in the baby's daily care (Hossain et al., 1994; Peláez-Nogueras et al., 1995; Smith & Howard, 2008). In addition, infant massage therapy—even as little as two days a week—can be used to help babies spend more time in active alert and active awake states, with less crying and lower stress hormone (cortisol) levels than infants who are simply rocked for the same amount of time. Infants who receive massage therapy also tend to gain more weight and show greater improvement on measures of emotional arousal, sociability, and soothability (Field et al., 1996, 2006).

Maltreatment: Abuse and Neglect

A second type of disturbed infant-caregiver relationship involves child **maltreatment,** which we discussed in Chapter 5. Even when maltreatment does not result in the death of a child, it may cause serious harm. For infants and children who survive maltreatment, negative effects are found in all developmental domains. Prolonged maltreatment is linked to higher levels of stress hormones than briefer exposure to abuse and neglect (De Bellis et al., 1999; Shonkoff & Phillips, 2000). In infancy, the quality of the infant-caregiver attachment relationship, which we discuss shortly, tends to be poor and subsequently jeopardizes other relationships in which children participate (Barnett, Ganiban, & Cicchetti, 1999; Cicchetti & Toth, 2006). As toddlers, children who are physically abused are more likely to be more aggressive and to have less awareness of and empathy toward others' emotions. They are also more likely to have learning and behavior problems in school.

Less is known about the effects of neglect (failure to meet a child's basic needs), but negative outcomes have also been reported for that form of maltreatment (Erickson & Egeland, 1996; Shonkoff & Phillips, 2000). Given that neglect is the most prevalent type of maltreatment experienced by infants younger than 1 year, with approximately one-third of reported cases involving babies younger than 4 days old, more research is needed to address the most common causes—parental drug abuse and abandonment (Brodowski et al., 2008).

Maltreatment has the most serious consequences when children and families are faced with multiple stressful life circumstances. The effects of child maltreatment can be buffered, however, by the presence of a nonabusive caregiver or another emotionally supportive adult upon whom the child can rely (Rutter, 2000; Werner, 2000). Nurse home visitation programs have had promising results by targeting parents before their child is born and offering parent education (Eckenrode et al., 2000; Olds et al., 1999). Other interventions focus on connecting at-risk parents with community resources and support groups (Cicchetti & Toth, 2006; Egeland, Jacobvitz, & Sroufe, 1988; Reynolds & Robertson, 2003).

When interventions do not succeed or cannot be implemented rapidly enough to protect children in abusive or neglectful homes, one option is to remove them from that setting. When this action is taken, they may be placed with relatives or in foster care with an unrelated family. These arrangements are generally preferable to group care in institutional settings, which are associated with a number of poor developmental outcomes.

Early Institutionalization and Social Deprivation

Interest in the effects of early institutionalization and social deprivation surged in the early 1990s, when approximately 40,000 Romanian children living in orphanages were adopted by U.S. families and families in Canada, England, and Western European countries (Johnson, 2000; Selman, 2002; Zeanah et al., 2003). Foreign-born adoptees are often referred to as orphans, but most have living biological parents who gave them up due to severe economic hardship (Johnson, 2000; Kreider, 2003). Many families who adopted these institutionalized children continue to see the consequences of their early caregiving experiences.

Caregivers in Romanian orphanages, like those in many traditional Baby Homes in Russia today, provided care that placed children at risk in all developmental domains. Typically, each caregiver was assigned to 10, or even 20 infants; infants were kept in their cribs as much as possible and received limited individual attention. Caregivers also propped bottles rather than holding them for younger babies and impersonally spoon-fed older infants and toddlers. Little or no time was spent in stimulating free play. As a result, children had significant delays in language, cognition, and motor skills; as we noted in Chapter 5, many failed to grow at normal rates before being adopted. The greater the amount of time children lived in the orphanage, the more severely stunted they were. In addition to neglect, many children suffered physical and sexual abuse, which left its own emotional and developmental scars, including impaired neural processing of faces and emotions (Moulson et al., 2009; Nelson, 2007; Smyke et al., 2007; Wismer Fries & Pollak, 2004).

Not all previously institutionalized children experienced negative consequences to the same degree, and in many cases marked improvement occurred after they were adopted. Researchers in Canada compared two groups of adoptees when they were 4 to 5 years of age: those adopted within 4 months of birth (Early Adopted, EA) and those adopted after 8 months or more of being cared for in an orphanage (Romanian Orphanage, RO). Median age at adoption in the RO group was 18 months, and time in the orphanage ranged from 8 to 53 months. These children were also compared with a group of Canadian born (CB) children living with their families of origin. The EA and CB groups were very similar to each other on most measures, whereas the RO group generally had more cognitive and emotional problems (Ames, 1997; Fisher et al., 1997; Morison, Ames, & Chisholm, 1995).

Many adoptees exhibited **indiscriminate friendliness**—"behavior that was affectionate and friendly toward all adults (including strangers) without the fear or caution characteristic of normal children. In these cases, a child's behavior toward other adults could not be discriminated from his or her behavior toward caregivers" (Chisholm, 1998, p. 1094; Chisholm et al., 1995). Indiscriminate friendliness, which children use to attract special attention from caregivers and visitors in an orphanage setting, contributed to parenting stress in a family setting, in part because of safety-related concerns that children would wander away or leave with a stranger without noticing or becoming distressed. Children in the RO group showed more indiscriminately friendly behavior than Canadian-born children and children in the EA group, even though they were between $4\frac{1}{2}$ and 9 years of age and had thus been in their adoptive homes for years. Parents reported that RO children were "overly friendly" and had shown no improvement in this behavior over time; high levels of parenting stress were found among parents who said that their child had not developed an emotionally close, preferential relationship with them.

Other researchers studied the cortisol (stress-hormone) responses of children approximately seven years after they had been adopted (Gunnar, 2000). RO children's early experience of social and physical adversity had lasting effects on their physiological stress-response system, making them react more strongly than other children to challenges or stressors (Gunnar, 2000;

Nelson, 2007). Early-adopted children who received reliable, sensitive, and responsive care in a family setting before the age of 1 year, however, often escaped many of the negative consequences of institutionalized care (Rutter, Kreppner, & O'Connor, 2001; Zeanah, 2000).

Studies of the effects of institutionalization in Russia showed similar effects of early deprivation and adversity, as well as differences between early adopted and later adopted children's subsequent development (Johnson, 2000; Juffer & Rosenboom, 1997; Juffer & van IJzendoorn, 2005). Parents who adopt previously institutionalized children thus need to be as concerned about their children's social and emotional well-being as they are about their physical and cognitive development (Shonkoff & Phillips, 2000).

Given the reality that not all children living in institutional settings are placed with new families at an early age, can anything be done to improve their early experience? Intervention studies suggest that a number of concrete changes promote both early physical growth and emotional health. These modifications include reducing the child-caregiver ratio and assigning caregivers to specific children to provide the greatest stability and continuity possible. Caregivers can also be trained to stimulate infants with toys and through face-to-face communication (Carlson & Earls, 1997). In some interventions in Russian Baby Homes, children have benefited from home-like living quarters with children of different ages, as would be found in an actual family. In these institutions, children also participate in enriched daily activities that may include massage, music classes, swimming, and dance (Groark et al., 2003, 2005; Gunnar, 2000). Children also show some improvement when placed in foster care following early institutionalization (Moulson et al., 2009).

An intervention in Baby Homes in St. Petersburg, Russia, compared developmental outcomes in three kinds of institutions: those in which caregivers had received training but no other changes had been made (Training Only), homes in which caregivers had been trained and structural changes in the living arrangements were put in place (Training and Structure), and Baby Homes in which no changes were made (Control). Initial findings from this controlled study echo those from other interventions; infants in the Training and Structure group grew better and showed fewer developmental delays than infants being reared in traditional Baby Homes (Chugani et al., 2001; Groark et al., 2003, 2005; Nelson, 2007; Zeanah et al., 2003). These findings provide hope that fewer children adopted from orphanages will experience the perturbations caused by early adversity and social deprivation, with the result that they and their new families will have a better chance of forming trusting, secure relationships.

DEVELOPING TRUST, BECOMING ATTACHED

In Erik Erikson's classic psychosocial theory, the initial task in infancy is to establish a sense of basic trust. Infants conclude this stage around the age of 18 months. At that time, if their care has been consistently nurturing and sensitive, they emerge with a sense of hope and a feeling that the world is a safe and supportive place. According to Erikson (1950), although a sense of trust is desirable, infants also need to retain an element of mistrust—a self-protective ability to differentiate between caregivers and all other individuals. These ideas were developed further in John Bowlby's attachment theory, which we discuss next.

Bowlby's Theory of Infant-Caregiver Attachment

John Bowlby's (1969/1982) theory of the infant-caregiver **attachment relationship** describes the special relationship that develops over the first year of life between infants and the people who care for them. Drawing from an eclectic mix of theories of his day, including those articulated by Erikson and by the ethologist Konrad Lorenz, Bowlby embraced the assumption that early experiences in a person's life profoundly affect the subsequent course of development. He asserted that human infants—like the young of many other mammals—possess a built-in repertoire of **attachment behaviors,** such as crying, cooing, smiling, looking at, and reaching for or moving toward caregivers, that attract attention and elicit care.

Bowlby noted that, over the course of the first year, infants' cognitive abilities increase and enable infants to form a representation of their relationship with their caregiver, based on specific memories of their experiences with him or her. Bowlby called these representations **internal working models.** He reasoned that infants with a working model of a caregiver who is consistently sensitive and effective would come to rely on that caregiver for comfort and assistance in novel or distressing situations. By contrast, infants with an insensitive, unpredictable, and ineffective caregiver would not seek out the caregiver when uncertain or distressed. If they did, the response that they received would not necessarily comfort or reassure them (Bowlby, 1969/1982, 1973, 1980, 1988).

In Bowlby's view (shown in Table 9.1), attachment develops gradually, beginning in the first two months with a stage in which there is no clear preference for familiar caregivers and finally reaching a stage where children's improving verbal abilities enable them to talk with caregivers about their relationship. As these stages indicate, attachment relationships emerge gradually over time and begin to be discernible in infants' behavioral preferences sometime between the ages of 6 and 9 months. Bowlby's theory thus makes it clear that infants do not become attached to their parents at birth. As the attachment relationship develops, infants are guided by two opposing forces—a drive to explore the world around them independently and feelings of uncertainty, wariness, even fear, as they move away from the security provided by the caregiver.

TABLE 9.1 Bowlby's Stages of the Development of Attachment

Age/Stage	Characteristics
Birth–2 months/Indiscriminate sociability	Attachment behaviors are displayed to both familiar and unfamiliar individuals. Infants are comforted equally well by primary caregivers and unfamiliar persons.
2–7 months/Discriminating sociability	Infants possess expectations about caregivers' behavior and respond differently to them than to unfamiliar persons. Caregivers' efforts to soothe and comfort infants tend to be more effective than other persons' attempts.
7–24 months/Directed attachment behaviors	Attachment behaviors are directed toward primary caregivers and are intended to maintain proximity to those caregivers. Primary caregivers are more effective than other persons at comforting distressed infants.
24 months+/Goal-corrected partnerships	Children's improving verbal abilities enable them to talk with caregivers about their relationship. Their growing awareness of others' thoughts and feelings also helps them understand caregivers' behavior and desires.

Source: Adapted from Bowlby (1969/1982).

Assessing Attachment Relationships

Bowlby's theoretical predictions were first tested empirically by Mary Ainsworth, who studied infant-caregiver interaction in Uganda as well as in the United States. Ainsworth observed that infants who experienced sensitive mother-infant interactions (such as those characterized by dyadic synchrony) usually had effective, positive attachment relationships (Ainsworth & Bell, 1969; Ainsworth, Bell, & Stayton, 1972; Ainsworth et al., 1978; Blehar, Lieberman, & Ainsworth, 1977). The most sensitive mothers—those who responded quickly and effectively when infants cried—were most likely to have children who showed a pattern of attachment behavior at the age of 12 months that reflected a **secure attachment relationship.** Numerous studies have subsequently supported Ainsworth's observations that maternal sensitivity is linked to security of attachment. These studies also indicate, however, that sensitivity is affected by environmental factors, such as changes in family structure and other life circumstances (De Wolff & van IJzendoorn, 1997; Harrist & Waugh, 2002; Posada et al., 2004; Susman-Stillman et al., 1996).

Attachment relationships from 12 months to 5 years of age can be assessed using a rating system known as the **Attachment Q-Sort (AQS)** (Waters, 1995; Waters & Deane, 1985). In the AQS, observers spend time with the family at home and then rate a set of statements according to how characteristic they are of the caregiver's behavior. Sensitive caregiving receives high ratings for statements such as, "monitors and responds to baby even when engaged in some other activity such as cooking or having a conversation with visitor," but not for statements such as, "leaves the room without any sort of 'signal' or 'explanation' to the baby (e.g., 'I'll be back in just a minute')." Observers also use their observations to rate statements about the child's behavior, indicating whether it is more true that, "if held in mother's arms, child stops crying and quickly recovers after being frightened or upset" or "when child is upset about mother leaving him, he sits right where he is and cries; doesn't go after her."

The majority of studies of attachment, however, use the **Strange Situation,** a laboratory procedure that Ainsworth developed for assessing attachment relationships at ages 12 to 24 months. As shown in Table 9.2, researchers observe how the infant behaves in a series of episodes designed to elicit increasing levels of stress and wariness; if and when the baby becomes distressed, researchers note the degree to which the caregiver is used as an effective source of comfort. Coordination of infant and parent behavior—rather than the presence or absence of any specific behavior, such as crying—during reunion is viewed as particularly significant.

Securely attached infants (also referred to as Type B) use the caregiver as a secure base during the Strange Situation. During the first three episodes, some secure infants may make eye contact with the caregiver and "check in" from time to time while playing on their own; other secure infants may vocalize or seek physical contact with the caregiver intermittently while they play. During the reunion portions (Episodes 5 and 8 in the table), some securely attached infants may seek contact with the caregiver by vocalizing, whereas others may move closer for a hug or other physical comforting. Regardless of the specific behaviors displayed during these episodes, securely attached infants generally show that they are happy to see the caregiver return and do not withhold contact from him or her. According to attachment theory, these positive feelings are based on months of interactions in which the caregiver responded to the infant's attachment behavior with sensitive, predictable, and effective actions.

Infants may be insecurely attached in one of several ways. Infants with **insecure-avoidant attachment** (Type A) tend to avoid the caregiver by failing to greet him or her or by delaying their response to the caregiver's return. Infants with **insecure-resistant attachment** (Type C, sometimes referred to as ambivalent), on the other hand, display contradictory behavior—despite

TABLE 9.2 Ainsworth's Strange Situation Procedure

Episode	Activity and Participants in Original Procedure	Episode	Activity and Participants in Sibling Procedure
1	Introduction to playroom (30 secs)	1	Parent and siblings play together (3 mins)
2	Parent and infant alone (3 mins)	2	Parent plays with only one sibling (3 mins)
3	Stranger enters, plays with infant	3	Parent plays with only the other sibling (3 mins)
4	Parent leaves room, baby and stranger remain	4	Parent leaves room, siblings remain together
5	Parent returns and stranger departs	5	Stranger enters room
6	Parent leaves room, baby remains alone	6	Stranger leaves room with older sibling, younger sibling remains alone
7	Stranger returns	7	Older sibling returns to room
8	Parent returns and stranger departs	8	Parent returns to room

Source: Based on information in Ainsworth et al., 1978; and Teti & Ablard, 1989.

appearing preoccupied with the caregiver, they may resist making contact or even show anger and distress when he or she returns. Infants classified as insecure (either Type A or Type C) may behave as they do because their caregivers have been unpredictable in their mood and reactions. To cope with this uncertainty, infants develop internal working models that make them alert and vigilant to the caregiver's current state, prepared to change their own behavior accordingly (Vondra & Barnett, 1999). Insecure-avoidant attachment may result when infants are overstimulated by intrusive caregivers. Insecure-resistant attachment, on the other hand, may develop when caregivers are rejecting or withdrawn, depressed, and unresponsive to infants' needs (Campbell et al., 2004; Isabella & Belsky, 1991; Teti et al., 1995).

As shown in Table 9.3, attachment classifications vary as a function of characteristics of infants, mothers, and the childrearing environment (Thompson, 2006; Vondra, Hommerding, & Shaw, 1999). In typical middle-class samples in North America, the majority of 12- to 18-month-old infants observed in the Strange Situation are classified as securely attached (Type B). Comparatively smaller proportions of infants in typical samples are classified as insecure-avoidant (Type A) or insecure-resistant (Type C) (Thompson, 1998; Vondra & Barnett, 1999).

Not all infants can be classified into attachment types A, B, or C. To address this problem, a fourth classification, **disorganized/disoriented attachment** (Type D), has been identified (Main & Solomon, 1986, 1990; van IJzendoorn, Schuengel, & Bakermans-Kranenburg, 1999). Type D infants may simultaneously display contradictory behavior, such as a mixture of anger and apparently calm play. They also may show unusual behaviors, such as "freezing" in mid-movement or showing fear when the caregiver returns. In typical middle-class samples, a relatively small proportion of infants are classified as Type D, but the percentages are significantly higher among lower income samples, children of teen mothers, abused and neglected children, and children whose mothers abuse alcohol and drugs or who report higher levels of depression or other psychiatric symptoms (Barnett et al., 1999; Macfie, Cicchetti, & Toth, 2001). Children in clinical samples, such as those with autism, Down syndrome, and neurological problems, tend to have a higher incidence of Type D attachment. This pattern is believed to be a reflection

TABLE 9.3	Attachment Classification in Relation to Characteristics of Infants, Mothers, and the Childrearing Environment	
Attachment Classification	**Sample**	**Incidence**
Secure (Type B)	Middle-class, North American	60–75%
Insecure-Avoidant (Type A)	Middle-class, North American	15–25%
Insecure-Resistant (Type C)	Middle-class, North American	10–15%
Disorganized/Disoriented (Type D)	Middle-class	15%
	Lower income	25%
	Teen mother	25%
	Abused/neglected child	48%
	Maternal alcohol/drug abuse	43%
	Maternal depression	19%
	Children in clinical samples (autism, Down syndrome, neurological problems)	35%

Source: Based on information in van IJzendoorn, Schuengel, & Bakermans-Kranenburg, 1999; and Thompson, 1998.

of these children's unusual social and cognitive abilities, however, and is not caused by mothers' behavior (Carlson, 1998; Lieberman & Zeanah, 1995; van Ijzendoorn et al., 1999).

Mothers of Type D infants may show unusual or disrupted emotional communication during the Strange Situation, appearing confused, frightened, or disoriented (Adam, Gunnar, & Tanaka, 2004; Lyons-Ruth, Bronfman, & Parsons, 1999). They may not greet the infant during the reunion episodes, or they may give contradictory cues, such as calling the infant to them but then moving away or holding them at arm's length. Some mothers of Type D infants fail to respond when the baby becomes distressed, or they behave inappropriately by mocking, teasing, or pulling the infant roughly by the wrist. Signs of role confusion may also be present, as when the parent tries to elicit comforting from the infant. Helping parents resolve feelings of trauma or loss is an important step in changing these behaviors and fostering a healthy parent-child relationship (Erickson, Korfmacher, & Egeland, 1992; Vondra & Barnett, 1999).

Another classification, **reactive attachment disorder (RAD),** has been proposed for maltreated and institutionalized children (Zeanah & Fox, 2004; Zeanah et al., 2004, 2005). These children tend to show unusual patterns of behavior, either emotionally withdrawn-inhibited or indiscriminately social-disinhibited. Current studies of attachment disorders are aimed at validating more fully the RAD classification and clarifying its relation to other attachment phenomena (Boris et al., 2004).

ATTACHMENT TO OTHER CAREGIVERS   Infants may be securely attached to one parent but insecurely attached to the other parent or another caregiver (Shonkoff & Phillips, 2000). Attachment to multiple caregivers tends to be similar when those adults cooperate in providing care, demonstrate and reinforce caregiving behaviors for each other, and discuss the child's behavior and personality, reinforcing a shared view (Sagi et al., 1995). Like mothers, fathers who are highly stressed, depressed, or who respond insensitively are more likely to have infants who are insecurely attached to them. Finally, reflecting the importance of the triadic infant-mother-father relationship, many researchers have found that the quality of the marital relationship and the degree of emotional support the father provides the mother in her role as caregiver are linked to the security of infant-caregiver attachment relationships (Belsky, 1996; Lamb & Lewis, 2004).

INFANTS' INFLUENCE ON ATTACHMENT   Thinking of the family as a system raises questions about the infant's own contributions to the attachment relationship. Is attachment security influenced by how easy or difficult infants are to take care of? Do fussier babies tend to develop insecure forms of attachment? A number of researchers have found that it is more challenging to provide sensitive, responsive care for some infants than for others (Atkinson et al., 1995, 1999; Capps, Sigman, & Mundy, 1994). The effect of most infant characteristics, however, is generally thought to be less important than the way parents respond to those characteristics (Bokhorst et al., 2003; van IJzendoorn et al., 1992, 2000). Put another way, attachment security is a product of both infant and maternal characteristics. Where there is a match between the baby's behaviors and the expectations or understanding of the caregiver, a phenomenon known as **goodness-of-fit,** there is a greater likelihood that sensitive, effective care can be provided (Chess & Thomas, 1996).

Mothers who are more sensitive and effective at soothing irritable 6-month-olds, for example, are more likely to have securely attached 12-month-olds than are mothers who are less sensitive and less effective (Susman-Stillman et al., 1996). Similar findings have been found in studies investigating links between security of attachment and maternal personality. Infants with a tendency to become distressed are more likely to be insecurely attached at 13 months if they have mothers with relatively rigid and constraining personalities. Distress-prone infants whose mothers are more flexible, by contrast, are more likely to be securely attached (Mangelsdorf et al., 1990). Parent education often helps new parents recognize infants' behavioral tendencies and learn to adjust their caregiving to meet their own child's specific needs, leading to more harmonious, effective interactions. One study of breastfeeding, sensitivity, and attachment found that mothers who were committed to breastfeeding and nursed their babies for much of the first year tended to have secure attachment relationships, possibly because they had learned to recognize and respond to the baby's behavioral signs of hunger and fullness (Britton, Britton, & Gronwaldt, 2006).

Low-risk preterm infants are just as likely as full-term babies to be securely attached (van IJzendoorn et al., 1992). For very low birthweight (VLBW) preterm infants, however, the risks may be elevated, as shown in a study of infants born more than four weeks early and weighing, on average, less than 1,000 grams. By the age of 19 months, VLBW infants were more likely to be insecurely attached, possibly due to their caregivers' ongoing psychological distress as their children fell behind full-term peers in achieving developmental milestones. The increase in insecure attachment in the VLBW group may also reflect diminishing social support provided to parents of preterm infants beyond the first birthday. These results, and similar findings from a study of families with triplets, suggest that parents of VLBW infants may require sustained support for the multiple challenges entailed in parenting high-risk children during infancy and beyond (Feldman, Eidelman, & Rotenberg 2004; Mangelsdorf et al., 1996).

CULTURE AND ATTACHMENT   Cross-cultural research examining parents' ideas about attachment behavior shows that both differences and similarities exist. In a study comparing lower-income Puerto Rican mothers with lower- and middle-income European American mothers, for example, the secure pattern in the Strange Situation was overwhelmingly preferred across cultures and socioeconomic groups. Mothers' judgments about insecure patterns, however, varied as a function of culture. Puerto Rican mothers gave negative ratings to the independent behavior of insecure-avoidant infants, whereas European American mothers responded negatively to the clinging, dependent behavior of insecure-resistant infants (Harwood, Miller, & Irizarry, 1995).

Mothers of 2- to 3-year-old children in six diverse cultures (China, Colombia, Germany, Israel, Japan, and the United States) also tended to agree about behaviors that are characteristic of an "ideally secure" child—namely, using the mother as a base for exploration. Cultural differences, however, were found in mothers' views about the importance of their children's maintaining physical contact with them, showing positive emotions when complying with their requests, and being willing to interact with other adults (Posada et al., 1995).

Even with the apparently universal appeal of secure-base behavior, there may also be variability *within* cultures and specific cultural communities (Howes & Guerra, 2009; Keller, 2008; Shweder et al., 2006; Thompson, 2006). A good example of this comes from studies of Israeli kibbutz-reared infants. When kibbutz-dwelling infants who experienced traditional communal sleeping arrangements apart from their parents were compared with infants also living in kibbutzes who slept at home, infants in the traditional group showed higher levels of insecure-resistant attachment (Sagi et al., 1985, 1994, 1995).

Attachment and Subsequent Development

Security of attachment affects children's expectations about relational partners, and children's internal working models guide them to interact with new individuals in ways that reflect and confirm their beliefs about social roles and relationships. Securely attached children thus tend to have positive expectations and to behave in ways that elicit positive behaviors from other people. Insecurely attached children, on the other hand, tend to have negative expectations and are more likely to enact familiar roles and display behaviors, such as dependency, hostility, or indifference, that negatively influence the behavior of new social partners (Sroufe, 1979; Sroufe, Carlson, & Schulman, 1993; Thompson, 1998).

According to attachment theory, securely attached children also have positive models of the self that make them curious and confident about exploring their environment, motivated to persevere when faced with challenges, and resilient enough to adapt to new situations and ask for assistance when they perceive the need for it. Insecurely attached children, by contrast, have incorporated their caregivers' negative views and reactions into their model of the self; at an early age, these children are less likely to explore their immediate environment, more likely to give up when confronted with challenges, and less able to monitor their own capabilities and seek help accordingly (Sroufe et al., 1993; Thompson, 1998; Verschueren, Marcoen, & Schoefs, 1996).

In the short-term, secure attachment relationships may protect children from the physiological effects of stress. When infants become distressed, fearful, or anxious, levels of the stress hormone cortisol tend to increase, just as they do in human adults and in nonhuman primates. In some stressful situations, however, including the Strange Situation, securely attached infants and young children do not experience increases in the amount of cortisol, even though they appear distressed, afraid, and worried, as long as their parent is nearby. By contrast, for insecurely attached children and especially for disorganized/disoriented children, the parent's presence does not have the same buffering effect on the child's stress-hormone system (Hertsgaard et al., 1995; Nachmias et al., 1996; Spangler & Grossmann, 1993).

Infants' attachment relationships also help them cope with the stress of adjusting to a new childcare arrangement. At 15 months of age, securely attached infants in one study had lower physiological stress responses than insecurely attached infants during the transition to nonparental childcare. Children's feelings of security were also enhanced when their mothers were sensitive to their feelings and spent time helping them adapt to the new arrangement (Ahnert et al., 2004). These findings support another facet of attachment theory, the notion that securely attached children may continue to thrive to a greater extent than insecurely attached children because securely attached children are more likely to continue receiving sensitive, warm, responsive care from their primary caregivers as they move into new settings and negotiate new tasks (Lamb, 1987; Thompson, 1998).

Secure and insecure attachment groups do not differ in basic cognitive abilities or intelligence, but there is a strong association between attachment and language, with securely attached children showing more competence than insecurely attached children. Researchers speculate that language development may be more optimally stimulated in secure attachment relationships because parents are better "teachers" and children are better motivated "students" (van IJzendoorn, Dijkstra, & Bus, 1995, p. 115). Put another way, secure children tend to be "more receptive to the parent's instruction, guidance, and teaching" (Corriveau et al., 2009; Shonkoff & Phillips, 2000, p. 238).

To the extent that securely attached children are receptive to other adults' instruction, guidance, and teaching, they would be predicted to adjust more easily to school and to receive more positive evaluations from teachers. These findings have been reported in longitudinal research comparing attachment classifications from infancy with measures (shown in Table 9.4) in early childhood and into late adolescence (Carlson, Sroufe, & Egeland, 2004; Erickson, Sroufe, & Egeland, 1985; Grossmann, Grossmann, & Zimmermann, 1999). In fact,

TABLE 9.4 Measures Used in the Mother-Child Longitudinal Study

Child Age	Measure
Prenatal	Maternal medical history
Birth–10 days	Infant medical history, Neonatal Behavioral Assessment Scale
	Maternal history of abuse and psychological problems, relationship status, risk status
3 months	Home observation of a feeding session
	Maternal rating of child's "personality" and behavioral tendencies (e.g., intensity, mood, adaptability, distractibility, persistence)
6 months	Home observation of play and teaching
12 & 18 months	Strange Situation
24 months	Laboratory problem-solving task with mother
42 months	Laboratory teaching task with mother
$4\frac{1}{2}$ – 5 years	Teacher and peer assessments of behavior grades 1, 2, 3, 6, and high school
10 & 15 years	Observation in four-week summer camp
13 years	Laboratory tasks with mother
$17\frac{1}{2}$ years	Self-assessment of affective disorders and schizophrenia
19 years	Self-assessment of dissociative disorders

Source: Based on information in Carlson, 1998, and Carlson et al., 2004.

as a result of a comprehensive study begun in 1975, researchers are now able to examine long-term effects of attachment in adolescence and are analyzing data from young adulthood (Carlson et al., 2004). The study, known as the Mother-Child Interaction Project, recruited a large sample of lower income mothers while they were receiving prenatal care at public health clinics.

At 12 and 18 months of age, infants and mothers were observed in the Strange Situation. A laboratory task at 24 months assessed mother-child interaction in a series of increasingly difficult problems. At 42 months of age, mothers were asked to teach children how to build specific types of block towers, name things with wheels, match colors and shapes, and follow a pattern on an Etch-a-Sketch® maze toy. Additional observations were carried out and information was gathered from teachers and peers from preschool through high school.

Over the years, children identified in infancy as securely attached generally have received higher ratings than insecurely attached children on a variety of measures of social skills and behaviors, self-confidence, and emotional health (Carlson et al., 2004; Sroufe, Egeland, & Carlson, 1999; Thompson, 1998). Securely attached children also tend to have more positive relationships with peers and friends than insecurely attached children. In adolescence, a history of insecure attachment, especially disorganized/disoriented attachment, is associated with greater susceptibility to the effects of stress, more behavior problems, and a higher risk of dissociative psychopathology (Branstetter, Furman, & Cottrell, 2009; Carlson, 1998; van IJzendoorn et al., 1999). Longitudinal data from this study also suggest that there is continuity of parenting across generations; the quality of caregiving that children experience during the first two years—whether sensitive and responsive or not—is correlated with the quality of parenting they provide for their own offspring (Kovan, Chung, & Sroufe, 2009).

Insecure attachment in infancy is not always a reliable predictor of later behavior problems and relationship difficulties, however (Belsky et al., 1996; van IJzendoorn et al., 1999). Lack of predictive power may be due to changes in the quality of the parent-child relationship over time or result from specific contributions of coexisting influences, such as maternal characteristics and behavior, social support, and infant characteristics (Shonkoff & Phillips, 2000; Thompson, 1998; Vondra et al., 1999). The possibility that attachment relationships may change on their own or improve through intervention provides hope for infants who experience adversity and instability early in life.

SIBLING RELATIONSHIPS

"Horizontal" relationships with siblings and peers vary along three basic dimensions—symmetry, closeness, and voluntariness (DeHart, 1999; Laursen, Hartup, & Koplas, 1996). Some brothers and sisters, such as twins, triplets, and other multiples, enter the family and grow up together, experiencing major milestones of development, including the development of attachment relationships, at the same time. Most siblings, however, do not experience development that is so closely synchronized. Table 9.5 compares sibling and peer relationships along these three dimensions.

Becoming a Sibling

It is not uncommon for firstborn children to experience the birth of a sibling negatively. Some preschool children become increasingly clingy, withdrawn, or aggressive or develop problems sleeping or using the toilet (Baydar, Greek, & Brooks-Gunn, 1997; Baydar, Hyle, & Brooks-Gunn,

TABLE 9.5	Sibling and Peer Relationships Differ in Symmetry, Closeness, and Voluntariness	
	Siblings	**Peers**
Symmetry	Many initial differences exist between siblings in physical, cognitive, and social abilities. These characteristics gradually change during early childhood, resulting in many fewer differences by the end of adolescence.	Relatively few differences exist between peers and friends in physical, cognitive, and social development and abilities. Peers and friends are typically more similar than different as they move from infancy to childhood and adolescence.
Closeness	More emotional intimacy and physical and emotional closeness exists between siblings than peers during early childhood (a pattern that reverses itself by adolescence).	There is less emotional intensity among peers and friends than among siblings, in both positive and negative ways.
Voluntariness	Siblings do not choose each other or create their relationship. Managing and maintaining mutually positive interactions is not generally a prominent concern for siblings. Siblings tend to play together more and have more conflicts than do peers and friends.	Peer relationships and friendships are typically based on mutually positive feelings and choice, with interactions characterized by more cooperation and flexibility than is true of most sibling interactions.

Source: Based on information in DeHart, 1999, and Laursen, Hartup, & Koplas, 1996.

1997; Brody, 1998). Not all firstborns react negatively, however. Children younger than 18 months tend to show little disruption and negativity in comparison with preschool-age firstborns. Whether the firstborn is a boy or girl may also make a difference in firstborns' reactions. Preschool-age boys, in particular, often react more negatively than preschool-age girls to the baby's birth (Dunn, Kendrick, & MacNamee, 1981).

Firstborn children's friendships may help buffer negative effects of the birth of a sibling, as shown in a study of 3- to 5-year-old firstborn children whose families were expecting a second child. Firstborns responded more positively to the birth of their sibling if they and their friends were able to manage conflicts when they arose and if they engaged in fantasy play, including pretense that involved sibling-related themes (Kramer & Gottman, 1992). This finding suggests that parents can ease firstborns' adjustment to siblinghood by supporting relationships with peers and friends.

Firstborns may also experience the arrival of a new baby more positively if parents reinforce the existing parent-child bond before the new sibling is born (Gottlieb & Mendelson, 1990; Teti et al., 1996). This may be difficult for parents who regard the new baby's arrival as unwanted and consequently give less positive emotional attention and support to older siblings (Barber & East, 2009). Mothers and fathers who are able to behave in positive, helpful, and emotionally supportive ways not only tend to form and reinforce a secure attachment relationship with their firstborns; they are also more likely to create a similarly secure relationship with their second-borns (Ward, Vaughn, & Robb, 1988). A securely attached older sibling is less likely than an insecurely attached older sibling to show hostility when the parent shows attention only to the younger child. In addition, as found in studies using a variation of the Strange Situation (shown in Table 9.2), in the parent's absence, securely attached older siblings are more likely to respond to younger siblings' distress by trying to soothe and comfort them (Stewart, 1983; Stewart & Marvin, 1984; Teti & Ablard, 1989).

Like parents, older siblings may provide a secure base and emotional comfort for infants and toddlers in new settings. When 2-year-olds and their mothers were observed with and without 4-year-old siblings in the backyard of an unfamiliar home, even during their first visit, younger siblings traveled greater distances from their mothers when older siblings were present. Very few younger siblings showed distress when the older sibling was present, but some younger siblings cried or indicated that they wanted to leave in the sibling-absent condition. The mere presence of older siblings also led to greater exploration of the space and the toys and other objects in it (Samuels, 1980).

When a second child is born, the existing family system evolves. The new sibling subsystem creates different issues for parents to consider, especially after the second child becomes more independently mobile and the possibility of conflicts over space and possessions increases (Dunn & Kendrick, 1982; Teti, 2002). Parents adapt to this new system by using a variety of means to influence their children's interactions and tailoring those methods to each child's developmental level (Kojima, 1999; Kreppner, 1988). These regulating behaviors appear to affect the quality of sibling interactions. If mothers refer to infant siblings' emotions or actions, for example, older siblings are more likely to direct positive behaviors toward them (Howe & Ross, 1990). Talking about and interpreting family members' feelings and actions also help link the existing parent-child relationship to the newer sibling relationship (Dunn, 1998, 2002).

How Siblings Contribute to Development

In many parts of the world, older siblings contribute directly to their younger siblings' development by serving as their primary caregivers when parents are working or caring for a newborn infant (Zukow-Goldring, 2002). Even where this is not a typical arrangement, siblings affect each

This girl's mother reinforces their relationship at the same time that she encourages her to form a positive relationship with her baby brother.

other through daily interactions. These interactions change over time, as the diagonal "slope" between siblings becomes less steep, and initially large differences in siblings' abilities begin to diminish (Abramovitch et al., 1986; DeHart, 1999; Dunn & Brown, 1996).

Sibling interactions are both intensely positive and intensely negative, and some of the most revealing studies have focused on conflicts between brothers and sisters in their own homes. One study began when the second-born child in each family was 14 months old and ended when that child was 24 months old. Sibling conflicts became more physically aggressive over time, with younger siblings increasingly joining their older siblings in initiating conflicts. By 18 months, younger siblings also showed increasing understanding of how to annoy the older sibling, especially through teasing. Younger siblings became aware of their parents' reactions to conflicts and learned to appeal to them for help when the older child had started the conflict but not when they themselves had been the aggressor (Dunn & Munn, 1985).

Children's early experience in family conflicts contributes to their understanding of others' feelings, thoughts, and actions. Sibling interactions are also linked to children's experience and competence in peer relationships (DeHart, 1999; Herrera & Dunn, 1997). Although siblings typically play complementary roles, in which the older child is more often the initiator and the younger child is more frequently the imitator and submitter, peer relationships can also be complementary when one child has the "home field advantage" (Abramovitch et al., 1986, p. 228). Rather than consistently playing the subordinate role, therefore, younger siblings learn both parts and can "step into a dominant role when the situation permits" (p. 228).

PEER RELATIONSHIPS AND FRIENDSHIP

Many interactions with peers and friends from birth to age 3 take place in what might be considered neutral territory, childcare settings and preschool classrooms. What do we know about infants' and very young children's capacity to interact with one another in the absence of either child's parent? Until relatively recently, many people—including experts in child development—believed that peer relationships and friendships among children younger than 2 years of age either did not exist or could not be studied due to verbal limitations. When researchers began to use reports from adults who spend time caring for infants and toddlers, as well as direct observations of young children's interactions, the study of children's earliest friendships and peer relationships blossomed (Howes, 1996, 2009; Rubin, Bukowski, & Parker, 1998, 2006).

Peer Interactions

Studies of interactions involving 12- to 18-month-old children show that groups of unacquainted peers behave differently with one another than do groups of peers who are well acquainted. Toddlers who know each other well have even been observed participating in unexpectedly advanced activities, such as coordinated games and cooperative fantasy play (Howes, 1985, 1988, 1996; Howes & Matheson, 1992; Howes & Unger, 1989). In one observation of groups of toddlers attending the same childcare centers, the youngest children (16 to 17 months of age) engaged in simple social play involving taking turns interacting with toys. A surprisingly advanced form of play—cooperative social pretend play—was observed in all of the children over 30 months of age and in half of the children just under the age of 24 months. Although other researchers had found that this form of play usually does not appear until at least 3 years of age, children's familiarity with one another appeared to support its earlier emergence in this sample (Howes, 1985, 2009).

In numerous ways, mothers and fathers influence children's peer relationships and social competence. High-quality play with fathers helps young children, especially boys, learn about the regulation of negative emotions that may arise during physical, competitive play. Fathers as well as mothers influence children's peer interactions by serving as advisors, social guides, and rule providers, giving advice, supervising play, and making or enforcing standards during play with peers. Like mothers, fathers are often managers of children's social opportunities, arranging play dates and choosing specific social activities (Parke & Buriel, 2006; Parke et al., 2004).

Friendship

Very young children have the capacity to form true friendships that involve companionship, mutual affection, intimacy, and closeness (Rubin et al., 2006). By approximately 12 months of age, toddlers who spend time together prefer some of their peers to others and seek them out. Children show their compatibility and mutual preference by spending significant amounts of time together and by frequently achieving a high level of interaction whenever social contact is made. Parents and other caregivers are often aware of their children's social preferences, especially when verbal skills advance enough to enable children to talk about their friends. There is also evidence that very young children's peer preferences tend to be stable. Many preschool children's friendships begin when they are toddlers, and they show the special connection that they feel through consistent efforts to play together and stay close to one another (Hay, Caplan, & Nash, 2008; Howes, 1996, 2009; Rubin et al., 2006).

Toddlers who are friends, like older children who are friends, tend to be similar in their activity levels, interaction styles, and social skills. Children show a preference for same-sex peers as early as 30 to 36 months of age and are thus more likely to become friends with same-sex peers (Serbin et al., 1994). Children who are friends often play familiar games and engage in favorite routines. As they develop the ability for social imitation, cooperation, and role reversal during play, young children who are friends build on their shared social skills and are able to play together at a more complex level than children who are not friends (Howes, 1996, 2009).

These girls have been friends for most of their young lives. Their interactions involve mutual affection, sharing, and a strong preference to play together.

Young children's mutual affection and intimacy with friends is reflected in a number of ways. Children who are friends tend to share emotions frequently, smiling or laughing together while looking at each other. The emotional significance of early friendships is also seen in the finding that children who are friends and move up to the next age grouping in a childcare setting together tend to adjust better than if they are moved alone (Howes, 1988). In addition, toddlers tend to respond to friends' emotional distress by attempting to comfort or help them, but they are less likely to do so if a nonfriend is distressed (Howes & Farver, 1987).

WRAPPING IT UP: Summary and Conclusion

Relationships are important in infancy and across the life span. Socialization goals and practices vary widely across cultural communities, as does the number and type of relationships beyond the infant-parent relationship. There are both differences and similarities in the roles and patterns of interaction that mothers and fathers enact with infants and very young children. Cross-cultural studies have highlighted differences between proximal and distal caregiving patterns.

Infants thrive when caregivers are sensitive and responsive to their needs. They are harmed, however, by early adversity, such as when the caregiving environment is affected by postpartum depression, maltreatment, and institutionalization. Early interventions that change these environments or remove the child from them may minimize some of the social and emotional harm.

Children are born ready to form attachment relationships with those who care for them—mothers, fathers, grandparents, older siblings, or unrelated caregivers. Infants' caregiving history influences the relationships that they develop within the family and in the greater world outside of the home. Longitudinal studies have shown that attachment security may have a long-lasting impact on children's relationships.

One of the greatest social challenges that very young children face is learning to control their emotional responses across different settings and with different partners. Parents, siblings, and peers all play a role in the socialization of emotion, a topic that we explore in our next chapter. We also consider when and how children develop a sense of themselves as coherent individuals who continue to exist despite situational variations in their behavior and feelings.

THINK ABOUT IT: Questions for Reading and Discussion

1. Are "vertical" and "horizontal" relationships equally important across the first three years of life? If not, how does their influence change?

2. A number of universal aspects of infant-caregiver relationships have been identified, but there are also many cross-cultural differences. What do these patterns tell you about social development from birth to age 3?

3. Compare the influence of mothers and fathers on babies during the first three years of life. To the extent that differences in these roles exist, how do they influence development in infancy and toddlerhood?

4. How do disturbances in the infant-caregiver relationship, such as postpartum depression or maltreatment, affect infants' development?

5. If you knew a couple considering adopting an infant from an orphanage, what advice would you give them? What sort of information would you suggest that they gather about the baby or the institution? How would that information be useful to them?

6. How does the attachment relationship affect physical, cognitive, and social development? Are there other aspects of development that might also be affected by the attachment relationship? How might you study those effects?

Key Words

Attachment behaviors (280)   Infants' built-in behaviors, such as crying, cooing, smiling, looking at, and reaching for caregivers, that attract attention and elicit care.

Attachment Q-Sort (AQS) (281)   A rating system that can be used outside of a laboratory setting to assess individual differences in infant-caregiver attachment relationships.

Attachment relationship (279)   The special relationship that develops over the first year of life between infants and the adults who care for them.

Bidirectional (267)   Interactions that involve reciprocal behaviors and responses between social partners.

Disorganized/disoriented attachment (282)   An infant-caregiver relationship that may develop when caregivers show contradictory, disrupted, or otherwise unusual emotional communication with their infants; also referred to as Type D.

Distal parenting (265)   A pattern of caregiving in which parents have physical contact with babies but emphasize face-to-face verbal and vocal interaction, and encourage infants to look at toys or other objects while they talk about and manipulate them together, reinforcing the value of independence and self-reliance.

Dyadic synchrony (267)   Interactions between infants and caregivers that are characterized by mutual attention and affective matching or regulation.

Effectance (267)   The feeling of influencing others or having an impact on the immediate environment, often in the pursuit of specific implicit or explicit goals.

Ethnotheories (265)   Implicit, coherent ideas about parenting and child development that reflect cultural communities' desired balance of characteristics such as independence/interdependence,

competitiveness/compliance, and self-expression/deference to others.

Goodness-of-fit (284)   A match between an infant's behaviors and the caregiver's expectations and understanding of those behaviors.

Indiscriminate friendliness (278)   Behavior that is affectionate and friendly toward all adults, including strangers, without the fear or caution characteristic of normal children; often observed in children adopted from orphanages or other institutional settings.

Insecure-avoidant attachment (281)   An infant-caregiver relationship that may develop when caregivers are overstimulating and intrusive when interacting with their infants; also referred to as Type A.

Insecure-resistant attachment (281)   An infant-caregiver relationship that may develop when caregivers are rejecting or withdrawn, depressed, and unresponsive to infants' needs and attachment behaviors; also referred to as Type C.

Internal working model (280)   Infants' mental representations of their relationship with their primary caregiver(s).

Maltreatment (277)   Neglect, medical neglect, physical abuse, sexual abuse, or psychological abuse.

Postpartum depression (275)   A sense of despair and sadness so pervasive that it affects a mother's ability to care for and interact effectively with her baby; approximately 15 percent of new mothers are affected in this way.

Proximal parenting (265)   A pattern of caregiving in which parents maintain close, nearly constant physical contact with babies, respond quickly when they cry or are hungry, and highlight the importance of social connections and interdependence among members of the family.

Reactive attachment disorder (RAD) (283)
A recently proposed type of attachment that may develop in institutionalized infants who are severely maltreated.

Secure attachment relationship (281)   An infant-caregiver relationship that develops when caregivers respond quickly and sensitively to their infant's signs of distress and other attachment behaviors; also referred to as Type B.

Sensitivity (269)   The degree to which parents and other caregivers are attentive to infants' signals, accurate in their perceptions, and responsive to their child's needs.

Strange Situation (281)   A laboratory procedure that Ainsworth developed to assess individual differences in infant-caregiver attachment relationships.

10

Temperament, Emotions, and the Self

In the United States in 2008, the three most popular names given to baby boys were Jacob, Michael, and Ethan, while the three most popular names for girls were Emma, Isabella, and Emily (Social Security Administration, 2009). Many thousands of parents chose these names for their babies, yet none of the 22,272 Jacobs or 18,587 Emmas will grow up to be the *same* Jacob or Emma. Each will be shaped by a unique

From birth, infants show differences in their emotional reactions to the people and situations they encounter. Some babies are drawn to novelty, whereas others are inhibited by it.

interaction of biologically based tendencies and environmental influences. In this chapter, we examine infants' early behavioral and emotional responses to the people and events they encounter. We also consider how infants' behaviors, and the responses those behaviors evoke, contribute to the development of a unique self.

If it had been possible in 2009 to gather together in an enormous playroom all of the Jacobs and all of the Emmas who were born in just one month in 2008, we would have noticed differences in their responses to the large crowd. Some babies would have been moving around, wide eyed with interest, joyfully taking in the sights and sounds, while others would have been looking timid or fearful, perhaps even crying. There would also have been differences in infants' ability to adjust to the unusual circumstances, with some children quickly appearing comfortable and happy, and others taking more time to feel at ease. These diverse responses reflect variations in temperament, a theoretical construct about which there has been vigorous and sustained research as well intense debate and disagreement.

TEMPERAMENT

The first source of disagreement in the study of temperament concerns how to define and measure it. At a basic level, there is agreement that **temperament** consists of qualities that parents as well as researchers are able to discern, including irritability, soothability, motor activity, sociability, attentiveness, adaptability, response to novelty, arousal, and regulation of states (Kagan, 1994; Wachs & Bates, 2001). Temperament has also been defined as "constitutionally based individual differences in emotional, motor, and attentional reactivity and self-regulation" (Rothbart & Bates, 1998, p. 109). Beyond these descriptions, there is no clear consensus about how many dimensions of temperament exist or how to measure them. We first consider the predominant ways in which researchers have defined and measured temperament in infancy. Then, because children's temperament influences interactions with caregivers, we explore links between temperament and attachment and, finally, discuss evidence of continuity between temperament in infancy and personality in childhood and beyond.

Defining and Measuring Temperament

There are remarkable individual differences in infants' patterns of sleeping, waking, feeding, fussing, and crying (St. James-Roberts & Plewis, 1996). As many parents confirm, these patterns often can be predicted from differences in fetal activity (DiPietro et al., 1996).

USING PARENTAL REPORTS   Most studies of temperament use parental report questionnaires, a practice with both strengths and limitations (Kagan, 1998; Rothbart & Bates, 2006; Wachs & Bates, 2001). The main advantage is that parents have a vast amount of experience with their infants across a wide range of settings. Only parents and other caregivers would know, for example, that a researcher observing an infant for the first time in a new setting is seeing behaviors that are not typical of that child in other settings. Parental reports and questionnaires are also less expensive to use than other methods of assessing temperament, such as observations in the laboratory or at home.

Disadvantages of using parental reports include low to moderate levels of agreement between mothers and fathers as well as low to moderate levels of agreement between parents and researchers (Atella et al., 2003; Bornstein, Gaughran, & Segui, 1991). Lack of agreement between parents suggests that reports about temperament may contain a subjective element or bias. This possibility is also reflected in correlations found in some studies between parental characteristics, such as parental preconceptions and maternal depression, and ratings of infant difficultness (Clarke-Stewart et al., 2000). Temperament ratings are affected to some degree by parental perceptions, psychological functioning, experience, and preferences, and are thus cultural and personal constructions that may or may not resemble more objective descriptions of infants' behavior (Kagan, 1998; Kiang, Moreno, & Robinson, 2004; Shwalb et al., 1996).

To address these concerns, some researchers have added parental diaries in which patterns of sleeping, crying, and fussing are recorded over several days (Atella et al., 2003; St. James-Roberts & Plewis, 1996). One study of parents' reports of "difficultness" in 6-week-old infants used a multimethod approach combining maternal and paternal ratings, diary records of babies' state behaviors, and laboratory observations. Although mothers and fathers interpreted some infant behaviors differently, for mothers, reports of difficult temperament appeared to correspond to other measures of infants' crying and fussing behaviors (Atella et al., 2003).

In a study of 8- to 10-month-olds, researchers compared parental reports about infants' temperament with their responses during a laboratory procedure designed to elicit the emotions of joy, fear, anger, and distress (discomfort to aversive stimulation). They also observed infants' emotional tone during naturalistic interactions with their mothers. Elicited emotions in the laboratory were consistent with fathers' temperament ratings and with infants' emotional tone during interactions with mothers, providing support for the validity of parent reports (Kochanska et al., 1998).

As shown in Table 10.1, all definitions of temperament include basic dimensions of infants' activity level and emotional responsiveness, but some go on to make additional behavioral distinctions (Goldsmith et al., 1987; Rothbart & Bates, 2006). These different approaches can make it difficult to make comparisons across studies of temperament, especially given the tendency for similar phenomena to be labeled differently by different researchers (Frick, 2004; Rothbart, 2004; Wachs & Bates, 2001). Although several models have been proposed, four views of temperament have dominated research in this area.

THOMAS AND CHESS'S MODEL   The first approach comes from the New York Longitudinal Study (NYLS) by Thomas, Chess, and their colleagues (Chess & Thomas, 1996; Thomas, Chess, & Birch, 1968; Thomas et al., 1963). As shown in Table 10.1, they used nine dimensions to assess infants. Approximately 35 percent of the infants in the NYLS sample could not be categorized and were thus described as "average." Based on their observations of the remaining infants, the researchers identified three major temperament classifications comprised of ratings on the set of nine dimensions: "easy," "difficult," and "slow to warm up."

TABLE 10.1	Models of Infant and Toddler Temperament	
Key Proponent(s)	**Dimensions**	**Assessment Instrument**
Thomas & Chess (1977)/Carey & McDevitt (1978)	Activity level Approach-withdrawal Adaptability Quality of mood Attention span/persistence Distractibility Rhythmicity/regularity Intensity of reactions Threshold of responsiveness	Revised Infant Temperament Questionnaire (RITQ)
Bates, Freeland, & Lounsbury (1979)	Fussy-difficult Unadaptable Dull Unpredictable	Infant Characteristics Questionnaire (ICQ)
Rothbart (1981)	Activity level Fear Distress to limitations Smiling and laughter Soothability Duration of orienting	Infant Behavior Questionnaire (IBQ)
Rothbart (2004)	Surgency/extraversion Negative affectivity Orienting/regulation	
Buss & Plomin (1984)	Activity level Negative emotionality Sociability	Emotionality Activity Sociability Questionnaire (EAS)
Goldsmith (1996)	Anger proneness Pleasure Interest-persistence Activity level Social fearfulness	Toddler Behavior Assessment Questionnaire (TBAQ) and Lab-TAB Observation Procedure

Source: Based on Bates, Freeland, & Lounsbury, 1979; Buss & Plomin, 1984; Carey & McDevitt, 1978; Goldsmith, 1996; Goldsmith et al., 1987; Rothbart, 1981, 2004; Rothbart & Bates, 1998, 2006; Thomas & Chess, 1977.

Thinking about our hypothetical baby party, Jacobs and Emmas who are "easy" babies (approximately 40 percent of the NYLS sample) would tend to show positive emotions, adapt well to the new situation, and react at a low or moderately intense level. "Difficult" Jacobs and Emmas, by contrast (approximately 10 percent of the NYLS sample), would be more likely to display negative moods, adjust slowly to the new situation and people, and show a high level of intensity in their reactions. Slow-to-warm-up babies (approximately 15 percent of the NYLS sample) would be likely to show negative emotions and adjust slowly to the new situation but would be only moderately intense in their reactions and low in activity level.

Bates, Freeland, and Lounsbury (1979) developed the Infant Characteristics Questionnaire (ICQ) to explore "difficultness," conceptualized as four components shown in Table 10.1. Questions on the ICQ include "How much does your baby fuss in general?" and "When your baby gets upset, how vigorously does he/she cry and fuss?" Not all temperament researchers agree with the "difficultness" classification system. Rothbart (1984), for example, whose system we discuss next, does not measure a dimension of "difficulty" and has questioned whether the term "difficult" is useful or even desirable when studying temperament. Behavior that is difficult in one setting, she points out, may not be problematic in other settings, and behavior that some researchers define as difficult may not be perceived in the same way by caregivers or even by other researchers (Goldsmith et al., 1987).

Thomas and Chess advocate assessing children's temperament by observing them in a variety of naturalistic settings for an extended period of time. One temperament rating that incorporates the Thomas and Chess dimensions is the Revised Infant Temperament Questionnaire (RITQ) (Carey & McDevitt, 1978). In the Thomas and Chess account, temperament reflects innate, genetic aspects of the "wiring" of the newborn's brain, but these early traits change over time as the child develops cognitively and as the family and other caregiving environments influence the child. As a result, temperament is viewed as being only relatively stable over time (Goldsmith et al., 1987). One implication of this view is that parents and caregivers can respond to children's temperamentally based behaviors and preferences—as well as their own tendencies—and strive to achieve goodness-of-fit (Schoppe-Sullivan et al., 2007). As we discussed briefly in Chapter 9, goodness-of-fit is correlated with security of attachment and occurs when there is a match between the child's temperament and characteristics of the environment. Seen in this way, an infant with a high level of activity may be a good match for a parent who also has a high activity level but may require adjustments for a parent who usually prefers to be less active.

ROTHBART'S FRAMEWORK   In the second major approach, Rothbart defines temperament as relatively stable, biologically based "individual differences in reactivity and self-regulation, observed in the domains of emotionality, motor activity, and attention" (Rothbart, 2004, p. 82; Rothbart, Sheese, & Posner, 2007). Unlike some other temperament theorists, Rothbart believes that "temperament can be observed at all ages as individual differences in patterns of emotionality, activity, and attention" (Goldsmith et al., 1987, p. 510). In her view, "temperament and personality are seen as broadly overlapping domains of study, with temperament providing the primarily biological basis for the developing personality" (Goldsmith et al., 1987, p. 510). As shown in Table 10.1, Rothbart initially developed the Infant Behavior Questionnaire (IBQ) to assess Duration of Orienting as well as five behavioral dimensions (Rothbart, 1981). Questions on the IBQ ask parents to rate the frequency with which particular behaviors occur, such as how often their infants cry loudly while waiting to be fed.

The dimensions represented in the IBQ are regarded as being present from birth but may not be observable until several months later or even toward the end of the first year of life. Different dimensions may also become salient at different points in early development. Rothbart notes, for example, that there is a biobehavioral shift at 2 to 3 months of age in which all infants show sharp increases in attending to people around them, smiling, and laughing; thereafter, individual differences in smiling and laughing tend to become more stable. Levels of distress, by contrast, appear to show distinctive patterns within individuals after approximately 6 months of age (Goldsmith et al., 1987).

Rothbart's model emphasizes stability of temperament over time, but it also includes a role for caregiver sensitivity (Rothbart, Derryberry, & Hershey, 2000). This perspective recognizes, for example, that some highly unreactive infants may require more conscious stimulation in order to become engaged in face-to-face interaction and that infants who cry with greater intensity may need different amounts and types of comforting (Jahromi, Putnam, & Stifter, 2004).

Rothbart's recently revised model contains just three factors, shown in Table 10.1 (Rothbart, 2004). According to this model, infants who are high on "surgency/extraversion" show a high degree of positive emotions, seek out high-intensity activities, have a high activity level, tend to be impulsive, and are rarely shy. High scores on "negative affectivity" include a tendency to feel shy, to have difficulty being soothed, and to experience discomfort, fear, anger-frustration, and sadness. Scores for "orienting/regulation" reflect infants' perception and attention to the immediate setting and activities as well as the ease with which negative emotions can be influenced by cuddling and soothing (Derryberry & Rothbart, 1997; Rothbart, 2004; Rothbart et al., 2001; Rothbart & Bates, 2006). Additional exploration of these three factors may bring together the diverse set of models and terms generated thus far in the study of temperament.

BUSS AND PLOMIN'S APPROACH   A third major framework, proposed by Buss (1995; Buss & Plomin 1984; Goldsmith et al., 1987), focuses on three core dimensions that are included in the items on Buss and Plomin's (1984) Emotionality Activity Sociability (EAS) questionnaire. Within this system, "activity level" dimension ranges from lethargy to extreme rapidity of vocalizing or speaking and moving. "Emotionality" ranges from barely discernible reactions to intense reactions that are out of control; emotionality is initially defined as strong arousal in response to events in the environment but becomes differentiated into fear and anger by 12 months of age. The "sociability" dimension varies from a preference for being alone to a strong tendency to seek out others with whom to interact and share activities.

According to Buss, temperament is a set of genetically based personality traits that appear during the first two years of life, traits that are distinct from those that are acquired or appear later in life. The focus is on only those traits that have a lasting effect on later personality and the model excludes traits that are regarded as irrelevant, such as rhythmicity (regularity in infants' eating and sleeping). In this view, although there may be temporary environmental effects, such as an illness that makes a normally active child less so, temperamental traits are generally stable over time and experience.

GOLDSMITH'S MODEL   A fourth perspective, contributed by Goldsmith (1996; Goldsmith & Campos, 1990), defines temperament as early individual differences in five dimensions of emotionality. Goldsmith developed the Toddler Behavior Assessment Questionnaire (TBAQ) to measure these dimensions of temperament in children aged 16 to 36 months. The TBAQ (shown in Table 10.1) is intended to extend upward Rothbart's IBQ, and several of the dimensions are the toddler version of an infant dimension: Distress to Limitations/Anger Proneness; Smiling and Laughter/Pleasure; and Duration of Orienting/Interest-Persistence.

Parents complete the 108-item TBAQ by rating their child in terms of the frequency with which behaviors are exhibited. "Anger proneness" is assessed with questions such as "When you do not allow your child to do something for her/himself, for example, dressing or getting into the car seat, how often does your child try to push you away?" "Pleasure" is gauged with questions such as "When in the bathtub, how often does your child babble or talk happily?" "Interest-persistence" is measured with questions such as "How often does your child play alone with his/her favorite toy for 30 minutes or longer?" Questions such as "When playing with a movable toy, how often does your child attempt to go as fast as s/he could?" measure "activity level," while "When your child is being approached by an unfamiliar adult while shopping or out walking, how often does your child show distress or cry?" assess "social fearfulness."

To observe behavior directly, Goldsmith and colleagues incorporated elements of several researchers' procedures and developed Lab-TAB, a standardized laboratory assessment of early temperament. Three versions of Lab-TAB exist, one for prelocomotor infants, another for infants who have started to crawl, and a third for preschoolers. As shown in Table 10.2, Lab-TAB consists of 3- to 5-minute episodes that simulate everyday situations in which individual differences in

TABLE 10.2	Examples of Episodes in Three Versions of the Lab-TAB Observational Assessment of Temperament		
	Prelocomotor	**Locomotor**	**Preschool**
	Fear	*Fear*	*Fear*
	Parasol Opening: A parasol opens fairly rapidly and without warning as the infant sits in an enclosed booth.	*Remote Controlled Spider:* A large, remote controlled spider enters the room unexpectedly and approaches the toddler.	*Risk Room:* The child plays in a room filled with slightly "threatening" stimuli, including a gorilla mask, a cloth tunnel, and a balance beam.
	Unpredictable Mechanical Toy: A noisy and unpredictable remote controlled toy dog approaches the infant in a relatively nonsocial setting.	*Stranger Approach:* An adult male stranger approaches and stares at the toddler.	*Scary Mask:* A familiar friendly female stranger wears a wolf mask. Initially facing away from the door, when the child enters the room, the stranger turns toward the child and engages him/her in a scripted conversation.
	Anger	*Anger*	*Distress (Frustration, Anger, Sadness)*
	Gentle Arm Restraint by Parent: The infant is temporarily prevented from playing with a novel, attractive toy when the parent gently holds the baby's arm.	*Maternal Separation:* The mother and toddler are separated.	*Toy in Box:* The child selects one of two attractive toys, which is then locked inside a transparent plastic box. The child is given a set of keys and encouraged to try unlocking the box and retrieving the toy, although none of the keys fit the lock.
	Toy Behind Barrier: A toy with which the infant has been playing is placed behind a barrier.	*Car Seat Restraint:* The parent places the toddler in a car seat.	*Impossibly Perfect Green Circles:* The child is asked to draw circles repeatedly for $3\frac{1}{2}$ minutes. After completing each circle, the child is told that it is flawed in some way and must be redrawn.
	Joy/Pleasure	*Joy/Pleasure*	*Exuberance*
	Puppet Game: The infant interacts with a sociable hand-puppet.	*Sound and Light:* The toddler watches a nonsocial stimulus consisting of sounds and lights.	*Bubbles:* The child learns to blow bubbles using a special bubble gun and is then encouraged to pop bubbles that the experimenter generates.
	Peek-A-Boo Game: Mothers follow a script when playing peek-a-boo with their infant.	*Cognitive Assimilation (Train Game):* The toddler explores and plays with a toy train.	*Pop-Up Snakes:* The child surprises the parent with a "candy" container that actually contains pop-up snakes.

(continued)

302 Chapter 10 • Temperament, Emotions, and the Self

TABLE 10.2 Continued

Interest/Persistence

Block Play: The infant has an opportunity to play with a set of blocks.

Person Interest: A female experimenter acts out a scripted set of behaviors in the presence of the infant.

Activity Level

Quilt Time: The infant is placed on a quilt that is spread on the floor and partially covered with an array of novel, low-intensity toys.

Prone and Supine Placement: The infant is placed in both front- and back-lying positions.

—

Interest/Persistence

Toy Interest: The toddler has an opportunity to play with a toy that has an electronic sound and light display.

Repeated Visual Stimulation: The toddler views a series of slides shown on a screen but unaccompanied by any auditory stimulation.

Activity Level

Fidgeting: The toddler watches a video, shown in the absence of any other activity-eliciting stimuli or toys.

Free Play: The toddler has the opportunity to play with several different types of toys.

—

Interest/Persistence

Perpetual Motion: The child is invited to play with a space wheel toy consisting of a small silver spinner resting on two plastic tracks on a base.

Bead Sorting: The child is invited to sort red, white, and blue beads into different containers.

Activity Level

Hippity Hop: The experimenter demonstrates how a large, multicolor bouncing ball with a handle works and then gives the child the opportunity to play with it.

Workbench: The child plays with a small wooden workbench with many unique parts.

Inhibitory Control

Tower of Patience: The child and experimenter build a tower with large cardboard blocks, taking turns adding one block at a time. Before each turn, the experimenter waits for longer time increments before adding a block.

Snack Delay: The child is asked to wait for the experimenter's signal before eating a chocolate snack within reach.

Contentment

Story Time: The experimenter shows the child a storybook without words and asks the child to explain what happens in the book. The child is then invited to tell the story to the parent.

Making a Bookmark: The child decorates a construction paper animal shape with ink stamps and markers.

Source: Goldsmith, Rieser-Danner, & Briggs, 1991; Rothbart & Goldsmith, 1991.

fear, anger, joy/pleasure, interest/persistence, and activity level can be observed (Goldsmith, Rieser-Danner, & Briggs, 1991; Rothbart & Goldsmith, 1991).

Temperament and Biology

In recent years, interdisciplinary teams of researchers have explored new questions about infant temperament. These approaches supplement parental reports and observer ratings with biological evidence from neurobehavioral and genetic studies.

HEART RATE   Greater variability in fetal heart rate is correlated with greater emotional reactivity, as well as more irritability and difficulty in infancy (Porges, Doussard-Roosevelt, & Maiti, 1994). There are also links between fetal neurobehavior and temperament, and more active fetuses tend to be more difficult, less predictable, less adaptable, and more active infants (DiPietro et al., 1996). Comparing heart-rate responses, Kagan and colleagues reported that extremely shy children tend to have higher and less variable responses to unfamiliar people and events than do extremely bold children (Kagan & Fox, 2006; Kagan, Reznick, & Snidman, 1988).

THE STRESS-RESPONSE SYSTEM   There are also links between temperamental differences and activation of the stress-response system. Gunnar and colleagues, for example, found correlations between 9-month-old infants' tendency to be distressed and measured levels of salivary cortisol (Gunnar, 1994; Nachmias et al., 1996; Stansbury & Gunnar, 1994). Cortisol responses differ in familiar and unfamiliar settings, however, and are buffered when sensitive, responsive caregivers are available. Additional study of the role of cortisol is needed, since some studies have found that children who are rated as bold, outgoing, and even risk-taking also tend to show elevations of cortisol in novel settings when they are experiencing positive rather than negative emotions (Buss et al., 2004; Donzella et al., 2000).

REACTIVITY AND INHIBITION   In studies of 1- and 2-year-old children, Kagan and Snidman (1991a, 1991b; Kagan, 1994) explored individual differences in responses to novel situations that they created in the laboratory. Their studies, which provide additional evidence of neurophysiological differences in temperament, focused on two extreme groups of children. One group, termed **inhibited to novelty,** responded to unfamiliar people and places by consistently becoming "quiet, vigilant, restrained, and avoidant while they assess the situation and their resources before acting" (Kagan, 1994, p. 16). The second group of children, who were **uninhibited to novelty,** consistently responded to equally unfamiliar situations with spontaneous engagement and interest.

These groups were explored further in a longitudinal study of infants at 2, 4, 9, 14, and 21 months of age (Kagan & Snidman, 1991a, 1991b). Two extreme patterns of response to novel visual, auditory, and olfactory stimuli predicted which infants would be inhibited and which uninhibited at the age of 2 years. At 4 months, infants were presented with a series of novel stimuli, including mobiles, toys, the sound of an unfamiliar woman's voice, and a sample of dilute butyl alcohol presented on a cotton swab. Some infants were termed **high-reactive** and others were classified as **low-reactive.** High-reactive infants showed "extreme degrees of motor activity, combined with fretting or crying" (Kagan, 1994, p. 17). These infants moved their arms and legs vigorously, arched their backs, and sometimes cried in response to the unfamiliar sights, sounds, and smells. Low-reactive infants, by contrast, showed low levels of motor activity and rarely cried or fussed. Both groups of infants were tested again at 14 and 21 months of age, when stimuli included toys that moved, a blood pressure cuff, electrodes, a noisy spinning bingo wheel, an unfamiliar woman who tried to get children to taste an unidentified liquid from a medicine dropper, an unfamiliar woman whose face was obscured from the child's view by a gas mask, and an unfamiliar woman with a black cloth over her head and shoulders. A small proportion of the high-reactive infants (about 15 percent of the total sample) were extremely fearful and inhibited at 14 and 21 months, whereas a slightly larger subsample of infants who had been low reactive (approximately 25 percent of the total sample) responded with a degree of positive emotion and interest that led them to be classified as uninhibited.

In addition to behavioral responses, the researchers measured heart rates of children in their longitudinal study and found that high-reactive (but not low-reactive) 4-month-olds had had higher heart rates both before birth and two weeks after birth. There were also group differences in the rate at which children's heart rates increased in response to novel events during the laboratory sessions. Moreover, inhibited (as compared with uninhibited children) also showed greater pupillary dilation and larger changes in blood pressure in response to stimuli. Kagan interpreted these findings as evidence that high-reactive infants were genetically predisposed to have a lower threshold for activation of the sympathetic nervous system—the source of the "fight-or-flight" response—whereas low-reactive infants inherited a higher threshold (Kagan 1994; Kagan, Snidman, & Arcus, 1998). Subsequent findings of continuity between inhibition at age 2 years and social anxiety at age 13 years have supported Kagan's conclusions, at least for the extreme groups in his studies (Biederman et al., 2001; Kagan & Fox, 2006; Kagan & Snidman, 1999; Schwartz, Snidman, & Kagan, 1999). Genetic differences—specifically, the DRD4 gene—have been linked to differences in EEG activity as well as soothability and other behavioral styles, supporting the notion that infants' responses to environmental events and experiences are influenced by biological factors (Schmidt, Fox, Perez-Edgar, & Hamer, 2009).

One longitudinal study examined early inhibition in children whose mothers were depressed and in a comparison group of children whose mothers were not depressed. When the children were toddlers, the researchers assessed their inhibition to novel social and nonsocial events, and at the age of 5 years, children were observed interacting with an unfamiliar peer. Those who had been extremely socially inhibited as toddlers were more shy and inhibited with the peer, especially during the initial interaction, and they sought to be closer to their mothers than children who had not been inhibited at the first assessment. No differences in behavior were found as a function of maternal depression, suggesting that children's temperamental reaction to novelty played a more significant role in their behavior at age 5 (Kochanska & Radke-Yarrow, 1992).

Kagan's procedures were also used to study infants of mothers with a clinically diagnosed panic disorder. Researchers videotaped these infants and a comparison group as they encountered Kagan's stimuli at 4 and 14 months of age. Mothers used the IBQ temperament subscale to rate their infants' responses to sudden or novel stimuli at both 4 and 14 months. Infant salivary cortisol samples were also obtained at both ages. No behavioral differences between infants of mothers with panic disorder and comparison infants were observed in response to Kagan's stimuli. Infants of mothers with panic disorder had higher cortisol levels than comparison infants at both ages, however, suggesting that they were more distressed. Mothers with panic disorder appeared to be aware of their infants' susceptibility to distress and, despite the absence of behavioral differences, rated their 4-month-olds significantly higher on this dimension of the temperament questionnaire. Given that infants whose mothers have panic disorder may themselves be at higher risk for anxiety disorders, measures of cortisol response may offer a method for early detection and therapy (Warren et al., 2003).

Other studies of neurophysiological responses, fear, and temperament using less extreme or nonclinical samples have not uniformly supported Kagan's conclusions (Buss et al., 2003;

Schmidt et al., 1997, 1999). Additional research using more similar measures and comparable samples is needed to understand these connections (Buss et al., 2004). For now, it seems reasonable to conclude that even initial predispositions may be altered by subsequent experience, since not all high-reactive infants in Kagan's study became extremely inhibited 2-year-olds or socially anxious 13-year-olds.

Temperament and Attachment

In Chapter 9, we noted that some attachment theorists explain similarity in children's attachment to different caregivers as the result of the caregivers' shared goals and co-constructed views of the child, which then produce similar caregiving behavior. As might be expected, temperament researchers offer a different explanation. Pointing to modest but significant concordances between children's attachment classifications to mothers and fathers, they assert that the infant's temperament elicits similar responses from different caregivers during the Strange Situation and across many other settings, thereby contributing to similarity in attachment security (Fox, Kimmerly, & Schafer, 1991). In this account, infants who are distressed by separation from their mothers are also distressed by separation from their fathers, and it is their consistent distress that evokes similar responses from both parents.

Given that infants with a difficult temperament place greater demands on caregivers than do infants with an "easy" temperament, parents' sensitivity and responsiveness is thought to have a significant influence on security of attachment. The research literature on links between attachment and temperament indicates that it is possible for infants who are temperamentally difficult, irritable, or prone to distress to become securely attached to their caregivers, provided that those caregivers are sensitive, responsive, and emotionally warm (Mangelsdorf et al., 1990; Mangelsdorf & Frosch, 1999; Susman-Stillman et al., 1996; Vaughn & Bost, 1999). Parents of irritable newborns who do not respond consistently to their infants' crying, by contrast, are more likely to have insecurely attached infants (van den Boom, 1989, 1994, 2001).

In one study, infants who showed higher levels of irritability in the Neonatal Behavioral Assessment Scale were significantly more likely than nonirritable newborns to be insecurely attached when assessed in the Strange Situation at 12 months (van den Boom, 1989). There is also limited evidence of links between parent reports of dimensions of temperament (e.g., distress) and specific behaviors during the Strange Situation (e.g., fussiness or resistance), but links between temperament measures and Strange Situation attachment classification per se have seldom been found (Rothbart & Bates, 2006; Shaw & Vondra, 1995). When attachment has been assessed using the Attachment Q-Set (AQS), however, stronger correlations have emerged, especially for toddlers and children as old as 3 years (Seifer & Schiller, 1995; Seifer et al., 1996; Vaughn et al., 1992). In general, children who are rated higher on temperamental measures of negative emotional reactivity tend to be rated lower for attachment security in the AQS.

Temperamental "difficultness" has been linked to less optimal outcomes later in childhood. One study of infants adopted by Dutch families before the age of 6 months followed them until they were 7 years old. Attachment security was assessed in the Strange Situation at 12 months of age, and a Dutch version of the ICQ was used to measure temperament at 12, 18, and 30 months. Maternal sensitivity was assessed at 12, 18, and 30 months and once more at 7 years. Several additional measures of socioemotional and cognitive development were used at 7 years. Higher levels of maternal sensitivity and secure attachment led to better outcomes, suggesting that early caregiving interactions influenced subsequent development. There were still influences of temperament, however. Easy temperament was associated with better outcomes for cognitive, social, and personality development at age 7, whereas infants who were temperamentally difficult had poorer childhood outcomes. The combination of disorganized attachment and difficult temperament was associated with less optimal cognitive and personality development (Stams, Juffer, & van IJzendoorn, 2002).

Interventions to help parents of irritable, difficult infants become more skilled in noticing, interpreting, and responding to their infants' cries have proved effective in enhancing the development of secure attachment. This was found in one study with lower-income mothers whose infants were extremely irritable from birth. When mothers were instructed to notice, interpret, and respond promptly to their infants' cues at 6 and 9 months of age, security of attachment in the Strange Situation was higher than among a group of control mothers and infants. Infants in the intervention group were also more sociable in interacting with their mothers and had higher levels of exploration (van den Boom, 1989, 1994, 2001).

Some researchers have begun to explore whether certain positive or adaptable "easy" temperaments may provide protection from the effects of nonoptimal early caregiving in settings such as orphanages. Investigators involved in the Bucharest Early Intervention Project (a study of Romanian orphanages), for example, note that not all infants who experience serious maltreatment and environmental adversity in institutional settings develop reactive attachment disorder or other forms of psychopathology (Cicchetti & Toth, 2006; Zeanah & Fox, 2004). When developmental psychologists and clinicians collaborate, there are many important questions to pursue, and answers may be forthcoming if differences in definitions and methods can be overcome (Frick, 2004; Lahey, 2004).

Temperament and Personality

To varying degrees, the major models of temperament propose that infant temperament is related to later personality and behavior. Temperamental qualities related to irritability, negative affect, and difficultness are generally expected to predict behavior problems that include internalizing (e.g., withdrawal) and externalizing (e.g., aggression). Temperamental fearfulness in response to novelty, by contrast, is conceptually linked principally with internalizing and social anxiety. Positive affect, sociability, activity level, and surgency/extraversion are linked to lower levels of behavior problems (Rothbart & Bates, 1998, 2006).

Continuity from infancy into childhood has been reported for a variety of measures and dimensions of temperament. The results of numerous studies suggest that the longer the time between comparisons, and the older the ages being compared, the greater the degree of continuity (Bates et al., 1991; Buss, 1995; Caspi, 2000; Lemery et al., 1999).

As we have already seen, there is evidence that high-reactive infants who show extremely negative (fearful) reactions to novel objects are also more likely than low-reactive infants to become inhibited and distressed in response to novel objects and situations during childhood and early adolescence (Kagan, 1998). Theoretically compatible findings were reported in a different study using parental ratings rather than direct observations of behavior. Toddlers rated lower on sociability (higher on shyness) in Buss and Plomin's (1984) EAS questionnaire were more likely to be rated as socially withdrawn at 4 years of age (Hagekull, 1994). Similarly, a longitudinal study in Norway found that infants rated on the EAS as temperamentally shy and emotional had a higher risk of developing anxiety and depression at 12 to 13 years of age, particularly if the family experienced adversity due to problems in areas such as housing, employment, physical health, and substance abuse (Karevold et al., 2009).

Researchers studying 85 Swedish families examined links between infant temperament, attachment, and personality traits in middle childhood (approximately 8 to 9 years of age)

(Hagekull & Bohlin, 2003). Attachment to mother was assessed in the Strange Situation at 15 months, and parents used Buss and Plomin's (1984) EAS to rate their child's temperament at 20 months of age. Personality in middle childhood was rated by mothers and teachers using the Five Factor Model (FFM), a widely recognized system for studying the structure of personality (Rothbart, Ahadi, & Evans, 2000). Infants with higher activity and sociability ratings were rated higher in middle childhood on the FFM extraversion/surgency. In addition, securely attached infants were rated in childhood as being more extraverted, more open to experience, and more emotionally stable than children who had been insecurely attached as infants. The researchers interpreted their findings in terms of attachment theory, which holds that security of attachment produces internal working models promoting positive interactions and exploration.

A longitudinal study of 1,300 children from Finland provides additional relevant evidence, although the first temperament ratings were not made until children ranged from 3 to 12 years of age (Pesonen et al., 2002). Mothers completed Buss and Plomin's (1984) EAS questionnaire at the initial measurement, and 17 years later the now-adult children used the EAS to provide self-ratings. There was significant but weak evidence of continuity between childhood ratings and those provided in adulthood. Children who had been rated low in sociability (indicating perceived social maladjustment) tended to rate themselves higher on items measuring anger (irritability, aggressiveness, and impatience) in adulthood. A measure of difficult temperament in infancy (not part of the EAS per se) showed slightly stronger continuity with an adult measure of difficult temperament (conceptualized as a combination of high activity-tempo, high anger, and low sociability).

In keeping with these findings, other comparisons of early temperament ratings at age 3 and self-reported personality traits in adulthood have found that children who were more impulsive and showed less self-control tended to be less likely as adults to report avoiding harm and more likely to be socially alienated. Children who were inhibited, by contrast, were more likely as adults to avoid harm, less likely to be aggressive, and less likely to be socially powerful (Caspi & Silva, 1995).

Overall, these results generally indicate the long-term predictive value of early temperament measures. At the same time, evidence for continuity has not always been strong, and there is not agreement about how to interpret the findings. Although there appear to be relatively direct links between infant temperament and subsequent behavior and personality, many questions still exist about the process through which early constitutional qualities exert their influence. Many temperament researchers favor an explanation in which temperament is seen as providing a context for subsequent development. In this way, a difficult temperament makes a child more vulnerable for later problems but does not inevitably lead to poorer behavior and outcomes (Rothbart & Bates, 2006). There is still a need for studies using larger samples, longitudinal designs, and multiple measures of temperament and personality (Caspi, 1998; Caspi & Shiner, 2006).

EMOTIONS

All of the temperament measures we have discussed include at least one dimension of infants' emotionality. Questions about infants' typical emotional reactions and mood imply that parents and other caregivers who spend time with particular infants are able to discern and differentiate between their displays of emotions such as fear, anger, and distress. Considering that temperament assessments have been carried out as early as 6 weeks of age, on what do parents base their ratings? As we begin our examination of emotional life during the first three years of life, we answer this question by exploring a slightly different one; namely, on what do *researchers* base their ratings of infants' emotional expressions? We also consider whether infants' observable expressions of emotion correspond to their subjective emotional experiences.

Expressing Emotions

According to most theories of emotional development, infants are either born with or very quickly develop a set of **primary emotions.** Primary emotions are relatively easy for most adult caregivers to notice and interpret correctly. At least some of these emotions may have survival value because they occur, for example, when babies are in distress due to pain or hunger (Witherington, Campos, & Hertenstein, 2001). The configuration of facial muscle activity that usually accompanies infants' cries of distress corresponds to the subjective feeling of emotional distress in verbal children and adults (Izard, 1979; Oster, Hegley, & Nagel, 1992).

One pioneering infant emotion researcher, Carroll Izard (1977; Izard & Malatesta, 1987), asserted that there are eleven primary emotions: interest, joy, surprise, sadness, anger, disgust, contempt, fear, shame, guilt, and shyness. Lewis (1995, 2000), by contrast, proposed that infants have just three primary emotions at birth: distress, interest, and pleasure. As shown in Table 10.3, additional primary emotions emerge as these initial responses are differentiated: Distress gives rise to sadness, disgust, anger, and fear; interest evolves into surprise; and pleasure is transformed into joy.

Researchers looking for evidence of emotional experience at birth or in the first months of life usually rely on infants' facial expressions. As we learned in Chapter 6, newborns given sweet-tasting liquids smile with apparent pleasure, a facial expression that is not displayed when unpleasant smelling and bad tasting substances are presented. Observers who are unaware of what infants have just tasted or smelled are able to use facial expressions to judge infants' emotional reactions accurately (Ganchrow, Steiner, & Daher, 1983; Steiner, 1979).

Adults who watched videotapes of 1- to 9-month-olds in a wide range of settings, including playing with their mothers and receiving a shot in a doctor's office, were able to use infants' facial expressions to identify a range of corresponding discrete emotions, such as happiness, interest, fear, and anger (Izard et al., 1980). Other studies have confirmed what parents already know, namely, that young infants being given routine immunizations are in emotional distress, as their facial expressions indicate (Izard et al., 1983).

Infants begin to communicate anger, distinct from distress caused by pain, at a young age (Coie & Dodge, 1998; Dodge, Coie, & Lynam, 2006). This was shown in a study in which 1-, 4-, and 7-month-olds' forearms were restrained and held in front of them for a few minutes

TABLE 10.3	Proposed Timeline for the Development of Emotions (Birth to 3 Years)		
Birth	**By 6 months**	**By 18 months**	**By 24 months**
Distress	Sadness	Embarrassment	Guilt
	Disgust	Jealousy	Shame
	Anger		
	Fear		
Interest	Surprise		Pride
Pleasure	Joy		

Source: Based on Lewis, 1995.

(Stenberg & Campos, 1990). One-month-olds showed a variety of negative facial expressions, none of which matched widely recognized criteria for the emotion of anger, but nearly half of 4-month-olds displayed facial expressions that were unequivocally angry (Izard, 1979; Oster et al., 1992). Seven-month-olds in a different study consistently showed angry facial expressions when a desired object (a teething biscuit that they were eating) was removed against their wishes (Stenberg, Campos, & Emde, 1983).

As we saw in Chapter 9, babies whose mothers are depressed may show expressions of sadness themselves in early infancy, by 2 to 3 months of age. Sad facial expressions have also been observed in young infants whose mothers are not depressed but who suddenly "freeze"—with their faces expressing no emotion at all—in a well-known laboratory procedure that we discuss in greater detail shortly (Cohn & Tronick, 1983, 1987).

Infants show expressions of fear after the age of about 6 months. This is reflected in their increasing wariness around unfamiliar adults and in their reactions in laboratory procedures such as the Lab-TAB episodes that are intended to induce fear (Buss & Goldsmith, 1998; Hiatt, Campos, & Emde, 1979; Mangelsdorf, 1992).

Raised eyebrows and wide eyes with an open mouth are key criteria for facial expressions of surprise (Izard, 1979). Facial expressions matching these criteria have been seen in 5- to 7-month-old infants, but they may also be displayed when infants are engaged in exploring toys (Camras, Lambrecht & Michel, 1996).

Infants begin to show joyful facial expressions and smiling between 2 and 3 months of age (Izard et al., 1995). Parents and other caregivers not only notice these signs of joy but work hard to elicit smiling and laughter through face-to-face playful interactions and tickling (Fogel et al., 1997). Infants' first laughs usually appear after the age of 2 months and may then become a frequent part of face-to-face interactions (Nwokah & Fogel, 1993; Nwokah et al., 1999).

A set of **secondary emotions**—embarrassment, envy, empathy, pride, shame, and guilt—emerge in the second and third years of life as a result of cognitive development and the capacity for mental representation (Lewis, 1995, 2000). These emotions are also referred to as **self-conscious emotions** (or social emotions) because they require the ability to engage in self-reflective thought and to compare oneself or one's actions to standards and expectations that others hold. Each of the self-conscious emotions is associated with a unique set of body postures (Barret & Nelson-Goens, 1997; Stipek, Recchia, & McClintic, 1992). Children feeling shame, for example, seem to be trying to

This baby's attachment to his father is evident in his initial wariness toward his father's co-worker.

This girl's attempts to hide her face as she looks downward suggest that she is experiencing a negative self-conscious emotion, such as shame.

hide or disappear as they look downward and their body appears to collapse inward. Children who feel guilty, by contrast, may move around as if trying to repair or undo specific mistakes that they have made. When feeling embarrassed, children tend to smile while alternately looking away from and then looking at people who are nearby. Feelings of pride seem to be expressed by smiling broadly, "puffing up," and even raising the arms triumphantly. We examine evidence for the development of these emotions later in this chapter as we consider how they contribute to children's capacity for self-regulation and prosocial behavior. We turn now to consider the ability to recognize and understand emotions in others.

Perceiving Emotions

Just as the ability to express emotions appears to be functioning almost from birth, infants also appear to notice and respond differentially to facial and vocal expressions of emotion in others from an early age (Walker-Andrews, 1997). Two-month-old infants can discriminate between facial expressions of different emotions, such as happy versus sad or angry faces (Nelson & Horowitz, 1983). The ability to discriminate among variations within emotional categories, such as a closed-mouth smile versus an open-mouth smile, appears to develop by approximately 5 months of age (Bornstein & Arterberry, 2003).

Faces and voices normally appear together, and infants are able to engage in intermodal perception—matching expressions of emotion that they both see and hear. Across many different emotions, 7-month-olds tend to look longer at faces matching a soundtrack, suggesting that they recognize, for example, that happy faces and voices go together, just as angry faces and voices do (Walker-Andrews, 1986, 1997). The capacity for intermodal perception of emotion has been found even when the soundtrack does not match the videotaped display in any way except in its emotional valence and even when the visual information is extremely limited, as in studies in which only small white dots attached to the actor's face are visible in the videotape (Soken & Pick, 1992, 1999).

Studies adopting a different approach have investigated the impact of emotional stimuli on infants' own emotional experience. These experiments indicate that even newborns show **emotional contagion,** a phenomenon in which facial, vocal, or gestural cues of one person give rise to a similar or related state in another person (Saarni, Mumme, & Campos, 1998). Neonates in one study who heard another neonate's tape-recorded cry also tended to cry, a response that occurred significantly less often when they heard recordings of their own cry, an older infant's cry, or a chimpanzee's cry (Martin & Clark, 1982). Other experiments have shown that 10-week-old infants respond differentially to their mothers' happy, sad, and angry facial and vocal expressions, looking happier when their mothers expressed happiness, for example, than when they expressed sadness or anger (Haviland & Lelwica, 1987). This pattern is similar to the finding that infants of depressed mothers also appear "depressed" at an early age, apparently as a consequence of weeks and months of face-to-face interactions with a sad caregiver.

The emotional contagion response has also been observed when infants hear verbal and vocal messages, even if they cannot understand them. In a study of 5-month-olds, infants responded differentially to tape recordings of adults' expressions of approval and disapproval, whether they were presented in a familiar or unfamiliar language (Fernald, 1993). Infants' sensitivity to information about emotion that is not presented visually helps explain why parents offering comforting words to distressed infants who have awakened in the middle of the night are often able to soothe them and alter their emotional state without turning on a light, especially if they also offer a soothing touch or body contact.

Often when parents convey information with emotional cues, they hope to influence children's behavior as well as change their emotional state. This happens, for example, when parents abruptly change their emotional tone of voice to stop a child from crawling toward a household hazard, such as the top of the stairs or a fireplace. Parents who want to help their infant feel comfortable with a new babysitter may use a warm, friendly tone of voice and smile while talking to the unfamiliar caregiver in front of their child. Supportive, nurturing early social experiences like these, as well as harsh, punitive interactions, influence the development of the neural system underlying emotion processing, fine-tuning abilities that are present at birth (Leppänen & Nelson, 2006; Parker, Nelson, & The Bucharest Early Intervention Project Core Group, 2005; Pollak, 2008; Pollak et al., 2000).

Communicating with Emotions

Infants' early ability to both express emotions and perceive them in others enables them to engage in emotional communication with those around them. Functionalist theories of emotional development assert that emotions are relational rather than residing within the individual, meaning that emotional experiences occur in the context of some other person, object, or stimulus (Barrett & Campos, 1987; Campos, Campos, & Barrett, 1989; Campos et al., 1994; Fogel et al., 1997). We turn now to consider infants' ability to comprehend and respond to messages that caregivers and others convey through emotional communication.

The **still-face paradigm** is a laboratory procedure for studying emotional communication and regulation by disrupting the normal verbal and nonverbal signals that parents and infants use to communicate. In some early experiments using the still-face paradigm, researchers instructed nondepressed mothers of 3-month-old infants to adopt a withdrawn depressed expression for 3 minutes during face-to-face interactions, either before or after a 3-minute session of normal behavior. Infants responded to their mother's simulated depressed state by showing higher proportions of negative behaviors (protests, wariness, and looking away) than during a 3-minute session of normal interaction. Babies whose mothers simulated depression prior to the normal-behavior session tended to carry their negativity into the normal episode (Cohn & Tronick, 1983, 1987). In some subsequent studies, the still-face paradigm has been modified to involve the infant, mother, and father; after playing normally with the baby, both parents enact

Even very young infants notice and respond to caregivers' facial expressions of emotion.

the motionless, expressionless still-face for 2 minutes before reengaging with the infant and working together to "repair" the family's emotional connection (Khazan et al., 2008).

When mothers, fathers, or both parents show an expressionless, unresponsive "still face" in the midst of normal interactions, 2- and 3-month-old infants respond with negative emotions and physiological signs of distress, such as increased heart rate (Braungart-Rieker et al., 1998; Moore & Calkins, 2004; Moore, Cohn, & Campbell, 2001). Between the ages of 2 to 9 months, most infants respond to their parents' still face by showing less positive and more negative emotion themselves. They may attempt to reengage their parents by brief intervals of smiling and eye contact, alternating with averted gaze and self-comforting behaviors, such as thumb sucking. The emotional effects of a brief still-face episode do not cause lasting harm to the parent-infant relationship, but their short-term impact is often seen in subsequent interactions, even after parents have resumed their normal style of interaction (Moore et al., 2001; Weinberg & Tronick, 1996; Weinberg et al., 1999).

Across many different cultures, parents touch their babies at least 50 percent of the time during typical interactions (Keller et al., 2004a; Stack & Muir, 1990). When Canadian researchers in one study with 5-month-olds varied the still-face episode by allowing parents to continue touching their infants as usual, they found that infants were significantly less upset by their parent's silence and neutral facial expression (Stack & Muir, 1992). This finding suggests that some of the distress that infants experience during the still-face episode may be the result of the absence of normal tactile contact. It also suggests that tactile stimulation not only reinforces the emotional message that is conveyed through parents' vocal, verbal, and visual contact but may contribute in its own way to infant-parent emotional communication. For parent-infant dyads in which one or both participants are deaf, the combination of visual and tactile channels may be even more important ways of achieving and maintaining effective emotional communication (Koester, 1995; Koester et al., 2004).

As we learned in Chapter 9, across cultures, face-to-face interactions involving mutual eye contact occur at different rates (Bornstein, 2006; Bugental & Grusec, 2006; Shweder et al., 2006). In some cultures, such as in Greece and Germany, parents tend to view infants as equal communication partners and give them numerous opportunities to be the "leader" of their shared "conversation." Higher percentages of close body contact and stimulation, by contrast, are seen in other cultures, such as West Africa, India, and Costa Rica, which tend to follow a hierarchically structured apprentice model in which infants learn principally by maintaining close physical proximity and imitating examples that parents and other caregivers provide (Keller et al., 2004b). These differences in typical interaction patterns raise the intriguing possibility that the standard still-face paradigm might have different effects on infants as a function of their culture's implicit model of optimal infant-parent communication.

Infants communicate with their parents in settings other than face-to-face interaction, of course, and emotional signals are sent and received in a wide range of settings. Many studies have explored the phenomenon of **social referencing,** in which infants respond to emotional cues from parents and other adults. A commonly used procedure in studies of social referencing involves placing infants in unfamiliar or ambiguous settings and observing whether their parents' emotional expressions influence their behavior.

In an often-cited study using the visual cliff (originally developed by Walk & Gibson, 1961, to study depth perception), 12-month-old infants were placed on the "shallow" end of the apparatus while their mothers stood on the other side, near the "deep" end (Sorce et al., 1985). When mothers displayed fearful expressions, none of the infants were willing to cross the visual cliff, but when happy and interested emotions were expressed, the majority of infants crawled across. The visual information for support was equally ambiguous in both instances, but infants used mothers' facial expressions to impose either a "safe" or "dangerous" interpretation on it and then act accordingly.

In other studies, reminiscent of the Strange Situation, an unfamiliar adult enters a room. When mothers greet the stranger positively, 10-month-old infants are more likely to behave positively toward the stranger than when the stranger receives a negative response or no response at all from the mother (Boccia & Campos, 1989). These findings suggest that parents may be able to help their infants feel more comfortable when they meet strangers by expressing the emotions that they would like their infants to display.

The majority of social referencing studies have observed infants and parents in laboratory settings in which a novel object, usually a noisy or moving toy, is introduced. In many cases, parents are instructed to show either positive or negative emotions about the object, and researchers watch to see whether infants approach or avoid it. In a variation on this popular social referencing procedure, researchers showed 10- and 12-month-old infants a videotape in which an unfamiliar woman looked directly at one of two objects and expressed facial and vocal signals that were positive, negative, or neutral. Infants were then presented with the two objects and researchers observed how they interacted with each one. Ten-month-olds' behavior with the objects was not influenced by the emotional content of the videotape, but 12-month-old infants avoided objects about which the speaker in the videotape had expressed negative emotions. Positive emotions, by contrast, did not elicit more positive interactions with objects than did neutral emotions (Mumme & Fernald, 2003). These findings are consistent with other studies showing that the capacity to use emotional cues as a guide to behavior in potentially ambiguous settings emerges sometime between 10 and 12 months of age (Hornik, Risenhoover, & Gunnar, 1987; Moses et al., 2001; Mumme, Fernald, & Herrera, 1996).

By approximately 18 months of age, children become aware that emotions are not inherently linked with objects and people but reflect particular individuals' feelings about those objects and people (Repacholi & Meltzoff, 2007). An object that one person dislikes, therefore, might very well be liked by someone else. When an experimenter expressed disgust about a kind of food that the child liked and joy about a kind of food that the child did not like, 18-month-olds were more likely to give the experimenter the food about which she had expressed delight rather than disgust, even though they did not personally prefer it (Repacholi & Gopnik, 1997).

Recognition that different people like different kinds of food or toys is closely linked to young children's emerging theory of mind (ToM) knowledge, including the understanding that emotions are subjective, internal states linked to specific people, objects, and events (Dunn & Hughes, 1998; Wellman et al., 1995; Wellman & Wooley, 1990). Parents who frequently engage young children in conversations about beliefs, desires, and emotions support the development of emotion understanding and contribute to their ToM knowledge (Cutting & Dunn, 1999; Dunn, Brown, & Beardsall, 1991; Dunn et al., 1991; Taumoepeau & Ruffman, 2006).

Regulating Emotions

When parents attempt to change infants' emotions and behavior, they may hope to have an impact only at that precise moment, achieving the short-term goal of ending a tired child's temper tantrum, reassuring a timid toddler about entering a new playgroup, or soothing and distracting a fussy infant while waiting in line at the grocery store. At other times, parents are motivated by longer-term goals, such as helping young children learn to wait patiently for their turn and behave appropriately in a wide range of settings, even in the parents' absence. In both cases, parents' efforts contribute to the development of **emotion regulation,** an internal and external process through which emotions are monitored, appraised, and modified in relation to goals (Campos, Frankel, & Camras, 2004; Campos et al., 1994; Kopp, 1989; Thompson 1994). The emotions involved may be positive or negative, including joy, pleasure, distress, anger, and fear, but most research to date has explored the regulation of negative emotions. In keeping with the notion of emotions as relationship-based phenomena, successful self-regulation of emotion is typically defined by external criteria and standards for expressing emotion in particular situations or in particular cultures (Friedlmeier & Trommsdorff, 1999; Kopp, 1989). Children learn, for example, that a critical difference between "outside" and "inside" voices is not necessarily the emotion they experience, which may be positive in both settings, but the degree of arousal and exuberance that is expressed.

Self-regulation of emotion during the first three years of life develops gradually as children acquire behaviors that can be used in emotion-arousing situations, develop memory and language skills, and receive external support from caregivers. By the end of the first year, infants are able to shift their attention and use emerging motor, social-emotional, and cognitive skills to regulate feelings of wariness or to indicate that they want specific kinds of responses from caregivers. In contrast to young infants' limited repertoire of responses to feelings of sadness, frustration, or distress, older infants and toddlers are increasingly able to recall past experiences and choose from an array of possible behaviors, such as asking to be picked up or searching for a favorite stuffed animal to make themselves feel better (Kopp, 1989). It is not unusual to see toddlers hide behind their parent's legs when a stranger pays attention to them, peeking out at the unfamiliar adult to the degree that they feel comfortable.

Some strategies that infants and toddlers use, such as looking quickly to their parents, are quite brief; other reactions, such as turning away from an overwhelming fireworks display and covering their ears, may be maintained for a longer period of time (Mangelsdorf, Shapiro, & Marzolf, 1995). Not all strategies succeed in eliminating or even reducing strong negative emotions, however. Experiments in fear-eliciting episodes like those used in the Lab-TAB procedure have shown that infants as young as 6 months try to withdraw from the approaching objects and look to their parents when they are afraid, but these behaviors appear only to prevent the fear from growing stronger rather than diminish it (Buss & Goldsmith, 1998). As language develops, especially between 18 and 30 months, children are able to use words to refer more specifically to their emotions and talk with others about strategies for regulating their feelings (Bretherton et al., 1986).

As children become more cognitively, linguistically, and socially competent, caregivers increasingly embed socialization goals and lessons about self-regulation in their interactions, insisting, for example, that children use a pleasant-sounding voice instead of whining when they ask for something to eat. Young children are further socialized toward self-regulation when parents and other caregivers introduce and modify rules, making their expectations explicit. Rules for 13-month-olds often address safety and moral issues, such as climbing onto the coffee table or hitting other people. Three-year-old children are expected to meet those expectations as well as follow rules concerning social conventions—eating in appropriate areas of the home, putting away toys, using good manners—and self-care—washing one's own hands, getting dressed by oneself (Gralinski & Kopp, 1993). Children's growing awareness of these rules is reflected in their increasing levels of compliance and in their reactions to peers who violate caregivers' rules. Younger toddlers (approximately 20 months of age) notice and respond to peers' violations of moral rules but tend to disregard violations of social conventional rules, whereas older toddlers (approximately 30 months of age) notice and respond to both types of transgressions (Lamb & Zakhireh, 1997; Smetana, 1984).

Very young children who have cooperative, emotionally positive relationships with parents who explain the reasons for rules and prohibitions tend to become aware of standards for behavior and learn to differentiate situations allowing for autonomy from those requiring compliance. They are also more likely to display self-regulation, accepting and complying with their parents' expectations—even in their parents' absence—than are children whose parents are more power assertive and less emotionally supportive of their need for independence (Aksan & Kochanska, 2005; Kochanska, 2002; Kochanska & Aksan, 2004; Kochanska et al., 2008).

Parents may intervene in different ways with different children. One study of jealousy in sibling pairs in which the younger sibling was 16 months of age and the older sibling was a preschool-age child showed that older siblings were generally better able than younger siblings to wait for their turn to play with a new toy. Younger siblings rated as being more temperamentally negative and angry were especially likely to experience feelings of jealousy as they watched their older sibling play with the toy, if they had not yet had their own turn with it. Parents who recognize differences and take individual temperaments and cognitive maturity into account tend to be more successful at helping children manage negative feelings (Volling, McElwain, & Miller, 2002). In this example, parents could give the younger child the first turn, which might make it easier for him or her to watch the older sibling taking a turn next.

Differences in the regulation and socialization of emotion are seen across cultures in the actions that caregivers take (Bornstein, 2006; Bugental & Grusec, 2006; Friedlmeier & Tromsdorff, 1999; Hastings & Rubin, 1999). In Japan, for example, mothers tend to use soft, quiet vocalizations and physical contact to soothe infants and minimize crying and distress. Parents in the United States, by contrast, are more likely to follow a "let-them-cry-it-out" approach. To a greater degree than is typically seen in the United States, therefore, Japanese parents attempt to regulate infants' expressions of negative emotion (Miyake et al., 1986; Saarni et al., 1998; Shwalb et al., 1996).

Across cultures, most parents and children talk about children's past emotional and moral experiences (Laible, 2004a, 2004b). There are cross-cultural differences, however, in the extent to which parents highlight versus minimize negative emotions when discussing behavioral standards and expectations for future behavior (Miller, Fung, & Mintz, 1996; Miller et al., 1997; Shweder et al., 2006). A study of 2-year-olds, for example, found that Chinese parents were more likely than European American parents to remind children of the negative consequences and negative emotions associated with past violations of standards for behavior. European American parents, by contrast, tended to transform discussions about children's previous transgressions into emotionally positive, entertaining stories of affirmation in an effort to preserve their child's self-esteem (Miller et al., 1997).

There are also differences within cultures in parents' responsiveness to infants' emotional signals, and these differences influence infants' subsequent emotional expressiveness. Some mothers in a longitudinal study between 2 and 22 months of age smiled when their babies were distressed or ignored their expressions of sadness. Over time, these infants tended to express less joy than infants whose mothers had responded more appropriately and sensitively when they cried or looked sad (Malatesta et al., 1989). Researchers have also found that some mothers tend to smile more and be more emotionally expressive when interacting with daughters than with sons (Karraker & Coleman, 2002; Malatesta & Haviland, 1982). In these cases, longitudinal data from 2 to 22 months of age showed that infant daughters, but not sons, became more emotionally expressive over time (Malatesta et al., 1989).

New ideas are emerging about how to define and study emotion regulation (Bridges, Denham, & Ganiban, 2004; Cole, Martin, & Dennis, 2004; Eisenberg & Spinrad, 2004). Current directions include incorporating developmental neuroscience and psychobiology perspectives to examine links to genetics and the structure and functioning of the brain (Goldsmith, Pollak, & Davidson, 2008; Thompson, Lewis, & Calkins, 2008). Ongoing longitudinal studies of brain and behavior responses to distress and negative emotions, for example, are likely to shed light on changes in emotional reactivity and regulation as a result of the developing attention system and caregiver behaviors (Bell & Wolfe, 2004; Eisenberg, Fabes, & Spinrad, 2006; Goldsmith & Davidson, 2004). The convergence of these new perspectives with traditional behavioral approaches is a promising way to explore issues of change and continuity in emotion regulation and dysregulation (DelCarmen-Wiggins, 2008).

Developing and Using Social Emotions

In most U.S. and European cultural contexts, the toddler years are notorious for being a period of increasingly negative, oppositional behavior—the so-called "terrible twos." In many theories of social and emotional development, young children's striving for autonomy and self-directed behavior at the same time that parents introduce and reinforce societal expectations and standards is considered psychologically healthy. According to Erik Erikson (1950), for example, following the stage of trust versus mistrust, from approximately 18 months to 3 years they negotiate the stage of autonomy versus shame and doubt. In this stage, children begin to resist caregivers' control to some extent, asserting their own wishes and desire for independence.

Many parents and caregivers endorse the value of this stage and thus try to support young children's psychosocial development by offering choices, rather than ultimatums, when it is reasonable and possible to do so. At the same time, as children get older, parents often articulate new expectations and demand greater compliance than before. They also try to reinforce and encourage emotions that prompt prosocial behavior, such as sharing and helping others, and reduce undesirable emotions and behavior, such as jealousy and aggression.

By the age of 30 months, children engage in both physical and relational aggression (Hay, 2005; Ostrov & Crick, 2007). This means that in addition to using behaviors such as hitting, pushing, kicking, and biting, young children also inflict emotional harm on others by jeopardizing their well-being through relationship-based tactics such as social exclusion. In some cases, these forms of aggression are planned and goal directed (proactive), but at other times they occur in response to frustration or provocation (reactive). Patterns of aggression tend to be stable over time, with girls and socially dominant children more often using relational aggression and older children using less physical aggression than younger children (Murray-Close & Ostrov, 2009). The tendency for boys to display more physical aggression than girls is evident as early as 17 months of age, but researchers disagree about whether this pattern has a biological basis or is the result of differential socialization (Baillargeon et al., 2007).

Longitudinal studies strongly suggest that parents' pattern of responding to infants' emotions and behavior may have long-lasting effects on self-regulation and social functioning. In one such investigation, children whose parents were more power assertive (coercive, harsh, and heavy-handed) at 2 and 3 years of age tended to be more oppositional and antisocial (disruptive and aggressive) as older preschoolers, particularly if they were insecurely attached at 15 months of age (Kochanska et al., 2009). A study of low-income families found that children rated as temperamentally fussy at 1 year of age tended to experience more power assertive discipline that included spanking than did less fussy children. In comparison with children whose parents used less power assertive discipline, those who were spanked had higher rates of aggressive behavior problems at the age of 2 years and lower Bayley mental development scores at age 3 (Berlin et al., 2009).

In a longitudinal study of genetically identical twins, one twin in each pair received more maternal negativity and less emotional warmth, often beginning at birth, than the other twin. By the age of 5 years, twins who had been the target of mothers' negative emotions had more problems regulating their own emotions, as reflected in a greater number of antisocial behavior problems (Caspi et al., 2004). Other longitudinal twin studies have found that identical twins whose parents create different emotional environments at 2 to 3 years of age—directing positive emotions and noncoercive discipline to one child and negative emotions and coercive, harsh discipline to the other child—differ in their tendency to engage in prosocial behavior (being helpful, cooperative, and showing concern for others) throughout early childhood and at least up to age 7 (Knafo & Plomin, 2006). These twin studies have also identified a genetic contribution toward empathy and prosocial behavior, however, indicating that both environmental factors and biological predispositions need to be considered (Knafo, 2006; Knafo et al., 2008).

Children as young as 12 months show one element of prosocial behavior—empathy (concern)—when they observe others in distress and attempt to comfort them. With age, they acquire a broader range of comforting strategies and apply them with more flexibility and specificity (Eisenberg & Fabes, 1998; Zahn-Waxler et al., 1992). A related form of prosocial behavior, altruism—helping another person even when there is no benefit for doing so—has been documented in children as young as 14 months using laboratory tasks in which an experimenter tries to retrieve out-of-reach objects, encounters a physical obstacle, or has other problems trying to complete a task that the child is able to perform. Two versions of each task are presented, varying according to whether the experimenter unintentionally or deliberately creates the circumstances in which the child's help is needed. In a task using a marker, for example, the experimenter either appears to accidentally drop the marker on the floor and then unsuccessfully reach for it or intentionally throw it down, out of reach. Following each task, the experimenter first waits 10 seconds to see if the child will help; during the next 10 seconds, the experimenter silently alternates gaze between the object and the child; in the final 10 seconds, the experimenter makes a comment such as "Oh, my marker!" but never asks the child for help directly.

Nearly all young children participating in these experiments offer help quickly, often within the first 10 seconds. As shown in Figure 10.1, they help more frequently when the experimenter appears not to have acted intentionally. Eighteen-month-olds surpass 14-month-olds, however, in the range of tasks for which they offer assistance, presumably because they possess more advanced cognitive abilities and knowledge (Warneken & Tomasello, 2006, 2007). Some researchers think that, because chimpanzees tested in similar tasks perform comparably to 14-month-olds, the basic

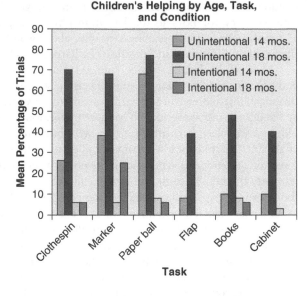

FIGURE 10.1 Children's Helping by Age, Task, and Condition. *Source:* Based on Warneken & Tomasello, 2007.

tendency to help others may be unlearned, part of an evolutionary predisposition among primates to cooperate and solve problems in social settings (Warneken, Chen, & Tomasello, 2006).

Environmental influences are clearly important, however, as seen in the increased tendency for 18-month-olds to help when they see cues hinting at social affiliation. In one experiment, the mere presence of two small dolls facing each other in the background of a photograph resulted in higher rates of helping in a subsequent task than did the presence of a single doll, two dolls facing away from each other, or two small stacks of blocks (Over & Carpenter, 2009). As we discuss next, there are many ways in which parents play an important role in shaping and expanding early prosocial tendencies.

When young children engage in antisocial behavior, such as biting another child in order to obtain a desired toy, parents, caregivers, and peers typically let them know that they have violated expectations and standards. Even toddlers are aware of rules (e.g., "We don't bite our friends"), and, by the age of 2 to 3 years, most children have begun to develop a moral code or **conscience**— an internal set of standards that guide behavior (Emde et al., 1991; Kochanska, 2002; Thompson, 2006). By the age of 2 years, most children show emotional distress and signs of guilt when they are responsible for a mishap that results in damage to objects or harm to other people. Researchers in some studies have observed 2-year-olds' emotional responses when they believe that they have broken a doll or spilled juice. In actuality, the experimenters rig the dolls and cups to make sure that these "accidents" will occur. Most 2-year-olds in such studies show signs of guilt through tension and frustration and try to repair the damage, attempting to fix the doll or clean up the juice (Cole, Barrett, & Zahn-Waxler, 1992).

Parents' emotional expressiveness helps children's social emotions become established as parents communicate their feelings, and these verbal and nonverbal emotional messages influence children's own emotional experience and knowledge (Barrett & Nelson-Goens, 1997). When children share their toys, for example, parents often show positive emotions and compliment them for their behavior, but when children throw their toys or take away other children's toys, parents show clear verbal and nonverbal disapproval.

Between 12 and 36 months of age, children become increasingly capable of complying with parents' requests and adjusting their behavior when asked to do so. Empathic parents who establish a **mutually responsive orientation (MRO)**—a "positive, close, mutually binding, cooperative, and affectively positive" relationship (Kochanska, 2002, p. 192)—increase the likelihood that children will not only become aware of standards and rules but also internalize and comply with them even when parents are not present (Aksan & Kochanska, 2005; Kochanska, Coy, & Murray, 2001; Kochanska & Murray, 2000).

Committed compliance is seen when children "embrace the maternal agenda, accept it as their own, and eagerly follow maternal directives in a self-regulated way" (Kochanska, Coy, & Murray, 2001, p. 1092). When asked to help clean up toys, children exhibiting committed compliance pick up toys throughout the play area without having to be prompted to move from one pile to another. They also tend to clap their hands when finished or show other nonverbal signs of pride in their accomplishment. **Situational compliance,** by contrast, "describes instances when children, although essentially cooperative, do not appear to embrace wholeheartedly the maternal agenda" (Kochanska et al., 2001, p. 1092). Children displaying situational compliance in a toy cleanup task usually pick up only a small number of toys or only those that they have been asked to pick up; they may even begin playing instead of putting the toys away.

Children with MRO relationships tend to display committed compliance, whereas the absence of an MRO relationship is more frequently associated with situational compliance (Kochanska, 2002). In a longitudinal study of MRO relationships, compliance, social emotions, and conscience, children were observed at 14 and 22 months as mothers tried to enlist them in acting out three pretend sequences (Clean the Table, Tea Party, and Feed the Bear). Conscience was assessed at 33 and 45 months of age by examining children's ability to resist playing with a set of prohibited toys and to resist cheating in an unwinnable game. The social emotion of guilt was also assessed at these ages, using rigged objects (Cole et al., 1992). In support of the MRO model, toddlers who were more willing and eager to comply with mothers during the imitation-of-pretense task showed more developed conscience (greater resistance to temptation) and higher levels of guilt as preschoolers (Forman, Aksan, & Kochanska, 2004).

There are individual differences in children's compliance. Children who are temperamentally more inhibited (according to CBQ ratings and as reflected in more fearful behavior in unusual settings resembling the Lab-TAB Risk Room), for example, show a higher rate of committed compliance when asked to resist playing with an attractive set of toys than children who are less temperamentally inhibited. Overall, however, longitudinal studies covering the ages 7 to 66 months strongly suggest that a sensitive, responsive parental relationship in infancy sets the stage for the development of social emotions, internalization of parental standards, conscience, and self-regulation (Kochanska, 2002; Kochanska & Murray, 2000; Laible & Thompson, 2000; Thompson, 2006). When parents' standards are internalized, children experience compliance and cooperation as self-generated regulation, reducing the oppositional behavior that is so often observed during the toddler years (Kochanska et al., 2001; Thompson, 2006).

THE SELF

Thinking about our hypothetical Jacob and Emma party, if we called out "Jacob! Emma!" at what age would we expect large numbers of infants to swivel their heads to see who had called their name? As it turns out, the ability to recognize one's own name develops relatively early, during the middle of the first year of life. It is so atypical for infants of this age not to respond when they hear their names, in fact, that those who do not show this reaction by 9 to 12 months of age may need to be seen by a pediatrician or infant mental health specialist to determine the extent and cause of this developmental delay. Although there may be other explanations, one study of home movies of infants later diagnosed with an autism spectrum disorder showed that these infants tended not to respond to their names, showed poor social attention, and lack of social smiling and appropriate facial expressions (Dawson et al., 2004; Werner et al., 2000). Assuming that all of the Jacobs and Emmas on hand oriented to the sound of their own name, would it be accurate to infer that they had a clear concept of themselves as objective, coherent individuals? As we will see, the development of a sense of self is a gradual achievement that takes place over the first three years of life (Harter, 1998, 2006; Thompson, 1998, 2006).

Recognizing the Self

Few researchers would conclude that a 7-month-old infant who consistently turns when her name is called understands that she is Emma. Over the course of the first year of life, however, infants gradually build a subjective sense of self. They do this by becoming aware of their ability to affect parents and other people through their daily interactions. In a sensitive and responsive caregiving environment, when infants cry, someone attends to their needs; when they roll over or sit up by themselves, someone exclaims enthusiastically about their achievement of a motor milestone. In games of peek-a-boo and other give-and-take activities, infants play a specific role that is inherently linked to their partners' actions. Infants also act upon objects in their environment, moving their hands, reaching toward objects, and bringing those objects to their mouth for oral exploration. All of these experiences, as well as a consistent subjective frame of reference, provide feedback to infants that they are distinct from others (Harter, 1998, 2006). By the age of about 12 months, they display social referencing and other forms of shared communication that many researchers assert signify a "dawning awareness of others (and oneself) as subjective entities with different and potentially shareable viewpoints" (Thompson, 1998, p. 76).

Objective awareness of the self—understanding of one's own characteristics and traits—does not emerge until later in the second year of life. To assess children's objective awareness of the physical self, Lewis and Brooks-Gunn (1979) developed a test of **visual self-recognition,** the rouge test. In this well-known laboratory procedure, a dot of rouge is surreptitiously applied to the child's nose and then he or she is placed in front of a mirror. If children touch the spot of rouge after seeing their reflection (as opposed to merely pointing at their reflection), they are credited with visual self-recognition. This reaction is seen reliably in most children by 18 months of age but may appear as early as 15 to 16 months or as late as 24 months (Asendorpf, & Baudonniere, 1993; Courage, Edison, & Howe, 2004; Lewis & Ramsay, 1997). Experiments in which surreptitious marking is accomplished by placing a sticker elsewhere, such as on young children's legs, show that self-recognition at 18 to 24 months of age is based on expectations about the appearance of their entire body, not just their face (Nielsen, Suddendorf, & Slaughter, 2006)

Soon after children show objective self-recognition, they begin to refer to themselves as specific individuals and comment on their own emotions and internal states. They also begin to use their own names and personal pronouns such as "me" and "mine" (Bertenthal & Fischer, 1978; Pipp, Fischer, & Jennings, 1987). Children become increasingly motivated to behave autonomously, rejecting offers of help with the often-heard assertion that they want to "do it myself." Around this same age, children also begin to engage in pretend play, which (as we discussed in Chapter 7) depends on the ability to think of objects and, at more advanced levels, the objective self as something other than what it really is (Kavanaugh, Eizenman, & Harris, 1997). One recent longitudinal study of children at 15, 18, and 21 months found that children who showed self-recognition in the rouge test used more personal pronouns and engaged in more advanced forms of pretend play than those who had not yet developed visual self-recognition. The nearly simultaneous emergence of these three measures suggests that they are linked to the

This toddler's sense of self is still developing, but her reaction to her own reflection shows that she knows that she is looking at herself.

development of an underlying objective representation of the self (Lewis & Ramsay, 2004). By approximately 30 months of age, children prefer playing with same-sex peers, indicating that they use their growing self-knowledge to guide their social behavior (Grace, David, & Ryan, 2008).

It is likely that links between self-representational awareness, **self-referential language,** social emotions, and socially desirable behavior are complex and multidirectional (Courage, Edison, & Howe, 2004). Investigations of early parent-child relationships appear to be a promising developmental context to explore (Bugental & Grusec, 2006; Parke & Buriel, 2006; Shweder et al., 2006; Thompson, 2006). Indeed, differences in caregiving experience at the age of 3 months appear to influence children's self-recognition and self-regulation at 18 to 20 months (Borke et al., 2007; Keller et al., 2004a, 2004b). In a cross-cultural study, infants of Nso farmers in Cameroon, who experience a proximal caregiving style, were compared with infants in urban Greek families, who experience a distal caregiving style. These groups were compared with a third group of infants, from middle-class Costa Rican families, in which caregiving blends aspects of proximal and distal styles. As shown in Table 10.4, infants in the Cameroon sample developed self-regulation (compliance with parents' requests to either perform particular actions or refrain from particular actions) earlier than infants in the other groups, whereas infants in the Greek sample developed self-recognition (assessed in the rouge test) earlier. As expected, infants in the Costa Rican sample were intermediate between the other groups of infants on both measures.

These findings suggest that early infant-caregiver interactions that emphasize shared feelings and physical interdependence (the proximal style) promote formation of a self that is viewed as "a communal agent who is basically interconnected with others, role oriented, and compliant" (Keller et al., 2004b, p. 1745). Infant-caregiver interactions that emphasize interpersonal distance and separateness, by contrast (the distal style), lead children to an earlier awareness of the self as

TABLE 10.4	Links between Caregiving Style, Self-Regulation, and Self-Recognition		
		Age at Assessment	
3 months		**18–20 months**	
Sample	**Caregiving Style**	**Frequency of Self-Regulation**	**Frequency of Self-Recognition**
Cameroon	Proximal	72%	3%
Costa Rica	Proximal and Distal	42%	50%
Greece	Distal	2%	68%

Source: Based on Keller et al., 2004b.

"an individual agent who is bounded, self contained, unique, and separate from others" (Keller et al., 2004b, p. 1745).

The objective self is thus a reflection of children's social and emotional experience. Parents' statements to and about their infants, as well as their emotional communication and actions, play a central role in the self that is constructed throughout infancy and childhood (Harter, 2006; Laible, 2004a; Miller et al., 1997; Shweder et al., 2006).

Evaluating the Self

At 2 and 3 years of age, children increasingly respond to and look for evaluative feedback about their actions from parents and other adults. In one study involving 13- to 39-month-old children, an experimenter introduced several new toys and demonstrated how they worked (Stipek et al., 1992). Children were then invited to take their turn and see if they could do it too. Children of all ages tended to smile both after the experimenter's demonstration and after their own performance, deriving pleasure directly from their actions. After the age of 21 months, however, and especially after 30 months of age, children were more likely to look up at the experimenter after they themselves had produced the outcome with the toy than after the effect had been produced by the experimenter. Whereas younger children do not anticipate or seek out adults' reactions to their performance, at 22 months and beyond, children increasingly look for acknowledgment when they have performed a task correctly and may even be expecting praise for their performance.

In a follow-up study of 24- to 60-month-old children, researchers compared reactions of children who succeeded at a task with reactions of children who failed (Stipek et al., 1992). The tasks consisted of puzzles as well as nesting cups that could be stacked from largest to smallest to form a tower. In the failure condition of each task, one puzzle piece was replaced with a piece from a different puzzle, and two same-sized cups were included in the set, making it impossible to stack them on top of each other in descending size as the experimenter had requested.

Children of all ages smiled more and were more emotionally positive in the success condition than in the failure condition. Many 2-, 3-, and 4-year-olds who succeeded showed "open" body postures consistent with feelings of pride. Following success, children were also more likely to look at the experimenter and call attention to their completion with comments such as "I did it" or "Done." Approximately half of the children in the success condition were praised for their performance, whereas the other half simply received a neutral comment noting that they had completed the task. Even without praise, children who succeeded showed positive emotions, but these emotions were heightened when praise was given following success.

Following failure, children of all ages tended to avoid eye or face-to-face contact with the experimenter by turning their heads or bodies in the opposite direction. "Closed" body postures indicative of negative self-consciousness or embarrassment were observed more frequently among children in the failure condition than in the success condition. When they encountered difficulty in the failure condition, older children tended to continue studying and working on the task, whereas younger children were more likely to lose interest and stop trying. After 32 months of age, children who failed were increasingly likely to express negative emotions by pouting or frowning. Children as young as 2 years of age reacted with negative emotion to failure in social settings, possibly because they equated failing at the tasks with failing to comply with the experimenter's instructions. Considering that 2-year-olds acted as if failure to complete the tasks was equivalent to failing to comply with a behavioral standard, the researchers caution that parents who are critical or demanding in one arena may inadvertently create anxiety in young children about evaluation in another arena. "If our analysis is correct, even parents who are careful not to criticize their young children's achievement 'failures' could contribute to achievement anxiety by expressing disapproval of behavior in other domains" (Stipek et al., 1992, p.74).

Children who hear comments like "You're a good listener!" or "Nice job picking up your toys!" show feelings of pride that are incorporated into the developing representation of the self. Parents who denigrate their children's efforts, by contrast, are more likely to induce feelings of shame or embarrassment that become incorporated into their self-representations. Children whose mothers praised them frequently during free play were more likely than children who were less frequently praised to call attention to their own achievements during free play. This observation led the investigators to assert that "[a] certain amount of praise may be essential for children to develop a sense of themselves as competent ... " (Stipek et al., 1992, p. 59).

This conclusion is also consistent with the findings of an important review of early intervention programs, which identified six psychosocial mechanisms consistently associated with positive cognitive, social, and emotional outcomes: (1) encouragement to explore the environment, (2) celebrating new skills, (3) protection from inappropriate punishment or ridicule for developmental advances, (4) mentoring in basic cognitive and social skills, (5) stimulation in language and symbolic communication, and (6) rehearsing and expanding new skills (Ramey & Ramey, 1998a, 1998b). When these experiences occur in children's lives on a daily basis, they and their parents co-construct self-representations that prepare them for subsequent developmental challenges and opportunities.

WRAPPING IT UP: Summary and Conclusion

Social and emotional development from birth to age 3 years is the result of the dynamic interplay between infants' inherent temperament and the sensitivity that parents and other caregivers show in trying to understand and respond to those qualities. There is a general consensus that temperament consists of infants' characteristic responses, such as irritability, soothability, motor activity, attentiveness, adaptability, response to novelty, arousal, and regulation of states. Continuity from infancy into later childhood exists for a variety of measures and dimensions of

temperament, including activity and sociability. Some studies have also found links between early temperamental "difficultness" and less optimal relationships and development at later ages. Social and cognitive development are buffered, however, when parents of "difficult" infants learn how to adjust caregiving behaviors to children's characteristics and behavioral tendencies.

Most major theories of emotional development suggest that infants are born with, or very quickly develop, a set of primary emotions. Some researchers assert that there are three primary emotions—distress, interest, and pleasure—and that this initial set subsequently becomes differentiated into multiple emotions, including sadness, anger, fear, surprise, and joy. Secondary emotions emerge in the second and third years of life as a result of cognitive development and the capacity for mental representation. These emotions are also referred to as self-conscious or social emotions because they require the ability to engage in self-reflective thought and to compare oneself or one's actions to external standards and expectations. Examples of secondary emotions are embarrassment, envy, empathy, pride, shame, and guilt.

The ability to both express emotions and perceive them in others enables infants to engage in emotional communication. Emotional experiences typically occur in relation to some other person, object, or event, rather than residing within the child per se. Infants notice and respond to parents' emotions from an early age and are increasingly able to engage in emotional "dialogues." Across infancy and the toddler period, parents raise their expectations for children's behavior and emotion regulation. As they do, they are increasingly likely to encourage and reinforce emotions that prompt prosocial behavior and discourage emotions and behavior that are undesirable, aggressive, or antisocial. Parents' emotional communication with infants and toddlers plays a central role in the development of social emotions and conscience, motivating children to follow an internalized set of standards for moral behavior.

A sense of self develops gradually over the first three years. Beginning in the first year, infants develop a subjective sense of self through daily interactions with parents and other caregivers. Objective self-recognition and awareness of the physical self typically emerges by the age of about 18 months, influenced by cognitive development as well as experiences with caregivers in specific cultural contexts. Other signs of children's growing sense of self are the appearance of self-referential language, social emotions, and socially desirable, self-regulated behavior.

Just as no two infants or toddlers are interchangeable, neither are all parents alike. As we discuss in the next chapter, all caregivers can benefit from education about children's needs from birth to age 3, and all children benefit from quality care.

THINK ABOUT IT: Questions for Reading and Discussion

1. How might parents and other caregivers differ in their behavior toward infants and toddlers if they believe that temperament is largely unchangeable, as opposed to believing that temperament can be modified by experience?

2. What are the advantages and disadvantages of using parent reports to study temperament? If you were going to conduct a study of temperament, how would you increase the usefulness of parent reports?

3. How does early dyadic emotional communication affect infants' and toddlers' functioning in other developmental domains? Put another way, what sorts of skill deficits would you expect to find in infants and toddlers who did not experience early dyadic emotional communication?

4. How do infants and toddlers learn to regulate their emotions?

5. How might the development and differentiation of emotions during the first three years of life coincide with or even contribute to the development of milestones in other domains? Consider examples as diverse as learning to walk, uttering first words, and forming an attachment relationship.

6. Which developmental milestones must be achieved before a child is capable of experiencing self-conscious (social) emotions?

7. How is development of the self related to development in other domains, such as cognition and language?

Key Words

Committed compliance (319)   Children's tendency to follow parents' directives and requests with a minimum of prompting and reminding.

Conscience (318)   An internal set of standards that guide behavior.

Emotional contagion (310)   A phenomenon in which facial, vocal, or gestural cues of one person give rise to a similar or related state in another person.

Emotion regulation (314)   A process through which emotions are monitored, appraised, and modified in relation to goals.

High-reactive (303)   Infants who respond to novelty by showing extreme degrees of motor activity, fretting, and crying.

Inhibited to novelty (303)   A constitutionally based tendency to respond to unfamiliar people and places by becoming quiet, vigilant, restrained, and avoidant.

Low-reactive (303)   Infants who respond to novelty by showing low levels of motor activity and a general absence of crying and fussing.

Mutually responsive orientation (MRO) (319)   A relationship quality that consists of positive emotions and close cooperative interactions.

Primary emotions (308)   A set of emotions—distress, interest, and pleasure—present at birth and differentiating into other emotions during infancy.

Secondary emotions (309)   A set of emotions—embarrassment, envy, empathy, pride, shame, and guilt—that emerges during the second and third years of life.

Self-conscious emotions (309)   Emotions that involve the comparison of oneself or one's actions to standards and expectations that others hold; also called social emotions.

Self-referential language (321)   An aspect of the self, seen in children's use of their own name, as well as personal pronouns, such as "me" and "mine."

Situational compliance (319)   Children's tendency to require prompting and reminding in order to follow parents' directives and requests.

Social referencing (313)   Attention that is focused on another person in order to gauge his or her emotional and behavioral response to an ambiguous situation.

Still-face paradigm (311)   A procedure for studying emotional communication and regulation by disrupting the normal verbal and nonverbal signals that parents and infants use to communicate.

Temperament (296)   A theoretical construct consisting of constitutionally based individual differences in emotionality, motor activity, attentiveness, adaptability, and self-regulation.

Uninhibited to novelty (303)   A constitutionally based tendency to respond to unfamiliar people and places by showing spontaneous engagement and active interest.

Visual self-recognition (320)   An early aspect of the self, measured by children's understanding that when they look in a mirror, the reflection that they see is their own.

Building Better Babies: Childcare and Early Intervention

Around the world, when women and men become mothers and fathers, whether by giving birth or through adoption, they look forward to spending time caring for their baby and getting to know him or her. In most of Europe and Scandinavia, as well as in

Canada and many other countries, new parents do these things while using a paid leave from their place of employment. Using a combination of paid and unpaid leaves, some working mothers and fathers do not resume full-time employment until their children are 1 or even 2 years old. As a result, families in those countries tend not to use nonparental childcare when their children are still very young.

In the United States, by contrast, one of the most significant and emotional decisions that new parents make concerns who will care for their baby. The majority of Americans believe that parents, especially mothers, should be the primary caregivers (Sylvester, 2001). Alternative arrangements are often needed, however, because mothers of infants in the United States tend to return to work before their children are 1 year old, often by 3 months after birth (Johnson, 2008). According to one survey of 324 new mothers, 83 percent stated a preference for childcare provided by a family member, but most (78 percent) were not able to achieve that type of arrangement (Riley & Glass, 2002). Deciding among feasible childcare options often becomes increasingly urgent as infants near the age of 3 months and mothers reach the end of their maternity leave. Besides the time limits imposed by maternity leave policies, what are the factors that influence new mothers' decisions about whether and when to return to work? How do parents of infants resolve these issues, and how different is their experience from the experience of parents in earlier years?

In this chapter we consider these questions by examining parental leave options in the United States and comparing them to policies available to parents in other parts of the world. Parents who have access to relatively lengthy paid leaves tend to make different decisions about returning to work and using nonparental childcare. Childcare for infants and toddlers has become common in the United States, and there is now evidence from numerous studies of its impact on physical, cognitive, and social and emotional development early in life. These studies provide a useful guide to the hallmarks of high-quality childcare—characteristics that parents should look for when choosing childcare arrangements. Finally, we consider studies of early intervention—a form of childcare that is designed either to compensate for or prevent developmental delays and deficits that may occur as a result of exposure to nonoptimal care-giving and high-risk environments.

CHILDCARE

The age at which children enter nonparental childcare is related to their mother's employment before birth and decisions about whether and when to begin working after birth. Since the 1960s, gains in women's education and delayed childbearing have changed the context in which families make these decisions. Women in the United States are more likely than in the past to work throughout their pregnancy and return to the same job after a brief maternity leave.

Maternal Employment

The need for nonparental childcare in the United States has grown, fueled by steady increases in the rate of participation in the paid labor force by all women, especially mothers of infants younger than 1 year (Downs, 2003). When the Census Bureau began recording labor force participation rates of mothers with infants in 1976, the rate was 31 percent among women who had had a child in the past year; before the economic downturn of 2008–2009, it hovered near 60 percent. Full-time employment (35 or more hours per week) is more common than part-time employment for all mothers of infants except those aged 15 to 19 years, who are more likely to be enrolled in high school (Downs, 2003; Hofferth & Curtin, 2003; Johnson, 2008).

Before we explore the range of possible childcare arrangements, let us compare the types of parental leaves that enable working women—and sometimes men—to take time off from work in the first place. Employees in the United States generally have a different set of options than workers in other countries. Even within the United States, there are differences in the amount of support new parents receive and in the factors that influence their decisions about whether and when to return to work.

Parental Leave Policies

Several types of parental leaves exist in developed, industrialized countries. **Maternity leaves** are job-protected leaves from work for employed women during the weeks after (and sometimes before) childbirth. For fathers, **paternity leaves** are job-protected leaves for employed men and are typically taken after childbirth, albeit for a much shorter time than maternity leaves. **Parental leaves** are job-protected leaves open to mothers or fathers and typically available as a supplement to maternity and paternity leaves; they may extend to cover children until they reach the age of 2 or even 3 years. **Family leaves** enable parents to take job-protected time off from work for a variety of reasons other than the birth of a child. Depending on the country and the employer, these leaves may be paid or unpaid (Kamerman, 2000; OECD, 2009; Ray, 2008).

In the United States, paid maternity leaves were once uncommon but have become more widespread, especially for women with higher levels of education (see Table 11.1). The largest increase in paid maternity leaves occurred between the early 1970s and the early 1980s, years straddling the **Pregnancy Discrimination Act of 1978,** which prohibited employment discrimination on the basis of pregnancy or childbirth (O'Connell, 1990; Smith & Bachu, 1999; Smith, Downs, & O'Connell, 2001). Maternal employment was also supported by changes in federal laws in 1976 that allowed families with dependent children to receive a tax credit for childcare (Johnson, 2008).

POLICIES IN THE UNITED STATES   The most uniform leave policy in the United States is the **Family and Medical Leave Act (FMLA),** which enables public and private workers to take up to 12 weeks of unpaid leave without risking the loss of their job. The law entitles workers to return to their previous job or its equivalent with the same pay, benefits, and other work conditions. It covers mothers or fathers who wish to care for a newborn infant, but any eligible worker can use an FMLA leave to care for a newly adopted child or a foster child, as well as a spouse or parent with a serious health condition. It can also be used by employees to take time off from work due to their own serious health condition or maternity-related disability.

Coverage by the FMLA is not universal. Private employers with fewer than 50 employees working within a 75-mile radius of their worksite are not required to provide FMLA leaves, and workers in eligible businesses must have worked for their employer for at least one year and for

TABLE 11.1   Proportion of Women Taking Paid Maternity Leaves, 1960s—Early 2000s

All Women*	All Women*	All Women*	College Graduates	Less than High School
(1961–1965)	(1986–1990)	(2000–2003)	(2002–2003)	(2002–2003)
16%	43%	49%	63%	22%

*These data are not disaggregated based on education.

Source: Based on information in Johnson, 2008; Smith, Downs, & O'Connell, 2001.

at least 1,250 hours (an average of 25 hours per week) during that year. In the end, approximately 55 percent of the workforce is covered by the FMLA. Those who are ineligible tend to be lower income, part-time workers, and new employees, including single women moving from welfare to work (Asher & Lenhoff, 2001; Kamerman, 2000). Twelve states—California, Connecticut, Hawaii, Maine, Minnesota, New Jersey, New York, Oregon, Rhode Island, Vermont, Washington, and Wisconsin—and the District of Columbia have expanded the FMLA to cover part-time employees or employees in smaller businesses (Asher & Lenhoff, 2001; Ray, 2008; U.S. Department of Labor, 2005).

Before the FMLA was passed in 1993, the majority of employed women did not receive paid maternity leaves, and new parents used other leave time, including paid sick leave, vacation leave, and short-term disability leave (Hofferth et al., 1991; Hofferth & Curtin, 2003). The proportion of women who return to work in the first 24 months after the birth of their child is higher now than before the FMLA. In addition, since 1993, women who take a leave after the birth of a child have been more likely to return to the same employer and working arrangements than was the case before the FMLA existed. These findings suggest that the FMLA has not been detrimental to most eligible employers and may even be associated with greater employee retention.

In 2000, only 17 percent of all employees took a leave for family or medical reasons. Out of those leaves, approximately 8 percent were taken as maternity leave, and 18 percent were used to care for a newborn, newly adopted, or newly placed foster child. Most employees do not use the entire 12-week period allowed; in 2000, the median leave length was only 10 days. The majority of employees who needed a leave but chose not to take it made their decision based on their need for continued income. Unsurprisingly, workers who have access to other forms of paid leave time are more likely to use those options and thus forego the opportunity to take an additional 12 weeks off from work without their usual income (Asher & Lenhoff, 2001; Cantor et al., 2001; Hofferth & Curtin, 2003; Waldfogel, 2001).

Employed women tend to return to work sooner now than they did before the FMLA was enacted. Table 11.2 shows that in the early 1960s, only a small proportion of all mothers with newborns had returned to work by the time their child was 6 months old, and only slightly more had returned by the time their child turned 1 year old. By the early 2000s, by contrast, more than half of new mothers returned to work by the sixth month (Johnson, 2008; Smith et al., 2001). Is the FMLA the reason for these trends? Not necessarily. Most of the available evidence suggests that other factors have played a more significant role.

One factor is the proportion of women who worked during their pregnancy, especially during the last trimester, and thus have prior work settings to which they can return after childbirth. As shown in Table 11.3, in the early 1960s, fewer than half of women worked during their pregnancy and less than one-fourth worked during the month before the birth of

TABLE 11.2 Proportion of Women Returning to Work as a Function of Child Age, 1960s—Early 2000s

1960s		Early 1990s		Early 2000s	
6 months	**1 year**	**6 months**	**1 year**	**6 months**	**1 year**
14%	17%	52%	52%	55%	64%

Source: Based on information in Johnson, 2008; Smith, Downs, & O'Connell, 2001.

TABLE 11.3	Proportion of Women Working During Pregnancy, Early 1960s—Early 2000s				
Early 1960s		**Early 1990s**		**Early 2000s**	
During pregnancy	*Within 1 month of birth*	*During pregnancy*	*Within 1 month of birth*	*During pregnancy*	*Within 1 month of birth*
44%	23%	67%	53%	67%	64%

Source: Based on information in Johnson, 2008; Smith, Downs, & O'Connell, 2001.

their first child. By the early 2000s, two-thirds of women worked during their pregnancy, and almost as many continued working to within 1 month of giving birth (Johnson, 2008; Smith et al., 2001).

Some of the other factors that determine how soon new mothers return to work after childbirth are women's wages, marital status, and family structure. Women with higher incomes tend to return to work sooner than women with lower paying jobs. Women whose spouses have high-paying jobs, however, tend to return less quickly because their own income is less critical to their family's economic well-being. Women with only one child return to work more quickly than women with more children, possibly because the cost of childcare for multiple children would be a greater economic drain on the family. Although single mothers may depend to a greater extent on the income from their jobs, married mothers tend to return to work more quickly than unmarried mothers. The presence of a spouse provides the opportunity for shared parental childcare, and a spouse's income can also help the couple pay for childcare more easily than a single mother's income (Hofferth & Curtin, 2003; Johnson, 2008).

Race and ethnicity are also related to new mothers' return to work. In the early 2000s, white non-Hispanic women (34 percent) were more likely to return to work within three months after the birth of their first child than African American women (26 percent), Hispanic/Latina women (25 percent), and Asian women (21 percent) (Johnson, 2008).

The proportion of women who work during the last month of pregnancy has increased dramatically.

Women's earlier return to work after childbirth may also be related to demographic changes in postsecondary education and the age at which women become first-time mothers. During the second half of the twentieth century, growing numbers of women completed undergraduate degrees (NCES, 2004). Women with higher levels of education, especially women with a college degree, are significantly more likely to return to the same job than mothers with lower levels of education. Education is also related to how quickly mothers return to work. Women with at least a bachelor's degree are more likely to return within three months than women with less than a high school education. A related finding is that older mothers tend to return to work sooner than younger mothers. Women aged 25 years and older at the time their first child was born are more likely to return within three months than women who are younger than 25. The increase in the proportion of first-time mothers who are age 30 or older may thus be another reason that women have tended to return to work earlier in the years since the FMLA was passed (Hofferth & Curtin, 2003; Johnson, 2008; Smith et al., 2001).

As we have seen, the FMLA does not cover all employees in the United States, and many eligible employees choose not to use it, either because they cannot afford to give up their income or because their employers provide them with more attractive paid leave options. The majority of women who work during pregnancy return to work within one year after their child's birth, with most mothers who return to work doing so by the time their child is 6 months old (Smith et al., 2001). These patterns result in large numbers of infants and toddlers in nonparental childcare. Would these trends be different if the FMLA were a paid leave?

In the late 1990s, there was growing interest in and public support for proposals that would strengthen the FMLA in this way (Walker, 1996). A survey of 3,000 adults in the United States found that 88 percent of parents of young children and 80 percent of all adults supported some form of paid parental leave. Forty percent of those surveyed supported a paid leave of three months or less for mothers, 25 percent supported four to 11 months, and almost 33 percent favored one year or more (Sylvester, 2001). Legislatures in several states have considered proposals to offer paid leaves for parents, but as of 2009, only California, Washington, and New Jersey had enacted paid family leave policies (National Partnership for Women & Families, 2009).

The California law, which went into effect in 2004 and was the first enacted, allows workers to take a partially paid family leave for up to six weeks to care for a newborn infant, a newly adopted child, or an ill family member. Employees may receive 55 percent of their usual wages during their absence (with a maximum of $917 per week in 2008) (U.S. Department of Labor, 2005). As of the law's fifth anniversary, fewer than 1 million of the estimated 13 million eligible workers had used it (Woolsey, 2009). It remains to be seen whether California's paid leave policy will result in more parents of newborns taking time off from work and whether it will be significantly better than the original FMLA at supporting working parents so that they can serve as their infants' primary caregivers.

POLICIES IN OTHER COUNTRIES   Women's rates of participation in the labor force in many other countries increased in parallel with rates in the United States; however, using a combination of paid and unpaid leaves, working mothers in many of those countries return to their jobs much later after the birth of a child (Kamerman, 2000). Maternity leave providing at least 50 percent (and sometimes 100 percent) of the mother's regular wages is offered in Austria, Belgium, Bulgaria, Cyprus, the Czech Republic, Denmark, Estonia, Finland, France, Germany, Greece, Hungary, Iceland, Ireland, Italy, Latvia, Lithuania, Luxembourg, the Netherlands, New Zealand, Norway, Poland, Portugal, Romania, the Slovak Republic, Slovenia, Spain, Sweden, Switzerland, Turkey, and the United Kingdom. It is also found in Canada, Israel, Japan, Korea, Malta, and Mexico. The Australian government initiated paid parental leave in 2011, offering mothers and fathers 18 weeks paid at minimum wage and 52 weeks unpaid leave, to be shared equally between the parents (Productivity Commission, 2009). With that action, the United States became the only one of the advanced industrialized countries known as the Organization for Economic Cooperation and Development (OECD) not to offer a paid maternity leave (Kamerman, 2000; OECD, 2001, 2009; Sagi et al., 2002).

New fathers are included in many parental leave policies. About one-third of the OECD countries offer some form of paid paternity leave, varying in length from just two days to three weeks. Parental leaves, which may be taken by either parent, are also available in many of these countries as a supplement to maternity and paternity leaves following the birth or adoption of a child. Parental leaves may provide partial payment but are often unpaid time that can be used until the child is 2 or 3 years old (Deven & Moss, 2002; Kamerman, 2000; O'Brien, 2004; OECD, 2009). Table 11.4 shows examples of parental leave policies in other countries.

Mothers in these countries usually take advantage of the leaves that are available to them, whereas fathers often do not use all of the paid time that they are entitled to take. Even using a portion of potential leave time in Sweden, however, means that fathers are on leave an average of 44 days (Kamerman, 2000).

How do these sorts of parental leave policies affect infants and their families? In Canada, like the United States, a high proportion (60 percent) of mothers with children under the age of 3 years are employed (Statistics Canada, 2003). Following the expansion of the parental leave policy, the median amount of time that Canadian mothers spent caring for their infants at home increased from six months in 2000 to 10 months in 2001. Mothers who used parental leave time but returned to work earlier than nine or 10 months in 2001 frequently had spouses who claimed a portion of paid parental leave as well. This pattern is reflected in a significant increase in the proportion of fathers who used paid parental benefits—3 percent in 2000 as compared with 10 percent in 2001 (Marshall, 2003).

Studies in other countries have found that more generous leaves following childbirth lead to healthier infants and children, as measured by birthweights, infant mortality rates, and rates of breastfeeding (Galtry, 2002; Ruhm, 1998). Policies that help parents remain at home with their infants for six, nine, or 12 months after birth also reduce maternal stress and may contribute to infants' cognitive and language development (Hill et al., 2005; Kamerman, 2000). As we discuss shortly, poor quality childcare places infants at risk. To the extent that parental leaves enable parents to avoid using inferior childcare, they also offer an attractive, direct way to promote infants' development (Kamerman et al., 2003; Lamb & Ahnert, 2006).

Childcare Arrangements

Whether they are working full- or part-time, the most basic choice new parents need to make is whether they want care provided by relatives or nonrelatives of their children. Relatives are defined as mothers, fathers, siblings, grandparents, and other relatives (aunts, uncles, cousins). Caregivers in the nonrelative category are in-home babysitters, neighbors, friends, and others providing care in any setting. Some nonrelatives are family childcare providers who care for one or more unrelated children in the caregiver's home. Other caregivers in the nonrelative category provide care in an organized childcare facility, such as a childcare center, nursery school, or preschool (Lamb & Ahnert, 2006; Mulligan, Brimhall, & West, 2005; U.S. Census Bureau, 2003).

When parents have a choice between two or more childcare settings, their selection may be affected by their beliefs about infants and their development. They may choose a childcare

TABLE 11.4	Examples of Parental Leave Policies in Other Countries
Country	**Parental Leave Policy**
Canada	Paid leave benefits exist for both parents up to one year. Mothers may claim 15–18 weeks of paid leave, and either parent can take up to 35 weeks of paid leave (at 55 percent of regular wages). Paid leave is available to almost all working mothers, including those employed part-time (as little as 12 hours per week).
Israel	Mothers receive three months of paid leave (six weeks of which may be taken before the birth of a child) at 100 percent of regular wages. They have the option of extending their leave with an additional nine months of unpaid maternity leave. Fathers may take parental leave instead of the mother, from the seventh week after the birth; they are also eligible for a parental allowance for a period of up to 42 days. By law, full-time working mothers may work one hour less per day during the four months following completion of maternity leave.
Japan	Mothers may take a 12-week paid leave and receive 60 percent of their usual wages. No paternity leave (paid or unpaid) exists.
Korea	Maternity leaves may last up to 15 weeks, with 100 percent of wages paid. No paternity leave (paid or unpaid) exists.
Norway	Six weeks of maternity leave are required to be taken as part of a paid parental leave that may last until the child is 12 months old. New fathers in Norway may take a 10-week paid leave. The rate of pay for mothers and fathers is 80 percent for 56 weeks or 100 percent for 46 weeks. Both parents are allowed to take an additional 12 months of unpaid parental leave.
Spain	New mothers are eligible for a paid 16-week maternity leave (at 100 percent of wages). Paternity leaves are 15 days long, paid at 100 percent of usual wages. An additional unpaid parental leave is available until children are 3 years old.
Sweden	Fathers may take a two-week paternity leave and receive 70 percent of regular wages. Maternity leave is available before birth only for women who are ill during their pregnancy, but both parents may take a parental leave (paid at 80 percent of usual wages) until their child is 16 months old. Both parents may also apply for an additional 18 months of unpaid parental leave.
United Kingdom	Mothers may take a 52-week leave: the first six weeks are paid at 90 percent of regular wages, pay for the next 20 weeks is determined by a different formula, and the final 26 weeks are unpaid. Fathers may take a leave of two weeks, taken in blocks of one week within eight weeks of the child's birth; the pay rate is up to 90 percent of regular wages.

Source: Based on Ben-Arieh, Zionit, & Krizak, 2003; Kamerman, 2000; Marshall, 2003a & 2003b: National Insurance Institute, 2003; Perusse, 2003; O'Brien, 2004; OECD, 2009; Rahn & Burch, 2002; Ray, 2008.

provider whose caregiving beliefs and practices are congruent with their own beliefs and practices, or they may look for childcare providers who can play a complementary role. Establishing a balance between the primary functions of home and childcare may be some parents' objective, with parental care emphasizing stress reduction and emotional regulation, while providers' care focuses on cognitive stimulation and learning to participate in a group with other children (Ahnert & Lamb, 2003; Lamb & Ahnert, 2006).

For some families, nonparental care may represent an opportunity to expose their children to peers who are likely to be similar in culture and language background. For other parents, nonparental care may be chosen because it provides early childhood education and enrichment, learning opportunities that their children might not otherwise have (Johnson et al., 2003). Parents may also choose a childcare arrangement for pragmatic reasons, such as the cost and convenience (Hofferth, 1991; Kisker & Maynard, 1991).

A survey of 324 working mothers six months after giving birth showed that the majority (53 percent) desired care provided by their child's father, while approximately one-fourth (24 percent) preferred at-home care provided by a relative or friend. Approximately 10 percent stated a preference for care at home provided by a paid sitter or nanny. As shown in Figure 11.1, however, only a small proportion of mothers were successful in arranging their most preferred type of childcare. Besides father-provided care (23 percent), the most commonly used childcare arrangements were **family childcare homes** (28 percent) and out-of-home care by relatives (20 percent), although these arrangements were not the ones that most mothers had preferred. Childcare centers were preferred the least (2 percent) but actually used by about 11 percent of all families in the survey (Riley & Glass, 2002).

The survey also found that a key determinant of whether mothers achieved their most desired childcare arrangements was their employment schedule. Mothers who worked evening or night shifts were more likely than mothers who worked daytime hours to use care by family members. Mothers who worked fewer hours were more likely to use a spouse or in-home sitter, whereas mothers working longer hours tended to use family childcare homes or daycare centers. Families' income per se did not ensure that the preferred childcare arrangement was achieved, but mothers with higher levels of education were more successful in achieving a match between their stated preference and their actual childcare arrangement. It is possible that these women had more flexible employment options or had family members and spouses who were either more willing or more able to participate in providing childcare in order to support mothers' employment. Changes in parental leave policies to reduce the number of hours parents work would be one way to enable more families to care for their own infants and achieve a match between their desired and actual childcare arrangements (Riley & Glass, 2002).

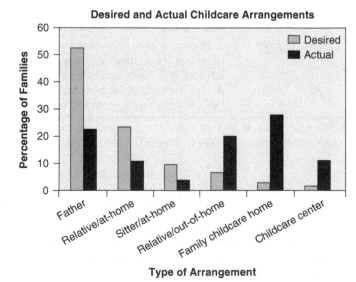

Desired and Actual Childcare Arrangements

FIGURE 11.1 A large percentage of working mothers in one survey reported differences between their desired and actual childcare arrangements. *Source:* Riley & Glass, 2002.

Many infants and toddlers with working parents are cared for by nonrelatives in a family childcare home.

According to the 2001 National Household Education Survey, 60 percent of children under age 5 with working parents are cared for by someone other than a parent. Overall, the most frequently used childcare arrangements are center-based care (33 percent) and care by relatives (22 percent), but mothers with higher levels of education (bachelor's degree or higher) are more likely to use childcare centers than mothers with lower levels of education. Among children under the age of 6 who are not enrolled in school, African American families are the most likely to use nonparental childcare of any type, while Hispanic families are the least likely (Mulligan et al., 2005).

The very youngest children, those under 2 years of age, are more likely to be cared for by relatives than in an organized childcare facility. Children from two-parent households are less likely than children from single-parent households to be cared for by relatives and more likely to be cared for by a parent (Sonenstein et al., 2002). Fathers provide approximately 20 percent of care for infants under the age of 1 year and for 1- to 2-year-old children; in some families with children younger than 2 years, parents arrange nonoverlapping work schedules in order to avoid nonparental care entirely. As shown in Figure 11.2, in 1999, the largest proportions of nonparental care for children younger than 2 years were provided by a grandparent or another relative, whereas nonrelative care, especially in an organized center, was more prevalent for 3- to 4-year-old children. (Lamb & Ahnert, 2006; U.S. Census Bureau, 2003).

One of the reasons many parents choose relative care is that nonparental care, especially high-quality care in an organized childcare setting, can be very expensive (Helburn & Howes, 1996). Childcare costs in the United States vary from state to state, and often differ in rural and urban areas. Full-time care for infants is the most expensive of all, with an average annual cost for infants as high as $15,895 for center care and $10,324 for family childcare homes. Overall, the average family spends more on infant care than on food each year, and in 49 states average childcare fees for two children of any age exceed the average rent cost. Childcare expenses tend to be lower for poor working families and families with lower levels of parental education, but families with fewer resources also spend a higher percentage of their income on childcare (Giannarelli, & Barsimantov, 2000; Mohan, Reef, & Sarkar, 2006; NACCRRA, 2009; Schulman, 2000).

Even when cost is not a primary consideration, parents of infants may wonder whether their infant will receive enough sensitive, responsive care in a childcare center or a family childcare

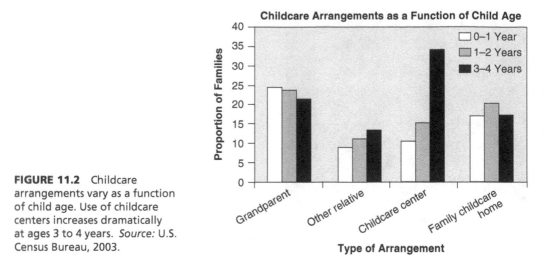

FIGURE 11.2 Childcare arrangements vary as a function of child age. Use of childcare centers increases dramatically at ages 3 to 4 years. *Source:* U.S. Census Bureau, 2003.

home. In our next section, we consider whether these concerns are supported by large-scale studies of early childcare and its effects on infants and toddlers. We also examine the characteristics that parents should look for in any nonparental childcare arrangement, qualities associated with more optimal developmental outcomes.

Effects of Childcare: The NICHD Study of Early Child Care and Youth Development

One of the most comprehensive sources of information about the effects of early childcare on infants and toddlers comes from the National Institute of Child Health and Human Development (NICHD). The **NICHD Study of Early Child Care and Youth Development (SECCYD)** was undertaken in 1991 as a seven-year longitudinal study of nearly 1,400 children in 10 sites across the United States. A team of researchers designed the study, ensuring that multiple methods and measures would be used. Information was gathered about the family environment and the characteristics of childcare arrangements, such as children's age of entry into nonparental care as well as the quantity, stability, quality, and type of care. Each childcare setting was assessed to determine caregivers' education and training, the child-to-adult ratio, and group size. The multiple methods used include observations, interviews, questionnaires, and standardized tests. In addition, rather than focus on just one domain of development, the NICHD Study of Early Child Care gathered information about children's social, emotional, cognitive, and language development, as well as behavior problems and physical health and development (Lamb & Ahnert, 2006; NICHD Early Child Care Research Network, 2005).

THE SAMPLE   To make the findings of the NICHD study as generalizable as possible, a diverse sample of children and families was selected, representing a range of socioeconomic, educational, and racial/ethnic backgrounds in the United States. The resulting sample is 76 percent white non-Hispanic, 13 percent African American, 6 percent Hispanic/Latino, 1 percent Asian/Pacific Islander/Native American, and 4 percent other minorities. Approximately 35 percent of children and families in the sample were living in or near poverty (NICHD Early Child Care Research Network, 2005).

PATTERNS OF CHILDCARE USE   The types of childcare included in the study were those chosen by families themselves and reflected the spectrum of childcare options available. In keeping with patterns of nonparental childcare use that others have reported, a large percentage of infants were cared for by relatives, whereas children older than 2 years were more likely to be in childcare centers (NICHD Early Child Care Research Network, 2005).

During the first year of life, children in the NICHD study spent an average of 33 hours per week in nonparental care. There were racial/ethnic differences in the amount of childcare, however, with African American infants experiencing the most hours and white non-Hispanic infants receiving the fewest. The majority of infants in the sample entered nonparental care before the age of 4 months, with most being cared for by relatives rather than in a family childcare home or a childcare center (NICHD Early Child Care Research Network, 2005).

Mothers with the highest incomes were more likely than other mothers to return to work and place their infants in care by the time they were 3 to 5 months old. These infants were more likely than other infants, however, to be cared for at home for the first 15 months after birth. Parents' own beliefs about the effects of early childcare affected their decisions about the best arrangements for their infants. Mothers who thought their children would benefit from childcare tended to return to work sooner and to use more hours of formal childcare in centers or family childcare homes, whereas mothers who were concerned that employment would harm their infants tended to choose informal family-based or in-home options (NICHD Early Child Care Research Network, 2005).

DEFINING QUALITY CHILDCARE   What should parents who are looking for high-quality childcare look for? Quality of childcare is typically measured by examining two kinds of variables. The first, *process* variables, are evident in the degree to which interactions between caregivers and children are stimulating and nurturing and promote children's development. The second type, *structural* variables, include the physical spaces in which children spend their time, the caregiver-to-child ratio, group size, and the education and experience of the caregivers. Although they are defined and measured separately, in most settings these components of quality are strongly linked—high-quality interactions tend to take place in settings that are safe and in which caregivers are well educated about and experienced in childcare.

Whether process and structural measures are examined separately or in combination, the quality of the average nonparental childcare arrangement has been described by many researchers as poor to mediocre (Helburn & Howes, 1996; Honig, 2002). No one knows with certainty how many young children are in unlicensed care of substandard quality, but one well-known study of 400 childcare centers in four states—the Cost, Quality and Child Outcomes in Child Care Centers (CQO) study—was both illuminating and discouraging. The research team found that only 14 percent of the centers provided interactions and care that were of high enough quality to support children's development, and 12 percent were of such low quality that they did not meet children's basic health and safety needs. Infants and toddlers received care that was rated lowest of all; only 8 percent of infant classrooms were judged to be high quality, and 40 percent were actually considered low quality (Cost, Quality, and Child Outcomes Study Team, 1995; National Center for Early Development and Learning, 1997).

A similar study of more than 200 family childcare homes in three states—the Study of Children in Family Child Care and Relative Care—found that only 9 percent of family childcare homes were providing care that could be considered good, while 56 percent was adequate or custodial, and 35 percent was inadequate (Kontos et al., 1994). Like the CQO study, the Study of Family Child Care and Relative Care also found that the majority of caregivers in both kinds of settings had low levels of formal education and experience in childcare.

To address these problems, early childhood education experts have proposed that federal regulations for childcare in the United States be established in order to ensure that all children have access to high-quality nonparental care (Brauner, Gordic, & Zigler, 2004). In the absence of such uniform, widely known, and enforced criteria, many parents focus on finding an affordable childcare arrangement that will meet their child's basic health and safety needs, while others intentionally look for more expensive options, based on the not-always-valid assumption that high cost is a reliable indicator of program quality (Helburn & Howes, 1996). Regardless of the criteria they use, many parents do not look specifically for childcare that also provides the benefits of high-quality early childhood education—"developmentally-appropriate curricula fostering a child's cognitive, social, and emotional development" (Brauner et al., 2004, p. 3).

Quality of care was a consideration in the NICHD study, which showed that high-quality childcare differed from lower quality care in three key ways: (1) a higher frequency of sensitive, responsive interaction between children and caregivers; (2) more adherence to recommended guidelines for group size, child-to-adult ratios, and aspects of the physical environment; and (3) the presence of caregivers with a higher level of education, specialized training, childcare experience, and more accurate beliefs about child development. Children from the highest and the lowest income levels were more likely than children from near-poverty income levels to experience high-quality childcare. Unlike affluent parents who could afford to pay for high-quality childcare and lower income parents who qualified for subsidized high-quality care, parents living near poverty had considerably fewer economic resources and thus fewer high-quality childcare choices (NICHD Early Child Care Research Network, 2005; Shonkoff & Phillips, 2000).

Some of the characteristics of quality—child-to-adult ratios, group size, teacher training, and teacher education—can be assessed through compliance with relevant state regulations. The NICHD study reported that most childcare centers included in its sample did not possess all four characteristics. The study found, however, that the greater the number of these characteristics present, the more advanced were children's language comprehension and school readiness and the fewer the number of behavior problems at ages 2 and 3 years (Lamb & Ahnert, 2006; NICHD Early Child Care Research Network, 2005).

The National Association for the Education of Young Children (NAEYC) reviews the quality of childcare programs by examining 10 components: child-teacher interactions, curriculum, family-teacher relationships, staff qualifications/professional development, administration, staffing ratios, physical environment, health/safety, nutrition/food service, and program evaluation. Parents looking for high-quality childcare can use NAEYC accreditation as a guide during their search, knowing that accredited programs conform to recommendations for age-appropriate child-to-adult ratios, group sizes, teacher training, and teacher education. In NAEYC-accredited programs, teachers are warm, responsive, supportive, and show respect for individuality. Teachers in NAEYC-endorsed programs are also likely to demonstrate cultural competence as a result of education and training in the areas of culture, language, and diversity. Staff in NAEYC-accredited programs are adults with recognized training and education; they understand early childhood development and are qualified to implement the program's curriculum. In NAEYC-accredited programs, ratios for the number of adults to children differ across age groups (1:4 for 0 to 12 months; 1:4 or 1:5 for 12 to 24 months, depending on total group size; 1:6 for 24 to 30 months; and 1:7 for 30 to 36 months) (NAEYC, 1995, 2002).

In addition to the measures we have already discussed, there are a number of formal systems for rating and evaluating the quality of early childhood environments. Among the most frequently used instruments are the Infant/Toddler Environment Rating Scale (Harms, Cryer, & Clifford, 1990), the Early Childhood Environment Rating Scale (Harms, Clifford, & Cryer, 1998), and the Classroom Practice Inventory (Hyson, Hirsh-Pasek, & Rescorla, 1990). These measures are consistent with

In high-quality childcare, interactions between caregivers and children are stimulating and nurturing and promote children's development. Structural variables, such as the caregiver-to-child ratio, group size, and the caregivers' education and experience, are also important indicators of quality.

NICHD definitions, NAEYC accreditation standards, and other well-known guidelines for developmentally appropriate practices (Bredekamp & Copple, 1997; Lamb & Ahnert, 2006).

Many studies have found that high-quality childcare is linked to more positive developmental outcomes than lower quality childcare. Program quality is affected by characteristics of families and children, however, including parenting skill, child temperament, and developmental disabilities. There is also variability in the age at which children enter nonparental childcare and in the quantity of care they receive each day. As we discuss next, the addition of these kinds of child-and-family variables has led to more complex results, but it also has clarified our understanding of the effects of childcare during the first three years of life.

EFFECTS ON THE INFANT-PARENT RELATIONSHIP   New parents may worry that full-time childcare will negatively affect the infant-parent attachment relationship. The NICHD study provides reassurance for these parents. Childcare per se neither jeopardizes nor promotes security of attachment, as measured by the Strange Situation (NICHD Early Child Care Research Network, 1997a, 1997b, 2005; Shonkoff & Phillips, 2000). Study results do indicate certain combinations of early care that were associated with insecure attachment, however. These combinations included poor quality care for more than 10 hours per week and multiple childcare arrangements during the first 15 months of life, but only when mothers themselves were less sensitive in their interactions with their infants; infants whose mothers were sensitive were significantly more likely to be securely attached, despite having the same childcare arrangements. Conversely, infants whose mothers were less sensitive were less likely to be insecurely attached if they were in high-quality childcare (NICHD Early Child Care Research Network, 2005).

Some infants experience a large number of caregiving arrangements and different caregivers as a result of staff turnover, which occurs in childcare positions at rates that are among the highest of all occupations in the United States (Shonkoff & Phillips, 2000). Even when there is not high turnover, however, most centers follow a practice of advancing children through different classrooms as they get older, leaving their previous caregivers behind. This practice fails to recognize the importance of the attachment relationship that forms between young children and their primary nonparental caregivers (Ahnert, Pinquart, & Lamb, 2006; Howes, 1999; Howes & Shivers, 2006). Alternatively, a small number of childcare centers strive for continuity of caregiver—having infants and toddlers remain with the same primary caregiver(s) during as much of their time in the center as possible (Cryer, Hurwitz, & Wolery, 2003).

There is some evidence from the NICHD study that infants who experience more hours of nonparental care in the first 6 months of life tend to have mothers who are less attentive, less responsive, and less affectionate. Greater amounts of nonparental care at an earlier age was associated with lower levels of positive child-parent interactions at the age of 3 years (Brooks-Gunn, Han, & Waldfogel, 2002). Quality of childcare made a difference, however, apart from the amount of time or age of entry into childcare. Children in high-quality childcare tended to have more positive interactions with nonparental caregivers and also had more positive interactions with their mothers at age 3. Mothers whose children were in high-quality childcare tended to show more sensitivity and positive involvement with their children when they were 15 and 36 months old. In the end, however, family variables, such as income, maternal sensitivity, maternal education, marital status, and maternal depression, had a stronger influence on the quality of mother-child interactions than did children's childcare experience (Lamb & Ahnert, 2006; Love et al., 2003; NICHD Early Child Care Research Network, 2005).

Researchers involved in a different large-scale study of approximately 760 Israeli infants, however, have obtained a different set of results. Investigators involved in the Haifa Study of Early Child Care found that center care per se increased the likelihood that infants in this large urban area would develop insecure attachment to their mothers, as assessed in the Strange Situation. Infants who were in center care beginning at the age of 3 months were significantly more likely to be insecurely attached than infants who were in group care in a family childcare home or in individual care provided by mothers, unpaid relatives, or paid nonrelatives. The highest rates of insecure attachment were found among infants whose mothers showed low levels of sensitivity toward them. The childcare characteristic that appeared to be the principal reason for the elevated incidence of insecure attachment was the higher average infant-to-adult ratio in center care as compared to a family childcare home (8:1 versus 4:1) (Sagi et al., 2002).

According to the researchers, center care in Israel is generally of poor quality, when evaluated according to NAEYC criteria, and there is significantly less variability in the quality of center care than is found in the United States. These findings suggest that, unlike most U.S. parents, Israeli parents have reason to be concerned about the potentially negative effects of center care for infants and to consider other individual or small-group arrangements for their infants when they return to work.

EFFECTS ON SOCIAL DEVELOPMENT   Consistent with evidence about infant-parent attachment, family and maternal characteristics exert a stronger influence than childcare experience per se on children's social behavior, compliance, and self-control. The most influential aspect of childcare experience, as we have already discussed for attachment and infant-parent interaction, is the quality of care provided. Infants in high-quality childcare tend to have emotionally positive, sensitive interactions with caregivers and are, in turn, less likely to have behavior problems at 2 and 3 years of age than are children in poor-quality childcare (NICHD Early Child Care Research Network, 1998; Peisner-Feinberg & Burchinal, 1997; Peisner-Feinberg et al., 2001). It has also been reported that children who spend more time in group care tend to display more cooperative behavior than children who spend less time in child care with peers, especially when providers have more than a high school level of education (Lamb & Ahnert, 2006; Loeb et al., 2004; NICHD Early Child Care Research Network, 2004, 2005).

Not all findings have been positive. Young children in the NICHD SECCYD who experienced multiple nonparental childcare arrangements within a typical week or on a single day, for example, tended to have more behavior problems and lower levels of prosocial behavior at ages 2 and 3 years, with the strongest effects seen among girls and younger children (Morrissey, 2009). A different NICHD SECCYD analysis found that the more time children spent in non-parental care, the more behavior problems and conflicts with adults they had at 54 months of age and in kindergarten. The effects of maternal sensitivity and family socioeconomic status played an even greater role in children's behavior problems during the transition to kindergarten, but children who had experienced a greater amount of any type of nonparental care still showed more social and emotional problems (NICHD Early Child Care Research Network, 2003, 2005). When the NICHD SECCYD sample was studied at the age of 15 years, children who had experienced higher levels of maternal insensitivity and spent more time in childcare centers had lower cortisol levels upon awakening in the morning, a tendency that has been found in other studies of children who experienced stress and adversity early in life (Roisman et al., 2009). The reasons for these patterns are not well understood; it is possible, for example, that individual differences, such as temperament or reactivity of the stress-response system, influence the way that early experience in childcare affects child development (Crockenberg, 2003; DeSchipper et al., 2004; Lamb & Ahnert, 2006).

Children with higher levels of physical, social, and emotional competence are better prepared for school than children who have difficulty controlling their emotions and relating to peers and teachers. According to current views, these skills are just as important as cognitive and academic readiness (Blair, 2002, 2003; Raver, 2002, 2003). On the whole, the NICHD study indicates that high-quality childcare promotes development in all of these domains, but it also appears that the more time children spend in any type of nonparental childcare, the more assertive, aggressive, and disobedient they are in kindergarten. It is unclear, even to many child development experts, how to interpret and respond to these findings. It is possible, for example, that being in childcare and amassing large amounts of experience in it causes children to behave in these ways. It is also possible, however, that parents tend to place certain kinds of children in childcare from an early age. This might occur if shyer, temperamentally inhibited toddlers are less likely to be placed in nonparental care than are more aggressive, temperamentally uninhibited toddlers. Given the nonexperimental design of the NICHD study, it is not possible to rule out either explanation, but the fact that some children with extensive early childcare experience have more behavior problems in kindergarten is a finding that deserves further exploration (Lamb & Ahnert, 2006; NICHD Early Child Care Research Network, 2005).

EFFECTS ON LANGUAGE AND COGNITIVE DEVELOPMENT   As we discussed in Chapter 8, language development is influenced by the family environment and parents' interactions with their children. In high-quality childcare, children receive emotionally positive care from caregivers who frequently engage them in stimulating conversations that support and reinforce early language development (Huttenlocher, 1998). The NICHD study has found that children in high-quality childcare tend to have better developed language abilities than children in poor-quality care at 15, 24, and 36 months, as well as more advanced cognitive abilities at 24 and 54 months (Burchinal et al., 2000; NICHD Early Child Care Research Network, 2000, 2005; NICHD Early Child Care Research Network & Duncan, 2003).

By 36 months, children who have been in higher quality childcare also tend to show higher levels of school readiness—skills and knowledge that help children do well in school, such as identification of colors, letters, and numbers, as well as counting ability, shape recognition, and the ability to make comparisons (NICHD Early Child Care Research Network, 2005; Peisner-Feinberg & Burchinal, 1997; Peisner-Feinberg et al., 2001). The association between school readiness and language abilities at age 36 months is stronger for children with moderate amounts of childcare (e.g., 10–30 hours/week), however, than for children with higher amounts (e.g., 30–40+ hours/week). These findings suggest that children with moderate amounts of high-quality nonparental care benefit from the combination of a stimulating childcare environment and adequate time to interact with and learn from parents in the home; when those parent-child interactions are of a high quality, they also contribute to children cognitive and linguistic gains (Adi-Japha & Klein, 2009).

Positive effects of high-quality, center-based care on cognitive growth and school readiness have also been found for low-income children whose mothers were enrolled in welfare-to-work programs (Loeb et al., 2004; Votruba-Drzal, Coley, & Chase-Lansdale, 2004). In fact, high-quality care has an even more profound positive impact on math and reading achievement in middle childhood (through 11 years of age) for children from lower-income families than it does on children from families with more socioeconomic resources (Brooks-Gunn, 2003; Dearing, McCartney, & Taylor, 2009; Fuller et al., 2002; Lamb & Ahnert, 2006; NICHD Early Child Care Research Network, 2005).

One study using data from the NICHD study found that children whose mothers worked typical daytime hours had higher cognitive test scores at 15, 24, and 36 months than children whose mothers had ever worked nonstandard hours, such as night shifts or jobs with variable schedules (Brooks-Gunn et al., 2002). This finding is consistent with other research suggesting that long hours of maternal employment in the first year of life may interfere with the time that parents can spend interacting with their infants and stimulating their cognitive and language development (Kamerman et al., 2003). The most negative effects were found when children were placed in lower quality childcare after their mothers began working 30 hours or more per week at 6 to 9 months. These negative effects were amplified among children whose mothers were rated as providing less sensitive care for their infants at 36 months (Brooks-Gunn et al., 2002).

Overall, it appears that early nonparental care is not in itself associated with negative child outcomes. Instead, characteristics of the family, including maternal sensitivity, appear to exert the predominant influence on early development. Nonparental childcare can have negative effects on children when the quality is low, and the most harmful situation involves the combination of maternal insensitivity with low-quality nonparental childcare. High-quality care is expensive, however, and not universally available. For one group of parents—those whose infants and toddlers have special needs—affordable, high-quality care is especially hard to secure (Kelly & Booth, 1999; Shonkoff & Phillips, 2000).

Including Children with Disabilities in Childcare

Children with disabilities or special needs have or are at risk for chronic physical, developmental, behavioral, or emotional conditions and typically need developmental, health, mental health, and related services that extend beyond those generally required by children (Child Care Law Center, 2003). Developmental disabilities may include autism spectrum disorders, cerebral palsy, hearing loss, cognitive disability, Down syndrome, spina bifida, and vision impairment (Centers for Disease Control & Prevention, 2005a).

Compared with mothers of typically developing children, mothers of children with disabilities tend to have more difficulty finding appropriate, affordable childcare and often return to work later after their children's birth. They also are more likely to work part-time and to choose individual care by a relative instead of group care in a family childcare home or childcare center (Kelly & Booth, 1999; Montes & Halterman, 2008). The greatest challenge in finding care for

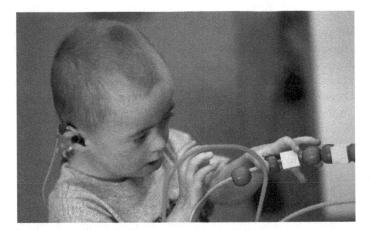

This boy has developmental disabilities, but he attends a childcare center with children who are not disabled and is included in all center activities.

infants and young children with disabilities is often the availability of childcare providers who are trained to work with children with special needs (Wolery & Odom, 2000). Federal legislation enacted since 1990 has led to the expansion of training and graduate programs in early childhood special education.

In 1990, the **Americans with Disabilities Act (ADA)** was passed to protect the civil rights of all individuals with disabilities. The ADA states that children cannot be excluded from services, such as childcare centers, private preschools, and other early childhood programs, because of their disability. Children with disabilities are also covered by the federal **Individuals with Disabilities Education Act (IDEA),** reauthorized in 2004. The final IDEA regulations specify two separate sections, Part B for children and youth ages 3 to 21 years and Part C, which explicitly covers services provided from birth to 2 years of age. In addition to other differences, this configuration reflects the possibility that some 3-year-old children may enter the public school system by participating in publicly funded early childhood programs, including pre-kindergarten, which we discuss later. Parts B and C both state that, to the greatest extent appropriate, children with disabilities must be included with peers who are not disabled, in the least restrictive environment possible (U.S. Department of Education, 2006).

Under the provisions of IDEA, children with disabilities in physical, cognitive, communication, or socioemotional development may qualify for **Early Intervention Services (EIS)** that include screening and assessment, family education and training, home visits, health and social services, speech-language therapy, and occupational and physical therapy, as well as assistive technology. Children and their families receive an Individualized Family Service Plan (IFSP) that describes services, providers, locations, and Individualized Education Plan (IEP) goals—a written statement of the child's present level of achievement and functioning, measurable annual goals, and a description of the education and services that will be provided to the child. In keeping with the concept of inclusion, services involve the family and are provided in the child's natural home and community environment (National Child Care Information Center, 1999).

Despite the progress that has been made in legislating more inclusive policies for children with disabilities, parents of children with special needs still face many challenges, in part because the supply of care for infants and young children with disabilities is still not adequate to meet the demand. In addition, although families living below the poverty level tend to have a higher percentage of children with disabilities or special needs, lower income neighborhoods tend to have fewer childcare options for children with special needs than higher income neighborhoods (NACCRRA, 2003; Shonkoff & Phillips, 2000).

Finally, within the childcare setting or preschool classroom, different models are used to achieve inclusion, resulting in varying degrees of coordination and collaboration among childcare providers and early childhood teachers. In some settings, there is little interaction and coordination, and an external consultant takes one or more children with special needs to a separate area of the classroom or even outside of the regular classroom to work with them on IFSP and IEP goals that may or may not coincide with the activities of the rest of the children in the class. In other cases, the preschool classroom teacher or childcare provider collaborates with and coordinates the efforts of a team of specialists who work with the child at different times during the day. A third approach, less commonly used but growing in popularity, employs a co-teaching model with significant classroom roles for both the early childhood teacher and an early childhood special education teacher (Wolery & Odom, 2000). The available evidence suggests that higher quality care is associated with more advanced development and optimal functioning for young children with disabilities, just as it is for typically developing infants and toddlers, but there is still much to be learned about the relative effectiveness of different models of care and early childhood special education (Booth & Kelly, 1998, 1999; Kelly & Booth, 1999).

Nearly all studies of early childcare have used nonexperimental designs. That is, mothers in the samples have not been randomly assigned to employment versus nonemployment, and type of childcare and its quality have not been controlled by researchers. It is likely, therefore, that preexisting differences in family characteristics, including income, education levels, and maternal sensitivity, lead parents to choose different childcare arrangements in the first place and contribute to different outcomes across childcare settings. Even with this caveat, however, the findings of the NICHD SECCYD and other research on the impact of high- versus low-quality early childcare are generally consistent with the results of studies using experimental designs to evaluate the effects of early interventions, which we discuss next.

EARLY INTERVENTION

The concept of **early intervention (EI)** is difficult to define succinctly because it encompasses a wide range of programs and philosophies. In some approaches, the goal is prevention of negative outcomes for children considered to be at risk due to family income, parent characteristics, birth experiences, or aspects of the environment, such as the intervention in Russian Baby Homes that we discussed in Chapter 9. In other interventions, the goal is the amelioration of existing identified conditions, such as developmental disabilities or developmental delays.

Some interventions focus on a specific developmental domain and objective, such as enhancing the quality of mother-infant interactions (Wendland-Carro et al., 1999), increasing young children's awareness of nutrition and disease prevention (Williams et al., 1998), or promoting reading and emergent literacy in low-income preschoolers (Weitzman et al., 2004; Whitehurst et al., 1994). Many comprehensive large-scale interventions, including several studies that we discuss shortly, address multiple developmental outcomes.

Intervention programs may involve direct interaction only with the target child or they may include parents and other family members, either in the home or in controlled childcare settings. The timing for initiating interventions is another dimension that varies; some programs begin while the mother is still pregnant, whereas others do not start until after the child is born (Cicchetti & Toth, 2006; Korfmacher, 2002; Lamb & Ahnert, 2006; Powell, 2006; Ramey et al., 2006).

Poverty as a Risk Factor: Implications for Prevention and Intervention

With the notion of prevention rather than intervention in mind, some early childhood experts have asserted that eligibility for IDEA services should be expanded from existing, diagnosed physical or mental conditions to include "family conditions that have a high probability of resulting in a developmental delay, such as significant parental mental illness (particularly maternal depression), parental substance abuse, and significant family violence" (NACCRRA, 2003). If eligibility were expanded in these ways, growing up in an environment of poverty could also be added to the list of risk factors for developmental disabilities and delays because it exerts significant stress on families. The poverty threshold in the United States varies according to region, household size, and composition; in 2008, it corresponded to an annual income of approximately $22,000 for a family of four (DeNavas-Walt, Proctor, & Smith, 2009).

In 2008, 21 percent of children under the age of 6 were living in poverty, a figure that is significantly higher than for 18- to 64-year-olds (12 percent) and those 65 years and older (10 percent). Poverty rates vary as a function of family structure; 54 percent of children under 6 living with an unmarried female adult lived in poverty in 2008, as compared with 11 percent of children living in married-couple families. Poverty rates were higher among African American and nonwhite Hispanic children than among Asian and white Hispanic children (DeNavas-Walt et al., 2009; Proctor & Dalaker, 2003).

Children living in poverty are more likely than children from higher income families to be exposed to family violence, chaos, and instability, and to live in more dangerous, polluted, and deteriorating neighborhoods with less access to healthcare. Children living in poverty are also more likely to attend less cognitively stimulating, lower quality childcare programs and schools and to have more limited access to books and computers (Evans, 2004; Federal Interagency Forum on Child and Family Statistics, 2009).

Rates of food insecurity (uncertain access to a healthy quantity and variety of food) are higher among children living in poverty than among children whose families have more resources. The home environments of children living in poverty are often different in other ways, too, as shown in studies using the **Home Observation for Measurement of the Environment (HOME),**

Growing up in poverty, especially in an environment of violence, chaos, and instability, exerts stress on families that increases children's risk of developmental delays and disabilities. Children exposed to risks due to earlier and more sustained poverty tend to have lower levels of cognitive and language development than children with briefer exposure.

a well-known tool that uses a combination of observer ratings and parental self-reports to assess the quality of a child's home environment (Caldwell & Bradley, 1984). From birth to 3 years of age, parents living in poverty are less likely than parents not living in poverty to speak to their children, respond to their children's speech, show affection to their children, keep their children in view where they can see them, and provide toys or interesting activities for them. They are more likely than parents not living in poverty to slap or spank their children, to interfere with or restrict their children from exploring, and less likely to provide a safe play environment (Bradley et al., 2001). Children exposed to cumulative risks at home and in other settings through early and sustained poverty tend to have significantly lower levels of cognitive and language development as well as higher levels of antisocial behavior than children who experience poverty more briefly (Bradley & Corwyn, 2002; Brooks-Gunn & Duncan, 1997; McLoyd, Aikens, & Burton, 2006).

Are these negative outcomes inevitable? Perhaps not, according to a study that compared more than 1,000 pairs of 5-year-old monozygotic (identical) and dizygotic (fraternal) twins in England and Wales, all of whom experienced significant socioeconomic deprivation. Some children had more positive outcomes than others and the effects of living in poverty varied as a function of both intrinsic child characteristics and caregiving experience. At least one child characteristic—temperament—appeared to buffer the effects of poverty, possibly because children with more sociable and outgoing temperaments elicited more cognitively stimulating interactions from child-care providers, exchanges that contributed to more positive cognitive, language, and behavioral outcomes. Caregiving experience in the family also played a role, however, and children whose mothers showed higher levels of warmth and engaged their children in stimulating activities appeared to promote positive adjustment, even in the face of socioeconomic deprivation (Kim-Cohen et al., 2004). These findings suggest that "if poor families are provided with the means to engage in stimulating activities with their young children, it may be possible to counteract some of the negative effects that living in a socioeconomically impoverished environment has on children's intellectual development" (Kim-Cohen et al., 2004, p. 662).

In addition to the positive influence of child temperament and parental involvement, child outcomes are enhanced when lower income parents are provided with economic resources, including direct income supplements (McLoyd, 1998, 2005; McLoyd et al., 2006). Public policies, however, such as the Personal Responsibility and Work Opportunity Reconciliation Act of 1996 and Temporary Assistance to Needy Families, require low-income mothers of infants and toddlers to leave home and enter the paid labor force, and there is relatively little support in the United States for providing parents with income supplements per se (Shonkoff & Phillips, 2000). As a result, most early interventions directly involve infants, toddlers, and their parents in behavioral and educational programs.

Early Intervention Through Childcare and Preschool

The strongest conclusions about the impact of early intervention can be made when children are randomly assigned to intervention and control groups, ensuring that there are no preexisting differences between groups at the beginning of the intervention. We look now at several of the most frequently cited studies in the early childhood intervention literature.

THE HIGH/SCOPE PERRY PRESCHOOL PROJECT   The Perry Preschool in Ypsilanti, Michigan, was the setting for an often-cited intervention project, the **High/Scope Perry Preschool Project,** carried out in the early 1960s. The target group—approximately 100 low-income African American 3- and 4-year-old children—received 2 hours of high-quality early childhood education each morning and 1 hour of home visits each afternoon. Participants were studied longitudinally and compared with a control group of similar children who did not participate in the 30-week preschool program. Initially, there were gains in measured IQ for the intervention group, but these differences diminished within a few years of participation in the program. Other long-lasting advantages for the intervention group were reported, however, including a lower likelihood of being placed in special education in elementary school, higher achievement test scores at age 14, higher rates of graduation from high school, higher earned incomes at age 27, and lower rates of juvenile delinquency and crime (Schweinhart, 2009; Schweinhart et al., 1993; Weikart, 1998).

THE ABECEDARIAN PROJECT AND PROJECT CARE   Long-term gains have also been reported in follow-up studies of participants in the **Abecedarian Project,** a study begun in 1972. In this study, approximately 100 low-income, primarily African American children were randomly selected to participate in a full-time, high-quality early childhood education program from the age of 6 weeks until 3 years. Periodic cognitive testing carried out between the ages of 3 and 21 years indicated that children who received the intervention had higher scores than a control group on cognitive and achievement tests, with differences found through age 21. Children in the intervention group also had lower rates of referral for special education and were less likely to repeat a grade, less likely to become adolescent parents, and more likely to complete high school (Campbell et al., 2001, 2002; Ramey & Ramey, 1998a, 1998b; Ramey et al., 2006). Similar results were found in a subsequent intervention, **Project CARE,** which began in 1978 and combined early childcare in a child development center, parent group meetings, and home visiting (Wasik et al., 1990).

THE INFANT HEALTH AND DEVELOPMENT PROJECT   In a more recent intervention using a larger sample, the **Infant Health and Development Project,** researchers conducted a longitudinal study of nearly 1,000 preterm, low-birthweight infants (Gross, Spiker, & Haynes, 1997; McCarton et al., 1997). All children participating in the project received healthcare and other community services, but one-third of the sample (the intervention group) was randomly selected to have home visits and to participate in full-day, high-quality childcare in child development centers from birth to age 3. Parents of this subsample also participated in a parent education component. At age 3, children who had participated in the intervention had higher measured intelligence, better vocabulary development, and fewer behavioral problems than children who were not part of the intervention. These gains were not sustained indefinitely, however. By age 8, the intervention group and the comparison group were no longer significantly different (Berlin et al., 1998; Gross et al., 1997).

THE CHICAGO LONGITUDINAL STUDY   The **Chicago Longitudinal Study (CLS)** is a federally funded investigation begun in 1986 to document the effects of early and extensive childhood intervention from ages 3 to 9 years (preschool to third grade) in an urban low-income, primarily African American sample of children and families. The intervention sample—approximately 1,000 children who attended or received services from 20 Child-Parent Centers—was compared with nearly 400 children who participated in an alternative all-day kindergarten program in five randomly selected Chicago public schools. The CLS used multiple sources of data, including teacher surveys, child surveys and interviews, parent surveys and interviews, school administrative records, standardized tests, and classroom observations. CLS parents' involvement in their children's education was enhanced through Child-Parent Centers, and benefits for child participants included higher levels of school achievement into adolescence, lower rates of grade retention and special education, lower rates of early school dropout, and lower rates of delinquent behavior (Reynolds,

2000, 2009). Follow-up studies of CLS participants have documented long-term positive educational and social outcomes, as well as cost-benefit analyses, through age 26 (Reynolds, Temple, & Ou, in press; Reynolds et al., in press).

Early Head Start

In 1994, the Administration on Children, Youth and Families (ACF) established **Early Head Start (EHS),** a national intervention program to provide services to low-income pregnant women and families with infants and toddlers. In addition to targeting children and families who meet income eligibility requirements, Early Head Start is guided by a policy of inclusion requiring that at least 10 percent of its programs are made available to children with disabilities, regardless of family income. Early Head Start services may be delivered in center-based or home-based settings, or a combination of these settings, and include quality early childhood education, parenting education, health and mental healthcare, nutrition education, and family support. The program has grown to over 700 programs serving more than 70,000 children and families across the United States (ACF, 2005; Kamerman et al., 2003; Powell, 2006).

From the beginning, Early Head Start was intended to be evaluated using a random-assignment design. The Early Head Start Research and Evaluation Project focused on 17 sites and studied 3,000 children and families, half of whom participated in Early Head Start and half of whom were randomly assigned to a control group. An array of assessments of cognitive, language, and social-emotional development were carried out when children were 14, 24, and 36 months old, and families were interviewed periodically about their use of services.

Benefits were found for both home- and center-based services, but the strongest effects were found for programs combining center-based care with home visits. Quality in Early Head Start centers was consistently high, as evaluated by NAEYC criteria. At 14 and 24 months of age, children in Early Head Start were three times more likely to receive their primary nonparental care in a good quality center than children in the control group (ACF, 2003a). As a result, children who participated in Early Head Start during its first three years had better outcomes on multiple measures at age 3 than children in the control group. In keeping with other studies of the impact of quality childcare on low-income children, more time in center care led to higher levels of cognitive development at 24 and 36 months and higher levels of language development at 36 months. Participation in Early Head Start also contributed to more involved object play and fewer negative interactions with parents (ACF, 2002; Love et al., 2002).

Children participating in Early Head Start were less likely than control group children to experience delays in cognitive and language functioning, but Early Head Start children with disabilities were more likely to receive screening and referral for Part C IDEA services than were control group children. Families of Early Head Start children with disabilities were more likely than other Early Head Start families to be highly involved in the program and to remain in the program longer than other families. This pattern may reflect the parent education and parent support groups that were provided in Early Head Start, as well as specialized training that many Early Head Start staff received to help them identify children who would benefit from a referral for Part C IDEA services. Not all families benefited to the same degree, however; many children in Hispanic/Latino families and children of teen mothers, as well as of children of parents with multiple demographic risk factors (e.g., lower levels of education) had lower functioning in cognitive and language development. These families were more likely than other Early Head Start families to be unaware of their children's disabilities, and their children were the least likely to receive Part C services, suggesting that different approaches may need to be used to help them understand the importance of early identification and intervention (ACF, 2003b).

Benefits were also found for parents who had received Early Head Start services; compared with parents of children in the control group, they were more emotionally supportive and less detached toward their children as well as more likely to report reading to their children every day. Early Head Start parents reported using fewer punitive discipline strategies and were less likely than control group parents to report spanking their children in the previous week. Parents in the Early Head Start group were also more likely to participate in education and job training activities and to be employed than were parents in the control group (Love et al., 2002, 2005; Powell, 2006).

Despite many positive outcomes, federal funding for EHS allows the program to reach only 3 percent of all eligible children, leaving states to develop local logistical and budgetary strategies to expand EHS (Peterson, Jones, & McGinley, 2008; Schumacher & DeLauro, 2008). As we discuss next, as additional initiatives are contemplated, researchers as well as members of the public are interested in knowing whether the funds spent on early intervention programs are a good investment (Cooper, 2008).

Measuring the Impact of Early Childhood Intervention

Does early intervention make a difference? A review of 38 studies of early childhood intervention and education programs, all of which provided high-quality, center-based early childhood education and family-oriented services, concluded that there are often lasting effects on achievement and academic success but few direct and lasting effects on measures of IQ per se (Barnett, 1998, 2009). A different review of early intervention programs came to similar conclusions, noting that positive effects of these programs are especially pronounced for lower income children whose parents have lower levels of education. Programs that do not continue as children make the transition to school, however, have relatively limited long-term effects, especially if children continue to live in lower income neighborhoods and attend poor-quality schools (Brooks-Gunn, 2003; McLoyd et al., 2006; Ramey et al., 2006). Finally, based on their review of the research literature, the primary investigators in the Abecedarian Project identified six principles (shown in Table 11.5) that underlie most successful interventions in early childhood, including Early Head Start and its predecessor Head Start (Ramey & Ramey, 1998b).

Even given these findings, some scholars, as well as policy makers and the general public, have asked whether the cost of interventions in infancy and early childhood is justified by the results. Funding provided for Head Start in 1999, for example, was $4.66 billion, but it is unclear whether this was too much or not enough (Shonkoff & Phillips, 2000). The cost of high-quality early intervention programs that incorporate the principles enumerated in Table 11.5 can surpass $8,000 to $10,000 per child annually. One year of the High/Scope Perry Preschool Project, for example, cost approximately $15,000 per child in 1998 dollars, making the total cost for the 100 participants in the Perry Preschool Project more than $1 million (Barnett, 1998; Shonkoff & Phillips, 2000). If this type of program were provided for tens of thousands of children and their families, how would we know whether the funds were invested wisely?

A relatively new perspective on this question has been provided through cost-benefit analyses of the High/Scope Perry Preschool Project. By comparing the costs of delivering the program with the value of the program to society as a whole, to taxpayers, and to program participants themselves, these analyses indicate that for every dollar of public funds invested in the intervention, there was a return to the public and participants of $8.74 (Schweinhart et al., 1993). This rate of return reflects savings that accrued, for example, because K-12 education could be provided more efficiently for program participants and with less need for special education or grade retention. There were also savings from the lower incidence of unemployment, welfare use, and criminal behavior by program participants (Barnett, 1998, 2009; Ramey et al., 2006; Shonkoff & Phillips, 2000).

TABLE 11.5	Principles of Successful Early Childhood Interventions
Principle	**Implications**
Developmental Timing	Interventions that begin earlier in development and are of longer duration tend to have larger effects than interventions that are briefer and begin later.
Program Intensity	Interventions that include more contact hours are most effective and families who participate most actively tend to receive the greatest benefits.
Direct Experience	Children who receive direct educational interventions have more positive and longer lasting outcomes than children who must wait to receive quality care until their parents have completed training and education interventions.
Program Breadth and Flexibility	Interventions that employ more services and multiple approaches have larger effects than narrower interventions.
Individual Differences	Some children and families experience greater benefits than other children and families, even when they are participants in the same intervention.
Ecological Dominion and Environmental Maintenance of Development	Positive early experiences must be reinforced with subsequent positive experiences and nurturing environments if early gains are to be maintained.

Source: Based on Ramey & Ramey, 1998b.

Two Federal Reserve economists performed a different analysis on the Perry Preschool data and concluded that the rate of return directly to the public was actually closer to 12 percent. They note that, not only is this a significantly higher rate than is usually expected from other public expenditures, such as new sports stadiums, but unlike sports stadiums, early childhood interventions can also reduce crime, increase earnings, and potentially break a chain of poverty (Rolnick & Grunewald, 2003). These and similar analyses, such as those calculating the return on investment for individual components of early interventions, raise thought-provoking questions about public funding for early childhood programs (Reynolds, Temple, & White, 2009).

Although there is mixed evidence about efficacy, some experts support a different model involving home visitation programs that combine healthcare, parenting education, child abuse prevention, and early intervention services (Astuto & Allen, 2009). Researchers as well as policy makers favor making evidence-based decisions about funding for early interventions, but many questions remain about the range of approaches and the contexts in which they are likely to have the greatest impact (McCall, 2009).

Pre-Kindergarten and Early Childhood Education

What does the future hold? A majority of states (38 as of 2002) have established and funded **pre-kindergarten (PK) programs**—programs or classes for 3- and 4-year-olds, housed in public schools, with a primary focus on enhancing disadvantaged children's school readiness (Pianta & Rimm-Kaufmann, 2006; Smith et al., 2003). In six states—Florida, Georgia, Massachusetts, New York, Oklahoma, and West Virginia—PK is more universally available, and all parents may choose to enroll their 4-year-old children. Education and training requirements for PK teachers vary across these states, however, as do family and school district participation rates.

An evaluation of Oklahoma's universal PK program, established in 1998, showed that families and school districts participate at high rates. Focusing on the PK program in the city of Tulsa, the researchers found that the PK student body was socioeconomically and racially/ethnically diverse. Even more importantly, the evaluation showed that all children benefited from PK attendance, especially in pre-reading skills, such as the identification of letters and words. Small gains were also reported for prewriting and spelling skills, as well as early math reasoning and problem-solving abilities (Gormley et al., 2005).

The evaluation does not demonstrate whether the Tulsa PK program—or other programs with a similar academic emphasis—is more beneficial than programs such as Early Head Start or its preschool counterpart Head Start (Henry, Gordon, & Rickman, 2006). Nor does it specifically address the longstanding debate among early childhood experts about the proportions of structured academic content and exploratory play that are appropriate for 3- and 4-year-old children (Pellegrini, 2009).

It is unclear how many other states will follow those that have already committed funds to PK readiness and whether universal PK will become coordinated at the national level. It is also unclear whether PK curricula will evolve to give greater attention to other dimensions of school readiness, such as self-regulation and social competence. Unlike other countries with PK programs, the United States does not have a unified approach or commitment, and more research is needed in several key areas: (1) understanding how to develop programs that will meet the needs of the growing population of immigrant children, Hispanic children, and other children who do not speak English as their first language; (2) understanding the ways in which child-teacher interactions and peer relationships are related to program outcomes; and (3) identifying a broad range of appropriate developmental outcomes (Farver, Lonigan, & Eppe, 2009; Garcia, 2009; Mashburn et al., 2009; Takanishi & Bogard, 2007).

There are still many things we do not know, but it is clear that a systems approach, such as the bioecological model articulated by Bronfenbrenner, is a valuable perspective for investigating the ways in which individuals are affected by, and have an effect on, a complex network of people and contexts (Bronfenbrenner & Morris, 1998; Foster & Kalil, 2005; Huston, 2005; Mashburn et al., 2009; Ramey et al., 2006). While the complexity of the model helps us consider multiple influences and measures, it reminds us, at the same time, that the task of connecting developmental science to public policy and applications in the field is not a simple one.

WRAPPING IT UP: Summary and Conclusion

Significant societal changes have occurred since the 1960s, with consequences for infants, toddlers, and families. An enormous childcare industry has developed and mushroomed to meet the demands created by increasing numbers of women with infants and toddlers participating in the paid labor force. Longitudinal studies, especially the NICHD SECCYD, have shown that early nonparental care is not the source of negative child outcomes per se. Quality of care makes a difference, however, and interacts with characteristics of the family, such as maternal sensitivity. Quality of childcare is measured by examining process variables and structural characteristics.

There is irrefutable evidence of the harm that children under the age of 3 years sustain when they experience poverty and deprivation, particularly when it is chronic. Infants and toddlers are resilient, however, and can benefit, as can their parents, from focused, intensive early interventions. The complexity and diversity of bioecological systems means that a one-size-fits-all approach is unlikely to succeed across all contexts.

THINK ABOUT IT: Questions for Reading and Discussion

1. Do you think that the United States will ever offer paid parental leaves for all parents? Why or why not? What are the pros and cons of paid leave policies for children as well as parents and society?

2. Is childcare good or bad for infants and toddlers? How do you know?

3. Have you had any direct experience in a childcare setting, either a family childcare home or a childcare center? If so, how would you evaluate the quality of the program and the care that children received in it?

4. If you could design the optimal intervention for infants and toddlers, what would you include in it and how would you measure the results?

5. What would be gained by legislating universal pre-K education that began before the age of 3 years? What would be the objections to this sort of nationwide initiative?

6. If you were able to shape the future simply by writing a chronology of childhood and child development for the next 25 years, what sorts of entries would you include and why? Do you think that those events will actually occur? Explain.

Key Words

Abecedarian Project (347)   An intervention in which approximately 100 low-income, primarily African American children participated in a full-time, high-quality early childhood program from the age of 6 weeks until 3 years.

Americans with Disabilities Act (ADA) (343) The federal civil rights act protecting individuals with disabilities.

Chicago Longitudinal Study (CLS) (347) A federally funded investigation begun in 1986 to document the effects of early and extensive childhood intervention in an urban low-income, primarily African American sample of children and families.

Early Head Start (EHS) (348)   A national intervention program that provides services to low-income pregnant women and families with infants and toddlers.

Early intervention (EI) (344)   Systematic efforts to either prevent or reduce the adverse developmental effects of family income, parent characteristics, birth experiences, or aspects of the environment. The strongest conclusions can be made when children are randomly assigned to intervention and control groups.

Early Intervention Services (EIS) (343)   Services provided through IDEA, including screening and assessment, family education and training, home visits, health and social services,

speech-language therapy, and occupational and physical therapy, as well as assistive technology.

Family childcare home (334)   Care that is provided for one or more unrelated children in the caregiver's home.

Family leave (328)   Job-protected time off from work for a variety of reasons other than the birth of a child.

Family and Medical Leave Act (FMLA) (328) The federal policy that allows certain categories of employees to take a 12-week, job-protected leave to care for a child, spouse, or parent or to take time off due to their own serious health condition.

High/Scope Perry Preschool Project (346) An intervention in which approximately 100 low-income African American preschoolers received high-quality early childhood education and home visits.

Home Observation for Measurement of the Environment (HOME) (345)   A tool for assessing the quality of a child's home environment, using a combination of observer rating and mother's reports.

Individuals with Disabilities Education Act (IDEA) (343)   The federal civil rights act covering children with disabilities; Part C explicitly covers services from birth to 24 months of age.

Infant Health and Development Project (347)
An intervention involving nearly 1,000 preterm, low birthweight infants, with one-third of the sample randomly selected to have home visits and to participate in full-day, high-quality childcare in child development centers from birth to age 3.

Maternity leave (328)   A job-protected leave from work for employed women during, and some times before, childbirth.

NICHD Study of Early Child Care and Youth Development (SECCYD) (336)   A longitudinal, multimethod and multimeasure study of approximately 1,400 children in childcare settings across the United States.

Parental leave (328)   A job-protected leave that is open to mothers or fathers, typically available as a supplement to maternity and paternity leaves.

Paternity leave (328)   A job-protected leave from work for employed men, typically taken after childbirth.

Pregnancy Discrimination Act of 1978 (328)
The federal act, passed in 1978, to prohibit employment discrimination on the basis of pregnancy or childbirth.

Pre-kindergarten (PK) Programs (350)
Programs or classes for 3- and 4-year-olds, housed in public schools, with a primary focus on enhancing disadvantaged children's school readiness.

Project CARE (347)   An intervention similar to the Abecedarian Project, in which low-income children participated in a full-time, high-quality early childhood program, supplemented with parent group meetings and home visiting.

12

Babies of Today and Tomorrow: Music, Media, and Computers

Our last chapter focuses on three prevalent influences in the lives of infants and toddlers today—music, media, and computers. Only one of these influences, music, is found on the list of Ten Things Every Child Needs, which we discussed briefly in Chapter 9 (Robert R. McCormick Foundation, 1997). As we review current studies and practices in this chapter, consider whether you think that the two other influences, media and computers, *should* be added to this list.

Listening to music is part of a typical day for most (81 percent) children younger than 2 years (Rideout, Vandewater, & Wartella, 2003). If there were a Toddler

Top 20, which songs would be on it? According to one informal survey of parents and caregivers, the song at the very top would be "The Itsy Bitsy Spider," while others making the list would include "Pat-A-Cake," "Row, Row, Row Your Boat," and "Twinkle, Twinkle Little Star," (Johnson-Green & Custodero, 2002). These songs (and others shown in Table 12.1) have been popular for generations, perhaps because they all have a simple melody, repetitive rhyming lyrics, and accompanying hand, arm, or whole-body movements that are easy for very young children to imitate. They are also easy for most adults to sing and can be used in almost any setting, including during diaper changing, while riding in the car, or during bath time. In this chapter, as we examine the role of music in young children's lives, we consider infants' and toddlers' ability to perceive the musical world around them as well as their developing ability to be involved in creating music of their own.

As Table 12.1 shows, one of the titles on our hypothetical Toddler Top 20 is a relatively newer song, "I Love You," which children are likely to hear for the first time while watching *Barney & Friends*. Many mothers and fathers who were themselves brought up watching *Sesame Street* and *Mister Rogers' Neighborhood* now direct their infants and toddlers to educational television programs created specifically for an under-3 audience. As a result, in many households, children younger than 3 not only turn on the TV by themselves and know how to change channels using the remote, but they also have favorite TV programs, TV channels, and DVDs that they ask to watch

TABLE 12.1	Popular Songs for Very Young Children: A Hypothetical Toddler Top 20
Popularity Ranking (1 = most popular)	**Song**
1	The Itsy Bitsy Spider
2	Pat-A-Cake
3	Row, Row, Row Your Boat
4	Twinkle, Twinkle Little Star
5	Wheels on the Bus
6	If You're Happy and You Know It
7	Open, Shut Them
8	Head, Shoulders, Knees, and Toes
9	The Hokey Pokey
10	Clean Up, Clean Up, Everybody Everywhere
11	If Your Name Is (child's name), Pop Right Up
12	Three Blind Mice
13	This Little Piggy
14	This Is the Way We . . .
15	Baa, Baa Black Sheep
16	The ABC Song
17	Mary Had a Little Lamb
18	Old MacDonald Had a Farm
19	Happy Birthday
20	I Love You

Source: Based on Johnson-Greene & Custodero, 2002.

and are able to start on their own (Anderson & Pempek, 2005; Rideout et al., 2003). How much television, DVDs, and videos do young children watch, and what are the effects of this activity on their behavior and development?

New and expectant parents are bombarded with advertisements encouraging them to boost their baby's brain by buying classical music CDs and DVDs designed to stimulate the senses of vision and hearing as well as lay a foundation for later language acquisition. It should not be surprising, then, that interactive media, and hybrid products that are part toy, part book, and part computer, have become pervasive in the lives of many young children in the United States. Even newborns and young infants are increasingly likely to play with "smart" toys and to fall asleep to the sounds of music by Mozart and other eighteenth-century composers being played on twenty-first century "music boxes."

Does Mozart's music have a unique and beneficial impact on infants, as has been asserted by individuals extrapolating from studies of college students (Rauscher, Shaw, & Ky, 1993, 1995)? Do allegedly brain-boosting products influence early development in the ways that their makers claim? Are infants whose parents cannot or choose not to buy and use them at a disadvantage developmentally? How will these experiences affect the babies of today and tomorrow?

MUSIC

As we have discussed in other chapters, the sense of hearing develops in advance of vision and is functioning well at birth. This means that even the very youngest infants are able to perceive an auditory world consisting of speech and nonspeech sounds, the latter of which may be produced by animals and, depending on where the child lives, machines and inanimate objects such as cars, airplanes, doorbells, and kitchen timers. Instrumental music is found in all human cultures and is the source of some of the other nonspeech sounds that infants hear. Cultural traditions and the availability of materials influence the size, construction, and purpose of instruments in a society, but nearly all cultures have instruments that can be blown, struck, bowed, or plucked. Given that the propensity to make music exists in all human cultures, many researchers have wondered whether the ability to perceive instrumental and vocal music might have evolved as a fundamental human skill, like the capacity to perceive and acquire language. As we discuss next, infants are born ready to detect many properties of the music and songs they hear (Papousek, 1996; Trehub, 2002). They soon use those abilities to make their own nonspeech sounds, which at first may be music only to their parents' ears.

Listening to Music

It seems that it is never too early to listen to and even benefit from music. Before birth, mothers generate a rhythmic "soundtrack" through their heartbeat. Fetuses also hear their mother's voice and, as we noted in Chapter 8, are able to learn the contours and intonations of their mother's speech. Women in the third trimester of pregnancy report that fetuses move and kick in response to music and other audible stimuli, and some experts think that prenatal exposure to music may stimulate infants' later cognitive and motor development (LaFuente et al., 1997). Studies confirm that infants respond differently to music that they heard in utero, as compared with other music that they have not heard previously (Hepper, 1991; Wilkin, 1995).

Infant-directed music has been used therapeutically with preterm infants in the neonatal intensive care unit, with mixed and sometimes inconclusive results (Cevasco, 2008; Hartling et al., 2009). More research is needed, but in a number of studies, instrumental or vocal music has prevented weight loss, reduced physiological stress, and helped stabilize preterm infants enough to allow them to gain weight, conserve energy, and spend fewer days in the hospital (Arnon et al.,

2006; Lubetzky et al., 2009; Neal & Lindeke, 2008; Standley, 2002; Whipple, 2008). These examples do not fit traditional definitions of "children's music," but most newborns do not have to wait very long before they hear instrumental and vocal music in more conventional settings.

MUSIC PERCEPTION   Researchers studying infants' music perception rely on many of the same procedures that are used to investigate infants' language perception. In some studies, researchers measure infants' attentiveness, emotional reactions, and motor responsiveness to musical stimuli played over loudspeakers. In other studies, a conditioned headturn procedure is used to reward infants with a pleasant visual sight, such as a fun animated toy, if they turn their head in a particular direction after a change in a musical soundtrack. Once infants have learned the contingencies involved in the procedure, researchers can present auditory stimuli with varying properties and determine whether babies notice the differences. Another method, the headturn preference procedure, involves presenting auditory stimuli on either the left or the right side. Researchers draw infants' attention by flashing a light and then playing music over a speaker located at that spot. If infants look longer when either speaker is playing a particular musical excerpt, researchers infer that the infant recognizes that excerpt. It is difficult to use these procedures with infants younger than 4 months; accordingly, most existing studies of music perception have focused on 6- to 12-month-olds (Ilari, 2002; Trehub, 2002).

Infants as young as 6 months are usually able to recognize recently heard melodies, despite changes in the pitch or tempo (Ilari, 2002; Trehub, 2002). In other words, if they are first familiarized with a sequence of notes, such as those in the song "Hot Cross Buns," they perceive that melody as familiar the next time it is played, even if it is slower or in a different musical key, as long as the relationship between the notes themselves does not change. When the distance between individual notes changes, however, infants respond as if the melody is a different one.

Infants also retain long-term memories of particular melodies. In studies with 6-month-olds, infants were able to recognize 30-second excerpts of melodies when they were tested 3 weeks later, provided that the excerpts had not changed (Trainor, Wu, & Tsang, 2004). Slightly older infants are able to store even longer and more complex melodies in memory. In one study, 7-month-olds heard two Mozart sonatas every day for two weeks. When subsequently presented with either the sonatas they had previously heard or similar but novel musical passages, babies recognized the familiar music and appeared to prefer it instead of the unfamiliar pieces (Saffran, Loman, & Robertson, 2000).

In a different study, 8-month-old infants heard one of two complex classical piano pieces three times a day for 10 days. Two weeks later, when infants were tested using the headturn preference procedure, they showed recognition for the music they had heard previously by looking longer at the speaker over which that piece was being played than they did when the speaker played unfamiliar music. Infants who had never heard either piece of music showed no difference in looking time (Ilari & Polka, 2006).

If you have ever heard a classical Chinese orchestra, you know that it sounds different from a Western orchestra. Although there are many similarities—such as the existence of families of woodwinds, brasses, strings, and percussion—different instruments as well as different musical scales and styles exist across cultures. By the age of about 12 months, infants know this too and are able to discriminate between features that belong in their own culture's music and features that do not belong. This auditory specialization for music, which is not found in 6-month-old infants, is similar to the specialization for speech sounds that occurs during the second half of the first year of life (Ilari, 2002).

Infants are sensitive to the rhythmic patterns in music that they hear. In an experiment with 6- to 9-month-olds, infants were familiarized with a rhythmic pattern consisting of several repetitions of two different tones. Subsequently, when the tones remained the same, but the rhythmic pattern and grouping had changed (e.g., from AAA BBB to AAAB BB or AA ABBB), infants were able to detect those differences (Thorpe & Trehub, 1989; Thorpe et al., 1988).

Taken together, these findings indicate that well before their first birthday, infants are able to remember both brief and relatively lengthy pieces of music of varying complexity. These studies do not reveal the basis for infants' auditory perception—the specific information that they remember about the music they have heard. Studies systematically manipulating the properties of musical stimuli may shed light on this early ability.

SINGING TO INFANTS   From Baby Mozart to Baby Beluga and the Wiggles, there is a diverse world of music for the very youngest listeners. Parents and caregivers have always sung to infants, of course, usually choosing different songs than they sing in other settings and modifying their singing as the situation demands. Mothers singing their favorite children's songs tend to use the same pitch level and tempo time after time, unless the infant's state indicates that they need a more or less arousing version (Bergeson & Trehub, 2002; Ilari, 2005).

As shown in Figure 12.1, when parents in one study were asked to sing a song of their choice to their 4- to 18-month-old infants, the most common songs performed were playsongs (e.g., "The Itsy Bitsy Spider"), followed by lullabies (e.g., "Rock-A-Bye Baby"), popular songs (e.g., "Mandy," a song made famous by pop singer Barry Manilow), invented songs (e.g., "It's Bath Time in Canada"), and other songs (including religious and unknown songs). Fathers in this study were less accustomed to singing to their infants than were mothers, which may be one reason that fathers chose to sing more popular and invented songs than traditional children's playsongs or lullabies (Trehub et al., 1997).

The presence of an infant elicits a specialized singing style. Mothers and fathers who were asked to sing to their infants and also to sing *as if* their infants were present were judged to be more intense and emotionally expressive in the former condition, regardless of the type of song they chose to sing (O'Neill, Trainor, & Trehub, 2001; Trehub, Hill, & Kamenetsky, 1997; Trehub et al., 1997). Like infant-directed speech, infant-directed singing is typically slower, higher in pitch, and more emotionally warm than singing that is not directed to infants (Trehub & Trainor, 1998). Older children, even those who are barely 3 years old, also alter their singing style when

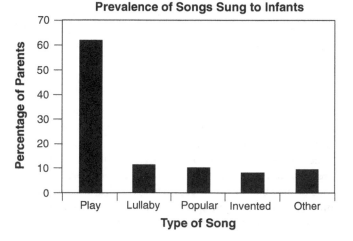

FIGURE 12.1   Out of all songs sung to infants, playsongs appear to be the most prevalent.
Source: Based on information in Trehub, Hill, & Kamenetsky, 1997.

singing to infant siblings, using a higher pitch level and a more "smiling" voice than when they cannot see their younger brothers and sisters (Trehub, Unyk, & Henderson, 1994).

Across a wide range of cultures, parents consistently use different kinds of music and songs to influence infants' behavior and states of arousal (Custodero, Britto, & Brooks-Gunn, 2003; Ilari, 2005; Trehub, Unyk, & Trainor, 1993a, 1993b; Unyk et al., 1992). While playsongs are intended to engage infants' attention and stimulate interaction, a quite different genre—the lullaby—is intended to soothe and calm infants as they fall asleep. If infants were able to understand the lyrics of "Rock-A-Bye Baby," which describe breaking tree boughs and falling cradles and babies, they might not find this lullaby very relaxing; fortunately, all they notice is its slow, gliding tempo and their parents' quiet, loving tone of voice.

Adults who hear recordings of lullabies, like "Rock-A-Bye Baby," describe them as "airy and flute-like," "smooth," and "soothing," even when the words have been electronically stripped away. Recordings of playsongs, by contrast, such as "The Itsy Bitsy Spider," tend to be described as "smiling," "brilliant and trumpet-like," "clipped," and "rhythmic" (Rock, Trainor, & Addison, 1999; Trehub et al., 1993a; Unyk et al., 1992). By the age of 9 months, infants respond differently to instrumental music that adults and older children characterize as "happy" versus "sad" (Flom, Gentile, & Pick, 2008). Even 5- to 7-month-old infants appear to notice some of these differences and respond by showing different behaviors to each genre. During lullabies, they are more likely to focus their attention on their own bodies and clothing, toys with which they are playing, and other nearby objects, such as pacifiers. When listening to playsongs, by contrast, they tend to show more outward-directed behavior, such as looking at their caregiver (Rock et al., 1999).

Infants respond positively to the modifications that parents make when singing to them, and they are more attentive to infant-directed singing than to other types of casual singing. This is especially true if the singer is their parent or another frequent caregiver. While recorded performances of unfamiliar adults engaged in infant-directed singing also elicit positive responses from infants, parents need not worry that their own singing is inadequate. Nor should they feel pressured by claims that commercially produced recordings of professional singers are the best way to stimulate their child's brain development. As one expert put it, "No one would suggest replacing maternal verbal interactions with recorded monologues or dialogues by professional actors. By the same token, professional singers are no substitute for live, maternal singing" (Trehub, 2002, p. 21). Instead, infants benefit most from emotionally rich, spontaneous singing, especially when it reflects and is sensitive to their changing states of arousal and emotional needs (Kuhl et al., 2003; Trehub, 2002).

Some songs that adults sing with or to children are used for specific routines and tasks. Personalized versions of "Good Morning" and "Hello, Everybody" signal the beginning of the day to children in group care, while the "Clean Up" song encourages "everybody everywhere" to "do their share" while picking up toys and books in the classroom or at home. Other songs, such as the "ABC" song, help children establish a foundation for learning the letters of the alphabet. Children who hear parents and other adults sing these songs on a regular basis soon begin to sing along with them (Ringgenberg, 2004). We turn now to consider the age at which young children begin to imitate songs that they hear, examining different approaches to music education for very young children.

Making Music

Music education has been part of preschool education in the United States since the nineteenth century, when it was imported from Europe with kindergarten and preschool movements. Frederic Froebel, the founder of kindergarten whom we mentioned in Chapter 1, presented many of his theories about young children's learning in *Mother-Play and Nursery Songs*, a book of songs, verses, games, and instructions to teachers. In Froebel's view, music was not an end in itself but served as a means of educating children, instilling a sense of order, and teaching self-discipline (McDonald & Simons, 1989).

In the 1920s, when child development studies began at child welfare stations in Iowa and elsewhere, researchers investigated music in order to determine the best pitch range for young children's voices. Most people today would probably be surprised to learn that the melody of "Twinkle, Twinkle Little Star" (originally composed in 1914) was modified as a result of this sort of research, repeating the first two lines at the end of the song to make it simpler for young children to sing. Researchers also made recommendations about the content of children's songs, which they asserted should be about common, everyday experiences (McDonald & Simons, 1989).

Today, organizations devoted to supporting development during infancy and early childhood, such as Zero to Three and the National Association for the Education of Young Children (NAEYC), encourage parents to sing to and with infants and toddlers. They also promote music and singing as teaching tools in the preschool classroom. Like kindergarten teachers from the nineteenth century, today's early childhood educators recognize that music is a natural and enjoyable way for children to learn. Preschool teachers can pair singing with movement or visual aids, modify familiar tunes in order to teach new vocabulary words, and encourage children to create their own songs and incorporate music into their play (Ringgenberg, 2004).

LEARNING TO SING   Like learning to talk, learning to sing does not happen overnight (as shown in Table 12.2). Around the age of 4 to 6 months, infants respond to music and singing with whole-body movements, but these movements are not synchronized to the properties of music, such as its rhythmic pattern. A period of "vocal contagion" begins at about 6 months of age; infants become so excited by other people's speaking and singing voices that they join in. Parents can encourage these "songs"—and support future speech development—by imitating their infants and responding with positive emotional feedback.

At 12 to 18 months, infants engage in vocal play and experiment with sound; brief but repetitive melodic and rhythmic patterns begin to appear in these vocalizations, making them

TABLE 12.2 Milestones in Learning to Sing	
Age	**Milestone**
4 to 6 months	Infants respond to music and singing with whole-body movements, usually not synchronized to properties of the music, such as its rhythmic pattern.
6 to 12 months	Infants display "vocal contagion," becoming so excited by other people's singing that they join in. Songs with corresponding gestures that parents and caregivers have used, such as those accompanying "The Itsy Bitsy Spider," become part of the child's performance too.
12 to 18 months	Infants engage in vocal play and experiment with brief but repetitive melodic and rhythmic patterns.
19 to 24 months	Infants create their own spontaneous songs, often while engaged in some other activity, such as playing with toys. Songs often contain recognizable elements of songs that they have heard.
30 to 36 months	Children imitate larger excerpts of songs, although their versions are not always accurate.

Source: Based on McDonald & Simons, 1989.

The National Association for the Education of Young Children promotes the use of music and singing as a teaching tool in the early childhood classroom. These children have a variety of percussion instruments available and are free to explore and use them in small groups or on their own.

sound like excerpts of songs. A listener who does not know the child well may only be able to guess that the child is "singing," whereas parents or other caregivers may be able to recognize bits of songs that the child and parents frequently listen to (such as the theme song from *Barney & Friends* or selections from a CD that is played during trips in the car).

From 19 to 24 months, infants experiment and create their own spontaneous songs, often while engaged in some other activity. Language and vocabulary develop rapidly during this period, and around 2 years of age, children's songs are often recognizable as derivations of specific songs. Strangers hearing 2-year-old children singing at the grocery store, for example, are now more likely to be able to identify the songs being performed.

Between 30 and 36 months of age, whole parts of songs may be imitated, although children's renditions may not be completely accurate. As children approach the age of 3 years, they are increasingly successful when trying to reproduce the words, rhythm, phrases, and melody of songs they have learned (McDonald & Simons, 1989).

Music education programs for children from birth to 3 years of age are often designed with parent involvement in mind. These programs usually feature playful interactions involving music, and help parents expand their knowledge of musical songs and games (Trehub, 2002). Typical music activities for infants and toddlers include rocking in time to rhythmic patterns, playing sound-imitation games, personalizing songs to include the child's name, and singing songs with accompanying actions. Two- to 3-year-olds can participate in more complex musical games involving group actions, such as the "Hokey Pokey," "Two Little Blackbirds," and "Farmer in the Dell," but they may have only limited success in singing or moving together as a group (McDonald & Simons, 1989).

PLAYING INSTRUMENTS Most infants are exposed to simple percussion instruments—rattles—at an early age, and many toddlers own toy xylophones, drums, or pianos. Regardless of whether they own toy instruments, all infants seem to enjoy banging with spoons on "drums" made out of high chair trays, plastic bowls, and any available overturned container. Infants also enjoy playing with toys that make noise, whether the sounds are produced by mechanical means (as when a ball containing jingle bells is rolled or shaken) or electronic systems (as occurs with devices that can be activated with the push of a button).

Children younger than 2 years typically interact with musical instruments such as pianos and xylophones by banging on the keys without any discernible rhythm pattern. Considering these tendencies, most early childhood educators recommend providing 2- to 3-year-olds with a variety of music-making materials but caution against musical activities that require children to perform together as a unit (McDonald & Simons, 1989).

Instead, emphasis is usually given to providing very young children with opportunities to explore materials in music-learning centers. In these designated areas of the early childhood classroom, children are able to listen to music, explore musical instruments, and create their own sounds in small groups or on their own. Percussion instruments in these centers usually include drums, rhythm sticks, sandblocks, woodblocks, tambourines, maracas, bells, cymbals, and gongs. The sounds that emanate from music-learning centers in early childhood classrooms may not always be melodious, but in many approaches to music education, they represent an important stage of development.

Listening to music, playing instruments, singing, and rhythmic movement are major components of most music education programs for young children, but not all forms of music education are alike. The Montessori Method, for example, developed in Italy in the early twentieth century, emphasizes self-directed learning within a predetermined sequence of experiences. In some activities, children as young as 2 years compare the sounds made by containers filled with different materials, such as sand, dried beans, and flour. In other activities, children learn about the relationship between size and sound by trying out a set of bells that gradually increase in size. Montessori's methods have been adapted and interpreted in many different ways over the years, and it is unlikely that many Montessori programs in the United States today follow the entire original music education curriculum (McDonald & Simons, 1989). What may be most important is the continued emphasis on exploration as a fundamental way of learning about music.

A different approach was developed in the 1940s by a Japanese music educator, Shinichi Suzuki. Suzuki Talent Education, often referred to simply as the **Suzuki Method,** is a method for teaching very young children (sometimes as early as 2 to 3 years) to play stringed instruments. Suzuki instructors use games to teach children about pitch, proper posture, arm position, and bow manipulations; many of the principles on which the approach is based can be generalized to

Some children learn to play a musical instrument at a very young age by using the Suzuki Method, observing others and eventually imitating and playing with them as a group.

music education more generally (McDonald & Simons, 1989). There are, however, a number of unique practices in the Suzuki Method.

The Suzuki Method explicitly compares learning to play an instrument to learning to speak a first language, with the result that imitation and feedback from parents, adults, and other children is the principal method used. Social interaction and being part of a group are also key elements of the Suzuki Method. Before children ever begin to play their own instrument, they attend classes and observe other children who have already begun their lessons.

Suzuki reasoned that, because humans do not learn to read before learning to speak, children learning to play an instrument should do so before learning to read music. Students memorize the pieces they are learning, and written musical notes are not introduced until a satisfactory skill level has been attained.

One consequence of Suzuki's beliefs about the importance of parent involvement is that parents who enroll their children in Suzuki classes are also enrolling themselves. According to Suzuki, parents must learn to play the instrument first and demonstrate their skills at home so that children will become interested and insist on playing too. Parents who have learned to play an instrument can reinforce the concepts and skills at home, and because they attend their children's weekly lessons, they are aware of and understand the teacher's instructions. Parents in the Suzuki Method also support their children's development by playing recordings of pieces they are learning, immersing them in the sounds outside of class and aiding memorization of the music (McDonald & Simons, 1989; Starr, 1976; Suzuki, 1973).

The Suzuki Method enables young children to develop a relatively high level of musical skills earlier than many traditional string instructors even begin formal lessons (Price, 1979). There is relatively little experimental research that clearly supports any one music education approach over all others, however, with respect to ultimate levels of skill development. Not all children are ready to begin an intensive study of an instrument at the age of 2 or 3 years, and not all parents are able to commit their families to a program that assumes that children will practice their instrument seven days a week. Still, many parents may feel compelled to make an early and significant investment in their children's musical development, increasingly because they have heard about the Mozart Effect. Awareness of this phenomenon has grown since it was first reported in 1993 by researchers studying college students (Rauscher et al., 1993). We now consider evidence for this well-publicized effect, especially as it pertains to infants and very young children.

The Mozart Effect

The **Mozart Effect** was the name given to findings reported in an experiment with 36 college students who listened to a 10-minute Mozart sonata. When these students took a spatial-temporal test, they scored higher than they had after experiencing 10 minutes of silence or listening to relaxation instructions (Rauscher et al., 1993). Some subsequent attempts to replicate this finding have not been successful, but even when it has been reproduced, the effect lasts for only about 10 minutes and appears to be limited to the kind of reasoning required for the spatial-temporal test (Rauscher et al., 1995).

As these research findings were disseminated to the general public, and even to professional audiences, however, many people jumped to the conclusion that listening to classical music, especially the music of Mozart, would enhance a wide range of cognitive abilities in both adults and children. There is no experimental evidence to support this conclusion (McKelvie & Low, 2002; Rauscher, 2003), but that has not prevented the proliferation of "brain-boosting" classical music CDs and DVDs, as well as Mozart Effect resources for parents and educators. There are many valid reasons to listen to Mozart and other classical music, and to introduce it to young children, but there is little reason to believe that it will increase their intelligence (Rauscher, 2003).

Parents and educators who wish to enhance children's spatial-temporal ability would do better to provide them with musical *training* (Schellenberg, 2004, 2005). Studies of children aged 3 to 12 years have found that music instruction results in better performance on spatial-temporal tasks, with the strongest effects occurring for the youngest children (Bilhartz, Bruhn, & Olson, 2000; Gromko & Poorman, 1998; Hetland, 2000; Rauscher, 2003).

In some of these studies, the effects of keyboard instruction have been compared with the effects of singing and with rhythm instruction. In an experiment involving 3- and 4-year-old children enrolled in Head Start, each of these musical experiences was associated with higher scores on spatial tasks than were found among children in a nonmusical control group. The group receiving rhythm instruction performed better than the others on sequencing and arithmetic tests, but no differences were found on tasks involving verbal ability, matching, or memory (Rauscher & LeMieux, 2003).

Other investigations have found that, although spatial-temporal reasoning underlies mathematical abilities, there is only limited support for a direct connection between music instruction and mathematics ability (Rauscher, 2003). Experimental studies of reading ability have failed to produce convincing evidence of a causal relationship between music instruction and reading scores, but there is correlational support for a link between music instruction and verbal memory ability (Rauscher, 2003).

Although the findings for an effect of music instruction on specific cognitive abilities have been mixed, there is less ambiguous evidence that music training may enhance overall intellectual ability, at least in school-age children (Schellenberg, 2005). In one experiment with 6-year-olds, for example, children were randomly assigned to 36 weeks of music lessons (keyboard or vocal), drama lessons, or no lessons. All of the groups showed increases in scores on standardized IQ tests by the end of the experiment, but the increase was greater for the two music groups (Schellenberg, 2004). Further research is needed in order to understand why and how music has these effects. Is it because music lessons are equivalent to gaining additional schooling? Does the activity help children develop intellectual abilities, such as attention, concentration, and memorization, that contribute to overall IQ? Perhaps the abstract nature of music itself—becoming aware of relationships that exist among a set of notes in a melody, regardless of the key in which it is played—is involved (Schellenberg, 2005).

Parents of very young children who wonder whether an early investment in music instruction is worthwhile may find encouragement in studies showing that the earlier children begin music instruction, the longer lasting are the benefits for spatial-temporal reasoning (Rauscher, 2002, 2003; Rauscher et al., 1997; Rauscher & Zupan, 2000). Children in one study who had begun piano instruction before the age of 5, for example, performed better on spatial ability tasks than children who started later and children who had had no music instruction (Costa-Giomi, 1999).

More research is needed, however, to illuminate the Music Lesson Effect and determine whether benefits found for preschool-age children receiving piano instruction also exist for young Suzuki students and children who begin other forms of music instruction before the age of 3. Regardless of the range of benefits ultimately found, and the age at which they occur, most music educators believe that it is important to employ developmentally appropriate methods and to instill in children (and parents) an appreciation that music is not just a tool for improving cognitive abilities but is valuable in and of itself (McDonald & Simons, 1989; Ringgenberg, 2004).

MEDIA

Is television valuable in and of itself? Providing entertainment, information, role models, and companionship, television is a staple in most U.S. children's daily media diet. Among children ages 2 to 17, the amount of television viewed per day (approximately 2.5 hours) has remained stable since 1997, even as computers and other media have joined TV sets in a high percentage of homes. A national survey of 1,000 parents of children younger than 6 years found that 99 percent owned at least one television. Nearly half (49 percent) had a video game player, although it was rarely used by children under the age of 2 years. In households where television was used heavily—in which the TV is always left turned on or is on most of the time—children were more likely than in other households to begin watching before the age of 1 (Rideout & Hamel, 2006; Rideout et al., 2003).

Among older children, television continues to be the medium with which they spend the most time each day (Comstock & Scharrer, 2006; Singer & Singer, 2001), but in a typical day children under 2 are more likely to listen to music (81 percent) and read or be read to (71 percent) than they are to watch television (59 percent) or watch videos and DVDs (42 percent). Still, in a typical day, children younger than 2 watch an average of 1 hour and 22 minutes of television and spend approximately the same amount of time (1 hour and 26 minutes) watching videos and DVDs (Rideout et al., 2003). Is time in front of television screens time well spent?

Some early childhood experts have expressed doubt about this possibility, while others have asserted that the message rather than the medium determines its value (Anderson et al., 2001; Center on Media and Child Health, 2005; Singer & Singer, 2001; Thakkar, Garrison, & Christakis, 2006). Among older children, there are a number of reasons that parents should be concerned about the amount and the content of television being watched (American Academy of Pediatrics Committee on Public Education, 2001). Children who spend many hours watching television or using other forms of media, such as video games and the Internet, may have disrupted or insufficient amounts of sleep, negatively affecting alertness and performance in school (Zimmerman, 2008). Heavy amounts of television viewing are associated with higher rates of overweight and consumption of unhealthy foods, whereas limiting the amount of time spent engaged in sedentary screen-based activities has been shown to prevent overweight and obesity, which has increased in recent years among children of all ages (Federal Interagency Forum on Child and Family Statistics, 2009). There is also strong evidence that among older children and adolescents, violent television increases the likelihood of short- and long-term aggressive and violent behavior (Anderson et al., 2003; Comstock & Scharrer, 2006). How does television affect the *youngest* viewers?

Television for Infants and Toddlers

No known benefits have been documented for infant TV viewing, and some experts believe that it may negatively affect early development in multiple domains (Christakis, 2009). In 2001, the American Academy of Pediatrics Committee on Public Education issued a policy statement on children's television viewing, asserting that children younger than 2 years of age should not watch any television, and children older than 2 should be limited to 2 hours of daily screen time. The primary rationale for this recommendation was that very young children benefit most from more active forms of learning, including play and conversations with adults and other children. Results from an experiment that we discussed in Chapter 8 are consistent with this view. In that study, 9-month-old infants who heard Mandarin Chinese produced in person by a native speaker were subsequently able to perceive Mandarin phoneme contrasts, but infants who saw only a videotape of the same speaker did not show this ability (Kuhl et al., 2003). Studies of verb learning by $2\frac{1}{2}$- to $3\frac{1}{2}$-year-olds have found a similar advantage, particularly for younger children, for live social interaction over video-only presentations of new vocabulary items (Roseberry et al., 2009).

Judging from the results of the national survey that we mentioned earlier, many parents of very young children have difficulty following the American Academy of Pediatrics recommendations. Not only is television present in nearly all homes, but 40 percent of children under the age of 3 years live in heavy-use households, in which the TV is always or usually on, even if no one is watching. In addition, 30 percent of children under the age of 3 in the survey sample had their own TV in their bedroom, and 58 percent reportedly watched TV daily. The survey also showed that even children younger than 2 years (26 percent) had a TV in their bedroom, with 43 percent watching it every day (Rideout & Hamel, 2006; Rideout et al., 2003). Other parent surveys of TV and DVD/video viewing have found that, by the age of 3 months, 40 percent of infants regularly watch TV, DVDs, and videos; the average reported viewing time increases from 1 hour per day for 12-month-olds to $1\frac{1}{2}$ hours per day for 24-month-olds (Zimmerman, Christakis, & Meltzoff, 2007).

Parents may not be aware of another regular source of screen time for some young children—the childcare setting. A survey of nearly 200 licensed childcare providers in four states found that children in family childcare homes were more likely to watch TV, DVDs, and videos than children in childcare centers; 70 percent of childcare homes, as compared with 36 percent of centers, reported having children watch TV daily. Preschoolers watched more TV, DVDs, and videos on average (2.4 hrs/day in childcare homes vs. 24 mins/day in centers) than either toddlers (1.6 hrs/day in childcare homes vs. 6 mins/day in centers) or infants (12 mins/day in childcare homes vs. 0 mins/day in centers) (Christakis & Garrison, 2009).

INFANT PERCEPTION OF VIDEO IMAGES   Most preschool children own a number of videos and DVDs, given to them as gifts or purchased by parents who consider them an important foundation for their children's cognitive development. Nearly one-third (27 percent) of children this age own at least one of the *Baby Einstein* videos designed for children ages 1 to 18 months (Rideout & Hamel, 2006; Rideout et al., 2003). When infants look at these programs on television screens, what do they see? On one level, they see a flat, two-dimensional surface—the television screen—but that surface is also a representation of people, animals, objects, and events occurring in a three-dimensional world.

Many studies, including some that we mentioned in previous chapters, have shown that even young infants are able to recognize depictions of real-world entities in pictures and video images. They are also able to differentiate video images from actual people, objects, and events. Two recent studies with 9-, 14-, and 19-month-old infants, however, show that they do not yet fully understand what the objects displayed on a video screen are (Pierroutsakos & Troseth, 2003). Infants were seated within reaching distance of a video monitor that displayed a video in which a woman presented a series of toys, tapped them on the tabletop shown in the video, and then placed them on the table, which happened to be the same table that the infant's seat was resting on. Some of the toys were stationary, while others could be made to rock or move. While each toy was shown resting, rocking, or moving slowly on the table, the woman's voice said, "Look at the TV" and "Wow, look at that!"

Whereas 9-month-old infants attempted to explore the toys shown on the video monitor, grasping, hitting, patting, and rubbing them as if they were actual objects, 14-month-olds were less likely to do so, and 19-month-olds rarely showed this response. Instead, 14-month-olds and, to an even greater extent, 19-month-olds were more likely to point to the toys shown on the screen. Infants who tried to touch the toys shown in the video did not appear surprised or upset when they failed to do so, suggesting that they may not have expected to be able to grasp them but were still exploring the video images in order to determine what they were (Pierroutsakos & Troseth, 2003).

In fact, researchers note, it takes many years for children to understand fully the properties of video images. Some 2- and 3-year-olds, for example, interact with televised images of people by talking to them, and children of this age may assert that objects shown in video images would be affected by actions in the room in which the video is being viewed, insisting, for example, that a video image of a ball shown at rest would move if the video monitor were tilted. These findings suggest that infants and very young children watching specially produced television programs and "brain-enhancing" videos and DVDs are unlikely to comprehend those materials in the ways that older children and adults would (Barr, 2008; Courage & Setliff, 2009; Garrison & Christakis, 2005; Pierroutsakos & Troseth, 2003).

Infants do perceive many kinds of information in videos, of course, including information about emotion. In Chapter 10, we discussed emotional contagion and social referencing. Studies exploring these phenomena further showed 10- and 12-month-old infants videotapes of a woman reacting to novel objects that had been created by the researchers. The woman first described the objects objectively (e.g., "Look, that's plastic. It has four legs. This thing is red.") while displaying neutral emotion. Infants were then given a chance to play with each object before the woman described another object while showing either positive or negative emotions about it. Twelve-month-olds, but not 10-month-olds, responded to the televised displays of negative emotion by showing more negative emotion themselves and by avoiding the objects to which the woman had responded negatively (Mumme & Fernald, 2003). These results are consistent with other studies showing that young children perceive and are affected by the emotional experiences of people with whom they spend time. Together, they suggest that parents should be aware that even 1-year-olds, and possibly younger infants, may experience emotional contagion in response to a range of negative emotions that they encounter in television programs, videos, and DVDs, including those not intended for child audiences (Courage & Setliff, 2009; Weber, 2006).

Most parents and caregivers do think carefully about the content of programs that children watch. A national survey of approximately 1,200 parents of children between the ages of 2 and 17 showed that 87 percent of parents of 2- to 5-year-olds had at least "some" concern about television's impact on their children. Regardless of their children's age, large proportions of parents who were surveyed agreed at least "somewhat" with statements about negative effects of television on children, including the belief that watching television decreases time spent reading (86 percent), increases materialism (83 percent), adds to loss of child innocence (77 percent), and increases stereotyped beliefs about gender (71 percent) and race (64 percent) (Woodward & Gridina, 2000). Are these and other concerns justified? To find out, let us examine studies of infants and very young children who watch TV, DVDs, and videos.

YOUNG CHILDREN'S RESPONSES TO TELEVISION   Some studies using parent reports have found a correlation between the amount of infant DVDs and videos watched and early language development; for 8- to 16-month-olds, each hour of baby DVDs and videos watched per day was associated with a loss of 17 points on the MacArthur CDI (Zimmerman et al., 2007). Although these results were correlational, they reinforced many experts' concerns (Courage & Setliff, 2009; Hirsh-Pasek & Golinkoff, 2008). Subsequently, the makers of one popular line of baby DVDs offered parents refunds, since they were unable to support claims that their products were educational (Lewin, 2009).

Children who live in homes where the television is almost always turned on are not only more likely to spend more time watching television than children in households where television

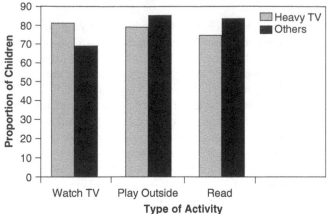

FIGURE 12.2 Children's activities are affected by household TV use. *Source:* Based on information in Rideout, Vandewater, & Wartella, 2003.

use is not as heavy, but as shown in Figure 12.2, they are also less likely to play outside or read. In heavy-TV homes, the percentage of children over 2 who can read is lower (24 percent versus 36 percent) than in homes where TV is used less (Rideout & Hamel, 2006; Rideout et al., 2003). This difference is consistent with the finding that preschool-age children who watch more than 2 hours of electronic media per day experience 1.6 fewer days per week of reading than children exposed to less than 2 hours of TV and related media per day (Tomopoulos et al., 2007).

Even the presence of "background television"—programs with adult content that is of little interest and largely incomprehensible to very young children—may be detrimental to early cognitive and language development and learning through active, engaged play (Anderson & Evans, 2001). Many children watch television at home while playing, shifting their attention back and forth, rather than having their attention completely "captured" by TV, DVDs, and videos (Anderson & Pempek, 2005). The ability to multitask in this way, however, may diminish the impact of nonscreen activities. A recent laboratory study found that 12- to 36-month-olds played less overall, engaged in shorter play episodes, and had shorter bouts of focused attention when a game show was on than when no television program was playing (Schmidt et al., 2008).

Whether adult- or child-focused, the presence of TV programs appears to interfere with parent-child interactions (Mendelsohn et al., 2008). In a study of more than 300 2- to 48-month-olds, for example, children wore digital recorders on random days for up to 24 months. Analysis of recordings showed that each hour of audible television noise was associated with significant reductions in the frequency and duration of child vocalizing, as well as reductions in the number of words produced by adults and conversational turns between children and adults (Christakis et al., 2009). Observations in a laboratory setting confirmed that adult-directed TV programs playing in the background negatively affected the quantity and quality of interactions between parents and 12- to 36-month-olds. Parents were less attentive, less actively involved, and less responsive during free play when a TV program was playing than when the TV in the room was not turned on (Kirkorian et sl., 2009).

Watching television does not inevitably replace or reduce the quantity and quality of all other activities, but the type of program watched influences the way that young children spend their time. Studies of children between 2 and 5 years of age have found that those who watch more hours of entertainment television, such as animated and other programs designed for a child audience without an informative purpose, tend to spend less time reading and experience fewer parental teaching activities at home, whereas children who watch more educational/informative programs do not show a reduction in reading and teaching time (Huston et al., 1999; Tomopoulos et al., 2007). One of the most significant findings about young children and television, therefore, may be that the message *is* more important than the medium.

This was also shown in a longitudinal study of 570 adolescents whose television use had been documented when they were 5 years old. The amount of television children had watched had less of an influence on later behavior and development than the content of programs they had watched (Anderson et al., 2001). Overall, preschoolers who watched more child informative programs with educational and prosocial themes, such as *Sesame Street* and *Mister Rogers' Neighborhood,* tended in adolescence to have higher grades, read more books, and place more value on achievement; they also showed greater creativity and exhibited lower levels of aggression than children who watched violent programs. These findings, although correlational, are in keeping with other studies of the intellectual benefits of educational television for preschool children (Wright et al., 2001).

The longitudinal study also showed, however, that the same programs may influence different children in different ways. Preschoolers who were especially likely to talk about television and incorporate television content into their play tended to show more negative and longer lasting effects of viewing violent programs when they were adolescents. For these children, the salience and vividness of superheroes and action and adventure themes may have led them to emphasize and practice violent and aggressive actions, increasing the likelihood that they would behave more aggressively throughout childhood and into adolescence (Anderson et al., 2001).

The analyses also showed that, even within the same category, different programs may be associated with different outcomes. Within the informative/educational category, there were differences between *Sesame Street* and *Mister Rogers' Neighborhood.* Different levels of creativity in adolescence among those who watched different educational/informative programs, for example, may have occurred because *Sesame Street* emphasizes and contributes to academic skills and knowledge, whereas *Mister Rogers' Neighborhood* stimulated imaginative and creative thinking. Alternatively, as with all correlational research, other explanations should be considered, including the possibility that differences among the children at age 5 drew them to some programs more than others and that children's characteristics were then reinforced—but not caused—by their TV viewing patterns (Anderson et al., 2001).

Parents of very young children monitor and manage their children's television viewing more than parents of older children (Huston et al., 1999). It may not be surprising in light of their influence on very young children's viewing choices, but most parents seem to find that television has more positive than negative effects and tend to believe that it is more helpful than harmful for children's learning. Whereas 70 percent of children 3 and younger were reported to have imitated positive behavior they had seen on television, such as sharing or helping, only 27 percent were reported to have imitated aggressive behavior, such as hitting or kicking (Rideout & Hamel, 2006; Rideout et al., 2003).

Parents are often aware of differences between television programs, in part because they watch many of those programs, especially when their children are young. According to one survey, the most popular co-viewed children's programs for parents and preschoolers were *Rugrats, Blues Clues, Barney & Friends,* and *Arthur.* Parents also reported that they encourage their children to watch educational channels and channels produced for child audiences, specifically, the Discovery Channel, PBS, The History Channel, The Learning Channel, and the Disney Channel. The top 10 encouraged children's programs (by the 57 percent of parents who were able to list any programs that they encouraged children to watch) included *Sesame Street, Blues Clues, Arthur, Barney & Friends, Rugrats,* and *Little Bear.* One program that is made for children, *Power Rangers,* was consistently mentioned as a program that parents did not want children to watch, presumably due to its themes of action and violence (Woodward & Gridina, 2000).

The first episode of *Sesame Street* was aired on PBS in 1969. Since then, it has been joined on an increasingly crowded television soundstage by a diverse range of human, animal, and uncategorizable performers who appear both on PBS and on a number of cable TV channels that offer programs for preschool children. One of the most controversial newcomers in the late 1990s was the program *Teletubbies,* developed with 2-year-old viewers in mind. Some parents were critical of the immature language models provided by the four Teletubbies—Tinky Winky, Dipsy, Laa-Laa, and Po. The program was aimed at children who are themselves in early stages of language development, however, and the show's developers deliberately gave each character a style of speaking that represented a particular stage (Teletubbies Frequently Asked Questions, 2002).

Given its young target audience, the pace of *Teletubbies* was designed to be much slower than the pace of programs that most parents enjoy sitting through, such as *Sesame Street.* The plots were also very simple, as seen in these descriptions of two typical episodes. In one, "a pair of boots appears in Teletubbyland," while in the other, "a door appears in Teletubbyland. The Tubbies have great fun opening and closing, knocking on and going through the door." Some parents were uncomfortable with elements of technology that were incorporated into Teletubbyland, including television screens built into each Teletubby's stomach. In every episode, one of the Teletubbies' screens turns on and video images of real children are displayed. The program was well received by its intended child audience, many of whom were undoubtedly drawn to the bright primary colors, simple musical melodies, and the Teletubbies' infantlike bodies and facial features.

The slow pace and immature language models in the *Teletubbies* may be one reason, however, that a longitudinal study of early television viewing and language outcomes found that watching greater amounts of *Teletubbies* was related to comprehending fewer vocabulary words and having less expressive language at the age of 30 months. Using data provided by parents' diaries of children's television exposure beginning at the age of 6 months, the researchers also found that children who had watched more of programs designed for older preschool audiences—*Dora the Explorer, Blues Clues, Arthur, Clifford,* and *Dragon Tales*—had larger receptive vocabularies and higher expressive language

This boy is a member of the target audience for *Teletubbies,* one of the first television programs developed with 2-year-old viewers in mind.

scores when they were 30 months old. Children who had watched larger amounts of *Sesame Street* had smaller expressive language, while those who had watched more *Barney & Friends*, a program that we discuss in greater detail shortly, had more expressive language but comprehended a smaller number of vocabulary words (Linebarger & Walker, 2005). Given that this study was correlational, not experimental, it is not clear how to interpret the results. While it is possible that program content caused children's language to develop—or fail to develop—in particular ways, it is also possible that children were attracted to programs that matched their language abilities.

Among the still-expanding options for very young viewers are new shows with new names and characters, such as *The Backyardigans* and *Boohbah*. In response to concerns that the downward age trend in children's television has created a new generation of ever-younger couch potatoes, themes of physical activity and physical fitness are evident in many of these programs, with most offering fun ways for children to be more active while they are watching (Singer & Singer, 2001, 2005).

One of the most physically active characters in children's television since 1993 has been a large purple dinosaur named Barney, a character adored by many 2- and 3-year-olds. As we discuss next, he is also a TV friend from whom they learn.

Barney & Friends

Singer and Singer (1998) evaluated the educational and entertainment value of *Barney & Friends* by studying the content of nearly 70 episodes produced between 1993 and 1995. They found that nearly every episode contained many elements that can prepare young children for school, including attention to cognitive skills and knowledge, emotional awareness, prosocial attitudes and behaviors, fine and gross motor skills and physical abilities, music and entertainment, and multicultural awareness.

The researchers also observed 3-year-old children's behaviors while they were watching episodes of *Barney & Friends* in early childhood classrooms. Episodes with the highest ratings for cognitive content tended to produce the greatest measurable cognitive effects in children, including the acquisition of new vocabulary and high levels of comprehension of the content. The content in the episodes included in the study was diverse, as is true of the program generally, and covered information about colors, animals, pirates, the alphabet, numbers, neighbors and neighborhoods, and music from around the world. The study showed that the most beneficial group context for learning the content in *Barney & Friends* occurred when children watched the program and then participated in teacher-led activities that reinforced important themes, skills, and vocabulary. Children who merely watched episodes of *Barney & Friends* benefited, albeit not to the same extent as children with a follow-up activity. Both of the groups that watched *Barney & Friends* benefited more than children in control groups, who were taught the follow-up lessons but did not watch any of the episodes.

Barney's impact was observed in other ways as well. Many children were observed participating along with Barney in singing, clapping, dancing, and marching during the program. Themes from the episodes were often subsequently incorporated into children's pretend play in the classroom. Children also resonated to the positive emotions displayed in *Barney & Friends*. They held hands, hugged, and sang "I Love You" along with Barney and his friends at the conclusion of each episode. Observations of 2-year-olds watching *Barney & Friends* and playing in the classroom later showed effects that were similar to those found for 3-year-old children. Two-year-olds were attentive during the episodes and subsequently showed a greater tendency to participate in symbolic play and to engage in more prosocial and less aggressive behavior (Singer & Singer, 1998).

Information about studies of *Barney & Friends* is available on the PBS website (PBSkids.org), along with suggestions for teachers and parents about how to provide children with fun, involving activities to follow up each episode. These activities, like the episodes themselves, reinforce cognitive skills at the same time that they promote pretend play, and the development of language, literacy, and prosocial behavior. Whether children love Barney or merely like him, parents can use these ideas to help get the most out of all of the television programs their children watch. In general, most experts also recommend that parents of toddlers limit TV time each day, watch with their children, participate together in activities during the show, and talk afterward about the positive and negative aspects of the program they have watched (Singer & Singer, 1998, 2005; Weber, 2006). This kind of active parental involvement, along with monitoring of the quantity and type of early TV exposure, may be one reason some studies, such as the longitudinal Project Viva, have found that TV viewing in infancy is not inevitably associated with language and visual-motor skill deficits at the age of 3 years (Schmidt et al., 2009).

COMPUTERS

Unlike television, today's parents of young children did not use computers during their own infant and toddler years. Nevertheless, the majority (72 percent) of parents of children age 6 and under believe that computers "mostly help" children's learning. Children today are often initiated into using computers by their parents; almost one-third (28 percent) have, at age 2 or younger, used a computer while sitting on a parent's lap (Rideout & Hamel, 2006; Rideout et al., 2003).

Computers in the Home

In households with children 3 years and under, most (71 percent) own computers and more than half (60 percent) are connected to the Internet. One-third of children 3 and under (31 percent) have ever used a computer, but regular computer use is relatively light among children in this age range; only 10 percent use a computer for any purpose in a typical day, usually to play games (Rideout & Hamel, 2006; Rideout et al., 2003).

The majority of households with infants and toddlers own computers, and many young children, like this girl, are initiated into using computers by a parent.

As a result of their experience, even very young children acquire a number of basic computer skills. According to their parents, they know how to turn it on by themselves (11 percent), load a CD-ROM without assistance (10 percent), and use a mouse to point and click (21 percent). Many young children who love Barney, Dora, Blue, and other characters from children's programs know that they can visit their television friends at websites offering online games and printable coloring pages. Twenty percent of children between the ages of 4 and 6 as well as 5 percent of children 3 years and under not only know about but also request specific Internet websites like these when using the computer in their home. In fact, according to a survey of parents, by the age of 2 years, 10 percent of children have visited websites for children (Rideout et al., 2003).

Computers in the Early Childhood Classroom

Early studies of young children's computer use in the preschool classroom addressed some educators' concerns that computers would isolate children from their peers. Observational research indicates that children tend to prefer using computers with peers or a teacher rather than alone. The software that teachers select, and the computer activities that children choose, provide them with numerous opportunities to cooperate as well as to ask questions and share their knowledge and opinions about the games and programs. Some 3- to 5-year-old children in one study even became computer experts who spontaneously tutored classmates (Rosengren, Gross, & Perlmutter, 1986).

There is a heated and ongoing debate about **"lapware"**—computer programs designed for parents to use with infants and children younger than 2 years of age (Alliance for Childhood, 2000; Cantor, 2001). Everyone agrees that more research is needed, but many experts believe that computer technology itself is neither inherently beneficial nor detrimental to young children's development (Clements, Nastasi, & Swaminathan, 1993). NAEYC takes the position that early childhood educators need to evaluate computer software just as they would evaluate books or other classroom materials, taking into account the age, individual, and cultural appropriateness. According to NAEYC and other experts, when computer technology is used appropriately by children 3 to 8 years of age, it can enhance cognitive and social development, especially if it is designed to encourage collaboration and communication between two or more children. Ideally, software for even younger children should also stimulate their creativity, problem solving, and language skills, while giving them control over the type and pace of activities they perform (Druin, 1999; Druin & Solomon, 1996). Developmentally appropriate uses of technology also include integrating computers into the regular learning environment and reinforcing learning that occurs in other parts of the classroom with more traditional learning tools, including books, art materials, and building toys (NAEYC, 1996).

Interactive Books and Toys

What is a computer? Although some computers and electronic toys look like computers, increasingly, the answer seems to be that a computer is any device that has microchip technology and responds when children act upon it. New computers for children are not simply boxy machines with glass screens and mice attached to a keyboard. Instead, they resemble books, traditional infant toys, and even stuffed animals (Druin, 1996; Druin & Solomon, 1996; Druin & Hendler, 2000). It can be difficult, therefore, for early childhood educators to differentiate between traditional learning tools and computers. Parents as well as early childhood educators need to evaluate these new products in light of available evidence about their effects on infants and young

Early childhood educators need to evaluate computer software just as they would evaluate other classroom materials. When used appropriately, computers can enhance young children's cognitive and social development, especially if programs are designed to encourage collaboration and communication between two or more children.

children, keeping in mind what we already know about supporting positive developmental outcomes from birth to age 3.

INTERACTIVE BOOKS   **Electronic books** have been developed that are more interactive than ordinary books, and young children can use them even if they do not yet know how to read. In most electronic books, touching the pages with a special wand activates a voice that reads the text of the story, states the names of objects on the page to which the child is pointing, and asks the child questions about the plot and characters. One potential advantage of many electronic books is that, as children get older, new pages that are even "smarter" can be inserted in place of the original, easier set of pages.

The extent to which educators choose or reject electronic books for their classrooms will be determined, in part, by their effects on young children's emerging literacy skills. Some studies have found that talking books enhance children's phonological awareness, but the experience of using electronic books does not necessarily result in better word reading or comprehension of the story's meaning (Chera & Wood, 2003; Medwell, 1998). In fact, children may even spend less time reading the text and more time activating other parts of the pages when they use electronic books. It is important, therefore, that nontext elements in electronic books be story-relevant, reinforcing key ideas in the text (Labbo & Kuhn, 2000; Wartella, Caplovitz, & Lee, 2004). In addition to illuminating the effects of interactive books on children's reading skills, more research is needed in order to understand whether and how they affect children's ability to create and tell their own stories.

"SMART" INFANT TOYS   Microchip technology has also entered today's toy boxes. For infants as young as 3 months, there are "smart" rattles that not only rattle when shaken but also light up, sing, laugh, and say hello in several languages. Other popular infant toys, like stacking rings, are now available in enhanced versions that respond, literally, with bells and whistles, as well as flashing lights, when the rings are stacked in the correct order. Blocks in one high-tech playset produce beautiful music, including Mozart, when arranged in different orders and with different sides placed into a recessed panel. There are also balls that emit music, letter names, and other sounds as children touch or roll them, and baby gyms in which each touch triggers music, lights, and phrases in foreign languages.

Technologically loaded toys may be expensive, but many manufacturers justify the cost by suggesting or even stating that they help infants learn more effectively than traditional, low-tech versions. Parents and other adults who purchase these toys may be drawn to the bells and whistles and may themselves enjoy playing with them. They should be aware, however, that there has been almost no independent, systematic research exploring the effects of these toys on early development. As a result, we do not know whether or how activating the smart stacking rings or playing with any toy that is designed to provide reinforcing feedback for only one correct solution influences exploration, play, and learning (Bergen, 2001; Hirsh-Pasek & Golinkoff, 2008; Wartella et al., 2004). Extrapolating from the evidence about the impact of TV, DVDs, and videos, however, to the extent that infants and toddlers sitting on an adult's lap enjoy playing on the computer or using high-tech toys together, and do so in moderation, it is reasonable to conclude that the activity is unlikely to either enhance or diminish their physical, cognitive, linguistic, or social development (Courage & Setliff, 2009).

WRAPPING IT UP: Summary and Conclusion

As described in this chapter, music, media, and computers are increasingly prevalent parts of children's everyday experiences from birth to age 3. There are intriguing similarities between the ability to perceive and produce instrumental music and the capacity to perceive and comprehend language, and music and singing are universally human phenomena. Media and computers, by contrast, are more recent, culturally specific inventions, and research has not kept up with the introduction of these technologies. As a result, parents, caregivers, and researchers alike proceed with varying amounts of interest, enthusiasm, skepticism, and alarm, often with unchecked or inaccurate assumptions about the factors that influence early development.

Throughout this book, we have seen that children are born ready to respond to and interact with people, objects, and events and that these experiences are an important foundation for subsequent development. We know that without adequate prenatal care, good nutrition, safe environments, sensitive and responsive caregivers, and stimulating experiences, infants are at risk for a range of immediate and long-lasting physical, cognitive, social, and emotional problems. We have also seen that infants and young children are resilient and that it is possible to compensate for early deprivation, although it becomes more difficult and more expensive to intervene as time passes. There is great potential to improve the future prospects for the most vulnerable and youngest members of society.

As a society, how can we most effectively use the resources and knowledge we have to promote the well-being of all infants and young children? Concerns about infants and toddlers who have too many smart, bossy toys diminish in significance as we consider that there are still many children living in poverty who do not own even a single book (Whitehurst et al., 1994). Debates about whether classical music is beneficial for early intellectual development pale in comparison to the reality that many infants and toddlers spend every day in childcare that provides a safe environment but fails to offer a well-rounded, age-appropriate foundation for learning and social and emotional development (Brauner et al., 2004). Parents who feel pressure to spend a small fortune on the latest technology-rich toys and learning materials need help, but so do parents who experience stress due to inadequate economic resources, poor or uncertain housing arrangements, and institutions that either ignore or misunderstand different cultural and ethnic backgrounds.

Many parents look to experts for guidance, but the experts too often have knowledge that applies only to specific developmental domains. Trained as scientists, most researchers will not draw conclusions or make recommendations that the available data cannot support, but this may have the unintended result of leaving the door open for unqualified individuals to interpret the findings as they wish. In addition, many academic experts are hesitant to disseminate their findings to broader audiences or to engage in public policy initiatives, although they may fully endorse the efforts of those who do incorporate these activities into their professional work (Huston, 2005; McCall, 2009). It is clear, however, that everyone with an interest in development from birth to 3 must share information across disciplinary and organizational boundaries, as suggested by a blue-ribbon panel of early childhood experts (Shonkoff & Phillips, 2000). The recommendations that this group published in an important book, *From Neurons to Neighborhoods*, are shown in Table 12.3.

Researchers supported by the National Institute of Child Health and Human Development, for example, must continue to share their findings not only with scholarly audiences but also through organizations, such as Zero to Three, the National Association for the Education of Young Children, and the Children's Defense Fund, that already serve as a bridge between developmental scientists, policy makers, educators, and parents. Parents are ultimately responsible for nurturing and guiding their children from birth to 3 and beyond, but they need and deserve to be educated about the best practices and how to apply them in their own children's lives.

TABLE 12.3   Promoting Healthy Development from Birth to 3

Recommendations

1. Provide the same amount of resources to foster socioemotional school readiness as are now provided to support literacy and numerical skills.
2. Evaluate schools' effectiveness in reducing disparities that exist at school entry among children from different socioeconomic and cultural backgrounds.
3. Invest resources to address young children's mental health needs by expanding efforts aimed at screening, early detection, treatment, and prevention.
4. Establish policies to provide more choices to more parents for allocating responsibility for early childcare.
5. Coordinate efforts and strategies among private, public, and philanthropic sectors to reduce environmental hazards that are known to pose risks for prenatal and postnatal development.
6. Develop funding to improve the quality of early childhood education by enhancing the skills, knowledge, and compensation of nonparental caregivers.
7. Review current public investments in childcare and early education in order to improve the quality of care that is provided for all young children, including those with developmental disabilities or chronic health conditions.
8. Ensure that children who are supported by a working adult do not live in poverty, and eliminate deep, persistent poverty regardless of employment status.
9. Document and ensure full implementation of effective interventions.
10. Coordinate state and local early childhood policies and agencies, especially those that pertain to mental health services and developmental-behavioral screening for neglected and maltreated children.
11. Create broad-based working groups involving professionals from the fields of education, health, and human services; charge them with the task of identifying professional training and development opportunities and challenges for individuals who work with young children and their families.

Source: Based on information in Shonkoff & Phillips, 2000.

THINK ABOUT IT: Questions for Reading and Discussion

1. What does the Toddler Top 20 and research in this chapter suggest to you about the characteristics of a "good" song for young children? If you wanted to write a new popular children's song, what would you include in it, and why?
2. How would you respond to a new parent who is considering buying CDs featuring Mozart for Babies in order to make her baby smarter?
3. Parents who have decided that their infant should have music lessons as early as possible come to you for advice. What would you tell them about the different methods of music instruction for very young children? What should they keep in mind about the early development of the ability to sing and play music?
4. Is television good or bad for infants and toddlers? How do you know? If you wanted to go beyond correlational research to study the effects of television viewing on children younger than 3 years of age, what sort of experiment would you design? What do you think you would find?
5. Many parents disregard the American Academy of Pediatrics recommendations about the use of television with young children. How would you convince parents in heavy-viewing households that they should minimize screen time, especially for children younger than 2 years of age?
6. With computers now in the majority of homes with children 3 years of age and under, is it more or less important than in the past to have computers in childcare and early childhood education settings? Explain.
7. What do infants and toddlers gain and lose from interacting with smart books and toys? How might these interactions affect their physical, cognitive, social, and emotional development?
8. If you had the opportunity to be an advocate for an issue affecting children from birth to age 3, which issue would you choose and why?

Key Words

Electronic books (374)   Interactive books containing a microchip that enables the reader to activate a voice that reads the text, states the names of objects on the page to which the reader is pointing, and asks the reader questions about the book's contents.

Lapware (373)   Computer programs designed for parents to use with infants and children younger than 2 years of age.

Mozart Effect (363)   The name given to findings of an experiment in which college students who listened to a Mozart sonata scored higher than they had after experiencing the same amount of silence or listening to relaxation instructions.

Suzuki Method (362)   A system developed in the 1940s by a Japanese music educator who believed that learning to play a musical instrument is like learning to speak a first language.

GLOSSARY

Abecedarian Project (347). An intervention in which approximately 100 low-income, primarily African American children participated in a full-time, high-quality early childhood program from the age of 6 weeks until 3 years.

Accommodation (197). Piaget's term for adjusting exploratory actions in response to an object's novel characteristics.

Accretion and deletion (167). The apparent appearance and disappearance of elements of a visual stimulus, such as its texture or pattern.

Active phase (100). The second phase of labor, with increasingly painful contractions coming more frequently as the cervix opens.

Allocentric framework (205). Spatial orientation that is based on external cues in the environment.

Americans with Disabilities Act (ADA) (343). The federal civil rights act protecting individuals with disabilities.

Amniocentesis (81). A procedure for prenatal diagnosis in which a small sample of fluid is taken from the amniotic sac and used to detect any genetic or chromosomal abnormalities.

Amodal properties (178). Information that exists redundantly across sense modalities, rather than being specific to just one modality, such as the synchrony of a sight and its accompanying sound.

Analgesic medication (112). Drugs that reduce pain without eliminating it.

Anesthetic medication (112). Drugs that eliminate pain by blocking nerves that send pain signals to the brain.

A-not-B error (200). Piaget's term for the tendency, first seen around 8 months of age, for infants to search for objects at locations from which they previously successfully retrieved objects, even though they saw the object being hidden at a different location.

Apgar Score (119). An assessment used at 1 and 5 minutes after birth to provide a profile of the infant's physical health.

Arbitrary relations (219). Steps in a sequence that may be performed in any order because they are not logically or practically linked.

Archival research (51). Research that replaces the direct observation or assessment of research participants with examination of records or artifacts.

Assent (54). Verbal agreement to participate in research, obtained when participants are unable to give informed consent.

Assessment of Preterm Infants' Behavior (APIB) (123). A modification of the NBAS that is designed to gauge the effects of interventions and treatments on preterm infants' motor, state, and other neurobehavioral responses (see Brazelton Neonatal Behavioral Assessment Scale).

Assimilation (197). Piaget's term for employing previously used actions to explore an object.

Assisted reproductive technology (ART) (68). Fertility treatments in which both egg and sperm are handled.

Attachment behaviors (280). Infants' built-in behaviors, such as crying, cooing, smiling, looking at, and reaching for caregivers, that attract attention and elicit care.

Attachment Q-Sort (AQS) (281). A rating system that can be used outside of a laboratory setting to assess individual differences in infant-caregiver attachment relationships.

Attachment relationship (279). The special relationship that develops over the first year of life between infants and the adults who care for them.

Auditory localization (171). The ability to detect the location of sound sources.

Autism (257). A syndrome characterized by disordered social interactions and problems with language and communication.

Autism spectrum disorder (ASD) (257). A cluster of five related syndromes that vary in terms of language skill deficits, children's IQ, and the appearance and course of symptoms.

Autosomes (62). Any of the chromosomes other than the sex-determining chromosomes.

Axon (131). A branchlike structure that conveys electrical messages outward from a neuron's cell body toward the synapse.

Babbling (236). Patterned but meaningless sequences of reduplicated sounds, such as strings of syllables.

Baby biography (40). Observational records made by parents or other caregivers of an infants' early development.

Bayley Scales of Infant Development (BSID) (222). A measure that is used to assess infant intelligence through motor, mental, and behavior rating scales.

Bayley Scales of Infant Development-Second Edition (BSID-II) (181). A widely use assessment that includes scales for measuring motor development from birth to 42 months of age.

Behavioral state (53). Any of 10 distinct levels of arousal observed in newborn infants, including four awake states, three transition states between sleep and waking, two sleep states, and one transition sleep state.

Bidirectional (267). Interactions that involve reciprocal behaviors and responses between social partners.

Binocular disparity (169). Slightly different retinal images that are produced when a viewer looks at a single object or visual stimulus.

Binocular vision (166). Visual input from two eyes that are aligned and move together.

Birth doula (116). A trained layperson who provides nonmedical assistance during labor and delivery.

Blastocyst (71). The hollow, spherical structure comprised of approximately 100 identical cells formed through mitosis during the first week after conception.

Body mass index (BMI) (128). A measure of weight in relation to height.

Brazelton Neonatal Behavioral Assessment Scale (NBAS) (122). A structured examination that is used with infants from birth until the age of 2 months to assess reflexes and social interactive behaviors.

Breech presentation (103). A birth in which the infant emerges feet or buttocks first.

Case study (40). Also referred to as the clinical method, this is an in-depth examination of a single individual.

Categorization (220). The ability to group aspects of the world according to shared attributes.

Cephalocaudal principle (71). The pattern of growth in which development begins in the anterior (head) and later occurs in the posterior (tail) of the organism.

Certified nurse-midwife (CNM) (115). Registered nurses who are trained to assist during labor and delivery.

Cesarean delivery (114). A surgical procedure performed when a vaginal delivery would be too dangerous for mother, baby, or both.

Chicago Longitudinal Study (CLS) (347). A federally funded investigation begun in 1986 to document the effects of early and extensive childhood intervention in an urban low-income, primarily African American sample of children and families.

Chorionic villus sampling (CVS) (81). A procedure for prenatal diagnosis in which cells are collected from the chorion, the fetal membrane that gives rise to the placenta.

Chromosomes (62). Physical structures consisting of DNA and supporting proteins.

Cohort (45). A particular group or generation of participants, such as infants born in the same year.

Cohort effects (46). A problem in cross-sectional research, in which age differences may actually stem from generational, or cohort, differences.

Colostrum (148). A thick, yellowish fluid, richer in protein and protective antibodies than the breast milk that is produced a few days after birth.

Committed compliance (319). Children's tendency to follow parents' directives and requests with a minimum of prompting and reminding.

Complementary feeding (152). The transition from exclusive breastfeeding or formula-feeding to the inclusion of solid food in an infant's diet.

Conditioned headturning (50). A technique in which infants are taught to turn their head every time they hear a particular signal—and only when they hear that signal. Once this headturning response has been conditioned and can be elicited reliably, a different stimulus is presented or alternated with the original signal. Infants who do not turn their head in response to the new stimulus are assumed to be able to discriminate between the signal used in conditioning and the new stimulus, whereas infants who turn their head are thought not to be able to make this discrimination.

Cones (165). Photoreceptors in the eye that respond to specific hues, or wavelengths of light.

Conscience (318). An internal set of standards that guide behavior.

Constrained statistical learning (235). The ability to extract recurring patterns from repeated experience with stimuli.

Continuous (5). Characterization of development as a gradual, smooth process of change.

Contrast sensitivity (166). The ability to perceive differences among the elements of an image or pattern under varying degrees of contrast between the pattern and its background (e.g., black patterns on a white background versus a grayish background).

Coordination of secondary schemes (198). Piaget's fourth substage of the sensorimotor period, in which infants perform two separate schemes in order to produce a desired outcome.

Cross-modal perception (180). The ability to transfer information about an object from one sense, such as vision, and use it when encountering the object later using a different sense, such as touch.

Cross-sectional research (45). A developmental design in which two or more age groups of participants are compared in terms of their behavior or ability at the same point in time.

Deferred imitation (199). The ability to remember and repeat an action that was observed earlier, in the absence of a model for those actions.

Dendrites (132). Branchlike structures that convey electrical messages from the synapse and toward a neuron's cell body.

Deoxyribonucleic acid (DNA) (62). Strands of molecules that carry the genetic code of a cell.

Dependent variable (38). The main behavior or response of interest in a study, this is the researchers' measure of the impact of the independent variable(s).

Depth perception (162). The ability to perceive a three-dimensional world.

Dilatation (99). Widening and opening of the cervix during labor.

Dishabituation (50). Infants' recovery of attention when a new stimulus is introduced.

Disorganized/disoriented attachment (282). An infant-caregiver relationship that may develop when caregivers show contradictory, disrupted, or otherwise unusual emotional communication with their infants; also referred to as Type D.

Distal parenting (265). A pattern of caregiving in which parents have physical contact with babies but emphasize face-to-face verbal and vocal interaction and encourage infants to look at toys or other objects while they talk about and manipulate them together, reinforcing the value of independence and self-reliance.

Dizygotic twins (67). Siblings resulting from two different eggs, also known as fraternal (DZ) twins.

Down syndrome (64). A congenital syndrome, also referred to as trisomy 21, in which there is an extra chromosome 21; individuals with Down syndrome have distinctive facial features and other physical characteristics and have mild to severe mental retardation.

Dyadic synchrony (267). Interactions between infants and caregivers that are characterized by mutual attention and affective matching or regulation.

Dynamic systems theories (164). Perspectives that describe development as the emergence of new forms of behavior due to self-organization and interactions of the components of a complex system operating on multiple levels.

Early Head Start (EHS) (348). A national intervention program that provides services to low-income pregnant women and families with infants and toddlers.

Early intervention (EI) (344). Systematic efforts to either prevent or reduce the adverse developmental effects of family income, parent characteristics, birth experiences, or aspects of the environment. The strongest conclusions can be made when children are randomly assigned to intervention and control groups.

Early Intervention Services (EIS) (343). Services provided through IDEA, including screening and assessment, family education and training, home visits, health and social services, speech-language therapy, and occupational and physical therapy, as well as assistive technology.

Ecological theory of perception (162). A theory that assumes that the visual system perceives meaningful information directly from the properties of the environment.

Ectoderm (72). The upper layer of the inner cell mass, which gives rise to the brain and spinal cord, sensory organs, and skin, nails, hair, and teeth.

Effacement (100). The thinning out of the cervix during labor.

Effectance (267). The feeling of influencing others or having an impact on the immediate environment, often in the pursuit of specific implicit or explicit goals.

Egocentric (197). Piaget's term for infants' tendency to understand the world through their own sensory and motor acts.

Egocentric framework (205). Spatial orientation that is based on one's own body and physical actions.

Egocentric speech (207). Verbal behavior that is directed toward oneself rather than others, with the purpose of enhancing concentration and performance during an activity.

Electroencephalogram (EEG) (130). A measure of the brain's activity that uses external electrodes placed on the scalp.

Electroencephalography (EEG) (49). A measurement of electrical activity and spontaneous natural rhythms in the brain.

Electronic books (374). Interactive books containing a microchip that enables the reader to activate a voice that reads the text, states the names of objects on the page to which the reader is pointing, and asks the reader questions about the book's contents.

Electronic fetal monitoring (EFM) (111). The use of external or internal sensors to monitor contractions and detect signs of fetal distress.

Embryonic stage (71). The second prenatal stage, lasting from 2 weeks to 8 weeks.

Emergentist coalition model (ECM) (251). A theory about early word learning that describes children shifting at approximately 12 months of age from a reliance on attentional cues such as perceptual saliency and temporal continuity to a greater dependency on social and linguistic cues such as eye gaze, social context, and grammar.

Emotional contagion (310). A phenomenon in which facial, vocal, or gestural cues of one person give rise to a similar or related state in another person.

Emotion regulation (314). A process through which emotions are monitored, appraised, and modified in relation to goals.

Enabling relations (219). A logically or practically necessary order between steps in a sequence.

Endoderm (72). The lower layer of the inner cell mass, from which the respiratory and digestive systems develop.

Episiotomy (113). A procedure in which an incision is made to widen the vaginal opening.

Ethnographic research (36). A technique for exploring the interaction of culture and biology, in which researchers from a Western culture make observations or conduct interviews in everyday settings in non-Western cultures.

Ethnotheories (265). Implicit, coherent ideas about parenting and child development that reflect cultural communities' desired balance of characteristics such as independence/interdependence, competitiveness/compliance, and self-expression/deference to others.

Event-related potential (ERP) (49). A measurement of electrical activity resulting in the brain from the presentation of discrete stimuli.

Event sampling (34). A technique in observational research in which a small number of behaviors are identified and the researcher makes a note each time they occur by making a mark on a prepared checklist.

Experience-dependent (133). Aspects of brain development that develop solely as a result of a person's experiences.

Experience-expectant (132). Aspects of brain development that "expect" to have certain kinds of stimulation and are ready to develop once they receive it.

Experimental design (42). A design that examines the influence of an independent variable on a dependent variable.

Explicit memory (218). Conscious awareness of specific information, such as events and facts.

External validity (39). The degree to which the findings of one study can be extended, or generalized, to other samples and settings.

Failure to thrive (FTT) (129). A condition, usually due to inadequate nutrition, in which a child's growth falters and weight gain is not as rapid as would be expected for his or her age.

Family childcare home (334). Care that is provided for one or more unrelated children in the caregiver's home.

Family leave (328). Job-protected time off from work for a variety of reasons other than the birth of a child.

Family and Medical Leave Act (FMLA) (328). The federal policy that allows certain categories of employees to take a 12-week, job-protected leave to care for a child, spouse, or parent or to take time off due to their own serious health condition.

Fetal alcohol syndrome (FAS) (85). A constellation of physical, behavioral, and cognitive abnormalities caused by prenatal exposure to alcohol.

Fetal stage (74). The third prenatal stage, lasting from 8 weeks until birth.

Fine motor skills (181). Skills, such as grasping small objects, that involve movements of the fingers and hands.

Forced-choice preferential looking (166). A research procedure in which infants are shown two visual stimuli simultaneously and the total amount of time they spend looking at each display is compared.

Fovea (166). The center of the eye.

Gaze following (213). A characteristic of social interaction in which one person shifts his or her visual attention in the direction another person has turned to look.

Genes (62). Units of hereditary information; each gene is a segment of DNA in a specific location on a chromosome.

Germinal stage (70). The first prenatal stage, beginning at conception and ending at approximately 2 weeks.

Goodness-of-fit (284). A match between an infant's behaviors and the caregiver's expectations and understanding of those behaviors.

Grammar (229). Systems of rules for combining words or signs

Gross motor skills (181). Skills, such as crawling and walking, that involve movements of the whole body and large muscle groups.

Guided participation (209). Patterns of social interaction and structured activity during joint problem solving involving people with different levels of skills and knowledge.

Habituation (50). The phenomenon in which infants gradually lose interest in a stimulus after repeated presentations.

Haptic information (180). Exploratory mouth or hand movements that go well beyond mere tactile contact with an object.

High/Scope Perry Preschool Project (346). An intervention in which approximately 100 low-income African American preschoolers received high-quality early childhood education and home visits.

High-reactive (303). Infants who respond to novelty by showing extreme degrees of motor activity, fretting, and crying.

Holophrase (243). Infants' first one-word utterances that name objects but also communicate other meanings.

Home Observation for Measurement of the Environment (HOME) (345). A tool for assessing the quality of a child's home environment, using a combination of observer rating and mother's reports.

Implicit memory (218). Unconscious learning, including conditioning and aspects of motor learning.

Independent variable (38). Aspects of a research setting that researchers identify or vary, such as presence or absence of an infant's mother, in order to determine their effect on behaviors of interest.

Indiscriminate friendliness (278). Behavior that is affectionate and friendly toward all adults, including strangers, without the fear or caution characteristic of normal children; often observed in children adopted from orphanages or other institutional settings.

Individuals with Disabilities Education Act (IDEA) (343). The federal civil rights act covering children with disabilities; Part C explicitly covers services from birth to 24 months of age.

Infant Health and Development Project (347). An intervention involving nearly 1,000 preterm, low birth-weight infants, with one-third of the sample randomly selected to have home visits and to participate in full-day, high-quality childcare in child development centers from birth to age 3.

Infant mortality rate (13). Number of infants who die before reaching the age of 1 year, usually reported as the number of deaths per 1,000 live births.

Infant school movement (23). An early nineteenth-century movement, imported to the United States from Europe, in which educators believed that children as young as 18 months could be educated and taught to read.

Infant-directed speech (233). Modifications that adults make when speaking (or signing) to infants, producing language that is shorter, more repetitive, higher-pitched, more variable in pitch, and less semantically and grammatically complex than language addressed to adults.

Informed consent (54). A key requirement in ethical research, based on research participants being able to understand the procedures involved in a study and any risks those procedures might entail and knowing that they are free to withdraw or decline to participate without any negative consequences.

Inhibited to novelty (303). A constitutionally based tendency to respond to unfamiliar people and places by becoming quiet, vigilant, restrained, and avoidant.

Insecure-avoidant attachment (281). An infant-caregiver relationship that may develop when caregivers are over-stimulating and intrusive when interacting with their infants; also referred to as Type A.

Insecure-resistant attachment (281). An infant-caregiver relationship that may develop when caregivers are rejecting or withdrawn, depressed, and unresponsive to infants' needs and attachment behaviors; also referred to as Type C.

Intermodal perception (178). The ability to integrate multiple simultaneous sources of sensory information, such as sights and sounds produced by a single object or event.

Internal validity (39). The degree to which differences in the dependent variable are actually due to differences in the independent variable.

Internal working model (280). Infants' mental representations of their relationship with their primary caregiver(s).

Intersensory redundancy hypothesis (179). The theoretical notion that intersensory redundancy in multimodal events promotes perception of amodal information, whereas unimodal events enhance perception of modality-specific properties.

Joint attention (214). Shared perceptual exploration during social interaction, in which gaze alternates between some aspect of the environment and another person involved in the interaction.

Kinematic depth cues (169). Information about perceptual depth that is carried by motion.

Kinesthetic sense (177). A sense that conveys information about the body's position and movement.

Labor induction (110). A procedure in which a hormone is administered in order to initiate uterine contractions leading to labor and delivery.

Laboratory setting (38). A specially designed research space that enables researchers to control or eliminate the influence of irrelevant or distracting factors.

Lapware (373). Computer programs designed for parents to use with infants and children younger than 2 years of age.

Latent phase (100). The initial phase of the first stage of labor, marked by widely spaced contractions that are not painful.

Lexical contrast (250). The ability to learn a new word's meaning by comparing it to words that are already known.

Literary evidence (9). Written information, including parents' diaries and letters, childrearing advice written by ministers and doctors, and children's books.

Longitudinal research (44). A developmental design in which investigators study the same sample of participants over time, taking measures of their behavior or ability at specified intervals.

Long-term memory (218). Information that is stored and available to be retrieved repeatedly over time.

Low birthweight (LBW) (107). A birthweight of less than $5\frac{1}{2}$ lb., or 2,500 grams.

Low-reactive (303). Infants who respond to novelty by showing low levels of motor activity and a general absence of crying and fussing.

Macrosomic birth (108). A birthweight of more than 8 lb. 13 oz., or 4,000 grams.

Magnetic resonance imaging (MRI) (131). An imaging technology that reveals the brain's structure.

Maltreatment (277). Neglect, medical neglect, physical abuse, sexual abuse, or psychological abuse.

Material culture (9). Physical evidence, such as toys, clothing, furniture, and works of art.

Maternal serum alpha fetoprotein (MSAFP) test (81). A screening test in which the level of alpha fetoprotein in the mother's bloodstream is measured; also known as the triple screen because it measures the amount of estriol and HCG present in the mother's blood.

Maternity leave (328). A job-protected leave from work for employed women during, and sometimes before, childbirth.

Mean length of utterance (MLU) (251). A measure of grammatical development that is based on the number of morphemes in speech.

Measurement equivalence (44). Correspondence between the measures, or dependent variables, used at two different points in time.

Meiosis (66). The process through which sex cells divide at conception.

Mental combinations (199). Piaget's sixth substage of the sensorimotor period, in which infants are able to think about their actions and select schemes in order to achieve a desired outcome.

Mental representation (197). The ability to remember and think about objects and events, even when those objects and events are not physically present.

Mesoderm (72). The middle layer of the inner cell mass, from which the circulatory and excretory systems, muscles, and skeleton develop.

Microgenetic research (46). A developmental design in which participants are observed over a period of time, perhaps 10 or more sessions, with the researchers gathering a rich set of data on which fine-grained analyses can be performed.

Micronutrient deficiency (155). A form of malnutrition that occurs when insufficient amounts of minerals and vitamins are consumed in the diet.

Mitosis (62). The life-long process of cell division in which a cell divides into two identical cells.

Monozygotic twins (67). Siblings resulting from a single egg, also known as identical (MZ) twins.

Morphemes (251). Minimal meaningful units in speech, such as words, parts of words, or word endings.

Mozart Effect (363). The name given to findings of an experiment in which college students who listened to a Mozart sonata scored higher than they had after experiencing the same amount of silence or listening to relaxation instructions.

Multifactorial transmission (65). The interaction of genes and the environment that produces most complex human characteristics.

Mutual exclusivity assumption (249). A constraint on learning that guides children to assume that objects will have only one name and to look for a nameless object when they hear a new word.

Mutually responsive orientation (MRO) (319). A relationship quality that consists of positive emotions and close cooperative interactions.

Myelin (132). A fatty covering that insulates axons and increases the efficiency of neural functioning.

Narrative record (34). A detailed description of the range of behaviors researchers observe.

Naturalistic observation (33). Studies in which researchers remain relatively passive observers in the sense that, apart from being physically present, they do not intervene in or try to influence the situation.

Naturalistic setting (33). Studies in which researchers observe infants in their usual surroundings, such as their own home or their regular childcare center.

Nature (5). Biological factors influencing development.

Neonatal Intensive Care Unit (NICU) (105). A specialized hospital setting for the care of medically vulnerable infants, including those born preterm and very preterm.

Neonatal Intensive Care Unit Network Neurobehavioral Scale (NNNS) (123). A measure designed to assess the functioning of at-risk infants, primarily those believed to have been exposed prenatally to alcohol, cocaine, or other teratogens.

Neonate (108). Newborns and infants younger than 1 month of age.

Neural tube defects (76). Birth defects that involve abnormal development of the neural tube during the first few weeks of the prenatal period.

Neurons (75). Nerve cells in the brain, comprised of a cell body, axons, and dendrites.

Neurotransmitters (132). Biochemical substances that transmit information between neurons through release and uptake at synapses.

NICHD Study of Early Child Care and Youth Development (SECCYD) (336). A longitudinal, multimethod and multimeasure study of approximately 1,400 children in childcare settings across the United States.

Nurture (5). Environmental and experiential factors influencing development.

Object permanence (199). Piaget's term for infants' gradually developing understanding that objects continue to exist even when they are not in sensory or motor contact with them.

Oblation (14). Medieval European practice involving the permanent "donation" of an infant or young child to a monastery.

Observer bias (34). The phenomenon in which researchers' expectations or beliefs influence the way they record or interpret behavior.

Obstetrician (115). A physician trained to assist and perform procedures during labor and delivery.

Operational definition (34). A clear, concrete verbal description that enables researchers to measure target behaviors and outcomes accurately.

Optical expansion and contraction (169). The increase and decrease in the size of an object's image on the retina.

Orienting response (50). Infants' behavior the first time a stimulus is presented, characterized by momentary cessation of any ongoing activity in order to give close attention to the new stimulus.

Overextension (243). A common error in which children use a word to refer to other objects that may be perceptually or functionally similar to the word's correct referent.

Overregularization (253). An error in which children apply grammatical morphemes to words for which a language makes an exception to the rule.

Ovum (66). Female sex cell.

Parental leave (328). A job-protected leave that is open to mothers or fathers, typically available as a supplement to maternity and paternity leaves.

Parental reports (51). Data provided about infants' behavior and development by their parents or caregivers.

Paternity leave (328). A job-protected leave from work for employed men, typically taken after childbirth.

Perceptual magnet effect (235). A phenomenon in which acoustic space is altered as a result of increasing sensitivity to native language phonemes and declining sensitivity to nonnative language phonemes.

Phonemes (234). Linguistically meaningful phonetic categories that signal differences in words through combinations of vowels and consonants.

Phonetics (234). A set of vowels and consonants that a particular language uses.

Phonology (229). Sound patterns of language.

Pictorial depth cues (170). Information about perceptual depth that is used in two-dimensional representations of the three-dimensional world, including relative size, linear perspective, texture gradients, and interposition.

Placenta (72). A network of blood vessels, formed from cells in the trophoblast and from cells in the uterine lining, the function of which is to convey oxygen and nutrients to the embryo and carry away waste products.

Play (192). Activity that is intrinsically motivated, focused on means rather than ends, different from purely exploratory behavior, nonliteral, and free from externally applied rules.

Positron emission tomography (PET) (131). An imaging technology that shows the amount of activity in the brain.

Postpartum depression (275). A sense of despair and sadness so pervasive that it affects a mother's ability to care for and interact effectively with her baby; approximately 15 percent of new mothers are affected in this way.

Practice effect (45). Improvement in participants' performance as a result of the repeated exposure to the measures of those abilities.

Pragmatics (229). Using language for particular purposes in specific social contexts.

Pregnancy Discrimination Act of 1978 (328). The federal act, passed in 1978, to prohibit employment discrimination on the basis of pregnancy or childbirth.

Preimplantation genetic diagnosis (PGD) (79). A procedure in which a biopsy is performed on blastocysts resulting from in vitro fertilization, with the purpose of selecting blastocysts that are not carriers of genetic mutations for disease for transfer to the woman's uterus.

Pre-kindergarten (PK) (350). Programs or classes for 3- and 4-year-olds, housed in public schools, with a primary focus on enhancing disadvantaged children's school readiness.

Premature rupture of membranes (PROM) (100). Condition occurring when the amniotic sac breaks open before contractions begin.

Preoperational thought (197). Piaget's second stage of cognitive development, from 2 to 6 years of age.

Pretend/symbolic play (195). Play that emerges after 12 months of age, in which children behave in a nonliteral way.

Preterm (103). A birth that occurs before 37 weeks gestation.

Primary circular reactions (198). Piaget's second substage of the sensorimotor period, in which sensory and motor schemes are activated by chance.

Primary emotions (308). A set of emotions—distress, interest, and pleasure—present at birth and differentiating into other emotions during infancy.

Project CARE (347). An intervention similar to the Abecedarian Project, in which low-income children participated in a full-time, high-quality early childhood program, supplemented with parent group meetings and home visiting.

Proprioceptive sense (177). A sense that conveys information from muscles, tendons, and joints about the body's position and movement.

Protein-energy malnutrition (PEM) (155). A form of malnutrition that occurs when insufficient amounts of protein and calories are consumed in the diet.

Proximal parenting (265). A pattern of caregiving in which parents maintain close, nearly constant physical contact with babies, respond quickly when they cry or are hungry, and highlight the importance of social connections and interdependence among members of the family.

Proximodistal principle (72). The pattern of growth in which development begins in the center of the body and moves toward the extremities of the organism.

Psychosocial short stature (130). A type of failure to thrive in which a child is both underweight and extremely short, often as a result of neglect or emotional and psychological trauma.

Quantitative archival evidence (9). Official sources of written information and data, including census data, tax records, and legislative and court records.

Quasi-experimental design (42). A design in which researchers collect information about groups of participants that are already formed before the study begins.

Random assignment (43). The equivalent of flipping a coin, this technique is used to ensure that each child has an equal chance of being placed into the different groups being compared on a specific dependent variable. As a result of this precaution, potentially important differences across children are distributed across the different groups.

Reactive attachment disorder (RAD) (283). A recently proposed type of attachment that may develop in institutionalized infants who are severely maltreated.

Recall memory (219). The ability to remember a previously presented stimulus or event in the absence of ongoing perceptual support.

Recognition memory (218). The ability to remember a previously presented stimulus or event when it is presented at a later time.

Referential cues (247). Verbal and nonverbal behaviors, such as gaze, facial expression, and head orientation, that reflect an individual's attentional focus, intentions, or expectations.

Reflexes (120). Involuntary responses to stimuli, present at birth and gradually diminishing during the first few months of life.

Reflex schemes (197). Piaget's first substage of the sensorimotor period, in which infants respond to the world with a limited set of preadapted behaviors.

Representational insight (206). Awareness of the relation between a space and a symbol for that space.

Research ethics (54). A set of principles and guidelines for conducting acceptable research activities.

Scaffolding (208). The process through which more capable individuals structure tasks to boost less capable individuals' performance.

Schemes (197). Piaget's term for actions used to explore and interact with the physical environment.

Secondary circular reactions (198). Piaget's third substage of the sensorimotor period, in which infants repeat schemes in order to achieve specific outcomes.

Secondary emotions (309). A set of emotions—embarrassment, envy, empathy, pride, shame, and guilt—that emerges during the second and third years of life.

Secure attachment relationship (281). An infant-caregiver relationship that develops when caregivers respond quickly and sensitively to their infant's signs of distress and other attachment behaviors; also referred to as Type B.

Self-conscious emotions (309). Emotions that involve the comparison of oneself or one's actions to standards and expectations that others hold; also called social emotions.

Self-referential language (321). An aspect of the self, seen in children's use of their own name, as well as personal pronouns, such as "me" and "mine."

Semantics (229). Meanings of words or signs.

Sensitivity (269). The degree to which parents and other caregivers are attentive to infants' signals, accurate in their perceptions, and responsive to their child's needs.

Sensorimotor intelligence (197). Piaget's first stage of cognitive development, from birth to 24 months of age.

Sex chromosomes (62). The pair of sex-determining chromosomes that each human possesses: XX in females and XY in males.

Sex-linked inheritance (63). Transmission of characteristics via the mother's X chromosome; sons but not daughters inherit the trait.

Shaken baby syndrome (SBS) (135). A subtype of abusive head trauma due to maltreatment, in which an angry or frustrated adult shakes an infant violently, resulting in brain damage or death.

Short-term memory (220). A limited storage system that holds information for only a few seconds if the information is not actively rehearsed.

Single-subject research (41). A variation of the case study, in which researchers intervene or study the effects of an experimental manipulation within a single participant.

Situational compliance (319). Children's tendency to require prompting and reminding in order to follow parents' directives and requests.

Social referencing (313). Attention that is focused on another person in order to gauge his or her emotional and behavioral response to an ambiguous situation.

Sociocultural contexts (207). Settings in which children spend time, including home, childcare, and school.

Sperm (66). Male sex cell.

Stagewise (4). Characterization of development as occurring in distinct phases, with qualitative differences between stages.

States of arousal (122). Distinct levels of alertness within the general behavioral categories of active sleep, quiet sleep, and wakefulness.

Stereoscopic depth information (169). Information about perceptual depth that is produced by binocular disparity.

Still-face paradigm (311). A procedure for studying emotional communication and regulation by disrupting the normal verbal and nonverbal signals that parents and infants use to communicate.

Strange Situation (281). A laboratory procedure that Ainsworth developed to assess individual differences in infant-caregiver attachment relationships.

Sudden infant death syndrome (SIDS) (144). The diagnosis given when an infant younger than 1 year dies and a complete investigation is unable to identify a specific cause.

Suzuki Method (362). A system developed in the 1940s by a Japanese music educator who believed that learning to play a musical instrument is like learning to speak a first language.

Syllables (236). Combinations of consonants and vowels, such as *baba* and *mama*.

Synapses (131). Spaces between neurons, in which biochemical messages are released and absorbed.

Synaptogenesis (132). Formation of synapses in a network of neurons.

Taxonomic assumption (249). A constraint on learning that guides children to assume that new words should be extended to objects within the same category rather than thematic associates.

Telegraphic speech (251). Early two-word and multiword utterances that sound like telegrams because they lack grammatical markers and extra words, such as articles, plural endings, prepositions, and auxiliary verbs.

Temperament (296). A theoretical construct consisting of constitutionally based individual differences in emotionality, motor activity, attentiveness, adaptability, and self-regulation.

Teratogens (69). Substances, such as alcohol, drugs, nicotine, and radiation, that are known to cause harm to the developing fetus.

Tertiary circular reactions (199). Piaget's fifth substage of the sensorimotor period, in which infants try different schemes to discover the effects of those actions.

Theory of mind (ToM) (216). A cognitive achievement that emerges around the age of 3 years, enabling children to understand others' feelings and beliefs.

Ultrasound (80). A prenatal diagnostic tool, also referred to as ultrasonography, that uses sound waves to create moving images of the fetus and detect any structural abnormalities.

Umbilical cord (72). The structure through which the embryo is connected to the placenta.

Underextension (243). An error in which children apply a word only to a specific instance or fail to use it to refer to other referents for which the word would be correct.

Uninhibited to novelty (303). A constitutionally based tendency to respond to unfamiliar people and places by showing spontaneous engagement and active interest.

Vertex position (101). A birth in which the infant is delivered head first.

Very low birthweight (VLBW) (107). A birthweight of less than $3\frac{1}{4}$ lb., or 1,500 grams.

Very preterm (104). A birth that occurs before 32 weeks gestation.

Vesicles (132). Neurotransmitter storage spaces at the end of the axon.

Vestibular sense (177). A sense that conveys information about physical balance and support.

Violation-of-expectation procedure (202). A procedure in which infants are shown possible and impossible events in order to test their understanding of physical phenomena and object properties.

Visual acuity (165). The smallest spacing that can be perceived between parts of a pattern.

Visual cortex (166). The area of the brain that processes visual information.

Visual fixation (49). Infants' looking behavior at stimuli presented in laboratory settings.

Visual preference method (49). A technique in which infants' looking behavior is used to determine their ability to perceive and notice differences between stimuli presented in a laboratory setting.

Visual self-recognition (320). An early aspect of the self, measured by children's understanding that when they look in a mirror, the reflection that they see is their own.

Whole object assumption (248). A constraint on learning that guides children to assume that new words refer to whole objects rather than actions, spatial location, or parts or features of objects.

Zone of proximal development (ZPD) (207). Vygotsky's term for the distance between a child's ability to solve a problem alone and how much better the child can solve the problem when guided or assisted by a more capable individual.

Zygote (67). The cell that results when an ovum is fertilized by a sperm cell.

REFERENCES

Abbott, A.L., & Bartlett, D.J. (2001). Infant motor development and equipment use in the home. *Child: Care, Health, and Development, 27,* 295–306.

Abbott, J.S.C. (1834/1972). *The mother at home; or, the principles of maternal duty familiarly illustrated.* New York: Arno Press & The New York Times.

Abels, M., Keller, H., Mohite, P., Mankodi, H., Shastri, J., Bhargava, S., et al. (2005). Early socialization contexts and social experiences of infants in rural and urban Gujarat, India. *Journal of Cross-Cultural Psychology, 36,* 717–738.

Abolyan, L.V. (2006). The breastfeeding support and promotion in Baby-Friendly maternity hospitals and not-as-yet Baby-Friendly hospitals in Russia. *Breastfeeding Medicine, 1,* 71–78.

Abramovitch, R., Corter, C., Pepler, D.J., & Stanhope, L. (1986). Sibling and peer interaction: A final follow-up and a comparison. *Child Development, 57,* 217–229.

Acredolo, L.P. (1978). Development of spatial orientation in infancy. *Developmental Psychology, 14,* 224–234.

Acredolo, L.P. (1990). Behavioral approaches to spatial orientation in infancy. In A. Diamond (Ed.), *The development and neural bases of higher cognitive functions* (pp. 596–607). New York: New York Academy of Sciences.

Acredolo, L.P., Goodwyn, S.W., Horobin, K., & Emmons, Y.D. (2000). The signs and sounds of early language development. In C. Tamis-LeMonda & L. Balter (Eds.), *Child psychology: A handbook of contemporary issues* (pp. 116–139). New York: Psychology Press.

Adam, E.K., Gunnar, M.R., & Tanaka, A. (2004). Adult attachment, parent emotion, and observed parenting behavior: Mediator and moderator models. *Child Development, 75,* 110–122.

Adams, R.J., Courage, M.L., & Mercer, M.E. (1991). Deficiencies in human neonates' color vision: Photoreceptoral and neural explanations. *Behavioural Brain Research, 43,* 109–114.

Adams, R.J., Courage, M.L., & Mercer, M.E. (1994). Systematic measurement of human neonatal color vision. *Vision Research, 34,* 1691–1701.

Adamson, L.B., Bakeman, R., & Deckner, D.F. (2004). The development of symbol-infused joint engagement. *Child Development, 75,* 1171–1187.

Adibi, J.J., Perera, F.P., Jedrychowski, W., Camann, D.E., Barr, D., & Whyatt, R.M. (2003). Prenatal exposures to phthalates among women in New York City and Krakow, Poland. *Environmental Health Perspectives, 111,* 1719–1722.

Adi-Japha, E., & Klein, P.S. (2009). Relations between parenting quality and cognitive performance of children experiencing varying amounts of childcare. *Child Development, 80,* 893–906.

ACF (Administration for Children and Families/U.S. Department of Health and Human Services). (2002). *Early Head Start benefits children and families.* Retrieved on September 1, 2005, from http://www.acf.hhs.gov/programs/core/ongoing_research/ehs/ehs_intro.html

ACF (Administration for Children and Families/U.S. Department of Health and Human Services). (2003a). *Research to practice: Child care.* Retrieved on September 1, 2005, from http://www.acf.hhs.gov/programs/core/ongoing_research/ehs/ehs_intro.html

ACF (Administration for Children and Families/U.S. Department of Health and Human Services). (2003b). *Research to practice: Children with disabilities in Early Head Start.* Retrieved on September 1, 2005, from http://www.acf.hhs.gov/programs/core/ongoing_research/ehs/ehs_intro.html

ACF (Administration on Children, Youth and Families/U.S. Department of Health and Human Services). (2005). About Early Head Start. Retrieved on September 1, 2005, from http://www.headstartinfo.org/infocenter/ehs_tkit3.htm

Adolph, K.E. (1995). Psychophysical assessment of toddlers' ability to cope with slopes. *Journal of Experimental Psychology, 21,* 734–750.

Adolph, K.E. (1997). Learning in the development of infant locomotion. *Monographs of the Society for Research in Child Development, 62*(3, Serial No. 251).

Adolph, K.E. (2000). Specificity of learning: Why infants fall over a veritable cliff. *Psychological Science, 11,* 290–295.

Adolph, K.E. (2008). Learning to move. *Current Directions in Psychological Science, 17,* 213–218.

Adolph, K.E., & Avolio, A.M. (2000). Specificity of learning: Why infants fall over a veritable cliff. *Psychological Science, 11,* 290–295.

Adolph, K.E., & Berger, S.E. (2006). Motor development. In W. Damon & R. Lerner (Series Eds.) & D. Kuhn & R. Siegler (Vol. Eds.), *Handbook of child psychology: Vol. 2. Cognition, perception, and language* (6th ed., pp. 161–213). New York: Wiley.

Adolph, K.E., Vereijken, B., & Denny, M.A. (1998). Learning to crawl. *Child Development, 69,* 1299–1312.

Adolph, K.E., Vereijken, B., & Shrout, P.E. (2003). What changes in infant walking and why. *Child Development, 74,* 475–497.

Aguiar, A., & Baillargeon, R. (2003). Perseverative responding in a violation-of-expectation task in 6.5-month-old infants. *Cognition, 88,* 277–316.

Ahluwalia, I.B., & Daniel, K.L. (2001). Are women with recent live births aware of the benefits of folic acid? *Morbidity and Mortality Weekly Report, 50(RR06),* 3–14.

Ahmed, A., & Ruffman, T. (1998). Why do infants make A not B errors in a search task, yet show memory for the location of hidden objects in a nonsearch task? *Developmental Psychology, 34,* 441–453.

Ahmed, S.F., & Hughes, I.A. (2002). The genetics of male undermasculinization. *Clinical Endocrinology, 56,* 1–18.

Ahnert, L., Gunnar, M.R., Lamb, M.E., & Barthel, M. (2004). Transition to child care: Associations with infant-mother attachment, infant negative emotion, and cortisol elevations. *Child Development, 75,* 639–650.

Ahnert, L., & Lamb, M.E. (2003). Shared care: Establishing a balance between home and child care settings. *Child Development, 74,* 1044–1049.

Ahnert, L., Pinquart, M., & Lamb, M.E. (2006). Security of children's relationships with nonparental care providers: A meta-analysis. *Child Development, 74,* 664–679.

Ainsworth, M.D.S. (1967). *Infancy in Uganda: Infant care and growth of love.* Baltimore: Johns Hopkins University Press.

Ainsworth, M.D.S., & Bell, S.M. (1969). Some contemporary patterns of mother-infant interaction in the feeding situation. In A. Ambrose (Ed.), *Stimulation in early infancy* (pp. 133–170). London: Academic Press.

Ainsworth, M.D.S., Bell, S.M., & Stayton, D.J. (1972). Individual differences in the development of some attachment behaviors. *Merrill-Palmer Quarterly, 18,* 123–143.

Ainsworth, M.D.S., Blehar, M.C., Waters, E., & Wall, S. (1978). *Patterns of attachment: A psychological study of the strange situation.* Oxford, UK: Erlbaum.

Akechi, H., Senjin, A., Kikuchi, Y., Tojo, Y., Osanai, H., & Hasegawa, T. (2009). Does gaze direction modulate facial expression processing in children with autism spectrum disorder? *Child Development, 80,* 1134–1146.

Akhtar, N., Dunham, F., & Dunham, P. J. (1991). Directive interactions and early vocabulary development: The role of joint attentional focus. *Journal of Child Language, 18,* 41–49.

Akhtar, N., & Gernsbacher, M.A. (2008). On privileging the role of gaze in infant social cognition. *Child Development Perspectives, 2,* 59–65.

Akhtar, N., & Tomasello, M. (2000). The social nature of words and word learning. In R.M. Golinkoff, K. Hirsh-Pasek, L. Bloom, L.B. Smith, A.L. Woodward, N. Akhtar, et al., *Becoming a word learner: A debate on lexical acquisition* (pp. 115–135). New York: Oxford University Press.

Aksan, N., & Kochanska, G. (2005). Conscience in childhood: Old questions, new answers. *Developmental Psychology, 41,* 506–516.

Aksoy, S., & Slobin, D.I. (1985). The acquisition of Turkish. In D.I. Slobin (Ed.), *The crosslinguistic study of language acquisition* (Vol. 1, pp. 15–68). Hillsdale, NJ: Erlbaum.

Alan Guttmacher Institute. (1999). *Sharing responsibility: Women, society, and abortion worldwide.* New York: AGI.

Al-Raees, G.Y., Al-Amer, M.A., Musaiger, A.O., & D'Souza, R. (2009). Prevalence of overweight and obesity among children aged 2–5 years in Bahrain: A comparison between two reference standards. *International Journal of Pediatric Obesity, 4,* 1–3.

Alexander, J.M., McIntire, D.D., & Leveno, K.J. (2001). Prolonged pregnancy: Induction of labor and Cesarean births. *Obstetrics & Gynecology, 97,* 911–915.

Allen, V.M., Baskett, T.F., O'Connell, C.M., McKeen, D., & Allen, A.C. (2009). Maternal and perinatal outcomes with increasing duration of the second stage of labor. *Obstetrics & Gynecology, 113,* 1248–1258.

Alliance for Childhood. (2000). *Fool's gold: A critical look at computers in childhood.* Retrieved December 27, 2009, from http://drupal6.allianceforchildhood .org/fools_gold

Allison, A. (1996). Producing mothers. In A.E. Imamura (Ed.), *Re-imaging Japanese women* (pp. 135–155). Berkeley, CA: University of California Press.

Almond, D., & Edlund, L. (2008). Son-biased sex ratios in the 2000 United States Census. *Proceedings of the National Academy of Science, 105,* 5681–5682.

Als, H., Butler, S., Kosta, S., & McAnulty, G. (2005). The Assessment of Preterm Infants' Behavior (APIB): Furthering the understanding and measurement of neurodevelopmental competence in preterm and full-term infants. *Mental Retardation and Developmental Disabilities Research Reviews. Special Issue: Neurodevelopmental Assessment of the Fetus and Young Infant, 11,* 94–102.

Als, H., Gilkerson, L., Duffy, F.H., McAnulty, G.B., Buehler, D.M., Vandenberg, K., et al. (2003). A three-center, randomized, controlled trial of individualized developmental care for very low birth weight preterm infants: Medical, neurodevelopmental, parenting, and caregiving effects. *Developmental and Behavioral Pediatrics, 24,* 399–408.

Als, H., Lester, B.M., Tronick, E., & Brazelton, T.B. (1982). Towards a research instrument for the assessment of preterm infants' behavior (APIB). In H.E. Fitzgerald, B.M. Lester, & M.W. Yogman (Eds.), *Theory and research in behavioral pediatrics* (Vol. 1, pp. 65–132). New York: Plenum.

Altimier, L. (2008). Shaken baby syndrome. *Journal of Perinatal and Neonatal Nursing, 22,* 68–76.

American Academy of Family Physicians. (1996). Fever in infants and children. *Family Health & Medical Guide.* Dallas, TX: Word Publishing. Retrieved July 27, 2009, from http://familydoctor.org/online/famdocen/ home/tools/symptom/504.printerview.html.

American Academy of Pediatrics. (1994). Prenatal genetic diagnosis for pediatricians, *Pediatrics, 93,* 1010–1015.

American Academy of Pediatrics. (2000a). Changing concepts of Sudden Infant Death Syndrome: Implications for infant sleeping environment and sleep position. *Pediatrics, 105,* 650–656.

American Academy of Pediatrics. (2000b). Fetal alcohol syndrome and alcohol-related neurodevelopmental disorders. *Pediatrics, 106,* 358–361.

American Academy of Pediatrics. (2000c). Molecular genetic testing in pediatric practice: A subject review. *Pediatrics, 106,* 1494–1497.

American Academy of Pediatrics. (2000d). Use of psychoactive medication during pregnancy and possible effects on the fetus and newborn. *Pediatrics, 105,* 880–887.

American Academy of Pediatrics Committee on Environmental Health (1997). Noise: A hazard for the fetus and newborn. *Pediatrics, 100,* 724–726.

American Academy of Pediatrics Committee on Environmental Health. (1999). Ultraviolet light: a hazard to children. *Pediatrics, 104,* 328–333.

American Academy of Pediatrics Committee on Fetus and Newborn. (2005). Underwater births. *Pediatrics, 115,* 1413–1414.

American Academy of Pediatrics Committee on Fetus and Newborn, American College of Obstetricians and Gynecologists, and Committee on Obstetric Practice. (2006). The Apgar score. *Pediatrics, 117,* 1444–1447.

American Academy of Pediatrics Committee on Fetus and Newborn, Committee on Drugs, Section on Anesthesiology, Section on Surgery. (2000). Prevention and management of pain and stress in the neonate. *Pediatrics, 105,* 454–461.

American Academy of Pediatrics Committee on Fetus and Newborn, Section on Surgery, and Section on Anesthesiology and Pain Medicine, Canadian Paediatric Society Fetus and Newborn Committee. (2006). Prevention and management of pain in the neonate: An update. *Pediatrics, 118,* 2231–2241.

American Academy of Pediatrics/Committee on Injury and Poison Prevention. (1993). Drowning in infants, children, and adolescents. *Pediatrics, 92,* 292–294.

American Academy of Pediatrics Committee on Injury and Poison Prevention. (2001a). Falls from heights: Windows, roofs, and balconies. *Pediatrics, 107,* 1188–1191.

American Academy of Pediatrics Committee on Injury and Poison Prevention. (2001b). Injuries associated with infant walkers. *Pediatrics, 108,* 790–792.

American Academy of Pediatrics Committee on Nutrition. (1999). Iron fortification of infant formulas. *Pediatrics, 104,* 119–123.

American Academy of Pediatrics Committee on Practice and Ambulatory Medicine and Section on Ophthalmology. (2002a). Use of photoscreening for children's vision screening. *Pediatrics, 109,* 524–525.

American Academy of Pediatrics Committee on Public Education. (2001). Children, adolescents, and television. *Pediatrics, 107,* 423–426.

American Academy of Pediatrics Committee on Sports Medicine. (1988). Infant exercise programs. *Pediatrics, 82,* 800.

American Academy of Pediatrics Joint Committee on Infant Hearing. (2007). Year 2007 position statement: Principles and guidelines for early hearing detection and intervention programs. *Pediatrics, 120,* 899–921.

American Academy of Pediatrics Section on Ophthalmology. (2002b). Red reflex examination in infants. *Pediatrics, 109,* 980–981.

American Academy of Pediatrics Section on Ophthalmology, American Academy of Ophthalmology, & American Association for Pediatric Ophthalmology and Strabismus. (2006). Screening examination of premature infants for retinopathy of prematurity. *Pediatrics, 117,* 572–576.

American Academy of Pediatrics, Shelov, S.P., & Hannemann, R.E. (Eds.). (1998). *Caring for your baby and young child: Birth to age 5.* New York: Bantam Doubleday Dell.

American Academy of Pediatrics Subcommittee on Hyperbilirubinemia. (2004). Management of hyperbilirubinemia in the newborn infant 35 or more weeks of gestation. *Pediatrics, 114,* 297–316.

American Academy of Pediatrics Task Force on Newborn and Infant Hearing. (1999). Newborn and infant hearing loss: Detection and intervention. *Pediatrics, 103,* 527–530.

American Academy of Pediatrics/Work Group on Breastfeeding. (1997). Breastfeeding and the use of human milk. *Pediatrics, 100,* 1035–1039.

American College of Obstetricians and Gynecologists. (1994). Exercise during pregnancy and the postpartum period. *ACOG Technical Bulletin, 189.*

American College of Obstetricians and Gynecologists. (2000). Perinatal viral and parasitic infections. *ACOG Practice Bulletin, Number 20.*

American College of Obstetricians and Gynecologists. (2003). Exercise during pregnancy and the postpartum period. *Clinical Obstetrics and Gynecology, 46,* 496–499.

American College of Obstetricians and Gynecologists Committee on Obstetric Practice. (2002). ACOG committee opinion. Mode of term singleton breech delivery. *International Journal of Gynecology and Obstetrics, 77,* 65–66.

American Speech-Language-Hearing Association. (2008). *Service provision to children who are deaf and hard of hearing, birth to 36 months [Technical report].* Retrieved July 31, 2009, from http://www.asha.org/docs/html/TR2008-00301.html.

Ames, E.W. (1997). *The development of Romanian orphan children adopted to Canada.* Burnaby, BC: Simon Fraser University.

Anderson, C.A., Berkowitz, L., Donnerstein, E., Huesmann, L.R., Johnson, J.D., Linz, D., Malamuth, N.M., & Wartella, E. (2003). The influence of media violence on youth. *Psychological Science in the Public Interest, 4,* 81–110.

Anderson, D.K., Lord, C., Risi, S., DiLavore, P.S., Shulman, C., Thurm, A., et al. (2007). Patterns of growth in verbal abilities among children with autism spectrum disorder. *Journal of Consulting and Clinical Psychology, 75,* 594–604.

Anderson, D.R., & Evans, M.K. (2001). Peril and potential of media for infants and toddlers. *Zero to three: National Center for Infants, Toddlers, and Families, 22,* 10–16.

Anderson, D.R., Huston, A.C., Schmitt, K.L., Linebarger, D.L., & Wright, J.C. (2001). Early childhood television viewing and adolescent behavior: The recontact study. *Monographs of the Society for Research in Child Development, 66*(1, Serial No. 264).

Anderson, D.R., & Pempek, T.A. (2005). Television and very young children. *American Behavioral Scientist, 48,* 505–522.

Andersson, K., Bohlin, G., & Hagekull, B. (1999). Early temperament and stranger wariness as predictors of social inhibition in 2-year-olds. *British Journal of Developmental Psychology, 17,* 421–434.

Anglin, J.M. (1977). *Word, object and conceptual development.* New York: Norton.

Anisfeld, M. (1996). Only tongue protrusion modeling is matched by neonates. *Developmental Review, 16,* 149–161.

Apgar, V. (1953). A proposal for a new method of evaluation of the newborn infant. *Current Research in Anesthesia and Analgesia, 32,* 260–267.

Ariagno, R.L., Thoman, E.B., Boeddiker, M.A., Kugener, B., Constantinou, J.C., Mirmiran, M., et al. (1997). Developmental care does not alter sleep and development of premature infants. *Pediatrics, 100,* e9–e15.

Ariès, P. (1962). *Centuries of childhood: A social history of family life* (R. Baldick, Transl.). New York: Knopf.

Armstrong, G.L., Billah, K., Rein, D.B., Hicks, K.A., Wirth, K.E., & Bell, B.P. (2007). The economics of routine childhood hepatitis A immunization in the United States: The impact of herd immunity. *Pediatrics, 119,* e22–e29.

Arnett, J.J. (2000). Emerging adulthood: A theory of development from the late teens through the twenties. *American Psychologist, 55,* 469–480.

Arnon, S., Shapsa, A., Forman, L., Regev, R., Bauer, S., Litmanovitz, I., et al. (2006). Live music is beneficial to preterm infants in the neonatal intensive care unit environment. *Birth, 33,* 131–136.

Arterberry, M.E. (2008). Infants' sensitivity to the depth cue of height-in-the-picture-plane. *Infancy,13,* 544–555.

Arterberry, M.E., & Bornstein, M.H. (2002). Infant perceptual and conceptual categorization: The roles of static and dynamic attributes. *Cognition, 86,* 1–24.

Asendorpf, J.B., & Baudonniere, P.M. (1993). Self-awareness and other-awareness: Mirror self-recognition and synchronic imitation among unfamiliar peers. *Developmental Psychology, 29,* 88–95.

Ashby, L. (1985). Partial promises and semi-visible youths: The Depression and World War II. In J.M. Hawes, & N.R. Hiner (Eds.), *American childhood: A research guide and historical handbook* (pp. 489–531). Westport, CT: Greenwood Press.

Asher, L.J., & Lenhoff, D.R. (2001). Family and Medical Leave: Making time for family is everyone's business. *The Future of Children, 11*(1), 115–121.

Ashmead, D.H., & Perlmutter, M. (1980). Infant memory in everyday life. In M. Perlmutter (Ed.), *New* directions for child development: Vol. 10. Children's memory (pp. 1–16). San Francisco: Jossey-Bass.

Ashton, D.M., Lawrence III, H.C., Adams III, N.L., & Fleischman, A.R. (2009). Surgeon General's Conference on the Prevention of Preterm Birth. *Obstetrics & Gynecology, 113,* 925–930.

Aslin, R.N. (1981). Development of smooth pursuit in human infants. In D.F. Fisher, R.A. Monty, & J.W. Senders (Eds.), *Eye movements: Cognition and visual perception* (pp. 31–51). Hillsdale, NJ: Erlbaum.

Aslin, R.N. (2007). What's in a look? *Developmental Science, 10,* 48–53.

Aslin, R.N., Jusczyk, P.W., & Pisoni, D.B. (1998). Speech and auditory processing during infancy: Constraints on and precursors to language. In W. Damon (Ed.) & D. Kuhn, & R.S. Siegler (Vol. Eds.), *Handbook of child psychology* (5th ed.): *Vol. 2.: Cognition, perception, and language* (pp. 147–198). New York: Wiley.

Aslin, R.N., & McMurray, B. (2004). Automated cornal-reflection eye tracking in infancy: Methodological developments and applications to cognition. *Infancy, 6,* 155–163.

Astuto, J., & Allen, L. (2009). Home visitation and young children: An approach worth investing in? *Social Policy Report, 23*(4).

Atella, L.D., DiPietro, J., Smith, B.A., & St. James-Roberts, I. (2003). More than meets the eye: Parental and infant contributors to maternal and paternal reports of early infant difficultness. *Parenting: Science and Practice, 3,* 265–284.

Atkinson, L., Chisholm, V.C., Scott, B., Goldberg, S., Blackwell, J., Dickens, S., & Tam, F. (1995). Cognitive coping, affective stress, and maternal sensitivity: Mothers of children with Down syndrome. *Developmental Psychology, 31,* 668–676.

Atkinson, L., Chisholm, V.C., Scott, B., Goldberg, S., Vaughn, B.E., Blackwell, J., Dickens, S., & Tam, F. (1999). Maternal sensitivity, child functional level, and attachment in Down syndrome. In J.I. Vondra, & D. Barnett (Eds.), Atypical attachment in infancy and early childhood among children at developmental risk. *Monographs of the Society for Research in Child Development, 64*(3, Serial No. 258), 45–66.

Au, T.K., Dapretto, M., & Song, Y. (1994). Input vs. constraints: Early word acquisition in Korean and English. *Journal of Memory and Language, 33,* 567–582.

Au, T.K., & Glusman, M. (1990). The principle of mutual exclusivity in word learning: To honor or not to honor? *Child Development, 61,* 1474–1490.

Bada, H.S., Das, A., Bauer, C.R., Shankaran, S., Lester, B., LaGasse, L., et al. (2007). Impact of prenatal cocaine exposure on child behavior problems through school age. *Pediatrics, 119,* e348–e359.

Badaly, D., & Adolph, K.E. (2008). Beyond the average: Walking infants take steps longer than their leg length. *Infant Behavior & Development, 31,* 554–558.

Badawy, A.M., Khiary, M., Sherif, L.S., Hassan, M., Ragab, A., & Abdelall, I. (2008). Low-molecular weight heparin in patients with recurrent early miscarriages of unknown aetiology. *Journal of Obstetrics and Gynaecology, 28,* 280–284.

Baddeley, A.D. (1992). Working memory. *Science, 255,* 556–559.

Baddeley, A.D. (2000). The episodic buffer: A new component of working memory? *Trends in Cognitive Sciences, 4,* 417–423.

Bahrick, L.E. (1987). Infants' intermodal perception of two levels of temporal structure in natural events. *Infant Behavior and Development, 10,* 387–416.

Bahrick, L.E., Flom, R., & Lickliter, R. (2002). Intersensory redundancy facilitates discrimination of tempo in 3-month-old infants. *Developmental Psychobiology, 41,* 352–363.

Bahrick, L.E., Hernandez-Reif, M., & Flom, R. (2005). The development of infant learning about specific face–voice relations. *Developmental Psychology, 41,* 541–552.

Bahrick, L.E., & Lickliter, R. (2000). Intersensory redundancy guides attentional selectivity and perceptual learning in infancy. *Developmental Psychology, 36,* 190–201.

Bahrick, L.E., Lickliter, R., & Flom, R. (2004). Intersensory redundancy guides the development of selective attention, perception, and cognition in infancy. *Current Directions in Psychological Science, Current Directions in Psychological Science, 13,* 99–102.

Bahrick, L.E., Lickliter, R., & Flom, R. (2006). Up versus down: The role of intersensory redundancy in the development of infants' sensitivity to the orientation of moving objects. *Infancy, 9,* 73–96.

Bahrick, L.E., Netto, D.S., & Hernandez-Reif, M. (1998). Intermodal perception of adult and child faces and voices by infants. *Child Development, 69,* 1263–1275.

Bahrick, L.E., & Watson, J.S. (1985). Detection of intermodal proprioceptive-visual contingency as a potential basis of self-perception in infancy. *Developmental Psychology, 21,* 963–973.

Baillargeon, R. (1994a). How do infants learn about the physical world? *Current Directions in Psychological Science, 3,* 133–140.

Baillargeon, R. (1994b). Physical reasoning in young infants: Seeking explanations for impossible events. *British Journal of Developmental Psychology, 12,* 9–33.

Baillargeon, R. (2002). The acquisition of physical knowledge in infancy: A summary in eight lessons. In U. Goswami (Ed.), *Blackwell handbook of child cognitive development* (pp. 46–83). Oxford: Blackwell.

Baillargeon, R., Spelke, E.S., & Wasserman, S. (1985). Object permanence in five-month-old infants. *Cognition, 20,* 191–208.

Baillargeon, R.H., Zoccolillo, M., Keenan, K., Côté, S., Pérusse, D., Wu, H., et al. (2007). Gender differences in physical aggression: A prospective population-based survey of children before and after 2 years of age. *Developmental Psychology, 43,* 13–26.

Bakker, E., & Wyndaele, J.J. (2000). Changes in the toilet training of children during the last 60 years: The cause of an increase in lower urinary tract dysfunction? *British Journal of Urology International, 86*(3), 248–252.

Baldwin, D.A. (1991). Infants' contribution to the achievement of joint reference. *Child Development, 62,* 875–890.

Baldwin, D.A., Markman, E.M., & Melartin, R. (1989). Infants' inferential abilities: Evidence from exploratory play. Paper presented at the Biennial Meeting of the Society for Research in Child Development, Kansas City, MO.

Baldwin, D.A., & Tomasello, M. (1998). Word learning: A window on early pragmatic understanding. In E.V. Clark (Ed.), *Proceedings of the 29th Annual Child Language Research Forum* (pp. 3–23). Stanford, CA: Center for the Study of Language and Information.

Baldwin, E.N. (2001). A current summary of breastfeeding legislation in the U.S. Retrieved October 11, 2002, from http://www.lalecheleague.org/LawMain.html

Baltimore, D. (2001). Our genome unveiled. *Nature, 409,* 814–816.

Baranek, G.T. (1999). Autism during infancy: A retrospective video analysis of sensory-motor and social behaviors at 9–12 months of age. *Journal of Autism & Developmental Disorders, 29,* 213–224.

Barber, J.S., & East, P.L. (2009). Home and parenting resources available to siblings depending on their birth intention status. *Child Development, 80,* 921–939.

Barbu-Roth, M., Anderson, D.I., Despres, A., Provasi, J., Cabrol, D., & Campos, J.J. (2009). Neonatal stepping in relation to terrestrial optic flow. *Child Development, 80,* 8–14.

Barlow, W.E., Davis, R.L., Glasser, J.W., Rhodes, P.H., Thompson, R.S., Mullooly, J.P., Black, S.B., Shinefield, H.R., Ward, J.I., Marcy, S.M., DeStefano, F., Chen, R.T., Immanuel, V., Pearson, J.A., Vadheim, C.M., Rebolledo, V., Christakis, D., Benson, P.J., & Lewis, N. (2001). The risk of seizures after receipt of whole-cell pertussis or measles, mumps, and rubella vaccine. *New England Journal of Medicine, 345,* 656–661.

Barnard, K.E., & Solchany, J. (2002). Mothering. In M.H. Bornstein (Ed.), *Handbook of parenting: Vol. 3 Status and social conditions of parenting* (2nd ed., pp. 3–25). Mahwah, NJ: Erlbaum.

Barnes, M.G., Grom, A.A., Thompson, S.D., Griffin, T.A., Pavlidis, P., Itert, L., et al. (2009). Subtype-secific peripheral blood gene expression profiles in recent-onset juvenile idiopathic arthritis. *Arthritis & Rheumatism, 60,* 2102–2112.

Barnett, D., Ganiban, J., & Cicchetti, D. (1999). Maltreatment, negative expressivity, and the development of Type D attachments from 12 to 24 months of age. In J.I. Vondra, & D. Barnett (Eds.), Atypical attachment in infancy and early childhood among children at developmental risk. *Monographs of the Society for Research in Child Development, 64*(3, Serial No. 258), 97–118.

Barnett, W.S. (1998). Long-term cognitive and academic effects of early childhood education on children in poverty. *Preventive Medicine, 27,* 204–207.

Barnett, W.S. (2009). *What do we know about the actual and potential effects of large-scale public preschool programs?* Invited symposium presented at the Biennial Meeting of the Society for Research in Child Development, Denver, CO. Retrieved December 22, 2009, from http://www.cehd.umn.edu/icd/CLS/SRCD2009.htm.

Baron-Cohen, S. (1995). *Mindblindness: An essay on autism and theory of mind.* Cambridge, MA: MIT Press.

Barr, R. (2008). Attention and learning from media during infancy and early childhood. In S.L. Calvert, & B.J. Wilson (Eds.), *Blackwell handbook of child development and the media.* Oxford, UK: Blackwell.

Barr, R.G., Barr, M., Fujiwara, T., Conway, J., Catherine, N., & Brant, R. (2009). Do educational materials change knowledge and behaviour about crying and shaken baby syndrome? A randomized controlled trial. *CMAJ, 180,* 727–733.

Barrett, K.C., & Campos, J.J. (1987). Perspectives on emotional development II.: A functionalist approach to emotions. In J.D. Osofsky (ed.), *Handbook of infant development* (2nd ed., pp. 555–578). New York: Wiley.

Barrett, K.C., & Nelson-Goens, G.C. (1997). Emotion communication and the development of the social emotions. *New Directions for Child Development, No. 77,* 69–88.

Basille, C., Frydan, R., Aly, A.E., Hesters, L., Fanchin, R., Tachdjian, G., et al. (2009). Preimplantation genetic diagnosis: State of the art. *European Journal of*

Obstetrics, Gynecology, and Reproductive Biology, 145, 9–13.

Bates, E., Bretherton, I., & Snyder, L. (1988). *From first words to grammar: Individual differences and dissociable mechanisms.* Cambridge, UK: Cambridge University Press.

Bates, E., Dale, P., & Thal, D. (1995). Individual differences and their implications for theories of language development. In P. Fletcher, & B. MacWhinney (Eds.), *The handbook of child language* (pp. 96–151). Oxford, UK: Blackwell.

Bates, E., Marchman, V., Thal, D., Fenson, L., Dale, P., Reznick, J.S., et al. (1994). Developmental and stylistic variation in the composition of early vocabulary. *Journal of Child Language, 21,* 85–124.

Bates, J., Freeland, C., & Lounsbury, M. (1979). Measurement of infant difficultness. *Child Development, 50,* 794–803.

Bates, J.E., Bayles, K., Bennett, D.S., Ridge, B., & Brown, M.M. (1991). Origins of externalizing behavior problems at eight years of age. In D. Pepler, & K. Rubin (Eds.), *Development and treatment of childhood aggression* (pp. 93–120). Hillsdale, NJ: Erlbaum.

Batki, A., Baron-Cohen, S., Wheelwright, S., Connellan, J., & Ahluwalia, J. (2000). Is there an innate module? Evidence from nonhuman neonates. *Infant Behavior & Development, 23,* 223–229.

Bauer, P.J. (2002). Long-term recall memory: Behavioral and neuro-developmental changes in the first 2 years of life. *Current Directions in Psychological Science, 11,* 137–141.

Bauer, P.J. (2005). New developments in the study of infant memory. In D.M. Teti (Ed.), *Handbook of research methods in developmental psychology* (pp. 467–488). Oxford, UK: Blackwell.

Bauer, P.J. (2006). Event memory. In W. Damon, & R. Lerner (Eds.) & D. Kuhn, & R. Siegler (Vol. Eds.), *Handbook of child psychology: Vol. 2. Cognition, perception, and language* (6th ed., pp. 373–425). New York: Wiley.

Bauer, P.J., Wenner, J.A., Dropik, P.L., & Wewerka, S.S. (2000). Parameters of remembering and forgetting in the transition from infancy to early childhood. *Monographs of the Society for Research in Child Development, 65*(4, Serial No. 263).

Bauer, P.J., Wiebe, S.A., Carver, L.J., Waters, J.M., & Nelson, C.A. (2003). Developments in long-term explicit memory late in the first year of life: Behavioral and electrophysiological indices. *Psychological Science, 14,* 629–635.

Bauer, P.J., Wiebe, S.A., Waters, J.M., & Bangston, S.K. (2001). Reexposure breeds recall: Effects of experience on 9-month-olds' ordered recall. *Journal of Experimental Child Psychology, 80,* 174–200.

Baydar, N., Greek, A., & Brooks-Gunn, J. (1997). A longitudinal study of the effects of the birth of a sibling during the first 6 months of life. *Journal of Marriage and the Family, 59,* 939–956.

Baydar, N., Hyle, P., & Brooks-Gunn, J. (1997). A longitudinal study of the effects of the birth of a sibling during preschool and early grade school years. *Journal of Marriage and the Family, 59,* 957–965.

Bayley, N. (1949). Consistency and variability in the growth of intelligence from birth to eighteen years. *Journal of Genetic Psychology, 75,* 165–196.

Bayley, N. (1969). *Bayley Scales of Infant Development.* New York: Psychological Corporation.

Bayley, N. (1993). *Bayley Scales of Infant Development: II.* New York: Psychological Corporation.

Beales, J.G. (1982). The assessment and management of pain in children. In P. Karoly, D.D. Steffer, & O'Grady (Eds.), *Child health psychology: Concepts and issues* (pp. 154–179). New York: Pergamon Press.

Beales, Jr. R.W., (1985). The child in seventeenth-century America. In J. M. Hawes, & N. R. Hiner (Eds.). (1985). *American childhood: A research guide and historical handbook* (pp. 15–56). Westport, CT: Greenwood Press.

Beauchamp, G.K., Cowart, B.L., Mennella, J.A., & Marsh, R.R. (1994). Infant salt taste: Developmental, methodological and contextual factors. *Developmental Psychobiology, 27,* 353–365.

Beck, L.F., Morrow, B., Lipscomb, L.E., Johnson, C.H., Gaffield, M., Rogers, M., & Gilbert, B.C. (2002). Prevalence of selected maternal behaviors and experiences, pregnancy risk assessment monitoring system (PRAMS), 1999. *Morbidity and Mortality Weekly Report, 51,* 1–26.

Becker, P.T., & Thoman, E.B. (1983). Organization of sleeping and waking states in infants: Consistency across contexts. *Physiology & Behavior, 31,* 405–410.

Beers, S.R., & De Bellis, M.D. (2002). Neuropsychological function in children with maltreatment-related posttraumatic stress disorder. *American Journal of Psychiatry, 159,* 483–486.

Behrend, D.A. (1995). Processes involved in the initial mapping of verb meanings. In M. Tomasello, & W. Merriman (Eds.), *Beyond names for things: Children's acquisition of verbs* (pp. 251–273). Hillsdale, NJ: Erlbaum.

Behrend, D.A., Scofield, J., & Kleinknecht, E.E. (2001). Beyond fast mapping: Young children's extensions of novel words and novel facts. *Developmental Psychology, 37,* 698–705.

Behrman, R.E., & Butler, A.S. (2006). *Preterm birth: Causes, consequences, and prevention.* Washington, DC: Institute of Medicine.

Behrman, R.E., Kliegman, R., & Jenson, H.B. (Eds.). (2000). *Nelson textbook of pediatrics* (16th ed.). Philadelphia: W.B. Saunders.

Beilin, Y. (2002). Advances in labor analgesia. *Mount Sinai Journal of Medicine, 69,* 38–44.

Bell, M.A., & Wolfe, C.D. (2004). Emotion and cognition: An intricately bound developmental process. *Child Development, 75,* 366–370.

Bellinger, D.C. (2005). Teratogen update: Lead and pregnancy. *Birth Defects Research and Clinical Molecular Teratology, 73,* 409–420.

Belluck, D. (January 18, 2009). Need a research subject? Check the crib. *New York Times.*

Belsky, J. (1996). Parent, infant, and social-contextual antecedents of father-son attachment security. *Developmental Psychology, 32,* 905–913.

Belsky, J., Campbell, S.B., Cohn, J.F., & Moore, G. (1996). Instability of infant-parent attachment security. *Developmental Psychology, 32,* 921–924.

Belteki, G., & Smith, G.C.S. (2009). Single versus multiple antenatal steroids in threatened preterm delivery: More benefit or harm? *Archives of Disease in Childhood. Fetal and Neonatal Edition, 94,* 5–7.

Belizá, J.M., Althabe, F., & Cafferata, M.L. (2007). Health consequences of the increasing caesarean section rates. *Epidemiology, 18,* 485–486.

Ben-Arieh, A., Zionit, Y., & Krizak, G. (Eds.) (2003). *Children in Israel: An annual statistical abstract.* Jerusalem: Center For Research and Public Education, National Council For The Child.

Bergen, D. (2001). Learning in the robotic world: Active or reactive? *Childhood Education, 77,* 249–250.

Berger, S.E., & Adolph, K.E. (2003). Infants use handrails as tools in a locomotor task. *Developmental Psychology, 39,* 594–605.

Berger, S.E., Adolph, K.E., & Lobo, S.A. (2005). Out of the toolbox: Toddlers differentiate wobbly and wooden handrails. *Child Development, 76,* 1294–1307.

Berger, S.E., Theuring, C., & Adolph, K.E. (2007). How and when infants learn to climb stairs. *Infant Behavior & Development, 30,* 36–49.

Bergeson, T.R., & Trehub, S.E. (2002). Absolute pitch and tempo in mothers' songs to infants. *Psychological Science, 13,* 71–74.

Bergström, M., Kieler, H., & Waldenström, U. (2009). Effects of natural childbirth preparation versus standard antenatal education on epidural rates, experience of childbirth and parental stress in mothers and fathers: A randomized controlled multicentre trial. *BJOG, 116,* 1167–1176.

Berkeley, G. (1901/1709). *An essay toward a new theory of vision.* Oxford, UK: Clarendon.

Berko, J. (1958). The child's learning of English morphology. *Word, 14,* 150–177.

Berkowitz, G.S., Wetmur, J.G., Birman-Deych, E., Obel, J., Lapinski, R.H., Godbold, J.H., Holzman, I.R., & Wolff, M.S. (2004). In utero pesticide exposure, maternal paraoxonase activity, and head circumference. *Environmental Health Perspectives, 112,* 388–391.

Berlin, L.J., Brooks-Gunn, J., McCarton, C., & McCormick, M.C. (1998). The effectiveness of early intervention: Examining risk factors and pathways to enhanced development. *Preventive Medicine, 27,* 238–245.

Berlin, L.J., Ispa, J.M., Fine, M.A., Malone, P.S., Brooks-Gunn, J., Brady-Smith, C., et al. (2009). Correlates and consequences of spanking and verbal punishment for low-income White, African American, and Mexican American toddlers. *Child Development, 80,* 1403–1420.

Bernard, P., & Harley, V.R. (2007). Wnt4 action in gonadal development and sex determination. *International Journal of Biochemistry and Cell Biology, 39,* 31–43.

Bernhardt, B.M., Kemp, N., & Werker, J.F. (2007). Early word-object associations and later language development. *Language, 27,* 315–328.

Berrol, S. (1985). Ethnicity and American children. In J.M. Hawes, & N.R. Hiner (Eds.), *American childhood: A research guide and historical handbook* (pp. 343–375). Westport, CT: Greenwood Press.

Bertenthal, B.I., & Clifton, R.K. (1998). Perception and action. In W. Damon (Editor-in-Chief), D. Kuhn, & R.S. Siegler (Vol. Eds.), *Handbook of child psychology: Vol. 2. Cognition, perception, and language* (5th ed., pp. 51–102). New York: Wiley.

Bertenthal, B.I., & Fischer, K.W. (1978). Development of self-recognition in the infant. *Developmental Psychology, 14,* 44–50.

Bertenthal, B.I., Proffitt, D.R., & Cutting, J.E. (1984). Infant sensitivity to figural coherence in biomechanical motions. *Journal of Experimental Child Psychology, 37,* 213–230.

Berthier, N.E. (1996). Learning to reach: A mathematical model. *Developmental Psychology, 32,* 811–823.

Bettes, B.A., Coleman, V.H., Zinberg, S., Spong, C.Y., Portnoy, B., DeVoto, E., et al. (2007). Cesarean delivery on maternal request: Obstetrician-gynecologists' knowledge, perception, and practice patterns. *Obstetrics & Gynecology, 109,* 57–66.

BFHI USA. (2009). Baby-Friendly hospitals and birth centers. Retrieved July 31, 2009, from http://www.babyfriendlyusa.org/eng/03.html

Bhat, A., Heathcock, J., & Galloway, J.C. (2005). Toy-oriented changes in hand and joint kinematics during the emergence of purposeful reaching. *Infant Behavior & Development, 28,* 445–465.

Bhatia, J., Greer, F., & Committee on Nutrition. (2008). Use of soy protein-based formulas in infant feeding. *Pediatrics, 121,* 1062–1068.

Bhatia, T.K., & Ritchie, W.C. (1999). The bilingual child: Some issues and perspectives. In W. C. Ritchie, & T. K. Bhatia (Eds.), *Handbook of child language acquisition* (pp. 569–643). San Diego: Academic Press.

Bhutta, A.T., Cleves, M.A., Casey, P.H., Cradock, M.M., & Anand, K.J.S. (2002). Cognitive and behavioral outcomes of school-aged children who were born preterm: A meta-analysis. *JAMA, 288,* 728–737.

Bhutta, Z.A., Darmstadt, G.L., Hasan, B.S., & Haws, R.A. (2005). Community-based interventions for improving perinatal and neonatal health outcomes in developing countries: A review of the evidence. *Pediatrics, 115,* 519–617.

Biederman, J., Hirshfeld-Becker, D.R., Rosenbaum, J.F., Herot, C., Friedman, D., Snidman, N., et al. (2001). Further evidence of association between behavioral inhibition and social anxiety in children. *American Journal of Psychiatry, 158,* 1673–1679.

Bilhartz, T.D., Bruhn, R.A., & Olson, J.E. (2000). The effect of early music training on child cognitive development. *Journal of Applied Developmental Psychology, 20*(4), 615–636.

Binns, H.J., Campbell, C., & Brown, M.J. for the Advisory Committee on Childhood Lead Poisoning Prevention. (2007). Interpreting and managing blood lead levels of less than 10 μg/dL in children and reducing childhood exposure to lead: Recommendations of the Centers for Disease Control and Prevention Advisory Committee on Childhood Lead Poisoning Prevention. *Pediatrics, 120,* e1285–e1298.

Birch, E.E., Garfield, S., Hoffman, D.R., Uauy, R., & Birch, D.G. (2000). A randomized controlled trial of early dietary supply of longchain polyunsaturated fatty acids and mental development in term infants. *Developmental Medicine and Child Neurology, 42,* 174–181.

Birch, E.E., & Wang, J. (2009). Stereoacuity outcomes after treatment of infantile and accommodative esotropia. *Optometry and Vision Science, 86,* 647–652.

Bishop, D.V.M., Price, T.S., Dale, P.S., & Plomin, R. (2003). Outcomes of early language delay: II. Etiology of transient and persistent language difficulties. *Journal of Speech, Language, and Hearing Research, 46,* 561–575.

Black, J.E. (1998). How a child builds its brain: Some lessons from animal studies of neural plasticity. *Preventive Medicine, 27,* 168–171.

Black, M.M., Dubowitz, H., Casey, P.H., Cutts, D., Drewett, R.F., Drotar, D., et al. (2006). Failure to thrive as distinct from child neglect. *Pediatrics, 117,* 1456–1458.

Black, M. M., Dubowitz, H., & Starr, R. H. (1999). African American fathers in low income, urban families: Development and behavior of their 3-year-old children. *Child Development, 70,* 967–978.

Blair, C. (2002). School readiness: Integrating cognition and emotion in a neurobiological conceptualization of child functioning at school entry. *American Psychologist, 57,* 111–127.

Blair, C. (2003). *Self-regulation and school readiness.* EDO-PS-03-7. Champaign, IL: Clearinghouse on Elementary and Early Childhood Education.

Blake, J., & de Boysson-Bardies, B. (1992). Patterns in babbling: A cross linguistic study. *Journal of Child Language, 19,* 51–74.

Blass, E.M., & Hoffmeyer, L.B. (1991). Sucrose as an analgesic for newborn infants. *Pediatrics, 87,* 215–218.

Blehar, M.C., Lieberman, A.F., & Ainsworth, M.D.S. (1977). Early face-to-face interaction and its relations to later infant-mother attachment. *Child Development, 48,* 182–194.

Block, R.W., Krebs, N.F., the Committee on Child Abuse and Neglect, & the Committee on Nutrition. (2005). Failure to thrive as a manifestation of child neglect. *Pediatrics, 116,* 1234–1237.

Bloom, K., Russell, A., & Wassenberg, K. (1987). Turn-taking affects the quality of infant vocalization. *Journal of Child Language, 14,* 211–227.

Bloom, L. (1970). *Language development: Form and function in emerging grammars.* Cambridge, MA: MIT Press.

Bloom, L. (1973). *One word at a time: The use of single word utterances before syntax.* The Hague: Mouton.

Bloom, L. (1993). *The transition from infancy to language.* New York: Cambridge University Press.

Bloom, L. (1998). Language acquisition in its developmental context. In W. Damon (Ed.) & D. Kuhn, & R.S. Siegler (Vol. Eds.), *Handbook of child psychology* (5th ed.): *Vol. 2. Cognition, perception, and language* (pp. 309–370). New York: Wiley.

Bloom, L., Tinker, E., & Margulis, C. (1993). The words children learn: Evidence against a noun bias in children's vocabularies. *Cognitive Development, 8,* 431–450.

Bloom, P. (1994). *Language acquisition: Core readings.* Cambridge, MA: MIT Press.

Bloom, P. (2000). *How children learn the meanings of words.* Cambridge, MA: MIT Press.

Boccia, M., & Campos, J.J. (1989). Maternal emotional signals, social referencing, and infants' reactions to strangers. In N. Eisenberg (Ed.), *New directions for child development* (Vol. 44, pp. 25–49). San Francisco: Jossey-Bass.

Bodrova, E., & Leong, D.J. (1996). *Tools of the mind: The Vygotskian approach to early childhood education.* Englewood Cliffs, NJ: Prentice Hall.

Bodrova, E., & Leong, D.J. (1998). Adult influences on play. In D.P. Fromberg, & D. Bergen (Eds.), *Play from birth to twelve and beyond: Contexts, perspectives, and meanings.* (pp. 277–282). New York: Garland Publishing.

Bojczyk, K.E., & Corbetta, D. (2004). Object retrieval in the 1st year of life: Learning effects of task exposure and box transparency. *Developmental Psychology, 40,* 54–66.

Bokhorst, C.L., Bakermans-Kranenburg, M.J., Fearon, R.M.P., van IJzendoorn, M.H., Fonagy, P., & Schuengel, C. (2003). The importance of shared environment in mother-infant attachment security: A behavioral genetic study. *Child Development, 74,* 1769–1782.

Booth, A.E. (2009). Causal supports for early word learning. *Child Development, 80,* 1243–1250.

Booth, A.E., & Waxman, S.R. (2009). A horse of a different color: Specifying with precision infants' mappings of novel nouns and adjectives. *Child Development, 80,* 15–22.

Booth, C.L., & Kelly, J.F. (1998). Child care characteristics of infants with and without special needs: Comparisons and concerns. *Early Childhood Research Quarterly, 13,* 603–622.

Booth, C.L., & Kelly, J.F. (1999). Child care and employment in relation to infants' disabilities and risk factors. *American Journal on Mental Retardation, 104,* 117–130.

Boris, N.W., Hinshaw-Fuselier, S.S., Smyke, A.T., Scheeringa, M.S., Heller, S.S., Zeanah, C.H. (2004). Comparing criteria for attachment disorders: Establishing reliability and validity in high-risk samples. *Journal of the American Academy of Child and Adolescent Psychiatry, 43,* 568–577.

Borke, J., Lamm, B., Eickhorst, A., & Keller, H. (2007). Father-infant interaction, paternal ideas about early child care, and their consequences for the development of children's self-recognition. *The Journal of Genetic Psychology, 168,* 365–379.

Bornstein, M., Gaughran, J., & Segui, I. (1991). Multimethod assessment of infant temperament: Mother questionnaire and mother and observer reports evaluated and compared at five months using the infant temperament measure. *International Journal of Behavioral Development, 14,* 131–151.

Bornstein, M.H. (1988). Mothers, infants, and the development of cognitive competence. In H.E. Fitzgerald, B.M. Lester, & M.W. Yogman (Eds.), *Theory and research in behavioral pediatrics* (Vol. 4, pp. 67–99). New York: Plenum.

Bornstein, M.H. (2006). Parenting science and practice. In W. Damon, & R. Lerner (Eds.) & K.A. Renninger, & I.E. Sigel (Vol. Eds.), *Handbook of child psychology: Vol. 4. Child psychology in practice* (6th ed., pp. 893–949). New York: Wiley.

Bornstein, M.H., & Arterberry, M.E. (2003). Recognition, discrimination and categorization of smiling by 5-month-old infants. *Developmental Science, 6,* 585–599.

Bornstein, M.H., Cote, L.R., Maital, S., Painter, K., Park, S., Pascual, L., et al. (2004). Cross-linguistic analysis of vocabulary in young children: Spanish, Dutch, French, Hebrew, Italian, Korean, and American English. *Child Development, 75,* 1115–1139.

Bornstein, M.H., Haynes, O.M., O'Reilly, A.W., & Painter, K. (1996). Solitary and collaborative pretense play in early childhood: Sources of individual variation in the development of representational competence. *Child Development, 67,* 2910–2929.

Bornstein, M.H., Haynes, O.M., Pascual, L., Painter, K.M., & Galperin, C. (1999). Play in two societies: Pervasiveness of process, specificity of structure. *Child Development, 70,* 317–331.

Bornstein, M.H., & Lamb, M.E. (1992). *Development in infancy: An introduction* (3rd ed.). New York: McGraw-Hill.

Bornstein, M.H., Putnick, D.L., Heslington, M., Gini, M., Suwalsky, J.T.D., Venuti, P., et al. (2008). Mother-child emotional availability in ecological perspective: Three countries, two regions, two genders. *Developmental Psychology, 44,* 666–680.

Bornstein, M.H., Slater, A., Brown, E., Roberts, E., & Barrett, J. (1997). Stability of mental development from infancy to later childhood: Three "waves" of research. In. G. Bremner, A. Slater, & G. Butterworth (Eds.), *Infant development: Recent advances* (pp. 191–215). East Sussex, UK: Psychology Press.

Borst, C.G. (1995). *Catching babies: The professionalization of childbirth, 1870–1920.* Cambridge, MA: Harvard University Press.

Borstelmann, L.J. (1983). Children before psychology: Ideas about children from antiquity to the late 1800s. In P.H. Mussen (Ed.) & W. Kessen (Vol. Ed.), *Handbook of child psychology* (4th ed.): *Vol. 1. History, theory, and methods*. New York: Wiley.

Boswell, J. (1988). *The kindness of strangers: The abandonment of children in Western Europe from late antiquity to the Renaissance*. Chicago: University of Chicago Press.

Bowden, K., Kessler, D., Pinette, M., & Wilson, E. (2003). Underwater birth: Missing the evidence or missing the point? *Pediatrics, 112*, 972–973.

Bowers, J.S., Mathys, S.L., & Gage, S.H. (2009). Preserved implicit knowledge of a forgotten childhood language. *Psychological Science, 20*, 1064–1069.

Bowlby, J. (1969/1982). *Attachment and loss: Vol. 1. Attachment*. (2nd ed.). New York: Basic Books.

Bowlby, J. (1973). *Attachment and loss: Vol. 2. Separation: Anxiety and anger*. New York: Basic Books.

Bowlby, J. (1980). *Attachment and loss: Vol. 3. Loss: Sadness and depression*. New York: Basic Books.

Bowlby, J. (1988). *A secure base: Parent-child attachment and healthy human development*. New York: Basic Books.

Bradley, R.H., & Corwyn, R.F. (2002). Socioeconomic status and child development. *Annual Review of Psychology, 53*, 371–399.

Bradley, R.H., Corwyn, R.F., McAdoo, H.P., & García Coll, C. (2001). The home environments of children in the United States: Part I: Variations by age, ethnicity, and poverty status. *Child Development, 72*, 1844–1867.

Brankston, G.N., Mitchell, B.F., Ryan, E.A., & Okun, N.B. (2004). Resistance exercise decreases the need for insulin in overweight women with gestational diabetes mellitus. *American Journal of Obstetrics and Gynecology, 190*, 188–193.

Branstetter, S.A., Furman, W., & Cottrell, L. (2009). The incidence of representations of attachment, maternal-adolescent relationship quality, and maternal monitoring on adolescent substance use: A 2-year longitudinal examination. *Child Development, 80*, 1448–1462.

Brauner, J., Gordic, B., & Zigler, E. (2004). Putting the child back into child care: Combining care and education for children ages 3–5. *Social Policy Report, 18*(3).

Braungart-Rieker, J.M., Garwood, M.M., Powers, B.P., & Notaro, P.C. (1998). Infant affect and affect regulation during the still-face paradigm with mothers and fathers: The role of infant characteristics and parental sensitivity. *Developmental Psychology, 34*, 1428–1437.

Brazelton, T.B., & Nugent, J.K. (1995). *Neonatal Behavioral Assessment Scale* (3rd ed.). Cambridge, UK: Cambridge University Press.

Brazelton, T.B., Christophersen, E.R., Frauman, A.C., Gorski, P.A., Poole, J.M., Stadtler, A.C., et al. (1999). Instruction, timeliness, and medical influences affecting toilet training. *Pediatrics, 103*, 1353–1358.

Bredekamp, S., & Copple, C. (1997). *Developmentally appropriate practice in early childhood programs* (Rev. ed.). Washington, DC: National Association for the Education of Young Children.

Bremner, R.H., Barnard, J., Hareven, T.K., & Mennell, R. (Eds.). (1970). *Children and youth in America: A documentary history: Vol. I, 1600–1865*. Cambridge, MA: Harvard University Press.

Bremner, R.H., Barnard, J., Hareven, T.K., & Mennell, R. (Eds.). (1971). *Children and youth in America: A documentary history: Vol. II, 1866–1932*. Cambridge, MA: Harvard University Press.

Brenner, R.A., Simons-Morton, B.G., Bhaskar, B., Revenis, M., Das, A., & Clemens, J.D. (2003). Infant-parent bed sharing in an inner-city population. *Archives of Pediatrics and Adolescent Medicine, 157*, 33–39.

Brenner, R.A., Taneja, G.S., Denise L. Haynie, D.L., Trumble, A.C., Qian, C., et al. (2009). Association between swimming lessons and drowning in childhood: A case-control study. *Archives of Pediatrics and Adolescent Medicine, 163*, 203–210.

Brent, R.L. (2004). Utilization of animal studies to determine the effects and human risks of environmental toxicants (drugs, chemicals, and physical agents). *Pediatrics, 113*, 984–995.

Brent, R.L., & Weitzman, M. (2004). The current state of knowledge about the effects, risks, and science of children's environmental exposures. *Pediatrics, 113*, 1158–1166.

Bretherton, I. (1992). The origins of attachment theory: John Bowlby and Mary Ainsworth. *Developmental Psychology, 28*, 759–775.

Bretherton, I., Fritz, J., Zahn-Waxler, C., & Ridgeway, D. (1986). Learning to talk about emotions: A functionalist perspective. *Child Development, 57*, 529–548.

Brewer, J., & Hunter, A. (1989). *Multimethod research: A synthesis of styles*. Newbury Park, CA: Sage.

Bridges, L.J., Denham, S.A., & Ganiban, J.M. (2004). Definitional issues in emotion regulation research. *Child Development, 75*, 340–345.

Bristow, D., Dehaene-Lambertz, G., Mattout, J., Soares, C., Gliga, T., Baillet, S., et al. (2008). Hearing faces: How the infant brain matches the face it sees with the speech it hears. *Journal of Cognitive Neuroscience, 21*, 905–921.

Britton, J.R., Britton, H.L., & Gronwaldt, V. (2006). Breastfeeding, sensitivity, and attachment. *Pediatrics, 118,* e1436–e1443.

Brodowski, M.L., Nolan, C.M., Gaudiosi, J.A., Yuan, Y.Y., Zikratova, L., Ortiz, M.J., et al. (2008). Nonfatal maltreatment of infants: United States, October 2005-September 2006. *Morbidity and Mortality Weekly Report, 57,* 336–339.

Brody, G.H. (1998). Sibling relationship quality: Its causes and consequences. *Annual Review of Psychology, 49,* 1–24.

Brody, J.E. (1999, Aug. 3). Success of toilet training still a matter of time. *The New York Times On the Web.* Retrieved September 30, 2000, from http://www .nytimes.com/library/national/science/ 080399hth-brody-children.html

Bronfenbrenner, U., & Morris, P.A. (1998). The ecology of developmental processes. In W. Damon (Ed.) & R.M. Lerner (Vol. Ed.), *Handbook of child psychology: Vol. 1. Theoretical models of human development* (pp. 993–1028). New York: Wiley.

Brooks, R., & Meltzoff, A.N. (2002). The importance of eyes: How infants interpret adult looking behavior. *Developmental Psychology, 38,* 958–966.

Brooks, R., & Meltzoff, A.N. (2005). The development of gaze following and its relation to language. *Developmental Science, 8,* 535–543.

Brooks-Gunn, J. (2003). Do you believe in magic?: What we can expect from early childhood intervention programs. *Social Policy Report, 17*(1).

Brooks-Gunn, J., & Duncan, G.J. (1997). The effects of poverty on children and youth. *The Future of Children, 7*(2), 55–71.

Brooks-Gunn, J., Han, W.J., & Waldfogel, J. (2002). Maternal employment and child cognitive outcomes in the first three years of life: The NICHD Study of Early Child Care. *Child Development, 73,* 1052–1072.

Brown, A. (2000). U.S. Consumer Product Safety Commission response to *The Future of Children* issue on unintentional injuries in childhood. Retrieved October 11, 2002, from http://www .futureofchildren.org/cpsc.htm

Brown, J.D., & Peuchaud, S.R. (2008). Media and breast-feeding: Friend or foe? *International Breastfeeding Journal, 3,* 15.

Brown, R. (1973). *A first language: The early stages.* Cambridge, MA: Harvard University Press.

Brown, R., & Hanlon, C. (1970). Derivational complexity and order of acquisition in child speech. In J. R. Hayes (Ed.), *Cognition and the development of language* (pp. 155–207). New York: Wiley.

Brown, R.W. (1957). Linguistic determinism and the parts of speech. *Journal of Abnormal and Social Psychology, 55,* 1–5.

Browne, J.V. (2008). Chemosensory development in the fetus and newborn. *Newborn & Infant Nursing Reviews, 4,* 180–186.

Bryce, J., Black, R.E., Walker, N., Bhutta, Z.A., Lawn, Joy E., Steketee, R.W. (2005). Can the world afford to save the lives of 6 million children each year? *Lancet, 365,* 2193–200.

Bucklin, B.A., Chestnut, D.H., & Hawkins, J.L. (2002). Intrathecal opioids versus epidural local anesthetics for labor analgesia: A meta-analysis. *Regional Anesthesis and Pain Medicine, 27,* 23–30.

Bugental, D.B., & Grusec, J.E. (2006). Socialization processes. In W. Damon, & R. Lerner (Eds.) & N. Eisenberg (Vol. Ed.), *Handbook of child psychology: Vol. 3. Social, emotional, and personality development* (6th ed., pp. 366–428). New York: Wiley.

Burchinal, M.R., Roberts, J.E., Riggins, Jr., R., Zeisel, S.A., Neebe, E., & Bryant, D. (2000). Relating quality of center-based child care to early cognitive and language development longitudinally. *Child Development, 71,* 339–357.

Burns, T.C., Yoshida, K.A., Hill, K., & Werker, J.F. (2007). The development of phonetic representation in bilingual and monolingual infants. *Applied Psycholinguistics, 28,* 455–474.

Bushnell, E.W., McKenzie, B.E., Lawrence, D.A., & Connell, S. (1995). The spatial coding strategies of one-year-old infants in a locomotor search task. *Child Development 66,* 937–958.

Busjahn, A., Knoblauch, H., Faulhaber, H., Aydin, A., Uhlmann, R., Tuomilehto, J., et al. (2000). A region on chromosome 3 is linked to dizygotic twinning. *Nature Genetics, 26,* 398–399.

Buss, A.H. (1995). *Personality, temperament, social behavior, and the self.* Boston: Allyn & Bacon.

Buss, K.A., Davidson, R.J., Kalin, N.H., & Goldsmith, H.H. (2004). Context-specific freezing and associated physiological reactivity as a dysregulated fear response. *Developmental Psychology, 40,* 583–594.

Buss, K.A., & Goldsmith, H.H. (1998). Fear and anger regulation in infancy: Effects on the temporal dynamics of affective expression. *Child Development, 69,* 359–374.

Buss, K.A., Malmstadt, Schumacher, J., Dolski, I., Kalin, N.H., Goldsmith, H.H., & Davidson, R.J. (2003). Right frontal brain activity, cortisol, and withdrawal behavior in 6-month-old infants. *Behavioral Neuroscience, 117,* 11–20.

Buss, K.A., & Plomin, R. (1984). *Temperament: Early developing personality traits*. Hillsdale, NJ: Erlbaum.

Butler, S.C., Berthier, N.E., & Clifton, R.K. (2002). Two-year-olds' search strategies and visual tracking in a hidden displacement task. *Developmental Psychology, 38*, 581–590.

Butterworth, G., & Hicks, L. (1977). Visual proprioception and postural stability in infancy: A developmental study. *Perception, 6*, 255–262.

Butterworth, G.E. (1995). Origins of mind in perception and action. In C. Moore, & P. Dunham (Eds.), *Joint attention: Its origins and role in development*. Hillsdale, NJ: Lawrence Erlbaum Associates.

Byrne, J.P., Crowther, C.A., & Moss, J.R. (2000). A randomised controlled trial comparing birthing centre care with delivery suite care in Adelaide, Australia. *Australian and New Zealand Journal of Obstetrics and Gynaecology, 40*, 268–274.

Bzach, K.R., & League, R. (1991). *Receptive-Expressive Emergent Language Test – Second edition (REEL-2)*. Austin, TX: Pro-Ed.

Cabrera, N.J., & Garcia Coll, C. (2004). Latino fathers: Uncharted territory in need of much exploration. In M.E. Lamb (Ed.), *The role of the father in child development* (4th ed., pp. 98–120). New York: Wiley.

Cabrera, N.J., Tamis-LeMonda, C.S., Bradley, R.H., Hofferth, S., & Lamb, M.E. (2000). Fatherhood in the twenty-first century. *Child Development, 71*, 127–136.

Cahan, E., Mechling, J., Sutton-Smith, B., & White, S.H. (1993). The elusive historical child: Ways of knowing the child of history and psychology. In G.H. Elder, Jr., J. Modell, & R.D. Parke (Eds.), *Children in time and place: Developmental and historical insights* (pp. 192–223). New York: Cambridge University Press.

Cairns, R.B. (1998) The making of developmental psychology. In W. Damon (Ed.) & R.M. Lerner (Vol. Ed.), *Handbook of child psychology (5th ed.): Vol. 1. Theoretical models of human development* (pp. 25–105). New York: Wiley.

Caldwell, B., & Bradley, R.H. (1984). *Home Observation for Measurement of the Environment*. Little Rock, AR: University of Arkansas at Little Rock.

Caldwell, K.L., Miller, G.A., Wang, R.Y., Jain, R.B., & Jones, R.L. (2009). Iodine status of the U.S. popuation, National Health and Nutrition Examination Survey 2003–2004. *Thyroid, 18*, 1207–1214.

Callaghan, W.M., MacDorman, M.F., Rasmussen, S.A., Qin, C., & Lackritz, E.M. (2006). The contribution of preterm birth to infant mortality rates in the United States. *Pediatrics, 118*, 1566–1573.

Calvert, K. (1992). *Children in the house: The material culture of early childhood, 1600–1900*. Boston: Northeastern University Press.

Cameron, C.E., & Hagen, J.W. (2005). Women in child development: Themes from the SRCD oral history project. *History of Psychology, 8*, 235–323.

Cammu, H., Martens, G., Ruyssinck, G., & Amy, J.J. (2002). Outcome after elective labor induction in nulliparous women: A matched cohort study. *American Journal of Obstetrics and Gynecology, 186*, 240–244.

Campbell, F.A., Pungello, E.P., Miller-Johnson, S., Burchinal, M., & Ramey, C.T. (2001). The development of cognitive and academic abilities: Growth curves from an early childhood educational experiment. *Developmental Psychology, 37*, 231–242.

Campbell, F.A., Ramey, C.T., Pungello, E.P., Sparling, J., & Miller-Johnson, S. (2002). Early childhood education: Young adult outcomes from the Abecedarian Project. *Applied Developmental Science, 6*, 42–57.

Campbell, S., Brownell, C., Hungerford, A., Spieker, S., Mohan, R., & Blessing, J. (2004). The course of maternal depressive symptoms and maternal sensitivity as predictors of attachment security at 36 months. *Development and Psychopathology, 16*, 231–252.

Campbell, S.B., Cohn, J.F., & Meyers, T. (1995). Depression in first-time mothers: Mother-infant interaction and depression chronicity. *Developmental Psychology, 31*, 349–357.

Campbell, T.F., Dollaghan, C.A., Rockette, H.E., Paradise, J.L., Feldman, H.M., Shriberg, L.D., et al. (2003). Risk factors for speech delay of unknown origin in 3-year-old children. *Child Development, 74*, 346–357.

Campos, J.J., Campos, R.G., & Barrett, K.C. (1989). Emergent themes in the study of emotional development and emotion regulation. *Developmental Psychology, 25*, 394–402.

Campos, J.J., Frankel, C.B., & Camras, L. (2004). On the nature of emotion regulation. *Child Development, 75*, 377–394.

Campos, J.J., Mumme, D.L., Kermoian, R., & Campos, R.G. (1994). A functionalist perspective on the nature of emotion. In N.A. Fox(Ed.), The development of emotion regulation: Biological and behavioral considerations. *Monographs of the Society for Research in Child Development, 59*(2–3, Serial No. 240), 284–303.

Campos, J.J., Witherington, D., Anderson, D.I., Frankel, C.I., Uchiyama, I., & Barbu-Roth, M. (2008). Rediscovering development in infancy. *Child Development, 79*, 1625–1632.

Camras, L.A., Lambrecht L., & Michel, G.F. (1996). Infant "surprise" expressions as coordinative motor structures. *Journal of Nonverbal Behavior, 20,* 183–195.

Canfield, M.A., Ramadhani, T.A., Shaw, G.M., Carmichael, S.L., Waller, D.K., Mosley, B.S., et al. (2009). Anencephaly and spina bifida among Hispanics: Maternal, sociodemographic, and acculturation factors in the National Birth Defects Prevention Study. *Birth Defects Research. Part A, Clinical and Molecular Teratology, 85,* 637–646.

Cannon, E.A., Schoppe-Sullivan, S.J., Mangelsdorf, S.C., Brown, G.L., & Sokolowski, M.S. (2008). Parent characteristics as antecedents of maternal gatekeeping and fathering behavior. *Family Processes, 47,* 501–519.

Cantor, D., Waldfogel, J., Kerwin, J., Wright, M., Levin, K., Rauch, J., et al. (2001). *Balancing the needs of families and employers: Family and Medical Leave surveys, 2000 update.* Rockville, MD: Westat.

Cantor, P. (2001). Computers and the very young. *Focus on Infants & Toddlers, 13*(4). Retrieved December 29, 2009, from http://www.udel.edu/bateman/acei/inf.vol.13.4.htm

Capps, L., Sigman, M., & Mundy, P. (1994). Attachment security in children with autism. *Development and Psychopathology, 6,* 249–261.

Carayol, M., Blondel, B., Zeitlin, J., Breart, G., & Goffinet, F. (2007). Changes in the rates of caesarean delivery before labour for breech presentation at term in France: 1972–2003. *European Journal of Obstetrics & Gynecology and Reproductive Biology, 132,* 20–26.

Carey, S., & Bartlett, E. (1978). Acquiring a single new word. *Papers and Reports on Child Language Development, 15,* 17–29.

Carey, W., & McDevitt, S. (1978). Revision of the infant temperament questionnaire. *Pediatrics, 61,* 735–739.

Carlson, A., Lino, M., Gerrior, S., & Basiotis, P.P. (2001). Report card on the diet quality of children ages 2 to 9. *Nutrition Insight, 25.* Alexandria, VA: USDA Center for Nutrition Policy and Promotion.

Carlson, E.A. (1998). A prospective longitudinal study of attachment disorganization/disorientation. *Child Development, 69,* 1107–1128.

Carlson, E.A., Sroufe, L.A., & Egeland, B. (2004). The construction of experience: A longitudinal study of representation and behavior. *Child Development, 75,* 66–83.

Carlson, M., & Earls, F. (1997). Psychological and neuroendocrinological sequelae of early social deprivation in institutionalized children in Romania. *Annals of the New York Academy of Sciences, 807,* 419–426.

Carlson, S.M., Mandell, D.J., & Williams, L. (2004). Executive function and theory of mind: Stability and prediction from ages 2 to 3. *Developmental Psychology, 40,* 1105–1122.

Carpenter, M., Nagell, K., & Tomasello, M. (1998). Social cognition, joint attention, and communicative competence from 9 to 15 months of age. *Monographs of the Society for Research in Child Development, 63*(4, Serial No. 255).

Carter, A.S., Garrity-Rokous, F.E., Chazan-Cohen, R., Little, C., & Briggs-Gowan, M.J. (2001). Maternal depression and comorbidity: Predicting early parenting, attachment security, and toddler social-emotional problems and competencies. *Journal of the American Academy of Child and Adolescent Psychiatry, 40,* 18–26.

Casasola, M., Cohen, L.B., & Chiarello, E. (2003). Six-month-old infants' categorization of containment spatial relations. *Child Development, 74,* 679–693.

Casper, M.J. (1998). *The making of the unborn patient: A social anatomy of fetal surgery.* New Brunswick, NJ: Rutgers University Press.

Caspi, A. (1998). Personality development across the life course. In W. Damon (Series Ed.) & N. Eisenberg (Vol. Ed.), *Handbook of child psychology: Vol. 3. Social, emotional, and personality development* (5th ed., pp. 311–388). New York: Wiley.

Caspi, A. (2000). The child is father of the man: Personality continuities from childhood to adulthood. *Journal of Personality and Social Psychology, 78,* 158–172.

Caspi, A., Moffitt, T.E., Morgan, J., Rutter, M., Taylor, A., Arseneault, L., Tully, L., Jacobs, C., Kim-Cohen, J., & Polo-Tomas, M. (2004). Maternal expressed emotion predicts children's antisocial behavior problems: Using monozygotic-twin differences to identify environmental effects on behavioral development. *Developmental Psychology, 40,* 149–161.

Caspi, A., & Shiner, R.L. (2006). Personality development. In W. Damon, & R. Lerner (Eds.) & N. Eisenberg (Vol. Ed.), *Handbook of child psychology: Vol. 3. Social, emotional, and personality development* (6th ed., pp. 300–365). New York: Wiley.

Caspi, A., & Silva, P.A. (1995). Temperamental qualities at age three predict personality traits in young adulthood: Longitudinal evidence from a birth cohort. *Child Development, 66,* 486–498.

Caughey, A.B., & Musci, T.J. (2004). Complications of term pregnancies beyond 37 weeks of gestation. *Obstetrics & Gynecology,103,* 57–62.

Center on Media and Child Health. (2005). *The effects of electronic media on children ages zero to six: A history of research.* Menlo Park, CA: The Henry J. Kaiser Family Foundation.

Centers for Disease Control and Prevention. (1995). Ectopic pregnancy, United States, 1990–1992. *Morbidity and Mortality Weekly Report, 44,* 46–48.

Centers for Disease Control and Prevention. (2000a). Birth defects. *National Vital Statistics Reports, 50*(5).

Centers for Disease Control and Prevention. (2000b). Blood levels in young children, United States and selected states, 1996–1999. *Morbidity & Mortality Weekly Report, 49,* 1133–1137.

Centers for Disease Control and Prevention. (2000c). Contribution of assisted reproductive technology and ovulation-inducing drugs to triplet and higher-order multiple births, United States, 1980–1997. *Morbidity and Mortality Weekly Report, 49,* 535–538.

Centers for Disease Control and Prevention. (2000d). Public Health Service Task Force recommendations for the use of antiretroviral drugs in pregnant women infected with HIV-1 for maternal health and for reducing perinatal HIV-1 transmission in the United States. Revisions to the 1998 recommendations. *Morbidity and Mortality Weekly Report, 47*(RR–2), 1–30.

Centers for Disease Control and Prevention. (2001). *1999 Assisted reproductive technology success rates: National summary and fertility clinic reports.* Atlanta, GA.

Centers for Disease Control and Prevention. (2002a). Birth defects: Having a healthy pregnancy. Retrieved December 4, 2004, from http://www.cdc .gov/ncbddd/bd/abc.htm

Centers for Disease Control and Prevention. (2002b). Infant mortality and low birth weight among black and white infants: United States, 1980–2000. *Morbidity & Mortality Weekly Report, 51,* 589–592.

Centers for Disease Control and Prevention. (2002c). Progress toward elimination of perinatal HIV infection, Michigan, 1993–2000. *Morbidity and Mortality Weekly Report, 51,* 93–97.

Centers for Disease Control and Prevention. (2002d). Public Health Service Task Force recommendations for use of antiretroviral drugs in pregnant HIV-1-infected women for maternal health and interventions to reduce perinatal HIV-1 transmission in the United States. Revisions to the 1998 recommendations. *Morbidity and Mortality Weekly Report, 51*(RR18), 1–38.

Centers for Disease Control and Prevention. (2002e). Use of assisted reproductive technology—United States, 1996 and 1998. *Morbidity and Mortality Weekly Report, 51,* 97–101.

Centers for Disease Control and Prevention. (2002f). West Nile virus and breastfeeding. *Morbidity & Mortality Weekly Report, 51,* 877–878.

Centers for Disease Control and Prevention. (2004). Spina bifida and anencephaly before and after folic acid mandate: United States, 1995–1996 and 1999–2000. *Morbidity & Mortality Weekly Report, 53,* 362–365.

Centers for Disease Control and Prevention. (2005a). Developmental disabilities. Retrieved December 28, 2005 from http://www.cdc.gov/ncbddd/dd/aic/resources/

Centers for Disease Control and Prevention. (2005b). 2005 National immunization survey. Retrieved November 30, 2006, from http://www.cdc.gov/breastfeeding/data/NNIS_data/data_2005.htm

Centers for Disease Control and Prevention. (2006). Improved national prevalence estimates for 18 selected major birth defects: United States, 1999–2001. *Morbidity & Mortality Weekly Report, 54,* 1301–1305.

Centers for Disease Control and Prevention. (2008). *Sudden Infant Death Syndrome (SIDS) and Sudden Unexpected Infant Death (SUID): Home.* Atlanta, GA: Author. Retrieved July 28, 2009, from http://www.cdc .gov/SIDS/

Centers for Disease Control and Prevention. (2009a). Alcohol use among pregnant and nonpregnant women of childbearing age—United States, 1991–2005. *Morbidity & Mortality Weekly Report, 58,* 529–532.

Centers for Disease Control and Prevention. (2009b). Immunization schedules. Retrieved July 27, 2009, from http://www.cdc.gov/vaccines/recs/schedules/default.htm#child

Cevasco, A.M. (2008). The effects of mothers' singing on full-term and preterm infants and maternal emotional responses. *Journal of Music Therapy, 45,* 273–306.

Chadwick, D.L., Bertocci, G., Castillo, E., Frasier, L., Guenther, E., Hansen, K., Herman, B., & Krous, H.F. (2008). Annual risk of death resulting from short falls among young children: Less than 1 in 1 million. *Pediatrics, 121,* 1213–1224.

Chahin, J., Villarruel, F.A., & Viramontez, R.A. (1999). Dichos y refranes: The transmission of cultural values and beliefs. In H.P. McAdoo (Ed.), *Family ethnicity: Strength in diversity* (2nd ed., pp. 153–167). Thousand Oaks, CA: Sage.

Chakrabati, B., Dudbridge, F., Kent, L., Wheelwright, S., Hill-Cawthorne, G., Allison, C., et al. (2009). Genes related to sex steroids, neural growth, and social-emotional behavior are associated with autistic traits, empathy, and Asperger syndrome. *Autism Research, 2,* 157–177.

Chakrabati, B., & Fombonne, E. (2001). Pervasive developmental disorders in preschool children. *Journal of the American Medical Association, 285,* 3093–3099.

Chamayou, S., Alecci, C., Ragolia, C., Giambona, A., Siciliano, S., Maggio, A., Fichera, M., & Guglielmino, A. (2002). Successful application of preimplantation genetic diagnosis for B-thalassaemia and sickle cell anaemia in Italy. *Human Reproduction, 17,* 1158–1165.

Chan, K.C., Ding, C., Gerovassili, A., Yeung, S.W., Chiu, R.W., Leung, T.N., et al. (2006). Hypermethylated RASSF1A in maternal plasma: A universal fteal DNA marker that improves the reliability of noninvasive prenatal diagnosis. *Clinical Chemistry, 52,* 2211–2218.

Chan, L.Y., Leung, T.Y., Fok, W.Y., Chan, L.W., & Lau, T.K. (2002). High incidence of obstetric interventions after successful external cephalic version. *BJOG, 109,* 627–631.

Charman, T., Drew, A., Baird, C., & Baird, G. (2003). Measuring early language development in pre-school children with autism spectrum disorder using the MacArthur Communicative Development Inventory (Infant Form). *Journal of Child Language, 30,* 213–236.

Chasan-Taber, L., Marcus, B.H., Stanek, E. 3rd, Ciccolo, J.T., Marquez, D.X., Solomon, C.G., et al. (2009). A randomized controlled trial of prenatal physical activity to prevent gestational diabetes: Design and methods. *Journal of Women's Health, 18,* 851–859.

Chatoor, I., Surles, J., Ganiban, J., Beker, L., Paez, L.M., & Kerzner, B. (2004). Failure to thrive and cognitive development in toddlers with infantile anorexia. *Pediatrics, 113,* e440–e447.

Chen, A., & Rogan, W.J. (2004). Breastfeeding and the risk of postneonatal death in the United States. *Pediatrics, 113,* e435–e439.

Chera, P., & Wood, C. (2003). Animated multimedia "talking books" can promote phonological awareness in children beginning to read. *Learning and Instruction, 13,* 33–52.

Chescheir, N.C. (2009). Maternal-fetal surgery: Where are we and how did we get here? *Obstetrics and Gynecology, 113,* 717–731.

Chess, S., & Thomas, A. (1996). *Temperament: Theory and practice.* Philadelphia: Brunner/Mazel.

Child Care Law Center. (2003). *Caring for children with special needs: The Americans with Disabilities Act (ADA) and child care.* San Francisco: CCLC.

Children's Environmental Health Initiative. (2002a). Children's environmental health. Retrieved September 1, 2003, from http://www.env.duke.edu/cehi/health/lead.htm

Children's Environmental Health Initiative. (2002b). *Children's environmental health: Lead poisoning.* Retrieved July 23, 2009, from http://nicholas.duke.edu/cehi/health/lead.htm

Chiriboga, C.A., Brust, J.C.M., Bateman, D., & Hauser, W.A. (1999). Dose-response effect of fetal cocaine exposure on newborn neurologic function. *Pediatrics, 103,* 79–85.

Chisholm, K. (1998). A three year follow-up of attachment and indiscriminate friendliness in children adopted from Romanian orphanages. *Child Development, 69,* 1092–1106.

Chisholm, K., Carter, M., Ames, E.W., & Morison, S.J. (1995). Attachment security and indiscriminately friendly behavior in children adopted from Romanian orphanages. *Development and Psychopathology, 7,* 283–294.

Cho, G.E., Miller, P.J., & Bracey, J.R. (2009). Self-esteem. In R.A. Shweder, T.R. Bidell, A.C. Dailey, S.D. Dixon, P.J. Miller, & J. Modell (Eds.), *The child: An encyclopedic companion* (pp. 876–878). Chicago: University of Chicago Press.

Cho, G.E., Miller, P.J., Sandel, T., & Wang, S. (2005). What do grandmothers think about self-esteem? American and Taiwanese folk theories revisited. *Social Development, 14,* 701–721.

Choi, S., & Gopnik, A. (1995). Early acquisition of verbs in Korean: A cross-linguistic study. *Journal of Child Language, 22,* 497–529.

Chomsky, N. (1958). Review of *Verbal Behavior* by B. F. Skinner. *Language, 35,* 26–58.

Chomsky, N. (1965). *Aspects of the theory of syntax.* Cambridge, MA: MIT Press.

Chomsky, N. (1980). Rules and representations. *Behavioral and Brain Sciences, 3,* 1–61.

Chomsky, N. (1986). *Knowledge of language: Its nature, origin, and use.* New York: Praeger.

Chow, J.F., Yeung, W.S., Lau, E.Y., Lam, S.T., Tong, T., Ng., E.H., et al. (2009). Singleton birth after preimplantation genetic diagnosis for Huntingon disease using whole genome amplifiation. *Fertility and Sterility, 92,* 828.e7–828.e10.

Christakis, D.A. (2009). The effects of infant media usage: What do we know and what should we learn? *Acta Paediatrica, 98,* 8–16.

Christakis, D.A., & Garrison, M.M. (2009). Preschool-aged children's television viewing in child care settings. *Pediatrics, 124,* 1627–1632.

Christakis, D.A., Gilkerson, J., Richards, J.A., Zimmerman, F.J., Garrison, M.M., Xu, D., et al. (2009). Audible television and decreased adult words, infant vocalizations, and conversational turns: A population-based study. *Archives of Pediatrics and Adolescent Medicine, 163,* 554–558.

Christian, C.W., Block, R., & the Committee on Child Abuse and Neglect. (2009). Abusive head trauma in infants and children. *Pediatrics, 123,* 1409–1411.

Chugani, H.T., Behen, M.E., Muzik, O., Juhasz, C., Nagy, F., & Chugani, D.C. (2001). Local brain functional activity following early deprivation: A study of postinstitutionalized Romanian orphans. *Neuroimage, 14,* 1290–1301.

Cicchetti, D., & Toth, S.L. (2006). Developmental psychopathology and preventive intervention. In W. Damon, & R. Lerner (Eds.) & K.A. Renninger, & I.E. Sigel (Vol. Eds.), *Handbook of child psychology: Vol. 4. Child psychology in practice* (6th ed., pp. 497–547). New York: Wiley.

Clapp, J. (1996). Morphometric and neurodevelopmental outcome at age five years of the offspring of women who continued to exercise regularly throughout pregnancy. *Journal of Pediatrics, 129,* 856–863.

Clarke-Stewart, K., Fitzpatrick, M., Allhusen, V., & Goldberg, W. (2000). Measuring difficult temperament the easy way. *Developmental and Behavioral Pediatrics, 21,* 207–223.

Clarkson, M.G. (1996). Infants' perception of intensity: Spectral profiles. *Infant Behavior and Development, 19,* 181–190.

Clarkson, M.G., Martin, R.L., & Miciek, S.G. (1996). Infants' perception of pitch: Number of harmonics. *Infant Behavior and Development, 19,* 191–197.

Clarkson, M.G., & Montgomery, C.R. (2000, July). Precision of infants' localization of brief sounds. Paper presented at the Biennial International Conference on Infancy Studies, Brighton, UK.

Clement, P.F. (1997). *Growing pains: Children in the industrial age, 1850–1890.* New York: Twayne/Prentice Hall International.

Clements, D.H., Nastasi, B.K., & Swaminathan, S. (1993). Young children and computers: Crossroads and directions from research. *Young Children, 48,* 56–64.

Cleveland, A., & Striano, T. (2007). The effects of joint attention on object processing in 4- and 9-month-old infants. *Infant Behavior & Development, 30,* 499–504.

Clifton, R.K., Rochat, P., Litovsky, R.Y., & Perris, E.E. (1991). Object representation guides infants' reaching in the dark. *Journal of Experimental Psychology: Human Perception and Performance, 17,* 323–329.

Clifton, R.K., Rochat, P., Robin, D.J., & Berthier, N.E. (1994). Multimodal perception in human infants. *Journal of Experimental Psychology: Human Perception and Performance, 20,* 876–886.

Cohen, L.B., & Cashon, C.H. (2006). Infant cognition. In W. Damon, & R. Lerner (Eds.) & D. Kuhn, & R. Siegler (Vol. Eds.), *Handbook of child psychology: Vol. 2. Cognition, perception, and language* (6th ed., pp. 214–251). New York: Wiley.

Cohen, L.B., & Marks, K.S. (2002). How infants process addition and subtraction events. *Developmental Science, 5,* 186–201.

Cohen, R., Mrtek, M.B., & Mrtek, R.G. (1995). Comparison of maternal absenteeism and infant illness rates among breastfeeding and formula-feeding women in two corporations. *American Journal of Health Promotion, 10,* 148–153.

Cohen, R.D. (1985). Child-saving and progressivism, 1885–1915. In J.M. Hawes, & N. R. Hiner (Eds.), *American childhood: A research guide and historical handbook* (pp. 273–309). Westport, CT: Greenwood Press.

Cohn, J.F., & Tronick, E.Z. (1983). Three-month-old infants' reaction to simulated maternal depression. *Child Development, 54,* 185–193.

Cohn, J.F., & Tronick, E.Z. (1987). Mother-infant face-to-face interaction: The sequence of dyadic states. *Developmental Psychology, 23,* 66–77.

Coie, J.D., & Dodge, K.A. (1998). Aggression and antisocial behavior. In W. Damon (Series Ed.) & N. Eisenberg (Vol. Ed.), *Handbook of child psychology: Vol. 3. Social, emotional, and personality development* (5th ed., pp. 779–862). New York: Wiley.

Cole, P.M., Barrett, K.C., & Zahn-Waxler, C. (1992). Emotion displays in two-year-olds during mishaps. *Child Development, 63,* 314–324.

Cole, P.M., Martin, S.E., & Dennis, T.A. (2004). Emotion regulation as a scientific construct: Methodological challenges and directions for child development research. *Child Development, 75,* 317–333.

Colombo, J. (1993). *Infant cognition: Predicting later intellectual functioning.* Thousand Oaks, CA: Sage.

Colombo, J. (2001). The development of visual attention in infancy. *Annual Review of Psychology, 52,* 337–367.

Colombo, J. (2002). Infant attention grows up: The emergence of a developmental cogntive neuroscience perspective. *Current Directions in Psychological Science, 11,* 196–200.

Colombo, J., & Janowsky, J.S. (1998). A cognitive neuroscience approach to individual differences in infant cognition. In J.E. Richards (Ed.), *Cognitive neuroscience of attention* (pp. 363–391). Mahwah, NJ: Erlbaum.

Colombo, J., Kannass, K.N., Shaddy, D.J., Kundurthi, S., Maikranz, J.M., Anderson, C.J., et al. (2004). Maternal DHA and the development of attention infancy and toddlerhood. *Child Development, 75,* 1254–1267.

Colombo, J., & Mitchell, D.W. (1990). Individual and developmental differences in infant visual attention. In J. Colombo, & J.W. Fagen (Eds.), *Individual differences in infancy* (pp. 193–227). Hillsdale, NJ: Erlbaum.

Colombo, J., Shaddy, D.J., Richman, W.A., Maikranz, J.M., & Blaga, O. (2004). Developmental course of visual habituation and preschool cognitive and language outcome. *Infancy, 5,* 1–38.

Colón, A.R., & Colón, P.A. (2001). *A history of children: A socio-cultural survey across millennia.* Westport, CT: Greenwood Press.

Colón, J.M. (1997). Assisted reproductive technologies. In M.L. Sipski, & C.J. Alexander (Eds.), *Sexual function in people with disability and chronic illness: A health professional's guide* (pp. 557–575). Gaithersburg, MD: Aspen Publishers.

Committee on Infectious Diseases. (2009). Recommended childhood and adolescent immunization schedules—United States, 2009. *Pediatrics, 123,* 189–190.

Committee to Reexamine IOM Pregnancy Weight Guidelines. (2009). *Weight gain during pregnancy: Reexamining the guidelines.* Washington, DC: National Academies Press.

Comstock, G., & Scharrer, E. (2006). Media and popular culture. In W. Damon, & R. Lerner (Eds.) & D. Kuhn, & R. Siegler (Vol. Eds.), *Handbook of child psychology: Vol. 2. Cognition, perception, and language* (6th ed., pp. 817–863). New York: Wiley.

Connolly, K.J., & Dalgleish, M. (1989). The emergence of a tool-using skill in infancy. *Developmental Psychology, 25,* 894–912.

Cooper, H. (2008). The search for meaningful ways to express the effect of interventions. *Child Development Perspectives, 2,* 181–186.

Cooper, R.P., & Aslin, R.N. (1990). Preference for infant-directed speech in the first month after birth. *Child Development, 61,* 1584–1595.

Corbetta, D., & Bojczyk, K.E. (2002). Infants return to two-handed reaching when they are learning to walk. *Journal of Motor Behavior, 34,* 83–95.

Corriveau, K.H., Harris, P.L., Meins, E., Fernyhough, C., Arnott, B., Elliott, L., et al. (2009). Young children's trust in their mother's claims: Longitudinal links with attachment security in infancy. *Child Development, 80,* 750–761.

Cosans, C. (2004). The meaning of natural childbirth. *Perspectives in Biology and Medicine, 47,* 266–272.

Cost, Quality, and Child Outcomes Study Team. (1995). Cost, quality, and child outcomes in child care centers: Key findings and recommendations. *Young Children, 50*(4), 40–44.

Costa-Giomi, E. (1999). The effects of three years of piano instruction on children's cognitive development. *Journal of Research in Music Education, 47,* 198–212.

Courage, M.L., Edison, S.C., & Howe, M.L. (2004). Variability in the early development of visual self-recognition. *Infant Behavior & Development, 27,* 509–532.

Courage, M.L., & Howe, M.L. (2001). Long-term retention in 3.5-month-olds: Familiarization time and individual differences. *Journal of Experimental Child Psychology, 79,* 271–293.

Courage, M.L., Reynolds, G.D., & Richards, J.E. (2006). Infants' attention to patterned stimuli: Developmental change from 3 to 12 months of age. *Child Development, 77,* 680–695.

Courage, M.L., & Setliff, A.E. (2009). Debating the impact of television and video material on very young children: Attention, learning, and the developing brain. *Child Development Perspectives, 3,* 72–78.

Cox, J.L., Holden, J.M., & Sagovsky, R. (1987). Detection of postnatal depression. Development of the 10-item Edinburgh Postnatal Depression Scale. *British Journal of Psychiatry, 150,* 782–786.

Crago, M., Annahatak, B., & Ningiuruvik, L. (1993). Changing patterns of language socialization in Inuit homes. *Anthropology and Educational Quarterly, 24,* 205–223.

Craig, S., McCall, E., Bell A., & Tubman, R. (2009). Improving survival for infants of <26 weeks' gestation, 1995–2005. *Archives of Disease in Childhood. Fetal and Neonatal Edition, 94,* F229-F230.

Crain, W. (2000). *Theories of development: Concepts and applications.* Upper Saddle River, NJ: Prentice Hall.

Cravens, H. (1985). Child-saving in the age of professionalism, 1915–1930. In J.M. Hawes, & N.R. Hiner (Eds.). (1985). *American childhood: A research guide and historical handbook* (pp. 415–488). Westport, CT: Greenwood Press.

Crockenberg, S.C. (2003). Rescuing the baby from the bathwater: How gender and temperament (may) influence how child care affects child development. *Child Development, 74,* 1034–1038.

Crockenberg, S.C. & Leerkes, E.M. (2005). Infant temperament moderates associations between childcare type and quantity and externalizing and internalizing behaviors at $2\frac{1}{2}$ years. *Infant Behavior and Development, 28,* 20–35.

Cryer, D., Hurwitz, S., & Wolery, M. (2003). *Continuity of caregiver for infants and toddlers.* EDO-PS-03-17. Champaign, IL: Clearinghouse on Elementary and Early Childhood Education.

Cummings, E.M., & Davies, P.T. (1999). Depressed parents and family functioning: Interpersonal effects and children's functioning and development. In T. Joiner, & J.C. Coyne (Eds.), *Advances in interpersonal approaches: The interactional nature of depression* (pp. 299–327). Washington, DC: American Psychological Association Press.

Cunniff, C., & Committee on Genetics. (2004). Pediatrics prenatal screening and diagnosis for pediatricians. *Pediatrics, 114,* 889–894.

Cunningham, D., Xiao, Q., Chatterjee, A., Sulik, K., Juriloff, D., Elder, F., et al. (2002). exma: An X-linked insertional mutation that disrupts forebrain and eye development. *Mammalian Genome, 13,* 179–185.

Curtiss, S. (1977). *Genie.* New York: Academic Press.

Custodero, L.A. Britto, P.R., & Brooks-Gunn, J. (2003). Musical lives: A collective portrait of American families. *Journal of Applied Developmental Psychology, 24,* 553–572.

Cutting, A.L., & Dunn, J. (1999). Theory of mind, emotion understanding, language, and family background: Individual differences and interrelations. *Child Development, 70,* 853–865.

Dale, P.S., Price, T.S., Bishop, D.V.M., & Plomin, R. (2003). Outcomes of early language delay: I. Predicting persistent and transient language difficulties at 3 and 4 years. *Journal of Speech, Language, and Hearing Research, 46,* 544–560.

Dale, P.S., Simonoff, E., Bishop, D.V.M., Eley, T.C., Oliver, B., Price, T.S., et al. (1998). Genetic influence on language delay in two-year-old children. *Nature Neuroscience, 1,* 324–328.

Damewood, M.D. (2001). Ethical implications of a new application of preimplantation diagnosis. *JAMA, 285,* 3143–3144.

Darwin, C. (1877). A biographical sketch of an infant. *Mind, 2,* 285–294.

Dawson, G., & Ashman, S.B. (2000). On the origins of a vulnerability to depression: The influence of the early social environment on the development of psychobiological systems related to risk for affective disorder. In C.A. Nelson (Ed.), The effects of early adversity on neurobehavioral development. *The Minnesota Symposia on Child Psychology* (Vol. 31, pp. 245–279). Mahwah, NJ: Erlbaum.

Dawson, G., Frey, K., Self, J., Panagiotides, H., Hessl, D., Yamada, E., & Rinaldi, J. (1999). Frontal brain electrical activity in infants of depressed and nondepressed mothers: Relation to variations in infant behavior. *Development and Psychopathology, 11,* 589– 605.

Dawson, G., Meltzoff, A. N., Osterling, J., Rinaldi, J., & Brown, E. (1998). Children with autism fail to orient to naturally occurring social stimuli. *Journal of Autism & Developmental Disorders, 28,* 479–485.

Dawson, G., Munson, J., Estes, A., Osterling, J., McPartland, J., Toth, K., et al. (2002). Neurocognitive function and joint attention ability in young children with autism spectrum disorder versus developmental delay. *Child Development, 73,* 345–358.

Dawson, G., Panagiotides, H., Klinger, L.G., & Spieker, S. (1997). Infants of depressed and nondepressed mothers exhibit differences in frontal brain electrical activity during the expression of negative emotions. *Developmental Psychology, 33,* 650–656.

Dawson, G., Toth, K., Abbott, R., Osterling, J., Munson, J., Estes, A., & Liaw, J. (2004). Early social attention impairments in autism: Social orienting, joint attention, and attention to distress. *Developmental Psychology, 40,* 271–283.

De Bellis, M.D., Keshavan, M.S., Clark, D.B., Caseey, B.J., Giedd, J.B., Boring, A.M., Frustaci, K., & Ryan, N.D. (1999). Developmental traumatology, Part 2: Brain development. *Biological Psychiatry, 45,* 1271–1284.

De Leeuw, J.W., de-Wit, C., Kuijken, J.P.J.A., Bruinse, H.W. (2008). Mediolateral episiotomy reduces the risk for anal sphincter injury during operative vaginal delivery. *British Journal of Obstetrics and Gynaecology, 115,* 104–108.

de Moraes Barros, M.C., Guinsburg, R., Mitsuhiro, S., Chalem, E., & Laranjeira, R.R. (2008). Neurobehavioral profile of healthy full-term newborn infants of adolescent mothers. *Early Human Development, 84,* 281–287.

de Onis, M., Garza, C., Onyango, A.W., & Borghi, E. (2007). Comparison of the WHO Child Growth Standards and the CDC 2000 Growth Charts. *The Journal of Nutrition, 137,* 144–148.

de Onis, M., & Onyango, A.W. (2003). The Centers for Disease Control and Prevention 2000 growth charts and the growth of breastfed infants. *Acta Paediatrica, 92,* 413–9.

de Villiers, J.G., & de Villiers, P.A. (1973). A cross-sectional study of the acquisition of grammatical morphemes. *Journal of Psycholinguistic Research, 2,* 267–278.

de Villiers, P.A., & de Villiers, J.G. (1978). *Language acquisition.* Cambridge, MA: Harvard University Press.

De Wolff, M.S., & van IJzendoorn, M.H. (1997). Sensitivity and attachment: A meta-analysis on parental antecedents of infant attachment. *Child Development, 68,* 571–591.

Deák, G., Flom, R., & Pick, A.D. (2000). Effects of gesture and target on 12- and 18-month-olds' joint visual attention to objects in front of or behind them. *Developmental Psychology, 36,* 511–523.

Dearing, E., McCartney, K., & Taylor, B.A. (2009). Does higher quality early childcare promote low-income children's math and reading achievement in middle childhood? *Child Development, 80,* 1329–1349.

DeCasper, A.J., Lecanuet, J.P., Busnel, M.C., Granier-Deferre, C., & Maugeais, R. (1994). Fetal reactions to recurrent maternal speech. *Infant Behavior and Development, 17,* 159–164.

Declercq, E., Barger, M., Cabral, H.J., Evans, S.R., Kotelchuck, M., Simon, C., et al. (2007). Maternal outcomes associated with planned primary cesarean births compared with planned vaginal births. *Obstetrics & Gynecology, 109,* 669–677.

Dee, D.L., Sharma, A.J., Cogswell, M.E., Grummer-Strawn, L.M., Fein, S.B., & Scanlon, K.S. (2008). Sources of supplemental iron among breastfed infants during the first year of life. *Pediatrics, 122,* S98–S104.

DeHart, G.B. (1999). Conflict and averted conflict in preschoolers' interactions with siblings and friends. In W.A. Collins, & B. Laursen (Eds.), Relationships as developmental contexts. *The Minnesota Symposia on Child Psychology* (Vol. 30, pp. 281–303). Mahwah, NJ: Erlbaum.

deJong, T.R., Chauke, M., Harris, B.N., & Saltzman, W. (2009). From here to paternity: Neural correlates of the onset of paternal behavior in California mice (Peromyscus californicus). *Hormones & Behavior, 56,* 220–231.

DelCarmen-Wiggins, R. (2008). Introduction to the special section: Transformative research on emotion regulation and dysregulation. *Child Development Perspectives, 2,* 121–123.

Della Grotta, S., LaGasse, L.L., Arria, A.M., Derauf, C., Grant, P., Smith, L.M., et al. (2009). Patterns of methamphetamine use during pregnancy: Results from the Infant Development, Environment, and Lifestyle (IDEAL) Study. *Maternal and Child Health Journal.*

DeLoache, J., & Gottlieb, A. (2000). *A world of babies: Imagined childcare guides for seven societies.* New York: Cambridge University Press.

DeLoache, J.S. (2000). Dual representation and young children's use of scale models. *Child Development, 71,* 329–338.

DeLoache, J.S., & Burns, N.M. (1994). Early understanding of the representational function of pictures. *Cognition, 52,* 83–110.

DeLoache, J.S., Pierroutsakos, S.L., Uttal, D.H., Rosengren, K.S., & Gottlieb, A. (1998). Grasping the nature of pictures. *Psychological Science, 9,* 205–210.

DeLoache, J.S., Uttal, D.H., & Rosengren, K.S. (2004). Scale errors offer evidence for a perception-action dissociation. *Science, 304,* 1027–1029.

Deloukas, P., Matthews, L.H., Ashurst, J., Burton, J., Gilbert, J.G., Jones, M., et al. (2001). The DNA sequence and comparative analysis of human chromosome 20. *Nature, 414,* 865–871.

DeNavas-Walt, C., Proctor, B., & Smith, J.C. (2009). Income, poverty, and health insurance coverage in the United States: 2008. *Current Population Reports, P60-236.* Washington, DC: U.S. Census Bureau.

Dencker, A., Berg, M., Bergqvist, L., Ladfors, L., Thorsen, L.S., & Lilja, H. (2008). Early versus delayed oxytocin augmentation in nulliparous women with prolonged labour—a randomized controlled trial. *BMOJ, 116,* 530–536.

Dennis, C., & Gallagher, R. (2001). *The human genome.* New York: Palgrave.

D'Entremont, B., Yazbeck, A., Morgan, A., & MacAulay, S. (2007). Early gaze-following and the understanding of others. In R. Flom, K. Lee, & D. Muir (Eds.), *Gaze-following: Its development and significance* (pp. 77–93). Mahwah, NJ: Lawrence Erlbaum Associates.

Derryberry, D., & Rothbart, M.K. (1997). Reactive and effortful processes in the organization of temperament. *Development and Psychopathology, 9,* 633–652.

DeSchipper, J.C., Tavecchio, L.W.C., van IJzendoorn, M.H., & van Zeijl, J. (2004). Goodness of fit in day care: Relations of temperament, stability, and quality of care with child's adjustment. *Early Childhood Research Quarterly, 19,* 257–272.

deUngria, M., Rao, R., Wobken, J.D., Luciana, M., Nelson, C.A., & Georgieff, M.K. (2000). Perinatal iron deficiency decreases cytochrome oxidase (CytOx) activity in selected regions of neonatal rat brain. *Pediatric Research, 48,* 169–176.

Deven, F., & Moss, P. (2002). Leave arrangements for parents: overview and future outlook. *Community, Work and Family, 5,* 237–256.

Diamond, A. (1991). Neuropsychological insights into the meaning of object concept development. In S. Carey, & R. Gelman (Eds.), *Biology and knowledge: Structural constraints on development* (pp. 37–80). Hillsdale, NJ: Erlbaum.

Diamond, A. (1998). Understanding the A-not-B error: Working memory vs. reinforced response, or active trace vs. latent trace. *Developmental Science, 1,* 185–189.

Diamond, A., Werker, J.F., & Lalonde, C. (1994). Toward understanding commonalities in the development of object search, detour navigation, categorization, and speech perception. In G. Dawson, & K. Fischer (Eds.), *Human behavior and the developing brain* (pp. 380–426). New York: Guilford Press.

Dias, M.S., Smith, K., deGuehery, K., Mazur, P., Li, V., & Shaffer, M.L. (2005). Preventing abusive head trauma among infants and young children: A hospital-based, parent education program. *Pediatrics, 115,* e470–e477.

DiGirolamo, A.M., Grummer-Strawn, L.M., & Fein, S.B. (2008). Effect of maternity-care practices on breast-feeding. *Pediatrics, 122,* S43–S49.

Dimmock, D., Kobayashi, K., Iijima, M., Tabata, A., Wong, L-J., Saheki, T., et al. (2007). Citrin deficiency: A novel cause of failure to thrive that responds to a high-protein, low-carbohydrate diet. *Pediatrics, 119,* e773–e777.

Dionne, G., Dale, P.S., Boivin, M., & Plomin, R. (2003). Genetic evidence for bidirectional effects of early lexical and grammatical development. *Child Development, 74,* 394–412.

DiPietro, J., Hilton, S., Hawkins, M., Costigan, K., & Pressman, E. (2002). Maternal stress and affect influence fetal neurobehavioral development. *Developmental Psychology, 38,* 659–668.

DiPietro, J.A. (2004). The role of prenatal maternal stress in child development. *Current Directions in Psychological Science, 13,* 71–74.

DiPietro, J.A., Hodgson, D.M., Costigan, K.A., & Johnson, T.R.B. (1996). Fetal antecedents of infant temperament. *Child Development, 67,* 2568–2583.

Dodge, K.A., Coie, J.D., & Lynam, D. (2006). Aggression and antisocial behavior in youth. In W. Damon, & R. Lerner (Eds.) & N. Eisenberg (Vol. Ed.), *Handbook of child psychology: Vol. 3. Social, emotional, and personality development* (6th ed., pp. 719–788). New York: Wiley.

Donzella, B., Gunnar, M.R., Krueger, W.K., & Alwin, J. (2000). Cortisol and vagal tone responses to competitive challenge in preschoolers: Associations with temperament. *Developmental Psychogiology, 37,* 209–220.

Doulas of North America. (2002). *What is a doula?* Retrieved January 10, 2003, from http://www.dona.org/faq.html

Douvan, E. (1985). The age of narcissism, 1963–1982. In J.M. Hawes, & N. R. Hiner (Eds.), *American childhood: A research guide and historical handbook* (pp. 587–617). Westport, CT: Greenwood Press.

Downs, B. (2003). Fertility of American women: June 2002. *Current Population Reports, P20–548.* Washington, DC: U.S. Census Bureau.

Draper, E.S., Zeitlin, J., Fenton, A.C., Weber, T., Gerrits, J., Martens, G., et al. (2009). Investigating the variations in survival rates for very preterm infants in 10 European regions: The MOSAIC birth cohort. *Archives of Disease in Childhood. Fetal and Neonatal Edition, 94,* F158–F163.

Dreher, M.C., Nugent, K., & Hudgins, R. (1994). Prenatal marijuana exposure and neonatal outcomes in Jamaica: An ethnographic study. *Pediatrics, 93,* 254–260.

Dromi, E. (1986). The one-word period as a stage in language development: Quantitative and qualitative accounts. In I. Levin (Ed.), *Stage and structure: Reopening the debate* (pp. 220–245). Norwood, NJ: Ablex.

Druin, A. (Ed.). (1999). *The design of children's technology.* San Francisco, CA: Morgan Kaufmann Publishers.

Druin, A., & Hendler, J. (Eds.). (2000). *Robots for kids: Exploring new technologies for learning.* San Diego, CA: Morgan Kaufmann Publishers.

Druin, A., & Solomon, C. (1996). *Designing multimedia environments for children: Computers, creativity, and kids.* New York: Wiley.

Dunham, I., et al. (1999). The DNA sequence of human chromosome 22. *Nature, 402,* 489–495.

Dunn, J. (1998). Siblings, emotion and the development of understanding. In S. Bråten (Ed.), *Intersubjective communication and emotion in early ontogeny. Studies in emotion and social interaction,* 2nd series (pp. 158–168). New York: Cambridge University Press.

Dunn, J. (2002). Sibling relationships. In P.K. Smith, & C.H. Hart (Eds.), *Blackwell handbook of childhood social development. Blackwell handbooks of developmental psychology* (pp. 223–237). Malden, MA: Blackwell.

Dunn, J., & Brown, J. (1996). Children's family relationships between two and five: Developmental changes and individual differences. *Social Development, 5,* 230–250.

Dunn, J., Brown, J., & Beardsall, L. (1991). Family talk about feeling states and children's later understanding of others' emotions. *Developmental Psychology, 27,* 448–455.

Dunn, J., Brown, J., Slomkowski, C., Tesla, C., & Youngblade, L. (1991). Young children's understanding of other people's feelings and beliefs: Individual differences and their antecedents. *Child Development, 62,* 1352–1366.

Dunn, J., & Hughes, C. (1998). Young children's understanding of emotion in close relationships. *Cognition and Emotion, 12,* 171–190.

Dunn, J., Kendrick, C., & MacNamee, R. (1981). The reaction of first-born children to the birth of a sibling: Mothers' reports. *Journal of Child Psychology and Psychiatry, 22,* 1–18.

Dunn, J., & Kendrick, C. (1982). Siblings and their mothers: Developing relationships within the family. In M.E. Lamb, & B. Sutton-Smith (Eds.), *Sibling relationships: Their nature and significance across the lifespan* (pp. 39–60). Hillsdale, NJ: Erlbaum.

Dunn, J., & Munn, P. (1985). Becoming a family member: Family conflict and the development of social understanding in the second year. *Child Development, 56,* 480–492.

Durkin, E.F., & Shaaban, A. (2009). Commonly encountered surgical problems in the fetus and neonate. *Pediatric Clinics of North America, 56,* 647–669.

Dwyer, J.B., McQuown, S.C., & Leslie, F.M. (2009). The dynamic effects of nicotine on the developing brain. *Pharmacology & Therapeutics, 122,* 125–139.

Ebrahim, S.H., & Gfroerer, J. (2003). Pregnancy-related substance use in the United States during 1996–1998. *Obstetrics and Gynecology, 101,* 374–379.

Eckenrode, J., Ganzel, B., Henderson, C.R., Smith, E., Olds, D.L., Powers, J., Cole, R., Kitzman, H., & Sidora, K. (2000). Preventing child abuse and neglect with a program of nurse home visitation. *JAMA, 284,* 1385–1391.

Ecker, J.L., Chen, K.T., Cohen, A.P., Riley, L.E., & Lieberman, E.S. (2001). Increased risk of cesarean delivery with advancing maternal age: Indications and associated factors in nulliparous women. *American Journal of Obstetrics and Gynecology, 185,* 883–887.

Eckerman, C.O., & Didow, S.M. (1989). Toddlers' social coordinations: Changing responses to another's invitation to play. *Developmental Psychology, 25,* 794–804.

Edwards, M. (1999). Pollution in the former Soviet Union: Lethal legacy. *National Geographic, 186*(2), 70–115.

Effer, S.B., Moutquin, J.M., Farine, D., Saigal, S., Nimrod, C., Kelly, E., & Niyonsenga, T. (2002). Neonatal survival rates in 860 singleton live births at 24 and 25 weeks gestational age. *BJOG, 109,* 740–745.

Egeland, B., Jacobvitz, D., & Sroufe, L.A. (1988). Breaking the cycle of abuse. *Child Development, 59,* 1080–1088.

Ehrenberg, H.M., Dierker, L., Milluzzi, C., & Mercer, B.M. (2003). Low maternal weight, failure to thrive in pregnancy, and adverse pregnancy outcomes. *American Journal of Obstetrics and Gynecology, 189,* 1726–1730.

Eickhorst, A., Lamm, B., Borke, J., & Keller, H. (2008). Fatherhood in different decades: Interactions between German fathers and their infants in 1977 and 2001. *European Journal of Developmental Psychology, 5,* 92–107.

Eide, B.I., Nilsen, A.B.V., & Svein Rasmussen, S. (2009). Births in two different delivery units in the same clinic: A prospective study of healthy primiparous women *BMC Pregnancy and Childbirth, 9,* 25–45.

Eimas, P.D., & Corbit, J.D. (1973). Selective adaptation of linguistic feature detectors. *Cognitive Psychology, 4,* 99–109.

Eisenberg, N., & Fabes, R.A. (1998). Prosocial development. In W. Damon, & N. Eisenberg (Eds.), *Handbook of child psychology: Vol. 3. Social, emotional, and personality development* (5th ed., pp. 701–778). New York: Wiley.

Eisenberg, N., Fabes, R.A., & Spinrad, T.L. (2006). Prosocial development. In W. Damon, & R. Lerner (Eds.) & N. Eisenberg (Vol. Ed.), *Handbook of child psychology: Vol. 3. Social, emotional, and personality development* (6th ed., pp. 646–718). New York: Wiley.

Eisenberg, N., & Spinrad, T.L. (2004). Emotion-related regulation: Sharpening the definition. *Child Development, 75,* 334–339.

Ekström, A., Widström, A., & Nissen, E. (2003). Duration of breastfeeding in Swedish primiparous and multiparous women. *Journal of Human Lactation, 19,* 172–178.

Elder, Jr. G.H., (1974). *Children of the Great Depression: Social change in life experience.* Chicago: University of Chicago Press.

Elder, Jr., G.H., & Hareven, T.K. (1993). Rising above life's disadvantage: From the Great Depression to war. In G.H. Elder, Jr., J. Modell, & R.D. Parke (Eds.). *Children in time and place: Developmental and historical insights* (pp. 47–72). New York: Cambridge University Press.

Elder, G.H., Jr., Modell, J., & Parke, R.D. (Eds.). (1993). *Children in time and place: Developmental and historical insights.* New York: Cambridge University Press.

Ellemberg, D., Lewis, T.L., Maurer, D., & Brent, H.P. (2000). Influence of monocular deprivation during infancy on the later development of spatial and temporal vision. *Vision Research, 40,* 3283–3295.

Emde, R.N. (1992). Individual meaning and increasing complexity: Contributions of Sigmund Freud and René Spitz to developmental psychology. *Developmental Psychology, 28,* 347–359.

Emde, R.N., Biringen, A., Clyman, R.B., & Oppenheim, D. (1991). The moral self in infancy: Affective core and procedural knowledge. *Developmental Review, 11,* 251–270.

Engle, P.L., & Breaux, C. (1998). Fathers' involvement with children: Perspectives from developing countries. *Social Policy Report, XII*(1), 1–21.

Engle, W.A., & the Committee on Fetus and Newborn. (2008). Surfactant-replacement therapy for respiratory distress in the preterm and term neonate. *Pediatrics, 121,* 419–432.

Engle, W.A., Tomashek, K.M., Wallman, C., and the Committee on Fetus and Newborn. (2007). "Late-preterm" infants: A population at risk. *Pediatrics, 120,* 1391–1401.

Ennouri, K., & Bloch, H. (1996). Visual control of hand approach movements in newborns. *British Journal of Developmental Psychology, 14,* 327–338.

Erickson, M.F., & Egeland, B. (1996). Child neglect. In J. Briere, & L. Berliner (Eds.), *The APSAC handbook on child maltreatment* (pp. 4–20). Thousand Oaks, CA: Sage.

Erickson, M.F., Korfmacher, J., & Egeland, B. (1992). Attachments past and present: Implications for therapeutic intervention with mother-infant dyads. *Development and Psychopathology, 4,* 495–507.

Erickson, M.F., Sroufe, L.A., & Egeland, B. (1985). The relationship between quality of attachment and behavior problems in a high risk sample. In I. Bretherton, & E. Waters (Eds.), Growing points in attachment theory and research. *Monographs of the Society for Research in Child Development, 50*(1/2, Serial No. 209), 147–166.

Erikson, E.H. (1950). *Childhood and society.* New York: Norton.

Erting, C.J., Prezioso, C., & O'Grandy Hynes, M. (1990). The interactional context of deaf mother-infant communication. In V. Voltera, & C.J. Erting (Eds.), *From gesture to language in hearing and deaf children* (pp. 97–106). Berlin: Springer.

ESHRE PGD Consortium Steering Committee. (2002). ESHRE Preimplantation Genetic Diagnosis Consortium: Data collection III (May 2001). *Human Reproduction, 17,* 233–246.

Eskenazi, B., & Castorina, R. (1999). Association of prenatal maternal or postnatal child environmental tobacco smoke exposure and neurodevelopmental and behavioral problems in children. *Environmental Health Perspectives, 107,* 991–1000.

Eugenín, J., Otárola, M., Bravo, E., Coddou, C., Cerpa, V., Reyes-Parada, M., et al. (2008). Prenatal to early postnatal nicotine exposure impairs central chemoreception and modifies breathing pattern in mouse neonates: A probable link to sudden infant death syndrome. *Journal of Neuroscience, 28,* 13907–13917.

Evans, G.W. (2004). The environment of childhood poverty. *American Psychologist, 59,* 77–92.

Evans, M.I., Harrison, M.R., Flake, A.W., & Johnson, M.P. (2002). Fetal therapy. *Clinical Obstetrics & Gynaecology, 16,* 671–683.

Evans, M.I., & Wapner, R.J. (2005). Invasive prenatal diagnostic procedures 2005. *Seminars in Perinatology, 29,* 215–218.

Evans, M.J., Gurer, C., Loike, J.D., Wilmut, I., Schnieke, A.E., Schon, E.A., et al. (1999). Mitochondrial DNA genotypes in nuclear transfer-derived cloned sheep. *Nature Genetics, 23,* 90–93.

Eyler, F.D., Behnke, M., Conlon, M., Woods, N.S., & Wobie, K. (1998). Birth outcome from a prospective, matched study of crack/cocaine use: II. Interactive and does effects on neurobehavioral assessment. *Pediatrics, 101,* 237–241.

Fagard, J., Spelke, E., & von Hofsten, C. (2009). Reaching and grasping a moving object in 6-, 8-, and 10-month-old infants: Laterality and performance. *Infant Behavior & Development, 32,* 137–146.

Fan, H-Y., Liu, Z., Shimada, M., Sterneck, E., Johnson, P.F., Hedrick, S.M., et al. (2009). MAPK3/1 (ERK1/2) in ovarian granulosa cells are essential for female fertility. *Science, 324,* 938–941.

Fannin, M. (2003). Domesticating birth in the hospital: "Family-centered" birth and the emergence of "homelike" birthing rooms. *Antipode, 35,* 513–535.

Fantz, R.L. (1961). The origin of form perception. *Scientific American, 204,* 66–72.

Fantz, R.L., Fagan, J.F., & Miranda, S.B. (1975). Early visual selectivity. In L.B. Cohen, & P. Salapatek (Eds.), *Infant perception: From sensation to cognition* (Vol. 1, pp. 249–345). New York: Academic Press.

Farley, T.F., Hambidge, S.J., & Daley, M.F. (2002). Association of low maternal education with neural tube defects in Colorado, 1989–1998. *Public Health, 116,* 89–94.

Farver, J.M., & Howes, C. (1993). Cultural differences in American and Mexican mother-child pretend play. *Merrill-Palmer Quarterly, 39,* 344–358.

Farroni, T., Csibra, G., Simion, F., & Johnson, M.H. (2002). Eye contact detection in humans from birth. *Proceedings of the National Academy of Sciences USA, 99,* 9602–9605.

Farver, J.M., Kim, Y.K., & Lee, Y. (1995). Cultural differences in Korean- and Anglo-American preschoolers' social interaction and play behaviors. *Child Development, 66,* 1088–1099.

Farver, J.M., Lonigan, C.J., & Eppe, S. (2009). Effective early literacy skill development for young Spanish-speaking English language learners: An experimental study of two methods. *Child Development, 80,* 703–719.

Farver, J.M., & Wimbarti, S. (1995). Indonesian toddlers' social play with their mothers and older siblings. *Child Development, 66,* 1493–1513.

Federal Interagency Forum on Child and Family Statistics. (2009). *America's children: Key national indicators of well-being, 2009.* Retrieved September 5, 2009, from http://childstats.gov/americaschildren/

Fei, C., McLaughlin, J.K., Lipworth, L., & Olsen, J. (2009). Maternal levels of perfluorinated chemicals and subfecundity. *Human Reproduction, 1,* 1–6.

Fein, S.B., Mandal, B., & Roe, B.E. (2008). Success of strategies for combining employment and breast-feeding. *Pediatrics, 122,* S56–S62.

Feinbloom, R.I. (1993). *Pregnancy, birth, and the early months: A complete guide* (2nd ed.). Reading, MA: Perseus Books.

Feldman, R. (2006). Biological rhythms to social rhythms: Physiological precursors of mother-infant synchrony. *Developmental Psychology, 41,* 175–188.

Feldman, R., Eidelman, A.I., & Rotenberg, N. (2004). Parenting stress, infant emotion regulation, maternal sensitivity, and the cognitive development of triplets: A model for parent and child influences in a unique ecology. *Child Development, 75,* 1774–1791.

Fennell, C.T., & Werker, J.F. (2003). Early word learners' ability to access phonetic detail in well-known words. *Language and Speech, 46,* 245–264.

Fennell, C.T., Byes-Heinlen, K., & Werker, J.F. (2007). Using speech sounds to guide word learning: The case of bilingual infants. *Child Development, 78,* 1510–1525.

Fenson, L., Bates, E., Dale, P.S., Goodman, J., Reznick, J.S., & Thal, D. (2000). Measuring variability in early child language: Don't shoot the messenger. *Child Development, 71,* 323–328.

Fenson, L., Dale, P.S., Reznick, J.S., Bates, E., Thal, D.J., & Pethick, S.J. (1994). Variability in early communicative development. *Monographs of the Society for Research in Child Development, 59*(5, Serial No. 242).

Fenwick, J., Staff, L., Gamble, J., Creedy, D.K., & Bayes, S. (2008). Why do women request caesarean section in a normal, healthy first pregnancy? *Midwifery*.

Ferber, S.G., & Makhoul, I.R. (2004). The effect of skin-to-skin contact (kangaroo care) shortly after birth on the neurobehavioral responses of the term newborn: A randomized, controlled trial. *Pediatrics, 113,* 858–865.

Ferber, S.G., & Makhoul, I.R. (2008). Neurobehavioural assessment of skin-to-skin effects on reaction to pain in preterm infants: A randomized, controlled within-subject trial. *Acta Paediatrica, 27,* 171–176.

Fernald, A. (1993). Approval and disapproval: Infant responsiveness to vocal affect in familiar and unfamiliar languages. *Child Development, 64,* 657–674.

Fernald, A., & Mazzie, C. (1991). Prosody and focus in speech to infants and adults. *Developmental Psychology, 27,* 209–221.

Fernald, A., & Morikawa, H. (1993). Common themes and cultural variations in Japanese and American mothers' speech to infants. *Child Development, 64,* 637–656.

Fernald, A., & O'Neill, D.K. (1993). Peekaboo across cultures: How mothers and infants play with voices, faces, and expectations. In K. MacDonald (Ed.), *Parent-child play* (pp. 259–285). Albany, NY: State University of New York Press.

Fernald, A., Perfors, A., & Marchman, V.A. (2006). Picking up speed in understanding: Speech processing efficiency and vocabulary growth across the 2nd year. *Developmental Psychology, 42,* 98–116.

Fernald, A., Pinto, J.P., Swingley, D., Weinberg, A., & McRoberts, G.W. (1998). Rapid gains in speed of verbal processing by infants in the 2nd year. *Psychological Science, 9,* 228–231.

Ferrari, P.F., Paukner, A., Ruggiero, A., Darcey, L., Unbehagen, S., & Suomi, S.J. (2009). Interindividual differences in neonatal imitation and the development of action chains in rhesus monkeys. *Child Development, 80,* 1057–1068.

Field, T. (1998a). Early interventions for infants of depressed mothers. *Pediatrics, 102,* 1305–1310.

Field, T. (1998b). Maternal depression effects on infants and early interventions. *Preventive Medicine, 27,* 200–203.

Field, T., Diego, M., & Hernandez-Reif, M. (2006). Prenatal depression effects on the fetus and newborn: A review. *Infant Behavior & Development, 29,* 445–455.

Field, T., Diego, M., & Hernandez-Reif, M. (2007). Massage therapy research. *Developmental Review, 27,* 75–89.

Field, T., Diego, M., Hernandez-Reif, M., Dieter, J.N.I., Kumar, A.M., Schanberg, S., & Kuhn, C. (2008). Insulin and insulin-like growth factor-1 increased in preterm neonates following massage therapy. *Journal of Dev Behav Pediatr, 29,* 463–466.

Field, T., Diego, M., Hernandez-Reif, M., Schanberg, S., & Kuhn, C. (2003). Depressed mothers who are "good interaction" partners versus those who are withdrawn or intrusive. *Infant Behavior & Development, 26,* 238–252.

Field, T., Fox, N.A., Pickens, J., Nawrocki, T., & Soutollo, D. (1995). Right frontal EEG activation in 3- to 6-month-old infants of depressed mothers. *Developmental Psychology, 31,* 358–363.

Field, T., Grizzle, N., Scafidi, F., Abrams, S., Rchardson, S., Kuhn, C., & Schanberg, S. (1996). Massage therapy for infants of depressed mothers. *Infant Behavior and Development, 19,* 107–112.

Field, T., Healy, B., Goldstein, S., Perry, S., Bendell, D., Schanberg, S., Zimmerman, E.A., & Kuhn, C. (1988). Infants of depressed mothers show "depressed" behavior even with nondepressed adults. *Child Development, 59,* 1569–1579.

Field, T., Hernandez-Reif, M., & Freedman, J. (2004). Stimulation programs for preterm infants. *Social Policy Report, 18*(1), 1–19.

Field, T., Schanberg, S., Scafidi, F., Bower, C., Vega-Lahr, N., Garcia, R., et al. (1986). Tactile/kinesthetic stimulation effects on preterm neonates. *Pediatrics, 77,* 654–658.

Filipek, P.A., Accardo, P.J., Ashwal, S., Baranek, G.T., Cook, E.H., Dawson, G., et al. (2000). Practice parameter: Screening and diagnosis of autism: Report of the Quality Standards Subcommittee of the American Academy of Neurology and the Child Neurology Society. *Neurology, 55,* 468–479.

Finkelstein, B. (1985). Casting networks of good influence: The reconstruction of childhood in the United States, 1790–1870. In J.M. Hawes, & N.R. Hiner (Eds.). *American childhood: A research guide and historical handbook* (pp. 111–152). Westport, CT: Greenwood Press.

Fisher, K.R., Hirsh-Pasek, K., Golinkoff, R.M., & Gryfe, S.G. (2008). Conceptual split? Parents' and experts' perceptions of play in the 21st century. *Journal of Applied Developmental Psychology, 29,* 305–316.

Fisher, L., Ames, E.W., Chisholm, K., & Savoie, L. (1997). Problems reported by parents of Romanian orphans adopted to British Columbia. *International Journal of Behavioral Development, 20,* 67–82.

Fivaz-Depeursinge, E., & Corboz-Warnery, A. (1999). *The primary triangle: A developmental systems view of mothers, fathers, and infants.* New York: Basic Books.

Fivush, R., Brotman, M., Buckner, J.P., & Goodman, S. (2000). Gender differences in parent-child emotion narratives. *Sex Roles, 42,* 233–254.

Fivush, R., Haden, C.A., & Reese, E. (2006). Elaborating on elaborations: Role maternal of reminiscing style in cognitive and socioemotional development. *Child Development, 77,* 1568–1588.

Fjeld, E., Siziya, S., Katepa-Bwalya, M., Kankasa, C., Moland, K.M., & Tylleskär, T., for the PROMISE-EBF Study Group. (2008). 'No sister, the breast alone is not enough for my baby' a qualitative assessment of potentials and barriers in the promotion of exclusive breastfeeding in southern Zambia. *International Breastfeeding Journal, 3,* 26.

Flanagan, K.D., & Park, J. (2005). *American Indian and Alaska Native children: Findings from the base year of the Early Childhood Longitudinal Study, birth cohort (ECLS-B).* Washington, DC: U.S. Department of Education.

Fletcher, K.L., Huffman, L.F., Bray, N.W., & Grupe, L.A. (1998). The use of the microgenetic method with children with disabilities: Discovering competence. *Early Education and Development, 9,* 357–373.

Flom, R., & Bahrick, L.E. (2007). The development of infant discrimination of affect in multimodal and unimodal stimulation: The role of intersensory redundancy. *Developmental Psychology, 43,* 238–252.

Flom, R., Deák, G.O., Phill, C.G., & Pick, A.D. (2004). Nine-month-olds' shared visual attention as a function of gesture and object location. *Infant Behavior & Development, 27,* 181–194.

Flom, R., Gentile, D.A., & Pick, A.D. (2008). Infants' discrimination of happy and sad music. *Infant Behavior & Development, 31,* 716–728.

Flom, R., & Pick, A.D. (2003). Verbal encouragement and joint attention in 18-month-old infants. *Infant Behavior & Development, 26,* 121–134.

Flom, R., & Pick, A.D. (2007). Increasing specificity and the development of joint visual attention. In R. Flom, K. Lee, & D. Muir (Eds.), *Gaze-following: Its development and significance* (pp. 95–111). Mahwah, NJ: Lawrence Erlbaum Associates.

Flynn, E., O'Malley, C., & Wood, D. (2004). A longitudinal, microgenetic study of the emergence of false belief understanding and inhibition skills. *Developmental Science, 7,* 103–115.

Fogel, A. (2000). Developmental pathways in close relationships. *Child Development, 71,* 1150–1151.

Fogel, A., Dickson, K.L., Hsu, H.C., Messinger, D., Nelson-Goens, G.C., & Nwokah, E. (1997). Communication of smiling and laughter in mother-infant play: Research on emotion from a dynamic systems perspective. *New Directions for Child Development, No. 77,* 5–24.

Fogel, A., Nwokah, E., & Karns, J. (1993). Parent-infant games as dynamic social systems. In K. MacDonald (Ed.), *Parent-child play.* Albany, NY: State University of New York Press.

Folven, R.J., & Bonvillian, J.D. (1991). The transition from nonreferential to referential language in children acquiring American Sign Language. *Developmental Psychology, 27,* 806–816.

Fombonne, E. (2003). The prevalence of autism. *JAMA, 289,* 87–89.

Fontaine, P., Adam, P., & Svendsen, K.H. (2002). Should intrathecal narcotics be used as a sole labor analgesic? A prospective comparison of spinal opioids and epidural bupivacaine. *Journal of Family Practice, 51,* 630–635.

Fontanel, B., & d'Harcourt, C. (1997). *Babies: History, art, and folklore.* New York: Harry N. Abrams.

Forget-Dubois, N., Dionne, G., Lemelin, J., Pérusse, D., Tremblay, R.E., & Boivin, M. (2009). Early child language mediates the relation between home environment and school readiness. *Child Development, 80,* 736–749.

Forman, D.R., Aksan, N., & Kochanska, G. (2004). Toddlers' responsive imitation predicts preschool-age conscience. *Psychological Science, 15*, 699–704.

Foster, E.M., & Kalil, A. (2005). Developmental psychology and public policy: Progress and prospects. *Developmental Psychology, 41*, 827–832.

Fox, M.A., Connolly, B.A., & Snyder, T.D. (2005). *Youth indicators, 2005: Trends in the well-being of American youth* (NCES 2005050). Washington, DC: U.S. Department of Education, National Center for Education Statistics.

Fox, M.K., Pac, S., Devaney, B., & Jankowski, L. (2004). Feeding Infants and Toddlers study: What foods are infants and toddlers eating? *Journal of the American Dietetic Association, 104*, 22–30.

Fox, N.A., Kimmerly, N.L., & Schafer, W.D. (1991). Attachment to mother/attachment to father: A meta-analysis. *Child Development, 62*, 210–225.

Francis, D., Diorio, J., Plotsky, P.M., & Meaney, M.J. (2002). Environmental enrichment reverses the effects of maternal separation on stress reactivity. *Journal of Neuroscience, 22*, 7840–7843.

Franco, P., Scaillet, S., Wermenbol, V., Valente, F., Grosswasser, J., & Kahn, A. (2000). The influence of a pacifier on infants' arousals from sleep. *The Journal of Pediatrics, 136*, 775–779.

Frank, D.A., Brown, J., Johnson, S., & Cabral, H. (2002). Forgotten fathers: An exploratory study of mothers' report of drug and alcohol problems among fathers of urban newborns. *Neurotoxicology & Teratology, 24*, 339–347.

Frankenburg, W., Dodds, J.B., & Archer, P. (1990). *Denver II: Technical manual.* Denver: Denver Developmental Materials.

Frasier, D. (1991). *On the day you were born.* Orlando, FL: Harcourt Brace & Co.

Freed, J. (2004, April 10). Rare disorder robs toddler of pain. *Associated Press.*

Freeman, T., Jadva, V., Kramer, W., & Golombok, S. (2009). Gamete donation: Parents' experiences of searching for their child's donor siblings and donor. *Human Reproduction, 24*, 505–516.

Freud, S. (1910). The origin and development of psychoanalysis. *American Journal of Psychology, 21*, 181–218.

Freudigman, K.A., & Thoman, E.B. (1998). Infants' earliest sleep/wake organization differs as a function of delivery mode. *Developmental Psychobiology, 32*, 293–304.

Frick, J.E., Colombo, J., & Saxon, T.F. (1999). Individual and developmental differences in disengagement of fixation in early infancy. *Child Development, 70*, 537–548.

Frick, P.J. (2004). Integrating research on temperament and childhood psychopathology: Its pitfalls and promise. *Journal of Clinical Child and Adolescent Psychology, 33*, 2–7.

Friedlmeier, W., & Trommsdorff, G. (1999). Emotion regulation in early childhood: A cross-cultural comparison between German and Japanese toddlers. *Journal of Cross-Cultural Psychology, 30*, 684–711.

Frith, L. (2001). Gamete donation and anonymity: The ethical and legal debate. *Human Reproduction, 16*, 818–824.

Frith, U. (2003). *Autism: Explaining the enigma.* Oxford: Blackwell Publishing.

Fujioka, T., Fujioka, A., Tan, N., Chowdhury, G., Mouri, H., Sakata, Y., et al. (2001). Mild prenatal stress enhances learning performance in the non-adopted rat offspring. *Neuroscience, 103*, 301–307.

Fuller, B., Kagan, S.L., Caspary, G.L., & Gauthier, C.A. (2002). Welfare reform and child care options for low-income families. *The Future of Children, 12*(1), 97–119.

Furman, L., Taylor, G., Minich, N., & Hack, M. (2003). The effect of maternal milk on neonatal morbidity of very-low-birth-weight infants. *Archives of Pediatrics and Adolescent Medicine, 157*, 66–71.

The Future of Children. (2000). Unintentional injuries in childhood: Executive summary. *The Future of Children, 10*(1), 2–7.

Galtry, J. (2002). Child health: An underplayed variable in parental leave policy debates? *Community, Work, & Family, 5*, 257–278.

Gamble, J., Creedy, D.K., McCourt, C., Weaver, J., & Beake, S. (2007). A critique of the literature on women's request for cesarean section. *Birth, 34*, 331–340.

Ganchrow, J.R., Steiner, J.E., & Daher, M. (1983). Neonatal facial expressions in response to different qualities and intensities of gustatory stimuli. *Infant Behavior and Development, 6*, 473–484.

Garcia, E. (2009). Young Hispanic children: Boosting opportunities for learning. *SRCD Social Policy Report Brief, 23*(2).

Garciaguirre, J.S., Adolph, K.E., & Shrout, P.E. (2007). Baby carriage: Infants walking with loads. *Child Development, 78*, 664–680.

Gardiner, H.W., Mutter, J.D., & Kosmitzki, C. (2002). *Lives across cultures: Cross-cultural human development* (2nd ed.). Boston: Allyn & Bacon.

Garfield, C.F., & Isacco, A. (2006). Fathers and the well-child visit. *Pediatrics, 117*, e637–e645.

Garner, B.P. (1998). Play development from birth to age four. In D.P. Fromberg, & D. Bergen (Eds.), *Play from birth to twelve and beyond: Contexts, perspectives, and meaning* (pp. 137–145). New York: Garland.

Garrett, M., McElroy, A.M., & Staines, A. (2002). Locomotor milestones and babywalkers: Cross sectional study. *BMJ, 324,* 1494.

Garrison, M.M., & Christakis, D.A. (2005). *A teacher in the living room? Educational media for babies, toddlers and preschoolers.* Menlo Park, CA: The Henry J. Kaiser Family Foundation.

Gaskins, S. (1999). Children's daily lives in a Mayan village: A case study of culturally constructed roles and activities. In A. Goncu (ed.), *Children's engagement in the world* (pp. 25–81). Cambridge, UK: Cambridge University Press.

Gawande, A. (2004, January 12). The mop-up: Eradicating polio from the planet, one child at a time. *The New Yorker,* 34–40.

Geissbuhler, V., & Eberhard, J. (2005). Experience of pain and analgesia with water and land births. *Journal of Psychosomatic Obstetrics and Gynaecology, 26,* 127–133.

Geissbuhler, V., Stein, S., & Eberhard, J. (2004). Waterbirths compared with landbirths: An observational study of nine years. *Journal of Perinatal Medicine, 32,* 308–314.

Gelman, S.A., & Kalish, C.W. (2006). Conceptual development. In W. Damon, & R. Lerner (Eds.) & D. Kuhn, & R. Siegler (Vol. Eds.), *Handbook of child psychology: Vol. 2. Cognition, perception, and language* (6th ed., pp. 687–733). New York: Wiley.

Gentner, D. (2007). Spatial cognition in apes and humans. *Trends in Cognitive Sciences, 11,* 192–194.

George, V.K., Li, H., Teloken, C., Grignon, D.J., Lawrence, W.D., & Dhabuwala, C.B. (1996). Effects of long-term cocaine exposure on spermatogenesis and fertility in peripubertal male rats. *Journal of Urology, 155,* 327–331.

Gerken, L., & Aslin, R.N. (2005). Thirty years of research on infant speech perception: The legacy of Peter W. Jusczyk. *Language Learning and Development, 1,* 5–21.

Germo, G., Chang, E., Keller, M.A., & Goldberg, W.A. (2007). Family sleep arrangements and family life: Perspectives from mothers and fathers. *Infant and Child Development (special issue on Parent-Child Co-Sleeping), 16,* 433–456.

Gernsbacher, M.A., & Frymiare, J. (2005). Does the autistic brain lack core modules? *Journal of Developmental and Learning Disorders, 9,* 3–16.

Gernsbacher, M.A., Stevenson, J.L., Khandakar, S., & Goldsmith, H.H. (2008). Why does joint attention look atypical in autism? *Child Development Perspectives, 2,* 38–45.

Gershkoff-Stowe, L., & Smith, L.B. (2004). Shape and the first hundred nouns. *Child Development, 75,* 1098–1114.

Gesell, A. (1946). The ontogenesis of infant behavior. In L. Carmichael (Ed.), *Manual of child psychology.* New York: Wiley.

Gianino, A., & Tronick, E.Z. (1988). The mutual regulation model: The infant's self and interactive regulation and coping defensive capacities. In T.M. Field, P.M. McCabe, & N. Schneiderman (Eds.), *Stress and coping across development* (pp. 47–68). Hillsdale, NJ: Erlbaum.

Giannarelli, L., & Barsimantov, J. (2000). Child care expenses of America's families. *Assessing the New Federalism.* Washington, DC: Urban Institute. Retrieved August 15, 2005, from http://www.urban.org/url.cfm?ID=310028

Gibbins, S., Stevens, B., Beyene, J., Chan, P.C., Bagg, M., & Asztalos, E. (2008). Pain behaviours in extremely low gestational age infants. *Early Human Development, 84,* 451–458.

Gibson, E.J. (1969). *Principles of perceptual learning and development.* New York: Appleton-Century-Crofts.

Gibson, E.J. (1984). Perceptual development from an ecological approach. In M. Lamb, A. Brown, & B. Rogoff (Eds.), *Advances in developmental psychology* (Vol. 3, pp. 243–285). Hillsdale, NJ: Erlbaum.

Gibson, E.J., & Walk, R.D. (1960). The visual cliff. *Scientific American, 202,* 64–71.

Gibson, E.J., & Walker, A.S. (1984). Development of knowledge of visual-tactual affordances of substance. *Child Development, 55,* 453–460.

Gibson, E.J., Riccio, G., Schmuckler, M.A., Stoffregen, T.A., Rosenberg, D., & Taormina, J. (1987). Detection of the traversability of surfaces by crawling and walking infants. *Journal of Experimental Psychology: Human Perception and Performance, 13,* 533–544.

Gibson, J.J. (1966). *The senses considered as perceptual systems.* Boston: Houghton Mifflin.

Gibson, J.J. (1979). *The ecological approach to visual perception.* Boston: Houghton Mifflin.

Gilbert, R. (2002). Water birth: A near-drowning experience. *Pediatrics, 110,* 409.

Gilbert, S.F. (2000). *Developmental biology* (6th ed.). Sunderland, MA: Sinauer Associates.

Gill, J.H. (2002). *Native American worldviews: An introduction.* Amherst, NY: Humanity Books.

Glanz, J.M., McClure, D.L., Magid, D.J., Daley, M.F., France, E.K., Salmon, D.A., et al. (2009). Parental refusal of pertussis vaccination is associated with an increased risk of pertussis infection in children. *Pediatrics, 123,* 1446–1451.

Gleitman, L. (1990). The structural sources of verb meanings. *Language Acquisition, 1,* 3–55.

Gnidovec, B., Neubauer, D., & Zidar, J. (2002). Actigraphic assessment of sleep-wake rhythm during the first 6 months of life. *Clinical Neurophysiology, 113,* 1815–1821.

Gold, S.J. (1999). Continuity and change among Vietnamese families. In H.P. McAdoo (Ed.), *Family ethnicity: Strength in diversity* (2nd ed., pp. 225–234). Thousand Oaks, CA: Sage.

Goldberg, J., Holtz, D., Hyslop, T., & Tolosa, J.E. (2002). Has the use of routine episiotomy decreased? Examination of episiotomy rates from 1983 to 2000. *Obstetrics & Gynecology, 99,* 395–400.

Goldberg, W.A., & Keller, H. (2007). Co-sleeping during infancy and early childhood: Key findings and future directions. *Infant and Child Development, 16,* 457–469.

Goldenberg, R.L., Culhane, J.F., Iams, J.D., & Romero, R. (2008). Epidemiology and causes of preterm birth. *The Lancet, 371,* 75–84.

Goldenberg, R.L., & Jobe, A.H. (2001). Prospects for research in reproductive health and birth outcomes. *JAMA, 285,* 633–639.

Goldfield, B. (1987). The contributions of child and caregiver to referential and expressive language. *Applied Psycholinguistics, 8,* 267–280.

Goldfield, B.A., & Reznick, J.S. (1990). Early lexical acquisition: Rate, content and the vocabulary spurt. *Journal of Child Language, 17,* 171–183.

Goldin-Meadow, S. (2006). Nonverbal communication: The hand's role in talking and thinking. In W. Damon, & R. Lerner (Eds.) & D. Kuhn, & R. Siegler (Vol. Eds.), *Handbook of child psychology: Vol. 2. Cognition, perception, and language* (6th ed., pp. 336–369). New York: Wiley.

Goldin-Meadow, S. (2007). Pointing sets the stage for learning language – and creating language. *Child Development, 78,* 741–745.

Goldin-Meadow, S. (2009). How gesture promotes learning throughout childhood. *Child Development Perspectives, 3,* 106–111.

Goldin-Meadow, S., Goodrich, W., Sauer, E., & Iverson, J. (2007). Young children use their hands to tell their mothers what to say. *Developmental Science, 10,* 778–785.

Goldin-Meadow, S., Mylander, C., & Franklin, A. (2007). How children make language out of gesture: Morphological structure in gesture systems developed by American and Chinese deaf children. *Cognitive Psychology, 55,* 87–135.

Goldman, L., Falk, H., Landrigan, P.J., Balk, S.J., Reigart, J.R., & Etzel, R.A. (2004). Environmental pediatrics and its impact on government health policy. *Pediatrics, 113,* 1146–1157.

Goldsmith, H.H. (1996). Studying temperament via construction of the Toddler Behavior Assessment Questionnaire. *Child Development, 67,* 218–235.

Goldsmith, H.H., Buss, A.H., Plomin, R., Rothbart, M.K., Thomas, A., Chess, S., Hinde, R.A., & McCall, R.B. (1987). Roundtable: What is temperament? Four approaches. *Child Development, 58,* 505–529.

Goldsmith, H.H., & Campos, J.J. (1990). The structure of infant temperamental dispositions to experience fear and pleasure: A psychometric perspective. *Child Development, 61,* 1944–1964.

Goldsmith, H.H., & Davidson, R.J. (2004). Disambiguating the components of emotion regulation. *Child Development, 75,* 361–365.

Goldsmith, H.H., Pollak, S.D, & Davidson, R.J. (2008). Developmental neuroscience perspectives on emotion regulation. *Child Development Perspectives, 2,* 132–140.

Goldsmith, H., Rieser-Danner, L., & Briggs, S. (1991). Evaluating convergent and discriminant validity of temperament questionnaires for preschoolers, toddlers, and infants. *Developmental Psychology, 27,* 566–579.

Goldstein, M.H., Schwade, J.A., & Bornstein, M.H. (2009). The value of vocalizing: Five-month-old infants associate their own noncry vocalizations with responses from caregivers. *Child Development, 80,* 636–644.

Golinkoff, R.M., & Hirsh-Pasek, K. (2007). Language development: The view from the radical middle. In H. Caunt-Nulton, S. Kulatilake, & I. Woo (Eds.), *Proceedings of the 31st Annual Boston University Conference on Language Development* (pp. 1–25). Somerville, MA: Cascadilla Press.

Golinkoff, R.M., & Hirsh-Pasek, K. (2008). How toddlers begin to learn verbs. *Trends in Cognitive Sciences, 12,* 397–403.

Golinkoff, R.M., Hirsh-Pasek, K., Cauley, K.M., & Gordon, L. (1987). The eyes have it: Lexical and syntactic comprehension in a new paradigm. *Journal of Child Language, 14,* 23–45.

Golinkoff, R.M., Shuff-Bailey, M., Olguin, R., & Ruan, W. (1995). Young children extend novel words at the basic level: Evidence for the principle of categorical scope. *Developmental Psychology, 31,* 494–507.

Gonzalez, A.P., Vasquez-Mendoza, G., García-Vela, A., Ramirez, A.G., Salazar-Torres, M., & Romero-Gutierrez, G. (2009). Weight gain in preterm infants following parent-administered vimala massage:

A randomized controlled trial. *American Journal of Perinatology, 26,* 247–252.

Gonzalez, E., Fekany-Lee, K., Carmany-Rampey, A., Erter, C., Topczewski, J., Wright, C.V.E., & Solnica-Krezel, L. (2000). Head and trunk in zebrafish arise via coinhibition of BMP signaling by *bozozok* and *chordino. Genes & Development, 14,* 3087–3092.

Goodluck, C.T. (1999). Necessary social work roles and knowledge with Native American: Indian Child Welfare Act. In H.P. McAdoo (Ed.), *Family ethnicity: Strength in diversity* (2nd ed., pp. 293–300). Thousand Oaks, CA: Sage.

Goodman, J.H. (2004). Paternal postpartum depression, its relationship to maternal postpartum depression, and implications for family health. *Journal of Advanced Nursing, 45,* 26–35.

Goodman, S.H., & Gotlib, I.H. (1999). Risk for psychopathology in the children of depressed mothers: A developmental model for understanding mechanisms of transmission. *Psychological Review, 106,* 458–490.

Goodwyn, S.W., & Acredolo, L.P. (1998). Encouraging symbolic gestures: A new perspective on the relationship between gesture and speech. In J. M. Iverson, & S. Goldin-Meadow (Eds.), *The nature and functions of gesture in children's communication* (pp. 61–73). San Francisco: Jossey-Bass.

Goodwyn, S.W., Acredolo, L.P., & Brown, C.A. (2000). Impact of symbolic gesturing on early language development. *Journal of Nonverbal Behavior, 24,* 81–103.

Gormley Jr., W.T., Gayer, T., Phillips, D., & Dawson, B. (2005). The effects of universal pre-K on cognitive development. *Developmental Psychology, 41,* 872–884.

Gossman, G.L., Joesch, J.M., & Tanfer, K. (2006). Trends in maternal request cesarean delivery from 1991 to 2004. *Obstetrics & Gynecology, 108,* 1506–1516.

Gottesman, I.I. (2001). Psychopathology through a life span-genetic prism. *American Psychologist, 56,* 867–878.

Gottlieb, A. (2000). Luring your child into this life: A Beng path for infant care. In J. DeLoache, & A. Gottlieb (Eds.), *A world of babies: Imagined childcare guides for seven societies* (pp. 55–89). New York: Cambridge University Press.

Gottlieb, L.N., & Mendelson, M.J. (1990). Parental support and firstborn girls' adaptation to the birth of a sibling. *Journal of Applied Developmental Psychology, 11,* 29–48.

Goubet, N., & Clifton, R.K. (1998). Object and event representation in 6½-month-old infants. *Developmental Psychology, 34,* 63–76.

Grab, D., Paulus, W.E., Bommer, A., Buck, G., & Terinde, R. (1999). Treatment of fetal erythroblastosis by intravascular transfusions: Outcome at 6 years. *Obstetrics and Gynecology, 93,* 165–168.

Grace, D.M., David, B.J., & Ryan, M.K. (2008). Investigating preschoolers' categorical thinking about gender through imitation, attention, and the use of self-categories. *Child Development, 79,* 1928–1941.

Graham, S.A., Nilsen, E.S., & Nayer S.L. (2007). Following the intentional eye: The role of gaze cues in early word learning. In R. Flom, K. Lee, & D. Muir (Eds.), *Gaze-following: Its development and significance* (pp. 193–216). Mahwah, NJ: Lawrence Erlbaum Associates.

Gralinski, J.H., & Kopp, C.B. (1993). Everyday rules for behavior: Mothers' requests to young children. *Developmental Psychology, 29,* 573–584.

Grammatopoulos, D.K., & Hillhouse, E.W. (1999). Role of corticotropin-releasing hormone in onset of labour. *Lancet, 354,* 1546–1549.

Grandjean, H., Larroque, D., & Levi, S. (1999). The performance of routine ultrasonic screening of pregnancies in the Eurofetus study. *American Journal of Obstetrics and Gynecology, 181,* 446–454.

Granrud, C.E., Yonas, A., Smith, I.M., Arterberry, M.E., Blicksman, M.L., & Sorknes, A.C. (1984). Infants' sensitivity to accretion and deletion of texture as information for depth at an edge. *Child Development, 55,* 1630–1636.

Gray, L., Watt, L., & Blass, E. (2000). Skin-to-skin contact is analgesic in healthy newborns. *Pediatrics, 105,* 1–6.

Greer, F.R., Krebs, N.F., & Committee on Nutrition. (2006). Optimizing bone health and calcium intakes of infants, children, and adolescents. *Pediatrics, 117,* 578–585.

Greer, F.R., Sicherer, S.H., Burks, A.W., & the Committee on Nutrition and Section on Allergy and Immunology. (2008). Effects of early nutritional interventions on the development of atopic disease in infants and children: The role of maternal dietary restriction, breastfeeding, timing of introduction of complementary foods, and hydrolyzed formulas. *Pediatrics, 121,* 183–191.

Groark, C.J., McCall, R.B., Muhamedrahimov, R.J., Nikiforova, N.V., & Palmov, O.I. (2003). *The effects of improving caregiving on early development.* Pittsburgh, PA: Office of Child Development, University of Pittsburgh.

Groark, C.J., McCall, R.B., Muhamedrahimov, R.J., Nikiforova, N.V., Palmov, O.I., & Fish, L. (2005). The developmental consequences of improvements in social-emotional environments in St. Petersburg (Russia) orphanages. Paper presented at the Biennial

Meeting of the Society for Research in Child Development, Atlanta, GA.

Gromko, J.E., & Poorman, A.S. (1998). The effect of music training on preschoolers' spatial-temporal task performance. *Journal of Research in Music Education, 46,* 173–181.

Gross, R.T., Spiker, D., Haynes, C.W. (Eds.). (1997). *Helping low birth weight, premature babies: The Infant Health and Development Program.* Stanford, CA: Stanford University Press.

Grossmann, K.E., Grossmann, K., & Zimmermann, P. (1999). A wider view of attachment and exploration: Stability and change during the years of immaturity. In J. Cassidy, & P.R. Shaver (Eds.), *Handbook of attachment: Theory, research, and clinical applications* (pp. 760–787). New York: Guilford Press.

Grummer-Strawn, L., Scanlon, K.S., Darling, N., & Conrey, E.J. (2006). Racial and socioeconomic disparities in breastfeeding—United States, 2004. *Morbidity and Mortality Weekly Report, 55*(12), 335–339.

Grummer-Strawn, L.M., Scanlon, K.S., & Fein, S.B. (2008). Infant feeding and feeding transitions during the first year of life. *Pediatrics, 122,* S36–S42.

Grunau, R.E., Weinberg, J., & Whitfield, M.F. (2004). Neonatal procedural pain and preterm infant cortisol response to novelty at 8 months. *Pediatrics, 114,* e77–e84.

Guise, J., Palda, V., Westhoff, C., Chan, B.K.S., Helfand, M., & Lieu, T.A. (2003). The effectiveness of primary care-based interventions to promote breastfeeding: Systematic evidence review and meta-analysis for the U.S. Preventive Services Task Force. *Annals of Family Medicine, 1,* 70–80.

Gunderson, V.M., Yonas, A., Sargent, P.L., & Grant-Webster, K.S. (1993). Infant macaque monkeys respond to pictorial depth. *Psychological Science, 4,* 93–98.

Gunnar, M.R. (1994). Psychoendocrine studies of temperament and stress in early childhood: Expanding current models. In J.E. Bates, & T.D. Wachs (Eds.), *Temperament, individual differences at the interface of biology and behavior* (pp. 175–198). Washington, DC: American Psychological Association Press.

Gunnar, M.R. (2000). Early adversity and the development of stress reactivity and regulation. In C. Nelson (Ed.), *Minnesota Symposium on Child Psychology: Vol. 31. The effects of adversity on neurobehavioral development* (pp. 163–200). Mahwah, NJ: Erlbaum.

Gunnar, M.R., Frenn, K., Wewerka, S.S., & Van Ryzin, M.J. (2009). Moderate versus severe early life stress: Associations with stress reactivity and regulation in 10–12-year-old children. *Psychoneuroendocrinology, 34,* 62–75.

Gunnar, M.R., Morison, S.J., Chisholm, K., & Schuder, M. (2001). Salivary cortisol levels in children adopted from Romanian orphanages. *Development and Psychopathology, 13,* 611–628.

Gunnar, M.R., & Quevedo, K. (2007). The neurobiology of stress and development. *Annual Review of Psychology, 58,* 145–173.

Gupta, R.S., Shuman, S., Taveras, E.M., Kulldorff, M., & Finkelstein, J.A. (2005). Opportunities for health promotion education in child care. *Pediatrics, 116,* e499–e505.

Haas, D.M., & Ramsey, P.S. (2008). Progestogen for preventing miscarriage. *Cochrane Database of Systematic Reviews, 2,* CD003511.

Hacein-Bey-Abina, S., Von Kalle, C., Schmidt, M., McCormack, M.P., Wulffraat, N., Leboulch, P., et al., (2003). LMO2-associated clonal T cell proliferation in two patients after gene therapy for SCID-X1. *Science, 302,* 415–419.

Hack, M., Klein, N.K., & Taylor, H.G. (1995). Long-term developmental outcomes of low birth weight infants. *The Future of Children: Low Birth Weight, 5(1),* 19–34. Los Altos, CA: Center for the Future of Children. The David and Lucile Packard Foundation.

Haddow, J.E., Palomaki, G.E., Allan, W.C., Williams, J.R., Knight, G.J., Gagnon, J., et al. (1999). Maternal thyroid deficiency during pregnancy and subsequent neuropsychological development of the child. *New England Journal of Medicine, 341,* 549–555.

Hadjikhani, N., Chabris, C.F., Joseph, R.M., Clark, J., McGrath, L., Aharon, I., et al. (2004). Early visual cortex organization in autism: An fMRI study. *Neuroreport: For Rapid Communication of Neuroscience Research, 15,* 267–270.

Haehl, V., Vardaxis, V., & Ulrich, B. (2000). Learning to cruise: Bernstein's theory applied to skill acquisition during infancy. *Human Movement Science, 19,* 685–715.

Hagekull, B. (1994). Infant temperament and early childhood functioning: Possible relations to the Five-Factor Model. In C.J. Halverson, Jr., G.A. Kohnstamm, & R.P. Martin (Eds.), *The developing structure of temperament and personality* (pp. 227–240). Hillsdale, NJ: Erlbaum.

Hagekull, B., & Bohlin, G. (2003). Early temperament and attachment as predictors of the Five Factor Model of personality. *Attachment & Human Development, 5,* 2–18.

Haith, M.M., & Benson, J.B. (1998). Infant cognition. In W. Damon (Editor-in-Chief), D. Kuhn, & R.S. Siegler (Vol. Eds.), *Handbook of child psychology:*

Vol. 2. Cognition, perception, and language (5th ed., pp. 199–254). New York: Wiley.

Hakuta, K. (1986). *Mirror of language: The debate on bilingualism.* New York: Basic Books.

Hale, C.M., & Tager-Flusberg, H. (2005). Social communication with children with autism: The relationship between theory of mind and discourse development. *Autism, 9,* 157–178.

Halgunseth, L.C. (2004). Continuing research on Latino families: El pasado y el futuro. In M. Coleman, & L.H. Ganong (Eds.), *Handbook of contemporary families: Considering the past, contemplating the future* (pp. 333–351). Thousand Oaks, CA: Sage.

Hall, D., & Kirsten, G. (2008). Kangaroo mother care: A review. *Transfusion Medicine, 18,* 77–82.

Hall, D.G., Lee, S.C., & Belanger, J. (2001). Young children's use of syntactic cues to learn proper names and count nouns. *Developmental Psychology, 37,* 298–307.

Hall, D.G., & Waxman, S.R. (2004). *Weaving a lexicon.* Cambridge, MA: MIT Press.

Halle, T. (2002). *Charting parenthood: A statistical portrait of fathers and mothers in America.* Washington, DC: Child Trends.

Halpern, S.A. (1988). *American pediatrics: The social dynamics of professionalism, 1880–1980.* Berkeley, CA: University of California Press.

Halpern, S.H., & Carvalho, B. (2009). Patient-controlled epidural analgesia for labor. *Anesthesia and Analgesia, 108,* 921–928.

Halverson, H.M. (1931). An experimental study of prehension in infants by means of systematic cinema records. *Genetic Psychology Monographs, 10,* 107–286.

Halverson, H.M. (1932). A further study of grasping. *Journal of Genetic Psychology, 7,* 34–64.

Hamilton, B.E., Martin, J.A., & Ventura, S.J. (2009). Births: Preliminary data for 2007. *National Vital Statistics Reports, 57*(12). Hyattsville, MD: National Center for Health Statistics.

Hamilton, B.E., Martin, J.A., Ventura, S.J., Sutton, P.D., & Menacker, F. (2005). Births: Preliminary data for 2004. *National Vital Statistics Reports, 54*(8). Hyattsville, MD: National Center for Health Statistics.

Hampson, J., & Nelson, K. (1993). The relation of maternal language to variation in rate and style of language acquisition. *Journal of Child Language, 20,* 313–342.

Hareven, T. (1985). Historical change in the family and the life course: Implications for child development. In A.B. Smuts, & J.W. Hagen (Eds.), History and research in child development. *Monographs of the Society for Research in Child Development, 50* (4–5, Serial No. 211), 8–23.

Hareven, T.K. (2000). *Families, history, and social change.* Boulder, CO: Westview Press.

Harjo, S.S. (1999). The American Indian experience. In H.P. McAdoo (Ed.), *Family ethnicity: Strength in diversity* (2nd ed., pp. 63–71). Thousand Oaks, CA: Sage.

Harkness, S., Moscardino, U., Blom, M.J.M., Huitrón, B., Vesely, C., Johnston, C., et al. (in press). Mothers' ideas and practices related to infant development in Italy, Spain, the Netherlands, and the US. *Journal of Developmental Processes.*

Harkness, S., & Super, C.M. (2001). Culture and parenting. In M.H. Bornstein (Ed.), *Handbook of parenting* (2nd ed., pp. 253–280). Hillsdale, NJ: Lawrence Erlbaum Associates.

Harkness, S., Super, C.M., Moscardino, U., Rha, J.-H., Blom, M.J.M., Huitrón, B., et al. (2007). Cultural models and developmental agendas: Implications for arousal and self-regulation in early infancy. *Journal of Developmental Processes, 1,* 5–39.

Harms, T., Clifford, R.M., & Cryer, D. (1998). *Early Childhood Environment Rating Scale—Revised (ECERS-R).* New York: Teachers College Press.

Harms, T., Cryer, D., & Clifford, R.M. (1990). *Infant/Toddler Environment Rating Scale.* New York: Teachers College Press.

Harris, B. (1979). Whatever happened to little Albert? *American Psychologist, 34,* 151–160.

Harris, G. (1997). Development of taste perception and appetite regulation. In G. Bremner, A. Slater, & G. Butterworth (Eds.), *Infant development: Recent advances* (pp. 9–30). East Sussex, UK: Psychology Press.

Harris, G., Thomas, A., & Booth, D.A. (1990). Development of salt taste in infancy. *Developmental Psychology, 26,* 534–538.

Harris, L.J. (1985). James Mark Baldwin on the origins of right- and left-handedness: The story of an experiment that mattered. In A.B Smuts, & J.W. Hagen (Eds.), History and research in child development. *Monographs of the Society for Research in Child Development, 50*(4–5, Serial No. 211), 44–64.

Harris, P.L., & Kavanaugh, R.D. (1993). Young children's understanding of pretense. *Monographs of the Society for Research in Child Development, 58* (1, Serial No. 231).

Harrison, D.M. (2008). Oral sucrose for pain management in the paediatric emergency department: A review. *Australasian Emergency Nursing Journal, 11,* 72–79.

Harrison, M.R., Keller, R.I., Hawgood, S.B., Kitterman, J.A., Sandberg, P.L., Farmer, D.L., et al. (2003). A randomized trial of fetal endoscopic tracheal occlusion for severe fetal congenital diaphragmatic hernia. *New England Journal of Medicine, 349,* 1916–1924.

Harrist, A.W., & Waugh, R.M. (2002). Dyadic synchrony: Its structure and function in children's development. *Developmental Review, 11,* 555–592.

Hart, B., & Risley, T.R. (1995). *Meaningful differences in the everyday experience of young American children.* Baltimore: Paul H. Brookes Publishing.

Hart, B., & Risley, T.R. (1999). *The social world of children learning to talk.* Baltimore: Paul H. Brookes Publishing.

Harter, S. (1998). The development of self-representations. In W. Damon (Series Ed.) & N. Eisenberg (Vol. Ed.), *Handbook of child psychology: Vol. 3. Social, emotional, and personality development* (5th ed., pp. 553–617). New York: Wiley.

Harter, S. (2006). The self. In W. Damon, & R. Lerner (Eds.) & N. Eisenberg (Vol. Ed.), *Handbook of child psychology: Vol. 3. Social, emotional, and personality development* (6th ed., pp. 505–570). New York: Wiley.

Hartling, L., Shaik, M.S., Tjosvold, L., Leicht, R., Liang, Y., & Kumar, M. (2009). Music for medical indications in the neonatal period: a systematic review of randomised controlled trials. *Archives of Disease in Childhood. Fetal and Neonatal Edition, 94,* F349–F354.

Hartup, W.W. (1989). Social relationships and their developmental significance. *American Psychologist, 44,* 120–126.

Hartup, W.W. (1996). The company they keep: Friendships and their developmental significance. *Child Development, 67,* 1–13.

Harwood, R., Leyendecker, B., Carlson, V., Asencio, M., & Miller, A. (2002). Parenting among Latino families in the U.S. In M.H. Bornstein (Ed.), *Handbook of parenting: Vol. 4. Social conditions and applied parenting* (2nd ed., pp. 21–46). Mahwah, NJ: Erlbaum.

Harwood, R.L., Miller, J.G., & Irizarry, N.L. (1995). *Culture and attachment.* New York: Guilford Press.

Harwood, R.L., Schöelmerich, A., Schulze, P.A., & Gonzalez, Z. (1999). Cultural differences in maternal beliefs and behaviors: A study of middle-class Anglo and Puerto Rican mother-infant pairs in four everyday situations. *Child Development, 70,* 1005–1016.

Harwood, R.L., Schöelmerich, A., Ventura-Cook, E., Schulze, P.A., & Wilson, S.P. (1996). Culture and class influences on Anglo and Puerto Rican mothers' beliefs regarding long-term socialization goals and child behavior. *Child Development, 67,* 2446–2461.

Hastings, P.D., & Rubin, K.H. (1999). Predicting mothers' beliefs about preschool-aged children's social behavior: Evidence for maternal attitudes moderating child effects. *Child Development, 70,* 722–741.

Hatchett, S.J., & Jackson, J.S. (1999). African American extended kin systems: An empirical assessment in the National Survey of Black Americans. In H.P. McAdoo (Ed.), *Family ethnicity: Strength in diversity* (2nd ed., pp. 171–190). Thousand Oaks, CA: Sage.

Hatem, M., Sandall, J., Devane, D., Soltani, H., & Gates, S. (2008). Midwife-led versus other models of care for childbearing women. *Cochrane Database of Systematic Reviews, 4,* CD004667.

Hatsu, I.E., McDougald, D.M., & Anderson, A.K. (2008). Effect of infant feeding on maternal body composition. *International Breastfeeding Journal, 3,* 18.

Hattori, M., Fujiyama, A., Taylor, T.D., Watanabe, H., Yada, T., Park, H.S., et al. (2000). The DNA sequence of human chromosome 21. *Nature, 405,* 311–319.

Hauck, F.R., Moore, C.M., Herman, S.M., Donovan, M., Kalelkar, M., Christoffel, K.K., et al. (2002). The contribution of prone sleeping to the racial disparity in sudden infant death syndrome: The Chicago Infant Mortality Study. *Pediatrics, 110,* 772–780.

Hauck, F.R., Omojokun, O.O., & Siadaty, M.S. (2005). Do pacifiers reduce the risk of sudden infant death syndrome? A meta-analysis. *Pediatrics, 116,* e716–e723.

Hauck, F.R., Signore, C., Fein, S.B., & Raju, T.N.K. (2008). Infant sleeping arrangements and practices during the first year of life. *Pediatrics, 122,* S113–S120.

Hauser, M.D., Newport, E.L., & Aslin, R.N. (2001). Segmentation of the speech stream in a nonhuman primate: Statistical learning in cotton-top tamarins. *Cognition, 78,* B53–B64.

Hausman, B.L. (2005). Risky business: Framing childbirth in hospital settings. *Journal of Medicine and Humanities, 26,* 23–38.

Haviland, J.M., & Lelwica, M. (1987). The induced affect response: 10-week-old infants' responses to three emotional expressions. *Developmental Psychology, 23,* 97–104.

Hawes, J.M., & Hiner, N.R. (Eds.). (1985). *American childhood: A research guide and historical handbook.* Westport, CT: Greenwood Press.

Hawkins, A.J., Lovejoy, K.R., Holmes, E.K., Blanchard, V.L., & Fawcett, E. (2008). Increasing fathers' involvement in child care with a couple-focused intervention during the transition to parenthood. *Family Relations, 57,* 49–59.

Hay, D.F. (2005). The beginnings of aggression in infancy. In R.E. Tremblay, W.W. Hartup, & J. Archer (Eds.), *Developmental origins of aggression* (pp. 107–132). New York: Guilford Press.

Hay, D.F., Caplan, M., & Nash, A. (2009). The beginnings of peer interaction. In K.H. Rubin, W. Bukowski, &

B. Laursen, B. (Eds.), *Handbook of peer interactions, relationships, and groups.* New York: Guilford Press.

Hay, D.F., Pawlby, S., Angold, A., Harold, G.T., & Sharp, D. (2003). Pathways to violence in the children of mothers who were depressed postpartum. *Developmental Psychology, 39*, 1083–1094.

Hayes, M.J., Fukumizu, M., Troese, M., Sallinen, B.J., & Gilles, A.A. (2007). Social experiences in infancy and early childhood co-sleeping. *Infant & Child Development, 16*, 403–416.

Hayne, H., Barr, R., & Herbert, J. (2003). The effect of prior practice on memory reactivation and generalization. *Child Development, 74*, 1615–1627.

He, F., Lidow, I.A., & Lidow, M.S. (2006). Consequences of paternal cocaine exposure in mice. *Neurotoxicology & Teratology, 28*, 198–209.

Hediger, M.L., Overpeck, M.D., Ruan, W.J., & Troendle, J.F. (2002). Birthweight and gestational age effects on motor and social development. *Paediatric and Perinatal Epidemiology, 16*, 33–46.

Hedrick, D., Prather, E., & Tobin, A. (1984). *The Sequenced Inventory of Communication Development.* Seattle: University of Washington Press.

Heibeck, T.H., & Markman, E.M. (1987). Word learning in children: An examination of fast mapping. *Child Development, 58*, 1021–1034.

Heikkilä, M., Peltoketo, H., & Vainio, S. (2001). Wnts and the female reproductive system. *Journal of Experimental Zoology, 290*, 616–623.

Heikkilä, M., Prunskaite, R., Naillat, F., Itäranta, P., Vuoristo, J., Leppäluoto, J., et al. (2005). The partial female to male sex reversal in Wnt-4-deficient females involves induced expression of testosterone biosynthetic genes and testosterone production, and depends on androgen action. *Endocrinology, 146*, 4016–4023.

Heimstad, R., Skogvoll, E., Mattsson, L.-A., Johansen, O.J., Eik-Nes, S.H., & Salvesen, K.A. (2007). Induction of labor or serial antenatal fetal monitoring in postterm pregnancy: A randomized controlled trial. *Obstetrics & Gynecology, 109*, 609–617.

Helburn, S.W., & Howes, C. (1996). Child care cost and quality. *The Future of Children, 6*(2), 62–82.

Held, R., Birch, E.E., & Gwiazda, J. (1980). Stereoacuity of human infants. *Proceedings of the National Academy of Sciences, 77*, 5572–5574.

Helfand, W. H., Lazarus, J., & Theerman, P. (2001). ". . . So that others may walk": The March of Dimes. *American Journal of Public Health, 91*(8), 1190.

Henry, G., Gordon, C.S., & Rickman, D.K. (2006). Early education policy alternatives: Comparing quality and outcomes of Head Start and state prekindergarten. *Education Evaluation and Policy Analysis, 28*, 77–97.

Hepper, P.G. (1991). An example of fetal learning before and after birth. *Irish Journal of Psychology, 12*, 95–107.

Hernandez, D.J. (1997). Child development and the social demography of childhood. *Child Development, 68*, 149–169.

Heron, M. (2007). Deaths: Leading causes for 2004. *National Vital Statistics Reports, 56*(5). Retrieved July 28, 2009, from http://www.cdc.gov/nchs/nvss/new_mortality.htm.

Herrera, C., & Dunn, J. (1997). Early experiences with family conflict: Implications for arguments with a close friend. *Developmental Psychology, 33*, 869–881.

Herrmann, D.N. (2008). Experimental therapeutics in hereditary neuropathies: The past, the present, and the future. *Neurotherapeutics, 5*, 507–515.

Hertsgaard, L., Gunnar, M., Erickson, M.F., & Nachmias, M. (1995). Adrenocortical responses to the strange situation in infants with disorganized/disoriented attachment relationships. *Child Development, 66*, 1100–1106.

Hespos, S.J., & Baillargeon, R. (2008). Young infants' actions reveal their developing knowledge of support variables: Converging evidence for violation-of-expectation findings. *Cognition, 107*, 304–316.

Hetland, L. (2000). Learning to make music enhances spatial reasoning. *Journal of Aesthetic Education, 34*, 179–238.

Hewlett, B.S. (1987). Intimate fathers: Patterns of paternal holding among Aka pygmies. In M.E. Lamb (Ed.), *The father's role: Cross-cultural perspectives* (pp. 295–330). Hillsdale, NJ: Lawrence Erlbaum Associates.

Hetzel, B.S. (1999). Iodine deficiency and fetal brain damage. *New England Journal of Medicine, 331*(26), 1770–1771.

Hewlett, B.S. (2004). Fathers in forager, farmer, and pastoral cutlures. In M.E. Lamb (Ed.), *The role of the father in child development* (4th ed., pp. 182–195). New York: Wiley.

Hewlett, B.S., Lamb, M.E., Shannon, D., Leyendecker, B., & Schölmerich, A. (1998). Culture and early infancy among central African foragers and farmers. *Developmental Psychology, 34*, 653–661.

Hiatt, S., Campos, J.J., & Emde, R.N. (1979). Facial patterning and infant emotional expression: Happiness, surprise and fear. *Child Development, 50*, 1020–1035.

Higgins, S.T., Heil, S.H., Badger, G.J., Skelly, J.M., Solomon, L.J., & Bernstein, I.M. (2009). Educational disadvantage and cigarette smoking during pregnancy. *Drug and Alcohol Dependence, 104 Supplement 1,* S100-S105.

Hill, J.L., Waldfogel, J., Brooks-Gunn, J., & Han, W. (2005). Maternal employment and child development:

A fresh look using newer methods. *Developmental Psychology, 41,* 833–850.

Hill, N.E., Bush, K.R., & Roosa, M.W. (2003). Parenting and family socialization strategies and children's mental health: Low-income Mexican-American and Euro-American mothers and children. *Child Development, 74,* 189–204.

Hinds, T.S., West, W.L., Knight, E.M., & Harland, B.F. (1996). The effect of caffeine on pregnancy outcome variables. *Nutrition Reviews, 54,* 203–207.

Hirsh-Pasek, K., & Golinkoff, R. (1996). *The origins of grammar: Evidence from early language comprehension.* Cambridge, MA: MIT Press.

Hirsh-Pasek, K., & Golinkoff, R.M. (2008). Brains in a box: Do new age toys deliver on the promise? In R. Harwood (Ed.), *Child development in a changing society.* Hoboken, NJ: Wiley.

Hirsh-Pasek, K., Trieman, R., & Schneiderman, M. (1984). Brown and Hanlon revisited: Mothers' sensitivity to ungrammatical forms. *Journal of Child Language, 11,* 81–88.

Ho, D.Y.F. (1987). Fatherhood in Chinese culture. In M.E. Lamb (Ed.), *The father's role: Cross-cultural perspectives* (pp. 227–245). Hillsdale, NJ: Lawrence Erlbaum Associates.

Hodges, C.A., Ilagan, A., Jennings, D., Keri, R., Nilson, J., & Hunt, P.A. (2002). Experimental evidence that changes in oocyte growth influence meiotic chromosome segregation. *Human Reproduction, 17,* 1171–1180.

Hodnett, E.D. (2001). Home-like versus conventional institutional settings for birth. *Cochrane Database of Systematic Reviews, 4,* CD000012.

Hodnett, E.D., Downe, S., Edwards, N., & Walsh, D. (2005). Home-like versus conventional institutional settings for birth. *Cochrane Database of Systematic Reviews, 1,* CD000012.

Hodnett, E.D., Lowe, N.K., Hannah, M.E., Willan, A.R., Stevens, B., Weston, J.A., Ohlsson, A., Gafni, A., Muir, H.A., Myhr, T.L., & Stremler, R. (2002). Effectiveness of nurses as providers of birth labor support in North American hospitals. *JAMA, 288,* 1373–1381.

Hoehl, S., Reid, V.M., Parise, E., Handl, A., Palumbo, L., & Striano, T. (2009). Looking at eye gaze processing and its neural correlates in infancy—Implications for social development and autism. *Child Development, 80,* 968–985.

Hoff, E. (2003). The specificity of environmental influence: Socioeconomic status affects early vocabulary development via maternal speech. *Child Development, 74,* 1368–1378.

Hofferth, S.L. (1991). *National Child Care Survey, 1990.* Washington, DC: The Urban Institute.

Hofferth, S.L., Brayfield, A., Deich, S., & Holcomb, P. (1991). *National Child Care Survey 1990.* Washington, DC: The Urban Institute.

Hofferth, S.L., & Curtin, S.C. (2003). The impact of parental leave on maternal return to work after childbirth in the United States. *OECD Social, Employment and Migration Working Papers No. 7,* 1–26.

Hoff-Ginsberg, E. (1997). *Language development.* Pacific Grove, CA: Brooks/Cole.

Hofmeyr, G.J. (2002). Interventions to help external cephalic version for breech presentation at term. *Cochrane Database of Systematic Reviews, 2,* CD000184.

Hofstadter, M., & Reznick, J.S. (1996). Response modality affects human infant delayed-response performance. *Child Development, 67,* 646–658.

Hollich, G., Golinkoff, R.M., & Hirsh-Pasek, K. (2007). Young children associate novel words with complex objects rather than salient parts. *Developmental Psychology, 43,* 1051–1061.

Hollich, G.J., Hirsh-Pasek, K., & Golinkoff, R.M. (2000). Breaking the language barrier: An emergentist coalition model for the origins of word learning. *Monographs of the Society for Research in Child Development, (3,* Serial No. 262, 65).

Holmes, A.V., Chin, N.P., Kaczorowski, J., & Howard, C.R. (2009). A barrier to exclusive breastfeeding for WIC enrollees: Limited use of exclusive breastfeeding food package for mothers. *Breastfeeding Medicine, 4,* 25–30.

Holowka, S., Brosseau-Lapré, F., & Petitto, L.A. (2002). Semantic and conceptual knowledge underlying bilingual babies' first signs and words. *Language Learning, 52,* 205–262.

Holowka, S., & Petitto, L.A. (2002). Left hemisphere cerebral specialization for babies while babbling. *Science, 297,* 1515.

Holsti, L., Grunau, R.E., Oberlander, T.F., & Whitfield, M.F. (2004). Specific Newborn Individualized Developmental Care and Assessment Program movements are associated with acute pain in preterm infants in the neonatal intensive care unit. *Pediatrics, 114,* 65–72.

Homer, C.S., Davis, G.K., Cooke, M., & Barclay, L.M. (2002). Women's experiences of continuity of midwifery care in a randomised controlled trial in Australia. *Midwifery, 18,* 102–112.

Homer, C.S., Davis, G.K., Petocz, P., Barclay, L., Matha, D., & Chapman, M. (2000). Birth centre or labour ward? A comparison of the clinical outcomes of low-risk women in a NSW hospital. *Australian Journal of Advanced Nursing, 18,* 8–12.

Honig, A.S. (2002). Research on quality in infant-toddler programs. EDO-PS-02-19. Champaign, IL: Clearinghouse on Elementary and Early Childhood Education.

Hood, B., Cole-Davies, V., & Dias, M. (2003). Looking and search measures of object knowledge in preschool children. *Developmental Psychology, 39,* 61–70.

Hood, B., & Willatts, P. (1986). Reaching in the dark to an object's remembered position: Evidence for object permanence in 5-month-old infants. *British Journal of Developmental Psychology, 4,* 57–65.

Hopkins, B., & Rönnqvist, L. (2002). Facilitating postural control: Effects on the reaching behavior of 6-month-old infants. *Developmental Psychobiology, 40,* 168–182.

Hopkins, B., & Westra, T. (1990). Motor development, maternal expectations and the role of handling. *Infant Behavior and Development, 13,* 117–122.

Horbar, J.D., & Lucey, J.F. (1995). Evaluation of neonatal intensive care technologies. *The Future of Children: Low Birth Weight, 5(1),* 139–161. Los Altos, CA: Center for the Future of Children, The David and Lucile Packard Foundation.

Hornik, R., Risenhoover, N., & Gunnar, M. (1987). The effects of maternal positive, neutral, and negative affective communications on infant responses to new toys. *Child Development, 58,* 937–944.

Horst, J.S., Oakes, L.M., & Madole, K.L. (2005). What does it look like and what can it do? Category structure influences how infants categorize. *Child Development, 76,* 614–631.

Horta, B.L., Bahl, R., Martines, J.C., & Victora, C.G. (2007). *Evidence on the long-term effects of breast-feeding: Systematic reviews and meta-analyses.* Geneva, Switzerland: WHO.

Hossain, Z., & Roopnarine, J.L. (1994). African-American fathers' involvement with infants: Relationship to their functional style, support, education, and income. *Infant Behavior and Development, 17,* 175–184.

Hossain, Z., Field, T., Pickens, J., Gonzalez, A., Malphurs, J., & DelValle, C. (1994). Infants of depressed mothers interact better with their nondepressed fathers. *Infant Mental Health Journal, 15,* 348–357.

Hovarth, A., Korde, L., Greene, M.H., Libe, R., Osorio, P., Faucz, F.R., et al. (2009). Functional phosphodiesterase 11A mutations may modify the risk of familial and bilateral testicular germ cell tumors. *Cancer Research, 69,* 5301–5306.

Howe, C.M. (Spring 1998). Teething: The El Nino of childhood. Not For Kids Only, 1(2), p. 1.

Howe, N., & Ross, H.S. (1990). Socialization, perspective-taking, and sibling relationship. *Developmental Psychology, 26,* 160–165.

Howes, C. (1985). Sharing fantasy: Social pretend play in toddlers. *Child Development 56,* 1253–1258.

Howes, C. (1988). Peer interaction of young children. *Monographs of the Society for Research in Child Development, 53(1,* Serial No. 217).

Howes, C. (1996). The earliest friendships. In W.M. Bukowski, A.F. Newcomb, & W.W. Hartup (Eds.), *The company they keep: Friendship in childhood and adolescence* (pp. 66–86). Boston: Cambridge University Press.

Howes, C. (1999). Attachment relationships in the context of multiple caregivers. In J. Cassidy, & P.R. Shaver (Eds.), *Handbook of attachment theory and research* (pp. 671–687). New York: Guilford Press.

Howes, C. (2009). Friendship in early childhood. In K.H. Rubin, W.M. Bukowski, & B. Laursen (Eds.), *Handbook of peer interactions, relationships, and groups. Social, emotional, and personality development in context* (pp. 180–194). New York: Guilford Press.

Howes, C., & Farver, J. (1987). Toddlers' responses to the distress of their peers. *Journal of Applied Developmental Psychology, 8,* 441–452.

Howes, C., & Guerra, A.W. (2009). Networks of attachment relationships in low-income children of Mexican heritage: Infancy through preschool. *Social Development, 18,* 896–914.

Howes, C., Guerra, A.W., & Zucker, E. (2007). Cultural communities and parenting in Mexican-heritage families. *Parenting: Science and Practice, 7,* 235–270.

Howes, C., & Matheson, C.C. (1992). Sequences in the development of competent play with peers: Social and social pretend play. *Developmental Psychology, 28,* 961–974.

Howes, C., & Shivers, E.M. (2006). New child-caregiver attachment relationships: Entering childcare when the caregiver is and is not an ethnic match. *Social Development, 15,* 574–590.

Howes, C., & Unger, O.A. (1989). Play with peers in child care settings. In M. Bloch, & A. Pellegrini (Eds.), *The ecological contexts of children's play* (pp. 104–119). Norwood, NJ: Ablex.

Hsu, H.-C., & Fogel, A. (2003). Social regulatory effects of infant nondistress vocalization on maternal behavior. *Developmental Psychology, 39,* 976–991.

Hubbs-Tait, L., Nation, J.R., Krebs, N.F., & Bellinger, D.C. (2005). Neurotoxicants, micronutrients, and social environments: Individual and combined effects on children's development. *Psychological Science in the Public Interest, 6,* 57–121.

Hudelist, G., Gelle'n, J., Singer, C., Ruecklinger, E., Czerwenka, K., Kandolf, O., et al. (2005). Factors predicting severe perineal trauma during childbirth: Role of forceps delivery routinely combined with mediolateral episiotomy. *American Journal of Obstetrics and Gynecology, 192,* 875–881.

Hudson, J.A., & Sheffield, E.G. (1998). Déjà vu all over gain: Effects of reenactment on toddlers' event memory. *Child Development, 69,* 51–67.

Hughes, C., & Ensor, R. (2007). Executive function and theory of mind: Predictive relations from ages 2 to 4. *Developmental Psychology, 43,* 1447–1459.

Huizink, A., Mulder, E., & Buitelaar, J. (2004). Prenatal stress and risk for psychopathology: Specific effects or induction of general susceptibility? *Psychological Bulletin, 130,* 115–142.

Huizink, A., Robles de Medina, P., Mulder, E., Visser, G., & Buitelaar, J. (2002). Psychological measures of prenatal stress as predictors of infant temperament. *Journal of the American Academy of Chlid & Adolescent Psychiatry, 41,* 1078–1085.

Hulbert, A. (Winter 1999). The century of the child. Wilson Quarterly, 23(1), 14–29.

Hulbert, A. (2003). *Raising America: Experts, parents, and a century of advice about children.* New York: Alfred A. Knopf.

Hummel, P., & van Dijk, M. (2006). Pain assessment: Current status and challenges. *Seminars in Fetal & Neonatal Medicine, 11,* 237–245.

Hus, V., Pickles, A., Cook, E.H., Jr., Risi, S., & Lord, C. (2007). Using the Autism Diagnostic Interview-Revised to increase phenotypic homogeneity in genetic studies of autism. *Biological Psychiatry, 61,* 438–448.

Huston, A.C. (2005). Connecting the science of child development to public policy. *Social Policy Report, 19*(4), 1–19.

Huston, A.C., Wright, J.C., Marquis, J., & Green, S.B. (1999). How young children spend their time: Television and other activities. *Developmental Psychology, 35,* 912–925.

Huston, T.L., & Holmes, E.K. (2004). Becoming parents. In A.L. Vangelisti (Ed.), *Handbook of family communication* (pp. 105–133). Mahwah, NJ: Lawrence Erlbaum Associates.

Huttenlocher, J. (1998). Language input and language growth. *Preventive Medicine, 27,* 195–199.

Huttenlocher, J., Levine, S., & Vevea, J. (1998). Environmental input and cognitive growth: JA study using time-period comparisons. *Child Development, 69,* 1012–1029.

Huttenlocher, J., Vasilyeva, M., Cymerman, E., & Levine, S. (2002). Language input at home and at school: Relation to child syntax. *Cognitive Psychology, 45,* 337–374.

Hutton, E.K., Hannah, M.E., & Barrett, J. (2002). Use of external cephalic version for breech pregnancy and mode of delivery for breech and twin pregnancy: A survey of Canadian practitioners. *Journal of Obstetrics and Gynaecology Canada, 24,* 804–810.

Hutton, E.K., & Hassan, E.S. (2007). Late vs early clamping of the umbilical cord in full term neonates: Systematic review and meta-analysis of controlled trials. *JAMA, 297,* 1241–1252.

Hwang, V., Shofer, F.S., Durbin, D.R., & Baren, J.M. (2003). Prevalence of traumatic injuries in drowning and near drowning in children and adolescents. *Archives of Pediatrics and Adolescent Medicine, 157,* 50–53.

Hyson, M.C., Hirsh–Pasek, K., & Rescorla, L. (1990). The classroom practices inventory: An observation instrument based on the NAEYC's guidelines for developmentally appropriate practices for 4- and 5-year old children. *Early Childhood Research Quarterly, 5,* 475–494.

Iams, J.D., Newman, R.B., Thom, E.A., Goldenberg, R.L., Mueller-Heubach, E., Moawas, A., et al. (2002). Frequency of uterine contractions and the risk of spontaneous preterm delivery. *New England Journal of Medicine, 346,* 250–255.

Ilari, B. (2005). On musical parenting of young children: Musical beliefs and behaviors of mothers and infants. *Early Child Development and Care, 175,* 647–660.

Ilari, B., & Polka, L. (2006). Music cognition in early infancy: Infants' preferences and long-term memory for Ravel. *International Journal of Music Education, 24,* 7–20.

Ilari, B.S. (2002). Music perception and cognition in the first year of life. *Early Child Development and Care, 172,* 311–322.

Imai, M., & Gentner, D. (1997). A crosslinguistic study of early word meaning: Universal ontology and linguistic influence. *Cognition, 62,* 169–200.

Imren, S., Fabry, M.E., Westerman, K.A., Pawliuk, R., Tang, P., Rosten, P.M., et al. (2004). High-level B-globin expression and preferred intragenic integration after lentiviral transduction of human cord blood stem cells. *Journal of Clinical Investigation, 114,* 953–962.

The Infant Health and Development Program. (1990). Enhancing the outcomes of low-birth-weight premature infants. *Journal of the American Medical Association, 263,* 3035–3042.

Ingersoll, E.W., Thoman, E.B. (1999). Sleep/wake states of preterm infants: Stability, developmental change, diurnal variation, and relation with caregiving activity. *Child Development, 70,* 1–10.

Injury Data Analysis Leads to Baby Walker Ban. (2004). Retrieved July 19, 2009, from http://www.hc-sc.gc.ca/sr-sr/activ/consprod/baby-bebe-eng.php

Institute of Medicine Immunization Safety Review Committee. (2004). *Immunization safety review: Vaccines and autism.* Washington, DC: National Academies Press.

International Genome Sequencing Consortium. (2001). Initial sequencing and analysis of the human genome. *Nature, 409,* 860–921.

International Schizophrenia Consortium. (2009). Common polygenic variation contributes to risk of schizophrenia and bipolar disorder. *Nature, 460,* 748–752.

Ip, S., Chung, M., Kulig, J., O'Brien, R., Sege, R., Glicken, S., et al. (2004). An evidence-based review of important issues concerning neonatal hyperbilirubinemia. *Pediatrics, 113,* 130–153.

Ireton, H., & Thwing, E. (1974). *The Minnesota Child Development Inventory.* Minneapolis: Behavior Science Systems.

Isabella, R.A., & Belsky, J. (1991). Interactional synchrony and the origins of infant-mother attachment: A replication study. *Child Development, 62,* 373–384.

Ispa, J.M., Fine, M.A., Halgunseth, L.C., Harper, S., Robinson, J., Boyce, L., Brooks-Gunn, J., & Brady-Smith, C. (2004). Maternal intrusiveness, maternal warmth, and mother-toddler relationship outcomes: Variations across low-income ethnic and acculturation groups. *Child Development, 75,* 1613–1631.

Iverson, J.M., & Fagan, M.K. (2004). Infant vocal-motor coordination: Precursor to the gesture-speech system? *Child Development, 75,* 1053–1066.

Iverson, J.M., Capirci, O., Volterra, V., & Goldin-Meadow, S. (2008). Learning to talk in a gesture-rich world: Early communication in Italian vs. American children. *Language, 28,* 164–181.

Iverson, J.M., & Goldin-Meadow, S. (2005). Gesture paves the way for language development. *Psychological Science, 16,* 367–371.

Iverson, P., & Kuhl, P.K. (1995). Mapping the perceptual magnet effect for speech using signal detection theory and multidimensional scaling. *Journal of the Acoustical Society of America, 97,* 553–562.

Iverson, P., Kuhl, P.K., Akahane-Yamada, R., Diesch, E., Tohkura, Y., Kettermann, A., et al. (2003). A perceptual interference account of acquisition difficulties for non-native phonemes. *Cognition, 87,* B47–B57.

Iyasu, S., Randall, L.L., Welty, T.K., Hsia, J., Kinney, H.C., Mandell, F., McClain, M., Randall, B., Habbe, D., Wilson, H., & Willinger, M. (2002). Risk factors for sudden infant death syndrome among Northern Plains Indians. *JAMA, 288,* 2717–2723.

Izard, C.E. (1977). *Human emotions.* New York: Plenum Press.

Izard, C.E. (1979). *The Maximally Discriminative Facial Movement Coding System (MAX).* Newark, DE: Instructional Resources Center, University of Delaware.

Izard, C.E., Fantauzzo, C.A., Castle, J.M., Haynes, O.M., Rayias, M.F., & Putnam, P.H. (1995). The ontogeny and significance of infants' facial expressions in the first 9 months of life. *Developmental Psychology, 31,* 997–1013.

Izard, C.E., Hembree, E.A., Dougherty, L.M., & Spizzirri, C. (1983). Changes in 2- to 19-month-old infants' responses to acute pain. *Developmental Psychology, 19,* 418–426.

Izard, C.E., Hembree, E.A., & Huebner, R.R. (1987). Infants' emotion expressions to acute pain: Developmental change and stability of individual differences. *Developmental Psychology, 23,* 105–113.

Izard, C.E., Huebner, R., Risser, D., McGinnes, G., & Dougherty, L. (1980). The young infant's ability to produce discrete emotion expressions. *Developmental Psychology, 16,* 132–140.

Izard, C.E., & Malatesta, C.Z. (1987). Perspectives on emotional development: I. Differential emotions theory of emotional development. In J.D. Osofsky (Ed.), *Handbook of infant development* (2nd ed., pp. 494–554). New York: Wiley.

Jacobs, D.E., Clickner, R.P., Zhou, J.Y., Viet, S.M., Marker, D.A., Rogers, J.W., et al. (2002). The prevalence of lead-based paint hazards in U.S. housing. *Environmental Health Perspectives, 110,* A599–A606.

Jacobs, D.E., Wilson, J., Dixon, S.L., Smith, J., & Evens, A. (2009). The relationship of housing and population health: A 30-year retrospective analysis. *Environmental Health Perspectives, 117,* 597–604.

Jacobs, S., Sokol, J., & Ohlsson, A. (2002). The newborn individualized developmental care and assessment program is not supported by meta-analyses of the data. *Journal of Pediatrics, 140,* 699–706.

Jacobson, S.W., & Jacobson, J.L. (2000). Teratogenic insult and neurobehavioral function in infancy and childhood. In C.A. Nelson (Ed.), *The effects of early adversity on neurobehavioral development: The Minnesota Symposia on Child Psychology* (Vol. 31, pp. 61–112). Mahwah, NJ: Lawrence Erlbaum Associates.

Jaffe, J., Beebe, B., Feldstein, S., Crown, C.L., & Jasnow, M.D. (2001). Rhythms of dialogue in infancy. *Monographs of the Society for Research in Child Development, 66*(2, Serial No. 265).

Jahromi, L.B., Putnam, S.P., & Stifter, C.A. (2004). Maternal regulation of infant reactivity from

2 to 6 months. *Developmental Psychology, 40,* 477–487.

Jain, A., & Belsky, J. (1997). Fathering and acculturation: Immigrant Indian families with young children. *Journal of Marriage and the Family, 59,* 873–883.

Jana, A.K. (2009). Interventions for promoting the initiation of breastfeeding: RHL commentary. The WHO Reproductive Health Library; Geneva: World Health Organization. Retrieved July 30, 2009, from http://apps.who.int/rhl/pregnancy_childbirth/care_after_childbirth/cd001688_JanaAK_com/en/

Jankowiak, W. (1992). Father-child relations in urban China. In B.S. Hewlett (Ed.), *Father-child relations: Cultural and biosocial contexts* (pp. 345–363). New York: Aldine de Gruyter.

Jankowski, J.J., Rose, S.A., & Feldman, J.F. (2001). Modifying the distribution of attention in infants. *Child Development, 72,* 339–351.

Janni, W., Schiessl, B., Peschers, U., Huber, S., Strobl, B., Hantschmann, P., et al. (2002). The prognostic impact of a prolonged second stage of labor on maternal and fetal outcome. *Acta Obstetricia et Gynecologica Scandinavica, 81,* 214–221.

Jedrychowski, W., Bendkowska, I., Flak, E., Penar, A., Jacek, R., Kaim, I., et al. (2004). Estimated risk for altered fetal growth resulting from exposure to fine particles during pregnancy: An epidemiologic prospective cohort study in Poland. *Environmental Health Perspectives, 112,* 1398–1402.

Jevitt, C., Hernandez, I., & Groër, M. (2007). Lactation complicated by overweight and obesity: Supporting the mother and newborn. *Journal of Midwifery & Women's Health, 52,* 606–613.

Ji, B.T., Shu, X.O., Linet, M.S., Zheng, W., Wacholder, S., Gao, Y.T., et al. (1997). Paternal cigarette smoking and the risk of childhood cancer among offspring of nonsmoking mothers. *Journal of the National Cancer Institute, 89,* 238–244.

Johansen, A.M., Wilcox, A.J., Lie, R.T., Andersen, L.F., & Drevon, C.A. (2009). Maternal consumption of coffee and caffeine-containing beverages and oral clefts: A population-based case-control study in Norway. *American Journal of Epidemiology, 169,* 1216–1222.

Johanson, R.B., & Menon, B.K. (2000). Vacuum extraction versus forceps for assisted vaginal delivery. *Cochrane Database of Systematic Reviews, 2,* CD000224.

Johnson, D.E. (2000). Medical and developmental sequelae of early childhood institutionalization in Eastern European adoptees. In C.A. Nelson (Ed.), *Minnesota Symposium on Child Psychology: Vol. 31. The effects of adversity on neurobehavioral development*

(pp. 113–162). Mahwah, NJ: Lawrence Erlbaum Associates.

Johnson, D.E., Miller, L.C., Iverson, S., Thomas, W., Franchino, B., Dole, K., et al. (1993). Post-placement catch-up growth in Romanian orphans with psychosocial short stature. *Pediatric Research, 33,* 89A.

Johnson, D.J., Jaeger, E., Randolph, S.M., Cauce, A.M., Ward, J., & National Institute of Child Health and Human Development Early Child Care Research Network. (2003). Studying the effects of early child care experiences on the development of children of color in the United States: Toward a more inclusive research agenda. *Child Development, 74,* 1227–1244.

Johnson, K.C., & Daviss, B.-A. (2005). Outcomes of planned home births with certified professional midwives: Large prospective study in North America. *BMJ, 330,* 1416–1422.

Johnson, M.H. (1997a). Building a brain. In *Developmental cognitive neuroscience: An introduction* (pp. 23–67). London: Blackwell.

Johnson, M.H. (1998). The neural basis of cognitive development. In D. Kuhn, & R.S. Siegler (Eds.), *Handbook of Child Psychology* (5th ed.): *Vol. 2. Cognition, perception, and language* (pp. 1–49). New York: Wiley.

Johnson, M.H. (2000). Functional brain development in infants: Elements of an interactive specialization framework. *Child Development, 71,* 75–81.

Johnson, M.H. (2001). Functional brain development in humans. *Nature Reviews Neuroscience, 2,* 475–483.

Johnson, M.H. (2005). Developmental neuroscience, psychophysiology, and genetics. In M.H. Bornstein, & M.E. Lamb (Eds.), *Developmental science: An advanced textbook* (pp. 187–222). Mahwah, NJ: Lawrence Erlbaum Associates.

Johnson, M.H., & Farroni, T. (2007). The neurodevelopmental origins of eye gaze perception. In R. Flom, K. Lee, & D. Muir (Eds.), *Gaze-following: Its development and significance* (pp. 1–16). Mahwah, NJ: Lawrence Erlbaum Associates.

Johnson, S., Hennessy, E., Smith, R., Trikic, R., Wolke D., & Marlow, N. (2009). Academic attainment and special educational needs in extremely preterm children at 11 years of age: The EPICure study. *Archives of Disease in Childhood Fetal Neonatal Ed, 94,* F283–F289.

Johnson, S.P. (1997b). Young infants' perception of object unity: Implications for development of attentional and cognitive skills. *Current Directions in Psychological Science, 6,* 5–11.

Johnson, S.P., & Aslin, R.N. (1996). Perception of object unity in young infants: The roles of motion, depth, and orientation. *Cognitive Development, 11,* 161–180.

Johnson, S.P., & Mason, U. (2002). Perception of kinetic illusory contours by two-month-old infants. *Child Development, 73,* 22–34.

Johnson, T.D. (2008). Maternity leave and employment patterns: 2001–2003. *Current Population Reports, (pp. 70–113).* Washington, DC: U.S. Census Bureau.

Johnson-Green, E., & Custodero, L.A. (2002, September). The toddler top 40: Musical preferences of babies, toddlers, and their parents. *Zero to Three, 25,* 47–48.

Johnston, C.C., Filion, F., Campbell-Yeo, M., Goulet, C., Bell, L., McNaughton, K., & Byron, J. (2009). Enhanced kangaroo mother care for heel lance in preterm neonates: a crossover trial. *Journal of Perinatology, 29,* 51–56.

Johnston, S.L., & Openshaw, P.J.M. (2001). The protective effect of childhood infections. *BMJ, 322,* 376–377.

Jones, K.L., & Smith, D.W. (1973). Recognition of the fetal alcohol syndrome in early infancy. *Lancet, 2,* 999–1001.

Jones, N.A., Field, T., Fox, N.A., Lundy, B., & Davalos, M. (1997). EEG activation in one-month-old infants of depressed mothers. *Development and Psychopathology, 9,* 491–505.

Jones, S.S. (1996). Imitation or exploration? Young infants' matching of adults' oral gestures. *Child Development, 67,* 1952–1969.

Juffer, F., & Rosenboom, L.G. (1997). Infant-mother attachment of internationally adopted children in the Netherlands. *International Journal of Behavioral Development, 20,* 93–107.

Juffer, F., & van IJzendoorn, M.H. (2005). Behavior problems and mental health referrals of international adoptees: A meta-analysis. *JAMA, 293,* 2501–2515.

Jusczyk, P.W., & Hohne, E.A. (1997). Infants' memory for spoken words. *Science, 277,* 1984–1986.

Jusczyk, P.W., Hohne, E.A., Jusczyk, A.M., & Redanz, N.J. (1993). Do infants remember voices? *Journal of the Acoustical Society of America, 93,* 2373.

Jusczyk, P.W., & Krumhansl, C.L. (1993). Pitch and rhythmic patterns affecting infants' sensitivity to musical phrase structure. *Journal of Experimental Psychology: Human Perception and Performance, 19,* 627–640.

Kaandorp, S., Di Nisio, M., Goddijn, M., & Middeldorp, S. (2009). Aspirin or anticoagulants for treating recurrent miscarriage in women without antiphospholipid syndrome. *Cochrane Database of Systematic Reviews, 1,* CD004734.

Kagan, J. (1994). On the nature of emotion. In N.A. Fox (Ed.), The development of emotion regulation: Biological and behavioral considerations. *Monographs of the Society for Research in Child Development, 59*(2–3, Serial No. 240), 7–24.

Kagan, J. (1998). Biology and the child. In W. Damon (Series Ed.) & N. Eisenberg (Vol. Ed.), *Handbook of child psychology: Vol. 3. Social, emotional, and personality development* (5th ed., pp. 177–235). New York: Wiley.

Kagan, J. (2002). *Surprise, uncertainty, and mental structures.* Cambridge, MA: Harvard University Press.

Kagan, J. (2008). In defense of qualitative changes in development. *Child Development, 79,* 1606–1624.

Kagan, J., & Fox, N.A. (2006). Biology, culture, and temperamental biases. In W. Damon, & R. Lerner (Eds.) & N. Eisenberg (Vol. Ed.), *Handbook of child psychology: Vol. 3. Social, emotional, and personality development* (6th ed., pp. 167–225). New York: Wiley.

Kagan, J., Reznick, J.S., & Snidman, N. (1988). Biological bases of childhood shyness. *Science, 240,* 167–171.

Kagan, J., & Snidman, N. (1991a). Infant predictors of inhibited and uninhibited profiles. *Psychological Science, 2,* 40–44.

Kagan, J., & Snidman, N. (1991b). Temperamental factors in human development. *American Psychologist, 48,* 856–862.

Kagan, J., & Snidman, N. (1999). Early childhood predictors of adult anxiety disorders. *Journal of Biological Psychiatry, 46,* 1536–1541.

Kagan, J., Snidman, N., & Arcus, D. (1998). Childhood derivatives of high and low reactivity in infancy. *Child Development, 69,* 1483–1493.

Kaiser, L., Allen, L.H., & American Dietetic Association. (2008). Position of the American Dietetic Association: Nutrition and lifestyle for a healthy pregnancy outcome. *Journal of the American Dietetic Association, 108,* 553–561.

Kaler, S.G., Holmes, C.S., Goldstein, D.S., Tang, J., Godwin, S.C., Donsante, A., et al. (2008). Neonatal diagnosis and treatment of Menkes disease. *New England Journal of Medicine, 358,* 605–614.

Källen, B. (2004). Neonate characteristics after maternal use of antidepressants in late pregnancy. *Archives of Pediatrics & Adolescent Medicine, 158,* 312–316.

Kamerman, S.B. (2000). Parental leave policies: An essential ingredient in early childhood education and care policies. *Social Policy Report, 14*(2), 1–16.

Kamerman, S.B., Neuman, M., Waldfogel, J., & Brooks-Gunn, J. (2003). Social policies, family types and child outcomes in selected OECD countries. *OECD Social, Employment and Migration Working Papers No. 6,* 1–55.

Kamper-Jørgensen, M., Andersen, L.G., Simonsen, J., & Sørup, S. (2008). Child care is not a substantial risk factor for gastrointestinal infection hospitalization. *Pediatrics, 122,* e1168–e1173.

Kant, I. (1924/1781). *Critique of pure reason* (F. M. Muller, Transl.). New York: Macmillan.

Kaplan, P.S., Goldstein, M.H., Huckeby, E.R., Owren, M.J., & Cooper, R.P. (1995). Dishabituation of visual attention by infant- versus adult-directed speech: Effects of frequency modulation and spectral composition. *Infant Behavior and Development, 18,* 209–223.

Karasik, L.B., Tamis-LeMonda, C.S., Adolph, K.E., & Dimitropoulou, K.A. (2008). How mothers encourage and discourage infants' motor actions, *Infancy, 13,* 366–392.

Karevold, E., Røysamb, E., Ystrom, E., & Mathiesen, K.S. (2009). Predictors and pathways from infancy to symptoms of anxiety and depression in early adolescence. *Developmental Psychology, 45,* 1051–1060.

Karraker, K.H., & Coleman, P. (2002). Infants' characteristics and behaviors help shape their environments. In H.E. Fitzgerald, K.H. Karraker, & T. Luster (Eds.), *Infant development: Ecological perspectives* (pp. 165–191). New York: RoutledgeFalmer.

Kärtner, J., Keller, H., Lamm, B., Abels, M., Yovsi, R., & Chaudhary, N. (2007). Manifestations of autonomy and relatedness in mothers' accounts of their ethnotheories regarding child care across five cultural communities. *Journal of Cross-Cultural Psychology, 38,* 613–628.

Kärtner, J., Keller, H., Lamm, B., Abels, M., Yovsi, R., Chaudhary, N., et al. (2008). Similarities and differences in contingency experiences of 3-month-olds across sociocultural contexts. *Infant Behavior & Development, 31,* 488–500.

Kasari, C., Sigman, M., Mundy, P., & Yirmiya, N. (1990). Affective sharing in the context of joint attention interactions of normal, autistic, and mentally retarded children. *Journal of Autism and Developmental Disorders, 20,* 87–100.

Kavanaugh, R.D., Eizenman, D.R., & Harris, P.L. (1997). Young children's understanding of pretense expressions of independent agency. *Developmental Psychology, 33,* 764–770.

Kavanaugh, R.D., & Engel, S. (1998). The development of pretense and narrative in early childhood. In O.N. Saracho, & B. Spodek (Eds.), *Multiple perspectives on play in early childhood education* (pp. 81–99). Albany: State University of New York Press.

Kawasaki, N., Nishimura, H., Yoshimura, T. & Okamura, H. (2002). A diminished intrapartum amniotic fluid index is a predictive marker of possible adverse neonatal outcome when associated with prolonged labor. *Gynecologic and Obstetric Investigation, 53,* 1–5.

Kaye, C.I., & the Committee on Genetics. (2006). Newborn Screening Fact Sheets. *Pediatrics, 118,* e935–e963.

Keating, M.B., McKenzie, B.E., & Day, R.H. (1986). Spatial localization in infancy: Position constancy in a square and circular room with and without a landmark. *Child Development, 57,* 115–124.

Keenan, P. (2000). Benefits of massage therapy and use of a doula during labor and childbirth. *Alternative Therapies in Health and Medicine, 6,* 66–74.

Keller, H. (2003). Socialization for competence: Cultural models of infancy. *Human Development, 46,* 288–311.

Keller, H. (2008). Attachment—past and present. But what about the future? *Integrative Psychological and Behavioral Science, 42,* 406–415.

Keller, H., Abels, M., Borke, J., Lamm, B., Lo, W., Su, Y., et al. (2007). Socialization environments of Chinese and Euro-American middle-class babies: Parenting behaviors, verbal discourses and ethnotheories. *International Journal of Behavioral Development, 31,* 210–217.

Keller, H., Borke, J., Staufenbiel, T., Yovsi, R.D., Abels, M., Papaligoura, Z., et al. (2009). Distal and proximal parenting as alternative parenting strategies during infants' early months of life: A cross-cultural study. *International Journal of Behavioral Development, 33,* 412–420.

Keller, H., Lohaus, A., Kuensemueller, P., Abels, M., Yosvi, R.D., Voelker, S., et al. (2004a). The bio-culture of parenting: Evidence from five cultural communities. *Parenting: Science and Practice, 4,* 25–50.

Keller, H., Otto, H., Lamm, B., Yovsi, R., & Kärtner, J. (2008). The timing of verbal/vocal communications between mothers and their infants: A longitudinal cross-cultural comparison. *Infant Behavior & Development, 31,* 217–226.

Keller, H., Yovsi, R., Borke, J., Kärtner, J., Jensen, H., & Papaligoura, Z. (2004b). Developmental consequences of early parenting experiences: Self-recognition and self-regulation in three cultural communities. *Child Development, 75,* 1745–1760.

Keller, H., Yovsi, R.D., & Voelker, S. (2002). The role of motor stimulation in parental ethnotheories: The case of Cameroonian Nso and German women. *Journal of Cross-Cultural Psychology, 33,* 398–414.

Kelley, S.A., Brownell, C.A., & Campbell, S.B. (2000). Mastery motivation and self-evaluative affect in toddlers: Longitudinal relations with maternal behavior. *Child Development, 71,* 1061–1071.

Kellman, P.J. (1984). Perception of three-dimensional form by human infants. *Perception and Psychophysics, 36,* 353–358.

Kellman, P.J., & Arterberry, M.E. (1998). *The cradle of knowledge: Development of perception in infancy.* Cambridge, MA: MIT Press.

Kellman, P.J., & Arterberry, M.E. (2006). Infant visual perception. In W. Damon, & R. Lerner (Eds.) D. Kuhn, & R. Siegler (Vol. Eds.), *Handbook of child psychology: Vol. 2. Cognition, perception, and language* (6th ed., pp. 109–160). New York: Wiley.

Kellman, P.J., & Banks, M.S. (1998). Infant visual perception. In W. Damon (Editor-in-Chief), D. Kuhn, & R.S. Siegler (Vol. Eds.), *Handbook of child psychology: Vol. 2. Cognition, perception, and language* (5th ed., pp. 103–146). New York: Wiley.

Kellman, P.J., & Spelke, E.S. (1983). Perception of partly occluded objects in infancy. *Cognitive Psychology, 15,* 483–448.

Kellman, P.J., & von Hofsten, C. (1992). The world of the moving infant: Perception of motion, stability, and space. *Advances in Infancy Research, 7,* 147–184.

Kelly, J.F., & Booth, C.L. (1999). Child care for infants with special needs: Issues and applications. *Infants and Young Children, 12,* 26–33.

Kennedy, H.P., & Shannon, M.T. (2004). Keeping birth normal: Research findings on midwifery care during childbirth. *Journal of Obstetrical and Gynecological Neonatal Nursing, 33,* 554–560.

Kent, R., & Miolo, G. (1995). Phonetic abilities in the first year of life. In P. Fletcher, & B. MacWhinney (Eds.), *The handbook of child language* (pp. 302–334). Oxford, UK: Blackwell.

Kerac, M., Egan, R., Mayer, S., Walsh, A., & Seal, A. (2009). New WHO growth standards: Roll-out needs more resources. *The Lancet, 374,* 100–102.

Khazan, I., McHale, J.P., & Decourcey, W. (2008). Violated wishes about division of childcare labor predict early coparenting process during stressful and nonstressful family evaluations. *Infant Mental Health Journal, 29,* 343–361.

Kiang, L., Moreno, A.J., & Robinson, J.L. (2004). Maternal preconceptions about parenting predict child temperament, maternal sensitivity, and children's empathy. *Developmental Psychology, 40,* 1081–1092.

Kim-Cohen, J., Moffitt, T.E., Caspi, A., & Taylor, A. (2004). Genetic and environmental processes in young children's resilience and vulnerability to socioeconomic deprivation. *Child Development, 75,* 651–668.

King, S., & Laplante, D.P. (2005). The effects of prenatal stress on children's cognitive development: Project Ice Storm. *Stress, 8,* 35–45.

Kinney, H.C., Randall, L.L., Sleeper, L.A., Willinger, M., Belliveau, R.A., Zec, N., et al. (2003). Serotonergic brainstem abnormalities in Northern Plains Indians with the sudden infant death syndrome. *Journal of Neuropathology and Experimental Neruology, 62,* 1178–1191.

Kirkorian, H.L., Pempek, T.A., Murphy, L.A., Schmidt, M.E., & Anderson, D.R. (2009). The impact of background television on parent-child interaction. *Child Development, 80,* 1350–1359.

Kisilevsky, B.S., Hains, S.M.J., Lee, K., Xie, X., Huang, H., Ye, H.H., et al. (2003). Effects of experience on fetal voice recognition. *Psychological Science, 14,* 220–224.

Kisker, E., & Maynard, R. (1991). Quality, cost and parental choice of child care. In D.M. Blau (Ed.), *The economics of child care* (pp. 127–143). New York: Russell Sage Foundation.

Kjos, S. (1999). Gestational diabetes mellitus. *New England Journal of Medicine, 341,* 1749–1756.

Klaus, M.H., & Kennell, J.H. (1997). The doula: An essential ingredient of childbirth rediscovered. *Acta Paediatr, 86,* 1034–1036.

Kleberg, A., Warren, I., Norman, E., Mörelius, E., Berg, A.-C., Mat-Ali, E., et al. (2008). Lower stress responses after Newborn Individualized Developmental Care and Assessment Program care during eye screening examinations for retinopathy of prematurity: A randomized study. *Pediatrics, 121,* e1267–e1278.

Klein, M.C., Gauthier, R.J., Jorgensen, S.H., Robbins, J.M., Kaczorowski, J., Johnson, B., et al. (1992). Does episiotomy prevent perineal trauma and pelvic floor relaxation? *The Online Journal of Current Clinical Trials, 106,* 375–377.

Klein, P. J., & Meltzoff, A. N. (1999). Long-term memory, forgetting, and deferred imitation in 12-month-old infants. *Developmental Science, 2,* 102–113.

Klemm, R.D.W., Labrique, A.B., Christian, P., Rashid, M., Shamim, A.A., Katz, J., Sommer, A., & West, Jr., K.P. (2008). Newborn Vitamin A supplementation reduced infant mortality in rural Bangladesh. *Pediatrics, 122,* e242–e250.

Klemmt, L., & Scialli, A.R. (2005). The transport of chemicals in semen. *Birth Defects Research. Part B, Developmental and Reproductive Toxicology, 74,* 119–131.

Klin, A., Volkmar, F.R., & Sparrow, S. (1992). Autistic social dysfunction: Some limitations of the theory of mind hypothesis. *Journal of Child Psychology and Psychiatry, 33,* 861–876.

Klonoff-Cohen, H. (2005). Female and male lifestyle habits and IVF: What is known and unknown. *Human Reproduction Update, 11,* 179–203.

Klonoff-Cohen, H.S., & Natarajan, L. (2004). The effect of advancing paternal age on pregnancy and live birth rates in couples undergoing in vitro fertilization or gamete intrafallopian transfer. *American Journal of Obstetrics and Gynecology, 191,* 507–514.

Klonoff-Cohen, H., & Lam-Kruglick, P. (2001). Maternal and paternal recreational drug use and sudden infant death syndrome. *Archives of Pediatric and Adolescent Medicine, 155,* 765–770.

Knafo, A. (2006). The Longitudinal Israeli Study of Twins (LIST): Children's social development as influenced by genetics, abilities, and socialization. *Twin Research and Human Genetics, 9,* 791–798.

Knafo, A., & Plomin, R. (2006). Parental discipline and affection and children's prosocial behavior: Genetic and environmental links. *Journal of Personality and Social Psychology, 90,* 147–164.

Knafo, A., Zahn-Waxler, C., Van Hulle, C., Robinson, J.L., & Rhee, S.H. (2008). The developmental origins of a disposition toward empathy: Genetic and environmental contributions. *Emotion, 8,* 737–752.

Kochanek, K.D., Murphy, S.L., Anderson, R.N., & Scott, C. (2004). Deaths: Final data for 2002. *National Vital Statistics Reports, 53*(5), 1–116.

Kochanska, G. (2002). Mutually responsive orientation between mothers and their young children: A context for the early development of conscience. *Current Directions in Psychological Science, 11,* 191–195.

Kochanska, G., & Aksan, N. (2004). Conscience in childhood: Past, present, and future. *Merrill Palmer Quarterly, 50,* 299–310.

Kochanska, G., Aksan, N., Prisco, T.R., & Adams, E.E. (2008). Mother-child and father-child mutually responsive orientation in the first two years and children's outcomes at preschool age: Mechanisms of influence. *Child Development, 79,* 30–44.

Kochanska, G., Barry, R.A., Stellern, S.A., & O'Bleness, J.J. (2009). Early attachment organization moderates the parent-child mutually coercive pathway to children's antisocial conduct. *Child Development, 80,* 1288–1300.

Kochanska, G., Coy, K.C., & Murray, K.T. (2001). The development of self-regulation in the first four years of life. *Child Development, 72,* 1091–1111.

Kochanska, G., Coy, K.C., Tjebkes, T.L., & Husarek, S.J. (1998). Individual differences in emotionality in infancy. *Child Development, 69,* 375–390.

Kochanska, G., & Murray, K.T. (2000). Mother-child mutually responsive orientation and conscience development: From toddler to early school age. *Child Development, 71,* 417–431.

Kochanska, G., & Radke-Yarrow, M. (1992). Inhibition in toddlerhood and the dynamics of the child's

interaction with an unfamiliar peer at age five. *Child Development, 63,* 325–335.

Koester, L.S. (1995). Face-to-face interactions between hearing mothers and their deaf infants. *Infant Behavior & Development, 18,* 145–153.

Koester, L.S., Traci, M.A., Brooks, L.R., Karkowski, A.M., & Smith-Gray, S. (2004). In K.P. Meadow-Orlans, P.E. Spencer, & L.S. Koester (Eds.), *The world of deaf infants: A longitudinal study* (pp. 40–56). New York: Oxford University Press.

Koffka, K. (1935). *Principles of gestalt psychology.* New York: Harcourt, Brace & World.

Kofman, O. (2002). The role of prenatal stress in the etiology of developmental behavioral disorders. *Neuroscience and Biobehavioral Reviews, 26,* 457–470.

Koivurova, S., Hartikainen, A., Gissler, M., Hemminki, E., Sovio, U., & Jarvelin, M. (2002). Neonatal outcome and congenital malformations in children born after in-vitro fertilization. *Human Reproduction, 17,* 1391–1398.

Kojima, Y. (1999). Mothers' adjustment to the birth of a second child: A longitudinal study on use of verbal and nonverbal behaviors toward two children. *Psychological Reports, 84,* 141–144.

Konopka, G., Bomar, J.M., Winden, K., Coppola, G., Jonsson, Z.O., Gao, F., et al. (2009). Human-specific transcriptional regulation of CNS development genes by FOXP2. *Nature, 462,* 213–217.

Kontos, S., Howes, C., Shinn, M., & Galinsky, E. (1994). *Quality in family child care and relative care.* New York: Teachers College Press.

Kopp, C.B. (1989). Regulation of distress and negative emotions: A developmental view. *Developmental Psychology, 25,* 343–354.

Koren, G., Pastuszak, A., & Ito, S. (1998). Drugs in pregnancy. *New England Journal of Medicine, 338,* 1128–1137.

Korfmacher, J. (2002). Early childhood interventions: Now what? In H.E. Fitzgerald, K.H. Karraker, & T. Luster (Eds.), *Infant development: Ecological perspectives* (pp, 275–294). New York: RoutledgeFalmer.

Kovács, A.M., & Mehler, J. (2009). Flexible learning of multiple speech structures in bilingual infants. *Science, 325,* 611–612.

Kovan, N.M., Chung, A.L., & Sroufe, L.A. (2009). The intergenerational continuity of observed early parenting: A prospective, longitudinal study. *Developmental Psychology, 45,* 1205–1213.

Kozorovitskiy, Y., Hughes, M., Lee, K., & Gould, E. (2006). Fatherhood affects dendritic spines and vasopressin V1a receptors in the primate prefrontal cortex. *Nature Neuroscience, 9*, 1094–1095.

Kramer, L., & Gottman, J.M. (1992). Becoming a sibling: "With a little help from my friends." *Developmental Psychology, 28*, 685–699.

Kramer, M.S., Chalmers, B., Hodnett, E.D., Sevkovskaya, Z., Dzikovich, I., Shapiro, S., et al. (2001). Promotion of Breastfeeding Intervention Trial (PROBIT): A randomized trial in the Republic of Belarus. *Journal of the American Medical Association, 285*, 413–420.

Kramer, M.S., Goulet, L., Lydon, J., Sequin, L., McNamara, H., Dassa, C., et al. (2001). Socio-economic disparities in preterm birth: Causal pathways and mechanism. *Paediatric and Perinatal Epidemiology, 15*(Suppl. 2), 104–123.

Kreider, R.M. (2003). Adopted children and stepchildren: 2000. *Census 2000 Special Reports, CENSR-6RV.* Washington, DC: U.S. Census Bureau.

Kreider, R.M., & Elliott, D.B. (2009). America's families and living arrangements: 2007. *Current Population Reports (P20-561).* Washington, DC: U.S. Census Bureau.

Kreppner, K. (1988). Changes in parent-child relationships with the birth of the second child. *Marriage and Family Review, 12*, 157–181.

Kuczmarski, R.J., Ogden, C.L., Grummer-Strawn, L.M., Flegal, K.M., Guo, S.S., Wei, R., et al. (2000). CDC growth charts: United States. *Advance data from vital and health statistics, No. 314.* Hyattsville, MD: National Center for Health Statistics.

Kugelman, A., Reichman, B., Chistyakov, I., Boyko, V., Levitski, O., Lerner-Geva, L., et al. (2007). Postdischarge infant mortality among very low birth weight infants: A population-based study. *Pediatrics, 120*, e788–e794.

Kuhl, P.K. (1987). Perception of speech and sound in early infancy. In P. Salapatek, & L. Cohen (Eds.), *Handbook of infant perception: Vol. 1. From sensation of perception* (pp. 275–382). Orlando, FL: Academic Press.

Kuhl, P.K. (1991). Human adults and human infants show a "perceptual magnet effect" for the prototypes of speech categories, monkeys do not. *Perception & Psychophysics, 50*, 93–107.

Kuhl, P.K. (2000). A new view of language acquisition. *Proceedings of the National Academy of Sciences, 97*, 11850–11857.

Kuhl, P.K. (2004). Early language acquisition: Cracking the speech code. *Nature Reviews Neuroscience, 5*, 831–843.

Kuhl, P.K., Andruski, J.E., Chistovich, I.A., Chistovich, L.A., Kozhevnikova, E.V., Ryskina, E.I., Stolyarova, E.I.,

Sundberg, U., & Lacerda, F. (1997). Cross-language analysis of phonetic units in language addressed to infants. *Science, 277*, 684–686.

Kuhl, P.K., Coffey-Corina, S., Padden, D., & Dawson, G. (2005a). Links between social and linguistic processing of speech in preschool children with autism: Behavioral and electrophysiological measures. *Developmental Science, 8*, F1–F12.

Kuhl, P.K., Conboy, B.T., Padden, D., Nelson, T., & Pruitt, J. (2005b). Early speech perception and later language development: Implications for the "critical period." *Language Learning and Development, 1*, 237–264.

Kuhl, P.K., & Miller (1982). Discrimination of auditory target dimensions in the presence or absence of variation in a second dimension by infants. *Perception & Psychophysics, 31*, 279–292.

Kuhl, P.K., Tsao, F.M., & Liu, H.M. (2003) Foreign-language experience in infancy: Effects of short-term exposure and social interaction on phonetic learning. *Proceedings of the National Academy of Sciences, 100*, 9096–9101.

Kuhl, P.K., Williams, K.A., Lacerda, F., Stevens, K.N., & Lindblom, B. (1992). Linguistic experience alters phonetic perception in infants by 6 months of age. *Science, 255*, 606–608.

Kuhlmeier, V.A., Troje, N.F., & Lee, V. (in press). Young infants detect the direction of biological motion in point-light displays. *Infancy*.

Kuhn, L., Aldrovandi, G.M., Sinkala, M., Kankasa, C., Semrau, K., Mwiya, M., et al. (2008). Effects of early, abrupt weaning on HIV-free survival of children in Zambia. *New England Journal of Medicine, 359*, 130–141.

Kuliev, A., & Verlinsky, Y. (2008). Preimplantation genetic diagnosis: Technological advances to improve accuracy and range of applications. *Reproductive BioMedicine Online, 16*, 532–538.

Kumwenda, N.I., Hoover, D.R., Mofenson, L.M., Thigpen, M.C., Kafulafula, G., Li, Q., et al. (2008). Extended antiretroviral prophylaxis to reduce breast-milk HIV-1 transmission. *New England Journal of Medicine, 359*, 119–129.

Kunisaki, S.M., & Jennings, R.W. (2008). Fetal surgery. *Journal of Intensive Care Medicine, 23*, 33–51.

Kwee, A., Elferink-Stinkens, P.M., Reuwer, P.J.H.M., & Bruinse, H.W. (2007). Trends in obstetric interventions in the Dutch obstetrical care system in the period 1993–2002. *European Journal of Obstetrics & Gynecology and Reproductive Biology, 132*, 70–75.

Labbo, L.D., & Kuhn, M.R. (2000). Weaving chains of affect and cognition: A young child's understanding of CD-ROM talking books. *Journal of Literacy Research, 32,* 187–210.

Labiner-Wolfe, J., Fein, S.B., & Shealy, K.R. (2008). Infant formula handling education and safety. *Pediatrics, 122,* S85–S90.

LaFuente, M.J., Grifol, R., Segarra, J., Soriano, J., Gorba, M.A., & Montesinos, A. (1997). Effects of the Firstart method of prenatal stimulation on psychomotor development: The first six months. *Pre- and Peri-Natal Psychology Journal, 11,* 151–162.

Lahey, B.B. (2004). Commentary: Role of temperament in developmental models of psychopathology. *Journal of Clinical Child and Adolescent Psychology, 33,* 88–93.

Laible, D. (2004a). Mother-child discourse about a child's past behavior at 30 months and early socio-emotional development at age 3. *Merrill-Palmer Quarterly, 50,* 159–180.

Laible, D. (2004b). Mother-child discourse in two contexts: Links with child temperament, attachment security, and socioemotional competence. *Developmental Psychology, 40,* 979–992.

Laible, D.J., & Thompson, R.A. (2000). Mother-child discourse, attachment security, shared positive affect, and early conscience development. *Child Development, 71,* 1424–1440.

Lamb, M.E. (1987). Predictive implications of individual differences in attachment. *Journal of Consulting and Clinical Psychology, 55,* 817–824.

Lamb, M.E. (1997). The development of father-infant relationships. In M.E. Lamb (Ed.), *The role of the father in child development* (3rd ed., pp. 104–120). New York: Wiley.

Lamb, M.E., & Ahnert, L. (2006). Nonparental child care: Context, concepts, correlates, and consequences. In W. Damon & R. Lerner (Eds.) & K.A. Renninger, & I.E. Sigel (Vol. Eds.), *Handbook of child psychology: Vol. 4. Child psychology in practice* (6th ed., pp. 950–1016). New York: Wiley.

Lamb, M.E., & Lewis, C. (2004). The development and significance of father-child relationships in two-parent families. In M.E. Lamb (Ed.), *The role of the father in child development* (4th ed., pp. 272–306). Hoboken, NJ: Wiley.

Lamb, S., & Zakhireh, B. (1997). Toddlers' attention to the distress of peers in a daycare setting. *Early Education & Development, 8,* 105–118.

Lambert, E.B., & Clyde, M. (2003). Putting Vygotsky to the test. In J.L. Roopnarine (Series Ed.) & D. E. Lytle (Vol. Ed.), *Play and educational theory and practice. Play & culture studies* (Vol. 5, pp. 59–98). Westport, CT: Praeger.

Lamm, B., Keller, H., Yovsi, R., & Chaudhary, N. (2008). Grandmaternal and maternal ethnotheories about early child care. *Journal of Family Psychology, 22,* 80–88.

Lampl, M. (2009). Human growth from the cell to the organism: Saltations and integrative physiology. *Annals of Human Biology, 36,* 478–495.

Lampl, M., & Thompson, A.L. (2007). Growth chart curves do not describe individual growth biology. *American Journal of Human Biology, 19,* 643–653.

Lande, B., Andersen, L., Bæug, A., et al. (2003). Infant feeding practices and associated factors in the first six months of life: The Norwegian Infant Feeding Survey. *Acta Paediatrica, 92,* 152–161.

Landon, M.B., Spong, C.Y., Thom, E., Carpenter, M.W., Ramin, S.M., Casey, B., et al. (2009). A multicenter, randomized trial of treatment for mild gestational diabetes. *New England Journal of Medicine, 361,* 1339–1348.

Landy, H.J., & Keith, L.G. (1998). The vanishing twin: a review. *Human Reproduction Update, 4,* 177–183.

Langer, A., Campero, L., Garcia, C., & Reynoso, S. (1998). Effects of psychosocial support during labour and childbirth on breastfeeding, medical interventions, and mothers' wellbeing in a Mexican public hospital: A randomised clinical trial. *British Journal of Obstetrics and Gynaecology, 105,* 1056–1063.

Larson, M.C., White, B.P., Cochran, A., Donzella, B., & Gunnar, M.R. (1998). Dampening of the cortisol response to handling at 3 months in human infants and its relation to sleep, circadian cortisol activity, and behavioral distress. *Developmental Psychobiology, 33,* 327–337.

Laskin, C.A., Spitzer, K.A., Clark, C.A., Crowther, M.R., Ginsberg, J.S., Hawker, G.A., et al. (2009). Low molecular weight heparin and aspirin for recurrent pregnancy loss: Results from the randomized, controlled HepASA Trial. *Journal of Rheumatology, 36,* 279–287.

Laursen, B., Hartup, W.W., & Koplas, A.L. (1996). Towards understanding peer conflict. *Merrill-Palmer Quarterly, 35,* 281–297.

Lederman, S.A., Rauh, V., Weiss, L., Stein, J.L., Hoepner, L.A., Becker, M., et al. (2004). The effects of the World Trade Center event on birth outcomes among term deliveries at three lower Manhattan hospitals. *Environmental Health Perspectives, 112,* 1772–1778.

Lee, C., Barr, R.G., Catherine, N., & Wicks, A. (2007). Age-related incidence of publicly reported shaken baby syndrome cases: Is crying a trigger for shaking? *Journal of Developmental and Behavioral Pediatrics, 28,* 288–293.

Lee, D.N., & Aronson, E. (1974). Visual proprioceptive control of standing in human infants. *Perception & Psychophysics, 15*, 529–532.

Leekam, S., Lopez, B., & Moore, C. (2000). Attentional and joint attention in preschool children with autism. *Developmental Psychology, 36*, 261–273.

Leerkes, E.M., Blankson, A.N., & O'Brien, M. (2009). Differential effects of maternal sensitivity to infant distress and nondistress on social-emotional functioning. *Child Development, 80*, 762–775.

Lehmann, S., Børdahl, P.E., Rasmussen, S.A., Irgens, L.M. (2007). Norwegian midwives and doctors have increased cesarean section rates. *Acta Obstetricia et Gynecologica Scandinavica, 86*, 1087–1089.

Lemery, K.S., Goldsmith, H.H., Klinnert, M.D., & Mrazek, D.A. (1999). Developmental models of infant and childhood temperament. *Developmental Psychology, 35*, 189–204.

Lenneberg, E.H., Rebelsky, F.G., & Nichols, I.A. (1965). The vocalizations of infants born to deaf and hearing parents. *Human Development, 8*, 23–27.

Leppänen, J.M., & Nelson, C.A. (2006). The development and neural bases of recognizing of facial emotion. In R. Kail (Ed.), *Advances in child development and behavior* (pp. 207–246). Amsterdam: Elsevier.

Leslie, A.M., & Roth, D. (1993). What autism teaches us about metarepresentation. In S. Baron-Cohen, H. Tager-Flusberg, & D. Cohen (Eds.), *Understanding other minds: Perspectives from autism* (pp. 83–111). Oxford, UK: Oxford University Press.

Lester, B.M., Tronick, E.Z., LaGasse, L., Seifer, R., Bauer, C.R., Shankaran, S., et al. (2002). The Maternal Lifestyle Study: Effects of substance exposure during pregnancy on neurodevelopmental outcome in 1-month-old infants. *Pediatrics, 110*, 1182–1192.

Lester, B.M., Tronick, E.Z., LaGasse, L., Seifer, R., Bauer, C.R., Shankaran, S., et al. (2004). Summary statistics of Neonatal Intensive Care Unit Network Neurobehavioral Scale scores from the Maternal Lifestyle Study: A quasinormative sample. *Pediatrics, 113*, 668–675.

Lester, B.M., Tronick, E.A., Mayes, L., et al. (1994). Neurodevelopmental consortium, the NICHD Neonatal research network. A neurodevelopmental follow-up battery for substance exposed infants. *Pediatric Research, 35*, 23A.

Levine, E.M., Ghai, V., Barton, J.J., & Strom, C.M. (2001). Mode of delivery and risk of respiratory disease in newborns. *Obstetrics & Gynecology, 97*, 439–442.

LeVine, R.A., Dixon, S., LeVine, S., Richman, A., Leiderman, P.H., Keefer, C.H., & Brazelton, T.B. (1994). *Child care and culture: Lessons from Africa.* Cambridge: Cambridge University Press.

Levine, T.P., Liu, J., Das, A., Lester, B., LaGasse, L., Shankaran, S., et al. (2008). Effects of prenatal cocaine exposure on special education in school-aged children. *Pediatrics, 122*, e83–e91.

Levitt, P., Reinoso, B., & Jones, L. (1998). The critical impact of early cellular environment on neuronal development. *Preventive Medicine, 27*(2), 180–183.

Lewin, T. (2009, October 24). No Einstein in your crib? Get a refund. *The New York Times.* Retrieved December 2, 2009, from http://www.nytimes.com/2009/10/24/educationn/24baby.html

Lewis, M. (1995). Self-conscious emotions. *American Scientist, 83*, 68–78.

Lewis, M. (2000). The emergence of human emotions. In M. Lewis, & J. M. Haviland-Jones (Eds.), *Handbook of emotions* (2nd ed., pp. 265–280). New York: Guilford Press.

Lewis, M., & Brooks-Gunn, J. (1979). *Social cognition and the acquisition of self.* New York: Plenum.

Lewis, M., & Ramsay, D.S. (2004). Development of self-recognition, personal pronoun use, and pretend play during the 2nd year. *Child Development, 75*, 1821–1831.

Lewis, M., & Ramsay, D. (1997). Stress reactivity and self-recognition. *Child Development, 68*, 621–629.

Li, H., George, V.K., Bianco, Jr., F.J., Lawrence, W.D., & Dhabuwala, C.B. (1997). Histopathological changes in the testes of prepubertal male rats after chronic administration of cocaine. *Journal of Environmental Pathology, Toxicology, and Oncology, 16*, 67–71.

Li, R., Fein, S.B., Chen, J., & Grummer-Strawn, L.M. (2008). Why mothers stop breastfeeding: Mothers' self-reported reasons for stopping during the first year. *Pediatrics, 122*, S69–S76.

Li, R., Fein, S.B., & Grummer-Strawn, L.B. (2008). Association of breastfeeding intensity and bottle-emptying behaviors at early infancy with infants' risk for excess weight at late infancy. *Pediatrics, 122*, S77–S84.

Lickliter, R., & Bahrick, L.E. (2000). The development of infant intersensory perception: Advantages of a comparative convergent-operations approach. *Psychological Bulletin, 126*, 260–280.

Lieberman, A.F., & Zeanah, C.H. (1995). Disorders of attachment in infancy. *Infant Psychiatry, 4*, 571–587.

Lieu, J.E.C., & Feinstein, A.R. (2002). Effect of gestational and passive smoke exposure on ear infections in children. *Archives of Pediatrics & Adolescent Medicine, 156*, 147–154.

Liittschwager, J. C., & Markman, E. M. (1994). Sixteen- and 24-month-olds' use of mutual exclusivity as a default assumption in second label learning. *Developmental Psychology, 30*, 955–968.

Lillard, A.S., & Witherington, D.C. (2004). Mothers' behavior modifications during pretense and their possible signal value for toddlers. *Developmental Psychology, 40*, 95–113.

Lin, C., & Liu, W.T. (1999). Intergenerational relationships among Chinese immigrant families from Taiwan. In H.P. McAdoo (Ed.), *Family ethnicity: Strength in diversity* (2nd ed., pp. 235–251). Thousand Oaks, CA: Sage.

Lindegren, M.L., Byers, Jr., R.H., Thomas, P., Davis, S.F., Caldwell, B., Roger, M., et al. (1999). Trends in perinatal transmission of HIV/AIDS in the United States. *JAMA, 282*, 531–538.

Linebarger, D.L., & Walker, D. (2005). Infants' and toddlers' television viewing and language outcomes. *American Behavioral Scientist, 48*, 624–645.

Linnet, K.M., Wisborg, K., Secher, N.J., Thomsen, P.H., Obel, C., Dalsgaard, S., et al., (2009). Coffee consumption during pregnancy and the risk of hyperkinetic disorder and ADHD: A prospective cohort study. *Acta Paediatrica, 98*, 173–179.

Liston, F.A., Allen, V.M., O'Connell, C.M., & Jangaard, K.A. (2008). Neonatal outcomes with caesarean delivery at term. *Archives of Disease in Childhood. Fetal and Neonatal Edition, 93*, F176–F182.

Liu, D., Sabbagh, M.A., Gehring, W.J., & Wellman, H.M. (2009). Neural correlates of children's theory of mind development. *Child Development, 80*, 318–326.

Liu, H.M., Kuhl, P.K., & Tsao, F.M. (2003). An association between mothers' speech clarity and infants' speech discrimination skills. *Developmental Science, 6*, F1–F10.

Liu, S., Liston, R.M., Joseph, K.S., Heaman, M., Sauve, R., Kramer, M.S., et al. (2007). Maternal mortality and severe morbidity associated with low-risk planned cesarean delivery versus planned vaginal delivery at term. *Canadian Medical Association Journal, 176*, 455–460.

Liu, X., Jiang, Q., Mansfield, S.G., Puttaraju, M., Zhang, Y., Zhu, W., et al. (2002). Partial correction of endogenous DeltaF508 CFTR in human cystic fibrosis airway epithelia by spliceosome-mediated RNA trans-splicing. *Nature Biotechnology, 20*, 47–52.

Lively, S., Logan, J.S., & Pisoni, D.B. (1993). Training Japanese listeners to identify English /r/ and /l/. II. The role of phonetic environment and talker variability in learning new perceptual categories. *Journal of the Acoustical Society of America, 94*, 1242–1255.

Lively, S., Pisoni, D.B., Yamada, R.A., Tohkura, Y., & Yamada, T. (1994). Training Japanese listeners to identify English /r/ and /l/. III. Long-term retention of new phonetic categories. *Journal of the Acoustical Society of America, 94*, 2076–2087.

Lloyd, B., & Goodwin, R. (1995). Let's pretend: Casting the characters and setting the scene. *British Journal of Developmental Psychology, 13*, 261–270.

Lloyd, I.C., Ashworth, J., Biswas, S., & Abadi, R.V. (2007). Advances in the management of congenital and infantile cataract. *Eye, 21*, 1301–1309.

Lloyd-Fox, S., Blasi, A., Volein, A., Everdell, N., Elwell, C.E., & Johnson, M.H. (2009). Social perception in infancy: A near infrared spectroscopy study. *Child Development, 80*, 986–999.

Lo, Y.M. (2005). Recent advances in fetal nucleic acids in maternal plasma. *Journal of Histochemistry and Cytochemistry, 53*, 293–296.

Lo, Y.M. (2006). Recent developments in fetal nucleic acids in maternal plasma: Implications to noninvasive prenatal fetal blood group genotyping. *Transfusion Clinique et Biologique, 13*, 50–52.

Lobel, M., Cannella, D.L., Graham, J.E., DeVincent, C., Schneider, J., & Meyer, B.A. (2008). Pregnancy-specific stress, prenatal health behaviors, and birth outcomes. *Health Psychology, 27*, 604–615.

Lobel, M., & DeLuca, R.S. (2007). Psychosocial sequelae of cesarean delivery: Review and analysis of their causes and implications. *Social Science & Medicine, 64*, 2272–2284.

Lobo, M.A., & Galloway, J.C. (2008). Postural and object-oriented experiences advance early reaching, object exploration, and means-end behavior. *Child Development, 79*, 1869–1890.

Lobo, M.A., Galloway, J.C., & Savelsbergh, G.J.P. (2004). General and task-related experiences affect early object interaction. *Child Development, 75*, 1268–1281.

Locke, J.L. (1983). *Phonological acquisition and change.* New York: Academic Press.

Lockman, J.J. (2000). A perception-action perspective on tool use development. *Child Development, 71*, 137–144.

Loeb, S., Fuller, B., Kagan, S.L., & Carrol, B. (2004). Child care in poor communities: Early learning effects of type, quality, and stability. *Child Development, 75*, 47–65.

Lohaus, A., Keller, H., Ball, J., Voelker, S., & Elben, C. (2004). Maternal sensitivity in interactions with 3- and 12-month-old infants: Stability, structural composition, and developmental consequences. *Infant and Child Development, 13*, 235–252.

Lohaus, A., Keller, H., Lissmann, I., Ball, J., Borke, J., & Lamm, B. (2005). Contingency experiences of 3-month-old children and their relation to later developmental achievements. *The Journal of Genetic Psychology, 166,* 365–383.

Lorber, M.F., & Egeland, B. (2009). Infancy parenting and externalizing psychopathology from childhood through adulthood: Developmental trends. *Developmental Psychology, 45,* 909–912.

Lord, C., Risi, S., Lambrecht, L., Cook, E.H., Leventhal, B.L., DiLavore, P.S., et al. (2000). The Autism Diagnostic Observation Schedule-Generic: A standard measure of social and communication deficits associated with the spectrum of autism. *Journal of Autism and Developmental Disorders, 30,* 205–223.

Lord, C., Rutter, M., & LeCouteur, A. (1994). Autism Diagnostic Interview-Revised: A revised version of a diagnostic interview for caregivers of individuals with possible pervasive developmental disorders. *Journal of Autism and Developmental Disorders, 24,* 659–685.

Lott, K.R. (2002). Oral healthcare for infants. *Dentistry Today, 21,* 64–67.

Louis, J., Cannard, C., Bastuji, H., & Challamel, M.J. (1997). Sleep ontogenesis revisited: A longitudinal 24-hour home polygraphic study on 15 normal infants during the first two years of life. *Sleep, 20,* 323–333.

Lovaas, O.I., & Smith, T. (1989). A comprehensive behavioral theory of autistic children: Paradigm for research and treatment. *Journal of Behavior Therapy and Experimental Psychiatry, 20,* 17–29.

Love, J.M., Harrison, L., Sagi-Schwartz, A., van IJzendoorn, M.H., Ross, C., Ungerer, J.A., et al. (2003). Child care quality matters: How conclusions may vary with context. *Child Development, 74,* 1021–1033.

Love, J.M., Kisker, E.E., Ross, C.M., Brooks-Gunn, J., Schochet, P.Z., Boller, K., et al. (2002). *Making a difference in the lives of infants and toddlers and their families: The impacts of Early Head Start* (Report prepared for the Administration for Children and Families, U.S. Department of Health and Human Services). Princeton: NJ: Mathematica Policy Research.

Love, J.M., Kisker, E.E., Ross, C., Raikes, H., Constantine, J., Boller, K., et al. (2005). The effectiveness of Early Head Start for 3-year-old children and their parents: Lessons for policy and programs. *Developmental Psychology, 41,* 885–901.

Lovejoy, M., Graczyk, P., O'Hare, E., & Neuman, G. (2000). Maternal depression and parenting behavior: A meta-analytic review. *Clinical Psychological Review, 20,* 561–592.

Loveland, K., & Landry, S. (1986). Joint attention and language in autism and developmental language delay. *Journal of Autism and Developmental Disorders, 16,* 335–349.

Low, W.A., & Clift, V.A. (1984). *Encyclopedia of Black America.* New York: Da Capo Press.

Lu, N., Samuels, M.E., Shi, L., Baker, S.L., Glover, S.H., & Sanders, J.M. (2004). Child day care risks of common infectious diseases revisited. *Child: Care, Health, and Development, 30,* 361–368.

Lubetzky, R., Mimouni, F.B., Dollberg, S., Reifen, R., Ashbel, G., & Mandel, D. (2009). Effect of music by Mozart on energy expenditure in growing preterm infants. *Pediatrics, 125,* e24–e28.

Lubic, R.W. (2002). Introduction to international efforts. Retrieved October 12, 2003, from http://www .BirthCenters.org

Lucas-Thompson, R., Townsend, E.L., Gunnar, M.R., Georgieff, M.K., Guiang, S.F., Ciffuentes, R.F., et al. (2008). Developmental changes in the responses of preterm infants to a painful stressor. *Infant Behavior & Development, 31,* 614–623.

Luccioli, S., Ross, M., Labiner-Wolfe, J., & Fein, S.B. (2008). Maternally reported food allergies and other food-related health problems in infants: Characteristics and associated factors. *Pediatrics, 122,* S105–S112.

Luke, L., & Brown, M.B. (2006). The changing risk of infant mortality by gestation, plurality, and race: 1989–1991 versus 1999–2001. *Pediatrics, 118,* 2488–2497.

Luo, Y., & Baillargeon, R. (2007). Do 12.5-month-old infants consider what objects others can see when interpreting their actions? *Cognition, 105,* 489–512.

Luo, Y., Kaufman, L., & Baillargeon, R. (2009). Young infants' reasoning about physical events involving inert and self-propelled objects. *Cognitive Psychology, 58,* 441–486.

Luyster, R., & Lord, C. (2009). Word learning in children with autism spectrum disorders. *Developmental Psychology, 45,* 1774–1786.

Lyons-Ruth, K., Bronfman, E., & Parsons, E. (1999). Maternal frightened, frightening, or atypical behavior and disorganized infant attachment patterns. In J.I. Vondra, & D. Barnett (Eds.), Atypical attachment in infancy and early childhood among children at developmental risk. *Monographs of the Society for Research in Child Development, 64*(3, Serial No. 258), 67–96.

Lytton, H., & Romney, D.M. (1991). Parents' differential socialization of boys and girl: A meta-analysis. *Psychological Bulletin, 109,* 267–296.

Ma, L., & Lillard, A. (2006). Where is the real cheese? Young children's understanding of pretense. *Child Development, 77,* 1762–1777.

MacDonald, H., & the Committee on Fetus and Newborn. (2002). Perinatal care at the threshold of viability. *Pediatrics, 110,* 1024–1027.

MacDonald, R., Anderson, J., Dube, W.V., Geckeler, A., Green, G., Holcomb, W., et al. (2006). Behavioral assessment of joint attention: A methodological report. *Research in Developmental Disabilities, 27,* 138–150.

MacDorman, M.F., & Kirmeyer, S. (2009). *Fetal and perinatal mortality, United States, 2005. National Vital Statistics Reports, 57*(8). Hyattsville, MD: National Center for Health Statistics.

MacDorman, M.F., & Mathews, T.J. (2008). Recent trends in infant mortality in the United States. *NCHS Data Brief, 9,* Hyattsville, MD: National Center for Health Statistics.

Macfie, J., Cicchetti, D., & Toth, S.L. (2001). The development of dissociation in maltreated preschool-aged children. *Development and Psychopathology, 13,* 233–254.

Mack, K.A., Gilchrist, J., & Ballesteros, M.F. (2008). Injuries among infants treated in emergency departments in the United States, 2001–2004. *Pediatrics, 121,* 930–937.

Macknin, M.L., Piedmonte, M., Jacobs, J., & Skibinski, C. (2000). Symptoms associated with infant teething: A prospective study. *Pediatrics, 105,* 747–752.

MacLeod, A.A., & Stoel-Gammon, C. (2005). Are bilinguals different? What VOT tells us about simultaneous bilinguals. *Journal of Multilingual Communication Disorders, 3,* 118–127.

MacPherson, A.C., & Moore, C. (2007). Attentional control by gaze cues in infancy. In R. Flom, K. Lee, & D. Muir (Eds.), *Gaze-following: Its development and significance* (pp. 53–75). Mahwah, NJ: Lawrence Erlbaum Associates.

MacWhinney, B., & Snow, C.E. (1990). The Child Language Data Exchange System: An update. *Journal of Child Language, 17,* 457–472.

Maddocks, D.G., Alberry, M.S., Attilakos, G., Madgett, T.E., Choi, K., Soothill, P.W., et al., (2009). The SAFE project: Towards non-invasive prenatal diagnosis. *Biochemical Society Transactions, 37*(Pt. 2), 460–465.

Maguire, C.M., Walther, F.J., van Zwieten, P.H.T., Le Cessie, S., Wit, J.M., Veen, S., et al. (2008). No change in developmental outcome with incubator covers and nesting for very preterm infants in a randomised controlled trial. *Archives of Disease in Childhood. Fetal and Neonatal Edition, 94,* F92-F97.

Main, M., & Solomon, J. (1986). Discovery of a disorganized disoriented attachment pattern. In T.B. Brazelton, & M.W. Yogman (Eds.), *Affective development in infancy* (pp. 95–124). Norwood, NJ: Ablex.

Main, M., & Solomon, J. (1990). Procedures for identifying infants as disorganized/disoriented during the Ainsworth Strange Situation. In M. Greenberg, D. Cicchetti, & E.M. Cummings (Eds.), *Attachment in the preschool years: Theory, research, and intervention* (pp. 121–160). Chicago: University of Chicago Press.

Malatesta, C.Z., Culver, C., Tesman, J.R., & Shepard, B. (1989). The development of emotion expression during the first two years of life. *Monographs of the Society for Research in Child Development, 54*(1–2, Serial No. 219).

Malatesta, C.Z., & Haviland, J.M. (1982). Learning display rules: The socialization of emotion expression in infancy. *Child Development, 53,* 991–1003.

Malloy, M.H., & Freeman, D.H. (2004). Age at death, season, and day of death as indicators of the effect of the Back to Sleep Program on Sudden Infant Death Syndrome in the United States, 1992–1999. *Archives of Pediatrics & Adolescent Medicine, 158,* 359–365.

Malone, F.D., Canick, J.A., Ball, R.H., Nyberg, D.A., Comstock, C.H., Bukowski, R., et al. (2005). First-trimester or second-trimester screening, or both, for Down's Syndrome. *New England Journal of Medicine, 353,* 2001–2011.

Malpani, A., Malpani, A., & Modi, D. (2002). Preimplantation sex selection for family balancing in India. *Human Reproduction, 17,* 11–12.

Malphurs, J., Larrain, C., Field, T., Pickens, J., Peláez-Nogueras, M., Yando, R., et al. (1996). Altering withdrawn and intrusive interaction behaviors of depressed mothers. *Infant Mental Health Journal, 17,* 152–160.

Mandel, D.R., Jusczyk, P.W., & Pisoni, D.B. (1995). Infants' recognition of the sound patterns of their own names. *Psychological Science, 6,* 314–317.

Mandler, J.M. (1992). How to build a baby. II. Conceptual primitives. *Psychological Review, 99,* 587–604.

Mandler, J.M. (1998). Representation. In W. Damon (Editor-in-Chief), D. Kuhn, & R.S. Siegler (Vol. Eds.), *Handbook of child psychology: Vol. 2. Cognition, perception, and language* (5th ed., pp. 255–308). New York: Wiley.

Mandler, J.M., & McDonough, L. (1998). On developing a knowledge base in infancy. *Developmental Psychology, 34,* 1274–1288.

Mangan, P., Franklin, A., Tignor, T., Bolling, L., & Nadel, L. (1994). Development of spatial memory abilities in young children. *Society for Neuroscience Abstracts, 20,* 363.

Mangelsdorf, S.C. (1992). Developmental changes in infant-stranger interaction. *Infant Behavior and Development, 15,* 191–208.

Mangelsdorf, S.C., & Frosch, C.A. (1999). Temperament and attachment: One construction or two? In H.W. Reese (Ed.), *Advances in child development and behavior* (pp. 181–220). San Diego, CA: Academic.

Mangelsdorf, S.C., Gunnar, M., Kestenbaum, R., Lang, S., & Andreas, D. (1990). Infant proneness-to-distress temperament, maternal personality, and mother-infant attachment: Associations and goodness of fit. *Child Development, 61,* 820–831.

Mangelsdorf, S.C., Plunkett, J.W., Dedrick, C.F., Berlin, M., Meisels, S.J., McHale, J.L., et al. (1996). Attachment security in very low birth weight infants. *Developmental Psychology, 32,* 914–920.

Mangelsdorf, S.C., Shapiro, J.R., & Marzolf, D. (1995). Developmental and temperamental differences in emotion regulation in infancy. *Child Development, 66,* 1817–1828.

Maples, W.C., & Bither, M. (2006). Treating the trinity of infantile vision development: Infantile esotropia, amblyopia, anisometropia. *Optometry and Vision Development, 37,* 123–130.

Maratsos, M. (1998). The acquisition of grammar. In W. Damon (Ed.) & D. Kuhn, & R.S. Siegler (Vol. Eds.), *Handbook of child psychology* (5th ed.): *Vol. 2. Cognition, perception, and language* (pp. 421–466). New York: Wiley.

March of Dimes. (2002). *HIV and AIDS in pregnancy.* Retrieved October 2, 2005, from http://www .modimes.org

Marchman, V.A., & Fernald, A. (2008). Speed of word recognition and vocabulary knowledge in infancy predict cognitive and language outcomes in later childhood. *Developmental Science, 11,* F9–F16.

Marcovitch, S., & Zelazo, P.D. (1999). The A-not-B error: Results from a logistic meta-analysis. *Child Development, 70,* 1297–1313.

Marcus, G.F., Pinker, S., Ullman, M., Hollander, M., Rosen, T.J., & Xu, F. (1992). Overregularization in language acquisition. *Monographs of the Society for Research in Child Development, 57*(4, Serial No. 228).

Marcus, G.F., Vijayan, S., Bandi Rao, S., & Vishton, P.M. (1999). Rule learning by seven-month-old infants. *Science, 283,* 77–80.

Markman, E.M. (1989). *Categorization and naming in children: Problems of induction.* Cambridge, MA: MIT Press.

Markman, E.M., & Hutchinson, J.E. (1984). Children's sensitivity to constraints on word meaning: Taxonomic versus thematic relations. *Cognitive Psychology, 16,* 1–27.

Markman, E.M., Wasow, J.L., & Hansen, M.B. (2003). Use of the mutual exclusivity assumption by young word learners. *Cognitive Psychology, 47,* 241–275.

Marlier, L., & Schaal, B. (2005). Human newborns prefer human milk: Conspecific milk odor is attractive without postnatal exposure. *Child Development, 76,* 155–168.

Marlier, L., Schaal, B., & Soussignan, R. (1998). Bottle-fed neonates prefer an odor experienced in utero to an odor experienced postnatally in the feeding context. *Developmental Psychobiology, 33,* 133–145.

Marshall, K. (2003). Benefiting from extended parental leave. *Perspectives on Labour and Income, 4*(3), 5–11. Statistics Canada, Cat. No. 75-001-XIE.

Martin, G.B., & Clark, R.D. (1982). Distress crying in neonates: Species and peer specificity. *Developmental Psychology, 18,* 3–9.

Martin, J.A., Hamilton, B.E., Ventura, S.J., Menacker, F., & Park, M.M. (2002). Births: Final data for 2000. *National Vital Statistics Reports, 50*(5). Hyattsville, MD: National Center for Health Statistics.

Martin, J.A., Hamilton, B.E., Sutton, P.D., Ventura, S.J., Menacker, F., Kirmeyer, S., et al. (2009). Births: Final data for 2006. *National Vital Statistics reports, 57*(7). Hyattsville, MD: National Center for Health Statistics.

Martin, J.A., Hamilton, B.E., Sutton, P.D., Ventura, S.J., Menacker, F., & Munson, M.L. (2005). Births: Final data for 2003. *National Vital Statistics Reports, 54*(2). Hyattsville, MD: National Center for Health Statistics.

Martin, J.A., MacDorman, M.F., Mathews, T.J. (1997). Triplet births: trends and outcomes, 1971–94. *Vital Health Statistics, 21*(55). Hyattsville, MD: National Center for Health Statistics.

Martin, J.A., Park, M.M., & Sutton, P.D. (2002). Births: Preliminary data for 2001. *National Vital Statistics Reports, 50*(10). Hyattsville, MD: National Center for Health Statistics.

Martinez, E.A. (1999). Mexican American/Chicano families: Parenting as diverse as the families themselves. In McAdoo, H.P. (Ed.), *Family ethnicity: Strength in diversity* (2nd ed., pp. 121–134). Thousand Oaks, CA: Sage.

Martinez, G.M., Chandra, A., Abma, J.C., Jones, J., & Mosher, W.D. (2006). Fertility, contraception, and fatherhood: Data on men and women from Cycle 6 (2002) of the National Survey of Family Growth. *Vital Health Statistics, 23(26).*

Martins, C., & Garffan, E. (2000). Effects of early maternal depression on patterns of infant-mother attachment: A meta-analytic investigation. *Journal of Child Psychology & Psychiatry, 41,* 737–746.

Martinson, K., & Nightingale, D. (2008). *Ten key findings from Responsible Fatherhood Initiatives: Urban Institute.* Retrieved December 4, 2009, from http://aspe.hhs.gov/hsp/07/PFF/KeyFindings/

Masataka, N. (1996). Perception of motherese in a signed language by 6-month-old deaf infants. *Developmental Psychology, 32,* 874–879.

Masataka, N. (1998). Perception of motherese in Japanese Sign Language by 6-month-old hearing infants. *Developmental Psychology, 34,* 241–246.

Mash, C. (2007). Object representation in infants' coordination of manipulative force. *Infancy, 12,* 329–341.

Mash, C., Arterberry, M.E., & Bornstein, M.H. (2007). Mechanisms of visual object recognition in infancy: Five-month-olds generalize beyond the interpolation of familiar views. *Infancy, 12,* 31–43.

Mash, C., Novak, E., Berthier, N.E., & Keen, R. (2006). What do two-year-olds understand about hidden-objects? *Developmental Psychology, 42,* 263–271.

Mashburn, A.J., Justice, L.M., Downer, J.T., & Pianta, R.C. (2009). Peer effects on children's language achievement during pre-kindergarten. *Child Development, 80,* 686–702.

Massaro, A.N., Hammad, T.A., Jazzo, B., & Aly, H. (2009). Massage with kinesthetic stimulation improves weight gain in preterm infants. *Journal of Perinatology, 29,* 352–357.

Massi Lindsey, L.L., Silk, K.J., Von Friederichs-Fitzwater, M.M., Hamner, H.C., Prue, C.E., & Boster, F.J. (2009). Developing effective campaign messages to prevent neural tube defects: A qualitative assessment of women's reactions to advertising concepts. *Journal of Health Communication, 14,* 131–159.

Masur, E. (1982). Mothers' responses to infants' object-related gestures: Influences on lexical development. *Journal of Child Language, 9,* 23–30.

Mathews, T.J. (2003). Trends in spina bifida and anencephalus in the United States, 1991–2002. National Center for Health Statistics eStat. Retrieved December 10, 2005, from http://www.cdc.gov/nchs/products/pubs/pubd/hestats/spine_anen.htm

Mathews, T.J. (2009). Trends in spina bifida and anencephalus in the United States, 1991–2006. *NCHS Health E-Stat.* Retrieved June 22, 2009, from http://www.cdc.gov/nchs/products/pubs/pubd/hestats/spine_anen.htm

Mathews, T.J., MacDorman, M.F., & Menacker, F. (2002). Infant mortality statistics from the 1999 period linked birth/infant death data set. *National Vital Statistics Reports, 50(4).* Hyattsville, MD: National Center for Health Statistics.

Maurer, D., Lewis, T.L., Brent, H.P., & Levin, A.V. (1999). Rapid improvement in the acuity of infants after visual input. *Science, 286,* 108–110.

Maurer, D., Mondloch, C.J., & Lewis, T.L. (2007). Effects of early visual deprivation on perceptual and cognitive development. In C. von Hofsten, & K. Rosander (Eds.), *Progress in Brain Research, 164,* 87–104.

Mayberry, R.I., & Nicoladis, E. (2000). Gesture reflects language development: Evidence from bilingual children. *Current Directions in Psychological Science, 9,* 192–196.

Maye, J., Weiss, D.J., & Aslin, R.N. (2008). Statistical phonetic learning in infants: Facilitation and feature generalization. *Developmental Science, 11,* 122–134.

Maynard, A.E. (2002). Cultural teaching: The development of teaching skills in Maya sibling interactions. *Child Development, 73,* 969–982.

McAdoo, H.P. (Ed.). (1999). *Family ethnicity: Strength in diversity* (2nd ed.). Thousand Oaks, CA: Sage.

McBride, B.A., & Lutz, M.M. (2004). Intervention: Changing the nature and extent of father involvement. In M.E. Lamb (Ed.), *The role of the father in child development* (4th ed., pp. 446–475). New York: Wiley.

McCall, R.B. (2009). Evidence-based programming in the context of practice and policy. *Social Policy Report, 23(3).*

McCall, R.B., & Carriger, M.S. (1993). A meta-analysis of infant habituation and recognition memory performance as predictors of later IQ. *Child Development, 64,* 57–79.

McCarton, C.M., Brooks-Gunn, J., Wallace, I.F., & Bauer, C.R. (1997). Results at age 8 years of early intervention for low-birth-weight premature infants: The infant health and development program. *JAMA, 277,* 126–132.

McClure, E.M., Goldenberg, R.L., & Bann, C.M. (2007). Maternal mortality, stillbirth and measures of obstetric care in developing and developed countries. *International Journal of Gynecology and Obstetrics, 96,* 139–146.

McCreath, K.J., Howcroft, J., Campbell, K.H., Colman, A., Schnieke, A.E., & Kind, A.J. (2000). Production of gene-targeted sheep by nuclear transfer from cultured somatic cells. *Nature, 405,* 1066–1069.

McCrink, K., & Wynn, K. (2004). Large-number addition and subtraction by 9-month-old infants. *Psychological Science, 15,* 776–781.

McDonald, D.T., & Simons, G.M. (1989). *Musical growth and development: Birth through six.* New York: Schirmer Books.

McDowell, M.A., Lacher, D.A., Pfeiffer, C.M., Mulinare, J., Picciano, M.F., Rader, J.I., et al. (2008). Blood folate levels: The latest NHANES results. *NCHS Data Brief, 6,* 1–8.

McEachin, J.J., Smith, T., & Lovaas, O.I. (1993). Long-term outcome for children with autism who received early intensive behavioral treatment. *American Journal on Mental Retardation, 97,* 359–372.

McGraw, M.B. (1935). *Growth: A study of Johnny and Jimmy.* New York: Appleton-Century.

McGraw, M.B. (1940). Neuromuscular development of the human infant as exemplified in the achievement of erect locomotion. *Journal of Pediatrics, 17,* 747–771.

McGuigan, F., & Salmon, K. (2004). The time to talk: The influence of the timing of adult-child talk on children's event memory. *Child Development, 75,* 669–686.

McHale, J.P., Kazali, C., Rotman, T., Talbot, J., Carleton, M., & Lieberson, R. (2004). The transition to coparenthood: Parents' pre-birth expectations and early coparental adjustment at 3 months postpartum. *Development and Psychopathology, 16,* 711–733.

McKelvie, P., & Low, J. (2002). Listening to Mozart does not improve children's spatial ability: Final curtains for the Mozart effect. *British Journal of Developmental Psychology, 20*(2), 241–258.

McKenna, J.J., & Volpe, L.E. (2007). Sleeping with baby: An internet-based sampling of parental experiences, choices, perceptions, and interpretations in a western industrialized context. *Infant and Child Development, 16,* 359–385.

McLanahan, S., & Carlson, M.S. (2004). Fathers in fragile families. In M.E. Lamb (Ed.), *The role of the father in child development* (4th ed., pp. 368–396). New York: Wiley.

McLoyd, V.C. (1998). Socioeconomic disadvantage and child development. *American Psychologist, 53,* 185–204.

McLoyd, V.C. (2005). Economic context and childhood experience: Making the case for why and how race matters in children's development. Master lecture given at the Biennial Meeting of the Society for Research in Child Development, Atlanta, GA.

McLoyd, V.C., Aikens, N.L., & Burton, L.M. (2006). Childhood poverty, policy, and practice. In W. Damon, & R. Lerner (Eds.) & K.A. Renninger, & I.E. Sigel (Vol. Eds.), *Handbook of child psychology:* Vol. 4. *Child psychology in practice* (6th ed., pp. 700–775). New York: Wiley.

McMurray, B. (2007). Defusing the childhood vocabulary explosion. *Science, 317,* 631.

McMurray, B., Aslin, R.N., & Toscano, J.C. (2009). Statistical learning of phonetic categories: Insights from a computational approach. *Developmental Science, 12,* 369–378.

Mead, M. (1928). *Coming of age in Samoa.* New York: Morrow.

Mead, M. (1930). *Growing up in New Guinea.* New York: Blue Ribbon.

Meadows, M. (2001). Pregnancy and the drug dilemma. FDA Consumer Magazine. Retrieved January 12, 2002, from http://www.fda.gov/fdac/features/2001/301_preg.html

Medoff-Cooper, B., McGrath, J.M., & Shults, J.J. (2002). Feeding patterns of full-term and preterm infants at forty weeks postconceptional age. *Journal of Developmental and Behavioral Pediatrics, 23,* 231–236.

Medwell, J. (1998). The Talking Books Project: Some further insights into the use of talking books to develop reading. *Reading, 32,* 3–8.

Meier, P. (1999, March 14). Childbirth pioneer: Dr. Martha Ripley crusaded for safer childbirth and healthier infants and founded Ripley Maternity Hospital in 1886. *StarTribune,* pp. E1, E5.

Meltzoff, A.N. (1988a). Infant imitation and memory: Nine-month-olds in immediate and deferred acts. *Child Development, 59,* 217–225.

Meltzoff, A.N. (1988b). Infant imitation after a 1-week delay: Long-term memory for novel acts and multiple stimuli. *Developmental Psychology, 24,* 470–476.

Meltzoff, A.N., & Borton, R.W. (1979). Intermodal matching by human neonates. *Nature, 282,* 403–404.

Meltzoff, A.N., & Brooks, R. (2007). Eyes wide shut: The importance of eyes in infant gaze-following and understanding other minds. In R. Flom, K. Lee, & D. Muir (Eds.), *Gaze-following: Its development and significance* (pp. 217–241). Mahwah, NJ: Lawrence Erlbaum Associates.

Meltzoff, A.N., & Moore, M.K. (1983). Newborn infants imitate adult facial gestures. *Child Development, 54,* 702–719.

Meltzoff, A. N., & Moore, M. K. (1998). Object representation, identity, and the paradox of early permanence: Steps toward a new framework. *Infant Behavior & Development, 21,* 201–235.

Menacker, F., & Martin, J.A. (2008). Expanded health data from the new birth certificate, 2005. *National Vital Statistics Reports, 56*(13).

Hyattsville, MD: National Center for Health Statistics.

Mendelsohn, A.L., Berkule, S.B., Tomopoulos, S., Tamis-LeMonda, C.S., Huberman, H.S., Alvir, J., et al. (2008). Infant television and video exposure associated with limited parent-child verbal interactions in low socioeconomic status households *Archives of Pediatrics and Adolescent Medicine, 162,* 411–417.

Mendelson, C.R. (2009). Minireview: Fetal-maternal hormonal signaling in pregnancy and labor. *Molecular Endocrinology, 23,* 947–954.

Mendes, E.W., & Procianoy, R.S. (2008). Massage therapy reduces hospital stay and occurrence of late-onset sepsis in very preterm neonates. *Journal of Perinatology, 28,* 815–820.

Mennella, J.A., & Beauchamp, G.K. (1999). Experience with a flavor in mother's milk modifies the infant's acceptance of flavored cereal. *Developmental Psychobiology, 35,* 197–203.

Mennella, J.A., & Beauchamp, G.K. (2002). Flavor experiences during formula feeding are related to preferences during childhood. *Early Human Development, 68,* 71–82.

Mennella, J.A., Jagnow, C.P., & Beauchamp, G.K. (2001). Prenatal and postnatal flavor learning by human infants. *Pediatrics, 107,* E88–E93.

Mennella, J.A., Kennedy, J.M., & Beauchamp, G.K. (2006). Vegetable acceptance by infants: Effects of formula flavors. *Early Human Development, 82,* 463–468.

Menon, V., Shailesh, G., Sharma, P., & Saxena, R. (2008). Clinical trial of patching versus atropine penalization for the treatment of anisometropic amblyopia in older children. *Journal of AAPOS, 12,* 493–497.

Mercer, B.M. (2003). Preterm premature rupture of the membranes. *Obstetrics & Gynecology, 101,* 178–193.

Merewood, A., Mehta, S.D., Chamberlain, L.B., Philipp, B.L., & Bauchner, H. (2005). Breastfeeding rates in US baby-friendly hospitals: Results of a national survey. *Pediatrics, 116,* 628–634.

Merriman, W.E., & Schuster, J.M. (1991). Young children's disambiguation of object name reference. *Child Development, 62,* 1288–1301.

Merten, S., Dratva, J., & Ackermann-Liebrich, U. (2005). Do baby-friendly hospitals influence breastfeeding duration on a national level? *Pediatrics, 116,* e702–e708.

Messinger, D.S., Bauer, C.R., Das, A., Seifer, R., Lester, B.M., LaGasse, L.L., et al. (2004). The Maternal Lifestyle Study: Cognitive, motor, and behavioral outcomes of cocaine-exposed and opiate-exposed infants through three years of age. *Pediatrics, 113,* 1677–1685.

Messinger, D.S., & Fogel, A. (1998). Give and take: The development of conventional infant gestures. *Merrill-Palmer Quarterly, 44,* 566–590.

Michaelsen, K.F., Larsen, P.S., Thomsen, B.L., & Samuelson, G. (1994). The Copenhagen cohort study on infant nutrition and growth: Duration of breast feeding and influencing factors. *Acta Paediatrica, 83,* 565–571.

Miller, P.J., Fung, H., & Mintz, J. (1996). Self-construction through narrative practices: A Chinese and American comparison of early socialization. *Ethos, 24,* 237–280.

Miller, P.J., Wiley, A.R., Fung, H., & Liang, C.H. (1997). Personal storytelling as a medium of socialization in Chinese and American families. *Child Development, 68,* 557–568.

Miller, S.A. (1998). *Developmental research methods* (2nd ed.). Upper Saddle River, NJ: Prentice Hall.

Minami, M., & McCabe, A. (1995). Rice balls and bear hunts: Japanese and North American family narrative patterns. *Journal of Child Language, 22,* 423–445.

Miotti, P.G., Taha, T.E.T., Kumwenda, N.I., Broadhead, R., Mtimavalye, L.A., Van der Hoeven, L., et al. (1999). HIV transmission through breastfeeding: A study in Malawi. *JAMA, 282,* 744–749.

Mirmiran, M., Kok, J.H., Boer, K., & Wolf, H. (1992). Perinatal development of human circadian rhythms: Role of the fetal biological clock. *Neuroscience Biobehavioral Review, 16,* 371–378.

Mitchell, E.A., Thach, B.T., Thompson, J.M., & Williams, S. (1999). Changing infants' sleep position increases risk of sudden infant death syndrome. *Archives of Pediatrics & Adolescent Medicine, 153,* 1136–1141.

Mitka, M. (2000). Neonatal screening varies by state of birth. *JAMA, 284,* 2044–2046.

Mix, K.S., Huttenlocher, J., & Levine, S.C. (2002). Multiple cues for quantification in infancy: Is number one of them? *Psychological Bulletin, 128,* 278–294.

Miyake, K., Campos, J., Kagan, J., & Bradshaw, D. (1986). Issues in socioemotional development in Japan. In H. Azuma, K. Hakuta, & H. Stevenson (Eds.), *Kodomo: Child development and education in Japan* (pp. 238–261). San Francisco: Freeman.

Mizuno, K., & Ueda, A. (2004). Antenatal olfactory learning influences infant feeding. *Early Human Development, 76,* 83–90.

Moe, V., & Smith, L. (2003). The relation of prenatal substance exposure and infant recognition memory to later cognitive competence. *Infant Behavior & Development, 26,* 87–99.

Mohan, E., Reef, G., & Sarkar, M. (2006). *Breaking the piggy bank: Parents and the high cost of child care.*

Arlington, VA: National Association of Child Care Resource and Referral Agencies.

Mok, E., Multon, C., Piguel, L., Barroso, E., Goua, V., Christin, P., et al. (2008). Decreased full breastfeeding, altered practices, perceptions, and infant weight change of prepregnant obese women: A need for extra support. *Pediatrics, 121,* e1319–e1324.

Molloy, A.M., Kirke, P.N., Troendle, J.F., Burke, H., Sutton, M., Brody, L.C., et al. (2009). Maternal vitamin B$_{12}$ status and risk of neural tube defects in a population with high neural tube defect prevalence and no folic Acid fortification. *Pediatrics, 123,* 917–923.

Momoi, N., Tinney, J.P., Liu, L.J., Elshershari, H., Hoffmann, P.J., Ralphe, J.C., et al. (2008). Modest maternal caffeine exposure affects developing embryonic cardiovascular function and growth. *American Journal of Physiology. Heart and Circulatory Physiology, 294,* H2248–H2256.

Montes, G., & Halterman, J.S. (2008). Child care problems and employment among families with preschool-aged children with autism in the United States. *Pediatrics, 122,* e202–208.

Moon, C., Cooper, R.P., & Fifer, W.P. (1993). Two-day-olds prefer their native language. *Infant Behavior and Development, 16,* 495–500.

Moon, R.Y., Calabrese, T., & Aird, L. (2008). Reducing the risk of Sudden Infant Death Syndrome in child care and changing provider practices: Lessons learned from a demonstration project. *Pediatrics, 122,* 788–798.

Moon, R.Y., Kotch, L., & Aird, L. (2006). State child care regulations regarding infant sleep environment since the Healthy Child Care America-Back to Sleep Campaign. *Pediatrics, 118,* 73–83.

Moon, R.Y., Patel, K.M., & Shaefer, S.J. (2000). Sudden infant death syndrome in child care settings. *Pediatrics, 106,* 295–300.

Moore, C. (2008). The development of gaze following. *Child Development Perspectives, 2,* 66–70.

Moore, C., & Cocas, L.A. (2006). Perception precedes computation. *Developmental Psychology, 42,* 666–678.

Moore, G.A., & Calkins, S.D. (2004). Infants' vagal regulation in the still-face paradigm is related to dyadic coordination of mother-infant interaction. *Developmental Psychology, 40,* 1068–1080.

Moore, G.A., Cohn, J.F., & Campbell, S.B. (2001). Infant responses to maternal still-face at 6 months differentially predict externalizing and internalizing behaviors at 18 months. *Developmental Psychology, 37,* 706–714.

Moore, M.K., & Meltzoff, A.N. (2004). Object permanence after a 24-hr delay and leaving the locale of disappearance: The role of memory, space, and identity. *Developmental Psychology, 40,* 606–620.

Moran, G.F., & Vinovskis, M.A. (1985). The great care of godly parents: Early childhood in Puritan New England. In A.B. Smuts, & J.W. Hagen (Eds.), *History and research in child development* (pp. 24–37). *Monographs of the Society for Research in Child Development, 50*(4–5, Serial No. 211).

Mörelius, E., Theodorsson, E., & Nelson, N. (2009). Stress at three-month immunization: Parents' and infants' salivary cortisol response in relation to the use of pacifier and oral glucose. *European Journal of Pain, 13,* 202–208.

Morelli, G.A., Rogoff, B., Oppenheim, D., & Goldsmith, D. (1992). Cultural variation in infants' sleeping arrangements: Questions of independence. *Developmental Psychology, 28,* 604–613.

Morison, S.J., Ames, E.W., & Chisholm, K. (1995). The development of children adopted from Romanian orphanages. *Merrill-Palmer Quarterly, 41,* 411–430.

Morris, B.H., Oh, W., Tyson, J.E., Stevenson, D.K., Phelps, D.L., O'Shea, T.M., et al. (2008). Aggressive vs. conservative phototherapy for infants with extremely low birth weight. *New England Journal of Medicine, 359,* 1885–1896.

Morris, G., & Baker-Ward, L. (2007). Fragile but real: Children's capacity to use newly acquired words to convey preverbal memories. *Child Development, 78,* 448–458.

Morrissey, T.W. (2009). Multiple child-care arrangements and young children's behavioral outcomes. *Child Development, 80,* 59–76.

Mortensen, E.L., Michaelsen, K.F., Sanders, S.A., & Reinisch, J.M. (2002). The association between duration of breastfeeding and adult intelligence. *JAMA, 287,* 2365–2371.

Moses, L.J., Baldwin, D.A., Rosicky, J.G., & Tidball, G. (2001). Evidence for referential understanding in the emotions domain at twelve and eighteen months. *Child Development, 72,* 718–735.

Moss, W., Darmstadt, G.L., Marsh, D.R., Black, R.E., & Santosham, M. (2002). Research priorities for the reduction of perinatal and neonatal morbidity and mortality in developing country communities. *Journal of Perinatology, 22,* 484–495.

Moulson, M.C., Westerlund, A., Fox, N.A., Zeanah, C.H., & Nelson, C.A. (2009). The effects of early experience on face recognition: An event-related potential study of institutionalized children in Romania. *Child Development, 80,* 1039–1056.

Mouradian, L.E., & Als, H. (1994). The influence of neonatal intensive care unit caregiving practices on motor functioning of preterm infants. *The American Journal of Occupational Therapy, 48,* 527–533.

Mouradian, L.E., Als, H., & Coster, W.J. (2000). Neurobehavioral functioning of healthy preterm infants of varying gestational ages. *Developmental and Behavioral Pediatrics, 21*, 408–416.

Mouradian, W.E., Wehr, E., & Crall, J.J. (2000). Disparities in children's oral health and access to dental care. *JAMA, 284*, 2625–2631.

Muir, D., & Hains, S. (2004). The u-shaped developmental function for auditory localization. *Journal of Cognition and Development, 5*, 123–130.

Mulder, E., Robles de Medina, P., Huizink, A., Van den Bergh, B., Buitelaar, J., & Visser, G. (2002). Prenatal maternal stress: Effects on pregnancy and the (unborn) child. *Early Human Development, 70*, 3–14.

Müller, U., & Giesbrecht, G. (2008). Methodological and epistemological issues in the interpretation of infant cognitive development. *Child Development, 79*, 1654–1658.

Mulligan, G., Brimhall, D., & West, J. (2005). *Child care and early education arrangements of infants, toddlers, and preschoolers: 2001, NCES 2006–039.* Washington, DC: National Center for Education Statistics.

Mumme, D.L., & Fernald, A. (2003). The infant as onlooker: Learning from emotional reactions observed in a television scenario. *Child Development, 74*, 221–237.

Mumme, D.L., Fernald, A., & Herrera, C. (1996). Infants' responses to facial and vocal emotional signals in a social referencing paradigm. *Child Development, 67*, 3219–3237.

Munakata, Y. (1998). Infant perseveration and implications for object permanence theories: A PDP model of the AB task. *Developmental Science, 1*, 161–184.

Mundy, P., Sigman, M., Ungerer, J., & Sherman, T. (1986). Defining the social deficits in autism: The contribution of nonverbal communication measures. *Journal of Child Psychology and Psychiatry, 27*, 657–669.

Murray, L., & Trevarthen, C. (1985). Emotional regulation of interactions between two-month-olds and their mothers. In T.M. Field, & N.A. Fox (Eds.), *Social perception in infants* (pp. 177–197). Norwood, NJ: Ablex.

Murray-Close, D., & Ostrov, J.M. (2009). A longitudinal study of forms and functions of aggressive behavior in early childhood. *Child Development, 80*, 828–842.

NACCRRA. (2003). Issue paper: Reauthorization of the Individuals with Disabilities Education Act. Retrieved August 29, 2005, from http://www.naccrra.org/policy

NACCRRA. (2009). *Parents and the high price of child care: 2009 update.* Retrieved December 22, 2009, from http://issuu.comm/naccrra/docs.

Nachmias, M., Gunnar, M., Mangelsdorf, S., Parritz, R.H., & Buss, K. (1996). Behavioral inhibition and stress reactivity: The moderating role of attachment security. *Child Development, 67*, 508–522.

NAEYC. (1995). *NAEYC position statement. Where we stand: Many languages, many cultures: Respecting and responding to diversity.* Adapted from *Responding to linguistic and cultural diversity: Recommendations for effective early childhood education.* Washington, DC: NAEYC.

NAEYC. (1996). *NAEYC position statement on technology and young children: Ages 3 through 8.* Washington, DC: NAEYC.

NAEYC. (2002). NAEYC accreditation. Retrieved on October 23, 2002, from http://www.naeyc.org

Naigles, L.G. (1990). Children use syntax to learn verb meanings. *Journal of Child Language, 17*, 357–374.

Naigles, L.G. (1996). The use of multiple frames in verb learning via syntactic bootstrapping. *Cognition, 58*, 221–251.

Naigles, L.R., Hoff, E., & Vear, D. (2009). Flexibility in early verb use: Evidence from a multiple-n diary study. *Monographs of the Society for Research in Child Development, 74*(2, Serial No. 293). Boston: Wiley-Blackwell.

Namy, L., Acredolo, L.P., & Goodwyn, S.W. (2000). Verbal labels and gestural routines in parental communication with young children. *Journal of Nonverbal Behavior, 24*, 63–79.

Nanez, J. (1988). Perception of impending collision in 3- to 6-week-old infants. *Infant Behavior and Development, 11*, 447–463.

Nanez, J., & Yonas, A. (1994). Effects of luminance and texture motion on infant defensive reactions to optical collision. *Infant Behavior and Development, 17*, 165–174.

Napier, K., & Meister, K. (2000). *Growing healthy kids: A parents' guide to infant and child nutrition.* New York: American Council on Science and Health.

National Association of Childbearing Centers. (2002). The birth center concept. Retrieved January 12, 2002, from http://www.birthcenters.org

National Association for Sport and Physical Education. (2002). *Active start guidelines for exercise for infants and toddlers.* Reston, VA: NASPE.

National Center for Biotechnology Information. (2002). Genes and disease. Retrieved January 12, 2002, from http://www.ncbi.nlm.nih.gov/disease/

National Center for Early Development and Learning (1997). Quality in child care centers, *Briefs, 1*(1). Chapel Hill, NC: Frank Porter Graham Child Development Center.

National Center for Education in Maternal and Child Health. (2002). *Bright futures in practice: Nutrition pocket guide.* Washington, DC: Georgetown University.

National Center for Education Statistics (NCES). (2004). Participation in undergraduate education. Washington, DC: Author. Retrieved November 1, 2005, from http://nces.gov

National Center for Health Statistics. (2001). Births/natality. *National Vital Statistics Reports, 50(5).* Hyattsville, MD.

National Center for Health Statistics. (2002). *Health, United States, 2002. With chartbook on trends in the health of Americans.* Hyattsville, MD.

National Center for Health Statistics. (2005). *Health, United States, 2005. With chartbook on trends in the health of Americans.* Hyattsville, MD.

National Center for Health Statistics. (2009). *Health, United States, 2008, With Chartbook.* Hyattsville, MD: Author. Retrieved July 19, 2009, from http://www.cdc.gov/nchs/hus.htm.

National Center on Birth Defects and Developmental Disabilities. (2007). *Annual Early Hearing Detection and Intervention (EHDI) program data.* Atlanta, GA: National Center on Birth Defects and Developmental Disabilities, Centers for Disease Control and Prevention. Retrieved July 26, 2009, from http://www.cdc.gov/ncbddd/ehdi/data.htm.

National Child Care Information Center. (1999). Inclusive child care—Quality child care for all children. *Child Care Bulletin* (Jan./Feb., Issue 21). Retrieved September 1, 2005, from http://www.nccic.org/ccb/issue21.html

National Fatherhood Initiative. (2009). *Fatherhood statistics.* Retrieved December 4, 2009, from http://www.fatherhood.gov/statistics/index.cfm#father.

NICHD (National Institute of Child Health and Human Development) Early Child Care Research Network. (1997a). The effects of infant child care on infant-mother attachment security: Results of the NICHD Study of Early Child Care. *Child Development, 68,* 860–879.

NICHD (National Institute of Child Health and Human Development) Early Child Care Research Network. (1997b). Child care in the first year of life. *Merrill-Palmer Quarterly, 43,* 340–360.

NICHD (National Institute of Child Health and Human Development) Early Child Care Research Network. (1998). Early child care and self-control, compliance and problem behavior at twenty-four and thirty-six months. *Child Development, 69,* 1145–1170.

NICHD (National Institute of Child Health and Human Development) Early Child Care Research Network. (2000). The relation of child care to cognitive and language development. *Child Development, 71,* 960–980.

NICHD (National Institute of Child Health and Human Development) Early Child Care Research Network. (2003). Does amount of time spent in child care predict socioemotional adjustment during the transition to kindergarten? *Child Development, 74,* 976–1005.

NICHD (National Institute of Child Health and Human Development) Early Child Care Research Network. (2004). Trajectories of physical aggression from toddlerhood to middle childhood. *Monographs of the Society for Research in Child Development, 69*(4, Serial No. 278).

NICHD (National Institute of Child Health and Human Development) Early Child Care Research Network. (2005). *Child care and child development: Results from the NICHD Study of Early Child Care and Youth Development.* New York: Guilford Press.

NICHD (National Institute of Child Health and Human Development) Early Child Care Research Network & Duncan, G.J. (2003). Modeling the impacts of child care quality on children's preschool cognitive development. *Child Development, 74,* 1454–1475.

National Institute of Neurological Disorders and Stroke (2001). NINDS spina bifida information. Retrieved December 10, 2005, from http://www.ninds.nih.gov/disorders/spina_bifida/spina_bifida.htm

National Institute on Drug Abuse. (2002). Heroin: Abuse and addiction. Retrieved August 26, 2004, from http://www.nida.nih.gov/ResearchReports/heroin/heroin4.html

National Institute on Occupational Safety and Health. (2002). The effects of workplace hazards on male reproductive health. *DHHS (NIOSH) Publication No. 96–132.* Washington, DC: National Institute on Occupational Safety and Health.

National Organization on Fetal Alcohol Syndrome. (2006). What is Fetal Alcohol Syndrome? Retrieved October 6, 2009, from http://www.nofas.org/resource/factsheet.aspx

National Partnership for Women & Families. (2009). *2009 state action on paid family and medical leave.* Retrieved December 22, 2009, from http://www.nationalpartnership.org.

Nazzi, T., Jusczyk, P. W., & Johnson, E. K. (2000). Language discrimination by English-learning 5-month-olds: Effects of rhythm and familiarity. *Journal of Memory & Language, 43,* 1–19.

Neal, D.O., & Lindeke, L.L. (2008). Music as a nursing intervention for preterm infants in the NICU. *Neonatal Network, 27,* 319–327.

Neil, P.A., Chee-Ruiter, C., Scheier, C., Lewkowicz, D.J., & Shimojo, S. (2006). Development of multisensory spatial integration and perception in humans. *Developmental Science, 9,* 454–464.

Nelson, C.A. (1994). Neural correlates of recognition memory in the first postnatal year. In G. Dawson, & K. Fischer (Eds.), *Human behavior and the developing brain* (pp. 269–313). New York: Guilford Press.

Nelson, C.A. (1995). The ontogeny of human memory: A cognitive neuroscience perspective. *Developmental Psychology, 31,* 723–738.

Nelson, C.A. (2001). The development of neural bases of face recognition. *Infant and Child Development, 10,* 3–18.

Nelson, C.A. (2007). A neurobiological perspective on early human deprivation. *Child Development Perspectives, 1,* 13–18.

Nelson, C.A., & Bloom, F.E. (1997). Child development and neuroscience. *Child Development, 68,* 970–987.

Nelson, C.A., & Horowitz, F.D. (1983). The perception of facial expressions and stimulus motion by 2- and 5-month-old infants using holographic stimuli. *Child Development, 56,* 868–877.

Nelson, C.A., & Luciana, M. (Eds.). (2008). *Handbook of developmental cognitive neuroscience* (2nd ed.). Cambridge, MA: MIT Press.

Nelson, C.A., & Monk, C.S. (2001). The use of event-related potentials in the study of cognitive development. In C.A. Nelson, & M. Luciana (Eds.), *Handbook of developmental cognitive neuroscience* (pp. 125–136). Cambridge, MA: MIT Press.

Nelson, C.A., Thomas, K.M., & de Haan, M. (2006). Neural bases of cognitive development. In W. Damon, & R. Lerner (Eds.) & D. Kuhn, & R. Siegler (Vol. Eds.), *Handbook of child psychology: Vol. 2. Cognition, perception, and language* (6th ed., pp. 3–57). New York: Wiley.

Nelson, C.A., & Webb, S.J. (2002). A cognitive neuroscience perspective on early memory development. In M. de Haan, & M.H. Johnson (Eds.), *The cognitive neuroscience of development* (pp. 99–125). London: Psychology Press.

Nelson, K., Hampson, J., & Shaw, L. (1993). Nouns in early lexicons: Evidence, explanations and implications. *Journal of Child Language, 20,* 61–84.

Nelson, P.B., Adamson, L.B., & Bakeman, R. (2008). Toddlers' joint engagement experience facilitates preschoolers' acquisition of theory of mind. *Developmental Science, 11,* 840–845.

Newcombe, N., & Huttenlocher, J. (2006). Development of spatial cognition. In W. Damon, & R. Lerner (Eds.) & D. Kuhn, & R. Siegler (Vol. Eds.), *Handbook of child psychology: Vol. 2. Cognition, perception, and language* (6th ed., pp. 734–776). New York: Wiley.

Newcombe, N., Huttenlocher, J., Drummey, A.B., & Wiley, J.G. (1998). The development of spatial location coding: Place learning and dead reckoning in the second and third years. *Cognitive Development, 13,* 185–201.

Newcombe, N.S., Sluzenski, J., & Huttenlocher, J. (2005). Preexisting knowledge versus on-line learning: What do young infants really know about spatial location? *Psychological Science, 16,* 222–227.

Nguyen, S., Kushel, C., & Teele, R. (2002). Water birth: A near-drowning experience. *Pediatrics, 110,* 411–413.

Nicklaus, S. (2006). Workshop summary: Understanding the development of food preferences early in life: Focus on follow-up studies. *Food Quality and Preference, 17,* 635–639.

NIH/NIMH Human Genetics Initiative (2005). *Identifying autism susceptibility genes.* Retrieved October 18, 2005, from http://www.nimh.nih.gov/press/autismgenetics.cfm

Nielsen, M., Suddendorf, T., & Slaughter, V. (2006). Mirror self-recognition beyond the face. *Child Development, 77,* 176–185.

Nikodem, V.C. (2004). Immersion in water in pregnancy, labour and childbirth. In *The Cochrane Library* (Issue 1). Chichester, UK: Wiley.

Nishitani, S., Miyamura, T., Tagawa, M., Sumi, M., Takase, R., Doi, H., et al. (2009). The calming effect of a maternal breast milk odor on the human newborn infant. *Neuroscience Research, 63,* 66–71.

Norris, S.A., Griffiths, P., Pettifor, J.M., Dunger, D.B., & Cameron, N. (2009). Implications of adopting the WHO 2006 Child Growth Standards: Case study from urban South Africa, the Birth to Twenty cohort, *Annals of Human Biology, 36,* 21–27.

Noymer, A. (2002). The March of Dimes. *American Journal of Public Health, 92*(2), 158.

Nsamenang, B.A. (1992). Perceptions of parenting among the Nso of Cameroon. *Father-child relations: Cultural and biosocial contexts* (pp. 321–344). New York: de Gruyter.

Nugent, J.K., Petrauskas, B., & Brazelton, T.B. (Eds.). (2009). *The newborn as a person: Enabling healthy infant development worldwide.* New York: John Wiley & Sons.

Nwokah, E., & Fogel, A. (1993). Laughter in mother-infant emotional communication. *Humor: International Journal of Humor Research, 6,* 137–161.

Nwokah, E.E., Hsu, H., Davies, P., & Fogel, A. (1999). The integration of laughter and speech in vocal communication: A dynamic systems perspective. *Journal of Speech and Hearing Research, 42,* 880–894.

Nyqvist, K.H., & Kylberg, E. (2008). Application of the Baby Friendly Hospital Initiative to neonatal care: Suggestions by Swedish mothers of very preterm infants. *Journal of Human Lactation, 24,* 252–263.

O'Brien, M. (2004). Social science and public policy perspectives on fatherhood in the European Union. In M.E. Lamb (Ed.), *The role of the father in child development* (4th ed., pp. 121–145). New York: Wiley.

O'Brien, M.A., Prosser, L.A., Paradise, J.L., Ray, G.T., Kulldorff, M., Kurs-Lasky, M., et al. (2009). New vaccines against otitis media: Projected benefits and cost-effectiveness. *Pediatrics, 123,* 1452–1463.

O'Connell, J.M., Dibley, M.J., Sierra, J., Wallace, B., Marks, J.S., & Yip, R. (1989). Growth of vegetarian children: The farm study. *Pediatrics, 84,* 475–481.

O'Connell, M. (1990). Maternity leave arrangements: 1961–1985. In *Work and Family Patterns of American Women. Current Population Reports,* Special Studies series P–23, no. 165. Washington, DC: U.S. Census Bureau.

O'Neill, C., Trainor, L.J., & Trehub, S.E. (2001). Infants' responsiveness to fathers' singing. *Music Perception, 18,* 409–425.

O'Neill, M., Bard, K.A., Linnell, M.,& Fluck, M. (2005). Maternal gestures with 20-month-old infants in two contexts. *Developmental Science, 8,* 352–359.

Oakes, L.M. (2009). The "Humpty Dumpty Problem" in the study of early cognitive development: Putting the infant back together again. *Perspectives on Psychological Science, 4,* 352–358.

Oakes, L.M., Coppage, D.J., & Dingel, A. (1997). By land or by sea: The role of perceptual similarity in infants' categorization of animals. *Developmental Psychology, 33,* 396–407.

Oakes, L.M., & Madole, K.L. (2000). The future of infant categorization research: A process-oriented approach. *Child Development, 71,* 119–126.

OECD. (2001). *Starting strong: Early childhood education and care.* Paris, France: OECD.

OECD. (2009). *Key characteristics of parental leave systems, PF7.* Retrieved December 22, 2009, from http://www.oecd.org/

Office of Refugee Resettlement. (2007). Fiscal year 2007 refugee arrivals. U.S. Department of Health and Human Services, Administration for Children & Families. Retrieved June 3, 2009, from http://www.acf.hhs.gov/programs/orr/data/fy2007RA.htm

Offit, P.A., Quarles, J., Gerber, M.A., Hackett, C.J., Marcuse, E.K., Kollman, T.R., Gellin, B.G., & Landry, S. (2002). Addressing parents' concerns: Do multiple vaccines overwhelm or weaken the infant's immune system? *Pediatrics, 109,* 124–129.

Ogden, C.L., Kuczmarski, R.J., Flegal, K.M., Mei, Z., Guo, S., Wei, R., et al. (2002). Centers for Disease Control and Prevention 2000 Growth Charts for the United States: Improvements to the 1977 National Center for Health Statistics version. *Pediatrics, 109,* 45–60.

Oken, E., Wright, R.O., Kleinman, K.P., Bellinger, D., Amarasiriwardena, C.J., et al. (2005). Maternal fish consumption, hair mercury, and infant cognition in a U.S. cohort. *Environmental Health Perspectives, 113,* 1376–1380.

Olds, D.L., Henderson, C.R., Klitzman, H.J., Eckenrode, J.J., Cole, R.E., & Tatelbaum, R.C. (1999). Prenatal and infancy home visitation by nurses: Recent findings. *The Future of Children, 9,* 44–65.

Oller, D.K., & Eilers, R.E. (1988). The role of audition in infant babbling. *Child Development, 59,* 441–449.

Olson, D., Sikka, R.S., Hayman, J., Novak, M., & Stavig, C. (2009). Exercise in pregnancy. *Current Sports Medicine Reports, 8,* 147–153.

Onishi, K.H., Baillargeon, R., & Leslie, A.M. (2007). 15-month-old infants detect violations in pretend scenarios. *Acta Psychologica, 124,* 106–128.

Onunaku, N. (2005). *Improving maternal and infant mental health: Focus on maternal depression.* Los Angeles, CA: National Center for Infant Early Childhood Health Policy.

Opdal, S.H., & Rognum, T.O. (2004). The Sudden Infant Death Syndrome gene: Does it exist? *Pediatrics, 114,* e506–e512.

Ophir, E., Strulov, A., Solt, I., Michlin, R., Buryanov, I., & Bornstein, J. (2008). Delivery mode and maternal rehospitalization. *Archives of Gynecology and Obstetrics, 277,* 401–404.

Oshima-Takane, Y., Goodz, E., & Derevensky, J.L. (1996). Birth order effects on early language development: Do secondborn children learn from overheard speech? *Child Development, 67,* 621–634.

Oster, H., Hegley, D., & Nagel, L. (1992). Adult judgments and fine-grained analysis of infant facial expressions: Testing the validity of a priori coding formulas. *Developmental Psychology, 28,* 1115–1131.

Osterling, J., & Dawson, G. (1994). Early recognition of children with autism: A study of first birthday home videotapes. *Journal of Autism & Developmental Disorders, 24,* 247–257.

Ostrov, J.M., & Crick, N.R. (2007). Forms and functions of aggression during early childhood: A short-term longitudinal study. *School Psychology Review, 36,* 22–43.

Osypuk, T.L., & Acevedo-Garcia, D. (2008). Are racial disparities in preterm birth larger in hypersegregated areas? *American Journal of Epidemiology, 167,* 1295–1304.

Otsuka, Y., Konishi, Y., Kanazawa, S., Yamaguchi, M.K., Abdi, H., & O'Toole, A.J. (2009). Recognition of moving and static faces by young infants. *Child Development, 80,* 1259–1271.

Ou, Y.S., & McAdoo, H.P. (1999). The ethnic socialization of Chinese American children. In H.P. McAdoo (Ed.), *Family ethnicity: Strength in diversity* (2nd ed., pp. 252–276). Thousand Oaks, CA: Sage.

Over, H., & Carpenter, M. (2009). Eighteen-month-old infants show increased helping following priming with affiliation. *Psychological Science, 20,* 1189–1193.

Overpeck, M.D., Brenner, R.A., Trumble, A.C., Smith, G.S.. MacDorman, M.F., & Berendes, H.W. (1999). Infant injury deaths with unknown intent: What else do we know? *Injury Prevention, 5,* 272–275.

Owen, C.G., Whincup, P.H., Odoki, K., Gilg, J.A., & Cook, D.G. (2002). Infant feeding and blood cholesterol: A study in adolescents and a systematic review. *Pediatrics, 110,* 597–608.

Owens, Jr. R.E., (1984). *Language development: An introduction.* Columbus, OH: Charles E. Merrill Publishing.

Özcaliskan, S., & Goldin-Meadow, S. (2005a). Do parents lead their children by the hand? *Journal of Child Language, 32,* 481–505.

Özcaliskan, S., & Goldin-Meadow, S. (2005b). Gesture is at the cutting edge of early language development. *Cognition, 96,* B101–B113.

Palmer, C.F. (1989). The discriminating nature of infants' exploratory actions. *Developmental Psychology, 25,* 885–893.

Pandis, G.K., Papageorghiou, A.T., Ramanathan, V.G., Thompson, M.O., & Nicolaides, K.H. (2001). Preinduction sonographic measurement of cervical length in the prediction of successful induction of labor. *Ultrasound in Obstetrics and Gynecology, 18,* 623–628.

Pang, J.W.Y., Heffelfinger, J.D., Huang, G.J., Benedetti, T.J., & Weiss, N.S. (2002). Outcomes of planned home births in Washington state: 1989–1996. *Obstetrics & Gynecology, 100,* 253–259.

Pantoja, A.P.F., Nelson-Goens, G.C., & Fogel, A. (2001). A dynamical systems approach to the study of early emotional development in the context of mother-infant communication (pp. 901–920). In A.F. Kalverboer, & A. Gramsbergen (Eds.), *Brain and behavior in human development.* Dordrecht, The Netherlands: Kluwer Academic Publishers.

Papousek, H. (1996). Musicality in infancy research: Biological and cultural origins of early musicality. In I. Deliege, & J. Sloboda (Eds.), *Musical beginnings: Origins and development of musical competence* (pp. 37–87). Oxford: Oxford University Press.

Parise, E., Cleveland, A., Costabile, A., & Striano, T. (2007). Influence of vocal cues on learning about objects in joint attention contexts. *Infant Behavior & Development, 30,* 380–384.

Parish-Morris, J., Hennon, E.A., Hirsh-Pasek, K., Golinkoff, R.M., & Tager-Flusberg, H. (2007). Children with autism illuminate the role of social intention in word learning. *Child Development, 78,* 1265–1287.

Parke, R.D. (2002). Fathers and families. In M.H. Bornstein (Ed.), *Handbook of parenting: Vol. 3. Status and social conditions of parenting* (2nd ed., pp. 27–73). Mahwah, NJ: Erlbaum.

Parke, R.D., & Buriel, R. (2006). Socialization in the family: Ethnic and ecological perspectives. In W. Damon, & R. Lerner (Eds.) & N. Eisenberg (Vol. Ed.), *Handbook of child psychology: Vol. 3. Social, emotional, and personality development* (6th ed., pp. 429–504). New York: Wiley.

Parke, R.D., Dennis, J., Flyr, M.L., Morris, K.L., Killian, C., McDowell, D.J., et al. (2004). Fathering and children's peer relationships. In M.E. Lamb (Ed.), *The role of the father in child development* (4th ed., pp. 307–340). New York: Wiley.

Parker, K.J., Buckmaster, C.L., Sundlass, K., Schatzberg, A.F., & Lyons, D.M. (2006). Maternal mediation, stress inoculation, and the development of neuroendocrine stress resistance in primates. *Proceedings of the National Academy of Sciences, 103,* 3000–3005.

Parker, L., Pearce, M.S., Dickinson, H.O., Aitkin, M., & Craft, A.W. (1999). Stillbirths among offspring of male radiation workers at Sellafield nuclear reprocessing plant. *Lancet, 354,* 1407–1414.

Parker, S.W., Nelson, C.A., & The Bucharest Early Intervention Project Core Group. (2005). An event-related potential study of the impact of institutional rearing on face recognition. *Development and Psychopathology, 17,* 621–663.

Parmar, P., Harkness, S., & Super, C.M. (2008). Teacher or playmate? Asian immigrant an Euro-American parents' participation in their young children's daily activities. *Social Behavior and Personality: An International Journal, 36,* 163–176.

Pascalis, O., de Schonen, S., Morton, J., Dereulle, C., & Fabre-Grenet, M. (1995). Mother's face recognition by neonates: A replication and an extension. *Infant Behavior and Development, 18,* 79–85.

Pater, J., Stager, C.L., & Werker, J.F. (2004). The perceptual acquisition of phonological contrast. *Language, 80*, 384–402.

Paterson, S.J., Heim, Friedman, J.T., Choudhury, N., & Benasich, A.A. (2006). Development of structure and function in the infant brain: Implications for cognition, language and social behaviour. *Neuroscience and Biobehavioral Reviews, 30*, 1087–1105.

Pathak, S., & Lees, C.C. (2009). An update: Ultrasound structural fetal anomaly screening. *Archives of Disease in Childhood. Fetal and Neonatal Edition, 94*, F384–F390.

Pauen, S. (2002). Evidence for knowledge-based category discrimination in infancy. *Child Development, 73*, 1016–1033.

Paulson, J., Dauber, S., & Leiferman, J. (2006). Individual and combined effects of postpartum depression in mothers and fathers on parenting behavior. *Pediatrics, 118*, 659–669.

Pawliuk, R., Westerman, K.A., Fabry, M.E., Payen, E., Tighe, R., Bouhassira, E.E., et al. (2001). Correction of sickle cell disease in transgenic mouse models by gene therapy. *Science, 294*, 2368–2371.

Pearson, B.Z., & Fernández, S.C. (1994). Patterns of interaction in the lexical growth in two languages of bilingual infants and toddlers. *Language Learning, 44*, 617–653.

Pediatric Eye Disease Investigator Group. (2006). A randomized trial to evaluate 2 hours of daily patching for strabismic and anisometropic amblyopia in children. *Ophthalmology, 113*, 904–912.

Peek, G.J., & Elliott, M.J. (2004). Fetal surgery for congenital diaphragmatic hernia. *Pediatrics, 113*, 1810–1811.

Pegg, J.E., Werker, J.F., & McLeod, P.J. (1992). Preference for infant-directed over adult-directed speech: Evidence from 7-week-old infants. *Infant Behavior and Development, 15*, 325–345.

Peisner-Feinberg, E.S., & Burchinal, M.R. (1997). Relations between preschool children's child-care experiences and concurrent development: The Cost, Quality, and Outcomes Study. *Merrill-Palmer Quarterly, 43*, 451–477.

Peisner-Feinberg, E.S., Burchinal, M.R., Clifford, R.M., Culkin, M.L., Howes, C., Kagan, S.L., et al. (2001). The relation of preschool child-care quality to children's cognitive and social developmental trajectories through second grade. *Child Development, 72*, 1534–1553.

Peláez-Nogueras, M., Field, T., Cigales, M., Gonzalez, A., & Clasky, S. (1995). Infants of depressed mothers show less "depressed"

behavior with their nursery teachers. *Infant Mental Health Journal, 15*, 358–367.

Peláez-Nogueras, M., Field, T.M., Hossain, Z., & Pickens, J. (1996). Depressed mothers' touching increases infants' positive affect and attention in still-face interactions. *Child Development, 67*, 1780–1792.

Pellegrini, A.D. (1998). Rough-and-tumble play from childhood through adolescence. In D.P. Fromberg, & D. Bergen (Eds.), *Play from birth to twelve and beyond: Contexts, perspectives, and meaning* (pp. 401–408). New York: Garland.

Pellegrini, A.D. (2009). Research and policy on children's play. *Child Development Perspectives, 3*, 131–136.

Pellegrini, A.D., & Smith, P.K. (1998). Physical activity play: The nature and function of a neglected aspect of play. *Child Development, 69*, 577–598.

Pelucchi, B., Hay, J.F., & Saffran, J.R. (2009). Statistical learning in a natural language by 8-month-old infants. *Child Developmet, 80*, 674–685.

Perera, F.P., Rauh, V., Tsai, W.Y., Kinney, P., Camman, D., Barr, D.B., et al. (2002). Effects of transplacental exposure to environmental pollutants on birth outcomes in a multiethnic population. *Environmntal Health Perspectives, 111*, 201–205.

Perera, F.P., Rauh, V., Whyatt, R.M., Tsai, W.Y., Bernert, J.T., Andrews, H., et al. (2004). Molecular evidence of an interaction between prenatal environmental exposures and birth outcomes in a multiethnic population. *Environmental Health Perspectives, 112*, 626–630.

Perera, F.P., Tang, D., Tu, Y.H., Cruz, L.A., Borjas, M., Bernert, T., et al. (2004). Biomarkers in maternal and newborn blood indicate heightened fetal susceptibility to procarcinogenic DNA damage. *Environmental Health Perspectives, 112*, 1133–1136.

Perry, B.D., & Pollard, R. (1998). Homeostasis, stress, trauma, and adaptation: A neurodevelopmental view of childhood trauma. *Child and Adolescent Psychiatric Clinics of North America, 7*, 33–51.

Persing, J., James, H., Swanson, J., Kattwinkel, J., & Committee on Practice and Ambulatory Medicine; Section on Plastic Surgery; and Section on Neurological Surgery. (2003). Prevention and management of positional skull deformities in infants. *Pediatrics, 112*, 199–202.

Pérusse, D. (2003). New maternity and parental benefits. *Perspectives on Labour and Income, 4*(3), 12–15, Statistics Canada, Cat. No. 75–001-XIE.

Pesonen, A.K., Räikkönen, K., Keskivaara, P., & Keltikangas-Järvinen, L. (2002). Difficult temperament in childhood and adulthood: Continuity from maternal perceptions to self-ratings over 17 years. *Personality and Individual Differences, 34,* 19–31.

Peters, J.W.B., Koot, H.M., Grunau, R.E., de Boer, J., van Druenen, M.J., Tibboel, D., et al. (2003). Neonatal facial coding system for assessing postoperative pain in infants: Item reduction is valid and feasible. *The Clinical Journal of Pain, 19,* 353–363.

Peterson, C.C., Wellman, H.M., & Liu, D. (2005). Steps in theory of mind development for children with autism and deafness. *Child Development, 76,* 502–517.

Peterson, S., Jones, L., & McGinley, K.A. (2008). *Early learning guidelines for infants and toddlers: Recommendations to states.* Washington, DC: Zero to Three.

Petitto, L.A. (2007). Cortical images of early language and phonological development using near infrared spectroscopy. In A.M. Battro, K.W. Fischer, & P.J. Léna (Eds.), *The educated brain: Essays in neuroeducation.* Cambridge, MA: Haravard University Press.

Petitto, L.A., Holowka, S., Sergio, L.E., Levy, B., & Ostry, D.J. (2004). Baby hands that move to the rhythm of language: Hearing babies acquiring sign language babble silently on the hands. *Cognition, 93,* 43–73.

Petitto, L.A., Holowka, S., Sergio, & Ostry, D.J. (2001). Language rhythms in baby hand movements: Hearing babies born to deaf parents babble silently with their hands. *Nature, 413,* 35–36.

Petitto, L.A., Katerelos, M., Levy, B.G., Gauna, K., Tétreault, K., & Ferraro, V. (2001). Bilingual signed and spoken language acquisition from birth: Implications for the mechanisms underlying early bilingual language acquisition. *Journal of Child Language, 28,* 453–496.

Petitto, L.A., & Kovelman, I. (2003). The bilingual paradox: How signing-speaking bilingual children help us to resolve it and teach us about the brain's mechanisms underlying all language acquisition. *Learning Languages, 8,* 5–18.

Petitto, L.A., & Marentette, P. (1991). Babbling in the manual mode: Evidence for the ontogeny of language. *Science, 251,* 1493–1496.

Petitto, L.A., Zatorre, R.J., Gauna, K., Nikelski, E.J., Dostie, D., & Evans, A.C. (2000). Speech-like cerebral activity in profoundly deaf people processing signed languages: Implications for the neural basis of human language. *Proceedings of the National Academy of Sciences, 97,* 13961–13966.

Petrova, A., Gnedko, T., Maistrova, I., Zafranskaya, M., & Dainiak, N. (1997). Morbidity in a large cohort study of children born to mothers exposed to radiation from Chernobyl. *Stem Cells, 15*(Suppl. 2), 141–150.

Petterson, S., & Albers, A.B. (2001). Effects of poverty and maternal depression on early child development. *Child Development, 72,* 1794–1813.

Phipps, M.G., Blume, J.D., & DeMonner, S.M. (2002). Young maternal age associated with increased risk of postnatal death. *Obstetrics and Gynecology, 100,* 481–486.

Piaget, J. (1936/1952). *The origins of intelligence in children.* New York: Norton.

Piaget, J. (1937/1971). *The construction of reality in the child.* New York: Ballantine.

Piaget, J. (1946/1962). *Play, dreams and imitation in childhood.* New York: Norton.

Piaget, J. (1954). *The construction of reality in the child.* New York: Basic Books.

Pianta, R.C., & Rimm-Kaufmann, S. (2006). The social ecology of the transition to school: Classrooms, families, and children. In K. McCarthy, & D. Phillips (Eds.), *Handbook of early child development* (pp. 490–507). Oxford, UK: Blackwell.

Pick, A.D., Gross, D., Heinrichs, M., Love, M., & Palmer, C. (1994). Development of perception of the unity of musical events. *Cognitive Development, 9,* 355–375.

Pierroutsakos, S.L., & Troseth, G.L. (2003). Video verité: Infants' manual investigation of objects on video. *Infant Behavior & Development, 26,* 183–199.

Pikwer, M., Bergström, U., Nilsson, J.-Å., Jacobsson, L., Berglund, G., & Turesson, C. (2009). Breast feeding, but not use of oral contraceptives, is associated with a reduced risk of rheumatoid arthritis. *Annals of the Rheumatic Diseases, 68,* 526–530.

Pilu, G., & Hobbins, J.C. (2002). Sonography of fetal cerebrospinal anomalies. *Prenatal Diagnosis, 22,* 321–330.

Pinheiro, J.M.B. (2009). The Apgar cycle: A new view of a familiar scoring system. *Archives of Disease in Childhood. Fetal and Neonatal Edition, 94,* F70–F72.

Pinker, S. (1994). *The language instinct: How the mind creates langauge.* New York: William Morrow.

Pipp, S., Fischer, K.W., & Jennings, S. (1987). Acquisition of self- and mother knowledge in infancy. *Developmental Psychology, 23,* 86–96.

Pleck, J.H. (1997). Paternal involvement: Levels, sources, and consequences. In M.E. Lamb (Ed.), *The role of the father in child development* (pp. 66–103). New York: Wiley.

Pleck, J.H., & Masciadrelli, B.P. (2004). Paternal involvement by U.S. residential fathers: Levels, sources, and consequences. In M.E. Lamb (Ed.), *The role of the father in child development* (4th ed., pp. 272–306). New York: Wiley.

Poehling, K.A., Szilagyi, P.G., Grijalva, C.G., Martin, S.W., LaFleur, B., Mitchel, E., et al. (2007). Reduction of frequent otitis media and pressure-equalizing tube insertions in children after introduction of pneumococcal conjugate vaccine. *Pediatrics, 119,* 707–715.

Polka, L., & Bohn, O.S. (1996). Cross-language comparison of vowel perception in English-learning and German-learning infants. *Journal of the Acoustical Society of America, 100,* 577–592.

Polka, L., & Werker, J. F. (1994). Developmental changes in perception of non-native vowel contrasts. *Journal of Experimental Psychology: Human Perception and Performance, 20,* 421–435.

Pollack, L.A. (1983). *Forgotten children: Parent-child relations from 1500 to 1900.* New York: Cambridge University Press.

Pollak, S.D. (2008). Mechanisms linking early experience and the emergence of emotions: Illustrations from the study of maltreated children. *Current Directions in Psychological Science, 17,* 370–375.

Pollak, S.D., Cicchetti, D., Hornung, K., & Reed, A. (2000). Recognizing emotion in faces: Developmental effects of child abuse and neglect. *Developmental Psychology, 36,* 679–688.

Pollitt, E., Golub, M., Gorman, K., Gratham-McGregor, S., Levitsky, D., Schürch, B., et al. (1996). A reconceptualization of the effects of undernutrition on children's biological, psychosocial, and behavioral development. *Social Policy Report, 10*(5), 1–28.

Pollitt, E., Gorman, K.S., Engle, P.L., Martorell, R., & Rivera, J. (1993). Early supplementary feeding and cognition. *Monographs of the Society for Research in Child Development, 58*(7, Serial No. 235).

Ponce-Rivera, L.N.M., Blanco-Montero, A., Reyes-Vazquez, H., Lopez-Enriquez, C., & Fuentes-Lugo, D. (2008). Assessment of differences between the New World Health Organization Child-Growth Standards and the Centers for Disease Control and Prevention 2000 growth charts in Latin American children: Which reference should we use? *Pediatrics, 121,* S114.

Population Reference Bureau/Child Trends. (2002). *KIDS COUNT international data sheet summary.* Washington, DC: PRB/CT.

Porges, S.W., Doussard-Roosevelt, J.A., & Maiti, A.K. (1994). Vagal tone and the physiological regulation of emotion. In N.A. Fox (ed). Emotion Regulation: Behavioral and Biological Considerations. *Monograph of the Society for Research in Child Development, 59* (2–3, Serial No. 240), 167–186.

Porter, R.H., & Winberg, J. (1999). Unique salience of maternal breast odors for newborn infants. *Neuroscience and Biobehavioral Reviews, 23,* 439–449.

Posada, G., Carbonell, O.A., Alzate, G., & Plata, S.J. (2004). Through Colombian lenses: Ethnographic and conventional analyses of maternal care and their associations with secure base behavior. *Developmental Psychology, 40,* 508–518.

Posada, G., Gao, Y, Posada, R., Tascon, M., Schoelmerich, A., Sagi, A., et al. (1995). The secure-base phenomenon across cultures: Children's behavior, mothers' preferences, and experts' concepts. In E. Waters, B.E. Vaughn, G. Posada, & K. Kondo-Ikemura (Eds.), Caregiving, cultural, and cognitive perspectives on secure-base behavior and working models: New growing points in attachment theory and research. *Monographs of the Society for Research in Child Development, 60* (Serial No. 244), 27–48.

Poulin-Dubois, D., Demke, T.L., & Olineck, K.M. (2007). The inquisitive eye: Infants' implicit understanding that looking leads to knowing. In R. Flom, K. Lee, & D. Muir (Eds.), *Gaze-following: Its development and significance* (pp. 263–281). Mahwah, NJ: Lawrence Erlbaum Associates.

Powell, D.R. (2006). Families and early childhood interventions. In W. Damon, & R. Lerner (Eds.) & K.A. Renninger, & I.E. Sigel (Vol. Eds.), *Handbook of child psychology: Vol. 4. Child psychology in practice* (6th ed., pp. 548–591). New York: Wiley.

Powls, A., Botting, N., Cooke, R.W.I., Stephenson, G., & Marlow, N. (1997). Visual impairment in very low birthweight children. *Archives of Disease in Childhood. Fetal and Neonatal Edition, 76,* F82–F87.

Preissler, M.A. (2006). Play and autism: Symbolic understanding. In D.G. Singer, R.M. Golinkoff, & K. Hirsh-Pasek (Eds.), *Play = learning: How play motivates and enhances children's cognitive and social-emotional growth* (pp. 231–250). New York: Oxford University Press.

Pretorius, E., Naudé, H., & Van Vuuren, C.J. (2002). Can cultural behavior have a negative impact on the development of visual integration pathways? *Early Child Development and Care, 172,* 173–181.

Price, C.V.G. (1979). A model for the implementation of a Suzuki violin program for the day-care center environment: An evaluation of its effectiveness and impact. *Dissertation Abstracts International, 40,* 5357A.

Proctor, B.D., & Dalaker, J. (2003). Poverty in the United States: 2002. *Current Population Reports, P60–222.* Washington, DC: U.S. Census Bureau.

Productivity Commission. (2009). *Paid parental leave: Support for parents with newborn children, Report No. 47.* Canberra, Australia. Retrieved December 23, 2009, from http://www.pc.gov/au/projects/inquiry/parentalsupport/report

Pruden, S. M., Hirsh-Pasek, K., Golinkoff, R., & Hennon, E.A. (2006). The birth of words: Ten-month-olds learn words through perceptual salience. *Child Development, 77,* 266–280.

Pulverman, R., Golinkoff, R.M., Hirsh-Pasek, K., Sootsman Buresh, J. (2008). Manners matter: Infants' attention to manner and path in non-linguistic dynamic events. *Cognition, 108,* 825–830.

Putzar, L., Hötting, K., Rösler, F., & Röder, B. (2007). The development of visual feature binding processes after visual deprivation in early infancy. *Vision Research, 47,* 2616–2626.

Quine, W.V.O. (1960). *Word and object.* Cambridge, UK: Cambridge University Press.

Quinn, P.C. (2008). In defense of core competencies, quantitative change, and continuity. *Child Development, 79,* 1633–1638.

Quinn, P.C., & Bhatt, R.S. (2009). Transfer and scaffolding of perceptual grouping occurs across organizing principles in 3- to 7-month-old infants. *Psychological Science, 20,* 933–938.

Quinn, P.C., Doran, M.M., Reiss, J.E., & Hoffman, J.E. (2009). Time course of visual attention in infant categorization of cats versus dogs: Evidence for a head bias as revealed through eye tracking. *Child Development, 80,* 151–161.

Quinn, P.C., Eimas, P.D., & Rosenkranz, S.L. (1993). Evidence for representations of perceptually similar natural categories by 3-month-old and 4-month-old infants. *Perception, 22,* 463–475.

Rahn, S.L., & Burch, H.A. (2002). Paid maternal and parental leave legislation and primary prevention. *The Social Policy Journal, 1,* 75–86.

Raje, N., & Anderson, K. (1999). Thalidomide: A revival story. *New England Journal of Medicine, 341,* 1606–1609.

Rakison, D.H., & Poulin-Dubois, D. (2002). You go this way and I'll go that way: Developmental changes in infants' detection of correlations among static and dynamic features in motion events. *Child Development, 73,* 682–699.

Ramchandani, P.G., O'Connor, T.G., Evans, J., Heron, J., Murray, L., & Stein. A. (2008). The effects of pre- and postnatal depression in fathers: A natural experiment comparing the effects of exposure to depression on offspring. *Journal of Child Psychology and Psychiatry, 49,*1069–1078.

Ramchandani, P., & Psychogiou, L. (2009). Paternal psychiatric disorders and children's psychosocial development. *Lancet, 374,* 646–653.

Ramchandani, P., Stein, A., Evans, J., O'Connor, T.G., & ALSPAC Study Team. (2005). Paternal depression in the postnatal period and child development: A prospective population study. *Lancet, 365,* 2201–2205.

Ramchandani, P.G., Stein, A., O'Connor, T.G., Heron, J., Murray, L., & Evans, J. (2008). Depression in men in the postnatal period and later child psycho-pathology: A population cohort study. *Journal of the American Academy of Child and Adolescent Psychiatry, 47,* 390–398.

Ramadhani, T., Short, V., Canfield, M.A., Waller, D.K., Correa, A., Royle, M., et al. (2009). Are birth defects among Hispanics related to maternal nativity or number of years lived in the United States? *Birth Defects Research. Part A, Clinical and Molecular Teratology, 85,* 755–763.

Ramenghi, L.A., Evans, D.J., & Levene, M.I. (1999). "Sucrose analgesia": Absorptive mechanism or taste perception? *Archives of Disease in Childhood Fetal Neonatal Ed. 80,* F146–F147.

Ramey, C.T., & Campbell, F.A. (1991). Poverty, early childhood education, and academic competence. In A. Huston (Ed.), *Children reared in poverty* (pp. 190–221). Cambridge, UK: Cambridge University Press.

Ramey, C.T., Campbell, F.A., Burchinal, M., Skinner, M. L., Gardner, D. M., & Ramey, S. L. (2000). Persistent effects of early childhood education on high-risk children and their mothers. *Applied Developmental Science, 4,* 2–14.

Ramey, C.T., & Ramey, S.L. (1998a). Early intervention and early experience. *American Psychologist, 53,* 109–120.

Ramey, C.T., & Ramey, S.L. (1998b). Prevention of intellectual disabilities: Early interventions to improve cognitive development. *Preventive Medicine, 27,* 224–232.

Ramey, C.T., Ramey, S.L., & Lanzi, R.G. (2006). Children's health and education. In W. Damon, & R. Lerner (Eds.) & K.A. Renninger, & I.E. Sigel (Vol. Eds.), *Handbook of child psychology: Vol. 4. Child psychology in practice* (6th ed., pp. 864–892). New York: Wiley.

Rao, M.R., Hediger, M.L., Levine, R.J., Naficy, A.B., & Vi, K.T. (2002). Effect of breastfeeding on cognitive development of infants born small for gestational age. *Acta Paediatrica, 91,* 267–274.

Rao, R., & Georgieff, M.K. (2000) Early nutrition and brain development. In C.A. Nelson (Ed.), The effects of early adversity on neurobehavioral development. *The Minnesota symposia on child psychology, 31,* 1–30. Mahwah, NJ: Lawrence Erlbaum Associates.

Rao, R., & Georgieff, M.K. (2001). Neonatal iron nutrition. *Seminars in Neonatology, 6,* 425–435.

Rapin, I. (1997). Autism. *New England Journal of Medicine, 337,* 97–104.

Rattaz, C., Goubet, N., & Bullinger, A. (2005). The calming effect of a familiar odor on full-term newborns. *Journal of Developmental & Behavioral Pediatrics, 26,* 86–92.

Rauscher, F.H. (2002). Mozart and the mind: Factual and fictional effects of musical enrichment. In J. Aronson (Ed.), *Improving academic achievement: Impact of psychological factors on education* (pp. 267–278). San Diego: Academic Press.

Rauscher, F.H. (2003). Can music instruction affect children's cognitive development? *ERIC Digest,* EDO-PS-03-12.

Rauscher, F.H., & LeMieux, M.T. (2003, April). *Piano, rhythm, and singing instruction improve different aspects of spatial-temporal reasoning in Head Start children.* Poster presented at the annual meeting of the Cognitive Neuroscience Society, New York.

Rauscher, F.H., Shaw, G.L., & Ky, K.N. (1993). Music and spatial task performance. *Nature, 365,* 611.

Rauscher, F.H., Shaw, G.L., & Ky, K.N. (1995). Listening to Mozart enhances spatial-temporal reasoning: Towards a neurophysiological basis. *Neuroscience Letters, 185,* 44–47.

Rauscher, F.H., Shaw, G.L., Levine, L.J., Wright, E.L., Dennis, W.R., & Newcomb, R.L. (1997). Music training causes long-term enhancement of preschool children's spatial-temporal reasoning. *Neurological Research, 19*(1), 1–8.

Rauscher, F.H., & Zupan, M. (2000). Classroom keyboard instruction improves kindergarten children's spatial-temporal performance: A field experiment. *Early Childhood Research Quarterly, 15,* 215–228.

Raver, C.C. (2002). Emotions matter: Making the case for the role of young children's emotional development for early school readiness. *Social Policy Report, 16*(3), 3–19.

Raver, C.C. (2003). *Young children's emotional development and school readiness.* EDO-PS-03-8. Champaign, IL: Clearinghouse on Elementary and Early Childhood Education.

Ray, R. (2008). *A detailed look at parental leave policies in 21 OECD Countries.* Washington, DC: Center for Economic and Policy Research.

Rayburn, W.F., & Zhang, J. (2002). Rising rates of labor induction: Present concerns and future strategies. *Obstetrics & Gynecology, 100,* 164–167.

Reddy, U.M., & Mennuti, M.T. (2006). Incorporating first-trimester Down Syndrome studies into prenatal screening. *Obstetrics & Gynecology, 107,* 167–173.

Reese, E., & Newcombe, R. (2007). Training mothers in elaborative reminiscing enhances children's autobiographical memory and narrative. *Child Development, 78,* 1153–1170.

Reid, V., Striano, T., Kaufman, J., & Johnson, M. (2004). Eye gaze cueing facilitates neural processing of objects in 4-month-old infants. *Neuroreport, 15,* 2553–2555.

Reid, V.M., & Striano, T. (2005). Adult gaze influences infant attention and object processing implications for cognitive neuroscience. *European Journal of Neuroscience, 21,* 1763–1766.

Reis, H.T., & Collins, W.A. (2004). Relationships, human behavior, and psychological science. *Current Directions in Psychological Science, 13,* 233–237.

Reissland, N., & Snow, D. (1996). Maternal pitch height in ordinary and play situations. *Journal of Child Language, 23,* 269–278.

Repacholi, B.M., & Gopnik, A. (1997). Early reasoning about desires: Evidence from 14- and 18-month-olds. *Developmental Psychology, 33,* 12–21.

Repacholi, B.M., & Meltzoff, A.N. (2007). Emotional eavesdropping: Infants selectively respond to indirect emotional signals. *Child Development, 78,* 503–521.

Repka, M.X. (2002a). Eye drops and patches both in fact work for amblyopia. *BMJ, 324,* 1397.

Repka, M.X. (2002b). Ophthalmological problems of the premature infant. *Mental Retardation and Developmental Disabilities Research Reviews, 8,* 249–257.

Repka, M.X., Beck, R.W., Holmes, J.M., Birch, E.E., Chandler, D.L., Cotter, S.A., et al. (2003). A randomized trial of patching regimens for treatment of moderate amblyopia in children. *Archives of Ophthalmology, 121,* 603–611.

Repka, M.X., Holmes, J.M., Melia, B.M., Beck, R.W., Gearinger, M.D., Tamkins, S.M., et al. (2005). The effect of amblyopia therapy on ocular alignment. *Journal of AAPOS, 9,* 542–545.

Reproductive Health Technology Project. (2006). *Pre-implantation genetic diagnosis fact sheet.* Retrieved July 5, 2009, from http://www.rhtp .org/fertility/pgd/default.asp

Rescorla, L. (1989). The Language Development Survey: A screening tool for delayed language in toddlers. *Journal of Speech and Hearing Disorders, 54,* 587–599.

Rescorla, L., & Alley, A. (2001). Validation of the Language Development Survey (LDS): A parent report tool for identifying language delay in toddlers. *Journal of Speech, Language, and Hearing Research, 44,* 434–445.

Rescorla, L.A. (1980). Overextension in early language development. *Journal of Child Language, 7,* 321–335.

Reynell, J., & Gruber, C. (1990). *Reynell Developmental Language Scales—U.S. Edition.* Los Angeles: Western Psychological Services.

Reynolds, A.J. (2000). *Success in early intervention: The Chicago Child-Parent Centers.* Lincoln, NE: University of Nebraska Press.

Reynolds, A.J. (2009). *Economic returns of early childhood development programs.* Invited symposium presented at the Biennial Meeting of the Society for Research in Child Development, Denver, CO. Retrieved December 22, 2009, from http://www .cehd.umn.edu/icd/CLS/SRCD2009.htm

Reynolds, A.J., & Robertson, D.L. (2003). School-based early intervention and later child maltreatment in the Chicago Longitudinal Study. *Child Development, 74,* 3–26.

Reynolds, A.J., Temple, J.A., & Ou, S. (2010). Impacts and implications of the Child-Parent Center Preschool Program. In A.J. Reynolds, A. Rolnick, M.M. Englund, & J. Temple (Eds.), *Cost-effective early childhood programs in the first decade: A human capital integration.* New York: Cambridge University Press.

Reynolds, A.J., Temple, J.A., & White, B. (2009). *Cost-Effective Early Childhood Development Programs: A Synthesis of Evidence in the First Decade of Life.* Invited symposium presented at the Biennial Meeting of the Society for Research in Child Development, Denver, CO. Retrieved December 22, 2009, from http://www .cehd.umn.edu/icd/CLS/SRCD2009.htm

Reynolds, A.J., Temple, J.A., White, B., Ou, S., & Robertson, D.L (in press). Age-26 cost-benefit analysis of the Child-Parent Center Early Education Program. *Child Development.*

Reznick, J.S., Corley, R., & Robinson, J. (1997). A longitudinal twin study of intelligence in the second year. *Monographs of the Society for Research in Child Development, 62*(1, Serial No. 250).

Reznick, J.S., Morrow, J.D., Goldman, B.D., & Snyder, J. (2004). The onset of working memory in infants. *Infancy, 6,* 145–154.

Richards, J.E. (2001). Attention in young infants: A developmental psychophysiological perspective. In C.A. Nelson, & M. Luciana (eds.), *Handbook of developmental cognitive neurosciences* (pp. 321–338). Cambridge, MA: MIT Press.

Richards, J.E. (2005). Localizing cortical sources of event-related potentials in infants' covert orienting. *Developmental Science, 8,* 255–278.

Richman, A.L., Miller, P.M., & LeVine, R.A. (1992). Cultural and educational variations in maternal responsiveness. *Developmental Psychology, 28,* 614–621.

Richter, L., & Richter, D.M. (2001). Exposure to parental tobacco and alcohol use: Effects on children's health and development. *American Journal of Orthopsychiatry, 71,* 182–203.

Rideout, V.J., & Hamel, E. (2006). *The media family: Electronic media in the lives of infants, toddlers, preschoolers, and their parents.* Menlo Park, CA: The Henry J. Kaiser Family Foundation.

Rideout, V.J., Vandewater, E.A., & Wartella, E.A. (2003). *Zero to six: Electronic media in the lives of infants, toddlers and preschoolers.* Menlo Park, CA: The Henry J. Kaiser Family Foundation.

Rieser, J.J. (1979). Spatial orientation of six-month-old infants. *Child Development, 50,* 1078–1087.

Riley, L.A., & Glass, J.L. (2002). You can't always get what you want–Infant care preferences and use among employed mothers. *Journal of Marriage and Family, 64,* 2–15.

Ringgenberg, S. (2004). Singing as a teaching tool. Early years are learning years, Release # 04/1. Washington, DC: National Association for the Education of Young Children. Retrieved March 29, 2006, from http://www.naeyc.org/ece/2004/01.asp

Rivera-Gaxiola, M., Silva-Pereyra, J., & Kuhl, P.K. (2005). Brain potentials to native and non-native speech contrasts in 7- and 11-month-old American infants. *Developmental Science, 8,* 162–172.

Robert R. McCormick Foundation. (1997). *Ten things every child needs.* Chicago: McCormick Foundation.

Roberts, J.E., Rosenfeld, R.M., & Zeisel, S.A. (2004). Otitis media and speech and language: A meta-analysis of prospective studies. *Pediatrics, 113,* e238- 248.

Robin, D.J., Berthier, N.E., & Clifton, R.K. (1996). Infants' predictive reaching for moving objects in the dark. *Developmental Psychology, 32,* 824–835.

Rocha, N.A.C.F., dos Santos Silva, F.P., & Tudella, E. (2006). The impact of object size and rigidity on infant reaching. *Infant Behavior & Development, 29,* 251–261.

Rocha, N.A.C.F., & Tudella, E. (2008). The influence of lying positions and postural control on hand–mouth and hand–hand behaviors in 0–4-month-old infants. *Infant Behavior & Development, 31,* 107–114.

Rochat, P. (1989). Object manipulation and exploration in 2- to 5-month-old infants. *Developmental Psychology, 25,* 871–884.

Rochat, P., Querido, J.G., & Striano, T. (1999). Emerging sensitivity to the timing and structure of protoconversation in early infancy. *Developmental Psychology, 35*, 950–957.

Rochat, P., & Senders, S.J. (1991). Active touch in infancy: Action systems in development. In M.J.S. Weiss, & P.R. Zelazo (Eds.), *Newborn attention: Biological constraints and the influence of experience* (pp. 412–442). Norwood, NJ: Ablex.

Rock, A.M.L., Trainor, L.J., & Addison, T.L. (1999). Distinctive messages in infant-directed lullabies and playsongs. *Developmental Psychology, 35*, 527–534.

Roelants, M., Hauspie, R., & Hoppenbrouwers, K. (2009). Breastfeeding, growth and growth standards: Performance of the WHO growth standards for monitoring growth of Belgian children. *Annals of Human Biology, 37*, 2–9.

Rogoff, B. (1998). Cognition as a collaborative process. In W. Damon (Editor-in-Chief), D. Kuhn, & R.S. Siegler (Vol. Eds.), *Handbook of child psychology: Vol. 2. Cognition, perception, and language* (5th ed., pp. 679–744). New York: Wiley.

Rogoff, B., Mistry, J., Göncü, A., & Mosier, C. (1993). Guided participation in cultural activity by toddlers and caregivers. *Monographs of the Society for Research in Child Development, 58*(8, Serial No. 236).

Rogoff, B., & Morelli, G. (1989). Perspectives on children's development from cultural psychology. *American Psychologist, 44*, 343–348.

Rogoff, B., Topping, K., Baker-Sennett, J., & Lacasa, P. (2002). Mutual contributions of individuals, partners, and institutions: Planning to remember in Girl Scout cookie sales. *Social Development, 11*, 266–289.

Roisman, G.I., Susman, E., Barnett-Walker, K., Booth-LaForce, C., Owen, M.T., Belsky, J., et al. (2009). Early family and child-care antecedents of awakening cortisol levels in adolescence. *Child Development, 80*, 907–920.

Rolnick, A., & Grunewald, R. (2003). The ABCs of ECD: A discussion on the economics of early childhood development. *The Region, 17*(4), 6–11.

Romero, R., Gómez, R., Chaiworapongsa, T., Conoscenti, G., Kim, J.C., & Kim, Y.M. (2001). The role of infection in preterm labour and delivery. *Paediatric and Perinatal Epidemiology, 15*(Suppl. 2), 41–56.

Rönnqvist, L., & von Hofsten, C. (1994). Neonatal finger and arm movements as determined by a social and an object context. *Early Development & Parenting, 3*, 81–94.

Rooks, J.P. (1997). *Midwifery and childbirth in America.* Philadelphia: Temple University Press.

Roopnarine, J.L. (2004). African American and African Caribbean fathers: Level, quality, and meaning of involvement. In M.E. Lamb (Ed.), *The role of the father in child development* (4th ed., pp. 58–97). New York: Wiley.

Roopnarine, J.L., Hossain, Z., Gill, P., & Brophy, H. (1994). Play in the East Indian context. In J.L. Roopnarine, J.E. Johnson, & F.H. Hooper (Eds.), *Children's play in diverse cultures* (pp. 9–30). Albany: State University of New York Press.

Roopnarine, J.L., Johnson, J.E., & Hooper, F.H. (Eds.). (1994). *Children's play in diverse cultures.* Albany: State University of New York Press.

The Roots of SRCD. (2009). The Society for Research in Child Development. Retrieved June 3, 2009, from http://www.srcd.org/index.php?option=com_content&task=view&id=71&Itemid=495.

Ros, A., Felberbaum, R., Jahnke, I., Diedrich, K., Schmucker, P., & Hüppe, M. (2007). Epidural anaesthesia for labour: does it influence the mode of delivery? *Archives of Gynecology and Obstetrics, 275*, 269–274.

Rose, S.A., & Feldman, J.F. (1997). Memory and speed: Their role in the relation of infant information processing to later IQ. *Child Development, 68*, 630–641.

Rose, S.A., Feldman, J.F., & Jankowski, J.J. (2001). Visual short-term memory in the first year of life: Capacity and recency effects. *Developmental Psychology, 37*, 539–549.

Rose, S.A., Feldman, J.F., & Jankowski, J.J. (2009). A cognitive approach to the development of early language. *Child Development, 80*, 134–150.

Rose, S.A., Feldman, J.F., Jankowski, J.J., & Van Rossem, R. (2005). Pathways from prematurity and infant abilities to later cognition. *Child Development, 76*, 1172–1184.

Rose, S.R., the American Academy of Pediatrics Section on Endocrinology and Committee on Genetics, Brown, R.S., the American Thyroid Association Public Health Committee, & Lawson Wilkins Pediatric Endocrine Society. (2006). Update of newborn screening and therapy for congenital hypothyroidism. *Pediatrics, 117*, 2290–2303.

Roseberry, S., Hirsh-Pasek, K., Parish-Morris, J., & Golinkoff, R.M. (2009). Live action: Can young children learn verbs from video? *Child Development, 80*, 1360–1375.

Rosengren, K.S., Gross, D., & Perlmutter, M. (1986). Preschool children's computing activity. *ERIC document ED 264–953. Resources in Education.* Available at http://www.eric.ed.gov

Rosengren, K.S., Gutiérrez, I.T., Anderson, K.N., Schein, S.S. (2009). Parental reports of children's scale errors in everyday life. *Child Development, 80,* 1586–1591.

Rossetti, L. (1990). *The Rossetti Infant Toddler Language Scale: A measure of communication and interaction.* East Moline, IL: LinguiSystems.

Ross-Sheehy, S., Oakes, L.M., & Luck, S.J. (2003). The development of visual short-term memory capacity in infants. *Child Development, 74,* 1807–1822.

Rothbart, M., & Goldsmith, H. (1991). Contemporary instruments for assessing early temperament by questionnaire and in the laboratory. In J. Strelau, & A. Angleitner (Eds.), *Explorations in temperament: International perspectives on theory and measurement.* London: Plenum Press.

Rothbart, M.K. (1981). Measurement of temperament in infancy. *Child Development, 52,* 569–578.

Rothbart, M. K. (1984). Social development. In M. J. Hanson (Ed.), *Atypical infant development* (pp. 207–236). Baltimore, MD: University Park Press.

Rothbart, M.K. (2004). Commentary: Differentiated measures of temperament and multiple pathways to childhood disorders. *Journal of Clinical Child and Adolescent Psychology, 33,* 82–87.

Rothbart, M.K., Ahadi, S.A., & Evans, S.A. (2000). Temperament and personality: Origins and outcomes. *Journal of Personality and Social Psychology, 78,* 122–135.

Rothbart, M.K., Ahadi, S.A., Hershey, K., & Fisher, P. (2001). Investigations of temperament at three to seven years: The Children's Behavior Questionnaire. *Child Development, 72,* 1394–1408.

Rothbart, M.K., & Bates, J.E. (1998). Temperament. In W. Damon (Series Ed.) & N. Eisenberg (Vol. Ed.), *Handbook of child psychology: Vol. 3. Social, emotional, and personality development* (5th ed., pp. 105–176). New York: Wiley.

Rothbart, M.K., & Bates, J.E. (2006). Temperament. In W. Damon, & R. Lerner (Series Eds.) & N. Eisenberg (Vol. Ed.), *Handbook of child psychology: Vol. 3. Social, emotional, and personality development* (6th ed., pp. 99–166). New York: Wiley.

Rothbart, M.K., Derryberry, D., & Hershey, K. (2000). Stability of temperament in childhood: Laboratory infant assessment to parent report at seven years. In V.J. Molfese, & D.L. Molfese (Eds.), *Temperament and personality development across the life span* (pp. 85–119). Hillsdale, NJ: Lawrence Erlbaum Associates.

Rothbart, M.K., Sheese, B.E., & Posner, M.I. (2007). Executive attention and effortful control: Linking temperament, brain networks, and genes. *Child Development Perspectives, 1,* 2–7.

Rothbaum, F., Pott, M., Azuma, H., Miyake, K., & Weisz, J. (2000). The development of close relationships in Japan and the United Sttes: Paths of symbiotic harmony and generative tension. *Child Development, 71,* 1121–1142.

Rothman, K.J., Moore, L.L., Singer, M.R., Nguyen, U.S., Mannino, S., & Milunsky, A. (1995). Teratogenicity of high vitamin A intake. *New England Journal of Medicine, 333,* 1369–1373.

Rovee-Collier, C. (1999). The development of infant memory. *Current Directions in Psychological Science, 8,* 80–85.

Rovee-Collier, C., Hartshorn, K., & DiRubbo, M. (1999). Long-term maintenance of infant memory. *Developmental Psychobiology, 35,* 91–102.

Rowe, M.L., & Goldin-Meadow, S. (2009). Differences in early gesture explain SES disparities in child vocabulary size at school entry. *Science, 323,* 951–953.

Rowe, M.L., Özçaliskan, S., & Goldin-Meadow, S. (2008). Learning words by hand: Gesture's role in predicting vocabulary development. *Language, 28,* 182–199.

Rubin, K.H., Bukowski, W., & Parker, J.G. (1998). Peer interactions, relationships, and groups. In W. Damon (Series Ed.) & N. Eisenberg (Vol. Ed.), *Handbook of child psychology: Vol. 3. Social, emotional, and personality development* (5th ed., pp. 619–700). New York: Wiley.

Rubin, K.H., Bukowski, W., & Parker, J.G. (2006). Peer interactions, relationships, and groups. In W. Damon, & R. Lerner (Eds.) & N. Eisenberg (Vol. Ed.), *Handbook of child psychology: Vol. 3. Social, emotional, and personality development* (6th ed., pp. 571–645). New York: Wiley.

Rubin, K.H., Fein, G.G., & Vandenberg, B. (1983). Play. In E.M. Hetherington (Vol. Ed.) & P.H. Mussen (Series Ed.), *Handbook of child psychology* (Vol. 4, pp. 693–741). New York: Wiley.

Ruda, M.A., Ling, Q.-D., Hohmann, A.G., Peng, Y.B., & Tachibana, T. (2000). Altered nociceptive neuronal circuits after neonatal peripheral inflammation. *Science, 289,* 628–630.

Ruffman, T., Slade, L., & Crowe, E. (2002). The relations between children's and mothers' mental state language and theory-of-mind understanding. *Child Development, 73,* 734–751.

Ruffman, T., Slade, L., Sandino, J.C., & Fletcher, A. (2005). Are A-not-B errors caused by a belief about object location? *Child Development, 76,* 122–136.

Ruhm, C.J. (1998). Parental leave and child health. NBER Working Paper No. W6554. Cambridge, MA: National Bureau of Economic Research.

Russell, G., & Hwang, C.P. (2004). The impact of workplace practices on father involvement. In M.E. Lamb (Ed.), *The role of the father in child development* (4th ed., pp. 476–504). New York: Wiley.

Rutter, M. (1998). Developmental catch-up, and deficit, following adoption after severe global early privation. English and Romanian Adoptees (ERA) Study Team. *Journal of Child Psychology & Psychiatry, 39,* 465–476.

Rutter, M. (2000). Resilience reconsidered: Conceptual considerations, empirical findings, and policy implications. In J.P. Shonkoff, & S.J. Meisels (Eds.), *Handbook of early childhood intervention* (2nd ed., pp. 651–682). New York: Cambridge University Press.

Rutter, M., Kreppner, J., & O'Connor, T. (2001). Specificty and heterogeneity in children's responses to profound institutional privation. *British Journal of Psychiatry, 179,* 97–103.

Ryan, A.S., & Zhou, W. (2006). Lower breastfeeding rates persist among the Special Supplemental Nutrition Program for Women, Infants, and Children Participants, 1978–2003. *Pediatrics, 117,* 1136–1146.

Ryan, A.S., Zhou, W., & Acosta, A. (2002). Breastfeeding continues to increase into the new millennium. *Pediatrics, 110,* 1103–1109.

Ryan, R.M., Martin, A., & Brooks-Gunn, J. (2006). Is one good parent good enough? Mother and father parenting and child cognitive outcomes in the Early Head Start Research and Evaluation Project. *Parenting: Science and Practice, 6,* 211–228.

Rymer, R. (1993). *An abused child: Flight from silence.* New York: HarperCollins.

Saarni, C., Mumme, D.L., & Campos, J.J. (1998). Emotional development: Action, communication, and understanding. In W. Damon (Series Ed.) & N. Eisenberg (Vol. Ed.), *Handbook of child psychology: Vol. 3. Social, emotional, and personality development* (5th ed., pp. 237–309). New York: Wiley.

Sabbagh, M.A., Bowman, L.C., Evraire, L.E., & Ito, J.M.B. (2009). Neurodevelopmental correlates of theory of mind in preschool children. *Child Development, 80,* 1147–1162.

Sabbagh, M.A., Henderson, A.M.E., Baldwin, D.A. (2007). What infants' understanding of referential intentions tells us about the neurocognitive bases of early word learning. In R. Flom, K. Lee, & D. Muir (Eds.), *Gaze-following: Its development and significance* (pp. 171–191). Mahwah, NJ: Lawrence Erlbaum Associates.

Saffran, J.R. (2003). Statistical language learning: Mehanisms and constraints. *Current Directions in Psychological Science, 12,* 110–114.

Saffran, J.R., & Estes, K.G. (2006). Mapping sound to meaning: Connections between learning about sounds and learning about words. In R. Kail (Ed.), *Advances in child development and behavior* (pp. 1–38). New York: Elsevier.

Saffran, J.R., Loman, M.M., & Robertson, R.R.W. (2000). Infant memory for musical experiences. *Cognition, 77,* B15–B23.

Saffran, J.R., Senghas, A., & Trueswell, J.C. (2001). The acquisition of language by children. *Proceedings of the National Academy of Science, 98,* 12874–12875.

Saffran, J.R., & Thiessen, E.D. (2003). Pattern induction by infant language learners. *Developmental Psychology, 39,* 484–494.

Saffran, J.R., Werker, J.F., & Werner, L.A. (2006). The infant's auditory world: Hearing, speech, and the beginnings of language. In W. Damon, & R. Lerner (Eds.) & D. Kuhn, & R. Siegler (Vol. Eds.), *Handbook of child psychology: Vol. 2. Cognition, perception, and language* (6th ed., pp. 58–108). New York: Wiley.

Sagi, A., Koren-Karie, N., Gini, M., Ziv, Y., & Joels, T. (2002). Shedding further light on the effects of various types and quality of early child care on infant-mother attachment relationship: The Haifa Study of Early Child Care. *Child Development, 73,* 1166–1186.

Sagi, A., Lamb, M.E., Lewkowicz, K.S., Shoham, R., Dvir, R., & Estes, D. (1985). Security of infant-mother, -father, and -metapelet attachments among kibbutz-reared Israeli children. In I. Bretherton, & E. Waters (Eds.), Growing points of attachment theory and research. *Monographs of the Society for Research in Child Development, 50*(1/2, Serial No. 209), 257–275.

Sagi, A., van IJzendoorn, M.H., Aviezer, O., Donnell, F., Koren-Karie, N., Joels, T., & Harel, Y. (1995). Attachments in a multiple-caregiver and multiple-infant environment: The case of the Israeli kibbutzim. In E. Waters, B.E. Vaughn, G. Posada, & K. Kondo-Ikemura (Eds.), Caregiving, cultural, and cognitive perspectives on secure-base behavior and working models: New growing points in attachment theory and research. *Monographs of the Society for Research in Child Development, 60*(Serial No. 244), 71–91.

Sagi, A., van IJzendoorn, M.H., Aviezer, O., Donnell, F., & Mayseless, O. (1994). Sleeping out of home in a kibbutz communal arrangement: It makes a difference for infant-mother attachment. *Child Development, 65,* 992–1004.

Sai, F.Z. (2005). The role of the mother's voice in developing mother's face preference: Evidence for intermodal perception at birth. *Infant and Child Development, 14,* 29–50.

Salsberry, P.J., & Reagan, P.B. (2005). Dynamics of early childhood overweight. *Pediatrics, 116,* 1329–1338.

Samuels, H.R. (1980). The effect of an older sibling on infant locomotor exploration of a new environment. *Child Development, 51,* 607–609.

Sanchez-Ramos, L., Olivier, F., Delke, I., & Kaunitz, A.M. (2003). Labor induction versus expectant management for postterm pregnancies: A systematic review with meta-analysis. *Obstetrics & Gynecology, 101,* 1312–1318.

Sanders, C., Diego, M., Fernandez, M., Field, T., Hernandez-Reif, M., Roca, A. (2002). EEG asymmetry responses to lavender and rosemary aromas in adults and infants. *International Journal of Neuroscience, 112,* 1305–1320.

Santos, I.S., Victora, C.G., Huttly, S., & Carvalhal, J.B. (1998). Caffeine intake and low birthweight: A population-based case-control study. *American Journal of Epidemiology, 147,* 620–627.

Santos, I., Victora, C.G., Martines, J., Goncalves, H., Gigante, H.P., Valle, N.J., et al. (2001). Nutrition counselling increases weight gain among Brazilian children. *Journal of Nutrition, 131,* 2866–2873.

Satcher, D. (2000). *Oral health in America: A report of the Surgeon General.* Washington, DC: U.S. Department of Health and Human Services.

Savulescu, J., & Dahl, E. (2000). Sex selection and preimplantation diagnosis: A response to the Ethics Committee of the American Society of Reproductive Medicine. *Human Reproduction, 15,* 1879–1880.

Saxe, R.R., & Pelphrey, K.A. (2009). Introduction to a special section of developmental social cognitive neuroscience. *Child Development, 80,* 946–951.

Sayle, A.E., Savitz, D.A., Thorp, J.M., Hertz-Picciotto, I., & Wilcox, A.J. (2001). Sexual activity during late pregnancy and risk of preterm delivery. *Obstetrics & Gynecology, 97,* 283–289.

Schaal, B., Coureaud, G., Doucet, S., Delaunay-El Allam, M., Moncomble, A.-S., Montigny, D., et al. (2009). Mammary olfactory signalisation in females and odor processing in neonates: Ways evolved by rabbits and humans. *Behavioural Brain Research, 200,* 346–358.

Schaal, B., Marlier, L., & Soussignan, R. (1998). Olfactory function in the human fetus: Evidence from selective neonatal responsiveness to the odor of amniotic fluid. *Behavioral Neuroscience, 112,* 1438–1449.

Schaal, B., Marlier, L., Soussignan, R. (2000). Human foetuses learn odours from their pregnant mother's diet. *Chemical Senses, 25,* 729–737.

Scheers, N.J., Rutherford, G.W., & Kemp, J.S. (2003). Where should infants sleep? A comparison of risk for suffocation of infants sleeping in cribs, adult beds, and other sleeping locations. *Pediatrics, 112,* 883–889.

Schellenberg, E.G. (2004). Music lessons enhance IQ. *Psychological Science, 15,* 511–514.

Schellenberg, E.G. (2005). Music and cognitive abilities. *Current Directions in Psychological Science, 14,* 317–320.

Schenker, J.G., & Ezra, Y. (1994). Complications of assisted reproductive techniques. *Fertility and Sterility, 61,* 411–422.

Schieffelin, B.B. (1990). *The give and take of everyday life: Language socialization of Kaluli children.* Cambridge, UK: Cambridge University Press.

Schieve, L.A., Cogswell, M.E., Scanlon, K.S., Perry, G., Ferre, C., Blackmore-Price, C., et al. (2000). Prepregnancy body mass index and pregnancy weight gain: Associations with preterm delivery. *Obstetrics & Gynecology, 96,* 194–200.

Schlossman, S. (1985). Perils of popularization: The founding of *Parents Magazine.* In A. Smuts, & J.W. Hagen (Eds.), History and research in child development (pp. 65–77). *Monographs of the Society for Research in Child Development, 50*(4–5, Serial No. 211).

Schmidt, L.A., Fox, N.A., Perez-Edgar, K., & Hamer, D.H. (2009). Linking gene, brain, and behavior. *Psychological Science, 20,* 831–837.

Schmidt, L.A., Fox, N.A., Rubin, K.H., Sternberg, E.M., Gold, P.W., Smith, C.C., & Schulkin, J. (1997). Behavioral and neuroendocrine responses in shy children. *Developmental Psychobiology, 30,* 127–140.

Schmidt, L.A., Fox, N.A., Schulkin, J., & Gold, P.W. (1999). Behavioral and psychophysiological correlates of self-presentation in temperamentally shy children. *Developmental Psychobiology, 35,* 119–135.

Schmidt, M.E., Pempek, T.A., Kirkorian, H.L., Lund, A.F., & Anderson, D.R. (2008). The effect of background television on the toy play behavior of very young children. *Child Development, 79,* 1137–1151.

Schmidt, M.E., Rich, M., Rifas-Shiman, S.L., Oken, E., & Taveras, E.M. (2009). Television viewing in infancy and child cognition at 3 years of age in a US cohort. *Pediatrics, 123,* e370–e375.

Schmidt, N., Abelsen, B., & Øian, P. (2002). Deliveries in maternity homes in Norway: Results from a 2-year prospective study. *Acta Obstetricia et Gynecologica Scandinavica, 81,* 731–737.

Schmuckler, M. (1996). Development of visually guided locomotion: Barrier crossing by toddlers. *Ecological Psychology, 8,* 209–236.

Schmuckler, M.A., & Fairhall, J.L. (2001). Visual-proprioceptive intermodal perception using point light displays. *Child Development, 72,* 949–962.

Schmuckler, M.A., & Gibson, E.J. (1989). The effect of imposed optical flow on guided locomotion in young walkers. *British Journal of Developmental Psychology, 7,* 193–206.

Schneider, W., & Bjorklund, D.F. (1998). Memory. In W. Damon (Editor-in-Chief), D. Kuhn, & R.S. Siegler (Vol. Eds.), *Handbook of child psychology: Vol. 2. Cognition, perception, and language* (5th ed., pp. 467–522). New York: Wiley.

Schnieke, A.E., Kind, A.J., Ritchie, W.A., Mycock, K., Scott, A.R., Ritchie, M., Wilmut, I., Colman, A., & Campbell, K.H. (1997). Human factor IX transgenic sheep produced by transfer of nuclei from transfectee fetal fibroblasts. *Science, 278,* 2130–2133.

Schnitzer, P.G., & Ewigman, B.G. (2005). Child deaths resulting from inflicted injuries: Household risk factors ad perpetrator characteristics. *Pediatrics, 116,* e687–e693.

Schoppe-Sullivan, S.J., Brown, G.L., Cannon, E.A., Mangelsdorf, S.C., & Sokolowski, M.S. (2008). Maternal gatekeeping, coparenting quality, and fathering behavior in families with infants. *Journal of Family Psychology, 22,* 389–398.

Schoppe-Sullivan, S.J., Mangelsdorf, S.C., Brown, G.L., & Sokolowski, M.S. (2006). Goodness-of-fit in family context: Infant temperament, marital quality, and early coparenting behavior. *Infant Behavior & Development, 30,* 82–96.

Schott, J.J., Benson, D.W., Basson, C.T., Pease, W., Silberbach, G.M., Moak, J.P., et al. (1998). Congenital heart disease caused by mutations in the transcription factor NKX2-5. *Science, 281,* 108–111.

Schulman, K. (2000). *The high cost of child care puts quality care out of reach for many families.* Washington, DC: Children's Defense Fund.

Schulz, C.B. (1985). Children and childhood in the eighteenth century. In J.M. Hawes, & N.R. Hiner (Eds.), *American childhood: A research guide and historical handbook* (pp. 57–109). Westport, CT: Greenwood Press.

Schumacher, M., Zubaran, C., & White, G. (2008). Bringing birth-related paternal depression to the fore. *Women and Birth, 21,* 65–70.

Schumacher, R., & DeLauro, E. (2008). *Building on the promise: State initiatives to expand access to Early Head Start for young children and their families.* Washington, DC: Center for Law and Social Policy.

Schwartz, C.E., Snidman, N., & Kagan, J. (1999). Adolescent social anxiety as an outcome of inhibited temperament in childhood. *Journal of the American Academy of Child and Adolescent Psychiatry, 38,* 1008–1015.

Schwartz, R.G., & Leonard, L.B. (1980). Words, objects, and actions in early lexical acquisition. *Papers and Reports in Child Language Development, 19,* 29–36.

Schwarz, E.B., Ray, R.M., Stuebe, A.M., Allison, M.A., Ness, R.B., Freiberg, M.S., et al. (2009). Duration of lactation and risk factors for maternal cardiovascular disease. *Obstetrics & Gynecology, 113,* 974–982.

Schweinhart, L.J. (2009). *Highly effective preschool program practices.* Invited symposium presented at the Biennial Meeting of the Society for Research in Child Development, Denver, CO. Retrieved December 22, 2009, from http://www.cehd.umn.edu/icd/CLS/SRCD2009.htm

Schweinhart, L.J., Barnes, H., Weikart, D., Barnett, W.S., & Epstein, A. (1993). *Significant benefits: Vol. 10. The High/Scope Perry Preschool study through age 27.* Ypsilanti, MI: High/Scope Press.

Schweinle, A., & Wilcox, T. (2004). Intermodal perception and physical reasoning in young infants. *Infant Behavior & Development, 27,* 246–265.

Schwemberger, J.G., Mosby, J.E., Doa, M.J., Jacobs, D.E., Ashley, P.J., Brody, D.J., et al. (2005). Blood lead levels: United States, 1999–2002. *Morbidity and Mortality Weekly Report, 54,* 513–516.

Scott, J.A., Binns, C.W., Oddy, W.H., & Graham, K.I. (2006). Predictors of breastfeeding duration: Evidence from a cohort study. *Pediatrics, 117,* e646–e655.

Scott, K.D., Berkowitz, G., & Klaus, M. (1999). A comparison of intermittent and continuous support during labor: A meta-analysis. *American Journal of Obstetrics and Gynecology, 180,* 1054–1059.

Scott, K.D., Klaus, P.H., & Klaus, M.H. (1999). The obstetrical and postpartum benefits of continuous support during childbirth. *Journal of Women's Health and Gender Based Medicine, 8,* 1257–1264.

Scott, R.M., & Baillargeon, R. (2009). Which penguin is this? Attributing false beliefs about object identity at 18 months. *Child Development, 80,* 1172–1196.

Sears, R.R. (1975). Your ancients revisited: A history of child development. In E.M. Hetherington (Ed.), *Review of child development research* (Vol. 5, pp. 1–73). Chicago: University of Chicago Press.

Sebastián-Gallés, N., & Bosch, L. (2005). Phonology and bilingualism. In N. Kroll, & A.M.B. de Groot (Eds.), *Handbook of bilingualism: Psycholinguistic approaches* (pp. 68–87). New York: Oxford University Press.

Seifer, R., & Dickstein, S. (2000). Parental mental illness and infant development. In C.H. Zeanah, Jr. (Ed.), *Handbook of infant mental health* (2nd ed., pp. 145–160). New York: Guilford Press.

Seifer, R., & Schiller, M. (1995). The role of parenting sensitivity, infant temperament, and dyadic interaction in attachment theory and assessment. In E. Waters, B.E. Vaughn, G., Posada, & K. Kondo-Ikemura (Eds.), Caregiving, cultural, and cognitive perspectives on secure-base behavior and working models: New growing points in attachment theory and research. *Monographs of the Society for Research in Child Development, 60*(2/3, Serial No. 244), 146–174.

Seifer, R., Schiller, M., Sameroff, A.J., Resnick, S., & Riordan, K. (1996). Attachment, maternal sensitivity, and temperament during the first year of life. *Developmental Psychology, 32,* 3–11.

Sekizawa, A., Purwosunu, Y., Matsuoka, R., Koide, K., Okazaki, S., Farina, A., et al. (2007). Recent advances in non-invasive prenatal DNA diagnosis through analysis of maternal blood. *The Journal of Obstetrics and Gynaecology Research, 33,* 747–764.

Selman, P. (2002). Intercountry adoption in the new millennium: The "quiet migration" revisited. *Population Research and Policy Review, 21,* 205–225.

Senghas, A., & Coppola, M. (2001). Children creating language: How Nicaraguan Sign Language acquired a spatial grammar. *Psychological Science, 12,* 323–328.

Senghas, A., Kita, S., & Özyurek, A. (2004). Children creating core properties of language: Evidence from an emerging sign language in Nicaragua. *Science, 305,* 1779–1782.

Serbin, L.A., Moller, L.C., Gulko, J., Powlishta, K.K., & Colburne, K.A. (1994). The emergence of sex segregation in toddler playgroups. *New Directions in Child Development, 65,* 7–17.

Seress, L. (2001). Morphological changes of the human hippocampal formation from midgestation to early childhood. In C.A. Nelson, & M. Luciana (Eds.), *Handbook of developmental cognitive neuroscience* (pp. 45–58). Cambridge, MA: MIT Press.

Shackman, J.E., Shackman, A.J., & Pollak, S.D. (2007). Physical abuse amplifies attention to threat and increases anxiety in children. *Emotion, 7,* 838–852.

Shannon, J.D., Tamis-LeMonda, C.S., & Cabrera, N. (2006). Fathering in infancy: Mutuality and stability between 6 and 14 months. *Parenting, 6,* 167–188.

Shapiro-Mendoza, C.K., Kimball, M., Tomashek, K.M., Anderson, R.N., & Blanding, S. (2009). US infant mortality trends attributable to accidental suffocation and strangulation in bed from 1984 through 2004: Are rates increasing? *Pediatrics, 123,* 533–539.

Sharma, A.J., Grummer-Strawn, L.M., Dalenius, K., Galuska, D., Anandappa, M., Borland, E., et al. (2009). Obesity prevalence among low-income, preschool-aged children—United States, 1998–2008. *Morbidity and Mortality Weekly Report, 58(28),* 769–771.

Sharma, S.K., Alexander, J.M., Messick, G., Bloom, S.L., McIntire, D.D., Wiley, J., & Leveno, K.J. (2002). Cesarean delivery: A randomized trial of epidural analgesia versus intravenous meperidine analgesia during labor in nulliparous women. *Anesthesiology, 96,* 546–551.

Sharon, T., & DeLoache, J.S. (2003). The role of perseveration in children's symbolic understanding and skill. *Developmental Science, 6,* 289–297.

Shaw, D.S., & Vondra, J.I. (1995). Infant attachment security and maternal predictors of early behavior problems: A longitudinal study of low-income families. *Journal of Abnormal Child Psychology, 23,* 335–357.

Shea, S.L., & Aslin, R.N. (1990). Oculomotor responses to step-ramp targets by young human infants. *Vision Research, 30,* 1077–1092.

Shealy, K.R., Scanlon, K.S., Labiner-Wolfe, J., Fein, S.B., & Grummer-Strawn, L.M. (2008). Characteristics of breastfeeding practices among US mothers. *Pediatrics, 122,* S50–S55.

Sheiner, E., Levy, A., Feinstein, U., Hallak, M., & Mazor, M. (2002). Risk factors and outcome of failure to progress during the first stage of labor: a population-based study. *Acta Obstetricia et Gynecologica Scandinavica, 81,* 222–226.

Shepard, T.H., Brent, R.L., Friedman, J.M., Jones, K.L., Miller, R.K., Moore, C.A., & Polifka, J. E. (2002). Update on new developments in the study of human teratogens. *Teratology, 65,* 153–161.

Shields, B.J., & Smith, G.A. (2006). Success in the prevention of infant walker–related injuries: An analysis of national data, 1990–2001. *Pediatrics, 117,* e452–e459.

Shin, T., Kraemer, D., Pryor, J., Liu, L., Rugila, J., Howe, L., et al. (2002). Cell biology: A cat cloned by nuclear transplantation. *Nature, 415,* 859.

Shinn, M.W. (1900/1985). *The biography of a baby.* Reading, MA: Addison-Wesley.

Shirtcliff, E.A., Coeb, C.L., & Pollak, S.D. (2009). Early childhood stress is associated with elevated antibody levels to herpes simplex virus type 1. *Proceedings of the National Academy of Sciences of the United States of America, 106,* 2963–2967.

Shonkoff, J.P., & Phillips, D.A. (Eds.). (2000). *From neurons to neighborhoods: The science of early childhood development.* Committee on Integrating the Science of Early Childhood Development. Board on Children, Youth, and Families, Commission on Behavioral and Social Sciences and Education. Washington, DC: National Academy Press.

Shore, C. (1995). *Individual differences in language development.* Thousand Oaks, CA: Sage.

Shore, C.M. (Ed.). (2004). *The many faces of childhood: Diversity in development.* Boston: Pearson Education.

Shu, X.O., Perentesis, J.P., Wen, W., Buckley, J.D., Boyle, E., Ross, J.A., et al. (2004). Parental exposure to medications and hydrocarbons and ras mutations in children with acute lymphoblastic leukemia: A report from the Children's Oncology Group. *Cancer Epidemiology, Biomarkers and Prevention, 13,* 1230–1235.

Shwalb, D.W., Nakawaza, J., Yamamoto, T., & Hyun, J.H. (2004). Fathering in Japanese, Chinese, and Korean cultures: A review of the research literature. In M.E. Lamb (Ed.), *The role of the father in child development* (4th ed., pp. 146–181). New York: Wiley.

Shwalb, D.W., Shwalb, B.J., & Shoji, J. (1996). Japanese mothers' ideas about infants and temperament. In S. Harkness, & C.M. Super (Eds.), *Parents' cultural belief systems: Their origins, expressions, and consequences* (pp. 169–191). New York: Guilford Press.

Shwe, H.I., & Markman, E.M. (1997). Young children's appreciation of the mental impact of their communication signals. *Developmental Psychology, 33,* 630–636.

Shweder, R.A., Goodnow, J.J., Hatano, G., LeVine, R.A., Markus, H.R., & Miller, P.J. (2006). The cultural psychology of development: One mind, many mentalities. In W. Damon, & R. Lerner (Eds.) & R.M. Lerner (Vol. Eds.), *Handbook of child psychology: Vol. 1. Theoretical models of human development* (6th ed., pp. 716–792). New York: Wiley.

Siddiqui, A. (1995). Object size as a determinant of grasping in infancy. *Journal of Genetic Psychology, 156,* 345–358.

Siegel, A.C., & Burton, R.V. (1999). Effects of babywalkers on motor and mental development in human infants. *Journal of Developmental and Behavioral Pediatrics, 20,* 355–361.

Siegler, R.S. (1996). *Emerging minds: The process of change in children's thinking.* New York: Oxford University Press.

Siegler, R.S. (2006). Microgenetic analyses of learning. In W. Damon, & R. Lerner (Eds.) & D. Kuhn, & R. Siegler (Vol. Eds.), *Handbook of child psychology: Vol. 2. Cognition, perception, and language* (6th ed., pp. 464–510). New York: Wiley.

Siegler, R.S., & Crowley, K. (1991). The microgenetic method: A direct means for studying cognitive development. *American Psychologist, 46,* 606–620.

Sigman, M., & Ruskin, E. (1999). Social competence in children with autism, Down Syndrome and other developmental delays: A longitudinal study. *Monographs of the Society for Research in Child Development, 64*(1, Serial No. 256).

Silvey, L.E. (1999). Firstborn American Indian daughters: Struggles to reclaim cultural and self-identity. In H.P. McAdoo (Ed.), *Family ethnicity: Strength in diversity* (2nd ed., pp. 72–93). Thousand Oaks, CA: Sage.

Simion, F., Regolin, L., & Bulf, H. (2008). A predisposition for biological motion in the newborn baby. *Proceedings of the National Academy of Science, 105,* 809–813.

Simon, T. J., Hespos, S. J., & Rochat, P. (1995). Do infants understand simple arithmetic? A replication of Wynn (1992). *Cognitive Development, 10,* 253–269.

Simons, S.H.P., van Dijk, M., Anand, K.S., Roofthooft, D., van Lingen, R., & Tibboel, D. (2003). Do we still hurt newborn babies: A prospective study of procedural pain and analgesia in neonates. *Archives of Pediatrics & Adolescent Medicine, 157,* 1058–1064.

Sinal, S.H., Petree, A.R., Herman-Giddens, M., Rogers, M.K., Enand, C., & DuRant, R.H. (2000). Is race or ethnicity a predictive factor in shaken baby syndrome? *Child Abuse & Neglect, 24,* 1241–1246.

Singer, D.G., & Singer, J.L. (Eds.). (2001). *Handbook of children and the media.* Thousand Oaks, CA: Sage.

Singer, D.G., & Singer, J.L. (2005). *Imagination and play in the electronic age.* Cambridge, MA: Harvard University Press.

Singer, J.L., & Singer, D.G. (1998). Barney & Friends as entertainment and education: Evaluating the quality and effectiveness of a television series for preschool children. In J.K. Asamen, & G.L. Berry (Eds.), *Research paradigms, television, and social behavior* (pp. 305–367). Thousand Oaks, CA: Sage.

Singer, L.T., Arendt, R.E., Minnes, S., Farkas, K., Salvator, A., Kirchner, H.L., et al. (2002). Cognitive and motor outcomes of cocaine-exposed infants. *JAMA, 287,* 1952–1960.

Singh, G.K., & Kogan, M.D. (2007). Persistent socioeconomic disparities in infant, neonatal, and postneonatal mortality rates in the United States, 1969–2001. *Pediatrics, 119,* e928–e939.

Singhal, A., Cole, T.J., Fewtrell, M., & Lucas, A. (2004). Breastmilk feeding and lipoprotein profile in adolescents born preterm: Follow-up of a prospective randomised study. *The Lancet, 363,* 1571–1578.

Skinner, B.F. (1957). *Verbal behavior.* New York: Appleton.

Slater, A., Johnson, S.P., Brown, E., & Badenoch, M. (1996). Newborn infants' perception of partly occluded objects. *Infant Behavior and Development, 19,* 145–148.

Slater, A., & Morison, V. (1985). Shape constancy and slant perception at birth. *Perception, 14,* 337–344.

Slater, A., & Quinn, P.C. (2001). Face recognition in the newborn infant. *Infant and Child Development, 10,* 21–24.

Slobin, D.I. (Ed.). (1985). *The crosslinguistic study of language acquisition* (Vol. 2). Hillsdale, NJ: Lawrence Erlbaum Associates.

Slobin, D.I. (1992). Introduction. In D.I. Slobin (Ed.), *The crosslinguistic study of language acquisition* (Vol. 2, pp. 1–14). Hillsdale, NJ: Lawrence Erlbaum Associates.

Small, M.F. (1998). *Our babies, ourselves: How biology and culture shape the way we parent.* New York: Anchor Books.

Smetana, J.G. (1984). Toddlers' social interactions regarding moral and conventional transgressions. *Child Development, 55,* 1767–1776.

Smith, B.A., & Blass, E.M. (1996). Taste-mediated calming in premature, preterm, and full-term human infants. *Developmental Psychology, 32,* 1084–1089.

Smith, B.L. (1982). Some observations concerning pre-meaningful vocalizations: hearing-impaired infants. *Journal of Speech and Hearing Disorders, 47,* 439–442.

Smith, G.C.S., Pell, J.P., Cameron, A.D., & Dobbie, R. (2002). Risk of perinatal death associated with labor after previous Caesarean delivery in uncomplicated term pregnancies. *JAMA, 287,* 2684–2690.

Smith, K., & Bachu, A. (1999). Women's labor force attachment patterns and maternity leave: A review of the literature. *Population Division Working Paper No. 32.* Washington, DC: U.S. Bureau of the Census.

Smith, K., Downs, B., & O'Connell, M. (2001). Maternity leave and employment patterns: 1961–1995. *Current Population Reports P70(79)* (pp. 1–21). Washington, DC: U.S. Bureau of the Census.

Smith, L., & Yu, C. (2008). Infants rapidly learn word-referent mappings via cross-situational statistics. *Cognition, 106,* 1558–1568.

Smith, L.B. (2000). Learning how to learn words. In R.M. Golinkoff, K. Hirsh-Pasek, L. Bloom, L.B. Smith, A.L. Woodward, N. Akhtar et al. (Eds.), *Becoming a word learner: A debate on lexical acquisition* (pp. 51–80). New York: Oxford University Press.

Smith, L.E., & Howard, K.S. (2008). Continuity of paternal social support and depressive symptoms among new mothers. *Journal of Family Psychology, 22,* 763–773.

Smith, L.M., LaGasse, L.L., Derauf, C., Grant, P., Shah, R., Arria, A., et al. (2006). The infant development, environment, lifestyle study: Effects of prenatal methamphetamine exposure, polydrug exposure, and poverty on intrauterine growth. *Pediatrics, 118,* 1149–1156.

Smith, T., Kleiner, A., Parsad, B., & Farris, E. (2003). *Prekindergarten in U.S. public schools: 2000–2001, NCES 2003-019.* Washington, DC: National Center for Education Statistics.

Smuts, A.B., & Hagen, J.W. (Eds.) (1985). History and research in child development. *Monographs of the Society for Research in Child Development, 50*(4–5, Serial No. 211).

Smyke, A.T., Koga, S.F., Johnson, D.E., Fox, N.A., Marshall, P.J., Nelson, C.A., et al., (2007). The caregiving context in institution-reared and family-reared infants and toddlers in Romania. *Journal of Child Psychology and Psychiatry, 48,* 210–218.

Social Security Administration. (2009). *Popular baby names: Top 10 names for 2008.* Retrieved December 7, 2009, from http://www.ssa.gov/OACT/babynames/.

Society for Research in Child Development (2000). Ethical standards for research with children. *SRCD Directory of Members, 1999–2000* (pp. 283–284). Ann Arbor, MI: SRCD.

Soken, N.H., & Pick, A.D. (1992). Intermodal perception of happy and angry expressive behaviors by seven-month-old infants. *Child Development, 63,* 787–795.

Soken, N.H., & Pick, A.D. (1999). Infants' perception of dynamic affective expressions: Do infants distinguish specific expressions? *Child Development, 70,* 1275–1282

Sonenstein, F.L., Gates, G.J., Schmidt, S., & Bolshun, N. (2002). Primary child care arrangements of employed parents: Findings from the 1999 National Survey of America's Families. *Occasional Paper Number 59.* Washington, DC: The Urban Institute.

Song, H., & Baillargeon, R. (2008). Infants' reasoning about others' false perceptions. *Developmental Psychology, 44,* 1789–1795.

Song, H., Onishi, K.H., Baillargeon, R., & Fisher, C. (2008). Can an agent's false belief be corrected through an appropriate communication? Psychological reasoning in 18.5-month-old infants. *Cognition, 109,* 295–315.

Sorce, J.F., Emde, R.N., Campos, J.J., & Klinnert, M.D. (1985). Maternal emotional signaling: Its effects on the visual cliff behavior of 1-year-olds. *Developmental Psychology, 21,* 195–200. [cited in Harris, 1989]

Southgate, V., Senju, A., & Csibra, G. (2007). Action anticipation through attribution of false belief by two-year-olds. *Psychological Science, 18,* 587–592.

Spangler, G., & Grossmann, K.E. (1993). Biobehavioral organization in securely and insecurely attached infants. *Child Development, 64,* 1439–1450.

Spelke, E.S., Breinlinger, K., Jacobson, K., & Phillips, A. (1993). Gestalt relations and object perception: A developmental study. *Perception, 22,* 1483–1501.

Spelke, E.S., Breinlinger, K., Macomber, J., & Jacobson, K. (1992). Origins of knowledge. *Psychological Review, 99,* 605–632.

Spelke, E.S., & Kinzler, K.D. (2009). Innateness, learning, and rationality. *Child Development Perspectives, 3,* 96–98.

Spelke, E.S., & Newport, E.L. (1998). Nativism, empiricism, and the development of knowledge. In W. Damon (Editor-in-Chief) & R.M. Lerner (Vol. Ed.), *Handbook of child psychology: Vol. 1. Theoretical models of human development* (5th ed., pp. 275–340). New York: Wiley.

Spencer, J.P., Blumberg, M.S., McMurray, B., Robinson, S.R., Samuelson, L.K., & Tomblin, J.B. (2009). Short arms and talking eggs: Why we should no longer abide the nativist-empiricist debate. *Child Development Perspectives, 3,* 79–87.

Spencer, J.P., & Perone, S. (2008). Defending qualitative change: The view from dynamical systems theory. *Child Development, 79,* 1639–1647.

Spencer, J.P., Smith, L.B., & Thelen, E. (2001). Tests of a dynamic systems account of the A-not-B error: The influence of prior experience on the spatial memory abilities of two-year-olds. *Child Development, 72,* 1327–1346.

Spitz, R. (1945). Hospitalism. An inquiry into the genesis of psychiatric conditions in early childhood. In A. Freud, H. Hartmann, & E. Kris (Eds.), *The psychoanalytic study of the child* (pp. 53–74). New York: International Universities Press.

Spivak, L., Sokol, H., Auerbach, C., & Gershkovich, S. (2009). Newborn hearing screening follow-up: Factors affecting hearing aid fitting by six months of age. *American Journal of Audiology, 18,* 23–33.

Sroufe, L.A. (1979). The coherence of individual development: Early care, attachment, and subsequent developmental issues. *American Psychologist, 34,* 834–841.

Sroufe, L.A. (2005). Attachment and development: A prospective, longitudinal study from birth to adulthood. *Attachment and Human Development, 7,* 349–367.

Sroufe, L.A., Carlson, E., & Shulman, S. (1993). Individuals in relationships: Development from infancy through adolescence. In D.C. Funder, R.D. Parke, C. Tomlinson-Keasey, & K. Widaman (Eds.), *Studying lives through time: Personality and development* (pp. 315–342). Washington, DC: American Psychological Association Press.

Sroufe, L.A., Egeland, B., & Carlson, E. (1999). One social world: The integrated development of parent-child and peer relationships. In W.A. Collins, & B. Laursen (Eds.), *Minnesota Symposium on Child Psychology: Vol. 30. Relationships as developmental contexts* (pp. 241–262). Mahwah, NJ: Lawrence Erlbaum Associates.

Sroufe, L.A., Egeland, B., Carlson, E., & Collins, W.A. (2005). *The development of the person: The Minnesota Study of Risk and Adaptation from Birth to Adulthood.* New York: Guilford Press.

St. James-Roberts, I., & Plewis, I. (1996). Individual differences, daily fluctuations, and developmental changes in amounts of infant waking, fussing, crying, feeding, and sleeping. *Child Development, 67,* 2527–2540.

Stack, D.M., & Muir, D.W. (1990). Tactile stimulation as a component of social interchange: New interpretations for the still-face effect. *British Journal of Developmental Psychology, 8,* 131–145.

Stack, D.M., & Muir, D.W. (1992). Adult tactile stimulation during face-to-face interactions modulates five-month-olds' affect and attention. *Child Development, 63,* 1509–1525.

Stack, D.M., Muir, D.W., Sherriff, F., Roman, J. (1989). Development of infant reaching in the dark to luminous objects and 'invisible sounds.' *Perception, 18,* 69–82.

Stams, G.J., Juffer, F., & van IJzendoorn, M.H. (2002). Maternal sensitivity, infant attachment, and temperament in early childhood predict adjustment in middle childhood: The case of adopted children and their biologically unrelated parents. *Developmental Psychology, 38,* 806–821.

Standley, J.M. (2002). A meta-analysis of the efficacy of music therapy for premature infants. *Journal of Pediatric Nursing, 17,* 107–113.

Stansbury, K., & Gunnar, M.R. (1994). Adrenocortical activity and emotion regulation. In N.A. Fox (Ed.), The development of emotion regulation: Biological and behavioral considerations. *Monographs of the Society for Research in Child Development, 59*(2–3, Serial No. 240), 108–134.

Starr, W. (1976). *The Suzuki violinist.* Knoxville, TN: Kingston Ellis Press.

Statistics Canada. (2003). The people: Household and family life: Stress. In Statistics Canada. Canada e-book. Ottawa, Ontario: Statistics Canada; 2003. Retrieved December 22, 2005, from http://142.206.72.67/02/02d/02d_005_e.htm

Steiner, J.E. (1979). Human facial expressions in response to taste and smell stimulation. In H.W. Reese, & L.PJ. Lipsitt (Eds.), *Advances in child development and behavior* (Vol. 13, pp. 257–295). New York: Academic Press.

Stenberg, C., & Campos, J.J. (1990). The development of anger expressions in infancy. In N. Stein, T. Trabasso, & B. Leventhal (Eds.), *Concepts in emotion* (pp. 518–530). Hillsdale, NJ: Lawrence Erlbaum Associates.

Stenberg, C., Campos, J.J., & Emde, R.N. (1983). The facial expression of anger in 7-month-old infants. *Child Development, 54,* 178–184.

Steptoe, P.C., & Edwards, R.G. (1978). Birth after re-implantation of a human embryo. *Lancet, 2,* 366.

Stewart, C.E., Stephens, D.A., Fielder, A.R., Moseley, M.J., et al. (2007). Modeling dose-response in amblyopia: Toward a child-specific treatment plan. *Investigative Ophthalmology & Visual Science, 48,* 2589–2594.

Stewart, R.B. (1983). Sibling attachment relationship: Child-infant interactions in the strange situation. *Developmental Psychology, 19,* 192–199.

Stewart, R.B., & Marvin, R.S. (1984). Sibling relations: The role of conceptual perspective-taking in the ontogeny of sibling caregiving. *Child Development, 55,* 1322–1332.

Stilson, S.R., & Harding, C.G. (1997). Early social context as it relates to symbolic play: A longitudinal investigation. *Merrill-Palmer Quarterly, 43,* 682–693.

Stipek, D., Recchia, S., & McClintic, S. (1992). Self-evaluation in young children. *Monographs of the Society for Research in Child Development, 57*(1, Serial No. 226).

Stoffregen, T., Adolph, K.E., Thelen, E., Gorday, K.M., & Sheng, Y.Y. (1997). Toddlers' postural adaptations to different support surfaces. *Motor Control, 1,* 119–137.

Stolz, H.E., Barber, B.K., & Olsen, J.A. (2005). Toward disentangling fathering and mothering: An assessment of relative importance. *Journal of Marriage and Family, 67,* 1076–1092.

Stone, P.W., Zwanziger, J., Hinton Walker, P., & Buenting, J. (2000). Economic analysis of two models of low-risk maternity care: A freestanding birth center compared to traditional care. *Research in Nursing & Health, 23,* 279–289.

Streri, A., & Molina, M. (1993). Visual-tactual and tactual-visual transfer between objects and pictures in 2-month-old infants. *Perception, 22,* 1299–1318.

Striano, T., Reid, V.M., & Hoehl, S. (2006). Neural mechanisms of joint attention in infancy. *European Journal of Neuroscience, 23,* 2819–2823.

Striano, T., Stahl, D., Cleveland, A., & Hoehl, S. (2007). Sensitivity to triadic attention between 6 weeks and 3 months of age. *Infant Behavior & Development, 30,* 529–534.

Strickland, C.E., & Ambrose, A.M. (1985). The baby boom, prosperity, and the changing worlds of children, 1945–1963. In J.M. Hawes, & N.R. Hiner (Eds.), *American childhood: A research guide and historical handbook* (pp. 533–585). Westport, CT: Greenwood Press.

Strid, K., Tjus, T., Smith, L., Meltzoff, A.N., & Heimann, M. (2006). Infant recall memory and communication predicts later cognitive development. *Infant Behavior & Development, 29,* 545–553.

Stromswold, K. (2006). Why aren't identical twins linguistically identical? Genetic, prenatal and postnatal factors. *Cognition, 101,* 333–384.

Sturner, R., Layton, T., Evans, A., Heller, J., Funk, S., & Machon, M. (1994). Preschool speech and language screening: A review of currently available tests. *American Journal of Speech-Language Pathology, 3,* 25–36.

Suárez, Z.E. (1999). Cuban Americans in exile: Myths and reality. In H.P. McAdoo (Ed.), *Family ethnicity: Strength in diversity* (2nd ed., pp. 135–152). Thousand Oaks, CA: Sage.

Suddendorf, T. (2003). Early representational insight: Twenty-four-month-olds can use a photo to find an object in the world. *Child Development, 74,* 896–904.

Sun, L.C., & Roopnarine, J.L. (1996). Mother-infant, father-infant interaction and involvement in childcare and household labor among Taiwanese families. *Infant Behavior and Development, 19,* 121–129.

Sunderam, S., Chang, J., Flowers, L., Kulkarni, A., Sentelle, G., Jeng, G., et al. (2009). Assisted reproductive technology surveillance—United States, 2006. *Morbidity & Mortality Weekly Report Surveillance Summary, 58*(5), 1–25.

Suomi, S. J. (1991). Early stress and adult emotional reactivity in rhesus monkeys. In D. Barker (Ed.), *The childhood environment and adult disease* (Ciba Foundation Symposium #156, pp. 171–188). Chichester, UK: Wiley.

Super, C. (1976). Environmental effects on motor development: The case of African infant precocity. *Developmental Medicine and Child Neurology, 18,* 561–567.

Super, C.M., & Harkness, S. (2009). Culture and infancy. In G. Bremner, & T. D. Wachs (Eds.), *Blackwell handbook of infant development* (Vol. 1). Oxford, UK: Blackwell.

Super, C.M., Harkness, S., van Tijen, N., van der Vlugt, E., Fintelman, M., & Dijkstra, J. (1996). The three R's of Dutch childrearing and the socialization of infant arousal. In S. Harkness, & C.M. Super (Eds.), *Parents' cultural belief systems: Their origins, expressions, and consequences* (pp. 447–466). New York: Guilford Press.

Susman-Stillman, A., Kalkoske, M., Egeland, B., & Waldman, I. (1996). Infant temperament and maternal sensitivity as predictors of attachment security. *Infant Behavior and Development, 19,* 33–47.

Suzuki, S. (1973). Children can develop their ability to the highest standard. In E. Mills, & T.C. Murphy (Eds.), *The Suzuki concept: An introduction to a successful method for early music education* (pp. 9–16). Berkeley, CA: Diablo Press.

Swan, S.H. (2000). Intrauterine exposure to diethylstilbestrol: Long-term effects in humans. *APMIS, 108,* 793–804.

Sylvester, K. (2001). Caring for our youngest: Public attitudes in the United States. *The Future of Children, 11*(1), 53–61.

Symon, A., Winter, C., Inkster, M., & Donnan, P.T. (2009). Outcomes for births booked under an independent midwife and births in NHS maternity units: Matched comparison study. *BMJ, 338,* b2060–b2068.

Tabor, A., Vestergaard, C.H., & Lidegaard, O. (2009). Fetal loss rate after chorionic villus sampling and amniocentesis: An 11-year national registry study. *Ultrasound Obstetrics & Gynecology, 34,* 19–34.

Taddio, A., Shah, V., Atenafu, E., & Katz, J. (2009). Influence of repeated painful procedures and sucrose analgesia on the development of hyperalgesia in newborn infants. *Pain, 144,* 43–48.

Tager-Flusberg, H. (1993). What language reveals about the understanding of minds in children with autism. In S. Baron-Cohen, H. Tager-Flusberg, & D. Cohen (Eds.), *Understanding other minds: Perspectives from autism* (pp. 138–157). Oxford, UK: Oxford University Press.

Tager-Flusberg, H. (2004). Strategies for conducting research on language in autism. *Journal of Autism and Developmental Disorders, 34,* 75–80.

Takanishi, R., & Bogard, K.L. (2007). Effective educational programs for young children: What we need to know. *Child Development Perspectives, 1,* 40–45.

Talbot, J.A., Baker, J.K., & McHale, J.P. (2009). Sharing the love: Prebirth adult attachment status and coparenting adjustment during early infancy. *Parenting: Science and Practice, 9,* 56–77.

Talge, N.M., Neal, C., Glover, V., et al. (2007). Antenatal maternal stress and long-term effects on child neurodevelopment: How and why? *Journal of Child Psychology & Psychiatry, 48,* 245–261.

Tamis-LeMonda, C.S., & Bornstein, M.H. (1996). Variation in children's exploratory, nonsymbolic, and symbolic play: An exploratory multidimensional framework. In C. Rovee-Collier, & L.P. Lipsitt (Eds.), *Advances in infancy research* (Vol. 10, pp. 37–78). Norwood, NJ: Ablex.

Tamis-LeMonda, C.S., Bornstein, M.H., & Baumwell, L. (2001). Maternal responsiveness and children's achievement of language milestones. *Child Development, 72,* 748–767.

Tamis-LeMonda, C.S., Bornstein, M.H., Cyphers, L., Toda, S., & Ogino, M. (1992). Language and play at one year: A comparison of toddlers and mothers in the United States and Japan. *International Journal of Behavioral Development, 15,* 19–42.

Tamis-LeMonda, C.S., Chen, L.A., & Bornstein, M.H. (1997). Mothers' knowledge about children's play and language development: Short-term stability and interrelations. *Developmental Psychology, 34,* 115–124.

Tamis-LeMonda, C.S., Damast, A.M., & Bornstein, M.H. (1994). What do mothers know about the developmental nature of play? *Infant Behavior and Development, 17,* 341–345.

Tamis-LeMonda, C.S., Shannon, J.D., Cabrera, N.J., & Lamb, M.E. (2004). Fathers and mothers at play with their 2- and 3-year-olds: Contributions to language and cognitive development. *Child Development, 75,* 1806–1820.

Task Force on Sudden Infant Death Syndrome. (2005). The changing concept of sudden infant death syndrome: Diagnostic coding shifts, controversies regarding the sleep environment, and new variables to consider in reducing risk. *Pediatrics, 116,* 1245–1255.

Taumoepeau, M., & Ruffman, T. (2006). Mother and infant talk about mental states relates to desire language and emotion understanding. *Child Development, 77,* 465–481.

Taveras, E.M., Scanlon, K.S., Birch, L., Rifas-Shiman, S.L., Rich-Edwards, J.W., & Gillman, M.W. (2004). Association of breastfeeding with maternal control of infant feeding at age 1 year. *Pediatrics, 114,* e577–e583.

Taylor, H.S. (2000). The role of HOX genes in the development and function of the female reproductive tract. *Seminars in Reproductive Medicine, 18,* 81–89.

Taylor, I. (1990). *Psycholinguistics*. Englewood Cliffs, NJ: Prentice Hall.

Teinonen, T., Aslin, R.N., Alku, P., & Csibra, G. (2008). Visual speech contributes to phonetic learning in 6-month-old infants. *Cognition, 108,* 850–855.

Teletubbies Frequently Asked Questions. (2002). Retrieved November 20, 2002, from http://www.bbc.co/uk/cbeebies/teltubbies/information/faq/

Teller, D.Y., Peeples, D.R., & Sekel, M. (1978). Discrimination of chromatic from white light by 2-month-old infants. *Vision Research, 18,* 41–48.

Tessier, R., Charpak, N., Giron, M., de Calume, Z.F., & Ruiz-Pelaez, J.G. (2009). Kangaroo Mother Care, home environment and father involvement in the first year of life: A randomized controlled study. *Acta Paediatrica, 98,* 1444–1450.

Teti, D.M. (2002). Sibling relationships. In J. McHale, & W. Grolnick (Eds.), *Interiors: Retrospect and prospect in the psychological study of families* (pp. 193–224). Mahwah, NJ: Erlbaum.

Teti, D.M., & Ablard, K.E. (1989). Security of attachment and infant-sibling relationships: A laboratory study. *Child Development, 60,* 1519–1528.

Teti, D.M., Gelfand, D.M., Messinger, D.S., & Isabella, R. (1995). Maternal depression and the quality of early attachment: An examination of infants, preschoolers, and their mothers. *Developmental Psychology, 31,* 364–376.

Teti, D.M., Sakin, J., Kucera, E., Corns, K.M., & Eiden, R.D. (1996). And baby makes four: Predictors of attachment security among preschool-aged firstborns during the transition to siblinghood. *Child Development, 67,* 579–596.

Teti, D.M., & Teti, L.O. (1996). Infant-parent relationships. In N. Canzetti, & S. Duck (Eds.), *A lifetime of relationships* (pp. 77–104). Pacific Grove, CA: Brooks/Cole.

Tew, M., & Damstra-Wijmenga, S.M.I. (1991). The safest birth attendants: Recent Dutch evidence. *Midwifery, 7,* 55–65.

Thakkar, R.R., Garrison, M.M., & Christakis, D.A. (2006). A systematic review for the effects of television viewing by infants and preschoolers. *Pediatrics, 118,* 2025–2031.

Thelen, E., Fisher, D.M., & Ridley-Johnson, R. (1984). The relationship between physical growth and a newborn reflex. *Infant Behavior and Development, 7,* 479–493.

Thelen, E., & Smith, L. (1994). *A dynamic systems approach to the development of cognition and action.* Cambridge, MA: MIT Press.

Thelen, E., & Smith, L.B. (2006). Dynamic systems theories. In W. Damon, & R.M. Lerner (Eds.), R.M. Lerner (Vol. Eds.), *Handbook of Child Psychology: Vol. 1. Theoretical models of human development* (6th ed., pp. 258–312). New York: Wiley.

Thelen, E., & Spencer, J.P. (1998). Postural control during reaching in young infants: A dynamic systems approach. *Neuroscience and Biobehavioral Reviews, 22,* 507–514.

Thiessen, E.D., Hill, E.A., & Saffran, J.R. (2005). Infant-directed speech facilitates word segmentation. *Infancy, 7,* 53–71.

Thiessen, E.D., & Saffran, J.R. (2003). When cues collide: Use of stress and statistical cues to word boundaries by 7- to 9-month-old infants. *Developmental Psychology, 39,* 706–716.

Thiessen, E.D., & Saffran, J.R. (2007). Learning to learn: Infants' acquisition of stress-based strategies for word segmentation. *Language Learning and Development, 3,* 73–100.

Thoman, E.B. (1990). Sleeping and waking states in infants: A functional perspective. *Neuroscience & Biobehavioral Reviews, 14,* 93–107.

Thomas, A., & Chess, S. (1977). *Temperament and development.* New York: Brunner/Mazel.

Thomas, A., Chess, S., & Birch, H.G. (1968). *Temperament and behavior disorders in children.* New York: New York University Press.

Thomas, A., Chess, S., Birch, H.G., Hertzig, M.E., & Korn, S. (1963). *Behavioral individuality in early childhood.* New York: New York University Press.

Thompson, B.L., Levitt, P., & Stanwood, G.D. (2009). Prenatal exposure to drugs: Effects on brain development and implications for policy and education. *Nature Reviews Neuroscience, 10,* 303–312.

Thompson, R.A. (1990). Vulnerability in research: A developmental perspective on research risk. *Child Development, 61,* 1–16.

Thompson, R.A. (1994). Emotion regulation: A theme in search of definition. In N.A. Fox (Ed.), The development of emotion regulation: Biological and behavioral considerations. *Monographs of the Society for Research in Child Development, 59*(2–3, Serial No. 240), 25–52.

Thompson, R.A. (1998). Early sociopersonality development. In W. Damon (Editor-in-Chief) & N. Eisenberg (Vol. Ed.), *Handbook of child psychology Vol. 3. Social, emotional, and personality development* (5th ed., pp. 25–104). New York: Wiley.

Thompson, R.A. (2006). The development of the person: Social understanding, relationships, conscience, self. In W. Damon & R. Lerner (Eds.) & N. Eisenberg (Vol. Ed.), *Handbook of child psychology: Vol. 3. Social, emotional, and personality development* (6th ed., pp. 24–98). New York: Wiley.

Thompson, R.A., Lewis, M.D., & Calkins, S.D. (2008). Reassessing emotion regulation. *Child Development Perspectives, 2,* 124–131.

Thorpe, L.A., & Trehub, S.E. (1989). Duration illusion and auditory grouping in infancy. *Developmental Psychology, 25,* 122–127.

Thorpe, L.A., Trehub, S.E., Morrongiello, B.A., & Bull, D. (1988). Perceptual grouping by infants and preschool children. *Developmental Psychology, 24,* 484–491.

Timmons, P.M., Rigby, P.W. J., & Poirer, F. (2001). The murine seminiferous cycle is pre-figured in the Sertoli cells of the embryonic testis. *Development, 129,* 635–647.

Tikotzky, L., & Sadeh, A. (2009). Maternal sleep-related cognitions and infant sleep: A longitudinal study from pregnancy through the 1st year. *Child Development, 80,* 860–874.

Todman, D. (2007). Childbirth in ancient Rome: From traditional folklore to obstetrics. *Australian and New Zealand Journal of Obstetrics and Gynaecoloy, 47,* 82–85.

Tollånes, M.C., Thompson, J., Daltveit, A.K. & Irgens, L.M. (2007). Cesarean section and maternal education: Secular trends in Norway, 1967–2004. *Acta Obstetricia et Gynecologica Scandinavica, 86,* 840–848.

Tomasello, M. (2000). Do young children have adult syntactic competence? *Cognition, 74,* 209–253.

Tomasello, M. (2006). Acquiring linguistic constructions. In W. Damon, & R. Lerner (Eds.) & D. Kuhn, & R. Siegler (Vol. Eds.), *Handbook of child psychology: Vol. 2. Cognition, perception, and language* (6th ed., pp. 255–298). New York: Wiley.

Tomasello, M. (2007). Cooperation and communication in the 2nd year of life. *Child Development Perspectives, 1,* 8–12.

Tomasello, M., & Barton, M. (1994). Learning words in non-ostensive context. *Developmental Psychology, 30,* 639–650.

Tomasello, M., Carpenter, M., & Liszkowski, U. (2007). A new look at infant pointing. *Child Development, 78,* 705–722.

Tomasello, M., & Farrar, J. (1986). Joint attention and early language. *Child Development, 57,* 1454–1463.

Tomopoulos, S., Valdez, P.T., Dreyer, B.P., Fierman, A.H., Berkule, S.B., Kuhn, M., et al. (2007). Is exposure to media intended for preschool children associated with less parent-child shared reading aloud and teaching activities? *Ambulatory Pediatrics, 7,* 18–24.

Tong, V.T., Jones, J.R., Dietz, P.M., D'Angelo, D., Bombard, J.M., & Centers for Disease Control and Prevention. (2009). Trends in smoking before, during, and after pregnancy—Pregnancy Risk Assessment Monitoring System (PRAMS), United States, 31 sites, 2000–2005. *Morbidity & Mortality Weekly Report, 58,* 1–29.

Toth, S.L., Rogosch, F.A., Sturge-Apple, M., & Cicchetti, D. (2009). Maternal depression, children's attachment security, and representational development: An organizational perspective. *Child Development, 80,* 192–208.

Tournaye, H., & Van Steirteghem, A. (1997). Intracytoplasmic sperm injection: ICSI concerns do not outweigh its benefits. *Journal of NIH Research, 9,* 35, 39–40.

Townsend, N.W. (1997). Men, migration, and households in Botswana: An exploration of connections over time and space. *Journal of Southern African Studies, 23,* 405–420.

Tozzi, A.E., Bisiacchi, P., Tarantino, V., De Mei, B., D'Elia, L., Chiarotti, F., et al. (2009). Neuropsychological performance 10 years after immunization in infancy with thimerosal-containing vaccines. *Pediatrics, 123,* 475–482.

Trainor, L.J., Austin, C.M., & Desjardins, R.N. (2000). Is infant-directed speech prosody a result of the vocal expression of emotion? *Psychological Science, 11,* 188–195.

Trainor, L.J., Wu, L., & Tsang, C.D. (2004). Long-term memory for music: Infants remember tempo and timbre. *Developmental Science, 7,* 289–296.

Trainor, L.J., & Zacharias, C.A. (1998). Infants prefer higher-pitched singing. *Infant Behavior and Development, 21,* 799–806.

Trautmann-Villalba, P., Gschwendt, M., Schmidt, M.H., & Laucht, M. (2006). Father-infant interaction patterns as precursors of children's later externalizing behavior problems: A longitudinal study over 11 years. *European Archives of Psychiatry and Clinical Neuroscience, 256,* 344–349.

Travis, L.L., & Sigman, M.D. (2000). A developmental approach to autism. In A.J. Sameroff, M. Lewis, & S.M. Miller (Eds.), *Handbook of developmental psychopathology* (2nd ed., pp. 641–655). New York: Plenum.

Trehub, S.E. (September, 2002). Mothers are musical mentors. *Zero to Three, 23,* 19–20.

Trehub, S.E., Hill, D.S., & Kamenetsky, S.B. (1997). Parents' sung performances for infants. *Canadian Journal of Experimental Psychology, 51,* 385–396.

Trehub, S.E., & Trainor, L. (1998). Singing to infants: Lullabies and play songs. *Advances in Infancy Research, 12,* 43–77.

Trehub, S.E., Unyk, A.M., & Henderson, J.L. (1994). Children's songs to infant siblings: Parallels with speech. *Journal of Child Language, 21,* 735–744.

Trehub, S.E., Unyk, A.M., Kamenetsky, S.G., Hill, D.S., Trainor, L.J., Henderson, J.L., & Saraza, M. (1997). Mothers' and fathers' singing to infants. *Developmental Psychology, 33,* 500–507.

Trehub, S.E., Unyk, A.M., Trainor, L.J. (1993a). Adults identify infant-directed music across cultures. *Infant Behavior and Development, 16,* 193–211.

Trehub, S.E., Unyk, A.M., Trainor, L.J. (1993b). Maternal singing in cross-cultural perspective. *Infant Behavior and Development, 16,* 285–295.

Tremblay, H., & Rovira, K. (2007). Joint visual attention and social triangular engagement at 3 and 6 months. *Infant Behavior & Development, 30*, 366–379.

Trimble, E.L. (2001). Update on diethylstilbestrol. *Obstetrics and Gynecological Survey, 56*, 187–189.

Troisi, R., Hatch, E.E., Titus-Ernstoff, L., Hyer, M., Palmer, J.R., Robboy, S.J., et al. (2007). Cancer risk in women prenatally exposed to diethylstilbestrol. *International Journal of Cancer, 121*, 356–360.

Tronick, E.Z., & Weinberg, M.K. (1997). Depressed mothers and infants: Failure to form dyadic states of consciousness. In L. Murray, & P.J. Cooper (Eds.), *Postpartum depression and child development* (pp. 54–81). New York: Guilford Press.

Tsao, F.M., Liu, H.M., & Kuhl, P.K. (2004). Speech perception in infancy predicts language development in the second year of life: A longitudinal study. *Child Development, 75*, 1067–1084.

Tudge, J.R.H., Doucet, F., Odero, D., Sperb, T.M., Piccinini, C.A., & Lopes, R.S. (2006). A window into different cultural worlds: Young children's everyday activities in the United States, Brazil, and Kenya. *Child Development, 77*, 1446–1469.

Tudge, J.R., Lee, S., & Putnam, S. (1998). Young children's play in socio-cultural context: South Korea and the United States. In S. Reifel (Series Ed.), *Play and Culture Studies* (Vol. 1, pp. 77–90). Stamford, CT: Ablex.

U.S. Census Bureau. (2003). Who's minding the kids? Child care arrangements: Spring 1999. *Current Population Reports, Detailed Tables (PPL–168).* Washington, DC: U.S. Bureau of the Census.

U.S. Department of Agriculture. (2002). *How WIC helps.* Retrieved January 10, 2003, from http://www.fns.usda.gov/wic/ProgramInfo/howwichelps.htm

U.S. Department of Education. (2006). *Topical brief on the reauthorized Individuals with Disabilities Educaion Act (IDEA).* Retrieved December 21, 2009, from http://idea.ed.gov/explore/view/p/%2Croot%2Cdynamic%2CTopicalBrief%2C10%2C.

U.S. Department of Health and Human Services. (2000a). *Healthy people 2010: Understanding and improving health.* Washington, DC: U.S. Government Printing Office.

U.S. Department of Health and Human Services. (2000b, November 27). *HHS Fact Sheet: HHS on the forefront of autism research.* Retrieved May 2, 2001, from http://www.hhs.gov/news/press/2001pres/01fsautism.html

U.S. Department of Health and Human Services (2009). *Autism spectrum disorders fact sheet.* Retrieved September 10, 2009, from http://www.cdc.gov/actearly

U.S. Department of Health and Human Services, Administration on Children, Youth and Families.

(2009). *Child maltreatment 2007.* Washington, DC: U.S. Government Printing Office. Retrieved July 19, 2009, from http://www.acf.hhs.gov/programs/cb/pubs/cm07/index.htm

U.S. Department of Labor. (2005). Federal vs. state Family and Medical Leave laws. Retrieved August 23, 2005, from http://www.dol.gov/esa/programs/whd/state/fmla/index.htm

UNICEF. (2009). *State of the world's children, 2009.* New York: UNICEF. Retrieved July 27, 2009, from http://www.unicef.org/sowc09/index.php.

United Nations. (2008a). Goal 4: Reduce child mortality. *Millennium Development Goals Report, 2008.* New York: Author.

United Nations (2008b). The Millennium Development Goals report. New York: United Nations. Retrieved July 13, 2009, from http://www.un.org/millenniumgoals.

United States Food and Drug Administration. (1996). Folic acid fortification fact sheet. Retrieved September 10, 2001, from http://www.cfsan.fda.gov/~dms/wh-folic.html

Unyk, A.M., Trehub, S.E., Trainor, L.J., & Schellenberg, G. (1992). Lullabies and simplicity: A cross-cultural perspective. *Psychology of Music, 20*, 15–28.

Uygur, D., Kis, S., Tuncer, R., Ozcan, F., & Erkaya, S. (2002). Risk factors and infant outcomes associated with umbilical cord prolapse. *International Journal of Gynaecology and Obstetrics, 78*, 127–130.

Vagh, S.B., Pan, B.A., & Mancilla-Martinez, J. (2009). Measuring growth in bilingual and monolingual children's English productive vocabulary development: The utility of combining parent and teacher report. *Child Development, 80*, 1545–1563.

Valenti, C.A. (2006). Infant vision guidance: Fundamental vision development in infancy. *Optometry and Vision Development, 37*, 147–155.

Valenzuela, M. (1997). Maternal sensitivity in a developing society: The context of urban poverty and infant chronic undernutrition. *Developmental Psychology, 33*, 845–855.

Vallabha, G.K., McClelland, J.L., Pons, F., Werker, J.F., & Amano, S. (2007). Unsupervised learning of vowel categories from infant-directed speech. *Proceedings of the National Academy of Science, 104*, 13273–13278.

VanArsdale, J.L., Leiker, R.D., Kohn, M., Merritt, T.A., & Horowitz, B.Z. (2004). Lead poisoning from a toy necklace. *Pediatrics, 114*, 1096–1099.

Vance, M.R. (2006). Summary of breastfeeding legislation in the U.S. Retrieved May 12,

2006, from http://www.lalecheleague.org/Law/summary.html

Van de Velde, M., Vercauteren, M., & Vandermeersch, E. (2001). Fetal heart rate abnormalities after regional analgesia for labor pain: The effect of intrathecal opioids. *Regional Anesthia and Pain Medicine, 26*, 257–262.

van den Boom, D.C. (1989). Neonatal irritability and the development of attachment. In G.A. Kohnstamm, J.E. Bates, & M.K. Rothbart (Eds.), *Temperament in childhood* (pp. 299–318). Chichester, UK: Wiley.

van den Boom, D.C. (1994). The influence of temperament and mothering on attachment and exploration: An experimental manipulation of sensitive responsiveness among lower-class mothers with irritable infants. *Child Development, 65*, 1457–1477.

van den Boom, D.C. (2001). First attachments: Theory and research. In G. Bremner, & A. Fogel (Eds.), *Blackwell handbook of infant development* (pp. 296–325). Oxford, UK: Blackwell.

van IJzendoorn, M.H., Dijkstra, J., & Bus, A.G. (1995). Attachment, intelligence, and language: A meta-analysis. *Social Development, 4*, 115–128.

van IJzendoorn, M.H., Goldberg, S., Kroonenberg, P.M., & Frenkel, O.J. (1992). The relative effects of maternal and child problems on the quality of attachment: A meta-analysis of attachment in clinical samples. *Child Development, 63*, 840–858.

van IJzendoorn, M.H., Moran, G., Belsky, J., Pederson, D., Bakermans-Krannburg, M.J., & Kneppers, K. (2000). *Child Development, 71*, 1086–1098.

van IJzendoorn, M.H., Schuengel, C., & Bakermans-Kranenburg, M.J. (1999). Disorganized attachment in early childhood: Meta-analysis of precursors, concomitants, and sequelae. *Development and Psychopathology, 11*, 225–249.

Van Rheenen, P., & Brabin, B.J. (2006). A practical approach to timing of cord clamping in resource poor settings. *BMJ, 333*, 954–958.

Van Rheenen, P., de Moor, L., Eschbach, S., de Grooth, H., & Brabin, B. (2007). Delayed cord clamping and haemoglobin levels in infancy: A randomized controlled trial in term babies. *Tropical Medicine and International Health, 12*, 603–616.

vanDijk, C.E., & Innis, S.M. (2009). Growth-curve standards and the assessment of early excess weight gain in infancy. *Pediatrics, 123*, 102–108.

Varendi, H., Porter, R.H., & Winberg, J. (1992). Attractiveness of amniotic fluid odor: Evidence of prenatal olfactory learning? *Acta paediatrica, 85*, 1223–1227.

Vaughn, B.E., & Bost, K.K. (1999). Attachment and temperament: Redundant, independent, or interacting influences on interpersonal adaptation and personality development? In J. Cassidy, & P.R. Shaver (Eds.), *Handbook of attachment: Theory, research, and clinical applications* (pp. 198–225). New York: Guilford Press.

Vaughn, B.E., Stevenson-Hinde, J., Waters, E., Kotsaftis, A., Lefaver, G.B., Shouldice, A., Trudel, M., & Belsky, J. (1992). Attachment security and temperament in infancy in early childhood. *Developmental Psychology, 28*, 463–473.

Vaughn Van Hecke, A., & Mundy, P. (2007). Neural systems and the development of gaze-following and related joint attention skills. In R. Flom, K. Lee, & D. Muir (Eds.), *Gaze-following: Its development and significance* (pp. 17–51). Mahwah, NJ: Lawrence Erlbaum Associates.

Vennemann, M.M., Bajanowski, T., Brinkmann, B., Jorch, G., Sauerland, C., Mitchell, E.A., et al. (2009). Sleep environment risk factors for Sudden Infant Death Syndrome: The German Sudden Infant Death Syndrome Study. *Pediatrics, 123*, 1162–1170.

Vennemann, M.M., Bajanowski, T., Brinkmann, B., Jorch, G., Yücesan, K., Sauerland, C., et al. (2009). Does breastfeeding reduce the risk of Sudden Infant Death Syndrome? *Pediatrics, 123*, e406–e410.

Venter, J.C., Adams, M.D., Myers, E.W., Li, P.W., Mural, R.J., Sutton, G.G., et al. (2001). The sequence of the human genome. *Science, 291*, 1304–1351.

Ventura, S.J., Hamilton, B.E., Mathews, T.J., & Chandra, A. (2003). Trends and variations in smoking during pregnancy and low birth weight: Evidence from the birth certificate, 1990–2000. *Pediatrics, 111*, 1176–1180.

Vereijken, B., Pedersen, A.V., & Størksen, J.H. (2009). Early independent walking: A longitudinal study of load perturbation effects. *Developmental Psychobiology, 51*, 374–383.

Vereijken, B., & Thelen, E. (1997). Training infant treadmill stepping: The role of individual pattern stability. *Developmental Psychobiology, 30*, 89–102.

Verlinsky, Y., Cohen, J., Munne, S., et al. (2004). Over a decade of preimplantation genetic diagnosis experience—a multicenter report. *Fertility and Sterility, 82*, 292–294.

Verlinsky, Y., Rechitsky, S., Schoolcraft, W., Strom, C., & Kuliev, A. (2001). Preimplantation diagnosis for Fanconi anemia combined with HLA matching. *JAMA, 285*, 3130–3133.

Verlinsky, Y., Rechitsky, S., Verlinsky, O., Masciangelo, C., Lederer, K., & Kuliev, A. (2002). Preimplantation diagnosis for early-onset Alzheimer disease caused by V717L mutation. *JAMA, 287*, 1018–1021.

Verschueren, K., Marcoen, A., & Schoefs, V. (1996). The internal working model of the self, attachment, and competence in five-year-olds. *Child Development, 67,* 2493–2511.

Vestergaard, M., Wisborg, K., Henriksen, T.B., Secher, N.J., Ostergaard, J.R., & Olsen, J. (2005). Prenatal exposure to cigarettes, alcohol, and coffee and the risk for febrile seizures. *Pediatrics, 116,* 1089–1094.

Vihman, M.M., Thierry, G., Lum, J., Keren-Portnoy, T., & Martin, P. (2007). Onset of word form recognition in English, Welsh, and English-Welsh bilingual infants. *Applied Psycholinguistics, 28,* 475–493.

Vogel, C.A., Bradley, R., Raikes, H.H., Boller, K., & Shears, J. (2006). Relation between father connectedness and child outcomes. *Parenting Science and Practice, Special Issue Early Head Start Fathers and Children, 6,* 189–211.

Volden, J., & Lord, C. (1991). Neologisms and idiosyncratic language in autistic speakers. *Journal of Autism and Developmental Disorders, 21,* 109–131.

Volkmar, F.R., & Mayes, L.C. (1990). Gaze behavior in autism. *Development and Psychopathology, 2,* 61–69.

Volling, B.L., McElwain, N.L., & Miller, A.L. (2002). Emotion regulation in context: The jealousy complex between young siblings and its relations with child and family characteristics. *Child Development, 73,* 581– 600.

von Hofsten, C. (1983). Foundations for perceptual development. In L.P. Lipsitt, & C.K. Rovee-Collier (Eds.), *Advances in infancy research* (Vol. 2, pp. 241–264). Norwood, NJ: Ablex.

von Hofsten, C. (1991). Structure of early reaching movements: A longitudinal study. *Journal of Motor Behavior, 23,* 280–292.

Vondra, J.I., & Barnett, D. (Eds.). (1999). Atypical attachment in infancy and early childhood among children at developmental risk. *Monographs of the Society for Research in Child Development, 64*(3, Serial No. 258).

Vondra, J.I., Hommerding, K.D., & Shaw, D.S. (1999). Stability and change in infant attachment in a low-income sample. In J.I. Vondra, & D. Barnett (Eds.), Atypical attachment in infancy and early childhood among children at developmental risk. *Monographs of the Society for Research in Child Development, 64*(3, Serial No. 258), 119–144.

Votruba-Drzal, E., Coley, R.L., & Chase-Lansdale, P.L. (2004). Child care and low-income children's development: Direct and moderated effects. *Child Development, 75,* 296–312.

Vouloumanos, A., & Werker, J.F. (2004). Tuned to the signal: The privileged status of speech for young infants. *Developmental Science, 7,* 270–276.

Vouloumanos, A., & Werker, J.F. (2007). Listening to language at birth: Evidence for a bias for speech in neonates. *Developmental Science, 10,* 159–171.

Vygotsky, L.S. (1933/1978). The role of play in development (M. Lopez-Morillas, transl.). In M. Cole, V. John-Steiner, S. Scribner, & E. Souberman (Eds.), *L.S. Vygotsky: Mind in society.* Cambridge, MA: Harvard University Press.

Vygotsky, L.S. (1934/1986). *Thought and language* (A. Kozulin, transl.). Cambridge, MA: MIT Press.

Wachs, T.D., & Bates, J.E. (2001). Temperament. In G. Bremner, & A. Fogel (Eds.), *Blackwell handbook of infant development* (pp. 465–501). Oxford, UK: Blackwells.

Wachs, T.D., Black, M.M., & Engle, P.L. (2009). Maternal depression: A global threat to children's health, development, and behavior and to human rights. *Child Development Perspectives, 3,* 51–59.

Wagner, C.L., Greer, F.R., & the Section on Breastfeeding and Committee on Nutrition. (2008). Prevention of rickets and vitamin D deficiency in infants, children, and adolescents. *Pediatrics, 122,* 1143–1152.

Wakeley, A., Rivera, S., & Langer, J. (2000a). Can young infants add and subtract? *Child Development, 71,* 1525–1534.

Wakeley, A., Rivera, S., & Langer, J. (2000b). Not proved: Reply to Wynn. *Child Development, 71,* 1537–1539.

Waldfogel, J. (September 2001). Family and medical leave: Evidence from the 2000 surveys. *Monthly Labor Review,* 17–23.

Walk, R.D., & Gibson, E.J. (1961). A comparative and analytical study of visual depth perception. *Psychology Monographs, 75*(15).

Walker-Andrews, A.S. (1986). Intermodal perception of expressive behaviors: Relation of eye and voice? *Developmental Psychology, 22,* 373–377.

Walker-Andrews, A.S. (1997). Infants' perception of expressive behaviors: Differentiation of multimodal information. *Psychological Bulletin, 121,* 437–456.

Walker, C.N., & O'Brien, B. (1999). The relationship between method of pain management during labor and birth outcomes. *Clinical Nursing Research, 8,* 119–134.

Walker, J.R. (1996). Funding child rearing: Child allowance and parental leave. *The Future of Children, 6*(2), 5–25.

Wallace, M.T., & Stein, B.E. (2000). Onset of cross-modal synthesis in the neonatal superior colliculus is gated by development of cortical influences. *Journal of Neurophysiology, 83,* 3578–3582.

Wallace, M.T., & Stein, B.E. (2007). Early experience determines how the senses will interact. *Journal of Neurophysiology, 97,* 921–926.

Wang, Q. (2004). The emergence of cultural self-construct: Autobiographical memory and self-description in American and Chinese children. *Developmental Psychology, 40,* 3–15.

Wang, Q. (2006). Relations of maternal style and child self-concept to autobiographical memories in Chinese, Chinese immigrant, and European American 3-year-olds. *Child Development, 77,* 1794–1809.

Ward, M.J., Vaughn, B.E., & Robb, M.D. (1988). Social-emotional adaptation and infant-mother attachment in siblings: Role of the mother in cross-sibling consistency. *Child Development, 59,* 643–651.

Warneken, F., Chen, F., & Tomasello, M. (2006). Cooperative activities in young children and chimpanzees. *Child Development, 77,* 640–663.

Warneken, F., & Tomasello, M. (2006). Altruistic helping in human infants and young chimpanzees. *Science, 311,* 1301–1303.

Warneken, F., & Tomasello, M. (2007). Helping and cooperation at 14 months of age. *Infancy, 11,* 271–294.

Warren, S.L., Gunnar, M.R., Kagan, J., Anders, T.F., Simmens, S.J., Rones, M., et al. (2003). Maternal panic disorder: Infant temperament, neurophysiology, and parenting behaviors. *Journal of the American Academy of Child and Adolescent Psychiatry, 42,* 814–825.

Wartella, E., Caplovitz, A.G., & Lee, J.H. (2004). From Baby Einstein to Leapfrog, from Doom to the Sims, from instant messaging to Internet chat rooms: Public interest in the role of interactive media in children's lives. *Social Policy Report, 18*(4), 1–19.

Wasik, B.H., Ramey, C.T., Bryant, D.M., & Sparling, J.J. (1990). A longitudinal study of two early intervention strategies: Project CARE. *Child Development, 61,* 1682–1696.

Watamura, S.E., Kryzer, E.M., & Robertson, S.S. (2008). Cortisol patterns at home and child care: Afternoon differences and evening recovery in children attending very high quality full-day center-based child care. *Journal of Applied Developmental Psychology, 30,* 475–485.

Waters, E. (1995). Appendix A. The Attachment Q-set (Version 3). In E. Waters, B.E. Vaughn, G. Posada, & K. Kondo-Ikemura (Eds.), Caregiving, cultural, and cognitive perspectives on secure-base behavior and working models: New growing points in attachment theory and research. *Monographs of the Society for Research in Child Development, 60* (Serial No. 244), 234–246.

Waters, E., & Deane, K.E. (1985). Defining and assessing individual differences in attachment relationships: Q-methodology and the organization of behavior in infancy and early childhood. In I. Bretherton, & E. Waters (Eds.), Growing points of attachment theory and research. *Monographs of the Society for Research in Child Development, 50*(1/2, Serial No. 209), 41–65.

Watkins, M.L., Rasmussen, S.A., Honein, M.A., Botto, L.D., & Moore, C.A. (2003). Maternal obesity and risk for birth defects. *Pediatrics, 111,* 1152–1158.

Watson, J.B. (1928). *Psychological care of infant and child.* New York: Norton.

Watson, J.B., & Rayner, R.A. (1920). Conditional emotional reactions. *Journal of Experimental Psychology, 3,* 1–14.

Watson, J.D., & Crick, F.H.C. (1953). Molecular structure of nucleic acids. *Nature, 171,* 737–738.

Waxman, S.R., & Hall, D.G. (1993). The development of a linkage between count nouns and object categories: Evidence from fifteen- to twenty-one-month-old infants. *Child Development, 64,* 1224–1241.

Waxman, S.R., & Kosowski, T.D. (1990). Nouns mark category relations: Toddlers' and preschoolers' word learning biases. *Child Development, 61,* 1461–1473.

Waxman, S.R., & Lidz, J.L. (2006). Early word learning. In W. Damon, & R. Lerner (Eds.) & D. Kuhn, & R. Siegler (Vol. Eds.), *Handbook of child psychology: Vol. 2. Cognition, perception, and language* (6th ed., pp. 299–335). New York: Wiley.

Waxman, S.R., & Markow, D.B. (1995). Words as invitations to form categories: Evidence from 12- to 13-month-old infants. *Cognitive Psychology, 29,* 257–302.

Weber, D.S. (2006). Media use by infants and toddlers: A potential for play. In D.G. Singer, R.M. Golinkoff, & K. Hirsh-Pasek (Eds.), *Play = learning: How play motivates and enhances children's cognitive and social-emotional growth* (pp. 169–191). New York: Oxford University Press.

Weeks, J.D., & Kozak, L.J. (2001). Trends in the use of episiotomy in the United States: 1980–1998. *Birth, 28,* 152–160.

Weikart, D.P. (1998). Changing early childhood development through educational intervention. *Preventive Medicine, 27,* 233–237.

Weikum, W.M., Vouloumanos, A., Navarra, J., Soto-Faraco, S., Sebastián-Gallés, N., & Werker, J.F. (2007). Visual language discrimination in infancy. *Science, 316,* 1159.

Weinberg, M.K., & Tronick, E.Z. (1996). Infant affective reactions to the resumption of maternal interaction after stillface. *Child Development, 67*, 905–914.

Weinberg, M.K., Tronick, E.Z., Cohn, J.F., & Olson, K.L. (1999). Gender differences in emotional expressivity and selfregulation during early infancy. *Developmental Psychology, 35*, 175–188.

Weitzman, C.C., Roy, L., Walls, T., & Tomlin, R. (2004). More evidence for Reach Out and Read: A home-based study. *Pediatrics, 113*, 1248–1253.

Wellman, H.M., Cross, D., & Watson, J. (2001). Meta-analysis of theory of mind development: The truth about false belief. *Child Development, 72*, 655–684.

Wellman, H., Harris, P.L., Banerjee, M., & Sinclair, A. (1995). Early understanding of emotion: Evidence from natural language. *Cognition and Emotion, 9*, 117–149.

Wellman, H., & Wooley, J. (1990). From simple desires to ordinary beliefs: The early development of everyday psychology. *Cognition, 35*, 245–275.

Wendland-Carro, J., Piccinini, C.A., & Millar, W.S. (1999). The role of an early intervention on enhancing the quality of mother-infant interaction. *Child Development, 70*, 713–721.

Werker, J.F., & Byers-Heinlein, K. (2008). Bilingualism in infancy: First steps in perception and comprehension. *Trends in Cognitive Sciences, 12*, 144–151.

Werker, J.F., Cohen, L.B., Lloyd, V.L., Casasola, M., & Stager, C.L. (1998). Acquisition of word-object associations by 14-month-old infants. *Developmental Psychology, 34*, 1289–1309.

Werker, J.F., Fennell, C.T., Corcoran, K.M., & Stager, C.L. (2002). Infants' ability to learn phonetically similar words: Effects of age and vocabulary. *Infancy, 3*, 1–30.

Werker, J.F., Pegg, J.E., & McLeod, P.J. (1994). A cross-language investigation of infant preference for infant-directed communication. *Infant Behavior and Development, 17*, 323–333.

Werker, J.F. Pons, F., Dietrich, C., Kajikawa, S., Fais, L., & Amano, S. (2007). Infant-directed speech supports phonetic category learning in English and Japanese. *Cognition, 103*, 147–162.

Werker, J.F., & Tees, R.C. (1984). Cross-language speech perception: Evidence for perceptual re-organization during the first year of life. *Infant Behavior and Development, 7*, 49–63.

Werker, J.F., & Yeung, H.H. (2005). Infant speech perception bootstraps word learning. *Trends in Cognitive Sciences, 9*, 519–527.

Werner, E.E. (1989). Children of the garden island. *Scientific American, 260*, 106–111.

Werner, E. (2000). Protective factors and resilience. In J.P. Shonkoff, & S.J. Meisels (Eds.), *Handbook of early childhood intervention* (2nd ed., pp. 115–132). New York: Cambridge University Press.

Werner, E., Dawson, G., Osterling, J., & Dinno, N. (2000). Recognition of autism spectrum disorder before one year of age: A retrospective study based on home videotapes. *Journal of Autism & Developmental Disorders, 30*, 157–162.

Wertsch, J. (1979). From social interaction to higher psychological processes. *Human Development, 22*, 1–22.

Wertsch, J. (1985). *Vygotsky and the social formation of mind.* Cambridge, MA: Harvard University Press.

Wertsch, J.V., & Tulviste, P. (1992). L.S. Vygotsky and contemporary developmental psychology. *Developmental Psychology, 28*, 548–557.

Whipple, J. (2008). The effect of music-reinforced nonnutritive sucking on state of preterm, low birthweight infants experiencing heelstick. *Journal of Music Therapy, 45*, 227–272.

White, B., Gunnar, M.R., Larson, M.C., Donzella, B., & Barr, R.G. (2000). Behavioral and physiological responsivity, sleep, and patterns of daily cortisol production in infants with and without colic. *Child Development, 71*, 862–877.

Whitehurst, G.J., Arnold, D.S., Epstein, J.N., Angell, A.L., Smith, M., & Fischel, J.E. (1994). A picture book reading intervention in day care and home for children from low-income families. *Developmental Psychology, 30*, 679–689.

Whiting, J.W.M., Child, I.L., Lambert, W.W., Fischer, A.M., Fischer, J.L., Nydegger, C., et al. (1966). *Field guide for a study of socialization: Six cultures series (Vol. 1).* New York: Wiley.

Whyatt, R.M., Rauh, V., Barr, D.B., Camann, D.E., Andrews, H.F., Garfinkel, R., et al. (2004). Prenatal insecticide exposures, birth weight and length among an urban minority cohort. *Environmental Health Perspectives, 112*, 1125–1132.

Widdowson, E.M. (1951). Mental contentment and physical growth. *Lancet, 1*, 1316–1318.

Wiggins, P. (2000). Shaken Baby Syndrome: What caregivers need to know. *Texas Child Care, 23(4)*, 16–19.

Wilcox, T., Woods, R., & Chapa, C. (2008). Color-function categories that prime infants to use color information in an object individuation task. *Cognitive Psychology, 57*, 220–261.

Wilkin, P. (1995). A comparison of fetal and newborn responses to music and sound stimuli with and without daily exposure to a specific piece of music.

Bulletin of the Council for Research in Music Education, 27, 163–169.

Williams, A.L., Khattak, A.Z., Garza, C.N., & Lasky, R.E. (2009). The behavioral pain response to heelstick in preterm neonates studied longitudinally: Description, development, determinants, and components. *Early Human Development, 85,* 369–374.

Williams, C.L., Squillace, M.M., Bollella, M.C., Brotanek, J., Campanaro, L., D'Agostino, C., et al. (1998). *Healthy Start:* A comprehensive health education program for preschool children. *Preventive Medicine, 27,* 216–223.

Williams, K., & Umberson, D. (1999). Medical technology and childbirth: Experiences of expectant mothers and fathers. *Sex Roles, 41,* 147–168.

Williamson, D.M., Abe, K., Bean, C., Ferré, C., Henderson, Z., & Lackritz, E. (2008). Current research in preterm birth. *Journal of Women's Health, 17,* 1545–1549.

Willinger, M., Ko, C.W., Hoffman, H.J., Kessler, R.C., & Corwin, M.J. (2000). Factors associated with care-givers' choice of infant sleep position, 1994–1998: The National Infant Sleep Position Study. *JAMA, 283,* 2135–2142.

Willinger, M., Ko, C.W., Hoffman, H.J., Kessler, R.C., & Corwin, M.J. (2003). Trends in infant bed sharing in the United States, 1993–2000: The National Infant Sleep Position Study. *Archives of Pediatrics and Adolescent Medicine, 157,* 43–49.

Wilson, D.A., & Sullivan, R.M. (1994). Neurobiology of associative learning in the neonate: Early olfactory learning. *Behavioral and Neural Biology, 61,* 1–18.

Wilson, M.J.A., MacArthur, C., Cooper, G.M., & Shennan, A. (2009). Ambulation in labour and delivery mode: A randomised controlled trial of high-dose vs mobile epidural analgesia. *Anaesthesia, 64,* 266–272.

Wilson, R.D. (2002). Prenatal evaluation for fetal surgery. *Current Opinions in Obstetrical Gynecology, 14,* 187–193.

Wilson-Costello, D., Friedman, H., Minich, N., Siner, B., Taylor, G., Schluchter M., & Hack, M. (2007). Improved neurodevelopmental outcomes for extremely low birth weight infants in 2000–2002. *Pediatrics, 119,* 37–45.

Winikoff, B., Castle, M A., & Laukaran, V.H. (Eds.). (1988). *Feeding infants in four societies: Causes and consequences of mothers' choices.* New York: Greenwood Press.

Winston, F.K., Chen, I.G., Elliott, M.R., Arbogast, K.B., & Durbin, D.R. (2004). Recent trends in child restraint practices in the United States. *Pediatrics, 113,* e458–e464.

Winter C., Macfarlane, A., Deneux-Tharaux, C., Zhang, W-H., Alexander, S., Brocklehurst, P., et al. (2007). Variations in policies for management of the third stage of labour and the immediate management of postpartum haemorrhage in Europe. *BJOG: British Journal of Obstetrics and Gynaecology, 114,* 845–854.

Wismer Fries, A.B., & Pollak, S.D. (2004). Emotion understanding of post-institutionalized Eastern European children. *Development and Psychopathology, 16,* 355–369.

Wisner, K.L., Parry, B.L., & Piontek, C.M. (2002). Postpartum depression. *New England Journal of Medicine, 347,* 194–199.

Witcombe, N.B., Yiallourou, S.R., Walker, A.M., & Horne, R.S.C. (2008). Blood pressure and heart rate patterns during sleep are altered in preterm-born infants: Implications for Sudden Infant Death Syndrome. *Pediatrics, 122,* e1242–e1248.

Witherington, D.C., Campos, J.J., & Hertenstein, M.J. (2001). Principles of emotion and its development in infancy. In G. Bremner, & A. Fogel (Eds.), *Blackwell handbook of infant development* (pp. 427–464). Oxford, UK: Blackwell.

Wolery, R.A., & Odom, S.L. (2000). *An administrator's guide to preschool inclusion.* Chapel Hill, NC: University of North Carolina, FPG Child Development Center, Early Childhood Research Institute on Inclusion.

Wolf, A.W., Lozoff, B., Latz, S., & Paludetto, R. (1996). Parental theories in the management of young children's sleep in Japan, Italy, and the United States. In S. Harkness, & C. M. Super (Eds.), *Parents' cultural belief systems: Their origins, expressions, and consequences* (pp. 364–384). New York: Guilford Press.

Wolff, T., Witkop, C.T., Miller, T., Syed, S.B., & U.S. Preventive Services Task Force. (2009). Folic acid supplementation for the prevention of neural tube defects: An update of the evidence for the U.S. Preventive Services Task Force. *Annals of Internal Medicine, 150,* 632–639.

Wolfsberg, T.G., McEntyre, J., & Schuler, G.D. (2001). Guide to the draft human genome. *Nature, 409,* 824–826.

Wong, K. (July 2009). Hitching a ride—Crawling may be unnecessary for normal child development. *Scientific American,* 20–23.

Wood, D., Bruner, J., & Ross, G. (1976). The role of tutoring in problem solving. *Journal of Child Psychology and Psychiatry, 17,* 89–100.

Woodward, A.L. (2000). Constraining the problem space in early word learning. In R. Golinkoff, K. Hirsh-Pasek, N. Bloom, G. Hollich, L. Smith, A.L. Woodward, L. Akhtar, M. Tomasello, & G. Hollich (Eds.), *Becoming a word learner: A debate on lexical acquisition* (pp. 81–114). Oxford: Oxford University Press.

Woodward, A.L., & Markman, E.M. (1998). Early word learning. In W. Damon (Ed.) & D. Kuhn, & R.S. Siegler (Vol. Eds.), *Handbook of child psychology Vol. 2. Cognition, perception, and language* (5th ed., pp. 371–420). New York: Wiley.

Woodward, A.L., Markman, E.M., & Fitzsimmons, C.M. (1994). Rapid word learning in 13- and 18-month-olds. *Developmental Psychology, 30*, 553–566.

Woodward, E.H., & Gridina, N. (2000). *Media in the home, 2000: The fifth annual survey of parents and children.* Philadelphia, PA: The Annenberg Public Policy Center of the University of Pennsylvania. Available at http://www.appcpenn.org/mediainhome/survey/survey7.pdf

Woodward, J., & Kelly, S.M. (2004). A pilot study for a randomized controlled trial of waterbirth versus land birth. *BJOG, 111*, 537–545.

Woodworth, S., Belsky, J., & Crnic, K. (1996). The determinants of fathering during the second and third year of life: A developmental analysis. *Journal of Marriage and the Family, 58*, 679–692.

Woolsey, L. (2009). *Fifth anniversary of California's successful paid family leave law.* August 5th, 2009, Paid Family Leave California press release, retrieved December 22, 2009, from http://www.paidfamilyleave.org.

World Health Organization. (1996). Safe use of iodized oil to prevent iodine deficiency in pregnant women. *Bulletin of the World Health Organization, 74*, 1–3.

World Health Organization. (2000). WHO Global Data Bank on Breastfeeding. Retrieved December 10, 2002, from http://www.who.int/nut/db_bfd.htm

World Health Organization. (2001a). Assessment of iodine deficiency disorders and monitoring their elimination: A guide for programme managers (2nd ed.). Geneva: WHO.

World Health Organization. (2001b). Micronutrient deficiencies: Combating vitamin A deficiency. Retrieved December 10, 2002, from http://www.who.int/nut/vad.htm.

World Health Organization. (2002a). Complementary feeding: Report of informal technical meeting to review and develop indicators. Retrieved June 11, 2010, from http://www.who.int/child_adolescent_health/documents/a91059/en/index.html

World Health Organization. (2002b). Micronutrient deficiencies. Retrieved December 10, 2002, from http://www.who.int/nut/#mic

World Health Organization. (2009). *The WHO child growth standards.* Geneva: World Health Organization.

World Health Organization (WHO) Department of Making Pregnancy Safer. (2006). WHO Recommendations for the prevention of postpartum haemorrhage. Retrieved July 14, 2009, from http://www.who.int/making_pregnancy_safer/publications/WHORecommendationsforPPHaemorrhage.pdf.

World Health Organization and UNICEF. (2009). *Acceptable medical reasons for use of breast-milk substitutes.* Geneva, Switzerland: Author.

World Health Organization/United Nations Children's Fund. (1989). *Protecting, promoting and supporting breastfeeding: The special role of maternity services.* Geneva, Switzerland: World Health Organization.

Worley, K.C., McIntire, D.D., & Leveno, K.J. (2009). The prognosis for spontaneous labor in women with uncomplicated term pregnancies: Implications for cesarean delivery on maternal request. *Obstetrics & Gynecology, 113*, 812–816.

Wren, C., Birrell, G., & Hawthorne, G. (2003). Cardiovascular malformations in infants of diabetic mothers. *Heart, 89*, 1217–1220.

Wright, A.L., & Schanler, R.J. (2001). The resurgence of breastfeeding at the end of the second millennium. *The Journal of Nutrition, 131*, 421S–425S.

Wright, C.A., George, T.P., Burke, R., Gelfand, D.M., & Teti, D.M. (2000). Early maternal depression and children's adjustment to school. *Child Study Journal, 30*, 153–168.

Wright, C.F., & Burton, H. (2009). The use of cell-free fetal nucleic acids in maternal blood for non-invasive prenatal diagnosis. *Human Reproduction Update, 15*, 139–151.

Wright, C.M., Parkinson, K.N., & Drewett, R.F. (2006a). How does maternal and child feeding behavior relate to weight gain and failure to thrive? Data from a prospective birth cohort. *Pediatrics, 117*, 1262–1269.

Wright, C.M., Parkinson, K.N., & Drewett, R.F. (2006b). The influence of maternal socioeconomic and emotional factors on infant weight gain and weight faltering (failure to thrive): Data from a prospective birth cohort. *Archives of Disease in Childhood, 91*, 312–317.

Wright, J., Huston, A.C., Murphy, K.C., St. Peters, M., Piñon, M., Scantlin, R., et al. (2001). The relations of early television viewing to school readiness and vocabulary of children from low-income families: The Early Window Project. *Child Development, 72*, 1347–1366.

Wright, V.C., Chang, J., Jeng, G., Macaluso, M. & Centers for Disease Control and Prevention (CDC). (2008). Assisted reproductive technology surveillance—United States, 2005. *Morbidity & Mortality Weekly Report Surveill Summary, 57(5)*, 1–23.

Wynn, K. (2000). Findings of addition and subtraction in infants are robust and consistent: Reply to Wakeley, Rivera, and Langer. *Child Development, 71*, 1535–1536.

Wynne-Edwards, K.E. (2001). Hormonal changes in mammalian fathers. *Hormones and Behavior, 40*, 139–145.

Wynne-Edwards, K.E., & Reburn, C.J. (2000). Behavioral endocrinology of mammalian fatherhood. *Trends in Ecology and Evolution, 15*, 464–468.

Xu, K., Shi, Z.M., Veeck, L.L., Hughes, M.R., & Rosenwaks, Z. (1999). First unaffected pregnancy using preimplantation genetic diagnosis for sickle cell anemia. *JAMA, 281*, 1701–1706.

Yang, L., Nong, Q.Q., Li, C.L., Feng, Q.M., & Lo, S.K. (2007). Risk factors for childhood drowning in rural regions of a developing country: A case-control study. *Injury Prevention, 13*, 178–182.

Yang, Q., Khoury, M.J., & Mannino, D. (1997). Trends and patterns of birth defects and genetic diseases associated mortality in United States, 1979–1992: An analysis of multiple-cause mortality data. *Genetic Epidemiology, 14*, 493–505.

Yavas, M. (1995). Phonological selectivity in the first fifty words of a bilingual child. *Language and Speech, 38*, 189–202.

Yazigi, R.A., Odem, R.R., & Polakoski, K.L. (1991). Demonstration of specific binding of cocaine to human spermatozoa. *JAMA, 266*, 1956–1959.

Yeargin-Allsopp, M., Rice, C., Karapurkar, T., Doemberg, N., Boyle, C., & Murphy, C. (2003). Prevalence of autism in a US metropolitan area. *JAMA, 289*, 49–55.

Yeung, W.J., Sandberg, J.F., Davis-Kean, P., & Hofferth, S.L. (2001). Children's time with fathers in intact families. *Journal of Marriage and the Family, 63*, 136–154.

Yonas, A., Elieff, C.A., & Arterberry, M.E. (2002). Emergence of sensitivity to pictorial depth cues: Charting development in individual infants. *Infant Behavior & Development, 25*, 495–514.

Yoshida, K.A., Fennell, C.T., Swingley, D., & Werker, J.F. (2009). Fourteen-month-old infants learn similar-sounding words. *Developmental Science, 12*, 412–418.

Young, K.T. (1990). American conceptions of infant development from 1955 to 1984: What the experts are telling parents. *Child Development, 61*, 17–28.

Youngblade, L.M., & Dunn, J. (1995). Individual differences in young children's pretend play with mother and sibling: Links to relationships and understanding of other people's feelings and beliefs. *Child Development, 66*, 1472–1492.

Zafeiriou, D.I. (2004). Primitive reflexes and postural reactions in the neurodevelopmental examination. *Pediatric Neurology, 31*, 1–8.

Zahn-Waxler, C., Radke-Yarrow, M., Wagner, E., & Chapman, M. (1992). Development of concern for others. *Developmental Psychology, 28*, 126–136.

Zeanah, C.H. (2000). Disturbances of attachment in young children adopted from institutions. *Developmental and Behavioral Pediatrics, 21*, 230–236.

Zeanah, C.H., & Fox, N.A. (2004). Temperament and attachment disorders. *Journal of Clinical Child and Adolescent Psychology, 33*, 32–41.

Zeanah, C.H., Nelson, C.A., Fox, N.A., Smyke, A.T., Marshall, P., Parker, S.W., & Koga, S. (2003). Designing research to study the effects of institutionalization on brain and behavioral development: The Bucharest Early Intervention Project. *Development and Psychopathology, 15*, 885–907.

Zeanah, C.H., Scheeringa, M., Boris, N.W., Heller, S.S., Smyke, A.T., & Trapani, J. (2004). Reactive attachment disorder in maltreated toddlers. *Child Abuse and Neglect, 28*, 877–888.

Zeanah, C.H., Smyke, A.T., Koga, S.F., Carlson, E., & Bucharest Early Intervention Project Core Group. (2005). Attachment in institutionalized and community children in Romania. *Child Development, 76*, 1015–1028.

Zelazo, N.A., Zelazo, P.R., Cohen, K.M., & Zelazo, P.D. (1993). Specificity of practice effects on elementary neuromotor patterns. *Developmental Psychology, 29*, 686–691.

Zelazo, P.D., Carter, A., Reznick, J.S., & Frye, D. (1997). Early development of executive function: A problem-solving framework. *Review of General Psychology, 1*, 1–29.

Zelazo, P.D., Reznick, J.S., & Spinazzola, J. (1998). Representational flexibility and response control in a multistep, multilocation search task. *Developmental Psychology, 34*, 203–214.

Zentner, M.R., & Kagan, J. (1996). Perception of music by infants. *Nature, 383*, 29.

Zhang, J., Meikle, S., Grainger, D.A., & Trumble, A. (2002). Multifetal pregnancy in older women and perinatal outcomes. *Fertility and Sterility, 78*, 562–568.

Zhang, Y., Kuhl, P.K., Imada, T., Kotani, M., & Tohkura, Y. (2005). Effects of language experience: Neural commitment to language-specific auditory patterns. *NeuroImage, 26,* 703–720.

Zhao, Y., Sheng, H.Z., Amini, R., Grinberg, A., Lee, E., Huang, S., et al. (1999). Control of hippocampal morphogenesis and neuronal differentiation by the LIM homeobox gene Lhx5. *Science, 284,* 1155–1158.

Zhu, H., Kartiko, S., & Finnell, R.H. (2009). Importance of gene-environment interactions in the etiology of selected birth defects. *Clinical Genetics, 75,* 409–423.

Zimmerman, F.J. (2008). *Children's media use and sleep problems: Issues and unanswered questions.*

Menlo Park, CA: Henry J. Kaiser Family Foundation.

Zimmerman, F.J., Christakis, D.A., & Meltzoff, A.N. (2007). Television and DVD/video viewing in children younger than 2 years. *Archives of Pediatric and Adolescent Medicine, 161,* 473–479.

Zimmerman, I., Steiner, V., & Pond, P. (1991). *Preschool Language Scale—3.* San Antonio, TX: Psychological Corp.

Zukow-Goldring, P. (2002). Sibling caregiving. In M.H. Bornstein (Ed.), *Handbook of parenting: Vol. 3. Status and social conditions of parenting* (2nd ed., pp. 253–286). Mahwah, NJ: Erlbaum.

INDEX

Page numbers in **bold** indicate key word definitions.

PHOTO CREDITS